JUDICIAL REASONING UNDER THE
UK HUMAN RIGHTS ACT

Judicial Reasoning under the UK Human Rights Act is a collection of essays written by leading experts in the field, which examines judicial decision-making under the UK's *de facto* Bill of Rights. The book focuses both on changes in areas of substantive law and the techniques of judicial reasoning adopted to implement the Act. The contributors therefore consider first general Convention and Human Rights Act concepts – statutory interpretation, horizontal effect, judicial review, deference, the reception of Strasbourg case-law – since they arise across all areas of substantive law. They then proceed to examine, not only the use of such concepts in particular fields of law (privacy, family law, clashing rights,

ONE WEEK LOAN

JUDICIAL REASONING UNDER THE UK HUMAN RIGHTS ACT

Edited by

HELEN FENWICK

GAVIN PHILLIPSON

AND

ROGER MASTERMAN

CAMBRIDGE
UNIVERSITY PRESS

CAMBRIDGE UNIVERSITY PRESS
Cambridge, New York, Melbourne, Madrid, Cape Town,
Singapore, São Paulo, Delhi, Tokyo, Mexico City

Cambridge University Press
The Edinburgh Building, Cambridge CB2 8RU, UK

Published in the United States of America by Cambridge University Press, New York

www.cambridge.org
Information on this title: www.cambridge.org/9780521176590

© Cambridge University Press 2007

First published 2007
First paperback edition 2011

A catalogue record for this publication is available from the British Library

ISBN 978-0-521-87633-9 Hardback
ISBN 978-0-521-17659-0 Paperback

CONTENTS

LIST OF CONTRIBUTORS

Aaron Baker is a Senior Lecturer in Law at the University of Durham. He began his academic career after six years as a discrimination trial attorney in the US. He is a graduate of the Oxford University BCL programme and of St Louis University School of Law in the US. He has been a lecturer at Durham since 2002.

David Feldman is Rouse Ball Professor of English Law in the University of Cambridge (2004–), a Fellow of Downing College, Cambridge (2003–), a Judge of the Constitutional Court of Bosnia and Herzegovina (2002–), and an Academic Associate of Chambers at 39 Essex Street (2004–).

Helen Fenwick is Professor of Law and Joint Director of the Human Rights Centre at the University of Durham, Convenor of the SLS Civil Liberties and Human Rights Group and a member of the Editorial Board of the *Civil Liberties Law Journal*. She is a Human Rights Consultant to Doughty Street Chambers in London.

Sonia Harris-Short studied law at Christ Church, Oxford, graduating with a first-class honours degree. She obtained her Masters degree (by research) from the University of British Columbia, before returning to the UK where she qualified as a barrister. She began her academic career at Durham University and is now a Senior Lecturer in Law at the University of Birmingham. She has published widely in the areas of family law and international human rights and has a particular interest in the protection of the individual rights of family members when placed within the wider family or community setting.

Aileen Kavanagh is a Reader in Law at the University of Leicester, and has held visiting appointments at St John's College, Oxford and at the University of Toronto Law School. She has published articles on constitutional theory in international and national academic journals.

Sir David Keene is a Lord Justice of Appeal. He is also Chairman of the Judicial Studies Board and a bencher of the Inner Temple.

Ian Leigh has been a Professor of Law at the University of Durham since 1997 and is Co-Director of the Human Rights Centre. He has held appointments at several universities, including visiting appointments at Osgoode Hall Law School, Ontario, and the University of Otago, New Zealand. He is also a Solicitor of the Supreme Court (England and Wales).

Roger Masterman is a Lecturer in Law at the University of Durham. He is a graduate of King's College London, and has worked previously at the Constitution Unit, University College London. Between 2002 and 2005, he was Senior Research Associate at the University of Durham working on the AHRC-funded project, 'Judicial Reasoning and the Human Rights Act 1998'.

Gavin Phillipson is currently Professor of Law at the University of Durham, having previously held positions at King's College London and the Universities of Sussex and Essex, and qualified as a solicitor in 1995. He also currently holds the position of Senior Fellow at the Centre for Media and Communications Law, University of Melbourne.

Paul Roberts is Professor of Criminal Jurisprudence at the University of Nottingham School of Law. He teaches and writes in the fields of criminal law theory, international and comparative criminal justice, and criminal procedure and evidence.

Colin Warbrick is Professor of Public International Law at the University of Birmingham. He works in the fields of international law and human rights, and was previously Professor of Law at the University of Durham. He has been a consultant to the Council of Europe and the Organization for Security and Co-operation in Europe on human rights matters.

FOREWORD

In his celebrated work, *On Liberty*, John Stuart Mill commented:

> There is a limit to the legitimate interference of collective opinion with individual independence; and to find that limit, and maintain it against encroachment, is as indispensable to a good condition of human affairs as protection against political despotism.

But finding that limit, striking the balance between the public interest and individual rights, remains as difficult and elusive today as it was in 1859. It is an exercise which lies at the heart of much of our contemporary discussion and litigation arising from the incorporation into domestic law of the European Convention on Human Rights. Nearly six years after the Human Rights Act 1998 came into force, the courts are still grappling with some fundamental issues. For example, when is it for the court to decide for itself whether there would be a breach of one of the Articles, as opposed to deciding whether some other body's decision on that issue was a proper one, with which the court will not interfere? It is inevitable that, when legal rights are expressed in such general terms as one finds in the Articles of the European Convention on Human Rights, there will be much room for differences of opinion as to the application of those rights.

I write these comments a few days after the House of Lords divided four to three on the approach to be adopted to Article 8 in proceedings by a public authority landlord to obtain possession of property owned by it: *Kay and others* v. *Lambeth London Borough Council*, 8 March 2006. Such a division of opinion in our highest court illustrates how much further debate lies ahead on human rights issues. That makes the publication of the present work most welcome.

It reflects a series of seminars, organised by the Human Rights Centre at the University of Durham, which focused on the way in which the English courts have sought to apply the 1998 Act and the European Convention. Inevitably perhaps, the authors of the various chapters identify a number of differences in the judicial reasoning to be found in the decided cases. This is not altogether surprising in a new and rapidly developing area of the law. But it means that there is considerable value in the careful and detailed analyses which one finds in these chapters. Those who practise the law will derive great benefit from this thought-provoking work, and I have no doubt that its contribution to the continuing human rights debate will prove of enduring worth.

Lord Justice Keene
Royal Courts of Justice

PREFACE AND ACKNOWLEDGMENTS

The project from which this collection grew was undertaken by various members of the University of Durham Human Rights Centre and a number of collaborators between October 2002 and September 2005. The research was funded by the Arts and Humanities Research Council, which accorded it £139,000.

The project set out to examine emerging themes in judicial reasoning under the Human Rights Act 1998. It is the universal experience that states which choose to include a Bill of Rights within their constitutional arrangements confer on the judges a very wide power. To have legitimacy, the exercise of the power must be adequately reasoned and transparent to those beyond the legal community. The effectiveness of constitutional jurisprudence in securing acceptance among the multiple audiences to which it is addressed depends upon the courts being well informed, and in judgments, taken as a whole, demonstrating a degree of internal consistency. Academic commentary on judgments of this kind is an important element in the process. There is a danger under the HRA that much judicial decision-making would be reduced to an *ad hoc* 'balancing' exercise, which is both intellectually unsatisfying and practically of limited value, since it gives so little guidance to the primary decision-makers, whether they be lower courts or officials. Thus, it was intended that the project would aid in providing such guidance to judges, counsel and executive policy-makers.

The seminars and the symposium (details of which are given below) at which interim findings were presented therefore set out to identify the strands of interpretative approaches already manifest in judgments under the HRA and to compare them with the ECHR expectations. The project sought to identify the forms of legal argumentation and judicial reasoning used in HRA cases, looking in particular at the forms of justification that were being given for moving beyond the minimum 'compatibility' standard. The overarching questions underpinning the papers were as follows: is the Strasbourg jurisprudence being faithfully applied by domestic courts; are there signs of movement beyond such application towards a 'British Bill of Rights approach'; what other sources of law or principle are being used in judicial reasoning with the conscious or unconscious aim of resisting the Convention, or at least of supplementing it?

The project took shape around a series of seminars examining the developing domestic case-law under the HRA held between April 2003 and January 2005 at the offices of Allen & Overy in London. At these events, papers were delivered by Gavin Phillipson (on breach of confidence and privacy), Ian Leigh (on the standard of judicial review), Sonia Harris-Short (on family law), Helen Fenwick (on balancing conflicting rights) and Aaron Baker (on discrimination law); their chapters in this volume are based on the papers given at these events. We owe a debt of thanks to those members of the profession who gave up their time to offer responses to the presentations – respectively, Sir Stephen Sedley, Sir David Keene, Judith Parker QC, Cherie Booth QC and Dame Laura Cox. The chapters which finally emerged in this book each drew benefit from the thoughts and comments given by each of our respondents. Our thanks are also due to those who kindly chaired the proceedings – Iain Christie (on two occasions), Murray Hunt, Dame Jill Black and Stephen Grosz – and to David Mackie QC, Jonathan Hitchin, Christabel Kensit, Siobhan Lynas and Tina Menish at Allen & Overy for providing us with an excellent venue, and for helping us to organise the events with great efficiency.

The Human Rights Centre held an end-of-project symposium at Durham Castle on 8–9 April 2005, which was attended by a large number of the leading experts on the HRA from academia and the profession, including senior judges. The chapters written by Professor Colin Warbrick, Roger Masterman, Professor David Feldman, Dr Aileen Kavanagh and Professor Paul Roberts, along with Gavin Phillipson's chapter on horizontal effect, were all initially presented at this event. The symposium also saw presentations from a number of people whose contributions do not appear in this volume, but without whose input the event would not have been such a success; those people are: Professor Conor Gearty, Sir Michael Tugendhat, Jo Miles, Rabinder Singh QC and Professor G. R. Sullivan. Similarly, those who chaired sessions at the symposium in April 2005 – Aidan O'Neill QC, Professor Eric Barendt, Professor Michael Bohlander, Sir David Keene and Iain Christie – are owed our gratitude. Acknowledgment should also be made of the contributions made by those members of the profession and academics – too numerous to name individually – who attended the events throughout the course of the project.

Finally, we would also like to thank Finola O'Sullivan of Cambridge University Press, for her enthusiastic backing for the project, for securing its acceptance for publication, and for her patience and flexibility in relation to the timetable, and Helen Francis for her detailed help in dealing with the practical issues of the submission of the manuscript and its production.

The majority of the chapters in this volume were completed in the spring and early summer of 2006, and seek to reflect developments in the law up to that point in time. The contribution by Lord Justice Keene, demonstrative of developing judicial attitudes towards the Human Rights Act, reflects his contribution to the seminar series, delivered in December 2003.

TABLE OF CASES

TABLE OF LEGISLATION

United Kingdom

TABLE OF TREATIES

The Human Rights Act in contemporary context

HELEN FENWICK, ROGER MASTERMAN
AND GAVIN PHILLIPSON

Introduction

A number of commentators have pointed out that the inception of Bills
of Rights tends to have the effect, as in Canada, of requiring courts to
grapple with justifications for rights and freedoms, taking a more philosophical approach to legal reasoning as they attempt to resolve conflicts between individual rights and competing societal and individual
interests.[1] When countries adopt a document setting out a list of human
rights with special constitutional status ('a Bill of Rights'), the effect on
judicial reasoning tends to be dramatic – as it was in Canada when it
adopted the Charter of Rights. In 2000, the Human Rights Act came into
force – affording the European Convention on Human Rights further
effect in domestic law – and, while it does not have the entrenched status
of other Bills of Rights, there is agreement that it does have what
'constitutional' status UK law allows.[2]

Academics and lawyers agree that the introduction of the Act was one
of the most significant developments in the public law field in the last
100 years. The Act did not create a home-grown Bill of Rights for the
UK; instead, it gave further legal effect to the European Convention on
Human Rights. Thus, its impact on judicial reasoning was less predictable than was the case in the broadly equivalent situation in Canada.
This requires a word of explanation, since at first sight the effect on
judicial reasoning in the UK was *more* predictable since the judges could

[1] See e.g. R. J. Sharpe, 'The Impact of a Bill of Rights on the Role of the Judiciary:
A Canadian Perspective' and M. Darrow and P. Alston, 'Bills of Rights in Comparative
Perspective', both in P. Alston (ed.), *Promoting Human Rights Through Bills of Rights:
Comparative Perspectives* (Oxford: Oxford University Press, 1999).
[2] *Thoburn v. Sunderland City Council* [2003] QB 151, para. 62. See also *Brown v. Stott*
[2003] 1 AC 681, 703, *per* Lord Bingham.

rely on an already large and developed body of jurisprudence interpreting the Convention – that of the European Court of Human Rights (and previously the Commission) at Strasbourg. But judicial receptivity to the ECHR under the Human Rights Act was less consistent than was the case in Canada: broadly speaking, the Canadian judges gave the Charter quite a warm reception, given the widespread popular support for its adoption, whereas, among British judges, some resistance to the Convention was evident.[3] The judges had become accustomed to the Convention as an international instrument, while at the same time they were proud of their long-established common law and constitutional traditions, including deference to parliament and to the executive in judicial review cases, as manifested in the *Wednesbury* doctrine.[4] Many of them appeared to take the view that the common law was already providing an effective protection for human rights – and could continue to develop in ways that would strengthen the protection.[5] Indeed, a number of judges continue to take this view,[6] and it is possible to discern further developments in a common law human rights tradition, running parallel to the HRA and engaging in an uneasy and uncertain relationship with it. This resistance to the Convention can be noted in particular, albeit to varying degrees, in the chapters in the book by Gavin Phillipson,[7] Ian Leigh, Sonia Harris-Short and Paul Roberts. There is thus a certain ambivalence in the attitude of the judiciary to the HRA,[8] which is not paralleled in Canada where there is a patriotic

---

[3] For example, Lord McCluskey – a long-term opponent of incorporation (see J. H. McCluskey, *Law, Justice and Democracy* (London: Sweet & Maxwell, 1987)) – wrote in *Scotland on Sunday* (6 February 2000) that the Act would be a 'field day for crackpots, a pain in the neck for judges and legislators and a goldmine for lawyers'. Buxton LJ's article, written prior to the coming into force of the HRA, and attempting to refute the notion that it would have any impact on private law may also be seen as evidence of resistance to it, at least in that particular arena: see 'The Human Rights Act and Private Law' (2000) 116 LQR 48.

[4] See *Associated Provincial Picture Houses Ltd* v. *Wednesbury Corporation* [1948] 1 KB 223.

[5] See Sir John Laws, 'Is the High Court the Guardian of Fundamental Human Rights?' [1993] PL 57.

[6] See e.g. the judgment of Laws LJ in *R. (ProLife Alliance)* v. *BBC* [2002] 2 All ER 756, which is based largely on common law reasoning. Lord Woolf's comments in *Attorney General's Reference (No. 1 of 2004)* [2004] 2 Cr App R 27, para. 14, that 'Article 6 does no more than reflect the requirements of fairness which have long been a part of English law', are also apposite.

[7] That is, his chapter on horizontal effect, Chapter 6.

[8] In spite of the frequent reminders that UK officials played a major part in drafting the ECHR and, for example, Jack Straw's reminder that it is '[a] classical statement of what British people have taken for granted as their rights in relation to the state' (Joint Committee on Human Rights, Minutes of Evidence, 14 March 2001, Q3).

attachment among the judiciary, the people and policy-makers to the Charter as a home-grown, specifically *Canadian* achievement. As Peter Hogg has put it:

> [The Charter's] adoption in 1982 was the product of a widespread public debate, in which the inevitable risks of judicial review played a prominent role. Admittedly, the Charter was never put to and approved by a popular referendum, but it has always commanded widespread popular support. A poll taken in 1999, on the heels of two controversial Charter decisions by the Supreme Court of Canada, showed 82 per cent of those polled saying that the Charter was 'a good thing', and 61 per cent saying that the courts, not the legislatures, should have the last word when the courts decide that a law is unconstitutional.[9]

In contrast, the lack of solidly based political and popular support for the HRA is quite possibly also something which affects judicial responses to it. To say that popular backing for the HRA does not reach that evident in relation to the Canadian Charter or, for example, the Scotland Act, passed after a referendum, is to understate the matter.[10] Indeed, at the time of completing this Introduction, the HRA is in the midst of a firestorm of criticism, coming not only from the Prime Minister, but also from the main Opposition party, and Britain's most popular newspaper, *The Sun*, which has launched a campaign for the repeal of the HRA,[11] with, it claims, 35,000 readers giving immediate support.[12] Tony Blair appears to be increasingly frustrated with the constraints upon deporting foreign prisoners and terrorist suspects imposed by Article 3.[13] The leader of the main Opposition party, David Cameron, having pledged that the Conservatives would 'scrap,

---

[9] P. Hogg, 'The Charter Revolution: Is It Undemocratic?' (2002) 12 *Constitutional Forum* 1 (footnotes omitted). For a more sceptical view, see F. L. Morton and R. Knopff, *Charter Revolution and the Court Party* (Peterborough: Broadview Press, 2000).

[10] One commentator – a long-standing advocate of domestic human rights legislation – has welcomed the discussions which will be prompted by the Conservative's 'British Bill of Rights' initiative as the Human Rights Act has – 'in the absence of prior consultation' – 'failed to attract sufficient symbolic significance to become embedded in the national consciousness' (Francesca Klug, 'Enshrine These Rights', *Guardian*, 27 June 2006; and letter to the *Observer*, 'Parliament – A Danger to Freedom', 9 April 2006).

[11] See its 'Leader' of 15 May 2006: 'At last Tony Blair admits he needs to do something about the ludicrous Human Rights Act. He wants the Government to have the power to overturn judges' barmy rulings where a criminal's so-called rights come ahead of their victim's. The PM says this is one of his "most urgent policy tasks". He's not kidding . . . Rest assured, *The Sun* will continue to fight for the scrapping of this disgraceful piece of legislation.'

[12] www.thesun.co.uk/article/0,,2-2006220181,00.html   [13] See n. 18 below.

reform or replace' the Act,[14] repeating the manifesto pledge they gave at the 2005 General Election, announced, as one of his first solid policy pledges since becoming leader that the Conservatives now sought to repeal the Act and replace it with a British Bill of Rights;[15] the reform appears to be aimed at least in part at freeing the government from some of the more 'inconvenient' requirements of the Convention[16] thought to be hampering the 'war on terror' and the fight against crime. It is clear that Mr Cameron regards this is a popular stance: it is fair to say that the attack on the HRA in the pages of certain best-selling newspapers, particularly recently, has been quite relentless, and filled with damaging myths and misconceptions.

Certainly, the HRA currently exists in a climate very different from that prevailing in 2000. We no longer feel that we are at the beginning of a new dawn for civil liberties in the UK. The emphasis of policy-makers is often no longer on the benefits of the HRA; the post-9/11 debate tends to concern methods of avoiding its effects. Thus, the current Labour government derogated from Article 5 between 2001 and 2005,[17] and has actively floated the possibility of withdrawal from the ECHR, followed by re-entry, but with a reservation in relation to the *Chahal*[18] principle deriving from Article 3, which the government claims is hindering its fight against international terrorism.[19] Tony Blair, in an open letter to the new Home Secretary, John Reid, spoke of the need to 'look again at whether primary legislation is needed to address the issue of court rulings which overrule the Government

---

[14] See 'Cameron Calls for Repeal of Human Rights Act', *Guardian*, 12 May 2006.

[15] Announced in a speech to the Centre for Policy Studies, 26 June 2006. The full text can be found at www.conservatives.com/tile.do?def=news.story.page&obj_id=130572&speeches=1.

[16] The proposed reform has been widely criticised as incoherent and contradictory, partly because the Conservatives do not propose that the UK withdraw from the ECHR itself. Michael Mansfield QC has described it as 'totally misconceived and tabloid driven'. See 'Tories Bill of Rights Bill Slammed', news.bbc.co.uk/1/hi/uk_politics/5115912.stm.

[17] Human Rights Act (Designated Derogation) Order 2001, SI 2001 No. 3644: this was enacted in order to allow Parliament to pass Part IV of the Anti-Terrorism, Crime and Security Bill, allowing for detention without trial of foreign terrorist suspects.

[18] *Chahal* v. *United Kingdom* (1996) 23 EHRR 413. That is, the principle that a signatory to the ECHR is not only prohibited from directly inflicting treatment contrary to Article 3, but may not deport a person to a country where there is a real risk of such treatment.

[19] The government has considered at various points the idea of either denouncing the Convention and re-entering it while entering a reservation to Article 3, so that it can deport suspects to countries despite a risk of torture; it also suggested introducing legislation directing judges how to interpret Article 3 so that they would prioritise national security over individual rights in this context: for an analysis, see A. Lester and K. Beattie, 'Risking Torture' [2005] EHRLR 265.

in a way that is inconsistent with other EU countries' interpretation of the European Convention on Human Rights'.[20] The desire to free the executive from the handcuffs of human rights principles may be seen at present most vividly in the Government's attempt to have the *Chahal* principle overturned at Strasbourg,[21] so that it will be able to deport suspected terrorists even to countries where there is a risk of their being subject to torture.[22] Amongst commentators also, there is doubt not only as to the basic desirability of incorporation of the Convention,[23] but more importantly as to the approach that should be taken to its interpretation, in terms of the balance to be struck between the power of the judiciary and that of Parliament and the executive.[24] It is plausible to suggest that this lack of popular support may affect the attitude of the judiciary – there may be some awareness among them of the fact that, if they adopt too expansive an approach to interpreting and enforcing the HRA, it might be radically modified or even repealed. It is impossible to tell whether the current storm of criticism surrounding the Act is mere journalistic and Westminster froth, which will evaporate in a few weeks or months, leaving judicial attitudes untouched: the Prime Minister's calls for a 'profound rebalancing of the civil liberties debate'[25] certainly suggests that he sees this issue as a serious policy priority, rather than just short-term populist rhetoric.[26]

---

[20] See 'Blair Stung into Review of Human Rights Law', *Telegraph*, 15 May 2006. Confidence in the Prime Minister's loyalty to the Convention and the HRA is not inspired by this seeming blunder of confusing the Council of Europe with the European Union.

[21] For recent discussion, see the 19th Report of the Joint Committee on Human Rights, HL 185 I/HC 701-I (2005–6), at paras. 19–27.

[22] The government is intervening in a case brought against Holland: *Ramzy v. Netherlands*, No. 25424/05.

[23] See e.g. C. A. Gearty and K. D. Ewing, 'Rocky Foundations for Labour's New Rights' [1997] EHRLR 146. Gearty has since modified his position to one which endorses the HRA, provided it is read in the way he suggests in n. 30 below.

[24] See n. 30 below.

[25] See 'PM Calls for "Rebalancing" of Civil Liberties Debate', *Guardian*, 15 May 2006.

[26] His Lord Chancellor, Lord Falconer, has been much more circumspect and, indeed, has said that the UK will not withdraw from the Convention, nor scrap the HRA; he has admitted the possibility that it could be amended 'if necessary', though his preferred course seems to be to educate judges and others as to its proper construction: see 'Human Rights Act Will Not Be Axed, Says Falconer', *Independent*, 15 May 2006. His 2006 review of the HRA, completed after the immediate firestorm of criticism around it had dissipated, amounted to a strong defence of it: *Review of the Implementation of the Human Rights Act*, Department for Constitutional Affairs, http://www.dca.gov.uk/peoples-rights/human-rights/pdf/full_review.pdf.

The HRA project: problems, complexities and judicial responses

In addition to the somewhat precarious political position of the HRA, this book as a whole sets out to show that the position of the UK in relation to the ECHR under the HRA does not parallel the position in jurisdictions such as Canada, for a number of other important reasons. The application of the ECHR via the HRA is highly problematic on a number of levels. Strasbourg's jurisprudence is often notably under-theorised. The reasoning is frequently brief, and lacking in rigour. In particular, the effects of the doctrine of the margin of appreciation result in some decisions in an almost complete failure to examine in any meaningful way the proportionality of restrictions upon individual rights adopted by states.[27] Great variation in the intensity of review may be discerned; indeed, no single account of proportionality can be derived from the Strasbourg jurisprudence.[28] The purpose of the Strasbourg system is to provide a basic level of protection for human rights – a 'floor' not a 'ceiling' of rights – across a vast and disparate geographical area, one with hugely differing cultural sensitivities and governmental concerns. It is important, therefore, to be realistic about the limitations of the Strasbourg jurisprudence, lest it be thought that its 'application' in English law can cure all our current ills in human rights terms. Indeed, importation of the case-law without a keen awareness of its limitations, in particular the effect of the margin of appreciation doctrine, can actually have the effect of *legitimising* areas of law that were previously seen as increasingly untenable.[29] Certainly, application of the Strasbourg jurisprudence *simpliciter*, will not by itself necessarily result in a rights-driven reform of UK law.

---

[27] Notorious examples are *Müller* v. *Switzerland* (1991) 13 EHRR 212 and *Otto-Preminger* v. *Austria* (1994) 19 EHRR 34.

[28] For general discussion, see C. Gearty, *Principles of Human Rights Adjudication* (Oxford: Oxford University Press, 2003); J. Rivers, 'Proportionality and Variable Intensity of Review' (2006) 65(1) CLJ 174–207. In the context of Article 10, see also G. Phillipson and H. Fenwick, *Media Freedom under the Human Rights Act* (Oxford: Oxford University Press, 2006), Chapter 2.

[29] An example would be the finding by Strasbourg (in *Wingrove* v. *UK* (1996) 24 EHRR 1) that the UK law of blasphemy does not violate the Convention, despite its openly discriminatory nature and its lack of either a public good defence or a requirement of specific intent; this gives an appearance of human rights respectability to the offence, allowing the government to claim that it is Convention-compliant, and does not therefore require reform or abolition.

It is also the case that, in addition to the difficulties inherent in the Strasbourg jurisprudence, the HRA itself is highly problematic. Intense normative and doctrinal debate continues around the balance to be struck between the enhanced power of the judiciary under the Act and that of Parliament and the executive.[30] The Act is also analytically and doctrinally ambiguous in some key areas – those of horizontal effect,[31] the ambit of s.3(1)[32] and the public authority definition[33] in particular. These points are explored in greater detail in subsequent chapters of this book, but, briefly, the HRA, as an incorporating instrument, gives rise to interpretative difficulties on a number of levels. First of all, there is the need to interpret the Strasbourg jurisprudence itself, to draw out the principles to be applied, by no means an easy task in many instances, given the characteristics of that jurisprudence described above. Secondly, there is sometimes a question whether to apply the case-law in domestic law at all: it is non-binding and there may be arguments in particular cases that it should not be followed.[34] These issues are explored in detail by Roger Masterman in Chapter 3, but, in brief, a particular problem may arise where a Strasbourg decision follows and

---

[30] Thus, Professor Gearty has argued for an approach to the HRA which maximises those aspects of it which preserve both the unfettered sovereignty of Parliament and a measure of discretion of the executive in relation to human rights issues: see his *Principles of Human Rights Adjudication* (Oxford: Oxford University Press, 2003). For his most recent contribution, see *Can Human Rights Survive?* (Cambridge: Cambridge University Press, 2006), Chapter 3. See also T. Campbell, 'Incorporation through Interpretation', in T. Campbell, K. D. Ewing and A. Tomkins (eds.), *Sceptical Essays on Human Rights* (Oxford: Oxford University Press, 2001); Lord Steyn, 'Deference: A Tangled Story' [2005] PL 346; J. Jowell, 'Judicial Deference: Servility, Civility or Institutional Capacity?' [2004] PL 592; R. Edwards, 'Judicial Deference under the Human Rights Act' (2002) 65 MLR 859; F. Klug, 'Judicial Deference under the Human Rights Act' [2003] EHRLR 125; T. Hickman, 'Constitutional Dialogue, Constitutional Theories and the Human Rights Act 1998' [2005] PL 306; C. O'Cinneide, 'Democracy and Rights: New Directions in the Human Rights Era' (2004) 57 *Current Legal Problems* 175; D. Nicol, 'The Human Rights Act and the Politicians' (2004) 24(3) LS 451; D. Nicol, 'Are Convention Rights a No-Go Zone for Parliament?' [2002] PL 438–48.

[31] See Chapter 6.   [32] See Chapters 3 and 4.

[33] For criticisms of the judicial approach to this issue so far, see the Joint Committee on Human Rights, 'The Meaning of Public Authority under the Human Rights Act', HC 382, HL 39 (2003–4); H. Quane, 'The Strasbourg Jurisprudence and the Meaning of a "Public Authority" under the Human Rights Act' [2006] PL 106.

[34] Under s.2(1) HRA, it must be taken into account, but is not binding. See further R. Masterman, 'Taking the Strasbourg Jurisprudence into Account: Developing a "Municipal Law of Human Rights" under the Human Rights Act' (2005) 54 ICLQ 907.

appears to contradict a decision of an appellate court on the same point of interpretation of Convention articles. As discussed by Gavin Phillipson in Chapter 9, precisely this problem is raised in relation to the crucial decision on privacy in *Von Hannover* v. *Germany*,[35] which immediately followed, and appears inconsistent in some respects with, the decision of the House of Lords in *Campbell* v. *MGN Ltd.*[36] A further potential clash became evident in relation to the House of Lords decision in *Qazi*,[37] on the scope of Article 8, which was rapidly contradicted on point by the decision of the Strasbourg court in *Connors* v. *United Kingdom*.[38] The question in subsequent litigation[39] was whether a lower court should follow the potentially incompatible House of Lords decision, or whether that court might be discharged from applying strict rules of precedent due to the possible conflict with more recent Strasbourg authority. The House of Lords ruled that lower courts remained bound to follow the precedents set by the Appellate Committee.[40] Thirdly, even if agreement can be reached as to the principles to be applied from the Strasbourg jurisprudence, there is still the vexed question as to the extent that the courts should defer to a 'discretionary area of judgment', enjoyed by the executive and/or Parliament, and as to its relation (if any) with the international law doctrine of the margin of appreciation, an issue discussed further by Ian Leigh in Chapter 7. If the area of law in question is common law governing private relations, the role of the Convention rights remains unclear.[41] Finally, if dealing with a statute, there is the question whether its wording and overall scheme allows the courts to change its interpretation to achieve compliance, or whether instead a declaration of incompatibility should be made. This involves determining the scope of s.3(1) HRA, the crucial duty to interpret legislation compatibly with the Convention rights, if possible. As discussed in Chapters 3 and 4, the proper approach to this provision has given rise to a great deal of academic and judicial disagreement. Even where the judges agree in deciding that existing domestic law is incompatible as it stands, there

---

[35] [2004] EMLR 21.   [36] [2004] 2 AC 457.

[37] *Harrow London Borough Council* v. *Qazi* [2004] 1 AC 983 (HL).

[38] (2004) 40 EHRR 189.

[39] *Leeds City Council* v. *Price and Others* [2005] 1 WLR 1825.

[40] *Kay and Others* v. *Lambeth London Borough Council; Price* v. *Leeds City Council* [2006] UKHL 10; [2006] 2 WLR 570. On which, see the discussion in Chapter 14, pp. 437–40.

[41] As discussed further in Chapter 6.

still remains the question of the extent to which it needs to change in order to become compatible.[42]

We would therefore suggest that the HRA, through these layers of complexity, allows the judges plenty of scope to adopt either an 'activist' or 'minimalist' approach to judicial reform of domestic law:[43] broadly speaking, the latter would seek merely to achieve minimal compliance with the Strasbourg case-law; the former would seek to build upon it, and deploy more general Convention principles, in order to construct something much more like a Bill of Rights approach. Moreover, while the former approach would tend to emphasise deference to the role of Parliament and the executive, the latter would tend to exhibit a more muscular and expansive conception of the judicial role under the Act.

As observed above, different levels of enthusiasm are discernible towards the HRA by different members of the judiciary. It might appear possible therefore to place the senior judges in two different 'camps', depending on their attitude to the HRA – broadly the minimalist and activist camps. In fact, it is not possible to discern a neat polarisation between them, although some broad trends are evident. As the book indicates, certain senior members of the judiciary have been activist in one context but minimalist in another. For example, Lord Hoffmann's strikingly activist approach in the Belmarsh case,[44] in which he was prepared, alone amongst a seven-strong panel, to find that there was no 'state of emergency threatening the life of the nation' in the UK, differed markedly from the much-criticised[45] minimalist and deferential posture he adopted in *Prolife Alliance*.[46]

The above remarks are intended to indicate the main issues that this book seeks to address. It seeks to encapsulate, at this early point in the post-HRA era, after it has been in force for six years, the interaction that is occurring between the Convention rights and sometimes repressive legislation, between the rights and the common law and indeed between the rights and a more developed version of themselves – a nascent Bill of

---

[42] See e.g. A. Kavanagh, 'Statutory Interpretation and Human Rights After *Anderson*: A More Contextual Approach' [2004] PL 537.

[43] Generally, contrast the viewpoints taken in Chapters 2 and 3.

[44] *A (FC) and Others (FC)* v. *Secretary of State for the Home Department; X (FC) and Another (FC)* v. *Secretary of State for the Home Department* [2004] UKHL 56.

[45] For an unusual instance of direct criticism by a fellow Law Lord, see Lord Steyn, 'Deference: A Tangled Story' [2005] PL 346; see also J. Jowell, 'Judicial Deference: Servility, Civility or Institutional Capacity?' [2004] PL 592.

[46] *ProLife Alliance* v. *BBC* [2004] 1 AC 185 (HL).

Rights based upon, but going further than, the Convention as interpreted at Strasbourg. If the HRA *is* to be utilised to create such a Bill
of Rights, judges will have to look beyond the often meagre and
un-theorised Convention jurisprudence in doing so.[47] The book thus
focuses on both content and process since it considers changes in the
substantive law and the new processes of judicial reasoning being
adopted. Thus it asks: which strategies of judicial reasoning are the
judges adopting under the Act? Are the judges responding to the Act in
a minimalist fashion – which is arguably all that the European Convention
demands? Or are they using the Act to create – in effect – a domestic Bill
of Rights?

The judiciary at present shows, albeit in a patchy, inconsistent manner, some signs of taking the view that the HRA authorises the UK courts
to develop their own approach to the interpretation and application of
the Act in a manner that *promotes* Convention rights rather than merely
respects them. The book will seek to determine whether these early signs
indicate a deeper trend. If at least some of the judges see the HRA as
more than simply a Convention implementation Act, how do they
regard it? Are the standards of the Convention to be regarded as a
domestic Bill of Rights to be given a national gloss, through a 'constitutional' approach to interpretation? Since there might be complications if
this were the case, is the effect collateral in the sense that it will inspire
the development of an indigenous, informal Bill of Rights? On the basis
that the 'Bill of Rights' approach to the HRA has at least some support
amongst certain members of the senior judiciary as the proper one,
experience elsewhere suggests the need for some grounding for the
whole process in which the courts are engaged – a shared understanding
of the enterprise in which the judges are involved. This book sets out to
make a contribution to providing that grounding. It also seeks to point
up the areas in which the judiciary, through the resistance they are
exhibiting to a thorough and clear-cut acceptance of the interpolation
of Convention standards into areas of law which they themselves have
constructed, are, in effect, preserving a wide measure of discretion as to
how great a role to give to Convention standards in individual cases: the
case studies examining the judicial attitude towards horizontal effect[48]

---

[47] As one of the authors has argued elsewhere: R. Masterman, 'Taking the Strasbourg
Jurisprudence into Account: Developing a "Municipal Law of Human Rights" under the
Human Rights Act' (2005) 54 ICLQ 907.

[48] In Chapter 6.

and the *Wednesbury*/proportionality debate[49] illuminate this tendency particularly clearly.

The book, we hope, is well placed to tackle these questions because it arose out of a project which was specifically intended to bridge the gap between academics and the profession. While the papers given at the seminars and conference[50] covered specific areas of substantive law, they all set out to identify the principles and themes evident in judicial reasoning related to the HRA in a cross-cutting manner, and the contributions from the audience reflected that approach. The book therefore aims to identify the particular approach the judges are taking to reasoning under the HRA, regardless of the specific area under consideration. To this end, in Part I, it considers general Convention and HRA concepts since they arise across all areas of substantive law. It then proceeds in Part II to examine not only the use of such concepts in particular contexts, but also the modes of reasoning adopted as judges seek to straddle the divide between familiar common law and statutory concepts/doctrines and European ones. While cross-cutting themes emerge, it will also be found that there are interesting variations between substantive areas, due to particular judicial approaches that have become established in such areas, often for historical reasons.

A number of chapters in Part II of the book, including in particular Chapters 2, 7 and 13, look particularly at the extent to which the Convention rights are being afforded real efficacy in the face of a number of recent legislative measures in the areas of criminal justice and immigration/national security. In order to declare such statutes compatible with the Convention rights, it appears arguable in relation to some decisions that reliance is being placed on a minimalist interpretation of the Convention.[51] Thus, this book seeks to make the argument that at the beginning of the Human Rights Act era the danger of a decrease in state accountability and the creation of merely empty or tokenistic guarantees is apparent. However, in relation to uses of coercive state power, especially in the terrorism context, the judges have, in the Belmarsh decision,[52] discussed in Chapter 7, utilised the HRA to

---

[49] In Chapters 7 and 8.   [50] See the Preface, pp. xi–xiii.

[51] See e.g. the discussion of the judgment of Laws LJ in *R (Limbuela)* v. *Secretary of State for the Home Department* [2004] QB 1440; [2004] 3 WLR 561 (CA), by Colin Warbrick in Chapter 2, pp. 46–51.

[52] *A (FC) and Others (FC)* v. *Secretary of State for the Home Department; X (FC) and Another (FC)* v. *Secretary of State for the Home Department* [2004] UKHL 56. For discussion of the discrimination issues raised by this case, see Chapter 12, pp. 366–9.

scrutinise executive decisions much more intensively than they felt themselves able to do previously: in that already famous judgment, the House of Lords declared the detention without trial regime put in place by Part IV of the Anti-Terrorism, Crime and Security Act 2001 incompatible with the Convention. However, as Conor Gearty has pointed out, the Law Lords may have felt able to take this stance due to the *lack* of a strike-down power in the HRA. The responsibility for setting free possible terrorists was ultimately (and formally) passed to the government and to Parliament, since under s.4 HRA the legislation under which the men were held remained valid and of full effect, rendering their continued detention lawful, domestically: the executive was not *forced* to act. In Gearty's colourful phrase: '[The Law Lords'] liberal fingerprints would not be – could not be – the last to be found on these men should they be released; the Home Secretary's and/or Parliament's imprimatur would also have to be impressed.'[53] The HRA was set up (under ss.4, 6(2) and 3(2)) in order to allow the government to rely on incompatible legislation – and this is of especial importance in relation to the use of coercive state power. Nevertheless, the decision is widely seen as one of the most significant affirmations of human rights by a UK court in recent times.[54]

In contrast, as Chapter 13 points out, the effect of the HRA in the criminal justice context has been muted and patchy. The book will set out to consider some of the reasons for this. It looks particularly at the extent to which the Convention is having real efficacy. This is a central concern of this book, since it argues that, in an era of heightened pressure on rights, there are dangers of a *lower* standard of protection for freedom than we had in the pre-Human Rights Act era. There is a danger that the Act will be utilised in Parliament to give the impression that a process of human rights auditing has occurred, stifling political discourse and obscuring the rights-abridging effects of legislation. Its effects may be marginalised due to the reduction or exclusion of judicial scrutiny which tends to accompany the provision of a statutory basis for interferences with rights in order to introduce further coercive state powers. This book seeks therefore, at this turning point for individual liberty in Britain, to make a contribution to the debate that is currently under way as to processes of judicial reasoning under the HRA. It argues for an understanding of the dangers of a

---

[53] C. Gearty, 'Human Rights in an Age of Terrorism: Injurious, Irrelevant or Indispensable?' (2005) 58 CLP 25, 35.

[54] See e.g. *ibid.*, p. 25.

minimalist interpretation of the Convention[55] and for the full realisation in domestic law of its underlying principles.

The structure of this book

As has been indicated, although the genesis of this book lies in a research project conducted by the Human Rights Centre at the University of Durham, it should not be assumed that each chapter reflects a uniform interpretation of what the Human Rights Act is, does or, indeed, should be. Consequently, no wholly consistent argument regarding the processes of judicial reasoning under the Act can be found in what follows; each chapter reflects the particular view of its author. Many perspectives can be discerned from the works in this collection – to an extent, that is unsurprising; as a legislative rights instrument, the Human Rights Act remains at an early stage of what will hopefully be a long life (assuming the various threats to repeal, review or otherwise neuter the potential of the HRA are not forthcoming).

This book is split into two parts. Part I, entitled 'The Interpretation of the Human Rights Act', examines various facets of what might be called the technical aspects of reasoning under the Act: the status of the Act and the Strasbourg jurisprudence in domestic law, the interpretative obligations of courts and tribunals, the horizontal effects of the Act, the transition from *Wednesbury* review towards a more rigorous proportionality test and the constraints on the powers of the courts under the principle of deference to the elected arms of the state. It also asks fundamental questions about the role and purpose of the Act, in particular contrasting the views of Colin Warbrick and Roger Masterman. These themes of judicial creativity and restraint, and of confidence and uncertainty which emerge, are returned to in the chapters which form Part II, entitled 'The Human Rights Act and Substantive Law'. Each chapter in Part II seeks to examine the effects of the HRA on a specific and discrete area of the law, namely, family law, discrimination law, criminal law, the development of a common law privacy remedy, and the process of balancing competing rights in the context of reporting restrictions on judicial proceedings. While Part I might be said to approach the HRA from a constitutional perspective, as Paul Roberts notes in his chapter, it 'does not follow from its indubitably

---

[55] We include within this attempts by judges to reinterpret rights in a way which provides *less* protection than Strasbourg, and which is unsupported by any Strasbourg authority: see n. 51 above.

constitutional status that the exclusive, or even primary, juridical significance of the Human Rights Act must be located only in the self-consciously
constitutional pronouncements of the highest courts'.[56] Each of the chapters contained in Part II therefore attempts to prise out strands of reasoning
as apparent in subject-specific areas of the law; they are case studies of
judicial reasoning at the micro-level, in contrast to the macro-level analysis
contained in Part I.

The interpretation of the Human Rights Act

The book begins with an international lawyer's perspective on the status of
the Human Rights Act and of the role of domestic courts *vis-à-vis* the
Convention rights. Colin Warbrick's chapter begins with an analysis
of what might be termed the 'minimalist' approach to the status of the
Convention in domestic law, examining whether the UK courts can be said
to be discharging their obligation of giving faithful effect to the Convention
case-law in a number of controversial areas. Professor Warbrick explains
the nature of the Convention system and why the co-operation of all organs
of the state is vital for its operation. The chapter then examines recent UK
cases which have addressed the formal and substantive questions of what
rights are 'Convention rights' for the HRA and what is required of states by
'Convention rights'. It concludes that these decisions show a proper regard
for the demands of the principle of co-operation between UK law and the
law of the ECHR. The minimum task of judicial reasoning of HRA judgments is to show that the national court has adequately and accurately
taken into account the formal and substantive aspects of 'Convention
rights' as understood by the European Court of Human Rights.

In the context of the status given to the Strasbourg jurisprudence in
domestic law under this requirement lying upon domestic courts, Roger
Masterman examines judicial approaches to this obligation, which – during
the Parliamentary debates on the Human Rights Bill – was seen as going to
the heart of the question of whether the Act would amount to a domestic
Bill of Rights. The obligation to 'take into account' Strasbourg jurisprudence is argued to have been approached in different ways by the judiciary;
a number of leading House of Lords decisions point to an obligation to
follow Strasbourg jurisprudence where it is 'clear and constant', while other
dicta points to the conclusion that this might be a more rigorous, and
restricting, requirement than s.2(1) on its face appears to require. These

---

[56] Chapter 13, p. 378.

contrasting – although not entirely irreconcilable – interpretations of the status of Strasbourg jurisprudence post-HRA are argued to represent a conflict between the old order and the new, values of precedent and legal certainty versus ideas of constitutional adjudication and a realignment of the separation of powers.

The interpretative obligation imposed on courts and tribunals by s.3(1) of the HRA has spawned a huge range of academic analyses, befitting its status as a key provision of the Act.[57] Two of our contributors analyse s.3(1) and its requirements from different perspectives. In his chapter, David Feldman continues the idea that the judicial role – and the techniques employed by judges – should be re-examined in the light of the HRA in the specific context of the obligation to 'interpret' legislation compatibly with the Convention rights. Feldman explores the processes of 'statutory interpretation' by way of s.3(1) HRA, working from the proposition that 'interpretation' is not only a question of the meaning of words in their statutory context, but a question of the effects or outcomes that those words may give rise to.[58] Against this backdrop, he proposes that the constitutional and institutional competences of the various decision-makers required to make judgments under s.3(1) – whether they be judges, legislators or administrators – will necessarily shape the inquiry required of them by the HRA, and that without an appreciation of the myriad factors which might influence such decision-making we may not fully comprehend the requirements of s.3(1) itself.

Equally, the relationship between s.3(1) and the s.4 ability of the judiciary to declare legislation incompatible with 'the Convention rights' is also key to an understanding of the Human Rights Act as a whole. Using s.3(1) may lead to what might be argued to be the effective rewriting of a statutory provision,[59] while recourse to s.4 defers to the

---

[57] See e.g. C. Gearty, 'Reconciling Parliamentary Democracy and Human Rights' (2002) 118 LQR 248; G. Phillipson, '(Mis-)Reading Section 3 of the Human Rights Act' (2003) 119 LQR 183; C. Gearty, 'Revisiting Section 3 of the Human Rights Act' (2003) 119 LQR 551; A. Kavanagh, 'The Elusive Divide between Interpretation and Legislation under the Human Rights Act 1998' (2004) 24 OJLS 259; D. Nicol, 'Statutory Interpretation and Human Rights after *Anderson*' [2004] PL 274; A. Kavanagh, 'Statutory Interpretation and Human Rights after *Anderson*: A More Contextual Approach' [2004] PL 537; A. Kavanagh, 'Unlocking the Human Rights Act: The "Radical" Approach to Section 3(1) Revisited' [2005] EHRLR 259.

[58] A point endorsed in Aileen Kavanagh's discussion of *Bellinger* v. *Bellinger* [2003] 2 AC 467 (HL) in Chapter 5, pp. 128–9.

[59] See e.g. *R* v. *A (No. 2)* [2002] 1 AC 45.

enacted intention of Parliament in the legislation in question; the choice the judiciary are faced with may be seen as analogous to as a choice between 'juristocracy' and Parliamentary democracy.[60] In her examination of the relationship between ss.3 and 4 of the Act, Aileen Kavanagh emphasises – in line with David Feldman – that we should not simply conceive of s.3(1) in terms of finding an interpretation which is linguistically possible. Basing her reasoning on the decision of the House of Lords in *Ghaidan* v. *Godin-Mendoza*, Kavanagh suggests that 'the choice between sections 3 and 4 involves a much broader evaluative decision requiring an assessment of the limits of judicial law-making in the context of a particular case'.[61] But does this amount to a sea-change in the process of judicial reasoning? Kavanagh argues that it does not. Comparing *Ghaidan* with the pre-HRA decision of *Fitzpatrick* v. *Sterling Housing Association Ltd*,[62] this chapter concludes by finding that it is not the methods of judicial reasoning that have changed, but the judiciary's willingness – in the appropriate case – to utilise those methods in a more creative manner. Dr Kavanagh also stresses the broad, contextual approach that the courts have taken to s.3(1), in which a wide range of factors is considered in deciding whether to reinterpret a statutory provision using that section. While this is an approach with which she personally agrees,[63] it may be noted that it is also one which maximises judicial discretion in relation to the use of s.3(1), a theme which reoccurs in a number of other chapters in this book.

Prior to the implementation of the HRA, the potential horizontal effect of the Act was a matter of some controversy. Some saw the Act as the catalyst for the creative development of common law doctrines to ensure that full effect was given to Convention rights[64] in the face of significant loci of private power; others saw it as a mechanism which would allow private citizens to assert Convention rights independently of a pre-existing cause of action,[65] others still as a distortion of the Convention's role as between the individual and the state.[66] In chapter 6,

---

[60] K. D. Ewing, 'The Bill of Rights Debate: Democracy or Juristocracy in Britain?', in K. D. Ewing, C. A. Gearty and B. Hepple, *Human Rights and Labour Law* (London: Mansell, 1994).

[61] See Chapter 5, p. 141.   [62] [2001] 1 AC 27.

[63] See her 'Statutory Interpretation and Human Rights after *Anderson*: A More Contextual Approach' [2004] PL 537.

[64] M. Hunt, 'The "Horizontal Effect" of the Human Rights Act' [1998] PL 423.

[65] H. W. R. Wade, 'Horizons of Horizontality' (2000) 116 LQR 217.

[66] R. Buxton, 'The Human Rights Act and Private Law' (2000) 116 LQR 48.

Gavin Phillipson argues that this area of reasoning is marked by a judicial failure to engage effectively with the theoretical and practical justifications for this use of the Convention rights and their accompanying jurisprudence. Moreover, the judiciary has shown a marked and increasing preference to avoid resolving this issue at any general level, thus preserving effective judicial discretion in this area. Thus, one important question remains unanswered: as Phillipson argues; 'the courts have left themselves the *ability* to bring Convention principles into private law, but have not fully accepted a position in which they are bound to act compatibly with them'.[67]

In his chapter, 'The Standard of Review and Legal Reasoning after the Human Rights Act', Ian Leigh investigates emerging trends in judicial review decisions under the HRA. Two broad themes can be identified: expansionary tendencies which seek to engage with the Strasbourg jurisprudence to intensify the standard of review, and those which seek to limit or resist that expansion. In common with the preceding chapter, the under-theorised approach to the potential impact of the HRA is addressed in the context of the judicial review of administrative action through the effective reversion to the standards of *Wednesbury* review, the tendency to give variable weight to different rights, and the concept of 'indirect deference' to Parliament. By contrast, Sir David Keene provides a judicial perspective on the concept of deference as applied under the Human Rights Act, endorsing the principles enunciated by Laws LJ in the case of *International Transport Roth GmbH* v. *Secretary of State for the Home Department*.[68] This chapter emphatically endorses the notion that, in spite of the enthusiastic embrace of theoretical analysis of the Human Rights Act by the academic branch (particularly in its discussion of the concept of deference),[69] for the judiciary at least, charged with the task of applying principle in practice, there remains a vital sense of pragmatism. As Sir David notes in his

---

[67] Chapter 6, p. 172.   [68] [2002] 3 WLR 344, 376–8.

[69] See e.g. J. Jowell, 'Judicial Deference: Servility, Civility or Institutional Capacity?' [2003] PL 592; M. Hunt, 'Sovereignty's Blight: Why Contemporary Public Law Needs the Concept of "Due Deference"', in N. Bamforth and P. Leyland (eds.), *Public Law in a Multi-Layered Constitution* (Oxford: Hart, 2003); F. Klug, 'Judicial Deference under the Human Rights Act' [2003] EHRLR 125; R. Clayton, 'Judicial Deference and "Democratic Dialogue": The Legitimacy of Judicial Intervention under the Human Rights Act 1998' [2004] PL 33; K. D. Ewing, 'The Futility of the Human Rights Act' [2004] PL 829; A. Young, '*Ghaidan* v. *Godin-Mendoza*: Avoiding the Deference Trap' [2005] PL 23.

chapter, citing Lord Steyn's speech in *ex parte Daly*, 'in law context is everything'.[70]

The Human Rights Act and substantive law

The potential for domestic courts under the Human Rights Act to develop a remedy for invasions of personal privacy was one of the more controversial predicted effects of judicial reasoning under the Act.[71] Indeed, in the first substantive, 'privacy' case heard after the coming into effect of the Human Rights Act, one member of the Court of Appeal felt confident enough to assert that 'we have reached a point at which it can be said with confidence that the law recognises and will appropriately protect a right of personal privacy'.[72] The obvious contrast of this stance with the conservative approach adopted by the Court of Appeal in *Kaye* v. *Robertson*[73] appears to demonstrate an enthusiastic embrace of the Convention standards in an area in which domestic law was widely argued to be lacking. And, despite subsequent courts' less than convincing endorsements of Sedley LJ's *dicta*,[74] Gavin Phillipson argues that the effect of the HRA on the common law doctrine of breach of confidence in the *Campbell*[75] decision has been such that it can now be asserted that we have – in all but name – a tort of invasion of privacy. However, he goes on to suggest that this radical use of the Convention is in fact paradoxical: the House of Lords made vigorous use of it to develop breach of confidence into a new tort of misuse of private information, before there was even a clear Strasbourg precedent requiring such action. *Von Hannover* v. *Germany*[76] subsequently provided that precedent, but also appeared to expand the requirements of Article 8 beyond those catered for by *Campbell*. In response, Phillipson argues, the courts in subsequent cases have so far resolutely avoided recognition of this area of dissonance, let alone sought to address it – an example perhaps of both the ambivalence surrounding the importation of Strasbourg jurisprudence into the private

---

[70] R. v. *Secretary of State for the Home Department, ex parte Daly* [2001] 2 AC 532, para. 28.
[71] See e.g. Lord Irvine of Lairg's comments at HL Debs., 24 November 1997, cols. 784–6.
[72] *Douglas* v. *Hello!* [2001] QB 967, 997, *per* Sedley LJ.   [73] [1991] FSR 62.
[74] See e.g. the comments of Lord Hoffmann in *Wainwright* v. *Home Office* [2003] 3 WLR 1137, para. 30: 'I do not understand Sedley LJ to have been advocating the creation of a high-level principle of invasion of privacy. His observations are in my opinion no more (although certainly no less) than a plea for the extension and possibly renaming of the old action for breach of confidence.'
[75] [2004] 2 WLR 1232.   [76] [2004] EMLR 21.

common law, and the reluctance to revisit the decisions of superior courts in the light of subsequent Strasbourg judgments.

In the succeeding chapter, Helen Fenwick continues this assessment of the courts' ability to effectively resolve issues of competing rights. As Sir David Keene indicates in his foreword to this work, the courts are accustomed to the task of 'striking the balance between the public interest and individual rights'; the Human Rights Act changes the nature of this judicial inquiry in those cases where competing Convention rights are raised. Fenwick examines the emerging jurisprudence on conflicts of media free speech and the privacy of children, arguing that the results demonstrate the 'contradictory nature' of much judicial decision-making under the Act which can be seen to 'reveal ... a sophisticated understanding of the value of individual rights under the Convention' while simultaneously reflecting 'the determination of judges to resist the HRA where a particular strand of consequentialist thinking has become entrenched in a field of law'.[77]

Sonia Harris-Short analyses the impact of the Human Rights Act in the sphere of family law. In the context of the regulation of intimate adult relationships and public and private law disputes concerning children, this chapter explores the initial, stunted, impact of the HRA in this area of the law. Of all those examined in this part of the book, adjudication in the family law field has been marked by a judicial reluctance to engage with the Convention rights, and with rights-based reasoning more generally. Two major reasons are advanced for the minimal impact of the HRA in this field; first, a judicial and practitioner attachment to the domestic tradition which places the welfare principle and the concept of the family unit at its core, a frame-work which is felt to be threatened by the potential adoption of more 'individualistic' human rights standards.[78] Secondly, this initial reluc-tance to engage with Convention standards is compounded by the fact that family law cases frequently engage sensitive issues of public policy and resource allocation, issues which under the separation of powers are – rightly or wrongly – traditionally regarded as the domain of

---

[77] See Chapter 10, p. 304. This latter point is also drawn out by the analyses of Sonia Harris-Short and Paul Roberts in their respective chapters.

[78] Similar themes arise in Paul Robert's chapter, which also notes the judicial attachment to existing domestic standards as a potential reason for domestic courts failing to engage properly with Strasbourg.

Parliament, and not of the courts.[79] The tensions described in Part I over the correct constitutional position and role of the courts in the emerging judicial human rights discourse are again therefore apparent at the micro-level, as the decision of the House of Lords in *Bellinger* v. *Bellinger*[80] amply illustrates. But, again, the dangers of attempting to extract any themes common to specific areas of law are apparent in this analysis as, by way of contrast with the decision in *Bellinger*, the House of Lords decision in *Mendoza* – again a case involving sensitive policy concerns – nevertheless provoked a 'strong bout of judicial activism'.[81] This largely cautious approach to the HRA and the Convention rights is echoed in the case-law arising out of disputes involving children – especially those governed by private law – where it is argued that, 'whilst the poor quality of reasoning employed in these cases is disappointing, the concern of the judiciary at turning their back on the welfare approach is understandable, if essentially misplaced'.[82]

The changing nature of the judicial role is analysed further in Aaron Baker's chapter, 'Article 14 ECHR: A Protector, Not a Prosecutor'. In common with chapters before and after, Baker highlights the tensions in judicial decisions as the courts come to terms with a new anti-discrimination provision. Particular attention is given to the – incorrect – assumption that Article 14 is 'parasitic' and structural problems caused by this for the processes of reasoning in domestic discrimination cases. Further, Baker charts the courts' attempts to move towards the more victim-centred analysis required by Article 14 – an analysis which is again at odds with domestic law traditions in this field which require a focus to be placed on the reasons for a certain decision, rather than its effects.[83]

In Chapter 13, Paul Roberts analyses the presumption of innocence as a human right – an issue which has been the subject of considerable litigation in the appellate courts over recent years, and on which there appears to be very little in terms of judicial consensus. For that reason alone, Roberts argues, the concept of the presumption of innocence would be an apt case study on judicial reasoning in the post-HRA era; the issue is given further salience by the fact that, prior to the HRA, many of the points raised by appeals were considered well-settled issues of criminal procedure. Again therefore, the HRA can be seen as the

[79] See e.g. the discussion of *Bellinger* v. *Bellinger*, in Chapter 4, p. 122.
[80] [2003] 2 AC 467.   [81] Chapter 11, p. 317.   [82] *Ibid.*, p. 346.
[83] A tension paralleled in the movements towards a more intensive standard of judicial review, discussed by Ian Leigh in Chapter 7, pp. 179–91.

catalyst for a questioning of existing domestic standards previously –
and amongst some judges arguably still[84] – thought to provide satisfactory protection for 'rights'. So, Roberts argues, the interface of domestic
and European standards has brought about a 'liberating effect' on
judicial interpretation – one which extends beyond the apparent scope
of Article 6 ECHR – but argues that judicial reasoning in this sphere has
been blighted by conceptual uncertainty and a tendency towards
'results-oriented reasoning' which threatens to hamper the coherent
judicial articulation of the presumption of innocence.

From the above, it will be seen that this book ranges widely over both
procedural and substantive aspects of the HRA and its impact. We hope it
will stimulate further thought and debate on this centrally important topic.

[84] See n. 6 above.

PART I

The interpretation of the Human Rights Act 1998

2

The European Convention on Human Rights and the Human Rights Act: the view from the outside

COLIN WARBRICK[*]

Introduction

When, in the Human Rights Centre, we were first contemplating the ways in which cases under the Human Rights Act (HRA) were being (and should have been) disposed of, it was clear that we had different, in some cases, quite different, conceptions of what the HRA was about and what we could expect from UK judges in applying it. These differences were not restricted to more or less liberal views about what human rights were, or how human rights should be protected in the UK, but about whether the HRA was just another example of a domestic statute implementing the UK's treaty obligations or whether it had the capacity to go beyond the protection of a minimal/minimum understanding of human rights and fundamental freedoms as protected by the European Convention on Human Rights (ECHR) to provide some substitute for the 'missing' Bill of Rights in the British constitution.

I approach this matter as an international lawyer, and I take it that, at least, 'Bringing Rights Home'[1] meant improving UK co-operation with the ECHR system by providing a better means for resolving disputes about the meaning and application of the ECHR in the UK legal system. (I do not discuss here the matter of whether or not the HRA could or should provide more – or even different – protection than the ECHR requires, except to assert in a 'constitutional lawyer-in-pub' sort of way that, as a matter of principle, I doubt that the process for enacting the HRA was appropriate to the creation of a Bill of Rights and I am

---

* Parts of this chapter are based on the inaugurating lecture for the Durham Human Rights Centre, 'Human Rights: International, European, English', which I gave in October 2001.
[1] 'Rights Brought Home: The Human Rights Bill', Cm. 3782 (1997), paras. 1.18 and 1.19.

sure that the ECHR is not the right instrument to be a national Bill of Rights.)

The ECHR is one of the most exceptional documents in international law, and the ECHR system is one of the most singular achievements of the modern international legal system. Neither of these claims implies that the ECHR is a 'Bill of Rights' for some 'European Constitution' or that the ECHR system has supplanted national legal systems as the primary guarantor of the protection of the individual against the state. It is not only right in principle but necessary in practice that the European Court of Human Rights (ECtHR) understands the Convention system as 'subsidiary' to the national legal orders as the means for protecting the human rights and fundamental freedoms of individuals. The significance of the Convention in international law is, first, that it exists (and works) at all. It demonstrates that there is neither principled nor pragmatic objection to identifying individual rights in an international treaty or to providing an international mechanism to which individuals have access to protect those rights. We have come to regard the ECHR and the ECtHR as part of the international furniture but this should not lead us to underestimate the revolutionary nature of the Convention project when it was conceived. Its success has been hard won and there are very limited comparators to the Convention system which have emerged to emulate its manifest achievements. Even the European states themselves have seemed surprised about what they have done and have been resistant to copying the Convention system into other areas of their activities. One can contrast the much more limited nature of the rights and protective regime of the European Social Charter with that of the Convention.[2] One must not be too complacent. The ECHR is not an overly ambitious document in its substance. Expansion of the rights it protects has been limited. The middle period of the Convention system's life, from the late 1960s to the late 1980s, when it matured and consolidated itself, played out against a period of economic well-being and political stability in the western European states which allowed for the relatively easy accommodation by states to adverse judgments of the Court. Nonetheless, by the 1980s, it had become a commonplace event for an individual, dissatisfied with the

[2] See D. Harris and J. Darcy, *The European Social Charter* (2nd edn, Ardsley, NY: Transnational Publishers, 2001); and R. Churchill and U. Khaliq, 'The Collective Complaints System of the European Social Charter: An Effective Mechanism for Ensuring Compliance with Economic and Social Rights?' (2004) 15 EJIL 417.

enjoyment of his rights in his national legal system, to 'take his case to Strasbourg', where, if successful, he would obtain a judgment, binding in international law against his state. With the notable (and extensive) exception of the reaction of Italy to judgments finding breaches of the 'reasonable time' standard in the fair trial guarantee in Article 6,[3] the record of compliance by states with judgments against them was pretty good, grudging perhaps, the most minimal possible sometimes, but no outraged obduracy to doing what the judgment required. The successful individual litigant depended on the response of states to judgments of the Court. His victory had been won in the international legal system and there was seldom any automatic transformation of this right to redress and satisfaction in international law into an equivalent right in the national legal system, there directly enforceable.[4]

The development of the Convention system

Since then, the pressures on the Convention system have increased, partly simply because the number of states parties to the Convention has increased. There have been other factors.[5] The Council of Europe system, let alone the Convention system, has had to accommodate a substantial expansion of its membership since 1989 of states which were 'rejoining' Europe or joining for the first time, and whose immediately previous political traditions were not the democratic, rule-of-law, human-rights-respecting ones of those states which had previously signed up to the Convention. There were bound to be new problems, some of a structural nature, of the transition. Further, the long-running security problems of Turkey with respect to the control of its Kurdish areas confronted the Court with a task of a different order to any it had previously faced, a task more like those the drafters of the Convention had expected their new regime to have to deal with. The Turkish cases show the deficiencies of the Convention system in dealing with the structural failings of a state to protect human rights, particularly when confronted with defects which result from positive state policy and

---

[3] For the latest of a series of Committee of Ministers resolutions on this matter, see CM 190a (2005).

[4] See 'Ensuring the Effectiveness of the Implementation of the European Convention on Human Rights at National and European Levels, CM Declaration', 12 May 2004.

[5] Lord Woolf, 'Review of the Working Methods of the European Court of Human Rights' (2005), pp. 7–8, and Chart 1, giving an indication of the increase in the workload of the ECtHR and the growing backlog of cases, despite the reforms so far introduced.

which the state finds itself obliged to defend (rather than the interstitial failings to which states could accommodate, which were the typical cases before the Court). To the situation in Turkey, we can now add the ongoing conflict in Chechnya.[6] It is far from clear that the mechanism of individual application is, or is alone, the way to meet situations involving patterns of human rights violations. In the most serious cases, there is scope for the development of the 'collective guarantee', that is, of the political commitment of the Council of Europe states to seek a resolution which abates the fundamental cause of the discontent, and not one which merely provides an individual remedy for those people able to utilise the Strasbourg machinery.[7] Nonetheless, these cases are important to establish the reality of state policy and as an indication of the magnitude of the violations. Although the ECtHR may not have it within its sole power to terminate the breaches of the Convention, its role is significant and is a further reason why it should be spared so far as possible cases which are capable of resolution within national legal systems.

This has been a pervasive concern of the institutions which goes back to before 1989. The initially gradual and then huge increases in its workload have put the effectiveness of the Convention system under threat. The Court has taken some steps to modify its working practices and remedial orders to resolve persistent or widespread violations.[8] The Council of Europe states have agreed fundamental reform and have invested increased resources in the institutions. It is clear, though, that, if any serious alleviation of the Court's position is to be achieved, the national legal systems must carry more of the load.[9] However, there is a measure of insulation between the Convention system as a creature of international law and national legal systems. It should be emphasised that the Convention speaks to the state. The government is not the defendant in Strasbourg: the government is defending the state. Adverse judgments of the Court are directed to the state. In all cases where a breach is found, judgments are declarations that the state is in violation of its Convention obligations.[10] The reason for what might

---

[6] E.g. *Isayeva* v. *Russia*, ECtHR No. 57950/00 (2005).

[7] CM Resolution (2004) 3, 'Judgments Revealing a Systemic Problem'.

[8] P. Leach, 'Beyond the Bug River: A New Dawn for Redress before the European Court of Human Rights' [2005] EHRLR 148.

[9] Below, n. 18.

[10] Judgments may go further than a declaration of a violation with the award of 'just satisfaction' under Article 41. See P. Leach, *Taking a Case to the European Court of Human Rights* (2nd edn, Oxford: Oxford University Press, 2005), Chapter 9.

seem a fundamental omission from the ECHR mechanism, that its judgments are not directly effective in national law, goes to its very nature. The ECHR protects a minimum catalogue of human rights to a minimal standard – the rights and the standard representing what the states agreed in 1950 (and, where they have added to the list of rights by protocols, have agreed since then) are those required to constitute a 'European' state, in this context meaning a state able to comply with the standards for membership of the Council of Europe.

The nature of the Convention system

It was not the object of the Convention to establish a uniform set of human rights for all the party states, still less to set an optimum standard. First of all, the Convention is a treaty separate from the Statute of the Council of Europe, requiring a discrete act of ratification, as do each of the subsequent protocols; secondly, the Convention admits reservations; thirdly, many of the provisions of the Convention allow a conditional power of interference with many of the protected rights, which states may utilise differently or not at all; fourthly, Article 15 of the ECHR permits (but does not demand) states to derogate from many of their obligations in time of emergency. The result is that, even at the formal level, the actual obligations of states parties to the Convention (or, put another way, the rights of persons under the jurisdiction of each of the parties) vary considerably, depending upon what use each state has made of its various opportunities to modify its participation in and application of the Convention.[11]

In addition, the Court has used its powers to interpret the Convention in ways which sometimes reinforce these differences by interpreting rights in such a way as to leave substantive decisions to the states.[12] First, the Court has recognised that the Convention imposes obligations of result, requiring that, in the event, individuals enjoy the rights under the Convention rather than that they enjoy them through any particular arrangement in national law. An obvious example is the right to a fair trial, which is to be protected by the overall criminal procedure adopted

---

[11] For a consideration of some of these possibilities, see Y. Arai-Takahashi, *The Margin of Appreciation and the Principle of Proportionality in the Jurisprudence of the ECHR* (Antwerp: Intersentia, 2002), especially Part III, 'Assessment'.

[12] E.g. *Vo* v. *France*, ECtHR No. 53924/00 (2004); (2005) 40 EHRR 12 (status of the foetus); *Pretty* v. *UK*, ECtHR No. 2346/02 (2002); (2002) 35 EHRR 1 (euthanasia).

by a state, not that states are obliged to use, say, an inquisitorial process for criminal trials as the means to the end of fair trials.[13] Secondly, when assessing the application of the Convention, the Court accords to parties a 'margin of appreciation', in a limited way to determine what the rights mean but, in a much more significant way, to decide what measures of interference with or derogation from Convention rights is needed in the circumstances in which each state finds itself. This approach to the review of powers leads to the heterogeneous enjoyment of rights from one state to another and demonstrates most obviously that the Convention is not directed to creating a uniform human rights regime for all the European states.[14] In the ordinary case, the Strasbourg judgment cannot be directly effective,[15] but, even if it could, it may require consideration of wider consequential changes, which do not fall within the powers of courts to provide.[16]

The margin of appreciation is the most prominent of several strands of a conception the Court has of its role in the protection of human rights as 'subsidiary' to the part to be played by national institutions. First, the Convention, as an international treaty, is directed to states, not to any particular organ within the state. It is for each of the national institutions to take whatever action is within their constitutional powers to secure the end of the protection of Convention rights as set out in the Convention, as interpreted by the ECtHR.[17] Many of the judgments allow a state a margin within which it must respond. The reaction often requires consultation with interested parties, the assessment of information which emerges and the exercise of political judgment which is a feature of all legislative action. The ECtHR has wisely conceded that these are functions better carried out by national bodies. There are, in

---

[13] See S. Trechsel, *Human Rights in Criminal Proceedings* (Oxford: Oxford University Press, 2005), pp. 81–94 and 291–326.

[14] See Arai, above n. 11; and P. Mahoney, 'Marvellous Richness of Diversity or Invidious Cultural Relativism' (1998) 19 HRLJ 1.

[15] *R. v. Lyons* [2002] UKHL 44.

[16] A good example is *Goodwin v. UK*, ECtHR No. 28957/95 (2002); (2002) 35 EHRR 18, where the findings in the applicant's favour in Strasbourg could not easily have been turned into a self-executing judgment. See *Bellinger v. Bellinger* [2003] UKHL 21. A new regime was introduced by the Gender Recognition Act 2004, which dealt with some of the consequences of the Strasbourg judgment, as well as the matters decided in the particular case.

[17] This might arise where the response requires some kind of 'scheme' or regime which can be done only by the legislature (occasionally by the executive) (see above n. 12) or where the Strasbourg obligation demands the criminalisation of conduct, again a matter very likely to lie exclusively within the province of the legislature (e.g. *X and Y v. Netherlands*, ECtHR A/91, No. 8978/80; (1986) 8 EHRR 235).

addition, functional reasons why decisions are better taken by national institutions. The Strasbourg Court simply cannot be the court of last resort to decide what is 'in the best interests of the child' or whether there is a real risk of ill-treatment if a person is removed from the jurisdiction of a Convention party. A Strasbourg judgment is (usually) a single decision in favour of a single applicant. Even if this judgment were executed by the national courts, it would have no effect on others in like case, whereas a national judgment in many cases would have an *in rem* reach and offer a solution for other victims and protection to future victims. All these considerations lead to the idea of 'subsidiariness', that the Strasbourg Court simply does not have the capacity (even if it had the expertise) to act as a court of last resort for all the European states, taking appeals, as well as review, bailing out the state which wanted to pass on the responsibility for what it could see would be an expensive or unpopular result to the ECtHR and so on. Nonetheless, the ECtHR has not abdicated from its ultimate responsibility – the exercise of the margin of appreciation is subject to supervision by the Court to ensure that the state authorities have remained within the limits of their discretion, in particular that any measures which interfere with the enjoyment of human rights are proportionate to the protection of whichever public interest they are aimed at.

The Convention system under pressure

The limits of the capacity of the institutions of the Convention system became apparent as participation in the Convention increased during the 1970s (including a wider acceptance of the right of individual application, then an optional undertaking for a party state). The potential number of applicants increased dramatically at a time when the Court was showing greater confidence and imagination in its approach to the interpretation of the Convention, creating an ever-widening spiral of demand for its services.

The expansion in the participation of states in the Convention system in the 1980s was a continuation of what one might call its 'original condition' (that its to say, one in which the members largely had a vigorous tradition of democracy, the rule of law and the protection of human rights). The next stage was different. Radical change followed the end of the Cold War. As those European states recently under the hegemony of the USSR gained their *de facto* independence, they, with different degrees of enthusiasm and expedition, sought to re-engage with 'Europe' and to become again members of this society of states with which they had previously been identified. For many, the ultimate object was to become a member of the European Union. A step along the way was to join the Council of Europe. By this time, all the members of the Council of Europe were parties to the ECHR and all accepted the optional procedural obligations of individual application and the jurisdiction of the Court. An undertaking to do the same was required of all new entrants to the Council, though it was appreciated that establishing a flourishing domestic regime for the protection of human rights in these states would require substantial commitments. The expansion began in parallel with procedural reform of the Convention system, eventually formalised in Protocol No. 11 and which became the version of the Convention system to which subsequent newcomers would accede. The reforms of Protocol No. 11 were designed to meet the increasing backlog of cases at Strasbourg. While the changes resulted in quite remarkable increases in the productivity of the institutions, even so, the new system could not keep up. Further reform was instituted by Protocol No. 14,[18] not without some reservations from human rights groups,[19] and, recently, Lord Woolf has presented a report from an expert group suggesting further procedural innovations.[20] All those who have examined the problem are agreed that an essential ingredient in any reform is that the national legal systems must take a greater share of the load, that the subsidiary nature of the Convention system must be taken seriously. In particular, this approach puts weight on the states' obligations to strive consciously to make their laws and regulations compatible with the Convention and to have in place effective systems of national remedies to dispose of arguable claims that individuals' rights have been violated. This puts proper emphasis on the remedial obligations of states under the Convention, obligations more far-reaching than they might appear at first glance. In express terms, there are the duties to provide remedies to contest the legality of detention under Article 5 and to provide systems of fair trial in civil and criminal cases in Article 6. However, practically every interference with a protected right made, say, under Article 8(2) and comparable powers will require the

---

[18] M. Eaton and J. Schokkenbroek, 'Reforming the Human Rights Protection System Established by the European Convention on Human Rights' (2005) 26 HRLJ 1.

[19] Joint Committee on Human Rights, 'Protocol No. 14 to the European Convention on Human Rights' (2004) HL8/HC106.

[20] Woolf, above n. 5.

provision of a domestic procedure in order to keep the use of the power within its proper limits as an ingredient of the proportionality of the interference. Then, both overlapping with these other duties and as a fall-back provision, Article 13 creates an individual right to an effective national remedy.[21]

The Convention itself tries to institutionalise the co-operative link between the Convention system and the national legal orders. The right to remedies in national law is a prominent element in the way the protection of individuals is accomplished, with Article 13 as a catch-all requirement where the Convention does not require or allow another standard of remedy to apply. Individuals are required to exhaust these domestic remedies where they are available as a condition for admissibility of any claim in Strasbourg, an obligation which the Court has construed strictly.[22] In this way, it was anticipated, only cases the consideration of which by the ECtHR was necessary would reach it. The more adventurous interpretative approach of the Court has, it is true, pulled in the opposite direction. If the Convention is a 'living instrument',[23] an aggrieved complainant will often want the chance to argue that circumstances have changed to make what is a clearly insufficient case into at least an 'arguable' one. The necessity for cases to go to Strasbourg to resolve this kind of claim will be reduced if the national authorities keep their obligations under the ECHR under review.[24]

The fact that states with constitutions which seek to protect the rule of law will routinely be equipped with systems of adequate national remedies capable of giving proper consideration to ECHR claims should not disguise the centrality of the fact that these are obligations necessary to the working of the Convention enterprise – only if these remedies are pervasive, accessible, effective and, above all, responsive to individual judgments and the developing Strasbourg jurisprudence, will a tolerably efficacious Convention system be possible. Good systems of national remedies are those which reduce to a minimum the cases which need to

---

[21] Obligations to provide remedies are positive obligations, obligations requiring the state to act, to provide institutions and the resources for their operation. Such duties are neither simple nor cheap to discharge. They are indubitably civil and political rights but they do not correspond to the orthodox model of the easily satisfiable 'negative' obligation of traditional theory.

[22] ECHR, Article 35; *Akdivar* v. *Turkey*, ECtHR No. 21893/93 (1996); (1997) 23 EHRR 143.

[23] E.g. *Selmouni* v. *France* (1999) ECtHR No. 25803/94; (2000) 29 EHRR 403 (understanding of 'torture'); *Goodwin* v. *UK*, ECtHR No. 28957/95 (2002); (2002) 35 EHRR 18 (understanding of rights of transsexuals).

[24] Cf. *Goodwin*, above n. 23, paras. 89–93.

go to Strasbourg and which constantly renew their role by incorporating new elements in the Court's case-law into their own practice. In *Ullah*, Lord Bingham said:

> The duty of national courts is to keep pace with the Strasbourg jurisprudence as it evolves over time: no more, but certainly no less.[25]

The UK and co-operation in the fulfilment of international obligations

The obligation of co-operation was, of course, an obligation of the UK before the HRA was enacted, but the uncertainty about the powers of national courts to use the ECHR and serious limits about remedial measures against government diminished the effectiveness of UK co-operation with the ECHR system.[26] It was to give better effect to that duty than was provided by the previous crude and unpredictable arrangements that the HRA was enacted. Some of its supporters might have held pretensions for it beyond this confined objective[27] but, in Convention terms, it was a big contribution to the system as a whole. Of course, and in keeping with the decentralised way in which states identify and give effect to their Convention duties, the HRA stops short of being the *most* effective measure that could be imagined. Priority was given to preserving the fundamental principle of Parliamentary sovereignty by leaving to Parliament the recasting, if it chose, of legislation, which, even on the most generous approach, could not be read in a Convention-compatible way.[28] The courts were obliged to take the Convention jurisprudence 'into account' when interpreting 'Convention rights', those rights in the ECHR given effect in UK law by the HRA, rather than being bound by judgments of the ECtHR.[29] There was no provision making Strasbourg judgments domestically self-executing. But, read from the perspective of an international lawyer, the HRA does all the UK is obliged to do[30] – it provides for the better

---

[25] R. (Ullah) v. Special Adjudicator [2004] UKHL 26, para. 20.

[26] See M. Hunt, Using Human Rights Law in the English Courts (Oxford: Hart Publishing, 1997), especially Chapters 5 and 8.

[27] M. Hunt, 'The "Horizontal Effect" of the Human Rights Act' [1998] PL 423, 435–42.

[28] HRA, s.10.

[29] HRA, s.2; see Roger Masterman, Chapter 3 in this volume.

[30] See Ireland v. UK, ECtHR A/25 (1978); (1979–80) 2 EHRR 25, para. 239 (no obligation to make the Convention part of national law).

implementation of the UK's obligations, including its obligation under Article 13 (though that is not a Convention right in the terms of the HRA), both as an end in itself (quicker, cheaper, simpler relief for victims of human rights violations) and as a means to giving effect to the general principle of co-operation between national and European systems, in the interests of both.[31] It will be important, though, that Parliament plays its part, either by new primary legislation or by using the facility provided in s.10 HRA to respond to findings of incompatibility by national courts[32] or to adverse judgments of the ECtHR.[33]

The UK courts have over the years worked out an increasingly internationalist attitude to the interpretation of legislation designed to give domestic effect to international treaties – the law of international co-operation depends upon it.[34] Arguably, the language of the HRA – to interpret 'so far as possible'[35] the statutory language compatibly with Convention rights – goes further than the tests so far relied upon but not by much. In *The Eschersheim*, Lord Diplock said that the task of the courts was to interpret the treaty in accordance with the methods of international law and to lay the meaning which emerged against the meaning of the implementing statute interpreted according to the methods of domestic law. If the latter was 'reasonably capable' of being given the meaning which was attributed to the former, then so the court should interpret the statute.[36] Where it does go much further is in imposing this interpretative duty on the courts with respect to *all* legislation, not just the HRA itself. This is not to say that the role of the UK courts would be a mechanical one, merely looking up the Strasbourg case-law and seeing if the challenged domestic act were compatible with it. The Strasbourg case-law itself needs interpretation.[37] Where there is

---

[31] Describing the discharge of the co-operation obligation thus far in 2002, the Lord Chancellor referred to action by the courts and by Parliament, and reminded the executive of its consequent responsibilities: Lord Irvine of Lairg, 'The Impact of the Human Rights Act: Parliament, the Courts and the Executive' [2003] PL 308, 323–4.

[32] As it did respond to the judgment of the House of Lords in *A* (see below n. 38) with the Prevention of Terrorism Act 2005.

[33] As it did to the judgment of the ECtHR in *Goodwin* with the Gender Recognition Act 2004: see above, n. 16.

[34] R. Gardiner, *International Law* (London: Longman, 2003), pp. 138–61.

[35] HRA, s.3(1).   [36] [1976] 1 All ER 920, 924.

[37] The question of the extra-territorial reach of the ECHR is proving particularly troublesome: see *R (Al-Skeini)* v. *Secretary of State for Defence* [2005] EWCA Civ 1609 (in which the question will shortly be given further consideration by the House of Lords); and *R. (Al-Jedda)* v. *Secretary of State for Defence* [2006] EWCA Civ 327.

no jurisprudence, reference must be made to the Convention itself. In many cases, the national court will be exercising or supervising the exercise of the margin of appreciation, in deciding, for instance, whether or not there were an emergency within the terms of Article 15[38] or if a measure of interference were proportionate to the end for which the decision-maker claimed to act.[39]

Some problems of interpretation of the ECHR

The judgments of the ECtHR on what the reports call 'THE LAW' are often formulaic and brief. It is possible to discern certain 'principles' to which the Court has recourse to explain how it goes about interpreting the Convention,[40] but it cannot be pretended that these principles are always applied in consistent or transparent ways.[41] The process of interpretation is further complicated by the Court's invocation of certain persistent values which inform the Convention – the promotion of democracy, respect for the rule of law and the furtherance of the protection of human rights. Again, the precise content of these ideas is lacking, and the interrelationship between them seldom provides prescriptive guidance about the Convention meaning. These uncertainties are compounded by the infiltration of moral assertion into some judgments – for example in the decision in *Soering*.[42] One writer suggests that the Court has got the interpretative process upside down – what it should be doing is using a moral calculus to work out what rights individuals within the European jurisdictions actually do have, and then interpret the Convention accordingly, regardless of any practice to the contrary, no matter how widespread or deeply rooted.[43] So, the

---

[38] *A and Others* v. *Secretary of State for the Home Department* [2004] UKHL 56.

[39] *Evans* v. *UK*, ECtHR No. 6339/05 (2006); [2006] FCR 585, finding no breach as a result of the judgment in *Evans* v. *Amicus Healthcare* [2004] EWCA Civ 727 (deciding that a man's consent to the use of frozen fertilised eggs for IVF could be withdrawn, where the woman wished to use them).

[40] For a terse and accessible account, P. Leach, above n. 10, pp. 161–75.

[41] For example, the 'European consensus' appears to be little more than a form of words rather than as the outcome of a rigorous enquiry into the practices of the states parties (though allowing intervention by NGOs often improves the quality of the comparative information brought to the Court, e.g. *MC* v. *Bulgaria*, ECtHR No. 39272/98 (2004), intervention by Interights), and the justification for any 'proportionality' conclusion can be elusive.

[42] *Soering* v. *United Kingdom*, ECtHR A/161; (1989) 11 EHRR 439, para. 88.

[43] G. Lestas, 'The Truth in Autonomous Concepts: How to Interpret the ECHR' (2004) 15 EJIL 279, 295–305.

picture I have painted in the previous paragraphs of a national court's role in protecting Convention rights is too simple. Although the Court has cast itself as a 'subsidiary' player, it has also claimed for itself a constitutional dimension, not, I think, so much an institutional claim,[44] as an interpretative one – a claim that the object and purpose of the ECHR is the 'effective' protection of human rights and that the nature of the Convention is as a progressive instrument, to be understood in the light of changing social, economic and technical circumstances. So, to collaborate fully with the Court, national tribunals have to keep on top of developments in the Court's practice, and even anticipate how it might resolve an issue. This is necessarily the case when the Strasbourg Court has not dealt with a point.[45] There is also space for national courts to reconsider Strasbourg cases which appear 'wrong', either because they are founded on a misunderstanding of national law[46] or because they are poorly reasoned, though here a strong case would need to be made that this were the case.[47]

A particularly intractable problem arises when courts, national ones or the ECtHR, have to accommodate clashes between Convention-protected human rights.[48] This has become a more frequent occurrence as the ECtHR has expanded the 'horizontal' reach of Convention obligations to put on states the duty to provide rights and remedies (and, sometimes, preventative protection) against the interference with the enjoyment of a person's rights under the Convention by another non-state actor. These incompatibilities can arise both on the face of the Convention right (the possible conflict of different conceptions of the right to respect family life for different members of the same family – a father's right to live with his children against a child's right to be protected from a violent father) and as

---

[44] Though see (President) L. Wildhaber, 'A Constitutional Future for the European Court of Human Rights?' (2002) 23 *Human Rights Law Journal* 161, pondering an institutional, constitutional role for the ECtHR, though not identifying what would be the 'constitution' of which the ECtHR would be its court.

[45] *R. (Ullah)* v. *Special Adjudicator* [2004] UKHL 26. Cases like this must be distinguished from ones where the ECtHR has considered an issue and left it to the national legal systems to decide: see above n. 12.

[46] *Osman* v. *UK*, ECtHR No. 23452/94 (1998); (2000) 29 EHRR 245, on which see C. Gearty, 'Unravelling *Osman*' (2001) 64 MLR 159; followed by *Z and Others* v. *UK*, ECtHR No. 29392/95 (2001); (2002) 34 EHRR 3, reviewing *Osman* in the light of domestic case-law.

[47] E.g. *Salabiaku* v. *France*, ECtHR A/141-A (1988); (1991) 13 EHRR 379; *Saunders* v. *UK*, ECtHR No. 19187/91 (1996); (1997) 23 EHRR 313.

[48] For a more detailed analysis of these issues, see Chapters 9 and 10 below.

between different rights (an individual's right to respect for private life against a media corporation's right to freedom of expression). Until recently, the ECtHR had been respectful of the way the contest between the two claims had been resolved by the national authorities, so long as they had taken into account the substance of the two Convention arguments.[49] The recent case of *Von Hannover*[50] is a radical abandonment of this cautious approach. Here, the ECtHR was prepared to find a violation by Germany of the right to respect for the private life of the applicant in the face of intrusion by the media, which would, of course, have relied on its right to freedom of expression. Germany said that national law had decided how such conflicts should be resolved and had provided a Convention-compliant remedy for resolving claims which arose. The Court differed from the German courts about the value to be attached to the media's Article 10 rights with respect to people like the applicant, and concluded that, where the individual did not have a political or public role, 'freedom of expression calls for a narrower interpretation' – not, note, that there was no Article 10 right in play.[51] The ECtHR disagreed with the German court's characterisation of the 'public' character of the applicant's position and found that the decision to deny her a remedy did not give effective protection to her Article 8 right. It is not clear to me the calculus which the Court used (or could use) to resolve the conflict, once it was conceded that two rights were in opposition. What the judgment does do is to give a national court a peg on which to hang judgments which reject the balance struck by its legislature or even the courts themselves but without giving the national courts guidance on how these decisions are to be made. It is one thing for the European judge to say, 'I should have struck the balance between the competing rights in a different place'; it is quite another to say what is the normative explanation for this different outcome.[52]

The most sensitive (that is, from the point of view of the states) of the Court's judgments rest on the claim of 'effectiveness' where it concludes that there is a need to imply into the Convention a right not expressly provided for on the face of the ECHR. This might be a controversial power even in a national context – in the interpretation of an international treaty, it has a revolutionary aspect. It is now, though, a

---

[49] The leading case is the much criticised *Otto Preminger* v. *Austria*, ECtHR A/295-A (1994); (1995) 19 EHRR 34, which may be explained in this way, even if the result is unpalatable.

[50] *Von Hannover* v. *Germany*, ECtHR No. 59320/00 (2004); (2005) 40 EHRR 1.

[51] *Ibid.*, para. 66.   [52] For an explanation, see G. Phillipson, Chapter 6 in this volume.

familiar process. It begins with *Golder*.[53] The justification was necessity –
manifest in *Golder* where the applicant's Convention right to a fair trial
would have been quite worthless without the implication of a right of
access to a court. Since then, there has opened up a secondary market
in implied terms, that is, implied limitations on implied rights.[54]
Subsequent cases have not been quite so obvious as *Golder* and need
the acceptance of some premise or other in order for the argument from
effectiveness to work. This is most obvious with respect to the most
extensive examples of the implication of duties for states, those which
arise from Articles 2 and 3, on the one hand the preventative duties to
pre-empt violations,[55] on the other the investigatory and remedial
duties which arise when there is a suspicion that Article 2 or 3 might
have been breached.[56] The premise here is the distinct importance of
these rights in the Convention canon, the consequences of their violation for individuals being so severe that stringent measures of prevention and investigation to secure access to remedies are justified. A shared
characteristic of these implied duties is that they impose positive obliga
tions on states, duties requiring initiatives and resources, perhaps need-
ing institutional measures by one state organ against another. These
factors together account for the enhanced sensitivity of the role of the
Court in implying obligations for states. Courts are always conscious of
the charge of 'judicial law-making' with its implication that the courts
are exceeding their competence. Implying positive obligations is a particularly vulnerable aspect of judicial activity – 'law-making' with
expensive or intrusive consequences.[57]

The HRA and the duty of co-operation

In the light of this account of the necessary role of national institutions,
especially courts, in securing the efficacious operation of the ECHR
system in general, as well as the satisfaction of the claim in an individual

---

[53] *Golder* v. *UK*, ECtHR A/18 (1975); (1979–80) 1 EHRR 524.
[54] E.g. *Al-Adsani* v. *UK*, ECtHR No. 35763/97 (2001); (2002) 34 EHRR 11.
[55] *Osman*, above n. 46, is an example.
[56] E.g. *Kaya* v. *Turkey*, ECtHR No. 22729/93 (1998); (1999) 28 EHRR 1.
[57] For an extensive account, see A. Mowbray, *The Development of Positive Obligations
under the European Convention on Human Rights by the European Court of Human Rights*
(Oxford: Hart Publishing, 2004). Professor Mowbray generally welcomes this process,
without alluding much to the judicialisation of resource questions which is an inevitable
concomitant of the satisfaction of positive obligations.

case, it is necessary to turn to the understanding the UK courts have of 'Convention rights' in the HRA – not their content but their nature. The House of Lords and Court of Appeal have had to address this question head on recently and, in doing so, they may have resolved some ambiguities of the previous decisions.

From the external perspective, the national courts have done their bit if they provide a remedy for an individual in circumstances where the applicant would have won if the case had reached Strasbourg, always assuming that it lay within the court's competence to do so. Put the other way round, there is no obligation arising from the ECHR on a national court to provide a remedy if an application would not have succeeded before the ECtHR, for example, if the Court were to conclude that state action fell within its margin of appreciation. These generalities put in terms of the HRA mean that, if a claim brought to a UK court would fail in Strasbourg, then the applicant should have no remedy because there had been no violation of any 'Convention right' under HRA. The reverse is not true – a claim might succeed in Strasbourg but have been beyond the power of the national court to afford redress, for example, where the most that it could do would be to make a declaration of incompatibility[58] or where the courts' understanding of the application of retrospective effect to the HRA excluded the national court from granting relief to an applicant.[59] A case might fail in Strasbourg for a number of reasons. The first one is where the state successfully argues that there was no Convention right *at all* or no Convention right which binds the defendant state in this case. There are two questions here which shade into one another. The first looks to be a matter of interpretation: does 'criminal charge' in Article 6(1) cover extradition proceedings? If not, then there is *no* Convention right to an Article 6 hearing for an extradition suspect.[60] This might be called the absence of a substantive Convention right. The second looks to be a matter of formality: has the state ratified a protocol? Has it made a reservation? (These are matters which are taken care of by the HRA.[61]) Recently, the UK courts have had to address what appears to be a matter of formality as a matter of interpretation: to what extent can Convention rights

---

[58] See *A*, above n. 38.
[59] *In re McKerr* [2004] UKHL 12. Another possibility will arise if the courts were to find that the HRA had a narrower territorial reach than was required to give full effect to the UK's obligation under the Convention.
[60] *Farmakopoulos* v. *Greece*, ECmHR No. 11683/85 (1990); 64 DR 52.
[61] Section 1(4) (future ratification of protocols); ss.15 and 17 (reservations).

under the HRA be enjoyed with respect to conduct which takes its effect on the applicant outside the UK?[62]

Quark

The House of Lords dealt with this question in *Quark*,[63] where a detail of the ECHR and some recondite British colonial law came together. The House of Lords decided that a decision of a British official taken as Commissioner of South Georgia and the South Sandwich Islands (SGSSI) was taken in the exercise of authority within that Dependent Territory. It was alleged that the decision was incompatible with Article 1 of Protocol No. 1 to the ECHR, which is a 'Convention right' for the UK. Whilst the ECHR itself had been extended to SGSSI, Protocol No. 1 had not. Accordingly, the House of Lords held that there was no Convention right on which the applicant could rely under the HRA. Lord Bingham said:

> A party unable to mount a successful claim in Strasbourg can never mount a successful claim under sections 6 and 7 of the 1998 Act[64]

and he concluded that an application by Quark in Strasbourg would 'inevitably fail'. Lord Hope put the matter more narrowly:

> It is not the purpose of the 1998 Act to impose liability on a public authority where the complaint *would not be within the jurisdiction of the European Court in Strasbourg.*[65]

The distinction is between the merits of a claim (Lord Bingham) and the competence of the ECtHR to consider a case at all (Lord Hope). Lord Nicholls put it more broadly:

> The Act was intended to provide a domestic remedy where a remedy would have been available in Strasbourg. Conversely, the Act was not intended to provide a domestic remedy where a remedy would not have been available in Strasbourg.[66]

The first sentence is misleading. It does not cover the case where the domestic court is restricted to a declaration of incompatibility (unless Lord Nicholls regards that as a 'domestic remedy'), nor does it include cases where the non-retrospectivity of the HRA precludes a domestic

---

[62] *Al-Skeini*, above n. 37.
[63] *R. v. Secretary of State for Foreign and Commonwealth Affairs, ex parte Quark Fishing Limited* [2005] UKHL 57.
[64] *Ibid.*, para. 24.   [65] *Ibid.*, para. 88; and see *ibid.*, para. 92.   [66] *Ibid.*, para. 34.

remedy even though a claim might have succeeded before the ECtHR.[67] But, if we read the first sentence subject to these (slight) qualifications and in conjunction with the second sentence, we get to something like:

> The Act was intended to provide a remedy if and only if a claim at Strasbourg would have succeeded, subject to limitations (and no extensions) provided by the Act itself.

This would correspond with the international law view that the Act has the narrow and identifiable purpose of giving better effect to the UK's international obligations and to nothing else.

Al-Jedda

The Court of Appeal relied on *Quark* in *Al-Jedda*.[68] Very briefly, the case concerned the lawfulness of the detention of a person by the British authorities in Iraq. He argued the detention regime was in breach of his Convention rights under Article 5. The government, while not conceding the application of the ECHR or a decision on the merits, insisted that its action was justified by relying on Security Council Resolution 1546, a Chapter VII resolution which conferred a power on the UK (to detain people in Iraq) which took priority over its other treaty obligations because of Article 103 of the Charter. On the basis of *Quark*, Al-Jedda would have had a claim under the HRA only if a claim at Strasbourg would have succeeded, subject to the limitations in the HRA (which are not relevant here). Although the Court of Appeal had heard argument about how the case might go in Strasbourg, it did not clearly decide how it might have come out there but it did consider the question as a matter of general international law.[69] It decided that the UK would have been justified in detaining Al-Jedda in accordance with the authority under Resolution 1546, its obligations to the contrary under the ECHR (if any) notwithstanding. The Court of Appeal relied on *Al-Adsani* (which is a strong authority suggesting that the proper interpretation of the ECHR take account of its status as an instrument within the international legal order) but was not persuaded that the international law arguments applied differently to human rights treaties than they did to other international agreements.[70] Reasoned this way, the fact that the

---

[67] See above n. 58 and n. 59.

[68] *R. (Al-Jedda)* v. *Secretary of State for Defence* [2006] EWCA Civ 327.

[69] *Ibid.*, para. 87.   [70] *Ibid.*, para. 80.

Security Council resolution had no direct effect in UK law (the United Nations Act 1946 requires secondary legislation to give domestic effect to Security Council resolutions) could be side-stepped because the understanding of 'Convention right' in the HRA referred to the understanding of the denominated rights by the ECtHR (in this case, within their international legal context).[71]

So, the first level of enquiry to determine what Convention rights are is: what are Convention rights as understood by Strasbourg in the light of international law? Has the state ratified the appropriate treaty? Has the treaty been extended to the relevant overseas territory? Is a reservation valid? Is the defendant state bound by another international obligation which supersedes the Convention right? But the next question is: what does the Convention right mean as understood by Strasbourg, in the light of international law? The duty of the domestic court trying to discharge its obligation of co-operation is to try to answer the question the best it can – first by determining accurately (and unconstrained by any rules of UK law) what the applicable international law is, and then by trying to anticipate how the ECtHR would take account of the position in international law. This last is not a simple question. Although *Al-Adsani* shows a strong inclination to take international law into account, even though the result is to reduce the protected rights, this has not been so in every instance. In *Soering*, the ECtHR did not interpret Article 3 taking into account the UK's international obligations under the UK–US extradition treaty. One would hazard a pretty strong guess that the ECtHR would not interpret Article 3 of the ECHR taking into account a Convention state's obligation under Article 1 of the UN Convention Against Torture to conclude that the state's duty to criminalise acts of torture was restricted to acts of official torture. An explanation here might be that the international legal rules on clashes of treaty obligations are not well developed, whereas the rules on state immunity, at least as they applied to the facts in *Al-Adsani*, were clear, while the contrary argument relying on *ius cogens* was unconvincing.[72] Equally, the intention of the parties in drafting the UN Charter is

---

[71] Whether the Court of Appeal is right about how the ECtHR would treat Security Council resolutions can be decided by the ECtHR if the Court of Appeal judgment is confirmed by the House of Lords. Of course, if the final judgment goes the other way, the government will have no such possibility of referring the case to Strasbourg.

[72] Compare D. Lloyd-Jones, 'Article 6 and Immunities Arising in Public International Law' (2003) 52 ICLQ 463 with A. Orakhelashvili, 'State Immunity and International Public Order' (2002) 45 GYIL 227.

pretty clear – it was to create a hierarchy of obligations.[73] Nonetheless, there is nothing automatic about the outcome – quite apart from the arguments of Security Council competence (which the Court of Appeal said were not for it[74]) – the ECtHR is not bound by the UN Charter or any decisions under it but, just as in *Al-Adsani*, the UK was bound by the rule on state immunity, so here the UK is bound by Security Council Resolution 1546. One might imagine that the ECtHR would be more conscious than the Court of Appeal was of the power/duty distinction and seek the least human-rights-intrusive interpretation of Resolution 1546. The mere citing of the argument of coherence, that the ECtHR must reach a solution compatible with a state's other obligations in international law does not mean that the other obligation will prevail, as *Soering* shows.

Quark and *Al-Jedda* do point to the duty of consultation of Strasbourg authority in determining what Convention rights are and what they mean, even if not absolutely conclusively. In doing so, they provide a comprehensible method for the national courts which will ensure that they play their part in ensuring the co-operation of the UK with the ECHR system. The House of Lords has had occasion to take the same approach in cases involving positive obligations under the Convention, where opinions have been expressed by judges in lower courts and the Court of Appeal which seek to impress the idea of Convention right with a domestic imprint.

The HRA and positive obligations

I have already made it clear that positive obligations are central to the Convention scheme because the widest group of positive obligations consists of the various duties to provide remedies. The effective fulfilment of these obligations will keep cases in the national legal systems (or make it easier for the ECtHR to dismiss misconceived claims at the admissibility stage). Faithful compliance with the duties to provide remedies will be a major contribution to the discharge of the overall obligation of co-operation. Remedial obligations are sometimes express

---

[73] The judgment in *Al-Jedda* attaches considerable weight to Simma's commentary on the Charter (B. Simma (ed.), *The Charter of the United Nations: A Commentary* (2nd edn, Oxford: Oxford University Press, 2002)) for the effect of Article 103, judgment: paras. 69–70.
[74] *Al-Jedda*, above n. 68, para. 68.

and direct,[75] sometimes they are consequential,[76] increasingly in recent years they have been implied. The underlying rational in all cases is that they are necessary to secure the effective enjoyment of rights, usually (but not invariably) of Convention rights. In addition, there are substantive positive obligations on states. A major component of this group are those obligations which require the state to provide 'horizontal effect' to Convention rights, to see that individuals are protected against the activities of other private persons which have an adverse effect on the enjoyment of the interest protected by human rights.[77] Some substantive rights under the Convention require positive action by the state, notably the right to free and fair elections, less obviously but no less necessary, the right to marry.[78]

Sometimes, a positive obligation arises by way of interpretation of what looks on its face to be purely a negative duty. Such duties may be implied, for example the duty on the state to provide proper training for its security forces in the use of lethal weapons.[79] They may also be implied and consequential, that is, they arise because of some action taken by the state, for example the duty to inquire into the circumstances of deaths caused by the use of force by state agents. I now want to look at one of these implied, consequential duties to see how the English courts have dealt with this kind of claim under the HRA. The claim is that Article 3 of the ECHR – the right not to be tortured and so on – demands not only that the state abstain from action falling within its proscriptions but that, in some circumstances attributable to the state, it must act to supply resources to certain individuals because of the situation the state has created (the individual, putting it the other way, will have a right to support from the state). The claim was put in terms of a right to social support from the state, a difficult case to make. A proper analysis will reveal that the claim was not for a right to social assistance

---

[75] As in Articles 5 and 6, for instance.

[76] This means that they arise because of some action a state has taken which affects the enjoyment of a Convention right and the provision of a remedy is a necessary ingredient in securing the proportionality of that intervention: e.g. *Gaskin* v. *UK*, ECtHR A/160 (1989); (1990) 12 EHRR 36.

[77] See above n. 49.

[78] Positive obligations sometimes need schemes instead of or in addition to the expenditure of resources and, once an adequate scheme is established, the ECtHR will not regard every failure under it as a breach of the Convention. On medical treatment, see *Powell* v. *UK*, ECtHR No. 45305/99 (2000).

[79] *McCann* v. *UK*, ECtHR A/324 (1995); (1996) 21 EHRR 97, para. 156; *Nachova* v. *Bulgaria*, ECtHR (GC), No. 43577/98 (2005); (2006) 42 EHRR 43, para. 97.

under Article 3 but a right to have assistance to avoid degrading treatment resulting from state policy.

Limbuela

L was one of three applicants whose claims were taken as test cases against the application of the Home Secretary's powers under s.95 of the Asylum and Immigration Act 1999, as modified by s.55 of the Nationality, Immigration and Asylum Act 2002.[80] The provisions were part of a policy to diminish the entitlement to public assistance in the UK for asylum seekers, an entitlement which had originally been grounded in the National Assistance Act 1948. The benefits thereby provided were not high but even these were removed by a government determined on a policy of not so 'benign deterrence' of those who would seek refugee status in the UK. Section 95 provided:

> (1) The Secretary of State may provide . . . support for—
>   (a) asylum-seekers . . .
>   who appear to the Secretary of State to be destitute or to be likely
>   to become destitute within such period as may be prescribed.
>   . . .
> (3) For the purposes of this section, a person is destitute if—
>   (a) he does not have adequate accommodation or any means of
>   obtaining it (whether or not his essential living needs are met); or
>   (b) he has adequate accommodation or the means of obtaining it but
>   cannot meet his other essential living needs.

The Home Office had identified a loophole in its policy of defending the UK against 'bogus' asylum seekers. Would-be asylum-seekers did not always announce themselves at the port of entry and, the later they did so, the greater the chance that facts would have been created which made their removal more difficult, even if their claims to refugee status were eventually rejected. Section 55 of the 2002 Act was enacted to, shall we say, 'encourage' immediate declaration of an intention to apply for asylum. Failure to do so carried a formidable sanction. Section 55 reads:

> (1) The Secretary of State may not provide . . . support [under s.95 of the
>   1999 Act] to [an asylum-seeker] if . . .

---

[80] R. v. *Secretary of State for the Home Department, ex parte Limbuela* [2005] UKHL 66.

    (b) the Secretary of State is not satisfied that the claim was made
      as soon as reasonably practicable after the [asylum-seeker's]
      arrival in the [UK].
(5) This section shall not prevent—
    (a) the exercise of a power by the Secretary of State to the extent
      necessary for the purpose of avoiding a breach of an [asylum-
      seeker's] Convention rights [within the meaning of the
      Human Rights Act] . . .

The test of reasonable practicability was applied with great strictness but none of the Home Secretary's decisions on this issue were contested by the time the litigation reached its final stages. Furthermore, the Home Secretary had taken a narrow view of what was required of him under s.55(5). As the new practice began to take effect, an increasing number of people were caught by s.55(1) but were not granted any assistance under s.55(5). The number of emergency applications in the Administrative Court caused considerable disruption to its operations. The circumstances of the applicants had been dire. They had all had to spend nights sleeping on the street and had had to beg for food. Interim relief had been provided but, if there were no obligation on the Home Secretary to provide assistance, they and others like them would be returned to their state of destitution once their immediate and desperate needs had been dealt with.

It should be noted that asylum-seekers were forbidden to work in the UK and it should be emphasised that the Home Secretary was under a *duty* under s.55(1) not to provide support for asylum-seekers who delayed communication with the authorities. Section 55(5)(a), on the other hand, enabled the Home Secretary to fulfil his duty under s.6(1) HRA as a 'public authority' to act in conformity with the Convention rights of individuals within the UK's jurisdiction. Two questions then: what did any relevant Convention right require and what had the Home Secretary to do 'to avoid' a breach of that right?

I deal only with the Convention point raised by these cases and, as they were dealt with by the Court of Appeal, only with the judgment of Laws LJ. He was scathing about the technical qualities of the first-instance judgments. He said:

> We are left with a state of affairs in which our public law courts are driven
> to make decisions whose dependence on legal principle is at best fragile,
> leaving uncomfortable scope for the social and moral preconceptions of
> the individual judge.

Hardly sugaring the pill, he went on:

> (I mean no offence to the distinguished judges who have heard these
> cases); and law and fact are undistinguished. We need to see whether
> there is room for a sharper, more closely defined approach.[81]

To try to find this sharper approach, Laws LJ began by looking at the
obligations which arose under Article 3 of the ECHR. His inquiry was,
though, not so much to seek assistance from the Strasbourg case-law but
to leave his own mark on the understanding of the Convention right
under Article 3. Article 3 says:

> No one shall be subject to torture or to inhuman or degrading treatment
> or punishment.

Clearly, the central protection provided here is against exceptional
physical intervention against an individual by agents of the state: it is a
negative duty. The ECtHR has been gradually extending the reach of
Article 3.[82] Here, the applicants sought to establish that there were
circumstances when the state had some obligation to provide elementary support to persons within its jurisdiction who otherwise faced
destitution. In the only approximately relevant authority, *O'Rourke*,[83]
a claim for subsistence had been deemed inadmissible but in that case
the applicant had not taken advantage of such social assistance as was
available to him. *O'Rourke* did not decide whether or not there was a
general right to social assistance, nor did it decide that there might not
be special circumstances in which the state might be obliged to provide
assistance. In the present cases, the applicants maintained that there was
no source of support for them, from their own initiative because they
were forbidden to work, from private sources because there was effectively none available, nor from the state because the Home Office did not
regard them as falling within s.55(5).

Laws LJ drew a distinction between the deliberate infliction of violence by state agents (though he did so by collapsing the distinction
between Articles 2 and 3[84]) and the various duties beyond these negative
proscriptions, not to kill and not to torture and so on, established by the

---

[81] *Secretary of State for the Home Department* v. *Limbuela* [2004] EWCA Civ 540, para. 58.
[82] *Ireland* v. *UK*, above n. 30 (mental anguish); *Selmouni*, above n. 24, para. 101 ('increas-
      ingly high standard').
[83] *O'Rourke* v. *UK*, ECtHR No. 39022/97 (2003) (admissibility).
[84] *Limbuela* (CA), above n. 81, para. 59.

ECtHR in its cases.[85] In addition to his distinction between 'state violence' and 'other cases', Laws LJ referred to the difference between negative and positive obligations but noted that the two categories did not coincide.[86] This is undoubtedly correct – the negative duty not to return a person to a jurisdiction where there is a real risk that he will be tortured or suffer other treatment prohibited by Article 3 of the ECHR is not 'state violence' in Laws LJ's sense. Indeed, he uses D^{87} as an example. However, the remainder of his treatment of the Article 3 case-law has little to do with how it is regarded by the ECtHR. He described the various duties under Article 3 as a 'spectrum', running from unauthorised state violence against a person (absolutely forbidden) to circumstances where an individual must endure a 'marked degree of suffering' as a consequence of a state policy, which would only violate Article 3 in the somewhat elusive circumstances when the suffering

> reaches so high a degree of severity that the court is bound to limit the State's right to implement the policy on Article 3 grounds.[88]

Categories are collapsed – the duty on the state to protect against excessive private violence against persons at large is put in the same box as the duty on the state to protect those in its custody or care (whether against state violence or private injury)[89] but, although both are positive obligations, the circumstances in which they arise is different and so is their content – the state has duties to be aware of the conditions of those in its custody and must be prepared to supervise their detention in a way appropriate to any risk the authorities ought to have been aware of.[90] Laws LJ needed his distinctions because he wanted to take on the claim that Article 3 was 'absolute', a word, he said, that was 'misleading'.[91] It was, he said, not the case that Article 3 meant that

> the executive government *in no* case has any legitimate power of judgment whatever as regards the protection of individuals from suffering which is inhuman or degrading to the extent that Article 3 contemplates.[92]

---

[85] He relied on *Pretty* v. *UK* (2002) 35 EHRR 1, para. 50, for authority to limit a state's duty under Articles 2 and 3: judgment, para. 60.

[86] *Ibid.*, para. 61.

[87] *D* v. *UK*, ECtHR No. 30240/96 (1997); (1997) 24 EHRR 423; and compare *N* v. *Secretary of State for the Home Department* [2005] UKHL 31.

[88] *Limbuela* (CA), above n. 81, para. 70.   [89] *Ibid.*, para. 64.

[90] *Keenan* v. *UK*, ECtHR No. 27229/95 (1999); (1998) 26 EHRR CD64.

[91] *Limbuela* (CA), above n. 81, para. 67.   [92] *Ibid.*

An essential element in Laws LJ's analysis was that what was at stake for the Court of Appeal was to determine when a positive obligation on the authorities arose to provide support to asylum-seekers, given that their distress arose as a consequence of a legitimate policy – how to treat asylum-seekers in the context where a significant proportion of them were 'bogus'. That was wrong. The applicants were victims of state policy – neither allowed to support themselves by working nor allowed access to public assistance. Causing great distress (as it was agreed must ultimately have been the case in some instances) might not have fitted 'State violence' in Laws LJ's characterisation. However, the ECtHR has included denial of certain material necessities as elements in conditions amounting to inhuman treatment by sensory deprivation.[93] Laws LJ was prepared to concede in *Limbuela* that 'the State is *in part* the author of the asylum-seeker's misfortunes'![94] In reality, the state was entirely responsible for the predicament of the applicants – if it had done nothing, at least they would have been entitled to work. From a Convention perspective, the real vice with Laws LJ's reasoning is that it runs together the identification of the content of a duty with the issue of whether the non-performance of a duty can be excused or justified. The ECtHR has been consistent and vehement that breaches of duties under Article 3 may not be defended on the basis that the interferences were necessary for some public good. Of course, the British government takes a different view, at least where the complaint is of the removal of persons to states where there is a real risk of ill-treatment. *Chahal*[95] has established that the negative duty not to do so cannot be overcome by reference to the characteristics of the applicant or the threat to security in the expelling state. The British government will challenge this position (and the long list of cases in which *Chahal* has been followed) when it intervenes in *Ramzy* v. *Netherlands*,[96] but, for the present at least, the 'absolute' dispensation prevails. However, *if* it is established that a particular degree of deprivation of the necessities of life would violate Article 3, and the state has created a real risk that that state of affairs will arise for a particular individual, the state may not justify creating those conditions on the basis that it is a necessary consequence of its asylum

---

[93] *Ireland* v. *UK*, above n. 30, para. 167; *McGlinchey* v. *UK*, ECtHR No. 50390/99 (2003); (2003) 37 EHRR 41, paras. 46 and 57.
[94] *Limbuela* (CA), above n. 81, para. 74 (emphasis added).
[95] *Chahal* v. *UK*, ECtHR No. 22414/93 (1996); (1997) 23 EHRR 413.
[96] *Ramzy* v. *Netherlands*, No. 25424/05.

policy, such that only truly exceptional hardship would qualify for relief, that is to say, more severe suffering than adventitiously caused harm which would breach Article 3. This seems to be the object of Laws LJ's analysis – to set a much higher threshold for when destitution would involve a breach of the Convention. He suggested that:

> acts or omissions of the State which expose persons to suffering other than violence . . . even suffering which may in some instances be as grave from the victim's point of view as acts of violence which would breach Article 3 are not categorically unjustifiable.[97]

Laws LJ was seeking a clear line to provide guidance to the Home Office about its obligations and so avoiding for officials the need to make fact-based decisions which every disappointed applicant would then bring to the courts, but, in finding his line, he was driven to a standard of extreme hardship – extreme, that is, in the context of some, apparently justifiable destitution. His reference to the original intentions of the drafters of the Convention is resonant of Judge Fitzmaurice's narrow conception of the purpose of Article 3 in the *Tyrer*[98] case, an attitude long-since abandoned by the ECtHR.[99] His reliance on *O'Rourke*, though he was conscious of its limitations, does not help. It is true that Article 3 cannot be read to provide a general obligation of social assistance, particularly at any reasonable level of support, just as the Convention cannot be read to provide a right to housing or a job, but that was not the issue here. The applicants were victims of state action and there is nothing in substance to distinguish late-reporting asylum-seekers from those for whom the state certainly does have duties of support and protection, those in its custody, where the Convention does set minimum standards, even if they are not very high.[100]

When the case reached the House of Lords, the judges first set right the characterisation of the wrong of which the applicants complained – they recognised that the applicants were arguing that the state had created a risk that their Article 3 rights would be (in each of their cases, later actually had been) violated by the creation of circumstances which condemned them to conditions of life incompatible with Article 3. It was not an assertion that Article 3 created a general positive

---

[97] *Limbuela* (CA), above n. 81, para. 68.
[98] *Tyrer* v. *UK*, ECtHR A/26 (1978); (1979–80) 2 EHRR 1.
[99] See *Selmouni*, above n. 23.
[100] E.g. *Kalashnikov* v. *Russia*, ECtHR No. 47095/99 (2002); (2003) 36 EHRR 34.

obligation to provide assistance but that, where a person's predicament was a result of state action, however otherwise justifiable it was to take that action, the state could not use it to excuse a breach of Article 3.[101] For instance, the state will be justified in detaining certain people but their conditions of detention must satisfy Article 3 standards, so a severe medical condition does not necessarily require a person properly detained to be released[102] but that they receive adequate treatment.[103] Even more clear is the case where the state actually creates the conditions of custody which violate Article 3, such as overcrowding or isolation.[104] Lord Hope and Baroness Hale distanced themselves from Laws LJ's 'spectrum' analysis, expressly noting that it found no basis in the case-law of the ECtHR.[105]

Lord Bingham said that the duty not to treat a person in violation of Article 3 was 'absolute', admitting no space for arguments about the proportionality of the state action, measuring it against some public interest the state intended to pursue. So what is this minimum standard of conditions of life which Article 3 requires the state not to inflict on an individual? Lord Bingham went on:

> I have no doubt that the threshold may be crossed if a late applicant with no means and no alternative means to support himself is, *by the deliberate action of the State*, denied shelter, food or the most basic necessities of life.[106]

The Law Lords all had difficulty in getting beyond this, instead resorting to examples of the kind of conditions they thought would be comprehended by Lord Bingham's test. On the face of it the mere fact of denial or withdrawal of support would not amount to a violation – the applicant might find himself the fortunate recipient of charitable or community assistance (which the Home Office's evidence seemed to suggest was available in profusion if only the applicants would seek it out – Shelter, intervening, pointed out that the reality was considerably less comforting[107]). Equally, of course, the Home Secretary had to know about an applicant's circumstances. The government's argument seemed to be that only where applicants were reduced to prostitution or begging would their straits be

---

[101] *Limbuela* (HL), above n. 81, *per* Lord Hope, para. 47.
[102] *Mousiel* v. *France*, ECtHR No. 67263/01 (2002).
[103] *Price* v. *UK*, ECtHR No. 33394/96 (2001); (2002) 34 EHRR 53.
[104] E.g. *Peers* v. *Greece*, ECtHR No. 28524/95 (2001); (2001) 33 EHRR 51.
[105] *Limbuela* (HL), above n. 81, paras. 53 and 77.
[106] *Ibid.*, para. 7 (emphasis added).   [107] *Ibid.*, para. 35, *per* Lord Hope.

sufficiently dire to warrant help[108] – in particular, mere 'rough sleeping' would not be enough. There were some unfortunate remarks along the way from Lord Scott[109] and Baroness Hale[110] about this last contention, but eventually all seemed to accept that living on the streets created such humiliation and danger, especially for women, that the threshold of Article 3 would be passed – if the applicant found himself in a condition of 'rooflessness and cashlessness'.[111] Lord Scott said:

> information that a particular asylum seeker was having to sleep out of doors would be a very strong indication that the threshold had been reached.[112]

Most important was Lord Brown's conclusion that the *intention* to create street homeless without resources would be enough[113] – perhaps better would have been, as a 'foreseeable consequence' of state action, rather than 'intention'. This goes back to the precise formulation of the Home Secretary's obligation in s.55(5) – it is 'for the purpose of avoiding' a breach of an applicant's Convention rights. Of course, the ECHR may impose the self-same duty – it is a distinctive part of the Article 2 and Article 3 case-law that states have positive duties to prevent violations of individuals' rights. The *Soering* principle is one example (though by no means the only one – recent environmental cases have relied on this kind of duty[114]). This kind of duty involves a risk assessment that the prohibited conditions might occur; the actual realisation of the risk would be an independent violation (and not necessarily conclusive evidence that the risk had been sufficiently severe[115]). Section 55(5) might be doing no more than Article 3 demands – to have a system for pre-empting the creation by action by the state which 'risks' the infliction of conditions which would violate Article 3. 'Risks' is in inverted commas because the precise quality of the risk assessment test is

---

[108] *Ibid.*, para. 59.   [109] *Ibid.*, para. 71.   [110] *Ibid.*, para. 78.

[111] *Ibid.*, para. 71, *per* Lord Scott, pointing to the open-endedness of the conditions of destitution faced by the applicants; *ibid.*, para. 78, *per* Baroness Hale; and *ibid.*, para. 102, *per* Lord Brown ('imminent street homelessness').

[112] *Ibid.*, para. 72. Lord Scott added that the indefinite prospect of enduring sleeping out of doors was a factor contributing to its unacceptability: *ibid.*, para. 71.

[113] *Ibid.*, para. 101, *per* Lord Brown.

[114] *Fadeyeva* v. *Russia*, ECtHR No. 55723/00 (2005); *Taskin* v. *Turkey*, ECtHR No. 46117/99 (2005).

[115] Cf. *Vilvarajah* v. *UK*, ECtHR A/215 (1991); (1992) 14 EHRR 248, where the ECtHR held that there was no evidence of a sufficiently serious risk of torture if applicants were returned to Sri Lanka. They were returned and some of them were tortured but, of itself, this was not evidence that the Court (or the British authorities) had miscalculated the risk.

elusive – clearly, the requirement of certainty would emasculate the duty
and equally the existence of a possibility would impose too strict an
obligation. The Court has used the 'substantial evidence' of a 'real risk'
of Article 3 treatment in removal cases and it seems to me to be perfectly
adaptable to 'internal' cases, once the Court has determined that there is
a preventative duty on the state. The judges in the House of Lords
recognised that the condition of persons denied assistance would dete-
riorate over time but thought that some degree of imminence of the
Article 3 conditions would be needed before the ECHR would require
the Home Secretary to intervene. Lord Brown's position, though it is not
quite put in these terms, should have been enough to condemn the
Home Office policy – it was foreseeable (there was a real risk) that
persons denied the right to work and the right to public assistance
would be driven to a roofless and cashless existence, in the absence of
any benevolent intervention by private sources. To allow the policy to
survive so that, for a short time, all applicants could explore (and
exhaust) the possibilities of charity, is, given the paucity of resources
from these sources of aid, quite insufficient reason to allow it to prevail –
even with what little charity there is out there, there is still a 'real risk'
that an individual will face destitution of a kind which would surpass the
Article 3 threshold. Just as the actual infliction of torture does not
necessarily show that there was a real risk that it would happen, so the
actual obtaining of, say, private assistance at some later date does not
necessarily show that there was not a real risk of 'Article 3 destitution' at
an earlier stage. Nothing can put right the subsequent torture but public
assistance can always be stopped if it were shown that there is no need
for it at some later date. The 'bright line' does not need to be desperate
destitution, nor should it depend on special vulnerability of the applicant. The degradation attached to living on the street without any means
of support because of decisions by the state provides a bright enough
line for responsive state officials and for the policing of any contested,
marginal cases by the courts. The Strasbourg duty of co-operation
requires the enlistment of all the organs of the state for its effective
discharge. *Limbuela* shows how it can be done in hard cases.

Conclusion

The House of Lords judgment seems to me to be a good example of the
co-operation which is necessary from state organs to give the Convention
system a future, despite all the demands upon it. The analysis of the

national law practice in terms of the multiple duties in Article 3 is correct; the 2002 Act itself, or the House of Lords interpretation of it, addresses the matter of preventative obligations. In interpreting what Article 3 requires, the judges look at the developing case-law of the ECtHR and, in particular, put the unhelpful language in *O'Rourke* to one side after looking carefully at its facts. They reaffirm the absolute nature of the Article 3 obligation, so firmly insisted upon by the ECtHR (and, in the present atmosphere, an essential bulwark against the march of counter-terrorism policies). The House of Lords could not simply apply the jurisprudence of the ECtHR, because it was incomplete, given the questions which had to be answered but it did, as s.2 of the Human Rights Act requires, 'take into account' the case-law, in a way which even an international lawyer can appreciate.

Looking from the outside, the role of UK courts under the HRA is to take note of the formal and substantive aspects of 'Convention rights'. The first consideration will not arise frequently – though as *A, Quark, Al-Jedda, Al-Skeini* and *B*[116] show, whether there is a Convention right in this sense arises more often than one might have anticipated. In resolving the formal question (which the House of Lords did in *Quark*), the courts have given a clear indication of how the substantive question should be answered – the national courts should seek out as best it can the 'Strasbourg' meaning (this is what *Limbuela* did). As Roger Masterman's chapter shows at a general level, and most of the other chapters about the HRA show for their specific concerns, this is not a mechanical task and, whatever the quality of the Strasbourg decisions, it cannot be made so. The Article 13 cases show what is required – the domestic courts must give proper consideration to the substance of the Convention argument. In doing so, they not only satisfy Article 13 but reduce the need for cases to go to the ECtHR and give the European Court a reasoned explanation of why the case came out as it did. Especially where the cases concern the exercise of the margin of appreciation, if the national courts do this well, Strasbourg has the chance to deal more easily with these applications than if it has to construct the legal arguments for itself. All this helps the state to discharge its general duty of co-operation.

But should the national judges go further? From the outside, there is no reason why they should – and no reason why they should not.[117] If the

---

[116] *R. (B)* v. *Foreign Secretary* [2004] EWCA Civ 1344.

[117] Article 53 provides: 'Nothing in this Convention shall be construed as limiting or derogating from any of the human rights or fundamental freedoms which may be

national courts use the Human Rights Act as though it were 'like' a Bill of Rights and move beyond what the Convention requires or allows, then they cut themselves free of all restraints. The Convention does have an objective meaning in the same way that a constitutional Bill of Rights has an objective meaning, but moving away from the Convention meaning of 'Convention rights' would be a step not justified by the HRA. The obligation of judicial reasoning for the English courts is to show that they have given faithful effect to the UK's obligations under the Convention – in the UK's interest and in the interest of the Convention system.

ensured under the laws of any High Contracting Party or under any agreement to which it is a party.'

3

Aspiration or foundation? The status of the Strasbourg jurisprudence and the 'Convention rights' in domestic law

ROGER MASTERMAN*

Introduction

In *A Bill of Rights for Britain*, Ronald Dworkin advocated the incorporation of the European Convention on Human Rights into domestic law to halt the 'decline in the culture of liberty'[1] that had affected freedom in the UK since the 1970s. He rejected the idea of adopting a newly drafted domestic instrument on the ground that – with the Convention still enforceable at Strasbourg – 'potential conflict between the two fundamental charters of rights would be a source of wasteful confusion'.[2] That the incorporated Convention could be as powerful an instrument as such a Bill of Rights was not, however, in doubt:

> Incorporation would put the special skills of British lawyers and judges, and the heritage of British legal principle, at the service of the civilised world. Britain could become once again a leader in defining and protecting individual freedom, instead of a sullen defendant giving ground to liberty only when ordered to do so by a foreign court.[3]

Dworkin saw that, in the hands of the domestic judiciary, the framework provided by the Convention might be crafted to form a 'distinctly British scheme of human rights and liberty',[4] and that specifically:

---

* This chapter was originally presented as a paper at the Judicial Reasoning and the Human Rights Act 1998 Symposium, held at Durham Castle on 8–9 April 2005. My thanks are due to the participants – particularly Aidan O'Neill QC for chairing the session – and to Helen Fenwick and Colin Warbrick for their comments on an earlier draft.
[1] R. Dworkin, *A Bill of Rights for Britain* (London: Chatto and Windus, 1990), p. 1.
[2] *Ibid.*, pp. 24–5. [3] *Ibid.*, p. 22. [4] *Ibid.*, p. 23.

> British judges could certainly adopt ... a more generous interpretation, using the rich and special traditions of the British common law to develop out of the Convention a particularly British view of the fundamental rights of citizens in a democratic society.[5]

That such an outcome might be achieved via the incorporation of the ECHR is at least arguable on the ground that the Convention is not to be seen as a mere aspiration for domestic authorities, but as a foundation on which to build; as Grosz, Beatson and Duffy have commented on the expectations of the Strasbourg organs:

> there is no imperative that parties to the Convention should adopt a uniform approach, only that they should not fall below an irreducible minimum, which will be monitored by the Strasbourg institutions. It is therefore open to national courts to develop a domestic jurisprudence under the Convention which may be more generous to applicants than that dispensed in Strasbourg, while remaining broadly consistent with it.[6]

It is clear that, for effect to be given to 'a more generous interpretation' than that provided by the Strasbourg institutions, domestic courts should not be bound to follow or apply the case-law of those bodies; this is reflected in the flexible obligation to 'take into account' that jurisprudence imposed by s.2(1) of the Human Rights Act. And, while the approach to s.2(1) HRA adopted by the House of Lords – which declares that 'clear and constant' Strasbourg jurisprudence should be followed – also recognises that *states* might provide for a more generous protection than Strasbourg, it does so under the proviso that 'such provision should not be a product of interpretation by national *courts*'.[7] This interpretation of the role of the domestic court *vis-à-vis* the European Court of Human Rights ensures that – in the absence of action taken by the domestic legislative or executive branches – the Strasbourg Court, rather than domestic courts, will continue to define the scope of the domesticated versions of the 'Convention rights', a role which sits uneasily with the position of that court as auditor of domestic standards.

---

[5] *Ibid.*, p. 22.

[6] S. Grosz, J. Beatson and P. Duffy, *Human Rights: The 1998 Act and the European Convention* (London: Sweet and Maxwell, 2000), p. 20. Also see Lord Irvine's comments at HL Debs., 24 November 1997, vol. 583, col. 835.

[7] *R. (on the Application of Ullah)* v. *Special Adjudicator; Do* v. *Immigration Appeal Tribunal* [2004] UKHL 26, para. 20, *per* Lord Bingham (emphasis added).

Dworkin offered further comment on the potential of the incorporated Convention, writing that:

> The courts, charged with the responsibility of creating from the Convention a distinctly British scheme of human rights and liberty, might think in terms of *principle* and less in terms of narrow precedent.[8]

The approach to the s.2(1) obligation which advocates that 'clear and constant' Strasbourg jurisprudence be followed, arguably bears many of the characteristics of a precedential system.[9] However, further analysis of cases under the Human Rights Act reveals a willingness to treat the Strasbourg case-law less as binding authority, more as an elaboration of guiding principles. Drawing on the principles which underpin Convention decisions might arguably represent a more realistic interpretation of the s.2(1) obligation; by denying that domestic courts are obliged to follow or apply the Convention jurisprudence, this construction of s.2(1) suggests that the domestic courts should be guided by the aims and objectives which inform the Convention and its case-law, rather than applying, in a precedent-like manner, the decisions of an international court of review. While, in *Kebilene*, Lord Hope appeared to acknowledge that, 'in the hands of the national courts . . . the Convention should be seen as an expression of fundamental principles rather than as a set of mere rules',[10] this approach is not, however, at its most evident in the 'clear and constant' jurisprudence approach of the House of Lords. Rather, it is reflected more obviously in a number of decisions made by the Court of Appeal which suggest that the task of the judges is 'not to cast around in the European Human Rights Reports like blackletter lawyers seeking clues. In the light of s.2(1) of the Human Rights Act 1998 it is to draw out the broad principles which animate the Convention.'[11]

---

[8] R. Dworkin, *A Bill of Rights for Britain* (London: Chatto and Windus, 1990), p. 23 (emphasis added). Dworkin's conception of 'principles' in his work *Taking Rights Seriously* is as follows: 'a standard that is to be observed, not because it will advance or secure an economic, political or social situation deemed desirable, but because it is a requirement of justice or fairness or some other dimension of morality' (R. Dworkin, *Taking Rights Seriously* (London: Duckworth, 2005), p. 22). On the 'principles' which the European Court of Human Rights has indicated should guide the application and interpretation of the ECHR see R. Masterman, 'Taking the Strasbourg Jurisprudence into Account: Developing a "Municipal Law of Human Rights" under the Human Rights Act' (2005) 54 ICLQ 907, 920.

[9] See R. Masterman, 'Section 2(1) of the Human Rights Act: Binding Domestic Courts to Strasbourg?' [2004] PL 725.

[10] R. v. DPP, ex parte Kebilene [2000] 2 AC 326, 380–1, *per* Lord Hope of Craighead.

[11] *Aston Cantlow Parochial Church Council* v. *Wallbank* [2002] Ch 51, 65.

The first of these approaches places legal certainty at its core and aims to deter accusations of the judge acting without reference to legal authority.[12] The second – although allowing the domestic judge a greater degree of creative autonomy – allows the judiciary to respond to national *and* international developments and looks to the incremental development of common law standards to restrain the excessive judicial activism which some feared the HRA might cause.

The question of a domestic Bill of Rights

The government's White Paper, *Rights Brought Home*, made it clear that the Human Rights Bill would not take the form of a Bill of Rights in the United States or Canadian mould, empowering the courts to strike down primary legislation for want of compatibility with the Convention rights.[13] Parliamentary sovereignty was to be preserved by way of the declaration of incompatibility; a measure designed to ensure that – in the event of a finding of incompatibility – the final resolution of the matter would lie with the democratic arms of government and not the unelected and unaccountable judiciary.[14] Nevertheless, it was clear that a significant transfer of power from the elected arms of government to the judicial branch would take place. As Klug has noted:

> The courts are clearly given new powers of judicial review under the HRA that they did not have before. They can now review the decisions and actions of ministers and officials in substantive, human rights terms and they can even consider the compatibility of primary legislation with the Convention rights in the HRA, something they were effectively constitutionally barred from doing before. This, together with the fact that s.2 of the Act allows the courts to range wider than the ECHR and look at the jurisprudence of other human rights treaties, is what makes it effectively a bill of rights or 'higher law'.[15]

---

[12] See e.g. Loveland's criticisms of the Court of Appeal decision in *Ghaidan* v. *Godin-Mendoza* [2003] Ch 380: I. Loveland, 'Making It up As They Go Along? The Court of Appeal on Same Sex Spouses and Succession Rights to Tenancies' [2003] PL 222.

[13] *Rights Brought Home: The Human Rights Bill*, Cm. 3782 (October 1997), paras. 2.10–2.15.

[14] Section 4(4) HRA; on which see the chapters by David Feldman and Aileen Kavanagh in this volume.

[15] F. Klug, 'The Human Rights Act: A "Third Way" or "Third Wave" Bill of Rights' [2001] EHRLR 361, 370.

As Klug notes, the discretionary power bestowed upon the courts by s.2(1) is a wide one; the judiciary were to be charged with the task of 'taking into account' decisions of the Strasbourg organs in adjudication under the Act. Section 2(1) obliges a court or tribunal, in 'determining a question which has arisen in connection with a Convention right'[16] to 'take into account any' judgment, decision, declaration or opinion of the Strasbourg organs, 'whenever made or given, so far as, in the opinion of the Court or tribunal, it is relevant to the proceedings in which that question has arisen'.[17]

The peculiar challenge posed to judicial reasoning in this context is that s.2(1) does not reflect our traditional understanding of how the authority of a higher court should be treated. The duty imposed on the domestic court or tribunal is to 'take into account' – not to follow or apply – appropriate Convention jurisprudence, although only insofar as it holds it to be of relevance to the case in hand. The discretion afforded to the court or tribunal may be either with regard to the decision of whether or not to follow the jurisprudence of the Strasbourg court, or concern the weight to be afforded to the Convention jurisprudence in coming to a decision under the HRA: in the words of Buxton LJ in *R. (on the Application of Anderson)* v. *Secretary of State for the Home Department*, the courts:

> will take the [Strasbourg] court's jurisprudence into account whether we determine the case in accordance with it, or on the other hand decline, on a reasoned basis, to apply that jurisprudence.[18]

On the face of it, this obligation may appear to be relatively weak – 'since it is open to the judiciary to consider but disapply a particular decision'[19] – but equally it remains open to the domestic judiciary to directly apply the

---

[16] 'Convention rights' are defined in s.1(1) HRA.

[17] The full text of s.2(1) HRA is as follows: 'A court or tribunal determining a question which has arisen in connection with a Convention right must take into account any – (a) judgment, decision, declaration or advisory opinion of the European Court of Human Rights, (b) opinion of the Commission given in a report adopted under Article 31 of the Convention, (c) decision of the Commission in connection with Article 26 or 27(2) of the Convention, or (d) decision of the Committee of Ministers taken under Article 46 of the Convention, whenever made or given, so far as, in the opinion of the court or tribunal, it is relevant to the proceedings in which that question has arisen.'

[18] *R. (on the Application of Anderson)* v. *Secretary of State for the Home Department* [2001] EWCA Civ 1698, para. 88.

[19] H. Fenwick, *Civil Liberties and Human Rights* (3rd edn, London: Cavendish, 2002), pp. 146–7.

principles of a pertinent Strasbourg decision to domestic proceedings. In deceptively simple terms, s.2(1) creates a significant judicial discretionary power to apply Strasbourg jurisprudence directly, to take it 'into account' but fail to apply it, or to come to a decision somewhere between the two extremes by either applying (or being influenced by) the Convention jurisprudence to a greater or lesser degree.

During the Parliamentary debates on the Human Rights Bill, the question of the extent to which domestic courts should either take into consideration, or be bound by, the jurisprudence of the Strasbourg institutions was seen as going to the heart of the debate over whether the Act would in practice amount to a domestic Bill of Rights – something more than the mere transposition of Convention standards as tools of interpretation into domestic law. And the ability of domestic courts to depart from Strasbourg jurisprudence has been seen by a number of commentators as one of the characteristics of the HRA which most resembles such a Bill.[20]

As evidenced in the debates on what was clause 2 of the Human Rights Bill, there was a concern amongst the Conservative opposition that United Kingdom judges, in dealing with Convention matters, should be bound to follow decisions of the Strasbourg Court. In the House of Lords at Committee Stage, Lord Kingsland voiced his concerns that:

> if our judges only take account of the jurisprudence of the European Court of Human Rights, we cast them adrift from their international moorings. The Bill ... will have no accurate charts by which to sail because the judges are obliged only to take account of the provisions of the Convention. That means that the Bill is effectively a domestic Bill of Rights and not a proper incorporation of international rights. It means that the judges ... are not obliged to act on it and can go in whatever direction they wish. I have great confidence in Her Majesty's judges, but I believe that they need greater guidance than they receive from the expression 'take into account'.[21]

Yet, the intention of the Labour administration was clearly that in the consideration of Convention points by domestic courts the HRA should *not* implement a system of precedent emanating from the Strasbourg

[20] D. Bonner, H. Fenwick and S. Harris-Short, 'Judicial Approaches to the Human Rights Act' (2003) 52 ICLQ 549, 553. The circumstances in which domestic courts might 'depart' from Strasbourg are examined below.
[21] HL Debs., 18 November 1997, vol. 583, col. 514. See also HC Debs., 3 June 1998, vol. 313, cols. 397–8, *per* Edward Leigh MP.

organs.[22] A Conservative amendment to replace the words 'must take into account' in clause 2 with the words 'shall be bound by' was rejected in the House of Lords on the following grounds by the then Lord Chancellor, Lord Irvine of Lairg: 'the word "binding" is the language of precedent but the Convention is the ultimate source of law . . . I think that "binding" certainly goes further . . . than the Convention itself requires.'[23]

A judge's ability to 'go in whatever direction they wish' is of course constrained by s.3(1) – the duty to interpret legislation compatibly with the Convention rights – and s.6 – which includes the duty of the courts themselves to act compatibly with the rights given effect under the Act. That questions of compatibility are to be gauged by specific reference to 'the Convention rights' and – given that the primary source of authority as to the meaning of those rights is the Convention jurisprudence – the domestic judge is hardly given licence to 'govern society on the basis of his own philosophy, his own biases, or his own worldview'.[24] But, in failing to oblige domestic courts to follow the Strasbourg jurisprudence, the HRA leaves open the question of whether it would be legitimate for a domestic court to develop its own reading of the compatibility of a provision with the Convention right in question either by extension of the right in question, or by a restrictive interpretation of the accepted criteria for qualification of those rights.

Preserving judicial discretion under section 2(1)

As Lord Irvine has written of the general nature of human rights instruments, 'their linguistic texture and their evolutive nature necessarily leave the judges with a significant margin of interpretative autonomy'.[25] The European Convention on Human Rights – although framed

---

[22] The White Paper stated that, 'our courts will be required to take account of relevant decisions of the European Commission and Court of Human Rights (although these will not be binding)': *Rights Brought Home: The Human Rights Bill*, Cm. 3782 (October 1997), para. 2.4.

[23] HL Debs., 18 November 1997, vol. 583, col. 514.

[24] Justice Antonin Scalia, 'The Bill of Rights: Confirmation of Extent Freedoms or Invitation to Judicial Creation?', in G. Huscroft and P. Rishworth (eds.), *Litigating Rights: Perspectives from Domestic and International Law* (Oxford: Hart Publishing, 2002), p. 23.

[25] Lord Irvine of Lairg, 'Activism and Restraint: Human Rights and the Interpretive Process', in Cambridge Centre for Public Law, *The Human Rights Act and the Criminal Justice and Regulatory Process* (Oxford: Hart Publishing, 1999), p. 14.

in more precise language than, for example, the US Bill of Rights – is no exception to this rule. The provisions of the Convention are expressed in a 'broad and ample style'[26] which – in some cases – allow for qualification[27] and derogation[28] under certain circumstances. These provisions have, of course, been fleshed-out by over four decades of jurisprudence from the European Court of Human Rights and the Commission on Human Rights. But to think that this jurisprudence could be followed or applied in the manner of precedents would be a mistake: whether because a wide margin of appreciation has been afforded, that the relevant decisions of the Strasbourg court do not define the content of the right in question, or that the relevant authority exists only in admissibility decisions, the fact is that 'decisions of the European Court are not infrequently Delphic in character'.[29]

Equally, application of the legal tenets contained within the Convention's articles may not be a straightforward exercise. As to the condition that a restriction be 'necessary in a democratic society', the European Court of Human Rights has offered some assistance in defining the meaning of this nebulous phrase, ruling out the 'flexibility of such expressions as "admissible", "ordinary", "useful", "reasonable" or "desirable"' and noting that it implied the existence – rather circuitously – of a 'pressing social need'.[30] To utilise tests such as this in the domestic context necessarily demands a degree of flexibility to be preserved. This – and further reasons why the domestic courts should enjoy a margin of discretion in 'applying' Convention jurisprudence under the Act – were identified by the government during the passage of the Human Rights Bill.

The Lord Chancellor, Lord Irvine, pointed to a number of grounds why United Kingdom courts should not be bound to follow the jurisprudence of the Strasbourg Court. The first was that the Convention itself, not the jurisprudence of the Court, is the 'ultimate source of the relevant law',[31] and as such the Convention system has no strict rule of precedent. The Convention is a 'living instrument' which should be given a 'dynamic

---

[26] *Minister of Home Affairs* v. *Fisher* [1980] AC 319, 328, *per* Lord Wilberforce.

[27] Articles 8–11 ECHR.

[28] Article 15 provides that certain of the Convention rights may be derogated from 'in time of war or other public emergency threatening the life of the nation ... to the extent strictly required by the exigencies of the situation'.

[29] A. T. H. Smith, 'The Human Rights Act: the Constitutional Context', in Cambridge Centre for Public Law, *The Human Rights Act and the Criminal Justice and Regulatory Process* (Oxford: Hart Publishing, 1999), p. 6.

[30] *Handyside* v. *United Kingdom* (1979–80) 1 EHRR 737, para. 48.

[31] HL Debs., 18 November 1997, vol. 583, col. 514.

interpretation in the light of conditions prevailing at the time a matter falls to be considered'.[32] As Lord Browne-Wilkinson commented during the parliamentary debates, 'I see no reason that we should fetter ourselves in that way in dealing with a jurisprudence which is by definition a shifting one.'[33]

Secondly, the United Kingdom is, under the Convention, only bound to 'abide by' rulings of the Strasbourg Court in cases in which it has been involved as a party to the proceedings.[34] This argument recognises that decisions of the Court involving other states parties may well involve the Court allowing the state concerned a 'margin of appreciation' which will 'vary in its application according to local needs and conditions'.[35] Accordingly, the margin of appreciation 'is not available to national courts when they are considering Convention issues arising within their own countries'.[36] Requiring United Kingdom courts to follow or apply judgments of the Court not directly concerning the UK would be 'quite inappropriate ... since such cases deal with laws and practices which are not those of the United Kingdom'.[37] And the direct application of decisions addressed to other states parties could possibly involve the importation of a margin of appreciation devised for another state party to the Convention – and would consequently allow the application of such a margin to a national authority for which it was not specifically conceived.[38]

---

[32] S. Grosz, J. Beatson and P. Duffy, *Human Rights: The 1998 Act and the European Convention* (London: Sweet and Maxwell, 2000), p. 18. See e.g. *Tyrer v. United Kingdom* (1979–80) 2 EHRR 1, para. 31.

[33] HL Debs., 19 January 1998, vol. 584, col. 1268.

[34] Article 46(1) ECHR provides: 'The High Contracting Parties undertake to abide by the final judgment of the Court in any case to which they are the parties.' Article 46(2) provides the task of supervising the execution of such a judgment is exercised by the Committee of Ministers.

[35] *R. v. Director of Public Prosecutions, ex parte Kebilene* [2000] 2 AC 326, 380–1, *per* Lord Hope.

[36] *Ibid.* See also *Brown* v. *Stott* [2003] 1 AC 681, 702, *per* Lord Bingham. As Leigh observes, this rejection of the doctrine's applicability in domestic law would in theory 'enlarge the scope for creative judicial interpretation since ... domestic judges would have a freer hand to determine for themselves the meaning of Convention rights in a uniquely British context' (I. Leigh, 'The UK's Human Rights Act: An Early Assessment' in G. Huscroft and P. Rishworth (eds.), *Litigating Rights: Perspectives from Domestic and International Law* (Oxford: Hart Publishing, 2002), p. 328).

[37] HL Debs., 18 November 1997, vol. 583, col. 514. The Lord Chancellor went on to say that Convention cases involving other states were 'a source of jurisprudence indeed, but not binding precedents which we should follow or even necessarily desire to follow' (HL Debs., 18 November 1997, vol. 583, col. 515).

[38] An argument advanced by H. Fenwick and G. Phillipson in 'Public Protest, the Human Rights Act and Judicial Responses to Political Expression' [2000] PL 627, 643–4.

Finally, Lord Irvine proposed that 'our courts must be free to try to give a lead to Europe as well as to be led'.[39] This, along with the government's recognition that the Convention is to provide a 'floor of rights' protection rather than a ceiling[40] confirms the possibility that it was countenanced that domestic courts might legitimately depart from – or build on the foundation of – the Strasbourg jurisprudence in order to enhance domestic rights protection. Within the framework established by the HRA, therefore, it is suggested that – while it would be a legitimate act under s.6 for a court or tribunal to provide a greater degree of protection – it would not be within the limits of the court's discretion to depart from Strasbourg jurisprudence to interpret domestic law in a way which would provide a lesser protection than that afforded by the Convention.[41]

A further objection to the notion that the domestic courts could be bound to follow the decisions of the Strasbourg institutions is that many such rulings are not suitable to be 'followed' in strict terms. Judgments of the Strasbourg Court are 'essentially declaratory'[42] in nature – stating whether a given decision or action of domestic authorities is either compatible with the Convention standards (or falling within a state's margin of appreciation) or in breach of those standards – and are addressed to the domestic authorities of the state party in question. As such, 'it is difficult, sometimes, to read them as giving rise to any clear *ratio decidendi* of the kind sought and applied by common lawyers'.[43] Equally, for the purposes of the Strasbourg organs, a domestic court is 'not obliged to give [a decision

---

[39] HL Debs., 18 November 1997, vol. 583, col. 515. An example of when it might be appropriate to depart from the Convention case-law was given by Lord Irvine, who said that clause 2(1) 'would permit the United Kingdom courts to depart from Strasbourg decisions where there was no precise ruling on the matter and a Commission opinion which does so had not taken into account subsequent Strasbourg case law' (HL Debs., 18 November 1997, vol. 583, col. 514).

[40] HL Debs., 18 November 1997, vol. 583, col. 510.

[41] For example by following an older Strasbourg authority where there had been subsequent developments furthering the protection afforded by the Convention. Indeed, providing a lesser protection than that currently provided for by the Convention organs would arguably amount to the court or tribunal, as a public authority, acting unlawfully under s.6 HRA (acknowledged in *R. (on the Application of Ullah)* v. *Special Adjudicator; Do* v. *Immigration Appeal Tribunal* [2004] UKHL 26, para. 23, *per* Lord Bingham).

[42] D. J. Harris, M. O'Boyle and C. Warbrick, *Law of the European Convention on Human Rights* (London: Butterworths, 1995), p. 26.

[43] A. T. H. Smith, 'The Human Rights Act: The Constitutional Context', in Cambridge Centre for Public Law, *The Human Rights Act and the Criminal Justice and Regulatory Process* (Oxford: Hart Publishing, 1999), p. 6.

of the Strasbourg institutions] direct effect in the national law of the defendant state' as a party is free to implement such decisions 'in accordance with the rules of its national legal system'.[44]

All of these submissions are consistent with the view of the Strasbourg organs that the Convention is a secondary method of rights protection – the primary responsibility lying with domestic authorities. As the European Court of Human Rights explained in the judgment to the *Handyside* case:

> The court points out that the machinery of protection established by the Convention is subsidiary to the national systems regarding human rights. The Convention leaves to each contracting state, in the first place, the task of securing the rights and liberties it enshrines ... By reason of their direct and continuous contact with the vital forces of their countries, State authorities are in principle in a better position than the international judge to give an opinion on the exact content of these requirements as well as on the 'necessity' of a 'restriction' or 'penalty' intended to meet them.[45]

Yet, as will be argued below, for the most part domestic courts appear to see this role as that of the elected arms of government, preferring to take their lead from Strasbourg.

Judicial approaches to section 2(1): legal certainty versus judicial discretion

'*Clear and constant*' jurisprudence

As Tierney has observed, 'the injunction contained in s.2(1) HRA that courts should take Strasbourg jurisprudence into account is a flexible adjudicatory device but one which inevitably creates an area of uncertainty for judges'.[46] As described above, it was this area of 'uncertainty' which the opposition found objectionable during the debates on the Human Rights Bill, preferring an approach which would guarantee greater legal clarity and protect the domestic judge against accusations of unwarranted activism.

---

[44] D. J. Harris, M. O'Boyle and C. Warbrick, *Law of the European Convention on Human Rights* (London: Butterworths, 1995), p. 26, where the example given is of *Vermeire v. Belgium* (1993) 15 EHRR 488.

[45] *Handyside* v. *United Kingdom* (1979–80) 1 EHRR 737, para. 48. See also *Case Relating to Certain Aspects of the Laws on the Use of Languages in Education in Belgium* (1979–80) 1 EHRR 252, para. 9.

[46] S. Tierney, 'Devolution Issues and s.2(1) of the Human Rights Act 1998' [2000] EHRLR 380, 392.

In fact, the domestic courts' approach to the construction of s.2(1) has so far betrayed little of the progressive approach to the Convention jurisprudence which caused such concern amongst the Conservative members prior to the HRA entering into force. The Appellate Committee of the House of Lords has presented a clear line of authority on the role of courts and tribunals under s.2(1),[47] originating in the reasoning of Lord Slynn of Hadley in *Alconbury*:

> Although the Human Rights Act 1998 does not provide that a national court is bound by these decisions it is obliged to take account of them so far as they are relevant. In the absence of special circumstances it seems to me that the court should follow any clear and constant jurisprudence of the European Court of Human Rights. If it does not do so there is at least a possibility that the case will go to that court which is likely in the ordinary case to follow its own constant jurisprudence.[48]

Lord Slynn's approach was subsequently endorsed by Lord Bingham in the *Anderson* case; he stated:

> While the duty of the House under s.2(1) of the Human Rights Act 1998 is to take into account any judgment of the European Court, whose judgments are not strictly binding, the House will not without good reason depart from the principles laid down in a carefully considered judgment of the court sitting as a Grand Chamber.[49]

While there may be arguably more flexibility in the approach advocated by Lord Bingham – that Strasbourg 'principles' rather than 'jurisprudence' be followed – there still remains the issue that the language used by both hints at something more than the duty to 'take into account' Convention case-law.[50] The approaches of both Lord Slynn and Lord Bingham seem to mirror the language of the Strasbourg Court when

---

[47] See e.g. *R. (on the Application of Anderson)* v. *Secretary of State for the Home Department* [2002] UKHL 46, para. 18; *R.* v. *Secretary of State for the Home Department, ex parte Amin* [2003] UKHL 51, para. 44; *R. (on the Application of Ullah)* v. *Special Adjudicator; Do* v. *Immigration Appeal Tribunal* [2004] UKHL 26, para. 20; *N* v. *Secretary of State for the Home Department* [2005] UKHL 31, para. 24.

[48] *R. (on the Application of Alconbury Developments Ltd)* v. *Secretary of State for the Environment, Transport and the Regions* [2001] UKHL 23, para. 26.

[49] *R. (on the Application of Anderson)* v. *Secretary of State for the Home Department* [2002] UKHL 46, para. 18.

[50] It is interesting to note that s.4 of the Republic of Ireland's European Convention on Human Rights Act 2003 requires that 'a court shall, when interpreting and applying the Convention provisions, take due account of the *principles* laid down by those declarations, decisions, advisory opinions, opinions and judgments [of the Strasbourg bodies]' (emphasis added).

dealing with the issue of departing from its own previous decisions, as the Court stated in *Goodwin* v. *United Kingdom*:

> While the court is not formally bound to follow its previous judgments, it is in the interests of legal certainty, foreseeability and equality before the law that it should not depart, without good reason, from precedents laid down in previous cases.[51]

The approach of the Strasbourg Court is indicative of the fact that it has consistently stressed that the Convention is a living instrument which 'must be interpreted in the light of present-day conditions',[52] as the Court has noted, 'a failure by the Court to maintain a dynamic and evolutive approach would risk rendering it a bar to reform or improvement'.[53] On this construction of s.2(1), the domestic courts would be justified in departing from such 'clear and constant' jurisprudence in what the House of Lords has referred to as 'special circumstances' – illustrations of which are explored below.

'An over-rigid approach'

A second strand of reasoning is, however, discernible from the jurisprudence on s.2(1) HRA. This approach suggests the domestic judge take a more holistic view of the Strasbourg case-law – drawing not only on relevant decisions, but the principles which animate the Convention – and recognises that the Convention case-law is perhaps not suitable to be 'followed' as such. The words of Sir Andrew Morritt VC cited above[54] were echoed by Lord Sutherland in *Clancy* v. *Caird*:

> It is the duty of this court, while considering the interpretation of the Convention, to have regard to the decisions in the European Court of Human Rights ... and the Commission. These decisions, however, are not to be treated in the same way as precedents in our own law. Insofar as principles can be extracted from these decisions, those are the principles which will have to be applied.[55]

In common with the approach of Lord Bingham in *Amin*, Sir Andrew Morritt VC and Lord Sutherland identify the 'principles' inherent in the Convention as the correct persuasive authority; by contrast their

---

[51] *Goodwin* v. *United Kingdom* (2002) 35 EHRR 18, para. 74.
[52] *Tyrer* v. *United Kingdom* (1979–80) 2 EHRR 1, para. 31.
[53] *Stafford* v. *United Kingdom* (2002) 35 EHRR 32, para. 68.   [54] Above n. 11.
[55] *Clancy* v. *Caird* 2000 SLT 546, para. 3, *per* Lord Sutherland.

approach is not reflective of the language of precedent.[56] To follow such
an approach would avoid accusations of distorting, arguably fettering,
the s.2(1) discretion – and would better reflect Dworkin's vision that the
domestic judiciary 'might think in terms of principle, and less in terms
of narrow precedent' under the incorporated Convention.

The importance of the principles which underpin the Convention and
its case-law has been acknowledged in adjudication under the Act; Lord
Bingham addressed the issue in *Amin*, while Lord Woolf in *R. (on the
Application of Al-Hasan)* v. *Secretary of State for the Home Department*
remarked that it is 'the principles which are relevant and important'.[57]
And Lord Hope – writing extra-judicially – has observed that, although
s.2(1) demands a certain 'respect for precedents' in the name of 'consistency', this must also allow for 'growth and development . . . [A] strict
application of the doctrine of precedent will be out of place in this
field.'[58] As noted above, these sentiments sit uneasily with elements of
the 'clear and constant' jurisprudence approach as evidenced in a number of House of Lords decisions under the Act.

Perhaps the most emphatic rejection of the approach illustrated by
the House of Lords decisions discussed above can be found in the
reasoning of Laws LJ. In the Court of Appeal decision in *Runa Begum*
v. *Tower Hamlets LBC*, Laws LJ addressed the role of the Court under the
HRA, stating:

> the court's task under the HRA . . . is not simply to add on the Strasbourg
> learning to the corpus of English law, as if it were a compulsory adjunct
> taken from an alien source, but to develop a municipal law of human
> rights by the incremental method of the common law, case by case, taking
> account of the Strasbourg jurisprudence as HRA s.2 enjoins us to do.[59]

---

[56] This approach has also received support from Rabinder Singh QC (sitting as a Deputy
High Court Judge) in the case of *R. (on the Application of Amirthanathan)* v. *Secretary of
State for the Home Department* [2003] EWHC 1107, where, referring to the judgment of
Laws LJ in *Prolife Alliance*, he said: 'one is looking to make good an autonomous human
rights jurisprudence by reference to principles to be found animating the Convention
rather than an over-rigid approach. The end result will be a flourishing of Convention
principles which should take root in the fertile soil of our own long tradition of liberty.'

[57] *R. (on the Application of Al-Hasan)* v. *Secretary of State for the Home Department* [2002]
1 WLR 545, 566.

[58] Lord Hope, 'The Human Rights Act 1998: The Task of the Judges' (1999) Stat LR 185,
192. On the issue of the effect of the Human Rights Act 1998 on the domestic doctrine of
stare decisis, see the decision of the House of Lords in *Kay* v. *London Borough of Lambeth*;
Leeds City Council v. *Price* [2006] UKHL 10, paras. 40–5.

[59] *Runa Begum* v. *Tower Hamlets London Borough Council* [2002] 2 All ER 668, para. 17.

Returning to this theme in *R. (on the Application of Prolife Alliance) v. British Broadcasting Corporation*[60] – concerning restrictions on political broadcasts made prior to a general election – Laws LJ stated that:

> The English court is not a Strasbourg surrogate ... [O]ur duty is to develop, by the common law's incremental method, a coherent and principled domestic law of human rights ... [T]reating the ECHR text as a template for our own law runs the risk of an over-rigid approach.[61]

On appeal, however, the Law Lords overturned the decision of the Court of Appeal, but this specific point was not addressed.[62] What the *dicta* of Laws LJ in both cases does, is place emphasis on the point made by the text of s.2(1) – but arguably lacking from some judicial discussion of the provision – that under the HRA the Strasbourg case-law is to be taken as persuasive rather than determinative authority and that as such a domestic court might legitimately depart from decisions of the Convention bodies, so long as the outcome remains 'compatible' in the sense envisaged by s.6 HRA.

Departing from Strasbourg

During the Parliamentary debates on the Human Rights Bill, Lord Irvine suggested that clause 2(1) – as it was then drafted – was designed to 'permit the United Kingdom courts to depart from Strasbourg where there was no precise ruling on a matter and a Commission opinion which does so had not taken into account subsequent Strasbourg case law'.[63] At the report stage, he added:

> The Courts will often be faced with cases that involve factors perhaps specific to the United Kingdom which distinguish them from cases considered by the European Court ... [I]t is important that our courts have the scope to apply that discretion so as to aid the development of human rights law.[64]

---

[60] *R. (on the Application of Prolife Alliance)* v. *British Broadcasting Corporation* [2002] 2 All ER 756.

[61] *Ibid.*, paras. 33–4.

[62] *R. (on the Application of Prolife Alliance)* v. *British Broadcasting Corporation* [2003] UKHL 23.

[63] HL Debs., 18 November 1997, vol. 583, col. 514.

[64] HL Debs., 19 January 1998, vol. 584, cols. 1270–1.

As noted above, the then Lord Chancellor had intended that the courts 'must be free to try to give a lead to Europe as well as to be led'.[65] Some examples can be found of the 'special circumstances' which might justify such a departure from 'clear and constant' Strasbourg case-law. The House of Lords has, for example, indicated that it might not follow or adopt the reasoning of a Strasbourg judgment on an issue on which that court had not 'receive[d] all the help which was needed to form a conclusion'.[66] A further indication of a situation where a United Kingdom court might legitimately depart from the 'clear and constant' jurisprudence of the European Court was given by Lord Hoffmann in *Alconbury*:

> The House [of Lords] is not bound by the decisions of the European Court and, if I thought that . . . they compelled a conclusion fundamentally at odds with the distribution of powers under the British constitution, I would have considerable doubt as to whether they should be followed.[67]

Lord Hoffmann's *dicta* hints at a certain normative force to the principles on which the UK constitution is based which might justify a departure from the Strasbourg authorities. Significantly, it can also be read as suggesting that the s.2(1) obligation might also require an evaluation of the suitability of the relevant Strasbourg authority to be applied or relied on in the domestic context. However, by prescribing that 'special circumstances' must exist to legitimise a departure from Strasbourg jurisprudence, the House of Lords has imposed a hurdle to the effective discharge of the s.2(1) obligation; domestic courts must justify their departures as fitting within the boundaries set down by the House of Lords.

Some reluctance on the part of lower domestic courts either to invite Strasbourg to re-examine a point of law, or indeed to 'give a lead' to the Convention organs, can be illustrated by the decision of the Court of Appeal in *Anderson*.[68] The case concerned the entitlement of the Home Secretary to set minimum tariffs of imprisonment to be served by

---

[65] *Ibid.*   [66] *R.* v. *Spear and Others* [2003] 1 AC 734, para. 12, *per* Lord Bingham.

[67] *R. (on the Application of Alconbury Developments Ltd)* v. *Secretary of State for the Environment, Transport and the Regions* [2001] UKHL 23, para. 76.

[68] *R. (on the Application of Anderson)* v. *Secretary of State for the Home Department* [2001] EWCA Civ 1698.

mandatory life prisoners, and preceded the hearing of the *Stafford*[69] case by the European Court of Human Rights, in the estimate of the Court of Appeal, by a year.[70] And, in spite of the doubts in the Court of Appeal as to whether the then arrangements for the setting of tariffs would survive scrutiny by the Strasbourg Court,[71] there was a marked reluctance to offer either an invitation to Strasbourg to reconsider its position or to provide a lead to the Convention organs: in the words of Simon Brown LJ:

> Where ... as here, the ECtHR itself is proposing to re-examine a particular line of cases, it would seem somewhat presumptuous for us, in effect, to pre-empt its decision.[72]

The Court of Appeal followed the approach advocated by counsel for the Home Secretary – that the clear and constant jurisprudence of the European Court of Human Rights should be followed – while adopting an almost deferential attitude to the Strasbourg Court, with Buxton LJ offering the following as justification for restraint:

> where an international court has the specific task of interpreting an international instrument it brings to that task a range of knowledge and principle that a national court cannot aspire to.[73]

This rigid interpretation of s.2(1) is in stark contrast to the progressive approach to the Strasbourg jurisprudence seemingly envisaged by the government during the Parliamentary debates on the Human Rights Bill, and arguably undermines the role of national authorities as the primary mechanism for securing the protections afforded by the Convention.

A more positive development has been evident in the aftermath of the decision of the European Court of Human Rights in *Osman* v. *United*

---

[69] *Stafford* v. *United Kingdom* (2002) 35 EHRR 32. The case involved a challenge under Article 5 to the Home Secretary's discretionary power to refuse to release a mandatory life prisoner in spite of recommendations of the parole board to the contrary. In a demonstration of the language of precedent filtering down, one commentator has noted that by the time *Anderson* reached the House of Lords – after the decision of the European Court of Human Rights in *Stafford* – the Law Lords were 'no longer bound' by the previous decisions of the European Court of Human Rights on the involvement of members of the executive in sentencing (M. Amos, '*R.* v. *Secretary of State for the Home Department, ex parte Anderson*: Ending the Home Secretary's Sentencing Role' (2004) 67 MLR 108, 116).

[70] *R. (on the Application of Anderson)* v. *Secretary of State for the Home Department* [2001] EWCA Civ 1698, para. 22.

[71] *Ibid.*, para. 66.   [72] *Ibid.*, para. 66.   [73] *Ibid.*, para. 91.

Kingdom – Lord Steyn has called it a 'creative dialogue' between domestic courts and Strasbourg.[74] In an article published before the Human Rights Act came into force, Lord Hoffmann cast doubt on the utility of a domestic court 'taking into account' a Strasbourg judgment in which the European Court of Human Rights had seriously misunderstood the relevant UK law – with the example given that of *Osman* v. *United Kingdom* and its treatment of the duty of care under the English law of negligence.[75] In *R.* v. *Lyons (No. 3)*, Lord Hoffmann elaborated on this, after explicitly recognising that s.2(1) only obliged courts to 'take account' of the Convention jurisprudence, by saying that, '[i]f, for example, an English court considers that the ECtHR has misunderstood or been misinformed about some aspect of English law, it may wish to give a judgment which invites the ECtHR to reconsider the question ... There is room for dialogue on such matters.'[76] Lord Steyn's example of this 'creative dialogue' in action refers to the judgment of the European Court of Human Rights in *Z* v. *United Kingdom*, in which the Court 'resiled'[77] from its earlier decision in *Osman* on the grounds that:

> its reasoning in the *Osman* judgment was based on an understanding of the law of negligence which has to be reviewed in the light of the clarifications subsequently made by the domestic courts and notably the House of Lords.[78]

While such a dialogue is to be welcomed, in this instance it is at least debatable whether the Human Rights Act provided the impetus for the European Court of Human Rights to review its position as set down in *Osman* as the case in which the House of Lords addressed the issue – *Barrett* v. *Enfield LBC*[79] – had been decided before the Act came into force, in June 1999.[80]

---

[74] Lord Steyn, '2000–2005: Laying the Foundations of Human Rights Law in the United Kingdom' [2005] EHRLR 349, 361.

[75] Lord Hoffmann, 'Human Rights and the House of Lords' (1999) 62 MLR 159, 162–4 (see also R. Clayton, 'Developing Principles for Human Rights' [2002] EHRLR 175, 178).

[76] *R.* v. *Lyons (No. 3)* [2003] 1 AC 976, para. 46.

[77] Lord Steyn, '2000–2005: Laying the Foundations of Human Rights Law in the United Kingdom [2005] EHRLR 349, 361.

[78] *Z and Others* v. *United Kingdom* (2002) 34 EHRR 3, para. 100.

[79] [2001] 2 AC 550.

[80] For a more recent example, see the discussion of the Court of Appeal judgment in *Evans* v. *Amicus Healthcare Ltd* [2004] EWCA Civ 727; [2004] 3 WLR 681 in *Evans* v. *United Kingdom*, judgment of the European Court of Human Rights, 7 March 2006 (available at www.echr.coe.int).

Aspiration or foundation? The status of 'Convention rights' in domestic law

While it could be suggested that the phrase 'clear and constant' actually gives courts considerable scope to depart from Strasbourg case-law – in particular, in an area where that jurisprudence is rapidly developing[81] – a further related development will come as a blow to those who saw in the scheme of the HRA the potential for the Act to provide the courts with a mandate to develop and expand on those standards found in the European Convention in the domestic context. A corollary of the precedent-like approach to the Strasbourg jurisprudence adopted by the House of Lords is the danger of regarding the Strasbourg standard as the aspiration rather than the foundation for the development of a domesticated rights jurisprudence. While this constrained approach has been recognised as one of the potential hazards of transposing an international treaty into a national 'Bill of Rights', it also brings with it the potential to frustrate the object both of the ECHR itself – the 'further realisation' of the Convention rights – and of the HRA by running the risk of confining the domestic judiciary to a compatibility-only approach to the Convention rights. As Clapham has written:

> the problem is that judges or Governments may be tempted to point to such minimum standards as evidence of the limits of the human rights at stake. The challenge is to ensure that national courts treat the international human rights as a part of the national heritage and interpret them in the national context so as to give the appropriate maximum protection at the national level ... It is important that national courts have the autonomy to interpret the relevant international human rights so as to make them appropriate to the national culture.[82]

While it may be necessary in the interests of legal certainty and judicial legitimacy to articulate the method by which Strasbourg case-law is 'taken into account' – whether the court in question places reliance on, or distinguishes (to use the language of precedent), the Strasbourg jurisprudence – it would seem to be counter to the scheme of the HRA

---

[81] Compare, for example, *Sheffield and Horsham* v. *United Kingdom* (1999) 27 EHRR 163 with *Goodwin* v. *United Kingdom* (2002) 35 EHRR 18.

[82] A. Clapham, 'The European Convention on Human Rights in the British Courts: Problems Associated with the Incorporation of International Human Rights', in P. Alston (ed.), *Promoting Human Rights Through Bills of Rights* (Oxford: Oxford University Press, 1999), pp. 134–5.

and to the purpose of the ECHR to limit domestic courts to a precedent-like application of the Strasbourg jurisprudence. Nevertheless, Lord Bingham in *Attorney-General's Reference, No. 4 of 2002*, has stated not only that should domestic courts retain a firm grounding in the Convention jurisprudence, but also that 'the United Kingdom Courts must take their lead from Strasbourg'.[83]

Domesticated interpretations of 'Convention Rights'

The decisions of the House of Lords in *R. (on the Application of Ullah)* v. *Special Adjudicator* and *R. (on the Application of S)* v. *Chief Constable of South Yorkshire; R. (on the Application of Marper)* v. *Chief Constable of South Yorkshire* make explicit the link between s.2(1) HRA and the question of English courts providing for a domestic interpretation of one of the 'Convention rights'. These two decisions make the resounding point that a domestic court should not extend the protection offered to a Convention right through broadening the scope of the right in question unless clearly sanctioned to do so by Strasbourg. It is worth repeating the relevant extract from the speech of Lord Bingham in full so that the link with the interpretation of s.2(1) adopted by the House of Lords is evident:

> In determining the present question, the House is required by section 2(1) of the Human Rights Act 1998 to take into account any relevant Strasbourg case law. While such case law is not strictly binding, it has been held that the courts should, in the absence of some special circumstances, follow any clear and constant jurisprudence of the Strasbourg court: *R (Alconbury Developments Ltd)* v. *Secretary of State for the Environment, Transport and the Regions* . . . This reflects the fact that the Convention is an international instrument, the correct interpretation of which can be authoritatively expounded only by the Strasbourg court. From this it follows that a national court subject to a duty such as that imposed by section 2 should not without strong reason dilute or weaken the effect of the Strasbourg case law. It is indeed unlawful under section 6 of the 1998 Act for a public authority, including a court, to act in a way which is incompatible with a Convention right. It is of course open to member states to provide for rights more generous than those guaranteed by the Convention, but such provision should not be a product of

---

[83] *Attorney-General's Reference, No. 4 of 2002* [2004] UKHL 43, para. 33. See also *Douglas* v. *Hello! Ltd* [2001] QB 967, 989, *per* Brooke LJ.

interpretation of the Convention by national courts, since the meaning of
the Convention should be uniform throughout the states party to it. The
duty of national courts is to keep pace with the Strasbourg jurisprudence
as it evolves over time: no more, but certainly no less.[84]

This analysis of the position of the Convention rights in domestic law leaves
little scope for domestic courts to expand the scope of the protection
afforded to one of the Convention rights in domestic proceedings. Lord
Bingham's *dicta* endorses a minimalist interpretation of the Human Rights
Act – reflecting the tension described by Clayton between the domestic
courts' acknowledgment of the 'constitutional status' of the Human Rights
Act and charges of exceeding the legitimate judicial role.[85]

In contrast to the grounds given by the courts on which 'departure'
from Strasbourg might be legitimate, no such grounds appear to exist on
which to alter the scope of the primary right in the domestic context.
Even when confronted with Strasbourg authority which the Law Lords
have acknowledged 'is not in an altogether satisfactory state', 'lacks its
customary clarity' and displays reasoning that has not been 'entirely
convincing', the House of Lords has maintained its position.[86] In the
words of Lord Hope in *N* v. *Secretary of State for the Home Department*:

> Our task, then, is to analyse the jurisprudence of the Strasbourg court
> and, having done so and identified its limits, to apply it to the facts of this
> case . . . It is not for us to search for a solution . . . which is not to be found
> in the Strasbourg case law. It is for the Strasbourg court, not for us, to
> decide whether its case law is out of touch with modern conditions and
> to determine what further extensions, if any, are needed to the rights
> guaranteed by the Convention. We must take its case law as we find it, not
> as we would like it to be.[87]

---

[84] R. (on the Application of Ullah) v. Special Adjudicator; Do v. Immigration Appeal
Tribunal [2004] UKHL 26, para. 20, per Lord Bingham. For a discussion of the
compatibility of this statement with the findings of the House of Lords in Kay
v. London Borough of Lambeth; Leeds City Council v. Price [2006] UKHL 10, see
Chapter 14, pp. 437–40.

[85] R. Clayton, 'Judicial Deference and "Democratic Dialogue": The legitimacy of judicial
intervention under the Human Rights Act 1998' [2004] PL 33, 34.

[86] N v. Secretary of State for the Home Department [2005] UKHL 31, paras. 11, 14 (per Lord
Nicholls) and 91 (per Lord Browne of Eaton-under-Heywood).

[87] Ibid., para. 25. For a detailed analysis of the relationship between the 'Convention
rights' under the HRA and the Convention as interpreted at Strasbourg, see R. (on the
Application of Al-Jedda) v. Secretary of State for Defence [2005] EWHC Admin 1809,
paras. 33–74.

This interpretation of the courts' role under the Human Rights Act also arguably further limits the potential for domestic courts to – in Lord Irvine's words – 'give a lead' to Strasbourg. The adoption of this position is clearly intended to guard against accusations of excessive activism or of acting without sufficient legal authority – but it also arguably adopts an overly deferential attitude to the judgments of an international court of review. What is clear is that, in advising against both the dilution and the extension of the protections provided in the domestic context – in addition to specifying narrow grounds on which departure from 'clear and constant' jurisprudence might be justified – the House of Lords has reduced the scope of the discretion afforded on the face of s.2(1) almost to vanishing point.

Discretion as to the 'qualification' analysis

Lord Bingham's *dicta* in *Ullah* was subsequently endorsed by Lords Steyn and Rodger in *Marper*, with Baroness Hale in that case adding that 'we must interpret the Convention rights in a way which keeps pace with rather than leaps ahead of the Strasbourg jurisprudence as it evolves over time'.[88] The speech of Lord Steyn (with which Lords Rodger, Carswell and Browne were in agreement) does, however, endorse an interpretation of Lord Bingham's *dicta* which preserves an important area of discretion for the domestic judge. Lord Steyn held that, when considering the question of the engagement of the primary right in question, the domestic judge should not broaden (or weaken) the Strasbourg interpretation of the right.[89] He went on to address the comments made by Lord Woolf CJ in the Court of Appeal in *Marper*, who had said:

> so there can be situations where the standards of respect for the rights of the individual in this jurisdiction are higher than those required by the Convention. There is nothing in the Convention setting a ceiling on the level of respect which a *jurisdiction* is entitled to extend to personal rights.[90]

---

[88] *R. (on the Application of S)* v. *Chief Constable of South Yorkshire; R. (on the Application of Marper)* v. *Chief Constable of South Yorkshire* [2004] UKHL 39; [2004] 1 WLR 2196, paras. 27, 66 and 78, *per* Lords Steyn and Rodger and Baroness Hale respectively.

[89] *Ibid.*, para. 27.

[90] *R. (on the Application of S)* v. *Chief Constable of South Yorkshire; R. (on the Application of Marper)* v. *Chief Constable of South Yorkshire* [2002] 1 WLR 3223, para. 34, *per* Lord Woolf (emphasis added).

Lord Woolf had gone on to indicate that the 'cultural traditions' of member states were to be relevant considerations when assessing the scope of the primary right in question – in this assertion he was supported by Sedley LJ.[91] Lord Steyn, however – after endorsing the findings of the Senior Law Lord in *Ullah* – went on to observe:

> I do accept that when one moves on to consider the question of objective justification under Article 8(2) the cultural traditions in the United Kingdom are material. With great respect to Lord Woolf CJ the same is not true under Article 8(1) . . . [T]he question of whether the retention of fingerprints and [DNA] samples engages Article 8(1) should receive a uniform interpretation throughout member states, unaffected by different cultural traditions.[92]

In contrast to this, Lord Woolf had made no distinction between the powers of the respective branches of government in his assertion that there was no limit to the degree of respect that a 'jurisdiction' might afford a Convention right, leaving open the question of whether this might be within the power of the courts if 'cultural traditions' so demanded. The House of Lords decisions in *Ullah* and *Marper* clearly indicate that – at least as far as the courts are concerned – a clear limit is imposed on the scope of the rights under the Convention by the judgments of the European Court of Human Rights. It is not therefore within the powers of a domestic court to extend the scope of a right in a direction not provided for by Strasbourg. The issue therefore becomes one of separation of powers – although it would remain within the power of a legislature to extend the protection offered to a certain right, this is not a liberty afforded to the courts under the Human Rights Act. Where domestic courts do retain a significant discretion to take into account local conditions – according to Lord Steyn in *Marper* – is in the determination of whether restricting the enjoyment of the right in question is justified in the circumstances of the case.

It is worth noting that this limitation on the powers of the courts under the Human Rights Act is what might be called a 'self-denying ordinance'. Looking back to the decision of the European Court of Human Rights in the *Handyside* case, it seems that the Strasbourg

---

[91] *Ibid.*, para. 68, *per* Sedley LJ.

[92] *R. (on the Application of S) v. Chief Constable of South Yorkshire; R. (on the Application of Marper) v. Chief Constable of South Yorkshire* [2004] UKHL 39; [2004] 1 WLR 2196, para. 27.

institutions make no distinction between the respective competences of the branches of government within member states:

> *State authorities* are in principle in a better position than the international judge to give an opinion on the exact content of these requirements as well as on the 'necessity' of a 'restriction' or 'penalty' intended to meet them.[93]

As such – in the eyes of the Strasbourg institutions as in those of Lord Woolf – no distinction is made between the respective competences of member states' arms of government; '[t]here is nothing in the Convention setting a ceiling on the level of respect which a *jurisdiction* is entitled to extend to personal rights'.[94] Indeed, as one former judge of the European Court of Human Rights has specifically noted, the role of the domestic judiciary under the Convention system:

> goes further than seeing to it that the minimum standards in the ECHR are maintained. That is because the ECHR's injunction to further realise human rights and fundamental freedoms contained in the preamble is also addressed to domestic courts.[95]

Yet, in the domestic context, the perceived limitations on the courts' role can be traced back to the traditional account of the separation of powers doctrine, in which 'Parliament has a legally unchallengeable right to make whatever laws it thinks right ... The executive carries on the administration of the country ... The courts interpret the laws, and see that they are obeyed.'[96] To extend the scope of one of the 'Convention rights' in the absence of Strasbourg authority would exceed the boundaries of the proper judicial role under the Act. This arguably restrictive interpretation of the judicial role – bearing in mind the purpose of the HRA and its status as a constitutional instrument[97] – bears much in common with the courts' approach to the limitations of

---

[93] *Handyside* v. *United Kingdom* (1979–80) 1 EHRR 737, para. 48.

[94] *R. (on the Application of S)* v. *Chief Constable of South Yorkshire; R. (on the Application of Marper)* v. *Chief Constable of South Yorkshire* [2002] 1 WLR 3223, para. 34, *per* Lord Woolf (emphasis added).

[95] Judge Sibrand Karel Martens, 'Incorporating the European Convention: The Role of the Judiciary' [1998] EHRLR 5, 14.

[96] *R.* v. *Secretary of State for the Home Department, ex parte Fire Brigades Union* [1995] 2 AC 513, 567, *per* Lord Mustill.

[97] See e.g. *Brown* v. *Stott* [2003] 1 AC 681, 703, *per* Lord Bingham.

s.3(1) of the HRA; in spite of the 'broad and malleable'[98] language of that provision, which *might* permit 'an interpretation which linguistically may appear strained',[99] s.3(1) does *not* sanction courts to act as legislators.[100]

Of course, these two approaches do not rule out the possibility of providing for an increased protection beyond that provided by Strasbourg through a removal of the margin of appreciation from the equation,[101] or by the development of a 'broadly consistent' domestic standard where the Convention decisions are few and inconsistent or deal with the question of admissibility only.[102] In those circumstances where little guidance can be gleaned from the Strasbourg jurisprudence, a domestic court would be forced to play a more creative role, with the principles which underpin the Convention elevated to a position of increased importance. In the areas where the Strasbourg case law affords little or no direct guidance – either where the primary source of authority exists only in admissibility decisions,[103] or where the Court has deferred to the judgment of national authorities[104] – 'indirect guidance may be obtained from it, but only by a process of inference; therefore the

---

[98] R. Clayton, 'Judicial Deference and "Democratic Dialogue": The Legitimacy of Judicial Intervention under the Human Rights Act 1998' [2004] PL 33, 34.

[99] *R. v. A (No. 2)* [2002] 1 AC 45, 68, *per* Lord Steyn.

[100] For commentary on the developing case-law on s.3(1) HRA, see C. Gearty, 'Reconciling Parliamentary Democracy and Human Rights' (2002) 118 LQR 248; G. Phillipson, '(Mis-)Reading Section 3 of the Human Rights Act' (2003) 119 LQR 183; C. Gearty, 'Revisiting Section 3 of the Human Rights Act' (2003) 119 LQR 551; A. Kavanagh, 'The Elusive Divide between Interpretation and Legislation under the Human Rights Act 1998' (2004) 24 OJLS 259; D. Nicol, 'Statutory Interpretation and Human Rights after *Anderson*' [2004] PL 274; A. Kavanagh, 'Statutory Interpretation and Human Rights after *Anderson*: A More Contextual Approach' [2004] PL 537; A. Kavanagh, 'Unlocking the Human Rights Act: The "Radical" Approach to Section 3(1) Revisited' [2005] EHRLR 259. See also the chapters by David Feldman and Aileen Kavanagh in this volume.

[101] Which *may* extend to the question of the scope of the primary right between 'different cultural, traditional and religious environments' (*Secretary of State for Work and Pensions* v. *M* [2006] UKHL 11, *per* Lord Mance, paras. 135–6).

[102] As in, for example, the case-law on public protest, on which see H. Fenwick and G. Phillipson, 'Public Protest, the Human Rights Act and Judicial Responses to Political Expression' [2000] PL 627, 640–1.

[103] *Ibid.*

[104] Strasbourg decisions on restrictions on freedom of expression on grounds of morality provide useful examples: *Handyside* v. *United Kingdom* (1979–80) 1 EHRR 737; *Müller* v. *Switzerland* (1991) 13 EHRR 212.

principles deriving from the Strasbourg jurisprudence should generally be called upon to underpin and guide this inferential process'.[105]

Stretching the limits of the judicial role under the Act

It is argued that the above-described differences in stance as regards both the approach to be taken to the s.2(1) obligation and the potential for the judiciary to enhance the scope of the 'Convention rights' as protected in domestic law can be traced to differing conceptions of the judicial role under the HRA and the rights to which it gives further effect in domestic law. In seeming contrast to the conservative or minimalist perspective on the judicial role described in Colin Warbrick's chapter in this volume, important *dicta* can be found to challenge the view that the 'Convention rights', as applied in domestic law, should be constrained by the judgments of the Strasbourg Court. The case of *Re McKerr* – concerning the procedural rights adjunctive to Article 2 ECHR and the question of their existence at common law prior to the advent of the HRA – is a pertinent example, with the speech of Lord Hoffmann particularly revealing in terms of his assessment of the position of the Convention rights in domestic law. Although decided before the House of Lords heard either *Ullah* or *Marper*,[106] Lord Hoffmann's view of the status of the 'Convention rights' in domestic law is indicative of initial judicial uncertainty surrounding their character. Lord Hoffmann said of the rights under the HRA that:

> Although people sometimes speak of the Convention having been incorporated into domestic law, that is a misleading metaphor. What the Act has done is to create domestic rights expressed in the same terms as those contained in the Convention. But they are domestic rights, not international rights. Their source is the statute, not the Convention ... their meaning and application is a matter for domestic courts, not the court in Strasbourg.[107]

This statement is remarkable in that it seems to mark a backward step from the House of Lords' concerns that any decision on a Convention right which departed from 'clear and constant' Strasbourg jurisprudence

---

[105] H. Fenwick and G. Phillipson, 'Direct Action, Convention Values and the Human Rights Act' (2001) 21 LS 535, 564.

[106] See also the decision of the Court of Appeal in *R. (on the Application of Al-Jedda)* v. *Secretary of State for Defence* [2006] EWCA Civ 327, esp. paras. 88–99.

[107] *In re McKerr* [2004] UKHL 12, para. 65.

ran the risk of being overturned by the European Court of Human Rights.[108] It is also arguably inconsistent with, or at least strongly in tension with, the requirement to 'take into account' the jurisprudence of the Strasbourg organs under s.2(1). Moreover, it could be suggested that this approach to the HRA comes close to treating the Act as a UK Bill of Rights as it has the potential to separate the content of domestic human rights law almost completely from the Convention and its jurisprudence. In asserting that the 'meaning and application' of the rights under the HRA is a 'matter for domestic courts' – and explicitly denying this function to Strasbourg – Lord Hoffmann could be seen as laying claim to a more creativist role for domestic courts in rights litigation. Diverging the meaning of the rights under the HRA *completely* from the Convention and its jurisprudence would, under the auspices of an Act designed to 'give further effect to the rights and freedoms guaranteed under the European Convention on Human Rights', undoubtedly come into conflict with the scheme of the HRA.[109] But, in his recognition that the 'meaning and application' of the rights conferred by the HRA is a matter for domestic courts, Lord Hoffmann may tacitly acknowledge that, in giving meaning to those rights, domestic courts should not be constrained by the judgments of the Strasbourg organs.

Returning to the judgment of Laws LJ in *ProLife Alliance*, a significant difference in the notion of the judicial role under the Act is evident to that disclosed in *Ullah* and *Marper*. In that case, Laws LJ stated that:

> I would assert that as a matter of domestic law the courts owe a special responsibility to the public as the constitutional guardian of freedom of political debate. This responsibility is most acute at the time and in the context of a public election, especially a general election. It has its origin in a deeper truth, which is that the courts are ultimately the trustees of our democracy's framework. I consider that this view is consonant with the common law's general recognition, apparent in recent years, of a category of fundamental or constitutional rights.[110]

---

[108] *R. (on the Application of Alconbury Developments Ltd) v. Secretary of State for the Environment, Transport and the Regions* [2001] UKHL 23, para. 26, *per* Lord Slynn.

[109] Most obviously in terms of judging the 'compatibility' of an act or omission with the Convention rights under s.3(1) or s.6(1) HRA and in the potential making of a 'declaration of incompatibility' under s.4(2).

[110] *R. (on the Application of ProLife Alliance) v. British Broadcasting Corporation* [2002] 3 WLR 1080, para. 36.

While the implications of this statement are more wide-ranging than can be explored here, it can be observed that Laws LJ clearly envisages a role for the courts which goes beyond the traditional conception of the separation of powers doctrine – that the courts are mere interpreters of the law as passed by the sovereign parliament. He sees the courts as defenders of fundamental constitutional principles which appear to transcend Parliamentary sovereignty.[111] From Laws LJ's *dicta*, however, it is also clear that this role arises not out of the Human Rights Act, but from the common law. Yet the role played by the Human Rights Act is fundamentally important to this viewpoint – as Laws LJ has stated elsewhere, 'the Human Rights Act 1998 now provides a democratic underpinning to the common law's acceptance of constitutional rights, and important new procedural measures for their protection'.[112] Indeed, one way in which the domestic judiciary might legitimately provide for an enhanced protection – beyond the ambit of the primary Convention right – would be through the common law fundamental rights jurisdiction, rather than the domestic articulation of the 'Convention rights'. As Lord Mance argued in *Secretary of State for Work and Pensions* v. *M*:

> the ... 'margin of appreciation' ... is ... to be understood in another sense, as referring to the freedom of national courts, or member states, to provide for rights more generous than those guaranteed by the Convention, though not as the product of interpretation of the Convention. In this connection, the United Kingdom already has, quite apart from the Convention, a developing body of common law authority underlining the importance attaching to fundamental rights.[113]

While it might therefore be argued that the emerging themes in judicial reasoning in this sphere err on the side of conservatism, there remains an undeniable, and unresolved, tension between differing conceptions of the Act itself – and those rights to which it gives further effect in domestic law – and the traditional position of the judiciary within the separation of powers.

---

[111] On which see Sir John Laws, 'Law and Democracy' [1995] PL 72.

[112] *International Transport Roth GmbH* v. *Secretary of State for the Home Department* [2003] QB 728, para. 71.

[113] *Secretary of State for Work and Pensions* v. *M* [2006] UKHL 11, para. 136, *per* Lord Mance.

Conclusion

As regards the status of the Strasbourg jurisprudence in domestic law, it is suggested that the dominant trends in adjudication under the HRA can be put down to two factors: first, a wish to preserve legal certainty and avoid accusations of unwarranted judicial activism; secondly, a particular vision of the role of the judges – as defined by the separation of powers doctrine – in a system unaccustomed to 'constitutional' adjudication. The precedent-like interpretation of the s.2(1) obligation reflects the laudable desire on the part of the courts to retain a firm grounding in Strasbourg authority; yet, at the same time, it could be said to distort the nature of the judicial inquiry as prescribed by that section of the Human Rights Act. The minimalist approach to the scope of the protections afforded under the Human Rights Act, if the analysis of Lord Bingham in *Ullah* is correct – that the matter of defining the scope of the primary right is a matter expressly reserved to Strasbourg – confirms that domestic judges should not seek to expand the scope of the Convention rights as applied in domestic law. While this too reflects a desire to sustain legal certainty, this approach arguably sits uneasily with the Act's status as a constitutional instrument and with the intentions of the Strasbourg institutions that state authorities be the primary mechanism for realising the Convention rights.

While there is an acknowledgment that the constitutional status of the Human Rights Act demands that it be given a 'generous and purposive' interpretation so that individuals can benefit from the full effect of the rights it confers,[114] as Clayton observes, this is in tension with established perceptions of the judicial role.[115] The judicially cautious stance to s.2(1) and the scope of the Convention rights is perhaps entirely in keeping with the traditional role of the courts as interpreters of the law rather than legislators. However, this common law fiction had been questioned long before the passing of an Act which has had the effect of bringing the judicial role closer to those areas which had been said to be beyond its reach.[116] As a direct result of the 1998 Act, more

---

[114] For discussion, see R. Masterman, 'Taking the Strasbourg Jurisprudence into Account: Developing a "Municipal Law of Human Rights" under the Human Rights Act' (2005) 54 ICLQ 907, 913–15.

[115] R. Clayton, 'Judicial Deference and "Democratic Dialogue": The Legitimacy of Judicial Intervention under the Human Rights Act 1998' [2004] PL 33, 34.

[116] Lord Reid, 'The Judge as Law Maker' (1972) 12 JSPTL 22; A. Lester, 'English Judges as Law Makers' [1993] PL 269.

than ever the courts are questioning the policies of the democratically elected arms of government on human rights grounds;[117] the Human Rights Act has – through proportionality analysis – brought judicial scrutiny of executive action closer than ever before to the review of policy on its merits;[118] and the potential for the courts under s.3(1) of the Human Rights Act to in effect rewrite statutory language has been clearly demonstrated by the House of Lords decision in *R. v. A (No. 2)*.[119] The Human Rights Act has undeniably redefined the judicial role; and in so doing it has altered the balance of power between judiciary, legislature and executive as it is traditionally understood. Yet, as evidenced above, many facets of judicial reasoning under the Human Rights Act display an adherence to a conception of the separation of powers which does not reflect the new legal realities. Beyond the confines of adjudication under the Human Rights Act, the courts are not only beginning to exercise what might naturally be called a 'constitutional' jurisdiction, but are openly acknowledging that in doing so they are operating almost entirely without precedent.[120] It would be unusual to say the least if such a jurisdiction were to develop on the one hand, while on the other the traditional constraints on the exercise of judicial power were to restrict the development of a constitutional human rights jurisdiction where the mandate to do so had been bestowed on the judiciary by parliament.

---

[117] For two particularly well-publicised examples, see *A and Others* v. *Secretary of State for the Home Department* [2004] UKHL 56; *R. (on the Application of Q)* v. *Secretary of State for the Home Department* [2003] EWCA Civ 364 (on which see A. Bradley, 'Judicial Independence under Attack' [2003] PL 397.

[118] See Ian Leigh, Chapter 7 in this volume.   [119] *R. v. A (No. 2)* [2002] 1 AC 45.

[120] See the decision of the Court of Appeal in *R. (on the Application of Jackson and Others)* v. *Attorney General* [2005] QB 579, para. 12, where the then Lord Chief Justice acknowledged that the court was acting as a 'constitutional court' and that 'there was no precise precedent' for its so doing.

4

Institutional roles and meanings of 'compatibility' under the Human Rights Act 1998

DAVID FELDMAN*

The purpose of this paper

In a previous comment on s.3 of the Human Rights Act 1998, I wrote:

> we cannot now assume that there is a single 'right answer' to the question,
> 'What does a provision in legislation mean?' Instead, there is a range of
> possible answers, and only those which are not incompatible with
> Convention rights may normally be adopted. This recognizes the indeter-
> minate nature of language in a more explicit way than has usually been
> the case, except in relation to EU law.[1]

In fact, this is a problem encountered in all interpretation, but s.3 requires
us to confront it openly, instead of dealing with it in silence, or pretending
that there is usually a right answer to the question, 'What does legislation
mean?' This paper starts from two propositions. First, we have to assume
that legislation produces effects in the world. Were that not so, it would
have merely symbolic significance. Secondly, interpreters must focus on
the effects achieved, rather than on the meanings of words.

* This chapter is a revised version of a paper prepared for the symposium on Judicial
Reasoning and the Human Rights Act 1998 held at the University of Durham on 8–9
April 2005. Earlier versions of ideas outlined here were discussed at a meeting of the Civil
Liberties Subject Section of the Society for Public Teachers of Law (now the Society of Legal
Scholars) at the University of Glasgow on 13 September 2001, and at a round table of the
International Association of Constitutional Law at L'Université Montesquieu (Bordeaux IV)
in October 2004. I am grateful to the editors of this volume, the participants in the
discussions, particularly Aharon Barak, Eric Barendt, Conor Gearty, Stephen Grosz, Aileen
Kavanagh, Sir David Keene, Kevin Kerrigan, Francesca Klug, Ian Leigh, Jo Miles, Aidan
O'Neill, Rabinder Singh, Soli Sorabjee, Hugh Tomlinson, Sir Michael Tugendhat and Colin
Warbrick, and Edward Adams for illuminating the subject for me.
[1] David Feldman, *Civil Liberties and Human Rights in England and Wales* (2nd edn,
Oxford: Oxford University Press, 2002), p. 86.

In this paper, I offer a typology of the different ways in which a reading or effect of legislation may be compatible or incompatible with a Convention right, and develop an institutional analysis of the manner in which interpreters adopt a reading of legislation, arguing that their institutional positions inevitably affect their approach to the twin processes of reading and giving effect to legislation.

We are quite used to the idea that the constitutional position of the interpreter delimits the bounds of the 'possible' when deciding whether it is possible to adopt a particular reading of legislation in order to achieve compatibility with a Convention right. In particular, we have come to accept that it is not 'possible' for an institution with an adjudicative role under the constitution to act legislatively, rewriting rather than reading the legislative text.[2] This really means that it is not possible for the institution to adopt a legislative approach and remain within its constitutional authority. It is less obvious that the reader's institutional position also affects what one means by saying that a reading or effect is 'compatible' or 'incompatible' with a right.[3] The first purpose of this paper is to argue that one's view of the (in)compatibility of a legislative provision with a Convention right is shaped by one's institutional position, so that the notion of (in)compatibility of a reading with a Convention right depends on the constitutional role of the reader, just as the range of 'possible' readings does. The second purpose is to distinguish between different senses in which a provision may be (in)compatible with a right.

What are the requirements of section 3(1) of the Human Rights Act 1998, and who are subject to them?

Concerning the relationship between provisions of legislation and the requirements of Convention rights – those rights under the European Convention on Human Rights which became part of municipal law in the United Kingdom by virtue of the Scotland Act 1998, the Northern Ireland Act 1998, the Government of Wales Act 1998 and the Human Rights Act 1998 – s.3 of the Human Rights Act 1998 provides:

---

[2] See e.g. *In re S (Minors) (Care Order: Implementation of Care Plan)* [2002] 2 AC 291.
[3] However, I will not deal with legislation which is designed to protect a right by removing an incompatibility in other legislation or by remedying a violation of the right; such legislation presents special problems which fall outside the scope of the present paper.

(1) So far as it is possible to do so, primary legislation and subordinate legislation must be read and given effect in a way which is compatible with the Convention rights.

(2) This section—
   (a) applies to primary and secondary legislation whenever enacted;
   (b) does not affect the validity, continuing operation or enforcement of any incompatible primary legislation; and
   (c) does not affect the validity, continuing operation or enforcement of any incompatible subordinate legislation if (disregarding any possibility of revocation) primary legislation prevents removal of the incompatibility.

Section 3(1) is entirely general in the way it imposes its obligation. It binds anyone who has to read and give effect to legislation. It applies to legislators and administrators as much as to adjudicators, and to people and institutions that are not public authorities for the purposes of the Human Rights Act 1998 (such as the two Houses of Parliament) just as it does to public authorities. This has important consequences. For example, when there was a question in 2004 as to the legality of a marriage between the Prince of Wales, the heir to the United Kingdom throne, and Mrs Camilla Parker-Bowles (as she then was) in a civil ceremony in England, the Lord Chancellor advised, and the Registrar General of Marriages seems to have decided, that the legislation could be interpreted as permitting the marriage partly because the Marriage Act 1836 (which prohibits members of the royal family from marrying in a civil ceremony in the UK) and the Marriage Act 1949 (which consolidated the legislation relating to marriage) had to be read and given effect, so far as possible, in a manner compatible with the Convention right of the parties to marry and to be free of discrimination in the protection for their substantive Convention rights.[4]

The work of Social Fund Inspectors offers another example. When reviewing a decision of a Social Fund Officer in relation to a discretionary loan or grant from the Social Fund, an Inspector is bound by s.140(2) of the Social Security Contributions and Benefits Act 1992 to give effect to general directions issued by the Secretary of State. (See also s.66(7) of the Social Security Administration Act 1992 and s.38(7) of the Social Security Act 1998.) However, as the directions are a form of

---

[4] Written statement by Lord Falconer of Thoroton on 23 February 2005, HL Debs., 24 February 2005, vol. 669, cols. WS87–WS88.

subordinate legislation, the Inspector is also bound to read and give effect to those directions in a manner compatible with Convention rights so far as possible, for example to avoid giving effect to the direction in such a way as to deny support to a claimant who would be left destitute as a result in breach of the right to be free of degrading treatment. If it is impossible to read and give effect to the direction in that way, the Inspector is entitled to conclude that the direction is invalid and ineffective, because the primary legislation under which the directions are given does not require the power to give directions to be used in a manner incompatible with Convention rights.

Many people are thus subject to the requirements of s.3(1), which presents the interpreter with the following challenges:

- understanding the range of outcomes for the case that could be justified by reference to sustainable readings of the other legislative provision;
- reading the Convention right(s) in the light of the facts of the case, with a view to deciding which, if any, of the range of outcomes justifiable under the legislative provision could also be justified by reference to the Convention right(s) (or, in other words, deciding what is meant by 'possible' and '(in)compatible' in the particular context);
- choosing an outcome;
- justifying the outcome by reference to sustainable readings of the various norm-generating texts.

For present purposes, we will concentrate on the terms 'compatible', 'incompatible', 'incompatibility' and 'possible', which are central to the scheme of s.3. We will seek to tease out the complexities of the concepts which are wrapped up in them, placing them in the constitutional and institutional contexts of different kinds of decision-making.

Section 3 appears to contemplate a process of comparing two norms, one deriving from a Convention right and the other from a statute, in order to achieve (where possible) harmony, or a lack of disharmony, between them. At first glance, one might be misled into thinking that one need only adjust the meanings of the terms of either the right or the statute or both so as to avoid a disharmony of meaning. That idea is based on the misconception that the process of comparing norms for legal purposes is purely abstract. In reality, it is nearly always grounded firmly in a view of the social world from which the dispute, which makes it necessary to address the statute and the right, emerges. The three forms of decision-making which come closest to viewing the norms in abstraction are: first, legislating; secondly, abstract review of the constitutionality of legislation;[5] and, thirdly, academic commentary on legislation. Yet the first and second of these rely on the decision-makers having a vision of the range of social situations to which the norms should apply, and the kinds of social effects which should be encouraged or discouraged by the norms. It is possible to make conceptually beautiful and coherent legislation in the abstract, but it is unlikely to be useful unless the beauty and coherence are yoked to a clear view of the social contexts which are likely to be affected. Members of the third class of decision-makers about laws, academic commentators, are entitled to see abstract beauty as an intellectual virtue, but usually regard practicality as a virtue with at least equal value.

Other instances of legal decision-making are more obviously rooted in the social milieu from which the dispute springs. Applying a statute to decide a case usually involves creating a picture of the circumstances giving rise to the dispute and trying to understand the obligations of the parties in the light of a single legislative provision or set of provisions. This is never a straightforward process. The task of creating a picture – sometimes misleadingly described as 'establishing the facts of the case' – involves imagination and judgment, and the picture painted by the decision-maker is likely to be influenced by all kinds of factors affecting the decision-maker's perception of social reality. If one is unfamiliar with the social or political milieu in which the case is rooted, it is very difficult to assess the evidence or form a useful picture of the circumstances (as my experience as a judge in the unfamiliar surroundings of Bosnia and Herzegovina has taught me).

Next, there is the sometimes difficult task of placing one's picture in a normative framework to allow one to decide on the best possible outcome and to justify one's choice rationally. Where the decisive norms derive from statutes, the process of justification must refer to the statute. It is not a matter of defining the terms used in the statute (a descriptive process relating to the social meanings of individual words or phrases), but an attempt to show that one of a number of possible outcomes can

---

[5] It should be noted that courts empowered to conduct abstract constitutional review are not always empowered to utilise a 'réserve d'interprétation' (that is to say, that the law is constitutionally valid if and only if it is interpreted in a particular way) and thereby to impose an obligation on other courts to interpret it in that way.

most convincingly be regarded as being within the ambit of the text. In the context of applying the European Convention on Human Rights, this has been explained by Judge Zupancic of the European Court of Human Rights,[6] and the insight applies generally to normative decision-making in individual cases. The process is usually called 'statutory interpretation', but it requires the 'interpreter' to focus at least as much on social reality and what is socially desirable as on the words of the statutory text. It is a richly complex and multi-faceted undertaking.

However, when the case engages Convention rights, the demands of the process are still more complex. One must then place one's picture of the circumstances of the case within a multi-dimensional framework, made up of not only the ordinarily applicable municipal laws but also the standards of European human rights law derived from the European Convention. When the case arises under the Human Rights Act 1998, s.3(1) of that Act applies, and the task of the decision-maker is still more complicated. The decision-maker must try to bring three norm-generating texts into some sort of harmony: the text of s.3(1) itself; the text of the other legislative provision that appears to be relevant to the case; and the text (or texts) of the Convention right (or rights) with which that provision must, if possible, be made compatible.

The constitutional and institutional roles of decision-makers and their effect on the meaning of 'compatible' and 'possible'

As noted above, s.3(1) imposes its obligation equally on legislators, administrators, other public authorities, and other people and institutions, but that does not mean that the general and absolute obligation

---

[6] Oral presentation by Judge Zupancic at a Round Table of the International Association of Constitutional Law on 'Interpretation of the Constitution' organised by Le Centre d'études et de recherches comparatives sur les constitutions, le libertés et l'état at l'Université Montesquieu (Bordeaux IV) on 15 and 16 October 2004. The comments are noted by Francis Delpérée, the Rapporteur for the conference, in 'L'interprétation de la constitution ou la leçon de music', in Ferdinand Mélin-Soucramanien (ed.), *L'interprétation constitutionnelle* (Paris: Dalloz, 2005), pp. 241–8 at p. 245: 'Et je n'ai pas m'empêcher d'esquisser un mouvement de surprise lorsque le juge Zupancic a très honnêtement reconnu que le texte de la Convention européenne des droits de l'homme n'était pas vraiment un instrument de référence pour la Cour de Strasbourg.' See also Otto Pfersmann, *ibid.*, p. 87, and Lech Garlicki, another judge of the Strasbourg Court, *ibid.*, p. 140, stressing that translating the general language of the Convention into more specific rules and principles, while not allowing the Court to disregard the written text entirely, 'requires a certain degree of creativity'.

under s.3 requires everyone reading legislation to behave in exactly the same way, or to take the same approach when deciding whether a statute is compatible with a Convention right. Legislators, administrators and adjudicators have different constitutional roles and competencies, and they perform different functions. Legislators and administrators lack the constitutional authority to interpret legislation and Convention rights finally and authoritatively. It may be more difficult for an official administering a statutory scheme to justify giving effect to a statute in an unexpected way in order to achieve compatibility with a Convention right, both because the official has no constitutional authority to determine the effect of a Convention right and because the administrative role is normally to work within, rather than determine the lawfulness of, a statutory scheme. In other words, the role and constitutional position of the person reading the legislation may significantly affect both what may be said to amount to an incompatibility and what range of readings of the legislation it is 'possible' for the decision-maker to adopt in order to avoid producing an incompatible effect.

As a general principle, the task of the interpreter of legislation is always to produce the best possible effect that can be justified by reference to the text. There may be different views as to the criteria for deciding what the best possible effect is. For example, in a legal system without entrenched fundamental values, it may be difficult to agree on criteria of 'goodness'. To limit unpredictability and inconsistency, members of different decision-making institutions develop conventions or presumptions to guide their decision-making, both individually and collectively as members of the specific institution. It seems to me to be plausible, and for current purposes will be assumed, that legislators interpret legislative proposals – Bills and the like – in the way best calculated to achieve their policy objectives, given their understanding of the world and of the constitutional and legal competence of their own institutions. Similarly, we shall assume for the moment that adjudicators interpret legislation in the way best calculated to achieve the objectives of any adjudicator: fairness, consistency and (in the case of judicial adjudicators) the maintenance of the principles of the rule of law. To put the matter at its simplest, people can only view the world and their part in it from the point of view in which they find themselves. Legislators adopt a model of the constitution which puts the legislative process at the centre of the constitution; similarly, adjudicators, executive bodies and administrators conceive of the constitution as centred on adjudication, government and public administration respectively. This explains why they can easily develop different views of their own constitutional competence and those of other agencies and institutions.[7]

This affects the ways in which legislators, administrators and adjudicators approach the text of legislation or proposed legislation. A legislator examines the provisions of proposed legislation with a view to amending it (if necessary) to produce the text that is most likely to realise that legislator's view of the best possible effect in the world from a policy perspective. The parliamentary draftsman does not seek to encapsulate the will of Parliament in the text. A Bill contains the will of the government (or of the proposer of the Bill if he or she is not a member of the government). Parliament's role is to review and amend the text, not to initiate it. A judicial adjudicator is concerned to give effect to the legislation in the way that best safeguards rule of law standards and any other values that are for the time being regarded as an important element in the legitimacy of legal outcomes. An administrator is less concerned with the rule of law, but more concerned with administrative efficiency, effectiveness and, often, economy.

Judges and administrators are also more conscious than legislators of the facts of individual cases. Legislators may have an idea in their minds of the typical factual situation with which given provisions will deal, but in the nature of their role they do not have before them a set of concrete cases against which to test their legislation. The best legislators take advice to inform themselves about the possible effects of particular provisions in a range of circumstances that seem likely to arise, but they can never predict all the cases that may materialise or the ingenuity of the police, prosecutors and others in trying to make provisions apply to situations for which they were not originally designed. Any doubts on this score can be set at rest by considering, for example, the use made of s.5 of the Public Order Act 1936 during the half-century before it was replaced. Originally passed to deal with gatherings of Mosleyite Blackshirts in British cities and counter-demonstrations by anti-fascists, it prohibited threatening, abusive or insulting words or behaviour likely to cause a breach of the peace, or whereby a breach of the peace was likely to be occasioned. This wording demonstrates a characteristic governmental fear of under-inclusiveness in legislation, and it came to be applied to a wide range of situations unrelated to political violence. By

---

[7] See D. Feldman, 'None, One or Several? Perspectives on the UK's Constitution(s)' [2005] CLJ 329–51, esp. 340–50; D. Feldman, 'Factors Affecting the Choice of Techniques of Constitutional Interpretation', in Mélin-Soucramanien (ed.), above n. 6, pp. 131–5.

1964, the section was applied to aggressive behaviour by an individual directed against another individual without any large-scale gathering or political disorder.[8] In 1972, in *Brutus* v. *Cozens*, the House of Lords had to remind the Divisional Court that: 'Insulting means insulting and nothing else.'[9] The word 'insulting' could not be stretched to cover the behaviour of a lone anti-apartheid protester who went onto Court No. 2 at Wimbledon to demonstrate when a South African tennis player, Chris Drysdale, was playing in a men's doubles match. The behaviour annoyed many people and might have led to a breach of the peace, but one could be annoyed by behaviour that could not be characterised as insulting. Yet, in 1982, the Divisional Court held (without referring or being referred to *Brutus* v. *Cozens*) that a person who masturbated in a public toilet was insulting another person present at the time.[10] This shows that any provision that confers discretion on an official is also liable to be used for unexpected purposes, presenting adjudicators with problems in deciding (for example) whether it is being used for an improper purpose, as the saga of Dame Shirley Porter and Westminster City Council's homes-for-votes plan demonstrates.[11]

Adjudicators and administrators, by contrast, are brought face to face every day with the concrete situations to which legislation applies or might apply, and face the task of deciding what effect provisions should have in unexpected circumstances. The adjudicator's job can be expressed in different ways. Viewed mechanistically, it could be said to be to apply the rules to the case and to give effect to the result. But this fails to take account of two aspects of the adjudicator's role. First, he or she must use a rule only so far as it is properly applicable. Judgment is required to decide whether or not the rule is properly applicable. The rule itself cannot usually determine the scope of its own applicability. Once that judgment is made, the rule may be used to justify or legitimate an outcome, but it cannot determine it. Secondly, the adjudicator must produce an outcome that is going to work, as far as possible, not just in that case but in other similar cases. It must be practicable, and must either be enforceable or command the respect of the parties. It must also be sufficiently in tune with the moral beliefs of a significant number of people to avoid bringing the legislation into disrepute.

---

[8] *Ward* v. *Holman* [1964] 2 QB 580 (CA).   [9] [1973] AC 854, 863 (HL), *per* Lord Reid.
[10] *Parkin* v. *Norman; Valentine* v. *Lilley* [1983] QB 92 (DC).
[11] *Porter* v. *Magill* [2001] UKHL 67; [2002] 2 AC 357 (HL).

These factors impose constraints on the range of decisions adjudicators can make. They also force adjudicators to read and give effect to legislation in ways that take account of a variety of considerations arising from sources other than the legislative provisions. When we read judgments and decisions, they often do not appear to be reasoned in that way. This is because at the stage when they deliver their final opinions adjudicators are not usually still working out their conclusion. They have normally already decided what the outcome should be in the course of preparing for and conducting the hearing and (if there is time) reflecting on it subsequently. Their job at the stage of delivering their decisions or opinions is to show how the outcome is justifiable by reference to a sustainable reading of the relevant legal sources. Offering this form of legal justification in public for their decisions is a condition for the constitutional legitimacy of every exercise of adjudicators' powers. It is a discipline of rationality rather than policy, and in that respect is quite different from the disciplines that justify the exercise of legislative power by legislators whether elected or not. To achieve the necessary formal justification adjudicators have to construct their opinions in a linear way, as if reasoning from first principles to a conclusion, but that is not (necessarily) the process of reasoning that led them to their conclusion in the first place. One occasionally catches a glimpse of the original process in some published opinions which start with broad statements of value or assertions of fact which make it possible to predict the conclusions, even before one reaches the discussion of legal rules or the facts of the case. The predominant style in published adjudicative opinions, however (at least in the United Kingdom), is justificatory and linear: adjudicators typically present their justification in the form of an argument, dealing with counter-arguments but moving inexorably towards the preferred result.[12]

Administrative decision-makers are in a different position. Typically, they have to make decisions which are as far as possible consistent with each other, and do so reasonably speedily. They may be resolving competing claims on public resources or making decisions restricting people's freedom to exercise their rights (such as land-use planning controls on private property) within a framework of policy and law which takes account of a variety of social interests. The decision-making process must necessarily respect legal constraints, but within them it is often controlled by institutional and managerial imperatives: officials

[12] Feldman, 'Factors', above n. 7, pp. 121–3.

may be required to meet targets (for example, to make a given number of decisions each week) which constrain the time they can spend on any one case; the range of possible decisions may be limited by budgetary or other restrictions; and the ethos of the institution or office may also shape the attitude of the decision-maker to particular issues or claimants. The main influences are policies of different kinds rather than rule-of-law ideals. Furthermore, they usually operate within a hierarchy with rules and guidance laid down (like the Social Fund general directions mentioned earlier) to help them to decide cases consistently and in accordance with objectives including budgetary propriety. While a Social Fund Inspector may be entitled or even bound to reinterpret or even disregard a Secretary of State's general direction in order to avoid a violation of a Convention right, it is unlikely that such a step would be welcomed by the Social Fund Commissioner, who will have sound organisational reasons to impose controls on individual Inspectors' freedom to play fast and loose with the general directions. The Inspectors will have to set the demands of managerial control and day-to-day consistency and predictability of decision-making within the Social Fund Inspectorate against the terms of s.3(1). Their institutional position will affect the way they understand the idea of compatibility and their freedom to read and give effect to legislation in particular ways.

That is just one example of how an interpreter's institutional role and the conditions for the legitimacy of his or her decisions affect the way in which he or she decides whether a decision or rule should be read or given effect in the light of its compatibility (for his or her purposes) with a Convention right. The ways in which this occurs can be explored in more depth by looking at how the process of assessing (in)compatibility is affected by the difference between three institutional roles of the possible decision-makers: an executive or ministerial role, including policy formation and legislative drafting; a parliamentary role, specifically one involving scrutiny of legislative proposals; and a judicial role, adjudicating authoritatively between disputed understandings of the relationship between the right-defining norm and the effect of the legislative provision.

Institutional views of (in)compatibility 1: government ministers and departments

The institutional standpoint of the decision-maker is, if anything, even more important in affecting decisions about compatibility than the rational typology outlined at p. 107 *et seq.*, below. As noted earlier, when a Minister of the Crown contemplates introducing to one of the Houses of Parliament a Bill, or making an Order in Council under the royal prerogative, a statutory instrument treated as primary legislation for the purposes of the Human Rights Act 1998, or subordinate legislation, he or she has to consider whether its provisions will be compatible with the Convention rights. This obligation has several sources. One is necessity. The Minister will want to know what effect the provisions are likely to have. In order to assess this, he or she will have to read the legislation, and ought (by virtue of s.3(1) of the 1998 Act) to read it in a manner compatible with Convention rights (so far as it is possible to do so). If the legislation in question is subordinate legislation, and it is later held to be incompatible with a Convention right, it is likely (save in certain circumstances) to be invalid to the extent of the incompatibility, and so will fail to have the desired effect. The Minister thus has both normative and prudential reasons for seeking compatibility between the legislation and relevant Convention rights.

If the legislation takes the form of a Bill to be presented to either House of Parliament, there is a further normative reason for considering the provisions in the light of Convention rights: s.19 of the Human Rights Act 1998 requires the Minister to state in writing before Second Reading either that in his or her view the Bill as introduced to the House is compatible with Convention rights, or that he or she is unable to say that it is compatible but would nevertheless like the House to consider the Bill. If the proposed legislation is not a Bill but is nevertheless primary rather than subordinate, it will not be invalid to the extent of any incompatibility, but any risk of its being given effect in an unforeseen way in order to secure compatibility provides a further prudential reason for seeking to draft the legislation in a way that can be given effect so as to achieve the Minister's desired outcome while being read in a manner compatible with relevant Convention rights. In addition, the *Human Rights Act 1998 Guidance for Departments*[13] provided that a Minister should, as a matter of good practice, volunteer his or her view as to the compatibility of a statutory instrument or draft statutory instrument for which an affirmative resolution is required, and that should always be done in relation to subordinate legislation that amends primary legislation.

But Ministers have no constitutional authority to make final decisions as to the compatibility of provisions with Convention rights. These

---

[13] Second edition, now superseded by Cabinet Office, *Guide to Legislative Procedures*, s.10, accessible at http://www.cabinetoffice.gov.uk/secretariats/economic_and_domestic/legislative_programme/guide.asp, para. 40.

are matters of law, not politics. How then does a Minister approach the question of compatibility? Authoritatively deciding on compatibility is the prerogative of the judicial branch. The Minister has to make a judgment, but it can be no more than an assessment of the risk of an authorised adjudicator later authoritatively holding some provision to be incompatible with a Convention right. The Minister takes legal advice, but ultimately makes his or her own assessment, and does not purport to offer more than a personal opinion. Indeed, in relation to Bills, that is all that s.19 of the Human Rights Act 1998 requires. The opinion is intended to inform the relevant House of Parliament in very broad overview of the Minister's conclusion. It offers no reasons, and is not to be regarded as having any particular authority. The purposes of s.19 seem to be twofold: first, to force the Minister to consider the question of compatibility at an early stage; secondly, to alert the relevant House of Parliament to the issue of compatibility by providing it with a statement of the Minister's conclusion. In relation to other types of legislation, there is no statutory requirement for any statement as to compatibility, although Standing Orders impose certain obligations on the promoters of private Bills, and the government has given undertakings, which now amount to a constitutional convention, that a Minister will express his or her view as to the adequacy of the promoters' compatibility statement in relation to private Bills and private Members' Bills. In relation to private Members' Bills, *The Human Rights Act 1998 Guidance for Departments*[14] said that Ministers should, as a matter of good practice, express the government's views on compatibility during the Second Reading debate.

The Minister's assessment of the risk of incompatibility is still (we have to assume) made as contemplated by *The Human Rights Act 1998 Guidance for Departments* even though its replacement, the *Guide to Legislative Procedures*, is far less specific.[15] Paragraphs 35 and 36, so far as relevant, provided:

> 35. Once the Bill is drafted, a document analysing the ECHR points should be prepared, probably by departmental lawyers, consulting Law

[14] Above, n. 13 at para. 38. The *Guide to Legislative Procedures* does not deal with this.
[15] *The Human Rights Act 1998 Guidance for Departments*, paras. 32–40, and the further guidance, *Section 19 Statements: Revised Guidance for Departments*, replacing para. 39 of the original version in relation to information to be disclosed to Parliament relating to the compatibility assessment. Cf. *Guide to Legislative Procedures*, paras. 10.9 to 10.12. It is understood that a new edition of the *Guide*, currently in preparation, will include more detailed provisions covering matters previously included in the revised para. 39 of the *Guidance for Departments*.

Officers and the Foreign and Commonwealth Office as appropriate. That document should be cleared with Ministers and circulated for Legislation Committee [of the Cabinet] with the Bill. The same document, taking into account any points raised at Legislation Committee, can then be put to the Minister in charge of the Bill prior to Introduction as the basis for his section 19 statement. The document, amended as necessary to reflect any developments, can subsequently go to the Minister in the second House as the basis for his section 19 statement.

36. An important issue is the degree of certainty needed to justify a statement under section 19 that in a Minister's view a Bill is compatible with the Convention rights. A common approach is needed across government. The following guidance has been agreed:

- A section 19(1)(a) statement may be made where, in the view of the Minister, the provisions of the Bill are compatible with Convention rights. In other cases a section 19(1)(b) statement should be made: such a statement is not one that the provisions of the Bill are incompatible with the Convention rights but only one to the effect that the Minister is unable to make a statement of compatibility. A section 19(1)(a) statement is a positive statement of compatibility.

- If a section 19(1)(a) statement is to be made, a Minister must be clear that, at a minimum, the balance of arguments supports the view that the provisions are compatible. A Minister will form his view on the basis of appropriate legal advice. Departmental lawyers will advise, if necessary following consultation with the Law Officers, whether the provisions of the Bill are on balance compatible with the Convention rights. In doing so, they will consider whether it is more likely than not that the provisions of the Bill will stand up to challenge on Convention grounds before the domestic courts and the Strasbourg Court. A Minister should not be advised to make a statement of compatibility where legal advice is that on balance the provisions of the Bill would not survive such a challenge. The fact that there are valid arguments to be advanced against any anticipated challenge is not a sufficient basis on which to advise a Minister that he may make a statement of compatibility where it is thought that these arguments would not ultimately succeed before the courts.

This made it clear that the risk assessment was made on the basis of a balance of probabilities. Ministers took and, under the *Guide to Legislation*, still take legal advice, but they are responsible to Parliament and must be clear as to the probability of the provisions being held to be compatible or incompatible. While it is not true to say that the Minister should consider any provision which does not meet the balance of probabilities test to be incompatible, such a provision will at least not be stated to be compatible in the Minister's view. There are thus three levels of compatibility for the purpose of the Minister's risk assessment: probably compatible; very possibly compatible but not able to be stated to be compatible; and probably incompatible. The assessment is made by considering the norm-generating texts in relation to each other against the background of various sets of assumed or anticipated facts, but without presuming that the assessment can take account of all possible circumstances. In this respect, the assessment is abstract rather than concrete.

Since the Minister's statement is no more than the assertion of a personal opinion relating to a risk assessment, it has no particular authority as a matter of law. The statement informs the House of the Minister's opinion, but it lacks all authority as a legal and constitutional determination of compatibility. Only the courts have authority to make such determinations. In *R. v. Lichniak*,[16] discussing the compatibility of the mandatory sentence of life imprisonment for murder with the Convention rights under Articles 3 and 6 of the ECHR, Lord Bingham of Cornhill said: 'The fact that section 1(1) [of the Murder (Abolition of Death Penalty) Act 1965] is the settled will of a democratic assembly is not a conclusive reason for upholding it, but a degree of deference is due to the judgment of a democratic assembly as to how a particular social problem is best tackled.' However, this is a far cry from giving any weight to a s.19 statement. As a matter of constitutional law, it would be constitutionally inappropriate for a court to give any weight to them, for at least three reasons. First, the statement relates to the form of the Bill first introduced to each House, not to the final form in which the Bill is enacted. Secondly, the Minister's statement gives no reason for his or her opinion as to compatibility and no information about the process of reasoning that led the Minister to his or her conclusion. It is therefore impossible for a court to assess the adequacy of the opinion. Thirdly, it is the courts, not the Minister, who constitutionally have authority to make final, authoritative determinations on questions of law, including compatibility. It would be constitutionally inappropriate for the courts to defer to Ministers on questions of law.

Institutional (in)compatibility 2: the two Houses of Parliament and their committees

When one of the Houses of Parliament or a Parliamentary committee or an Officer of either House scrutinises a Bill from a human rights

---

[16] [2002] UKHL 47; [2003] 1 AC 903 (HL), para. 14.

standpoint, the position is subtly different. The purposes of this scrutiny are fourfold: to identify publicly and for the assistance of each House any way in which a Bill gives rise to an enhanced risk of causing or allowing violations of human rights; to elucidate and test the government's or promoter's reasons for thinking that the Bill is compatible, or (occasionally) to consider whether it is appropriate for either House to consider a Bill if the Minister has made a s.19(1)(b) statement, with a view to improving the quality of compatibility assessments within government departments; to make and publish an independent risk assessment supported by published reasons to inform debate on the Bill in each House of Parliament; and to make recommendations for amending the Bill or for extraneous safeguards against violations of rights, to improve the quality of the Bill and/or to offer protections for people's rights. The inquiry and assessment are necessarily conducted on an abstract basis, without reference to the concrete facts of any contested case.

Like Ministers, the two Houses of Parliament and their committees have no constitutional authority to decide questions of law, and questions of compatibility are always questions of law. Indeed, they are questions of pure law, because the issues cannot be determined in the light of concrete factual situations. For the main parliamentary body dealing with such matters, the Joint Committee on Human Rights (JCHR), the conclusion of the risk assessment is usually expressed not by reference to compatibility but instead by reference to degrees of risk of incompatibility. (Other committees dealing occasionally with questions of compatibility include the Joint Committee on Statutory Instruments, the Commons Home Affairs Committee, the Lords Delegated Powers and Regulatory Reform Committee, and the European Union committees of both Houses.) Only rarely can the JCHR say that a provision gives rise to a risk of either logical or unconditional incompatibility. Usually, the JCHR's scrutiny reports assess the risk of practical and/or conditional incompatibility, examining safeguards against the use of discretion in an incompatible way or the likelihood that the government's arguments for justifying an interference with a right will be acceptable to adjudicators. The JCHR's conclusion generally takes the form of a statement, with supporting reasons, that a provision gives rise to a significant, or substantial, or serious or severe risk that the provision will be held to be intrinsically incompatible with a Convention right or to have given rise to violations of Convention rights in operation. Other Bills or provisions will normally be dismissed in a sentence as not giving rise in the JCHR's view to any significant risk of incompatibility (although the matter is sometimes complicated by the fact that the JCHR assesses the risk of incompatibility with a very wide range of human rights treaty obligations of the United Kingdom, not merely Convention rights).[17] For Parliament, then, there are at least four levels of risk of incompatibility: no significant risk, a significant risk, a substantial risk, and a serious or severe risk.

It follows that a Minister may properly make a s.19(1)(a) statement of compatibility in respect of a Bill even after receiving legal advice, in line with the subsequent view of the JCHR, that a provision gives rise to a significant or, perhaps, substantial risk of being held to be incompatible with a Convention right.

Thus for both Ministers and Parliament compatibility and incompatibility are matters of risk rather than authoritative determination, and the purposes for which the risk is assessed and the terms in which it is assessed are different by reason of the institutional position and role of each body.

Institutional (in)compatibility 3: adjudicators, especially judges of superior courts

By contrast with Ministers and the Houses of Parliament, adjudicators are constitutionally empowered to make authoritative determinations of questions of law, including the best reading, effect and compatibility with Convention rights of legislative provision. The task here is not to make a risk assessment but to decide finally; a provision is either compatible or incompatible. While adjudicators, like Ministers and the Houses of Parliament, must grapple with the problems presented by the different logical and practical senses of (in)compatibility, an adjudicator's job is to a degree simpler (although carrying more responsibility), and adjudicators are helped by being able to view the various norm-generating texts through the prism of the facts of the case at bar.

This makes it unsurprising that the judges are unwilling to grant remedies in cases which seem to them to be of no practical importance, unless a statutory provision (such as s.4 of the Human Rights Act 1998

---

[17] For discussion, see Lord Lester of Herne Hill QC, 'Parliamentary Scrutiny of Legislation under the Human Rights Act 1998' [2002] EHRLR 432–51; D. Feldman, 'Parliamentary Scrutiny of Legislation and Human Rights' [2002] PL 323–48; D. Feldman, 'The Impact of Human Rights on the UK Legislative Process' (2004) 25 *Statute LR* 91–115.

relating to declarations of incompatibility) expressly require them to consider doing so. They have shown themselves unwilling to make declarations of lawfulness of conduct raising questions of compatibility hypothetically or in the abstract where on the facts of a case the compatibility could not realistically be said to have affected the person seeking a determination. In *R. (Rusbridger)* v. *Attorney-General*,[18] the House of Lords refused a declaration that s.3 of the Treason Felony Act 1948, making it a felony to 'imagine, invent, devise, or intend to deprive or depose our Most Gracious Lady the Queen . . . from the style, honour, or royal name of the imperial crown of the United Kingdom' (*inter alia*), would be incompatible with the right to freedom of expression under Article 10 of the ECHR if interpreted as criminalising a campaign to replace the monarchical system of government in the UK with a republic. The applicant (the editor of *The Guardian*, a newspaper which was conducting a campaign to replace the monarchy with a republican form of government for the UK) was in no immediate danger of prosecution; indeed, there had been no prosecution for the offence since 1883, in the extremely unlikely event that any prosecution would be brought, the House considered it certain that the 1848 Act would be interpreted, using s.3 of the Human Rights Act 1998, as not criminalising such a campaign. Similarly, in *Lancashire County Council* v. *Taylor (Secretary of State for the Environment, Food and Rural Affairs intervening)*,[19] the Court of Appeal declined, both on procedural grounds and on the merits, to make a declaration of incompatibility in respect of the Agricultural Holdings Act 1986. The defendant was the tenant of an agricultural holding owned by the claimant, and had received notice to quit. He argued that the Act discriminated against him on the ground of property, violating ECHR Article 14, because of a difference in treatment of tenants under the Act which had nothing to do with the reason for him being given notice to quit. The Court of Appeal held that he could not be regarded as a 'victim', within the meaning of s.7(7) of the Human Rights Act 1998 and Article 34 of the ECHR, of any such violation.

This is sensible in view of the courts' primary constitutional obligation to make decisions in contested cases that will produce workable and justifiable effects in the world, rather than resolving hypothetical questions which could never affect the parties: the court's approach is related

[18] [2003] UKHL 38; [2004] 1 AC 357 (HL).
[19] [2005] EWCA Civ 284; [2005] 1 WLR 2668 (CA).

to its constitutional role. Nevertheless, the approach in the *Rusbridger* case cannot be an invariable rule. In the European Court of Human Rights, a person may be a victim of a violation of a Convention right as a result of criminal law, and so entitled to a judgment in his or her favour on the merits, without being at substantial risk of being prosecuted. In *Dudgeon* v. *United Kingdom*,[20] the applicant was a practising male homosexual in Northern Ireland where, at the time, buggery was a criminal offence. Although no prosecution for such an offence had been brought for a number of years, and the responsible authorities said that the law was unlikely to be enforced against Mr Dudgeon, the European Court of Human Rights decided that his right to respect for private life under Article 8 of the Convention had been violated, because he was subject to an implied threat of prosecution and penalty as long as the law remained in force, even if it was not in practice enforced. In *Rusbridger*, indeed, Lord Steyn drew attention to the broad approach adopted by the Strasbourg Court to the concept of a 'victim'.[21] If there is a difference between *Dudgeon* and *Rusbridger*, it can only be the length of time since there had been any prosecution for the respective offences and the degree to which a future prosecution could be regarded as a thoroughly far-fetched possibility under the social and political conditions prevailing in the jurisdictions of Northern Ireland and England and Wales respectively.

Two other aspects of the institutional position of adjudicators affect the way they regard the idea of compatibility or incompatibility. The first is the need for adjudicators to define the scope of their constitutional authority *vis-à-vis* other institutions, including Parliament and government. Some judges have tried to deal with this factor by making use of such notions as institutional competence, deference, and discretionary area of judgment. Without going into any detail about these techniques, it is enough for present purposes to note that they all relate to notions of relative institutional authority. Properly applied, they ought not to affect the approach of judges to questions of logical or unconditional compatibility, as these are issues of pure law as to which only adjudicators have final constitutional authority. They become relevant to the determination of questions of practical (especially speculative) and conditional compatibility. Since the courts have turned their faces against determining compatibility speculatively (as noted above), the main field in which questions of relative institutional

[20] (1982) 4 EHRR 149.   [21] [2003] UKHL 38; [2004] 1 AC 357 (HL), para. 21.

authority can properly affect determinations of compatibility is in relation to issues concerning the aim of an interference with a right and the
legitimacy of that aim, the existence of a pressing social need for the
interference, and the proportionality of the interference (although, as
A v. *Secretary of State for the Home Department*[22] makes clear, proportionality is ultimately a question of law, not of fact or political judgment).

The other aspect of the institutional position of adjudicators affecting
their approach to questions of compatibility is the hierarchical structure
of authority within the adjudicative system, reflected in the doctrine of
precedent: tribunals lower in the hierarchy must usually follow decisions
of higher tribunals. This imposes a special constraint in respect of the
notion of compatibility not shared by other institutions. We observed
earlier that evaluating the logical compatibility of legislation with a
Convention right involved interpreting the Convention right in the
light of relevant Strasbourg case-law. The effect of that case-law cannot
be divorced from the structures of authority within, and between, the
Strasbourg Court and the various adjudicative bodies in the United
Kingdom. As there is no principle of *stare decisis* in the Strasbourg
system, Strasbourg judgments and decisions cannot have binding
authority as it is understood in common law systems. What is more,
admissibility decisions in Strasbourg are rather like an unreserved
county court judgment drafted by court officials rather than the judge.
This presents problems when adjudicators in the United Kingdom either
want to depart from the trend of authority in Strasbourg, as in
R. v. Spear,[23] where the House of Lords considered that a decision of
the Strasbourg court had been reached on the basis of incomplete
understanding of how the system of courts-martial operated in the
UK. Alternatively, a court might want to follow Strasbourg authority
but be constrained by an inconsistent decision of a municipal court
above it in the judicial hierarchy, as in *Price and others* v. *Leeds City
Council*.[24] Here, in an action for possession of land, the defendants who
had occupied it argued that moving them would violate their Convention
rights, including the right to respect for their homes and private and family
lives under ECHR Article 8. The Court of Appeal was faced with a conflict
between a recent decision of the House of Lords in *Harrow LBC
v. Qazi*,[25] holding that Article 8 rights could never be a defence to an

---

[22] [2004] UKHL 56; [2005] 2 AC 68 (HL).   [23] [2002] UKHL 31; [2003] 1 AC 734 (HL).
[24] [2005] EWCA Civ 289, *sub nom. Leeds City Council* v. *Price* [2005] 1 WLR 1825 (CA).
[25] [2003] UKHL 43; [2004] 1 AC 983 (HL).

action to exercise an absolute right to possession of land, and an even more recent decision of the European Court of Human Rights in *Connors* v. *UK*[26] to the opposite effect. The Court of Appeal followed the decision of the House of Lords, but gave permission to appeal so that the House could reconsider its earlier decision in the light of that of the Strasbourg Court.[27]

In such cases, as with the example of the administrative hierarchy of Social Fund decision-making mentioned earlier, the assessment of compatibility depends on the relationship between levels of institutional authority within the system of adjudicative bodies as much as on a reading of the various norm-generating texts. The courts are required to triangulate the legislation, the right, including its qualifications and the justifications for interfering with it, and the most desirable outcome on the facts in order to decide the question of compatibility.[28]

Forms of rational (in)compatibility

Cutting across the institutional differences between the positions of decision-makers and their approaches to s.3, there are a number of different senses in which a reading of legislation might be said to be compatible (or incompatible) with a right. There are related differences between ways in which it might be regarded as possible or impossible to give effect to legislation in a compatible manner. This section examines two perspectives in which to view compatibility and incompatibility. The first is rational, looking at the relationship between the right-defining norm and the legislative norm being tested against it. The second is institutional, based on the position within the state of the person making the assessment of (in)compatibility.

In assessing the rational (in)compatibility of a right-defining norm and a legislative norm, there are two possible approaches. One is logical, and comes into play when the norms are being compared *in abstracto*, in the absence of any need to use the assessment to decide a disputed issue between real parties in the light of concrete facts. The other is practical, and is seen when one has to compare the outcome of giving effect to the

---

[26] (2004) 40 EHRR 189.
[27] For a discussion of the House of Lords judgment in this case, see Chapter 14, pp. 437–40.
[28] See e.g. *Douglas* v. *Hello! Ltd* [2001] QB 967; [2001] 2 WLR 992; [2001] 2 All ER 289 (CA); and *Campbell* v. *MGN Ltd* [2004] UKHL 22; [2004] 2 AC 457 (HL).

legislative norm to concrete facts with the requirements of the right-
defining norm in those circumstances.

Rational (in)compatibilities: logical, practical, conditional and unconditional

What is involved in deciding whether one norm is compatible with
another norm? We can distinguish between several kinds of incompatibility. Two norms are *logically* incompatible to some degree if one of
them demands action that the other forbids, or denies a freedom that the
other guarantees. A statutory provision authorising indefinite detention
of foreigners, but not UK nationals, suspected of having links with
international terrorism would be logically incompatible with the right
to be free of discrimination on the ground of nationality in the enjoyment of liberty and security of the person, because it would be impossible in practice to give effect to the statutory power without infringing
the human rights norm. That is why the decision to amend the detention
regime in Part 4 of the Anti-Terrorism, Crime and Security Act 2001
in the light of the declaration of incompatibility made by the House
of Lords in *A* v. *Secretary of State for the Home Department*[29] made it
necessary to replace Part 4 entirely. (Its place was taken by the control-
order regime in the Prevention of Terrorism Act 2005.)[30]

Norms are *practically* incompatible if one norm imposes constraints
on action that make it extremely difficult for the subject to make use of
the freedom that the other norm guarantees. For example, the rule of
English law making a marriage void unless the contracting parties were
regarded respectively as a man and a woman (or boy and girl) at the time
of their births is not logically incompatible with the right to marry under
ECHR Article 12, but it reduced the value of the right to transsexuals so
significantly (because many transsexuals would be unable to marry
anyone of the sex opposite to their reassigned gender) that it was held
in *Goodwin* v. *United Kingdom*[31] and *Bellinger* v. *Bellinger*[32] to interfere
with the very essence of the right and so to be a violation of it. The same
might be true of the rule that members of the royal family could not
marry in a civil ceremony: it does not in itself constitute a violation of

---

[29] [2004] UKHL 56; [2005] 2 AC 68 (HL).
[30] See D. Feldman, 'Terrorism, Human Rights and Their Constitutional Implications'
(2005) 1 *European Constitutional Law Review* 531–552.
[31] (2002) 35 EHRR 18.   [32] [2003] UKHL 21; [2003] 2 AC 467 (HL).

the right to marry, but might infringe the rights of both a member of the royal family and his or her intended spouse if the rules of the Church of England forbid a church wedding for one or other of them.

We can also distinguish between *unconditional* incompatibility (for example, any norm that purports to authorise torture or inhuman or degrading treatment or punishment is automatically incompatible with the right under ECHR Article 3) and *conditional* incompatibility (such as a norm authorising a child to be taken into care, infringing the right to private and family life under ECHR Article 8(1) but incompatible with it only if the interference cannot be justified by reference to the criteria set out in Article 8(2)).

Logical, practical and unconditional incompatibilities can all be described as *intrinsic* to the norms under consideration. They do not require interpreters to consider factors extrinsic to the norms themselves (although, as noted above, the judgments involved in giving effect to the norms will usually involve consideration of the facts or predicted facts of actual or imagined cases and at least some norms of social and constitutional morality). Conditional incompatibility, by contrast, requires a formally different type of analysis, because it expressly requires the interpreter to assess compatibility partly by reference to *extrinsic* factors such as the aims that the interference with a right serves and the existence of a need for it in a democratic society.

The types of intrinsic and extrinsic incompatibilities described so far can be labelled as a rational typology, because the distinctions are concerned with the kinds of reasons needed to establish an incompatibility and the relationship between those reasons and the various norm-generating texts. These texts include the relevant case-law from the European Court of Human Rights (since s.2 of the Human Rights Act 1998 requires that this should be taken into account), case-law from courts in the jurisdiction (England and Wales, Scotland or Northern Ireland), and (perhaps) decisions from other jurisdictions in the UK on similar points. Indeed, because the European Convention on Human Rights is what is often called a living instrument, and its organic growth is achieved through the case-law, the focus often has to be on the case-law rather than on the text of the Convention. This feature is common to much interpretation of treaties and constitutions. This has two implications for determining questions of incompatibility.

First, a decision as to whether legislation is rationally compatible with a Convention right will require the evaluator to move back and forth between two norm-generating texts, reading them in the light of the

facts or imagined facts to which the legislation is said to apply. What is a
Convention right for the purposes of municipal law in the UK? There are
a number of controversies as to their nature. Some people regard them
as the product of legal rules; others consider them to be essentially
values, not rules. The significance of this is that a piece of legislation
may be incompatible with the values underpinning a right while
being compatible with its letter and attendant case-law, or *vice versa*.
Another division is between those who (like Lord Hoffmann and Roger
Masterman[33]) regard the rights as creatures of municipal law, and others
who (like Buxton LJ, Colin Warbrick[34] and Lord Bingham of Cornhill[35])
consider them to be rights under international law. This has important
implications for the scope of the Convention rights. If they are creatures
of municipal law, it is open to municipal authorities (including courts)
to use the text of the Convention as a living instrument in municipal law,
providing the basis for more wide-ranging legal protection for the
underlying values than has yet been accorded by the European Court
of Human Rights. If, on the contrary, the rights are creatures of public
international law, the rate of development of protection in municipal
law should not exceed that in public international law. The resulting
differences in the scope of the rights necessarily affects the compatibility
of legislative provisions with the rights as interpreted at a particular
moment.

Secondly, the Strasbourg approach to interpreting rights under the
ECHR is itself fact-dependent. The European Court of Human Rights
rarely engages in textual exegesis. Its normal approach is to consider
whether the facts of the case before it fall within the reach of the key
concepts by reference to which the right is formulated – for example,
private life, family life, expression, manifestation of belief, and so on –
and, if it does, how close to the core of the concept the case comes. This
is an inevitable consequence of treating the Convention as a living
instrument.[36] The Court does not move from a definition of the right
to an application of it, but rather compares the facts with the idea or

---

[33] See *In re McKerr* [2004] UKHL 12; [2004] 1 WLR 807 (HL), para. 63, *per* Lord
Hoffmann; and Roger Masterman, Chapter 3 in this volume.

[34] See Sir Richard Buxton, 'The Human Rights Act and Private Law' (2000) 116 LQR 48;
and Colin Warbrick, Chapter 2 in this volume.

[35] See *R (Ullah)* v. *Special Adjudicator* [2004] UKHL 26; [2004] 2 AC 323 (HL), para. 20.

[36] Lech Garlicki, 'The Methods of Interpretation', in Mélin-Soucramanien (ed.), above
n. 6, pp. 139–53.

ideal that is thought to underlie the textual expression of the right in question. This technique means that the scope of a right in the Strasbourg case-law depends on a concern with outcomes more than a concern with the details of the text. It makes the compatibility of a statutory provision with a Convention right less predictable.

What readings are 'possible'? The constitutional and institutional perspectives

Most discussions of the range within which a Convention-compatible reading of legislation is possible have so far concentrated on two issues. One is *linguistic*. Adjudicators have said that there is a limit to the extent to which language can be stretched in order to secure compatibility, and it can be assumed that legislators and Ministers and their advisers work on the same assumption. The other is *institutional*. Adjudicators have stressed that they should not rewrite legislation in a way that would amount to acting as legislators. They have also taken account of the possible knock-on effects of a new or strained Convention-compatible reading of the legislation; where there are significant effects of this kind it will usually be preferable to make a declaration of incompatibility under s.4 of the Human Rights Act 1998 and allow the government and legislature to take necessary corrective action, as in *Bellinger* v. *Bellinger*,[37] although the chapters by Aileen Kavanagh and Sonia Harris-Short in this volume show that opinions on this may differ.

For present purposes, I want to stress two points.

First, both the linguistic and the institutional considerations are outcome-centred in significant ways. The linguistic considerations are outcome-centred because one cannot avoid asking whether the outcome that would be produced for the parties affected by the decision by a reading of legislation could legitimately be seen as within the intendment of the legislation (although there are also other considerations). To this extent, the approach to reading the legislation has to be similar to the approach taken by the European Court of Human Rights to deciding whether a given case falls within the scope of one of the Convention rights, as outlined above. The institutional considerations are outcome-centred in a different way. Instead of focusing on the concrete effects of the decision for the parties, institutional issues are concerned with the

---

[37] [2003] UKHL 21; [2003] 2 AC 467 (HL).

effect of the process of reasoning on inter-institutional relationships within a constitutional matrix.

Secondly, the outcome-focused considerations do not operate in the same way in all institutions. Linguistic considerations do not affect all interpreters of legislation in the same way. A parliamentary body does not worry about the outcome of particular cases, because it does not have to deal with individual cases. Nor does it have to worry about inter-institutional relationships: when it legislates, the Queen in Parliament is usually the boss, and its understanding of the terms of its own proposed legislation does not depend on the notion that some other body might be more competent to make the sort of legislation in question. This attitude is reinforced by s.3(2) of the Human Rights Act 1998: incompatibility does not make primary legislation invalid or ineffective. Similarly, a Minister approaches linguistic considerations from the perspective of a desire to give effect to a broad policy, not to adjudicate on individual cases, although Ministers may be more sensitive to the risk of incompatibility in relation to those pieces of subordinate legislation that would be invalid if held to be incompatible with a Convention right.

For judges, however, the outcome of a particular case is a powerful consideration, and their whole approach to reading and giving effect to legislation is coloured by them. A further institutional consideration affecting the exercise by judges of their functions under s.3(1) is that it may be politically less contentious to make a declaration of incompatibility under s.4 than to impose a new reading of the legislation with unexpected side-effects. Here, too, their view of the outcome of a reading colours the approach. One may suspect that courts will be willing to take more risks with a compatibility decision when it will have no immediate effect on the rights and obligations of the people involved than when it will have immediate effects, particularly in fields of political sensitivity. We may see this not only in *A* v. *Secretary of State for the Home Department*[38] but also in a long line of cases where aspects of the Convention right to a fair hearing under ECHR Article 6, domestic legislation and possible outcomes are triangulated so as to avoid producing results that would be regarded by some people as outraging common sense, triangulating the various strands in the 'interpretative' process to produce the desired outcome.

---

[38] [2004] UKHL 56; [2005] 2 AC 68 (HL).

Conclusion

The main proposition for which I have argued here is that we can best understand the nature of the requirements of s.3(1) of the Human Rights Act 1998 by reference to the variations between these perspectives and their various dimensions. I have not attempted an exhaustive enumeration of the many perspectives and dimensions in which the compatibility of norms is assessed. For example, I have said nothing here specifically about the way that the role of an international, rather than national, tribunal affects the approach to making this evaluation, but there can be no doubt that factors specifically relevant to international tribunals like the European Court of Human Rights, such as the notion of subsidiarity, significantly affect the approach of those tribunals to the task of evaluating the compatibility of national norms with international standards.[39] Nor have I said anything about people performing other roles, such as advocates, legal advisers or academic commentators. Nevertheless, I hope that the limited number of examples and perspectives identified above have sufficiently established and illustrated the deep complexity of the notion of (in)compatibility of norms.

It follows from my approach that, so far as s.3 of the Human Rights Act 1998 is concerned with interpretation, interpretation is not concerned primarily with the meaning of words, but rather with the effect to be given to them in a particular institutional setting. This is common to all legal interpretation, which aims to achieve effects and justify them by reference to a tenable reading of the authoritative texts. It also follows that compatibility means different things to different people, or more precisely to different institutions, because of their different constitutional positions, functions and working methods. We will not fully understand the idea of compatibility or the role of Convention rights within different institutions (if we can ever understand it at all) unless we are constantly aware of the implications of different institutional perspectives for the ways in which norms, including human rights norms, are given effect.

---

[39] See e.g. D. Feldman, 'Establishing the Legitimacy of Judicial Procedures for Protecting Human Rights' (2001) 13 *European Review of Public Law* 139; Garlicki, above n. 36.

5

Choosing between sections 3 and 4 of the Human Rights Act 1998: judicial reasoning after *Ghaidan* v. *Mendoza*

AILEEN KAVANAGH[*]

The importance of judicial reasoning

Lord Justice Sedley has commented extra-judicially that, although the HRA's impact on modes of legal reasoning does not make headlines, it 'may well turn out to be one of the most fundamental changes worked by the Act'.[1] The HRA has brought the subject of judicial reasoning to centre stage, both in the decisions of the higher courts and in the academic commentary which sets out to analyse and understand them. This is largely a consequence of the fact that, when enacting the HRA, Parliament decided to place much of the burden of the Act's implementation on the interpretative function of the courts, by imposing on them the duty in s.3(1) to 'read and give effect' to all legislation in a way which is compatible with Convention rights, 'so far as it is possible to do so'. Lawyers of every hue must now confront the fact that issues of judicial reasoning, in particular interpretive reasoning, have become central to understanding, analysing and predicting the ways in which the HRA will impact on all areas of the law.

But how well equipped are lawyers to address these questions of interpretative methodology which are now of such immense practical importance? For many, their legal education will not provide very much in the way of preparation. The subject of statutory interpretation has

---

* I would like to thank the participants at the Symposium on Judicial Reasoning under the Human Rights Act in Durham in April 2005 for discussion and helpful feedback and on the first draft of this paper, and Robert Wintemute for valuable comments on the section comparing *Ghaidan* and *Fitzpatrick*.
1 Sir Stephen Sedley, 'The Rocks or the Open Sea: Where Is the Human Rights Act Heading?' (2005) 32 *Journal of Law and Society* 3, 9.

suffered from long-standing neglect on the law school curriculum where it is generally relegated (if it appears at all) to one or two perfunctory lectures in the 'Introduction to Law' courses for first year students. Ironically, this neglect has gone hand in hand with the enormous growth in importance of statute law. As Lord Steyn noted extra-judicially:

> interpreting and applying various pieces of legislation amounts to the major part of the legal work of English judges, perhaps as high as 90 per cent ... Universities in England have not entirely adjusted to the reality that statute law is the dominant source of law of our time.[2]

But not only is statutory interpretation sidelined in law teaching, it is also sorely neglected in academic writing. Despite a recent proliferation of books and articles on virtually every substantive aspect of the law, there are still only two major book-length treatments of the subject of statutory interpretation and very few articles.[3] Statutory interpretation is simply not part of the mainstream of academic legal research.[4]

For public lawyers, the neglect of statutory interpretation is even more serious than for other branches of the law because of the immense constitutional significance of the subject. Statutory interpretation involves an inter-institutional meeting between the judiciary and the elected branches of government, where judges get to decide what statutes mean. We know that this task goes well beyond looking up the dictionary definitions of words. It involves deciding how broadly or narrowly to interpret a provision, whether it should be 'read down' to avoid an apparent absurdity or unjust application, or whether words should be 'read in' to clarify, amplify or modify the ordinary statutory meaning. In other words, the courts have the power to limit, extend and modify the operation of statutes when interpreting them. It should therefore come as no surprise that, in cases which turn on issues of statutory interpretation, judges often justify one interpretation over another on explicitly constitutional grounds, i.e. on arguments based

---

[2] J. Steyn, 'Dynamic Interpretation Amidst an Orgy of Statutes' [2004] EHRLR 245, 246.

[3] J. Bell and G. Engles, *Cross on Statutory Interpretation* (London: Butterworths, 1995); F. Bennion, *Statutory Interpretation: A Code* (4th edn, London: Butterworths, 2002). However, interpretive reasoning is an important part of contemporary jurisprudential scholarship: see e.g. A. Marmor, *Interpretation and Legal Theory* (2nd edn, Oxford: Hart Publishing, 2005) and A. Marmor (ed.), *Law and Interpretation: Essays in Legal Philosophy* (Oxford: Clarendon Press, 1995).

[4] For a lament about the scholarly neglect of statutory interpretation in the US, see Justice Scalia (of the United States Supreme Court), *A Matter of Interpretation: Federal Courts and the Law* (Princeton: Princeton University Press, 1997), pp. 14ff.

on the constitutional framework of the state and the proper constitutional role of the judiciary within it.[5]

The failure to take statutory interpretation seriously as a subject of constitutional importance has had negative consequences for the development of public law doctrine. For one thing, it has contributed to a tendency to underestimate the considerable law-making power which judges exercise (and have always exercised) when they interpret statutes, and to overestimate the significance of the fact that judges in the UK do not have the power to 'strike down' Acts of Parliament. Thus, in the debates surrounding the enactment of the HRA, it was often argued that on no account could judges be given the power to strike down Acts of Parliament because this would clearly violate the principle of Parliamentary sovereignty. Considerably less energy was dedicated to exploring the various ways in which the interpretive powers of the courts (even before the HRA was enacted) challenge, limit and modify the Diceyan orthodoxy that Parliament can enact any law it wishes which cannot be overridden by another branch of government.[6]

One need only look at the way in which the so-called 'presumptions of statutory interpretation' operate to see how creative judges can be in statutory interpretation – how they are partners rather than servants when interpreting legislation.[7] Even in the absence of ambiguity in the statutory language, judges can rely on 'presumptions of general application' which are described in Sir Rupert Cross' classic work as not only supplementing the statutory text but also operating 'at a higher level as expressions of fundamental principles governing both Civil Liberties and the relations between Parliament, the executive and the courts. They operate here as constitutional principles which are not easily displaced by statutory text.'[8]

One such presumption is the principle of legality, which requires that, in the absence of express language or necessary implication to the

---

[5] In a discussion on the doctrine of proportionality, Gráinne de Búrca also notes that judicial statements about the proper standard of review tend to be 'explicitly constitutional in nature': see 'Proportionality and *Wednesbury* Unreasonableness: The Influence of European Legal Concepts on UK Law' (1997) 3 EPL 561, 562.

[6] Though Lord Lester subsequently queried whether the duty to adopt a strained reading of legislation in fact involves a greater inroad upon Parliamentary sovereignty than the power to strike down inconsistent legislation: 'Developing Constitutional Principles of Public Law' [2001] PL 684, 691. This argument has also been made in the American context: see F. Schauer, 'Ashwander Revisited' [1995] *Supreme Court Review* 71, 91.

[7] For further reflection on the way in which statutory interpretation involves 'power-sharing' between Parliament and the courts, see A. Ashworth, 'Interpreting Criminal Statutes: A Crisis of Legality' (1991) 107 LQR 419, 422–3.

[8] Bell and Engles, *Cross on Statutory Interpretation*, above n. 3, p. 166.

contrary, general words contained in statutes must be read subject to the basic rights of the individual. Relying on this principle in the pre-HRA case of *Simms*, Lord Hoffmann noted that these presumptions mean that the UK courts 'apply principles of constitutionality little different from those which exist in countries where the power of the legislature is expressly limited by a constitutional document'.[9] The role of these principles in statutory interpretation (and their constitutional function) has often been obscured by focusing too narrowly on the fact that UK judges do not have the power to 'strike down' legislation. More detailed study of the techniques of statutory interpretation can bring to the surface these less obvious, but no less significant, constitutional inter-actions (and sometimes confrontations) which take place when judges interpret statutes. Statutory interpretation is not just a set of technical rules. It is a matter of the extent and limits of the partly political choices which judges make when they opt for one interpretation or another.[10] Since the HRA places much of the constitutional responsibility for protecting rights on the interpretive function of the courts, the impor-tance of this study can no longer be avoided.

Judicial reasoning after *Ghaidan* v. *Mendoza*

According to the terms of the HRA, judges have a duty under s.3(1) to read and give effect to legislation 'if it is possible to do so'. Failing this, they have a discretion to issue a 'declaration of incompatibility' under s.4 which, in itself, has no legal effect on the statutory provision under consideration. Naturally, one of the key questions concerning judicial reasoning under the Act has been: 'How do judges determine when it is possible to give a Convention-compatible interpretation under s.3 and what factors influence that determination?' In other words, how do judges choose between s.3 and s.4 when faced with an apparent incompatibility with Convention rights?

The leading case on this issue is now the House of Lords decision in *Ghaidan* v. *Mendoza*.[11] There, the court found it possible (by a majority of four to one) to read the words 'living together as his or her wife or husband' in paragraph 2(2) of Schedule 1 to the Rent Act 1977 to

---

[9] *R. v. Secretary of State for the Home Department, ex parte Simms* [2000] 2 AC 115, 131, *per* Lord Hoffmann; see also *Matadeen v. Pointu* [1999] 1 AC 98, 110, where Lord Hoffmann suggested that the HRA created a 'modified form of constitutional review not much different than if it had been entrenched'.

[10] See further Ashworth, 'Interpreting Criminal Statutes', above n. 7, p. 445.

[11] [2004] 3 WLR 113.

include same-sex couples, so that, like cohabiting heterosexual couples, they could succeed to a statutory tenancy on the death of their partner. The first step in the reasoning process was to establish whether paragraph 2(2), as ordinarily understood, violated Convention rights. Only if this question was answered in the affirmative could they then go on to see if a s.3(1) interpretation was 'possible' to save it from the apparent incompatibility. This follows a now well-established pattern in the s.3(1) case-law whereby the courts initially construe legislation 'without reference to section 3',[12] before going on to construe it 'in accordance with section 3'.[13] Adopting this two-stage approach, the House of Lords in *Ghaidan* agreed unanimously that paragraph 2(2) was discriminatory towards same-sex couples and violated their rights under Article 14 taken together with Article 8.[14]

The next question was whether this apparent or *prima facie* discrimination could be eliminated by adopting a s.3(1) interpretation. In addressing this question, their Lordships had to consider two arguments which seemed to pose an obstacle to this route:

(1) that 'husband and wife' are gender-specific terms; and
(2) that when Parliament enacted paragraph 2(2) it never intended it to be extended to cover same-sex couples.

The majority rejected both these contentions, with Lord Nicholls and Lord Rodger giving full judgment on the s.3 point. Lord Steyn concurred with Lords Nicholls and Rodger but offered some brief, general statements of his own on the application of s.3.[15] Together, these judgments form a rich and complex analysis which raise as well as answer difficult questions about the relationship between s.3 and s.4 HRA. Since I have examined the role of Parliamentary intention in adjudication under the

---

[12] See e.g. *Ghaidan*, above n. 11, para. 24, *per* Lord Nicholls; *R (Fuller)* v. *Chief Constable of Dorset Constabulary* [2002] 3 WLR 1133, para. 39, *per* Stanley Burnton J; *International Transport Roth GmbH* v. *Secretary of State for the Home Department* [2002] 3 WLR 344, *per* Jonathan Parker LJ.

[13] *Roth*, above n. 12, para. 149. For further comment on this two-stage approach, see A. Kavanagh, 'The Elusive Divide Between Interpretation and Legislation' (2004) 24 OJLS 259, 274ff; see also C. Gearty, 'Reconciling Parliamentary Democracy and Human Rights' (2002) 118 LQR 248, 252.

[14] Lord Nicholls, para. 24; Lord Rodger, para. 128; Lord Millett, para. 55; Baroness Hale, para. 143; with Lord Steyn supporting the reasoning of the majority.

[15] Baroness Hale concurred with the three judges of the majority, but did not give any independent analysis of the s.3(1) issue beyond saying that *Ghaidan* was 'not even a marginal case of s.3(1)'s application': para. 144.

HRA elsewhere,[16] this chapter will concentrate on the question of whether, or to what extent, express statutory terms pose an obstacle to a s.3 interpretation. I will then go on to consider Lord Steyn's claim that s.3 should be understood as a remedial provision, before concluding with some general comments on the way in which the HRA has influenced or modified traditional forms of judicial reasoning.[17]

Express terms as a limit on section 3(1)

Giving the leading judgment in *Ghaidan*, Lord Nicholls began with a point on which there is now judicial consensus, namely, that s.3(1) may require the court to depart from the unambiguous meaning the legislation would otherwise bear.[18] Once we accept this fact, argued Lord Nicholls, it follows that the application of s.3(1) should not 'depend critically on the particular form of words adopted by the parliamentary draftsman ... that would make the application of section three something of a semantic lottery'.[19] Drawing a distinction between the language of a statute and the 'concept expressed in that language',[20] Lord Nicholls pointed to the injustice of a situation whereby, 'if the draftsman chose to express the concept being enacted in one form of words, section 3 would be available to achieve Convention compliance. If he chose a different form of words, section 3 would be impotent.'[21] Luckily, this injustice could be avoided because the terms of s.3(1) enabled the court to 'read in words which change the meaning of the enacted legislation, so as to make it Convention compliant'[22] and allowed the court to 'modify the meaning, and hence the effect, of primary and secondary legislation'.[23]

However, Lord Nicholls was keen to stress that this process of 'modification' was not without limits.[24] First, the courts should not adopt a meaning which is inconsistent with a 'fundamental feature' of the legislation under scrutiny. It must be compatible with 'the underlying thrust' of the legislation. Secondly, s.3(1) should not require the courts

---

[16] A. Kavanagh, 'The Role of Parliamentary Intention in Adjudication under the Human Rights Act 1998' (2006) 26 OJLS 179.

[17] Within the confines of this essay, I will not be able to consider the argument advanced by both Lord Steyn, paras. 48ff, and Lord Rodger, paras. 118ff, that the interpretive obligation under EC law provides a useful analogy for understanding s.3 HRA.

[18] Lord Nicholls, paras. 29–30; Lord Steyn, para. 44; Lord Rodger, para. 119; Lord Millett, para. 67.

[19] *Ibid.*, para. 31.   [20] *Ibid.*, para. 31.   [21] *Ibid.*, para. 31.   [22] *Ibid.*, para. 32.

[23] *Ibid.*, para. 32.   [24] These are outlined in *ibid.*, para. 33.

to make decisions for which they are not equipped because they would require 'legislative deliberation'. He cited *Anderson*[25] as an example of the first, *Bellinger*[26] as an example of the second and *Re S*[27] as an example of both.[28]

Lord Nicholls does not explain what he means by 'the concept' expressed in the legislation or how judges are to elicit what this 'concept' is. The implication seems to be that the 'concept' is something more abstract than the language of the statute. However, if we look at the way in which Lord Nicholls rendered paragraph 2(2) compatible with Convention rights, we get a better insight into what he had in mind. In applying s.3(1) to the facts of *Ghaidan*, Lord Nicholls argued that, although the language may seem gender-specific, the 'social policy underlying the Act'[29] (namely, that the survivor of a cohabiting heterosexual couple has security of tenure[30]) was equally applicable to stable homosexual couples because they have 'an equivalent relationship'.[31] He looked at the basic features of the relationship which qualified for a statutory tenancy (which he identified as the sharing of life and making a home together) and then established that same-sex couples shared those general features. So Lord Nicholls stated the purpose of the legislation at a relatively high level of abstraction, which then informed the way in which he 'read' the explicit terms of the Act. Although the terms 'husband and wife' are gender-specific, the 'concept' underlying the legislative provision (i.e. the purpose of protecting people who are in stable, loving relationships who have set up home together) could include same-sex couples.

Whilst this purposive approach was not clearly applied in the other judgments, Lord Rodger relied on a distinction which seems similar to Lord Nicholls' language/concept dichotomy. For Lord Rodger, what prevented a court from applying s.3(1) was not 'any mere matter of the linguistic form in which Parliament has chosen to express the obligation' but rather 'the entire substance of the provision'.[32] The courts are not entitled to 'change the substance of a provision entirely'.[33] Throughout his judgment, Lord Rodger stressed that what prevents the application of s.3(1) would be an inconsistency with the 'fundamental',[34] 'cardinal'[35] or 'essential principles'[36] of the legislation under

---

[25] R. *(Anderson)* v. *Secretary of State for the Home Department* [2002] 3 WLR 1800.
[26] *Bellinger* v. *Bellinger* [2003] 2 WLR 1174.   [27] *Re S, Re W* [2002] 2 AC 291.
[28] *Ghaidan* above n. 11, para. 34.   [29] *Ibid.*, para. 35.   [30] *Ibid.*, para. 17.
[31] *Ibid.*, para. 17.   [32] *Ibid.*, para. 110.   [33] *Ibid.*, para. 110.   [34] *Ibid.*, para. 117.
[35] *Ibid.*, para. 113.   [36] *Ibid.*, para. 121.

scrutiny. Echoing Lord Nicholls' fears about the semantic lottery, he warned that:

> attaching decisive importance to the precise adjustments required to the language of any particular provision would reduce the exercise envisaged by s.3(1) to a game where the outcome would depend in part on the particular turn of phrase chosen by the draftsman and in part on the skill of the court in devising brief formulae to make the provision compatible with convention rights ... Parliament was not out to devise an entertaining parlour game for lawyers, but, so far as possible, to make legislation operate compatibly with convention rights. This means concentrating on matters of substance, rather than on matters of mere language.[37]

Applying these general statements about the limits of s.3(1) to the facts of *Ghaidan*, Lord Rodger noted that there was 'no principle underlying the Act as a whole'[38] which would conflict with a s.3(1) interpretation which included same-sex couples, although he acknowledged that this 'would, of course, involve extending the reach of para. 2(2), but it would not contradict any cardinal principle of the Rent Act'.[39] So it seems that, although Lords Nicholls and Rodger did not believe that the application of s.3(1) was subject to the 'mere' textual or linguistic limits contained in the terms of the statute, it was limited by an obligation to ensure that it would not violate (variously) its 'fundamental features', 'essential principles', the underlying 'concept' or 'purpose', or its 'entire substance'.

What are we to make of this way of understanding the limits of s.3(1)? It seems to me that, in seeking to refute an argument that a s.3(1) interpretation was impossible in a case where the express legislative terms seem to violate the Convention, their Lordships went too far in the opposite extreme by seeming to deny that there were *any* textual limits to the operation of s.3(1). For the purpose of disposing of *Ghaidan*, it would have been sufficient to say that textual or linguistic limits are not the only ones relevant to the s.3(1) inquiry and that sometimes it will be necessary to modify the ordinary statutory meaning in order to achieve Convention-compatibility. In other words, even if we accept that rectification of express statutory terms is part of the power given to judges under s.3(1), that does not mean that those terms are of no relevance in determining the limits of a s.3(1) interpretation in a particular case.

---

[37] *Ibid.*, para. 123. These concerns were also voiced by Lord Steyn who lamented that there had been 'an excessive concentration on linguistic features of the particular statute': *ibid.*, para. 41.

[38] *Ibid.*, para. 128.   [39] *Ibid.*, para. 128.

I have argued elsewhere that a s.3(1) interpretation will not be desirable where the courts establish that the interpretation would involve a radical reform of a legislative provision or set of provisions which would be more suitable for Parliament to undertake.[40] An example of a case where this limit was reached is *Bellinger* v. *Bellinger*.[41] There, the House of Lords argued that the far-reaching ramifications of the proposed interpretation for many areas of the law meant that it was more appropriate for Parliament to tackle the issue of transsexual marriage than the courts. This led the court to issue a declaration of incompatibility. *Bellinger* highlights the point that the choice between s.3 and s.4 is not simply a matter of determining the linguistic possibilities in the text of the statute. Rather, it engages much broader considerations of political morality about the extent and limits of judicial law-making and the appropriate division of labour between the three branches of government.

But this is not to say that the statutory text has no bearing at all on that evaluation. Consider the *Anderson* case,[42] where the House of Lords refused to read s.29 of the Crime Sentences Act 1997 in a Convention-compliant way, because to do so would be to replace a scheme whereby the Home Secretary made the sentencing decision with an entirely different scheme. A declaration of incompatibility was issued instead. In *Ghaidan*, *Anderson* was cited by Lords Nicholls, Rodger and Steyn as a case which did not hinge on any linguistic difficulties in achieving a s.3(1) interpretation in that case, but rather because it would violate a 'fundamental feature' of the 1997 Act. However, this overlooks the fact that, in coming to this conclusion, the House of Lords in *Anderson* placed much emphasis on the express terms of s.29. For example, Lord Hutton noted in *Anderson* that 'it is clear *from the wording* of section 29 of the Crime Sentences Act 1997 that Parliament intended that the decisions ... are to be taken by the Home Secretary and not by the judiciary or by the parole board'.[43] Therefore, 'having regard to the *clear provisions of section 29*', it was not possible pursuant to s.3(1) to interpret s.29 so as to take away from the Home Secretary the power to decide on the length of the tariff period and to give it to the judiciary.

---

[40] See Kavanagh, 'The Elusive Divide Between Interpretation and Legislation', above n. 13, pp. 270–4 and 279–82. This is similar to Lord Nicholls' second limit on section 3 stated in *Ghaidan*, that the courts should not make decisions requiring 'legislative deliberation': *Ghaidan*, above n. 11, para. 33.

[41] [2003] 2 AC 467.   [42] [2003] 1 AC 837.   [43] *Anderson*, above n. 25, para. 80.

So, one of the factors leading the court to the conclusion that a s.3 interpretation was not possible in *Anderson* was the fact that the power to release a convicted murderer was expressly conferred on the Home Secretary.[44] In reasoning in this way, Lord Hutton was not concentrating on form *rather than* substance, or adhering in a legalistic way to 'linguistic niceties'. Rather, his Lordship was making a judgment about the degree of legal reform necessary to make s.29 Convention-compatible, taking into account, as one factor relevant to that judgment, the express terms of the statute under scrutiny.[45]

So, whilst it is certainly right to say that s.3(1) does not depend on linguistic possibilities alone, we should not be driven to the opposite extreme of denying that the express terms of the statute under scrutiny therefore have no role to play in determining whether a s.3(1) interpretation is appropriate in the context of a particular case. The express terms of the legislation partly determine whether a s.3(1) interpretation is more or less appropriate than a declaration of incompatibility. In fact, *Ghaidan* itself is an illustration of this point. Although a s.3(1) interpretation of the Rent Act was deemed possible there, Lord Rodger rightly noted that 'the position might well have been different if Parliament had not enacted para. 2(2) and had continued to confine the right to succeed to the husband or wife of the original tenant'.[46]

This reflects the insight of Lord Millett's dissenting judgment, namely, that, 'whilst the courts may look behind the words of the statute, they cannot be disregarded or given no weight, because they are the medium by which Parliament expresses its intention'.[47] In fact, in *Wilson* v. *First County Trust*,[48] Lord Nicholls describes this as a 'cardinal constitutional principle',[49] reinforced by Lord Hobhouse who in the same case declared that 'the constitutional means by which laws are made is by the entry of the statute in the statute book'.[50] It is significant that, in *Ghaidan*, neither Lord Nicholls nor Lord Rodger gave much emphasis to the constitutional status of statutory provisions, but rather referred throughout their judgments to the linguistic choices made by the parliamentary draftsman,[51] despite the fact that there was no

---

[44] Lord Bingham, *ibid.*, para. 30.
[45] In fact, it may be that Lord Rodger seems to acknowledge this implicitly when he commented in *Ghaidan* that the court in *Anderson* could not deprive the Home Secretary of 'the *express* power to release' and could not 'negative the *explicit* power of the Secretary of State': para. 111.
[46] Para. 128.   [47] Para. 70.   [48] [2003] 3 WLR 568.   [49] Para. 67.   [50] Para. 139.
[51] Lord Nicholls, para. 31; Lord Rodger, para. 123.

suggestion in *Ghaidan* that there had been a drafting error in the Rent
Act. Parliamentary draftsmen are professionally trained to accurately
reflect the will of Parliament in legislative form and that is the form
which Parliament authorises and votes on through the various stages
of the legislative process. So, as a conceptual matter, statutory terms
should not be characterised merely as the linguistic choices of whoever
happened to draft legislative provisions. Rather, they are the constitutionally authorised vehicle through which Parliament expresses its
intention. This is not to say that judges can never modify those terms,
but rather that, in so doing, the courts are aware that those terms partly
limit their powers of rectification and cannot be disregarded entirely in
the judicial law-making function. Moreover, one of the primary ways in
which we elicit what the 'fundamental features' of any piece of legislation are, is by reading its express terms.[52] So, the words of the statutory
provisions are important in applying this important limit to the application of s.3(1). This is not a matter of choosing substance over form,
but rather of acknowledging that statutory 'substance' is partly determined by statutory 'form', if by the latter we mean the terms in which
Parliament has chosen to express its intentions.

Nor does this conclusion reduce the judicial duty under s.3 to the
operation of a 'semantic lottery' or an entertaining parlour game for
lawyers. It is simply to acknowledge that the entitlements and rights
we have depends, in part, on the statutory provisions enacted by
Parliament, and there are limits to what judges can achieve even through
the most ingenious interpretation. By enacting s.3(1), Parliament chose
to implement the HRA, in part, through techniques of judicial interpretation, thus leaving in place this dependence. Although the HRA
gives judges more leeway than before to engage in a rectification of
statutory provisions, it does not eradicate all the limits which inevitably
beset the peculiarly judicial method of law reform. This will mean that
the way in which legislation is drafted impacts on how easy or difficult it
is to achieve a s.3(1) interpretation. Finding a suitable way of reading a
statutory provision which protects Convention rights, whilst simultaneously causing the least change possible to the existing legislation, is
one of the difficult tasks presented to judges under the HRA. To be sure,
this is no parlour game for the entertainment of lawyers. Serious rights

---

[52] Lord Millett also makes the point that the essential features of the legislative scheme
'must be gathered in part at least from the words that Parliament has chosen to use':
para. 77.

issues are involved. However, it *does* place a premium on the skill of judges to occasionally find neat ways around the language of the statute if that language seems on its face to violate Convention rights and a declaration of incompatibility is inappropriate.

Some comments on Lord Millett's dissenting judgment

Although Lord Millett's view that the limits of s.3(1) are partly contained in the express terms of the statute is supported here, this should not be taken as an endorsement either of the conclusion reached by his Lordship in *Ghaidan* or his overall way of reasoning to that conclusion. As regards his general comments on the extent and limits of s.3(1), they are just as noteworthy for their considerable conformity with the majority's view on s.3(1), as they are for his ultimate dissent on the facts of *Ghaidan*. Lord Millett agreed with the rest of the House that s.3(1) may require the courts to depart from the unambiguous meaning of the statutory provision[53] and give it 'an abnormal construction'.[54] He accepted that the courts can read in and read down and 'supply missing words so long as they are consistent with the fundamental features of the legislative scheme'.[55] He even went as far as to suggest that the courts can 'do considerable violence to the language and stretch it almost (but not quite) to breaking point'.[56] Finally, he joined the rest of the House in confirming that the interpretation adopted in *R. v. A* was a legitimate exercise of the court's powers under s.3(1). According to Lord Millett, the interpretation adopted there merely 'glossed but did not contradict anything in the relevant statute'.[57]

The main difference between Lord Millett and the rest of the House on the general issue of the limits of s.3(1) is Lord Millett's belief that the court must be constrained by the language of the statute.[58] On his reasoning, if the court is not so constrained, their powers become 'quasi-legislative' rather than 'interpretative',[59] where the former includes the power to 'modify' statutory language whereas the latter

---

[53] Para. 67.   [54] Para. 60.   [55] Para. 67.   [56] Para. 67.

[57] Para. 74. For further analysis of *R. v. A*, see A. Kavanagh, 'Unlocking the Human Rights Act: The "Radical" Approach to Section 3(1) Revisited' [2005] EHRLR 261.

[58] He also suggests that an interpretation cannot be an 'impossible' one, or that it must be 'intellectually defensible', or that it should not 'stretch the language to breaking point' (all at para. 67). Although these statements are unobjectionable, they are also too vague to shed any light on the precise limits of s.3(1).

[59] Para. 64.

does not. The distinction between legislation and interpretation is a complex one. I have argued elsewhere that it is in the nature of interpretation to include some modification of statutory meaning, such that it entails (rather than eschews) judicial law-making which shares some similarities with legislative law-making.[60] If this is correct, it would cast doubt on Lord Millett's distinction between a quasi-legislative and interpretative power. In fact, it is difficult to see exactly how Lord Millett can maintain this distinction whilst simultaneously arguing that s.3(1) entitles the court to depart from the unambiguous meaning of the statutory provision and 'do considerable violence' to statutory language.

Leaving these issues aside, I think the key to understanding Lord Millett's reasoning in *Ghaidan* is contained more in his application of s.3(1) to the facts of the case, rather than in his general pronouncements on the limits of s.3.[61] What prevented Lord Millett adopting a s.3(1) interpretation in *Ghaidan* was his view that both the language and legislative history showed that the phrase 'living together as his or her husband and wife' connoted 'an open relationship between persons of the opposite sex'.[62] By interpreting this phrase to include same-sex couples, the majority contradicted the 'essential features' of the relationship which Parliament had 'in contemplation'.[63] So, the difference between the majority and Lord Millett on the facts of *Ghaidan* turned on different views about the 'essential features' of the relationship referred to in paragraph 2(2). For the majority, the gender of the cohabitees was not significant, especially in light of their finding (supported by Lord Millett) that to exclude same-sex couples from the legislation would be discriminatory towards them. For Lord Millett, gender combined with a requirement of 'openness' were. Lord Millett's views on the 'openness' requirement seem out of touch with contemporary reality, since it is not uncommon for same-sex couples to set up home together and live openly in a stable, loving relationship which is, as Baroness Hale put it, 'marriage-like'. Moreover, these relationships are indistinguishable in form to cohabiting heterosexual couples

---

[60] Kavanagh, 'The Elusive Divide Between Interpretation and Legislation under the HRA', above n. 13, pp. 266–7.

[61] Alison Young also suggests that it is 'possible to account for Lord Millett's dissent as a difference in application as opposed to a fundamental disagreement about the nature of s.3(1)': see A. Young, '*Ghaidan* v. *Godin-Mendoza*: Avoiding the Deference Trap' [2005] PL 23, 26.

[62] Para. 78.   [63] Para. 78.

to which paragraph 2(2) already applied. On my analysis, the express terms of paragraph 2(2) allowed for an interpretation which would include these 'marriage-like' relationships, despite the fact that this was probably not envisaged when the paragraph was enacted. In fact, although the words 'husband' and 'wife' are gender-specific, the phrase as a whole, namely, 'living together as his or her husband or wife', was not. The key word here is 'as', which suggests living together in a marriage-like relationship, but not one based on actual marriage. This paved the way for a Convention-compatible interpretation without the need for any substantial rectification of the statutory terms.[64]

Rights and remedies under section 3(1)

A central theme in Lord Steyn's judgment in *Ghaidan* was the idea that, in order to understand s.3(1) properly, we need to appreciate its role in the 'remedial scheme'[65] of the 1998 Act. His Lordship emphasised repeatedly that s.3(1) is the 'prime remedial measure'[66] of the 1998 Act, whereas s.4 is 'a measure of last resort'.[67] In fact, this seems to provide Lord Steyn with his primary justification for eschewing 'linguistic arguments' in favour of a 'broad approach' to statutory interpretation under s.3(1), namely, that, 'if the core remedial purpose of s.3(1) is not to be undermined a broader approach is required'.[68] Although the idea of s.3(1) as a 'remedial' provision is not mentioned explicitly by any of the other judges in *Ghaidan*, it is interesting to note that counsel for Mr Mendoza[69] argued the case in these terms, i.e. by claiming that 'the *appropriate remedy* is for the court to exercise its interpretive obligation under s.3 of the 1998 Act to interpret legislation compatibly with the Convention rights'.[70]

---

[64] See *Fitzpatrick* v. *Sterling Housing Association Ltd* [1998] 2 WLR 225, *per* Ward LJ (CA): '"As" means "in the manner of" and suggests how the couple functioned, not what they were': *ibid.*, p. 338; see also Robert Wintemute, 'Same-Sex Partners, Living as Husband and Wife, and Section Three of the Human Rights Act 1998' [2003] PL 621, 627.

[65] Paras. 38, 40, 46 and 49.   [66] Paras. 46 and 50.   [67] Para. 46.   [68] Para. 49.

[69] Rabinder Singh QC and Paul Staddon.

[70] At 563 (emphasis added). Similarly, in Lord Steyn's judgment in *Anderson*, his consideration of whether it would be appropriate to adopt an interpretation under s.3(1) or issue a declaration of incompatibility under s.4 was carried out under the heading 'The Remedy': Anderson, above n. 25, paras. 58ff; see also Buxton LJ in *Ghaidan* v. *Mendoza* [2002] 4 All ER 1162, paras. 34–35.

Section 3(1) as a remedial provision

In my view, it is entirely correct to view the interpretive obligation under s.3(1) as a remedial provision, and this insight provides us with a key to understanding one important aspect of the interplay between s.3 and s.4.[71] The remedial nature of s.3 follows from the very nature of judicial interpretation. Statutory interpretation is not carried out in the abstract or for the pure intellectual satisfaction of discerning the meaning of unclear statutory provisions. Rather, it is carried out in order to reach a conclusion on the legal dispute before them. Judicial interpretations are instrumental to legal outcomes.[72] One of the factors influencing statutory interpretation is the judicial duty to strive to do justice for the individual litigant and apply the law fairly and equitably in the context of each case. Although this is not the only factor influencing judicial interpretation, it is certainly an important one, and, in the context of choosing between s.3(1) and s.4, it plays a significant role. In particular, it will sometimes create a strong judicial incentive to adopt a s.3(1) interpretation in situations where either a s.4 declaration of incompatibility would be unable to provide a remedy for the individual litigant, or where the court feels that a s.4 declaration is unlikely to result in legal change.

Take for example the difference of judicial approach in *Ghaidan* and *Bellinger*. If we accept that the linguistic impediment (or indeed lack of linguistic impediment) to adopting a s.3(1) interpretation was very similar in both cases, what explains the fact that a s.3 interpretation was adopted in *Ghaidan*, but the interpretive route was deemed inappropriate in *Bellinger*? The answer lies in the different remedial implications of the choice between s.3 and s.4 in both cases. If Mr Mendoza had received a declaration of incompatibility in *Ghaidan*, he could not have succeeded to a statutory tenancy. Nor could the Civil Partnership Bill going through Parliament at the time have been of any assistance to him, because his partner was dead.[73] However, although a s.4 declaration

---

[71] For a helpful overview of the issue of remedies under the HRA, see D. Feldman, 'Remedies for Violations of Convention Rights under the Human Rights Act' [1998] EHRLR 691–711; and I. Leigh and L. Lustgarten, 'Making Rights Real: The Courts, Remedies and the Human Rights Act' (1999) 58 CLJ 509, 536.

[72] Kavanagh, 'The Elusive Divide Between Interpretation and Legislation under the HRA', above n. 13, p. 262.

[73] Robert Wintemute also makes the point that a s.4 declaration would have been meaningless to Mr Mendoza: see Wintemute, 'Same-Sex Partners', above n. 64, p. 627. This point seems to be overlooked by Lord Millett in *Ghaidan*, when he queried whether it was appropriate for the House of Lords in *Ghaidan* to adopt a s.3(1) interpretation

provided no immediate remedy for Mrs Bellinger, the courts were assured that she could get married in the near future under the forth-coming legislation. Given the disadvantages of a s.3(1) interpretation in that case, the appropriate solution was to issue a declaration of incompatibility, whilst relying on assurances given to the court by the Secretary of State that Mrs Bellinger's rights would be protected in future legislation. Indeed, such legislation was provided shortly afterwards by the Gender Recognition Act 2004. Similar concerns were at work in *R. v. A.* In that case, a declaration of incompatibility would have provided no remedy for the defendant who risked undergoing an unfair trial. Only by adopting a s.3(1) interpretation was the court able to vindicate the defendant's rights.[74] Again, the remedial aspect of the judicial role under the HRA weighed strongly in favour of a s.3(1) interpretation rather than a s.4 declaration of incompatibility. This is not to say that the obligation to provide a remedy in the individual case overrides all other concerns. It is simply to say that it is one important factor bearing on the choice between s.3 and s.4.[75]

Section 4 as a 'measure of last resort'

This leads on to the second strand of Lord Steyn's analysis, namely, that a declaration of incompatibility ought to be 'a measure of last resort'.[76] In support of this conclusion, he relied on statements made by the two promoters of the Human Rights Bill as it was going through Parliament.[77] In the House of Lords, the Lord Chancellor observed that 'in 99 percent of the cases that will arise, there will be no need for judicial declaration of incompatibility',[78] and, in the House of Commons, the Home Secretary said '[w]e expect that, in almost all

---

'when the government had announced its intention to bring forward corrective legislation in the form of the Civil Partnership Act': *Ghaidan*, above n. 11, para. 56.

[74] I have argued that similar 'remedial' concerns were at work in *R. v. A*: see further Kavanagh, 'Unlocking the Human Rights Act: The 'Radical' Approach to Section 3(1) Revisited', above n. 57, p. 273.

[75] For the view that s.3(1) can be a vehicle for providing a remedy for violation of Convention rights, see also A. Henderson, 'Readings and Remedies: Section 3(1) of the HRA and Rectifying Constructions' [2000] *Judicial Review* 258ff; Wintemute, 'Same-Sex Partners', above n. 64, p. 627; Lester, 'Developing Constitutional Principles of Public Law', above n. 6, p. 691.

[76] Paras. 39 and 50. This view was also put forward by the Secretary of State for the Home Department (Mr Jack Straw) in the Parliamentary debates on the Human Rights Bill, *Hansard*, HC 3 June 1998, cols. 421–2.

[77] Cited in para. 46.   [78] *Hansard*, HL, 5 February 1998, col. 840 (3rd reading).

cases, the courts will be able to interpret the legislation compatibly with the Convention'.[79] Moreover, he attached an appendix to his judgment in *Ghaidan* which listed the cases where a breach of Convention rights was found and the courts had to consider whether to opt for s.3 or s.4. This revealed that the courts issued a declaration of incompatibility more often than they used their interpretive powers under s.3(1).[80] Lord Steyn argued that 'these statistics by themselves raise a question about the proper implementation of the 1998 Act'[81] and whether the case-law has taken a wrong turning, especially since the statistics in no way matched the ministerial predictions as the Human Rights Bill was going through Parliament.

There are reasons to doubt whether either of these arguments provide adequate support for Lord Steyn's conclusion. As regards the argument based on *Hansard*, it is worth questioning at the outset whether Lord Steyn's reliance on *Hansard* is compatible with his extra-judicial views[82] about the dangers and limited value of ministerial statements as an indication of a statute's true meaning, given that they are made by members of the executive driven by the political goal of winning support for what was in this case a controversial Bill.[83] Following the reconsideration of *Pepper* v. *Hart* by the House of Lords in *Wilson* v. *First County Trust*,[84] it seems that we can make the following statements about the status of ministerial statements made in the course of parliamentary debates. First, they do not *determine* the meaning of s.3(1) or its relationship with s.(4) and do not bind the courts in any way. At most, they can be viewed as background or contextual material which may or may not shed light on the meaning of these two complex sections of the HRA.[85] Secondly, the House of Lords in *Wilson* cast

---

[79] *Hansard*, HC, 16 February 1998, col. 778 (2nd reading).

[80] Section 3(1) was only used in ten cases, whereas a declaration of incompatibility was issued in fifteen cases, with five declarations reversed on appeal to the House of Lords.

[81] Para. 39.   [82] Lord Steyn, '*Pepper* v. *Hart*: A Re-examination' (2001) 21 OJLS 59–72.

[83] This is also questioned by Lord Phillips, 'The Interpretation of Contracts and Statutes', Lecture, 10 October 2001, www.keatingchambers.com/KEATING_LECTURE_Oct2001.doc.

[84] [2003] 3 WLR 568. For an analysis of the impact of *Wilson* on the rule in *Pepper* v. *Hart*, see further A. Kavanagh, '*Pepper* v. *Hart* and Matters of Constitutional Principle' (2005) 121 LQR 98, 112–21.

[85] As Lord Nicholls put it in *Wilson*, ministerial statements are 'no more than part of the background . . . [H]owever such statements are made and however explicit they may be, they cannot control the meaning of an act of Parliament.' Para. 58.

doubt on the plausibility of assuming that statements made by individual ministers should be attributed to Parliament as a whole.[86]

We have good reason to be wary of relying too heavily on statements made by members of the executive, whose main task is to push controversial Bills through Parliament.[87] The ministerial statements cited by Lord Steyn in *Ghaidan* may simply have been politically motivated pronouncements designed to assuage the fears of opponents to the Human Rights Bill that it would greatly expand judicial power, rather than any considered opinion on the complex interplay between s.3 and s.4. Alternatively, the executive's expectation that s.4 would be used only rarely may simply have rested on 'an unduly rosy view of British legislation'[88] in the early days of the Labour Government that very little of their legislation was in fact contrary to the Convention. Finally, whilst not overruling *Pepper* v. *Hart*, the House of Lords in *Wilson* were adamant that the limits on the admissibility of ministerial statements set out in *Pepper* should be strictly observed. Geoffrey Marshall has argued that the views of the parliamentary sponsors of the Human Rights Bill on the meaning of s.3 fail the test of clarity or unambiguity requisite for admissibility under *Pepper* v. *Hart*.[89] Relying on some cryptic ministerial statements in *Hansard* about the search for 'possible' meanings under s.3(1), combined with evidence of apparent conflict between statements made by the Lord Chancellor and those made by Lord Cooke of Thorndon, Marshall makes a very strong case for this conclusion.[90]

So the ministerial statements by members of the executive about Convention-compatible interpretations being possible in almost all cases may be insufficient, in themselves, to ground an argument about the appropriate judicial approach to s.3(1). But what about Lord Steyn's suggestion that the statistics on the judicial choice between s.3 and s.4 may reflect a wrong turning in the law? On my analysis, these statistics can tell us nothing about the appropriate application of s.3 and s.4. The reason for this goes back to the nature of the interpretive task. Judicial interpretation under the HRA requires judges to balance two sets of competing

---

[86] Lord Hobhouse, para. 139; Lord Nicholls, para. 67.

[87] Kavanagh, '*Pepper* v. *Hart*', above n. 84, pp. 105–7.

[88] Leigh and Lustgarten, 'Making Right Real', above n. 71, p. 536.

[89] Marshall, 'The Lynchpin of Parliamentary Intention: Lost, Stolen or Strained?' [2003] PL 236, 238–9.

[90] Interestingly, Lord Cooke stated in Parliament that 'strained interpretations' were not possible under s.3(1): see HL Debs., 18 November 1997, col. 533, although this is exactly what is now endorsed by the House of Lords in *Ghaidan*.

values. One weighs in favour of adopting an innovative or 'strained' interpretation (i.e. the values of doing justice in the instant case and the equitable development of the law). The other pulls in favour of a less innovative interpretation or a declaration of incompatibility, thus either partly or fully avoiding the need to engage in judicial law reform. These include legal certainty, stability and continuity in the law.[91] The relative weight of any of these factors or 'interpretative criteria'[92] varies according to the particular circumstances and context of the case at hand. In some cases (as in *Ghaidan*), the circumstances of the case combine to weigh in favour of an innovative interpretation. In *Bellinger*, they pull in the direction of a declaration of incompatibility. One cannot determine whether s.3 or s.4 will be appropriate in advance. All one can do is provide an analysis of the factors which influence the choice and then see how important they are in the context of a particular case. Therefore, statistics alone cannot inform us about the appropriateness of choosing between s.3 and s.4. Assessment of this issue can only properly come from an analysis of the choice in the context of particular cases.

Lord Nicholls rightly pointed out in *Ghaidan* that a 'comprehensive answer to [the question of when a s.3(1) interpretation is possible] is proving elusive'.[93] Such an answer is elusive not because of inadequate powers of understanding, but because of the necessarily evaluative nature of the task which judges have to undertake when applying s.3 by balancing two sets of values which pull in different directions. As experience in the application of the section accumulates, we may get a stronger sense of the relevant factors which tip the scales in favour of one option or the other. But this is far from identifying a single 'test' or 'standard' or 'criterion' which would determine the issue.[94] Such a test is impossible to devise, or, if

---

[91] For an analysis of interpretation as involving this type of balancing between different values, see J. Raz, 'On the Authority and Interpretation of Constitutions: Some Preliminaries', in L. Alexander (ed.), *Constitutionalism: Philosophical Foundations* (Cambridge: Cambridge University Press, 1998), pp. 152–93.

[92] Stefan Vogenauer argues that statutory interpretation involves the 'weighing of conflicting interpretative criteria': see S. Vogenauer, 'A Retreat from *Pepper* v. *Hart*? A Reply to Lord Steyn' (2005) 25 OJLS 629, 661.

[93] Para. 27.

[94] Lord Nicholls posed the question about the possibilities of s.3(1) in these terms: 'What is not clear is the *test* to be applied in separating the sheep from the goats. What is the *standard*, or the *criterion*, by which possibility is judged?' Para. 27. Similarly, Lord Steyn commented that he was 'not disposed to try to formulate precise rules about where section 3 may not be used'. Para. 50. In my view, the nature of statutory interpretation is such that it would be impossible to formulate such precise rules, even if his Lordship were disposed to do so.

attempted, would be so abstract that it would merely provide some general guidelines or indications of the factors relevant to that determination, but would not, in itself, determine the choice.[95]

So, should declarations of incompatibility be a measure of last resort for the judiciary, given the remedial nature of s.3(1)? After all, we have only shown that some of Lord Steyn's arguments in favour of this conclusion are problematic, not that the conclusion itself is without merit. At the very least, one can say (following the House of Lords in *Wilson*) that a s.3(1) interpretation is 'an essential preliminary step to making a declaration of incompatibility'.[96] This follows from the terms of s.4(1) which state that s.4(2) only applies to proceedings in which a court 'determines' whether a provision is compatible with a Convention right. Only when a court is 'satisfied'[97] that there is an incompatibility, may it then make a declaration of incompatibility. So, s.3(1) must be the courts' first resort because the possibility of a Convention-compatible interpretation must be explored before a declaration of incompatibility can be issued under s.4.

Moreover, if we draw on Lord Steyn's insight that s.3 has a remedial purpose then a further conclusion can be drawn. This is that, in cases where the rights violation is substantial and a remedy is required, there will be strong reasons in favour of a 'strained' interpretation under s.3 because a declaration of incompatibility would be of no remedial use to the person asserting a rights violation.[98] Whether those reasons win out in any particular case will depend on a variety of contextual factors such as how 'strained' that interpretation might be, whether it would be inconsistent with core features of the legislation under scrutiny or the legislative terms, whether it would have wide-ranging implications for the broader legislative context, and whether it would involve judges in making decisions which would be more appropriate for legislative

---

[95] The importance of context in determining the choice between s.3 and s.4 may have been acknowledged by Lord Rodger when he commented in *Ghaidan* that some questions about the application of s.3 'cannot be clear-cut and will involve matters of degree which cannot be determined in the abstract but only by considering the particular legislation in issue.' Para. 115.

[96] *Wilson, per* Lord Nicholls, para. 14.   [97] Section 4(2).

[98] This is not to assume that all litigants who bring human rights claims are seeking an immediate remedy. They may simply be using litigation as a way of raising the public profile of their grievance, thereby hoping to stimulate political resolution of the issue. My point is simply that, in some cases (as in *Ghaidan* or *R.* v. *A*) where the main aim of the litigation must have been to seek immediate redress through the courts, there will be strong arguments in favour of choosing s.3 over s.4.

deliberation. So not only must the s.3 line of inquiry be pursued first, there may well be added reasons for judges to choose s.3 over s.4. If this more contextual approach is adopted, the need to take sides between those who argue that s.3 should be used all or nearly all the time[99] and those who argue that s.4 should be used more often,[100] is obviated. On my analysis, one cannot determine this issue in the abstract. It all depends on the details and context of the cases which get litigated under the HRA. All one can say is that s.3 should be used when it is appropriate considering all the factors relevant to that issue in the case before the courts, and s.4 should be used when it is not.

Finally, Gavin Phillipson has argued that, included in the duty contained in s.3(1) to read 'primary and secondary legislation whenever enacted' compatibly with the Convention, is the judicial obligation to read s.3(1) itself in a Convention-compatible fashion.[101] If this premise is accepted, it follows (argues Phillipson) that s.3(1) 'should be read so as to give it maximum possible scope, so that it virtually always achieves Convention-compliance when reading other statutes'.[102] On this basis, he favours a reading of s.3(1) which 'maximises rather than minimises protection for Convention rights' such that the courts should strive to achieve a s.3(1) interpretation in almost all cases and minimise their use of s.4. The problem with this argument is that, even if we accept Phillipson's premise, it does not necessarily support his conclusion. Convention-compatibility can be achieved in different ways. One option is to secure compatibility through judicial interpretation. Another is to amend legislation through the Parliamentary process to remove any incompatibility. The HRA explicitly allows for both options. If Phillipson's premise is correct, then the whole of the HRA must be read in a Convention-compatible way, including s.4. The judicial obligation under s.3(1) should not be read in isolation, but rather in conjunction with the alternative option of issuing a declaration of incompatibility under s.4. The difficult judicial choice created by the interaction between s.3 and s.4 is not between maximising or

---

[99] See e.g. G. Phillipson, '(Mis-)reading Section Three of the Human Rights Act' (2003) 119 LQR 183ff.

[100] See e.g. T. Campbell, 'Incorporation through Interpretation', in T. Campbell, K. D. Ewing and A. Tomkins (eds.), *Sceptical Essays on Human Rights* (Oxford: Oxford University Press, 2002), pp. 99–100; Gearty, 'Reconciling Parliamentary Democracy and Human Rights', above n. 13, p. 250.

[101] See Phillipson, '(Mis-)reading Section Three', above n. 99, pp. 183ff.

[102] *Ibid.*, p. 187.

minimising Convention compatibility. Rather, it is about finding the most appropriate *way* of maximising protection of human rights in the context of a particular case. In some cases, this will be achieved by pursuing the interpretive route. In others, a better way of achieving Convention compatibility will be to issue a declaration of incompatibility. In the latter cases, the justification for the judicial choice in favour of s.4 may well be (as it was in *Bellinger, Anderson, Re S* and *Roth*) that legislative law reform was required to maximise the protection of Convention rights, a result which could not be achieved (or could not be achieved to the same degree) by way of judicial interpretation.

The argument from 'dialogue'

The idea that s.4 should be a 'measure of last resort' has attracted criticism from some of the leading academic commentators on the HRA. They argue that declarations of incompatibility should be used more often because they facilitate 'dialogue' between the courts and the elected branches of government. Encouraging such dialogue was one of purposes of the 1998 Act, to which judges can give effect by issuing declarations of incompatibility.[103] As Geoffrey Marshall put it:

> a declaration by the courts provides the legislature with a considered judicial view of the rights-compatibility of the legislation. It can then reflect on its actions and either take the remedial steps provided for in section 10 of the Act or exercise its retained sovereign prerogative to disagree with the judicial assessment and confirm its initial view of its legislation.[104]

It is necessary to make a few brief points in response to this argument. First, if what is meant by 'dialogue' is simply the interaction between the courts and the elected branches of government, this is nothing new and it is certainly not the exclusive property of the declaration of incompatibility mechanism under the HRA. The metaphor of 'dialogue' is equally applicable not only to s.3(1) but also to ordinary instances of

---

[103] Marshall, 'The Lynchpin of Parliamentary Intention', above n. 89, pp. 243–4; F. Klug, 'Judicial Deference under the Human Rights Act 1998' [2003] EHRLR 125, 130ff; F. Klug, 'The Human Rights Act: A "Third Way" or a "Third Wave" Bill of Rights' [2001] EHRLR 361, 370; D. Nicol, 'Statutory Interpretation and Human Rights after *Anderson*' [2004] PL 273, 281; D. Nicol, 'Gender Reassignment and the Transformation of the Human Rights Act' (2004) 120 LQR 195, 197; D. Nicol, 'Are Convention Rights a No-Go Zone for Parliament?' [2002] PL 438, 441.

[104] Marshall, 'The Lynchpin of Parliamentary Intention', above n. 89, pp. 243–4. The 'dialogue' argument is also supported by Klug and Nicol.

statutory interpretation, whereby Parliament enacts the legislation (sometimes intentionally leaving gaps for the judiciary to fill) and the courts interpret it by determining its meaning when applied to a particular case. Parliament then has a number of 'responses'. By far the most frequent response is to do nothing, i.e. to acquiesce in the interpretation. This may have more to do with the scarcity of Parliamentary time than any considered view about the correctness of the interpretation. But, of course, it also has the option (though rarely exercised) of changing the interpretation, either outright or in part. If this changed provision comes up again for interpretation in the courts, the process of so-called 'dialogue' can continue.[105]

This familiar interaction between the branches of government is simply an aspect of the general point made at the beginning of this paper, namely, that statutory interpretation involves an inter-institutional meeting between the courts and the legislature. Unsurprisingly, therefore, s.3(1) instantiates the same sort of 'dialogue'. Parliament enacts legislation, and, if the courts decide to interpret it using the s.3(1) mechanism, it is open to Parliament to do nothing or to change the interpretation by enacting new legislation (or open to the executive to exercise its power under s.10 HRA for fast-track amendment). The point is that, even if we accept that encouraging 'dialogue' is one of the purposes of the HRA to which the courts should give effect, this does not support the conclusion that s.4 is the only or even the primary way of fulfilling that purpose. It could also be carried out by adopting an interpretation under s.3.

Secondly, the argument from 'dialogue' (at least as presented by Geoffrey Marshall) overlooks the important remedial role of s.3(1). Whilst it is certainly true that, when carrying out their interpretive functions, judges ought to be sensitive to the constitutional division of labour between the three branches of government and which institution is best placed to carry out certain types of legal reform, this does not mean that judges should make their choice between s.3 and s.4 on the basis of which option would facilitate more 'dialogue' with the elected branches. Judges have to decide cases involving actual litigants whose

---

[105] Similarly, we are all aware of cases where the judiciary believe that it would be inappropriate (or impossible) for them to reform the law by way of interpretation despite an obvious injustice to the litigant before them, because this would exceed their constitutional role. Even in this situation, the courts can nonetheless highlight the injustice and (in *obiter* statements) urge the government or Parliament to reform the law and this is often sufficient to prompt Parliament to reconsider its legislation.

rights may have been violated, and they have an obligation to arrive at a just outcome in the context of that case. If, for example, Mr Mendoza had received a declaration of incompatibility (as Marshall recommends) he would have been left without an effective remedy for the violation of his Convention rights. It would have been poor consolation to him to discover that a judicial decision which failed to vindicate his rights was justified on the basis that it 'improved the quality of political discourse'.[106]

Finally, Francesca Klug has suggested that s.4 has come to be seen as a measure of last resort because of an assumption that it would '*force* the Executive and Parliament to change the legislation'.[107] But the opposite is in fact the case. It is precisely the weakness of s.4 as a remedial measure which sometimes encourages the courts to adopt an interpretation under s.3(1).[108] For example, one of the reasons for the judicial reluctance to issue a declaration of incompatibility in *R. v. A* was the fear that the government would not change the 'rape shield' provision in response to such a declaration.[109] Had the House of Lords had the option of striking down the legislation in *R. v. A*, they may well have done so, because it would have rendered the statutory provision inoperative for the purposes of the rape trial at issue, but would have simultaneously forced Parliament to reform the section so that it could protect fair trial rights in future cases. So, ironically, the fact that the declaration of incompatibility has no legal effect places pressure on the UK courts to be more robust and creative in exercising their interpretive powers, than if they had the power to strike down legislative provisions altogether.[110]

Contrasting *Ghaidan* and *Fitzpatrick*

One interesting aspect of *Ghaidan* was that it departed from the pre-HRA decision of *Fitzpatrick* v. *Sterling Housing Association Ltd*,[111] handed down only four years previously on facts very similar to those

---

[106] Nicol, 'Are Convention Rights a No-Go Zone for Parliament?', above n. 103, p. 442.

[107] Klug, 'Judicial Deference', above n. 103, p. 131 (emphasis added).

[108] This view is also shared by Lord Lester, 'Developing Constitutional Principles of Public Law', above n. 6, p. 691; see also Henderson, 'Readings and Remedies: Section 3(1) of the HRA and Rectifying Constructions', above n. 75, p. 261.

[109] The basis of this fear and the desirability of a declaration of incompatibility in *R v. A* is considered further in Kavanagh, 'Unlocking the Human Rights Act', above n. 57, p. 273.

[110] It is ironic because many of those who argued against including a striking-down power in what became the HRA were largely motivated by a concern to curb judicial power.

[111] [2001] 1 AC 27.

in *Ghaidan*. Therefore, the contrast between the two cases is instructive as a way of examining the difference s.3(1) has made to traditional methods of statutory interpretation. In *Fitzpatrick*, the House of Lords unanimously rejected the contention that the words 'living together as his or her husband or wife' could be read to include homosexual partners. Their rejection was based on the fact that the terms 'husband' and 'wife' are gender-specific[112] and that in using the words 'as his or her husband or wife' Parliament did not intend to include homosexual partners.[113] However, by a majority of three to two their Lordships held that homosexual partners could be considered 'a member of the original tenant's family' for the purposes of paragraph 3(1) of Schedule 1 to the Rent Act, thus enabling the plaintiff to succeed to an assured rather than a statutory tenancy.

It should be noted at the outset that, although counsel for Mr Fitzpatrick[114] argued that he should succeed to a statutory tenancy under paragraph 2(2) of the Rent Act, they seemed to place the weight of their submissions on the alternative argument that Mr Fitzpatrick qualified as a 'family member' of the original tenant under paragraph 3(1) of the Schedule.[115] This may have been because Mr Fitzpatrick was content with an assured tenancy, or because his lawyers believed that he had more chances of success on the 'family member' rather than the 'spouse' argument. Whatever the case may be, by the time we get to *Ghaidan*, Mr Mendoza was guaranteed an assured tenancy because of *Fitzpatrick*, but he also wanted a below-market rent that goes with a statutory tenancy.[116] Therefore, he based his legal arguments on paragraph 2(2). The different lines of argument adopted by the claimants in both cases no doubt had an impact on the judicial decisions which ultimately emerged. However, there are also more fundamental differences in the method of judicial reasoning adopted in both cases.

The first such difference is that, in *Fitzpatrick*, no issue of discrimination was raised,[117] whereas in *Ghaidan* the House of Lords was bound to consider whether paragraph 2(2) was *prima facie* discriminatory (and therefore violated Convention rights) as part of the 'first stage' of the judicial inquiry under s.3(1). So, the discriminatory aspect of paragraph

---

[112] As Lord Nicholls stated: 'A husband is a man and a wife is a woman', *ibid.*, p. 43, supported by Lord Clyde, *ibid.*, p. 47 and Lord Slynn, *ibid.*, p. 34.
[113] Lord Slynn, *ibid.*, p. 34.   [114] Nicholas Blake QC and Jan Luba.
[115] See the synopsis of these submissions at [2001] 1 AC 27, 29–30.
[116] See Wintemute, 'Same-Sex Partners', above n. 64, p. 621.
[117] Lord Slynn, [2001] 1 AC 27, 35; Lord Clyde, *ibid.*, p. 47.

2(2) was an essential aspect of the judicial reasoning in *Ghaidan* but played little or no role in *Fitzpatrick*.[118] This shows that, even before s.3(1) is directly engaged, the HRA has a bearing on judicial reasoning by bringing the rights-based dimension of the case to the fore. Thus, in *Fitzpatrick*, the question was whether same-sex partners could qualify either under paragraph 2(2) or under paragraph 3(1) of the Rent Act, whereas in *Ghaidan* the question was whether, *despite* a *prima facie* incompatibility with the Convention, the courts could *nonetheless* render paragraph 2(2) Convention-compatible by way of interpretation under s.3(1).

The second difference between the two cases follows from this. Once the court established a difference in treatment based on sexual orientation, this placed the onus on those defending the statutory provision to provide a cogent justification for the difference in treatment. As Lord Nicholls put it in *Ghaidan*, 'to be acceptable these distinctions should have a rational and fair basis'.[119] This highlights what some commentators have referred to as 'the culture of justification'[120] which attended the enactment of the HRA. Again, this changes the legal context in which judicial decisions are made and influences the judicial reasoning. A third and important distinction between *Fitzpatrick* and *Ghaidan* concerns the judicial approach to the terms of paragraph 2(2). In *Fitzpatrick*, the fact that 'husband and wife' connoted a relationship between two persons of the opposite sex led the court to reject Mr Fitzpatrick's claim without much discussion,[121] whereas in *Ghaidan* this did not mark the end of the interpretive inquiry. Post-HRA, the judiciary has more freedom to depart from both the express terms of legislation and the legislative purpose which lay behind those terms, and are more likely to exercise this freedom creatively if there is a serious rights violation and the only way of providing a remedy is to adopt an innovative interpretation. Fourthly, just before the House of Lords decision in *Ghaidan* was handed down, the ECtHR decided in *Karner v. Austria*[122]

---

[118] See also N. Bamforth, 'A Constitutional Basis for Antidiscrimination Protection?' (2003) 119 LQR 215, 217, who points out that the finding that Mr Mendoza's Convention rights were violated because the legislation was discriminatory meant that the court did not defer substantially to Parliament in approaching the issue of how the discrimination should be remedied.

[119] Paras. 9 and 19.

[120] See e.g. M. Hunt, 'Sovereignty's Blight: Why Contemporary Public Law Needs a Concept of Due Deference', in N. Bamforth and P. Leyland (eds.), *Public Law in a Multi-Layered Constitution* (Oxford: Hart, 2003), p. 351; see also Lord Steyn, 'Dynamic Interpretation', above n. 2, p. 254.

[121] Slynn, [2001] 1 AC 27, 34; Lord Nicholls, *ibid.*, p. 43.   [122] (2003) 2 FLR 623.

that legislation which prevented same-sex couples from gaining the same tenancy rights as unmarried different sex couples was unlawful sexual orientation discrimination in violation of Convention rights. Although the House of Lords in *Ghaidan* did not seem to place much weight on *Karner*, it is clear that, had the House of Lords found against him, Mr Mendoza would have been entitled to compensation from the Strasbourg Court for violation of his rights as established by *Karner*.[123] The existence of Strasbourg case-law bearing directly on an issue before a UK court can influence the resolution of the case at domestic level.

Last but not least, there is what might be called the 'legitimacy issue'. In *Fitzpatrick*, many of the judges were reluctant to interpret paragraph 2(2) to include same-sex couples because they believed that law reform in this area of 'social policy' should be carried out by Parliament rather than the courts.[124] However, the issue was framed in a different way in *Ghaidan*. Due to the existence of the HRA, the question was now presented as a rights issue (an area in which the judiciary has particular expertise), whereby the judiciary had to consider the means by which they could remedy the violation. Moreover, they had the added sense of legitimacy in tackling the violation by way of interpretation, due to the fact that Parliament had given them a mandate to do exactly that when it enacted s.3(1). This combined to reassure the courts that they were not usurping Parliament's powers, but rather were carrying out the will of Parliament as expressed in s.3(1) HRA, a belief further bolstered by the assurance from counsel for the Secretary of State (who intervened in *Ghaidan*) that the government had no objection to the application of s.3(1) in this case.[125]

Conclusion

In *Ghaidan* v. *Mendoza*, their Lordships stressed that, even when the express terms of the legislation or the legislative purpose which lies behind those terms, seem to be incompatible with the Convention,

---

[123] See further Wintemute, 'Same-Sex Partners', above n. 64, p. 627.

[124] See e.g. Slynn, [2001] 1 AC 27, 33–4; Hutton, *ibid.*, p. 66; Hobhouse, *ibid.*, p. 67. This was also an important factor leading the Court of Appeal in *Fitzpatrick* to refuse to interpret paragraph 2(2) to include same-sex couples, [1998] Ch 304, 319, *per* Waite LJ; *ibid.*, p. 324, *per* Roch LJ.

[125] Peter Sales QC. Robert Wintemute argues that, by adopting the s.3(1) interpretation in *Ghaidan*, thereby providing an immediate remedy to the claimant, the courts were saving the UK government and Parliament the work of removing the incompatibility and thus working in accordance with the 'division of labour' envisaged by s.3(1): Wintemute, 'Same-Sex Partners', above n. 64, p. 627.

this does not create an automatic barrier to the application of s.3(1). Under s.3(1), the courts have the power to 'modify' legislative meaning. *Ghaidan* emphasises that we should not view s.3(1) purely in terms of finding an interpretation which is linguistically possible. It clarifies that the choice between s.3 and s.4 involves a much broader evaluative decision requiring an assessment of the limits of judicial law-making in the context of a particular case, including its remedial dimension. This essay took issue not with these conclusions, but rather with the way in which some of their Lordships presented them in the course of their general remarks on the extent and limits of s.3. In particular, it was argued here that, although a departure from the express legislative terms is envisaged by s.3(1), it does not follow that those terms have no bearing on the limits of the s.3(1) inquiry. Nor does it mean that we should characterise the statutory provisions enacted by Parliament as the product of the accidental linguistic choices of the Parliamentary draftsmen.

The last section of the essay contained some reflections on the differences the HRA can make to judicial reasoning, as exemplified by the contrasting judicial approaches in *Fitzpatrick* and *Ghaidan*. It revealed that the House of Lords in *Ghaidan* was more willing to 'rectify' the terms of paragraph 2(2) than they were in *Fitzpatrick*. However, this does not mean that the HRA has ushered in a radically new type of judicial reasoning. The difference post-HRA lies more in the judiciary's willingness to use existing (creative) techniques of statutory interpretation and in their sense of legitimacy in doing so. It is not a fundamental difference in kind, but rather a different view of the appropriateness of relying on existing techniques which were formerly only used in exceptional circumstances.[126]

This can be illustrated by looking at the reasoning of the House of Lords in *Fitzpatrick* on the issue of whether a same-sex partner could be considered part of the original tenant's 'family'. Accepting this argument by a majority of three to two, their Lordships argued that, since the word 'family' was 'flexible',[127] they should identify the main characteristics of a family in order to see if a homosexual couple satisfied those characteristics.[128] These were identified as 'a degree of mutual interdependence, of the sharing of lives, of caring and love, of commitment and

---

[126] This view is shared by Laws LJ, 'The Impact of the Human Rights Act 1998 on the Interpretation of Enactments in the UK', in R. Bigwood (ed.), *The Statute: Making and Meaning* (Wellington: Lexis-Nexis, 2004), p. 245.
[127] Lord Nicholls, [2001] 1 AC 27, 41.   [128] Lord Slynn, *ibid.*, p. 35.

support'.[129] Since these features could be manifested by same-sex partners, they could therefore establish the necessary familial link to qualify for an assured tenancy. Lord Nicholls also added a purposive element to his reasoning, namely, that:

> the underlying legislative purpose [of the Rent Act] was to provide a secure home for those who share their lives together with the original tenant in the manner which characterises a family unit. This purpose would be at risk of being stultified if the courts could not have regard to changes in the way people live together and changes in the perception of relationships.[130]

This type of reasoning is not different in kind (in fact, is remarkably similar) to the approach adopted by the majority in *Ghaidan* on the issue of whether same-sex partners could live together 'as husband and wife'.[131] The main difference in *Ghaidan* was that the court was under a duty to consider the compatibility of paragraph 2(2) with Convention rights, and, once alert to a clear violation, had to consider the choice between s.3 and s.4 in light of their remedial duties. All of these contextual factors relevant in *Ghaidan* gave the House of Lords reasons to lean in favour of an innovative interpretation which were not present in *Fitzpatrick*.

So, the judicial reasoning which the courts undertake under the HRA does not differ fundamentally from that which took place prior to the HRA. It still involves the need to balance the arguments for and against judicial innovation on the facts of a particular case. The differences lie in the context in which this balancing takes place, including the heightened focus on the protection of Convention rights, the court's remedial duties, the appropriateness of judicial- versus legislative law reform and the anticipated effectiveness of a declaration of incompatibility. These choices must now be made in the spotlight thrown upon them by the HRA, where their immense constitutional significance is no longer hidden in the shadows of statutory interpretation, but rather in the centre-stage of constitutional law for all to see.

---

[129] *Ibid.*, p. 38.   [130] *Ibid.*, pp. 45–6.

[131] The fact that Ward LJ in the Court of Appeal in *Fitzpatrick* [1998] Ch 304, 324ff, was able to interpret the words 'living together as his or her husband' to include same-sex couples shows that this interpretation was possible using traditional methods of statutory interpretation even before the HRA came into force.

6

Clarity postponed: horizontal effect after *Campbell*

GAVIN PHILLIPSON[*]

Introduction

The issue of whether the Human Rights Act imports Convention rights –
or Convention principles – into private law is of great importance to the
judicial attitude towards the HRA project. This chapter seeks not simply
to analyse the doctrinal treatment of the issue by the courts, but to
suggest, tentatively, some considerations underlying the judicial approach
to it which might explain the result that, six years after the HRA came into
force, there is still considerable ambiguity surrounding this point. I start
with the following contention: that to allow what was hitherto
an international treaty to penetrate deep into the common law[1] was
something about which the judiciary was always likely to feel ambiva-
lent. It is one thing when Parliament simply *replaces* an area of common
law with a statutory code – though it may be noted that even the
enactment of a new statutory code in a particular area has not prevented
the judiciary from developing the common law in a way that arguably
circumvents or subverts it.[2] But for Parliament to enact a statute that

---

[*] An earlier version of this chapter was presented as a paper at the Judicial Reasoning and
the Human Rights Act 1998 Symposium, held at Durham Castle on 8–9 April 2005. I am
especially grateful to Eric Barendt, who chaired the session, and to the participants for
the discussion which followed.
[1] By which is meant the common law governing legal relationships between private parties.
[2] The classic example is the persistence of the judiciary in developing the crime of
conspiracy to corrupt public morals in the much criticised decisions in *Shaw* v. *DPP*
[1962] AC 220 and *Knuller* v. *DPP* [1973] AC 435, even though it arguably captured the
same mischief as the offences enacted by the Obscene Publications Act 1959: for discussion, see H. Fenwick and G. Phillipson, *Media Freedom under the Human Rights Act*
(Oxford: Oxford University Press, 2006), Chapter 8. The recent decision of the House of
Lords in *R.* v. *Rimmington* [2005] UKHL 63 firmly asserted the legitimacy of maintaining
common law criminal offences (of nuisance in that case) even where Parliament had
created offences covering substantially the same areas.

had the capacity to colonise whole swathes of the common law with general Convention principles was quite another matter: it threatened the whole traditional common law style of reasoning and the judiciary's autonomy in developing it. If Parliament chooses to enact in one statute – the HRA – a provision that clearly instructs the judges how to interpret other statutes,[3] that is one thing: Parliament is merely modifying the rules of interpretation applying to the laws that Parliament itself produces.[4] Even to enact a provision, such as s.12 HRA, which governs the test to be applied to the granting of a particular *remedy* in private law[5] and the procedures to be followed where it is applied for,[6] while affecting common law litigation, does not touch the principles of substantive common law. These remain in the hands of the judges, and determine, of course, whether any cause of action is arguably made out, so as to give rise to a possible remedy. But to give effect to the HRA so that it interpenetrated a set of treaty-derived principles into all the areas of common law that could be affected by the Convention would, to the judicial mind, be a momentous change indeed.

True it is that in the pre-HRA period the judges, perhaps searching for a way to remedy what Dawn Oliver once termed the 'ethical aimlessness' of the common law,[7] developed the notion that such law, where ambiguous, should be developed with the Convention in mind.[8] However, it is also well known that this principle was not consistently applied, to say the least. Indeed, aside from the Court of Appeal judgment in *Derbyshire* v. *Times Newspapers*,[9] and the seminal House of Lords decision in *Reynolds* v. *Times Newspapers*[10] – which was decided on the eve of the

---

[3] The effect of s.3(1) HRA.

[4] This is not to say that such a power is without controversy: plainly, the rules of interpretation are judge-made, and the HRA is an incursion into these rules: nevertheless, it is a different thing from imposing a set of principles directly into a body of *substantive law* created by the judiciary.

[5] That is, s.12(3) HRA, which modifies the test for the granting of interim injunctions which affect the right to freedom of expression.

[6] Section 12(2).

[7] D. Oliver, 'A Bill of Rights for the United Kingdom', in D. Oliver (ed.), *Government in the United Kingdom* (Milton Keynes: Open University Press, 1991), p. 151.

[8] See e.g. the *dicta* of Ralph Gibson LJ in *Attorney-General* v. *Newspaper Publishing plc* (1990) *The Times*, 28 February, in the context of contempt of court: 'If it is not clear in what terms the relevant law is to be formulated, and there is no binding authority upon the matter, this court should have regard to the terms of the Convention.' For general discussion, see M. Hunt, *Using Human Rights Law in English Courts* (Oxford: Hart, 1997), pp. 143–51 and 185–91.

[9] [1992] QB 770.   [10] [2001] 2 AC 127; [1999] 3 WLR 1010 (HL).

coming into force of the HRA – it is hard to find a decision of an appellate court on the common law on which the Convention had an important effect:[11] sometimes indeed it was virtually ignored,[12] while the failure of the courts to fashion a common law remedy to protect privacy, answering to Article 8 of the Convention, became notorious.[13] In relation to Article 10 – the most influential Convention right in this regard – rather than clearly changing existing common law doctrine by reference to the Convention, the fashion became to assert that there was no difference between the respect afforded to freedom of expression by the common law on the one hand, and the Convention, on the other,[14] as affirmed by Lord Goff in the *Spycatcher* litigation.[15] Thus the House of Lords in *Derbyshire* v. *Times Newspapers*[16] chose not to follow the Court of Appeal in relying on the Convention to develop the common law, relying instead on principles found to derive from the common law itself to decide that, in the interests of freedom of speech, governmental bodies could not maintain an action in defamation.

Thus, to this observer at least, calls for the HRA to be given full horizontal effect,[17] or even as importing an obligation to change the common law whenever it was found to be inconsistent with the Convention

---

[11] In terms of remedies, one could cite *Rantzen* v. *Mirror Group Newspapers Ltd* [1994] QB 670, 692, in which Article 10 had a direct effect upon the guidance given as to the assessment of the quantum of damages in libel cases; however, although this involved a common law action, the Court of Appeal was engaged in determining what was meant by the phrase 'excessive' awards of damages in a *statutory* provision.

[12] E.g. M. Beloff and H. Mountfield, 'Unconventional Behaviour? Judicial Uses of the European Convention in England and Wales' [1996] EHRLR 467, 487 and 488, cite as an example of the influence of the Convention the decision by Scott VC in *A-G* v. *Blake* [1997] Ch 84, in which the judge 'refused to enforce an alleged fiduciary duty which he considered was a breach of Article 10 having regard to the derogations contained in it'. However, this decision was overturned by the Court of Appeal, whose decision was upheld by the House of Lords in a judgment in which Article 10 merited only a brief, dismissive mention: [2001] 1 AC 268, 287, *per* Lord Nicholls, although the law report reveals that it was cited extensively in argument (see *ibid.*, pp. 271–5).

[13] Most particularly in *Kaye* v. *Robertson* [1991] FSR 62. On the common law and privacy, see further, Chapter 9.

[14] Thus the authors of one commentary note the approach taken in *John* v. *MGN Ltd* [1996] 2 All ER 37, *per* Sir Thomas Bingham MR, who said that the 'the same result [as in that case] was achieved by the application of Article 10, which, whilst not a free-standing source of law in the United Kingdom, was not in any way in conflict or discrepant with the common law and "reinforced and buttressed" the conclusions reached by the Court, independently of the Convention': Beloff and Mountfield, above, n. 12 p. 487, n. 7.

[15] *A-G* v. *Guardian Newspapers* (*No. 2*) [1990] 1 AC 109.

[16] [1993] AC 534; [1993] 2 WLR 449 (HL).   [17] See below, pp. 151 and 153.

rights,[18] always seemed unrealistic. It seemed likely instead that the judiciary would prefer a more open-ended interpretation, under which, while they should now *consistently take the Convention into account* in common law adjudication, its force or status would not there be clearly overriding. This would allow judges a measure of discretion as to the force given to Convention principles in any given case, thus preserving the essentially flexible and pragmatic nature of the common law. In terms of the case-law so far on point it is the tentative thesis of this chapter that the judiciary collectively has managed to *avoid* resolving the horizontal effect question decisively and that this avoidance has not been a question of chance or oversight, but rather is at least semi-deliberate. The question thus being left at large, it is one that can be dealt with by judges in individual cases, by giving the Convention as much or as little purchase as seems best, all things considered, in the particular case; but the hands of the judiciary are not tied generally to the Convention in private law cases.[19]

How, then, were the judiciary served, in their attempts to solve the horizontal effect conundrum, by its drafting and by academic commentary? The position, I would suggest, was somewhat paradoxical. On the one hand, the judiciary were *hindered* in the attempt correctly to construe the HRA in this area both by its ambiguous drafting and by the plethora of competing academic argument on the subject, of which more later. On the other hand, if, as I have suggested, the instinct of the judges was to *resist* too clear-cut and powerful an incursion of the Convention into private law, preferring instead to keep the issue openended, then this very ambiguity surrounding the issue was actually helpful. It is indeed now a trite observation that the question of the effect that the HRA gives to the Convention rights in relation to private common law has been one of its most controversial and contested aspects. This is partly because of its complexity and normative implications – the courts of virtually every country with a Bill of Rights have had to face this question, giving varying answers, depending only partly upon the text of the Bills of Rights themselves.[20] But it is also, as the

---

[18] See below, text to note 50.   [19] See below, pp. 153–4.

[20] See e.g. the decision of the Canadian Supreme Court in *Retail Wholesale and Department Store Union Local 580 et al.* v. *Dolphin Delivery Ltd* (1985) 33 DLR (4th) 174; of the South African Constitutional Court case on the horizontal effect of human rights under the Interim Constitution: *Du Plessis and Others* v. *De Klerk and Another* 1996 (3) SA 850, 900; discussion of the stance of the German Supreme Court in B. Markesenis, 'Privacy,

author has pointed out elsewhere,[21] because Parliament contrived to omit from the HRA any mention either of its effect upon private law, or upon the common law generally. All these questions were left to be dealt with by the bald provisions of ss.6(1)[22] and 6(3).[23] Section 6(1), which lays obligations only upon 'public authorities' to act compatibly with the Convention rights, on its face therefore rules out horizontal effect: private bodies, such as newspapers, landlords or employers are not bound by the Act to respect Convention rights. It is also the case that the Act does not, as such, incorporate the rights into UK law: rather, as is well known, it gives them particular effects in particular contexts: the two most important[24] are as interpretative aids where statutes apply[25] and as a duty binding upon public authorities. However, the courts, as 'public authorities' themselves,[26] have a duty not to act incompatibly with the Convention rights; if this duty applied even when dealing with private common law, it was bound to create *some* role for the rights even in common law litigation between private parties,[27] thus giving rise to a form of 'horizontal effect', though the HRA left it wholly unclear what this role should be. Other Bills of Rights offer at least more guidance,[28] whilst the Constitution of South Africa deals with the matter explicitly, by making plain that private persons *are* in principle bound by the constitutional rights and that the courts must develop the common law to give effect to these obligations.[29] The horizontal effect issue was raised in Parliament, during the passage of the Human Rights Bill, in relation to the fears the media had of being exposed to the development

Freedom of Expression, and the Horizontal Effect of the Human Rights Bill: Lessons from Germany' (1999) 115 LQR 47. For a more general comparative survey, see S. Gardbaum, 'The "Horizontal Effect" of Constitutional Rights' (2003) 102 *Michigan Law Review* 387.

[21] 'The Human Rights Act, the Common Law and "Horizontal Effect": A Bang or a Whimper?' (1999) 62 *Modern Law Review* 824.

[22] Section 6(1) provides: 'It is unlawful for a public authority to act in a way which is incompatible with a Convention right.'

[23] Section 6(3) provides that 'public authority includes a court or tribunal'.

[24] The other key provision is s.7, which gives a cause of action against a public authority that has acted incompatibly with a Convention right and s.8, which gives a power to award damages where such an action succeeds.

[25] Section 3 HRA.   [26] Section 6(3)(a) HRA.

[27] *Per* s.3(1) HRA, *all* statutes will also have to be interpreted 'so far as possible' in accordance with Convention rights.

[28] The Canadian Constitution, s.52 states that '*any law* that is inconsistent with the provisions of the Constitution is, to the extent of the inconsistency, of no force or effect'.

[29] See s.8 of the South African Bill of Rights.

of a common law action to protect the right to privacy enshrined in Article 8.[30] The government managed to fob off Lord Wakeham[31] and the press with s.12, which did probably make it a little harder to obtain interim injunctions[32] against the media, but other than that contained the, as it turns out, meaningless injunction to courts to have 'particular regard' to freedom of expression.[33]

Next, the academics turned their attention to the issue. It is by now well known what happened next: comprehensive polarisation of opinion. However, before turning to survey briefly the academic debate and its possible impact upon subsequent judicial approaches to the issue, it is necessary to look a little more closely at the notion of horizontal effect and the terms of the HRA itself.

Horizontal effect: the basic issues

It is important to start by pointing out that the notion of 'horizontal effect' signifies effects in the private sphere both upon the common law *and* upon the interpretation of statutes. Indeed, one of the major decisions on s.3(1), discussed by Aileen Kavanagh in Chapter 5, *Ghaidan* v. *Mendoza*,[34] was concerned with a dispute between two private parties – landlord and tenant – albeit one governed by statute. However, it has been accepted by the courts without hesitation that *all* statutes should be interpreted compatibly with Convention rights, regardless of whether they regulate the behaviour of public authorities or private persons. As the Court of Appeal said in *X* v. *Y*,[35] '[s]ection 3 draws no distinction between legislation

---

[30] See e.g. HL Debs., 18 November 1997, col. 473, *per* Lord Ackner.
[31] Then chair of the Press Complaints Commission.   [32] Section 12(3).
[33] Section 12(4). 'Meaningless' in that this provision has not resulted in the courts building in extra weight for freedom of expression, as emphatically confirmed in *Campbell* [2004] 2 WLR 1232; [2004] 2 AC 457 (see below). Indeed, Sedley LJ has interpreted s.12(4) as bringing *Article 8* into the frame: *Douglas v Hello!* [2001] QB 967, at 1003. His Lordship reasoned that Article 10 contains (in para. 2) the exceptions it is subject to, including Article 8, under the 'rights of others' exception. Therefore, 'you cannot have particular regard to article 10 without having equally particular regard at the very least to article 8'.
[34] [2004] 3 WLR 113. For general discussion of this aspect of the Act's horizontal effect, see further N. Bamforth, 'The True "Horizontal Effect" of the Human Rights Act' (2001) 117 LQR 34.
[35] [2004] ICR 1634, para. 57(2), in which the Court of Appeal accepted that employment law legislation had, in principle, to be interpreted and applied in a way that was compatible with any relevant Convention rights, though on the facts it was found that the claimed right (Article 8) was not engaged.

governing public authorities and legislation governing private individuals'. As suggested above, such an outcome was perhaps predictable: for the courts to accept a modification by Parliament of the rules of interpretation governing Parliament's statutes is quite a different matter from acceptance of a wholesale incursion through Act of Parliament of a set of detailed principles into the purely judicial realm – the common law. It is this, much more thorny issue upon which the discussion in this chapter concentrates.

The two levels of analysis

It is important to note at the outset that the issue of horizontal effect raises questions at two levels, which are logically and legally distinct: first, at the Convention level, as a matter of interpretation of the Convention and the Strasbourg Court's jurisprudence; secondly, at the local, domestic level, as a matter of interpretation of the particular instrument giving effect to the Convention – the Human Rights Act. To put it another way, the court must, first, determine whether there are any Convention obligations in play at all and, secondly, if so, how it is to give effect to them in domestic law. Section 2(1) HRA provides that a court, 'in determining any question . . . in connection with a Convention right, must take into account' any relevant Strasbourg jurisprudence. Plainly, the issue of the horizontal effect of the Convention under the HRA is a question 'in connection with a Convention right'. Thus, when considering whether to treat the Convention right as having any relevance at all to the particular situation, the court should examine whether Strasbourg has found the right to require positive state intervention between private parties.[36] In other words, it must ask: is there an obligation on the UK to provide a measure of protection for Convention rights in situations such as the one that has arisen in the litigation, which the court *could* discharge in this case? The Court of Appeal accepted in *X* v. *Y*[37] that s.2(1) HRA required it to examine relevant Strasbourg jurisprudence in deciding the horizontal effect point;[38] in that case, the issue was whether the dismissal of the applicant based on the concealment by him of his caution for an act of gross

---

[36] As it did, for example, in *A* v. *United Kingdom* (1998) 27 EHRR 611, in which an obligation to provide protection for a child against its parents in respect of physical discipline was found, under Article 3 of the Convention.

[37] [2004] ICR 1634. The case took the form of an action for unfair dismissal.

[38] *Ibid.*, paras. 39–42.

indecency with another male engaged his right to private life. It is important to note that this first level must be investigated in *all* cases, *including* those involving statutes, since the question here is whether there are any Convention obligations in play at all, not yet how the court is to give effect to them.

The second level is local and specific, and it derives from the particular instrument incorporating the Convention into UK law – the Human Right Act. This second level is logically distinct from the first, because a court *might* decide that, whilst it appeared that Strasbourg had interpreted a particular right as imposing a positive obligation to intervene between private parties, the particular provisions of the HRA – in particular, s.6(1) – precluded this, so that the UK government would have to legislate to provide the required protection. Lord Hoffmann, as discussed below,[39] made precisely this distinction. It is also suggested, however, that, when deciding the issue as to the interpretation of the HRA, the courts should take account of the Strasbourg jurisprudence on whether and when the Convention requires a horizontal application.[40] In other words, the answer given at the first level is relevant to that given at the second, though not determinative of it.

Direct effect, and 'strong' and 'weak' indirect effect

At the second level – in deciding how to provide in domestic law for any horizontal effect required by the Convention – a basic distinction may be drawn between what is often termed 'direct' and 'indirect' horizontal effect. A measure has 'direct' horizontal effect if it lays duties directly upon a private body to abide by its provisions and makes breach of these duties directly actionable at the instance of an aggrieved party. In contrast, if a measure has only *indirect* horizontal effect, this means that, whilst the rights cannot be applied directly to determine private relations and are not actionable *per se* in such a context, they may be relied upon indirectly, to govern or at least influence the interpretation and application of pre-existing law. It has been accepted by most scholars that the HRA does not give rise to direct horizontal effect,[41] a conclusion based primarily upon the fact that s.6(1) states: 'It is unlawful for a *public authority* to act in a way which is incompatible with one

---

[39] See the text to n. 111 below.   [40] This is required by s.2(1) HRA.
[41] Murray Hunt, 'The Horizontal Effect of the Human Rights Act' [1998] PL 423, 438, asserts that this is 'clear beyond argument'.

or more of the Convention rights' (emphasis added). However, it has been generally accepted that some degree of *indirect* horizontal effect arises from it. This is because the courts – and tribunals – are stated to be public authorities for the purposes of the Act[42] and, it is argued, are therefore themselves bound to apply Convention standards in giving judgment even in cases involving only private individuals. However, in an early indication of judicial attitudes towards this issue, Buxton LJ[43] rejected even this argument and contended trenchantly for the Convention rights to be given no horizontal effect at all within the common law.

In contrast, William Wade contended for a form of full horizontal effect. His view was that in practice it should make no difference whether the defendant is a public or private body, since the courts in giving judgment would have a duty to uphold Convention rights under s.6 regardless.[44] I have set out arguments elsewhere against this position,[45] and will not repeat them here, in a context in which not the *academic* but the judicial perspectives are my concern. It suffices to mention that Wade's view seems to raise the difficulty of the absence of a cause of action, given that a litigant has one against another party only if she can allege that they have acted, or are threatening to act, unlawfully. A private party like a newspaper will not have done so, solely by violating or threatening to violate Article 8. As the Court of Appeal said bluntly in *X* v. *Y*,[46] which concerned an action by a former employee against his employer relying on Article 8:

> The applicant did not assert any cause of action against the employer under the HRA. He does not have an HRA cause of action. The employer is not a public authority within section 6 of the HRA. It was not unlawful under section 6 of the HRA for the employer, as a private sector employer, to act in a way which was incompatible with article 8.[47]

---

[42] Section 6(3)(a); Hunt describes this provision as 'of great significance for the horizontality [of the Act]' (Hunt, above n. 41, p. 439); see also Wade, 'The United Kingdom's Bill of Rights', in J. Beatson, C. F. Forsyth and I. Hare (eds.), *Constitutional Reform in the United Kingdom: Practice and Principles* (Oxford: Hart, 1998), pp. 62–4.

[43] 'The Human Rights Act and Private Law' (2000) 116 LQR 48.

[44] Wade, 'The United Kingdom's Bill of Rights', above n. 42, pp. 62–3; see also his 'Horizons of Horizontality' (2000) 116 LQR 224; and, with C. F. Forsyth, *Administrative Law* (8th edn, Oxford: Oxford University Press, 2000), Appendix 2.

[45] See above n. 21. Hunt (above n. 41) and others (below nn. 52 and 53) have also contested Wade's view.

[46] [2004] ICR 1634.   [47] *Ibid.*, para. 54(2).

The court went on to say specifically that the fact that the employment tribunal, like a court, is itself a public authority under s.6(3) HRA and so must act compatibly with the Convention rights under s.6(1), '[does] not, however, give the applicant any cause of action under the HRA against an employer which is not a public authority'.[48] Contrary to Wade's view, then, s.6(1) gives the Convention rights no purchase in private law adjudication except upon existing causes of action.

Thus the courts have now more or less ruled out Wade's view – without much explanation, but doubtless motivated in part by a desire to protect private law from a full-scale takeover by the Convention. They have also rejected Buxton's approach.[49] Both of these positions, it should be noted, are extremes: each would deny the courts flexibility in the horizontal application of the Convention – Buxton's because it would *preclude* it, Wade's because it would *demand* it, in a particularly drastic way that would threaten whole swathes of the common law with replacement by private HRA actions. In contrast, a view that has received some support from the judiciary – and perhaps more than any other from commentators – is that put forward by Murray Hunt.[50] He argued for what he termed 'strong indirect horizontal effect': that the judges have a clear duty under s.6 to interpret and apply *existing law* to render it compatible with the Convention rights; once there was reliance by either party upon an existing cause of action, the judicial duty was activated. In an article published in 1999,[51] I argued, on a number of grounds, that the HRA does not impose this absolute duty, but rather a weaker one – the obligation to *take account* of Convention principles or values when engaging in common law adjudication, affording them a variable weight, depending on the context. A number of other commentators, including Lester and Pannick[52] and Grosz and Beatson,[53] appeared to back Hunt's view in favour of strong horizontal effect and at one point it looked as if there was at least a clear academic

---

[48] *Ibid.*, para. 58(3).

[49] Buxton LJ, 'The Human Rights Act and Private Law' (2000) 116 LQR 48. See e.g. the *dicta* of Butler Sloss P in *Venables and Another* v. *News Group Newspapers* [2001] 1 All ER 908, 916, and the approach taken in *Campbell* [2004] 2 WLR 1232; [2004] 2 AC 457 (below).

[50] 'The Horizontal Effect of the Human Rights Act' [1998] PL 423.

[51] 'The Human Rights Act, the Common Law and "Horizontal Effect": A Bang or a Whimper?' (1999) 62 MLR 824.

[52] A. Lester and D. Pannick, 'The Impact of the Human Rights Act on Private Law: The Knight's Move' (2000) 116 LQR 380.

[53] J. Beatson and S. Grosz, 'Horizontality: A Footnote' (2000) 116 LQR 385.

consensus building around indirect horizontal effect – in either its weaker or stronger forms. However, it is important to note that in fact this proved not to be the case: Jonathan Morgan[54] has argued for the Wade position of full or direct horizontal effect, though his article did not take account of a number of the arguments put forward against the Wade position.[55] Moreover, Professor Beyleveld and Shaun Pattinson have put forward a complex and sophisticated argument in favour of full or direct horizontal effect in the *Law Quarterly Review*,[56] engaging in a critique and analysis of most of the main academic arguments against such a position. Again, I do not seek here to refute the arguments put forward in this article. Rather, I confine myself to noting that, by the time the House of Lords decided *Campbell* v. *MGN*,[57] there was a rich and sophisticated academic literature on this subject, in which, whilst there was perhaps a consensus that the Buxton anti-horizontalist position was wrong, there was little agreement aside from that.

As far as the courts are concerned, since they have more or less ruled out the two extreme interpretations put forward by Buxton and Wade, the question has been whether they would adopt the strong version of horizontal effect put forward by Hunt or some weaker one, as suggested by the author. As I have pointed out previously,[58] the former, since the court is bound to act compatibly with the Convention in adjudicating upon existing law, suggests that only legal interests recognised as coming within paragraph 2 of the Convention right in question[59] could lawfully constitute reasons for overriding the right. This is so, because, if the court allowed an interest *other* than one recognised by the Convention to override a Convention right, it would not be acting compatibly with the Convention. In contrast, under the weak model, in which the Convention right figures only as a value, to be given a variable weight

---

[54] 'Questioning the True Effect of the HRA' (2002) 22 *Legal Studies* 159; see also his 'Privacy, Confidence and Horizontal Effect: "Hello" Trouble' (2003) 62 CLJ 444.

[55] He did not deal with those put forward in G. Phillipson, n. 51 above.

[56] 'Horizontality Applicability and Horizontal Effect' (2002) 118 LQR 623.

[57] [2004] 2 WLR 1232; [2004] 2 AC 457.

[58] Above, n. 51, 838–9.

[59] Assuming that one is dealing with one of Articles 8–11. In relation to the absolute rights (Articles 3, 4, 6, 7 and 12) there would of course be *no* lawful common law exceptions under this model, while in relation to the narrowly qualified rights (Articles 2 and 5) the exceptions would have to correspond only to those narrowly enumerated in the relevant articles.

depending upon the context, it only amounts to a reason for deciding a case in a particular way;[60] it may therefore be overridden by any other interest that the court finds compelling in a particular case. One might therefore expect the weaker model to be instinctively more attractive to the judiciary, as preserving the traditional flexibility of common law reasoning.[61] However, a more passive course – simply failing to resolve which of the two models was to be followed – would achieve the same result: the absence of a clear imperative to act compatibly with, rather than have regard to, the Convention right, would leave the courts with more flexibility. In this respect, it is interesting to note that some judicial disinclination to pin down this issue clearly and decisively was evident from the very beginning; as we shall see, it has persisted up to the most recent judicial pronouncements.

The pre-*Campbell* case-law on horizontal effect

In *Douglas* v. *Hello!*,[62] the first case to consider the matter, quite different language was used by the judges to refer to the duties generated by s.6: the effect was broadly to locate the court's stance within the camp in the middle, and that with the most academic support – indirect horizontal effect – but to refuse to clarify the matter further. Thus Brooke LJ spoke of the judges' obligation of '*taking into account* the positive duties identified by the court at Strasbourg when they develop the common law',[63] while Keene LJ similarly stated that the courts' approach must now be '*informed* by the jurisprudence of the Convention in respect of article 8'.[64] Sedley LJ, in contrast, appeared explicitly to approve Hunt's stronger approach.[65] His view was that, 'by virtue of s.6 of the Act, the courts of this country *must themselves act compatibly* with … the … Convention rights'.[66] *Venables*[67] also expressly endorsed the strong version: 'The duty on the court, in my view, is to act compatibly with Convention rights in adjudicating upon existing common law causes of action, and that includes a positive as well as a negative obligation.'[68]

---

[60] The parallel with Dworkin's concept of principles, rather than rules, is clear at this point: Dworkin, *Taking Rights Seriously* (London: Duckworth, 1978).
[61] See above, p. 146.
[62] *Douglas and Zeta Jones and Others* v. *Hello!* [2001] QB 967.
[63] *Ibid.*, pp. 993–4.   [64] *Ibid.*, p. 1012.   [65] *Ibid.*, p. 1002.
[66] *Ibid.*, p. 998. Sedley LJ's approach was followed in *Theakston* v. *MGN* [2002] EMLR 22.
[67] *Venables and Another* v. *News Group Newspapers* [2001] 1 All ER 908.   [68] *Ibid.*, p. 917.

The Court of Appeal in *Campbell*,[69] on the other hand, expressed the duty in the weaker form: Phillips MR, giving the judgment of the Court, held that 'the courts must *have regard* to' Articles 8 and 10[70] in a common law context; he did not speak of a duty to act compatibly with them. *A* v. *B plc*,[71] while endorsing a clear role for the Convention rights in private law cases, does not resolve the matter. Woolf CJ, giving the judgment of the court, simply stated, without more:

> Under section 6 of the [HRA], the court, as a public authority, is required not to act 'in a way which is incompatible with a Convention right.' The court is able to achieve this by absorbing the rights which articles 8 and 10 protect into the long-established action for breach of confidence.[72]

The first part of this *dicta*, it will be noted, simply quotes s.6(1). The second sentence plainly suggests a form of indirect horizontal effect, since Articles 8 and 10 are not to be applied directly between private parties, but instead 'absorbed' into breach of confidence. The metaphor of absorption is not an exact one, but Lord Woolf does seem to be suggesting that the imperative to act compatibly with Convention rights applies to doctrines of substantive law, something which sounds close to the Hunt position. However, as appears below, these dicta were cited by two of their Lordships in *Campbell* v. *MGN*, one of whom thought he was not deciding the question of horizontality at all,[73] while the other thought these *dicta* had already decided it:[74] the passage is evidently therefore not without ambiguity. Purportedly following this and the other Court of Appeal decisions, Lindsay J in *Douglas II* found that the 'scope' of breach of confidence now 'needs to be evaluated in the light of' the courts' obligations under s.6(1).[75] This sounds like 'weak' indirect effect: to assess one area of law 'in the light of' another, is to take that second area into account, rather than to act compatibly with it. Moreover, Sedley LJ has recently remarked in a different context, 'it is probable, though as yet undecided', that the s.6(1) duty lying on courts 'governs remedies and procedures, rather than doctrines of substantive law':[76] if this is the case, then horizontal effect would not apply to legal doctrines such as breach of confidence at all, only to consideration of

---

[69] [2003] QB 633 (CA).   [70] *Ibid.*, p. 658 (emphasis added).
[71] [2002] 3 WLR 542.   [72] *Ibid.*, p. 546.
[73] [2004] 2 WLR 1232; [2004] 2 AC 457, *per* Lord Nicholls, para. 17.
[74] *Ibid.*, *per* Lord Hope, para. 86.   [75] [2003] 3 All ER 996, para. 186(i).
[76] *R. (on the Application of Wooder)* v. *Feggetter* [2003] QB 219, para. 48.

what remedies should be granted under it. However, if this is so, why did Lord Woolf in *A* v. *B plc* talk of 'absorbing' Articles 8 and 10 into breach of confidence?

Thus, taken together, these cases do *not* disclose what one commentator[77] ascribed to the judgment in *Douglas* – 'a complete acceptance of the judicial duty to act compatibly with Convention rights', although they do amount to a clear rejection of the Buxton view. Rather, they leave a range of options open: in the realm of private common law, the HRA requires, first, only a modification of the approach to remedies and procedures; or, secondly, it requires the courts to take into account the Convention when developing and applying the common law; or, thirdly, it requires the court to act compatibly with the Convention when so doing. We may note also the readiness of the judges to disagree freely with each other on the issue, without seeking to resolve it, and Sedley LJ's frank admission in *Feggetter* that the issue had not been resolved. We may finally mention again *X* v. *Y*.[78] Since the case was not concerned with common law, but with a statute, it is not of direct relevance to our focus here, but certain remarks made by the Court of Appeal are of interest. Noting the academic debate, the court said, disarmingly:

> The general question of horizontality has not yet been resolved by a court. Indeed, *it may never be resolved judicially* at the same high level of abstraction on which the debate has been conducted for the most part in the law books and legal periodicals. The facts of particular cases and the legal contexts in which they fall to be decided tend to put very general propositions into a more limited and manageable perspective.[79]

The language here is remarkable: the use of the passive voice – 'it may never be decided' – seems perhaps designed to veil the rather surprising meaning: it would sound more startling if the judges had said, of an important point of law, 'we may never decide this'. The effect is, curiously, to suggest to the reader that, while the issue may not be resolved, this is not a question of judicial *choice*, but rather a somehow inevitable result of the judicial perspective, which deals always with the 'particular facts' and particular 'context'. In other words, its intention seems to have been to lower expectations of a decisive judicial resolution of the horizontal effect issue, suggesting instead that the judges will deal

---

[77] I. Hare, 'Vertically Challenged: Private Parties, Privacy and the Human Rights Act' [2001] EHRLR 526, 533.
[78] [2004] ICR 1634.   [79] *Ibid.*, para. 45 (emphasis added).

with it contextually rather than as a question of overarching legal principle; simultaneously the language used seeks to deflect attention from the deliberate judicial choice to avoid resolution.

This then was the backdrop to the House of Lords decision in *Campbell*: an issue of crucial importance to the interpretation and the impact of the HRA; left largely ambiguous by Parliament; fiercely contested in leading academic articles; substantially – almost deliberately – unresolved by the lower courts. All this uncertainty of course existed four years after the HRA came into force and six years after it was passed. One might have thought that legal certainty, if nothing else, required that the question be given a definitive answer, despite the just-noted remarks of the Court of Appeal in *X* v. *Y*. This backdrop, I would suggest, makes how the Law Lords actually handled the horizontal effect point in *Campbell* all the more remarkable.

Campbell and horizontal effect

Turning now to look at the case itself, the facts should very briefly be noted, in order to indicate the context in which the case was decided. Naomi Campbell complained of the publication of details of her treatment at Narcotics Anonymous for drug addiction, including a photograph of her taken outside the clinic. She relied upon an existing cause of action, breach of confidence; however, to provide her with a remedy required a substantial extension of the law as it stood, in reliance on Article 8;[80] therefore the application of the Convention to the case was a highly significant issue. I will consider their Lordships' approach to the issue in two ways: first, by looking at their formal *dicta* on the matter, and, secondly, by looking briefly at what their actual approach to Convention jurisprudence and principle was.

The analysis of the majority

We may start with Lady Hale, who was the only member of the House to take a clear and unambiguous position on the matter:[81]

> Neither party to this appeal has challenged the basic principles which have emerged from the Court of Appeal in the wake of the Human Rights Act 1998. The 1998 Act does not create any new cause of action between

---

[80] As argued in Chapter 9.   [81] [2004] 2 WLR 1232; [2004] 2 AC 457 para. 132.

private persons. But if there is a relevant cause of action applicable, the court
as a public authority must act compatibly with both parties' Convention
rights. In a case such as this, the relevant vehicle will usually be the action for
breach of confidence, as Lord Woolf CJ held in *A* v. *B plc*, para. 4.[82]

These *dicta* appear both to rule out the Wade position, *and* to endorse
that of Hunt: the court must act compatibly with the rights themselves –
there is no talk of having regard to the values underlying the rights.
Having taken this position, Lady Hale then very much proceeds to put it
into practice: her judgment amounts to a careful analysis of relevant
Convention jurisprudence and principles and a reformulation of the law
to reflect them, in particular in relation to the correct approach to
balancing Articles 8 and 10.[83] We will come back to the fact that a
viewpoint which her Ladyship says is agreed upon by the parties is
actually disputed by both Lord Nicholls and Lord Hoffmann in their
speeches. It is almost as if Lady Hale is pretending that the point is well
settled in order to decide it without appearing to – deciding it almost by
default.

Next we come to Lord Hope (Lord Carswell simply agreed with Lords
Hope and Hale, and so his speech adds nothing to the analysis of this
point). Lord Hope is by no means as clear as Lady Hale; indeed, he takes
up no explicit position on this matter. Rather, his Lordship first of all
makes a somewhat ambiguous reference to the *dicta* of Lord Woolf
already cited: 'As Lord Woolf CJ said in *A* v. *B plc*, para. 4, new breadth
and strength is given to the action for breach of confidence by [Articles 8
and 10].'[84] Since paragraph 4 of *A* v. *B* also contains Lord Woolf's *dicta*
about acting compatibly with the Convention rights cited with approval
by Lady Hale (above), and since Lord Hope voices no criticism or
dissent from them, his Lordship *seems* at this point to be endorsing
Lady Hale's view. But it is rather striking that, in pronouncing upon
such an important point, his Lordship does not make himself rather
clearer. Lord Hope then goes on to make his own comment:

> In the present case it is convenient to begin by looking at the matter from
> the standpoint of the respondents' assertion of the article 10 right and the
> court's duty as a public authority under section 6(1) of the Human Rights

---

[82] See text to n. 72 above.
[83] Here she builds upon the approach she had sketched out in the Court of Appeal decision
in *Re S* [2003] 2 FCR 577.
[84] [2004] 2 WLR 1232; [2004] 2 AC 457, para. 86.

Act 1998, which section 12(4) reinforces, not to act in a way which is
incompatible with *that* Convention right.[85]

This passage is notable in being specifically confined in application to
Article 10; it does suggest a reading of it whereby courts must act
compatibly with it in private law cases, rather than merely have particular regard to its importance, but it does not seek to resolve the
horizontal effect conundrum generally.

What is the more strange, especially in contrast to the view of Lord
Hoffmann, discussed below, is that, having seemingly decided that
Articles 8 and 10 must be applied in this context, Lord Hope goes on
to deny that this makes any difference, save in terms of semantics:

> *The language* has changed following the coming into operation of the
> Human Rights Act 1998 and the incorporation into domestic law of
> article 8 and article 10 of the Convention. We now talk about the right
> to respect for private life and the countervailing right to freedom of
> expression. The jurisprudence of the European Court offers important
> guidance as to how these competing rights ought to be approached and
> analysed. I doubt whether the result is that the centre of gravity, as my
> noble and learned friend Lord Hoffmann says, has shifted. It seems to me
> that the balancing exercise to which that guidance is directed is essentially
> the same exercise, although it is plainly now more carefully focussed and
> more penetrating.[86]

As will appear below, Lord Hoffmann takes precisely the opposite view
on both counts: while Lord Hope seems to contend that there *is* horizontal effect under the HRA but says that it makes little difference, Lord
Hoffmann argues that there is *no* horizontal effect arising from the HRA,
but that the values underlying Articles 8 and 10 are applicable anyway
and make a fundamental difference to this area of common law – 'a shift
in the centre of gravity', as he terms it.

However, having said that the difference between the common law
and the Convention in this area is more or less semantic, Lord Hope
then goes on, like Lady Hale, to engage in a detailed analysis of
Convention jurisprudence: he does so in relation to the existence of a
privacy interest – decided by reference to *Z* v. *Finland*[87] – its strength,
and the manner in which that interest should be weighed against the
competing freedom of speech interest. Thus his principal objection to

---

[85] *Ibid.*, para. 114 (emphasis added).   [86] *Ibid.*, para. 86 (emphasis added).
[87] (1997) 25 EHRR 371.

the Court of Appeal decision which he, as part of the majority, over-turned, is that '[the judges] do not appear to have attempted to balance the competing Convention rights against each other'. In working out how to carry out this exercise, Lord Hope then quotes extensively from *Bladet Tromso* v. *Norway*,[88] *Jersild* v. *Denmark*,[89] *Observer and Guardian* v. *United Kingdom*,[90] and *Fressoz and Roire* v. *France*.[91] He concludes that the weight of both rights in the particular context must be subject to searching scrutiny, as must the necessity for their restriction and the need to ensure that such restriction goes no further than is necessary. In doing so he observes:

> The jurisprudence of the European Court of Human Rights explains how these principles are to be understood and applied in the context of the facts of each case.[92]

In carrying out the balancing act, Lord Hope uses decisions such as *Dudgeon* v. *United Kingdom*[93] in order to establish that interference with more intimate areas of private life require a weightier justification – an important decision that had notably been omitted from consideration in earlier privacy decisions to which it had clear relevance, such as *A* v. *B*, *Theakston*,[94] and the Court of Appeal decision in *Campbell*.[95] He also uses cases on 'low value speech' such as *Tammer* v. *Estonia*,[96] to find that there were no political or democratic values at stake in the case and that no pressing social need to interfere with Campbell's privacy rights had been identified, contrasting Campbell's case with *Goodwin* v. *United Kingdom*.[97] In scrutinising the privacy value at stake in the decision, he relied on *PG and JH* v. *United Kingdom*[98] and *Peck* v. *United Kingdom*.[99]

In short, both Lord Hope and Lady Hale appear to engage in what can be termed strong indirect horizontal effect reasoning, which the author has described elsewhere as meaning that 'breach of confidence [is] treated simply as an empty shell into which Article 8 principles [are] poured'.[100] Indeed, as discussed in Chapter 9,[101] they also changed the shape of the shell – remoulding breach of confidence so radically that it

---

[88] (2000) 29 EHRR 125.   [89] (1994) 19 EHRR 1.   [90] (1992) 14 EHRR 153.
[91] (2001) 31 EHRR 28.   [92] *Campbell*, para. 113   [93] (1981) 4 EHRR 149.
[94] *Theakston* v. *MGN* [2002] EMLR 22.   [95] [2003] QB 633 (CA).
[96] (2001) 37 EHRR 857, para. 59.   [97] (1996) 22 EHRR 123.
[98] App. No. 44787/98, para. 57.   [99] (2003) 36 EHRR 719.
[100] G. Phillipson, 'Transforming Breach of Confidence? Towards a Common Law Right to Privacy under the Human Rights Act' (2003) 66 MLR 726, 731.
[101] See esp. pp. 221–7.

now makes more sense to speak of the tort of misuse of private information, as Lord Nicholls did.[102] The difference between the two is that, while Lady Hale expressly accepted the application of strong horizontal effect as a duty that must be carried out in each case involving common law actions that are in the sphere of Convention rights, Lord Hope did not.

The analysis of the minority

Turning now to the minority, we may consider the comments of Lord Nicholls first. Lord Nicholls at first struck a note that sounded very much in harmony with the speech of Lady Hale:

> The time has come to recognise that the values enshrined in articles 8 and 10 are now part of the cause of action for breach of confidence [citing Lord Woolf CJ's *dicta* in *A* v. *B plc*, para. 4]. Further, it should now be recognised that for this purpose these values are of general application. The values embodied in articles 8 and 10 are as much applicable in disputes between individuals or between an individual and a non-governmental body such as a newspaper as they are in disputes between individuals and a public authority.[103]

Two things are noteworthy about these *dicta*: first, it is the *values underlying the rights* that are to be applicable in resolving disputes between private individuals; this is very different from pronouncing that there is a duty to act compatibly with the rights themselves. To find that some values are applicable to the situation is simply to identify some broad principles that should be taken into account: this differs sharply from saying that the individuals have rights, which the court must manipulate the law to satisfy. In other words, Lord Nicholls, like Lady Hale, cites the same *dicta* of Lord Woolf, but draws from them a different conclusion; it is also one that is apt to leave future courts far more flexibility in applying Convention principles in common law reasoning.

Whatever his differences with Lady Hale, however, it seems at least that Lord Nicholls has decided the question of horizontal effect. However, a surprise lies in wait when one moves to the next paragraph of his speech:

---

[102] [2004] 2 WLR 1323; [2004] 2 AC 457, para. 14: 'The essence of the tort is better encapsulated now as misuse of private information.'

[103] *Ibid.*, para. 17.

In reaching this conclusion it is not necessary to pursue the controversial
question whether the European Convention itself has this wider effect.
Nor is it necessary to decide whether the duty imposed on courts by
section 6 of the Human Rights Act 1998 extends to questions of substantive law as distinct from questions of practice and procedure. It is
sufficient to recognise that the values underlying articles 8 and 10 are not
confined to disputes between individuals and public authorities.[104]

In other words, Lord Nicholls asserts that neither of the two questions
raised by horizontal effect – whether Article 8 is applicable horizontally
and whether s.6(1) requires or precludes the court from giving it this
effect – are relevant. The former proposition at least must be seriously
questionable – why would the courts give effect to Article 8 in a case
concerning two private parties if, in Strasbourg terms, it was a guarantee
applicable only against direct state intrusion into private life? His
Lordship also refers back to, and leaves entirely open the question raised
by Sedley LJ[105] as to whether the HRA gives the Convention rights any
purchase at all in private law, or affects only remedies and procedures.
The question that these *dicta* wholly avoid is, *why* values underlying
Articles 8 and 10 should have any application in private law if it is not for
the Human Rights Act? And how, in a case concerned directly with the
effect of the Convention on private common law, could Lord Nicholls
state that it was unnecessary to decide the question of the horizontal
effect of the Convention under section 6 HRA?

The remainder of his Lordship's speech is all the more surprising.
Having found it unnecessary to decide the applicability of the
Convention, Lord Nicholls then proceeds to apply the Convention, in
some detail:

In applying this approach, and giving effect to the values protected by
article 8, courts will *often* be aided by adopting the structure of article 8
in the same way as they now habitually apply the Strasbourg court's
approach to article 10 when resolving questions concerning freedom of
expression.[106] When both [Articles 8 and 10] are engaged a difficult
question of proportionality may arise. This question is distinct from the
initial question of whether the published information engaged article 8 at
all by being within the sphere of the complainant's private or family life.
    Accordingly, in deciding what was the ambit of an individual's 'private
life' in particular circumstances courts need to be on guard against using

---

[104] *Ibid.*, para. 18.   [105] Above, text to n. 76.
[106] [2004] 2 WLR 1323; [2004] 2 AC 457, para. 19.

as a touchstone a test which brings into account considerations which should more properly be considered at the later stage of proportionality. *Essentially the touchstone of private life is whether in respect of the disclosed facts the person in question had a reasonable expectation of privacy.*[107]

His Lordship thus adopts a quite specific approach, based on proportionality, to balancing the two articles, and also carefully distinguishes those factors which go to proportionality and those which go to the scope of the right – to whether there is a *prima facie* cause of action in privacy. Like Lady Hale and Lord Hope, he also adopts a specific doctrinal test to be used in the common law – the reasonable expectation of privacy test – something which comes, in fact, from Strasbourg jurisprudence.[108] In other words, Lord Nicholls' speech is something of an enigma on this point. He appears to back a particular view of horizontal effect (weak indirect effect) but then states that it is unnecessary to decide the issue; he then goes on to apply, if anything, strong indirect effect, by changing the common law so as to make it compatible with the relevant Convention rights. One wonders if the apparent contradictions in the reasoning here are explicable by the considerations suggested earlier: Lord Nicholls seemingly wanted, like the Court of Appeal in *X* v. *Y*, to avoid resolution of the horizontal issue in general terms; however, he was also keen to find some robust principle to drive the development of breach of confidence into the 'tort of misuse of private information':[109] hence, perhaps, his use of the Convention to remould an area of private law, coupled with a denial that the horizontal effect issue was raised.

Lord Hoffmann, in contrast to Lord Nicholls' view that it was unnecessary to decide the horizontal effect point, does decide it. He seemingly does so in favour of the view of Buxton LJ,[110] which, it had been generally thought, had been ruled out some time ago:

> Even now that the equivalent of article 8 has been enacted as part of
> English law, it is not directly concerned with the protection of privacy

---

[107] *Ibid.*, paras. 20 and 21 (emphasis added).
[108] *PG and JH* v. *United Kingdom*, ECHR 2001-IX, para. 57: 'a person's reasonable expectations as to privacy may be a significant, though not necessarily conclusive factor'; applied in *Peck* v. *UK* (2003) 36 EHRR 719, para. 62: 'As a result, the relevant moment was viewed to an extent which far exceeded any exposure to a passer-by or to security observation ... and to a degree surpassing that which the applicant could possibly have foreseen when he walked in Brentwood on 20 August 1995.'
[109] See para. 14 of his speech.
[110] 'The Human Rights Act and Private Law' (2000) 116 LQR 48.

against private persons or corporations. It is, by virtue of section 6 of the
1998 Act, a guarantee of privacy only against public authorities. Although
the Convention, as an international instrument, may impose upon the
United Kingdom an obligation to take some steps (whether by statute or
otherwise) to protect rights of privacy against invasion by private individuals, it does not follow that such an obligation would have any counterpart in domestic law.[111]

Note that this last sentence explicitly draws a distinction between the
matter as it may stand at Strasbourg and the position under domestic
law, what we referred to as the first and second levels. This passage
overall seems flatly opposed to the views of Lady Hale, who accepted a
clear obligation *on the domestic courts* to give effect to a right of privacy
against private bodies. However, having seemingly ruled out any form of
horizontal effect, the next part of Lord Hoffmann's speech is rather
surprising:

What human rights law has done is to identify private information as
something worth protecting as an aspect of human autonomy and dignity. And this recognition has raised inescapably the question of why it
should be worth protecting against the state but not against a private
person. I can see no logical ground for saying that a person should have
less protection against a private individual than he would have against the
state for the publication of personal information for which there is no
justification.[112]

While it may be the case in principle that there is no reason to make such
a statement, as a matter of law, there are two very obvious reasons for
doing so. First, the Convention binds state parties only; secondly, the
HRA binds only 'public authorities'. These legal facts surely provide the
'logical ground' that his Lordship cannot see. We appear to have an
acceptance of horizontal effect without its being attributed to either the
HRA or indeed the ECHR – a kind of free-standing moral argument for
horizontality. And indeed this acceptance is, oddly, manifest in Lord
Hoffmann's speech, in which the influence of the Convention appears to
be just as strong as in the speeches of his brethren:

As Sedley LJ observed in ... *Douglas* v. *Hello! Ltd* [2001] QB 967, 1001,
the new approach takes a different view of the underlying value which the
law protects. Instead of the cause of action being based upon the duty of

[111] [2004] 2 WLR 1323; [2004] 2 AC 457, para. 49.   [112] *Ibid.*, para. 50.

good faith applicable to confidential personal information and trade secrets alike, it focuses upon the protection of human autonomy and dignity – the right to control the dissemination of information about one's private life and the right to the esteem and respect of other people.[113]

... As for human autonomy and dignity, I should have thought that the extent to which information about one's state of health, including drug dependency, should be communicated to other people was plainly something which an individual was entitled to decide for herself: compare *Z* v. *Finland*.[114]

His Lordship also cited *Fressoz and Roire* v. *France*[115] and *Peck* v. *UK*;[116] in particular, he relied upon *Fressoz* to decide that Article 10 requires a margin of latitude to be granted to journalists as to the manner in which they present their stories and that the conduct of *The Mirror* in the instant case was within that margin. In other words, despite Lord Hoffmann's apparent invocation of a view similar to that of Buxton LJ, he proceeds to do precisely what that view precludes – namely, give effect to Convention principles in private law.[117] The paradoxical approach his Lordship takes is similar to that of Lord Nicholls, save that, in this case, it appears that Lord Hoffmann wants generally to resist horizontal effect: it is just that he also wants to inject Convention principles into this particular area of law.

Finally, having seen above the apparent strong disagreement amongst their Lordships on this issue in *Campbell*, it is worth noting Lord Hoffmann's assertion that there is in fact no difference of significance between them:

> But the importance of this case lies in the statements of general principle on the way in which the law should strike a balance between the right to privacy and the right to freedom of expression, on which the House is unanimous. The principles are expressed in varying language but speaking for myself I can see no significant differences.[118]

---

[113] *Ibid.*, para. 51.   [114] *Ibid.*, para. 53.

[115] (1999) 5 BHRC 654.   [116] (2003) 36 EHRR 719.

[117] Buxton LJ argued that the HRA would have no effect on private common law, not even as a set of values, since the Convention rights 'remain, stubbornly, values whose content lives in public law'. 'The Human Rights Act and Private Law' (2000) 116 LQR 48, 59.

[118] [2004] 2 WLR 1323; [2004] 2 AC 457, para. 36.

This myth of unanimity is also echoed by Lady Hale:

> This case raises some big questions ... How do [Articles 8 and 10] come into play in a dispute between two private persons? But the parties are *largely agreed* about the answers to these. They disagree [only] about where that balance is to be struck in the individual case.[119]

Note that her Ladyship, in the second sentence, specifically claims agreement upon the horizontal effect issue, without mentioning the strong *disagreement* between her brethren on point. All were indeed plainly averse to the Wade view – with Lady Hale expressly ruling it out. But it seems perverse to ignore wholly the clear differences that remained in the formal answer that their Lordships give to the question of horizontal effect. It gives the impression, again, that a clear resolution of the issue, which grapples clearly with the different arguments and resolves them, is being avoided.

Campbell *and horizontal effect: conclusions*

A few concluding points may be made about the treatment of this issue in *Campbell*. First, there is citation of not a single academic article on this crucial point, despite the very rich literature that this issue has generated, nor any discussion of comparative jurisprudence. Secondly, there is no engagement with any of the arguments raised in the literature or comparative case-law – and this is in a very long and complex judgment that squarely raised the horizontality issue. Thirdly, with the exception of Lady Hale, there is the seeming desire on the part of their Lordships to dodge the question or to fudge it. Thus Lord Hope does not answer it clearly, but in this instance relies heavily upon Convention principles. Lord Nicholls appears to endorse a weak version of horizontal effect – but then says that he is deciding nothing and it is unnecessary to do so. Lord Hoffmann states that he is ruling out horizontal effect altogether – but then gives the Convention articles a central role to play in deciding the matter. Lord Carswell avoids the issue altogether. Fourthly, none of the judges even begin to engage with what we identified as the first level of the horizontal effect enquiry – the question whether Article 8 itself and its associated jurisprudence *requires* the protection between private parties that the judgment gives, for the first time, in English law. In this sense, remarkably, they pre-empted the

---

[119] *Ibid.*, para. 126.

Strasbourg Court, which had, at the time of the *Campbell* judgment, given no clear answer to that question.

What can be said with confidence is that all their Lordships applied the Convention jurisprudence to resolve the case. What cannot be said is that there was any agreement between them as to why they took this course of action. There was of course nothing to stop the courts using such jurisprudence to develop the common law even prior to the HRA, as they did in cases such as *Derbyshire*[120] and *Reynolds*,[121] in relation to defamation. Therefore the mere use of the Strasbourg case-law in *Campbell* cannot, without more, be taken to have settled the point of the horizontal effect generated by the *HRA*. Perhaps Lord Hoffmann, who specifically stated that Article 8 did not impose obligations in the private sphere, simply regarded the Strasbourg case-law as a useful source of inspiration for what in formal terms he saw as purely common law development,[122] akin to looking to decisions of the Canadian or Australian courts for guidance. What is clear is that the total effect of the speeches delivered in *Campbell* was, remarkably, to leave the horizontal effect issue as unresolved as it had been before: the Wade position was once again implicitly ruled out by all, but nothing further was agreed upon.

Post-*Campbell* case-law on horizontal effect

The House of Lords appeared to reconsider the horizontal effect issue in a decision taken soon after *Campbell*, namely the appeal of *Re S (A Child)*.[123] The facts are not material; the decision concerned what is known as the 'inherent jurisdiction' of the High Court to restrain reporting on matters relating to children.[124] The limits of this jurisdiction, and the different categories of case in which it would arise were considered in the leading pre-HRA case of *Re Z*.[125] In the course of giving the unanimous judgment of the House, Lord Steyn said this:

---

[120] In the Court of Appeal judgment: *Derbyshire County Council v. Times Newspapers Ltd* [1992] 3 WLR 28, esp. 60–1, *per* Butler-Sloss LJ.

[121] [1999] 3 WLR 1010.

[122] That is, common law development absent any constitutionalising effect of the HRA upon it.

[123] [2005] 1 AC 593. The decision is analysed in detail in Chapter 10.

[124] *Re X (A Minor) (Wardship: Restriction on Publication)* [1975] Fam 47, esp. at 57

[125] *Re Z (A Minor) (Identification: Restrictions on Publication)* [1996] 2 WLR 88.

> The House unanimously takes the view that since the 1998 Act came into force in October 2000, the earlier case law about the existence and scope of inherent jurisdiction need not be considered in this case or in similar cases. The foundation of the jurisdiction to restrain publicity in a case such as the present is now derived from Convention rights under the ECHR. This is the simple and direct way to approach such cases. In this case the jurisdiction is not in doubt.[126]

This is a remarkable passage. First of all, it is plain from the words, 'since the 1998 Act came into force', that Lord Steyn regards the change in approach he outlines *as brought about by the HRA*. There is thus no ambiguity, as there is in some of the speeches in *Campbell*, as to the *reason* for applying Convention principles. Secondly, the *dicta* above, rather than referring to the Convention rights being 'absorbed into' an existing cause of action, or being 'taken into account' in deciding the result of such a case, appear rather to conceptualise the Convention rights as giving rise to a new jurisdiction: the previous basis for the jurisdiction, Lord Steyn declares, no longer needs to be considered. This sounds very much like the Convention rights not influencing but *replacing* the old cause of action, and thus like direct horizontal effect: the jurisdiction derives directly from the Convention rights themselves, as Lord Steyn puts it. The equivalent would have been for their Lordships in *Campbell* to say that there was no longer any need, in privacy cases like Campbell's, to bother with the common law of confidence; instead, the action could found directly on Article 8 itself. Such an approach (if that is what his Lordship meant) would plainly run directly counter to that taken by the House in *Campbell* and to previous *dicta* ruling out the direct application of the Convention rights.[127] It would be remarkable if the House of Lords had, in *Re S*, announced such a radical and controversial development without full discussion of their reasons for doing so. More implausible still is the notion that the House intended to overrule a key aspect of its decision in *Campbell*, handed down only a few months before *Re S*, to the effect that breach of confidence was the primary vehicle for protecting privacy – in other words that *indirect* horizontal effect, of some form, was to be the key to developing privacy rights. Whilst the House of Lords has the power to overrule its previous decisions, it exercises it very sparingly; it would be astonishing if it were

---

[126] *Ibid.*, para. 23. [127] E.g. *Venables* [2001] 1 All ER 908, 917; *X* v. *Y* [2004] ICR 1634.

to overrule a decision taken so recently and without any acknowledgment of what it was doing.[128]

The better reading of *Re S*, therefore, is that it is dealing only with the application of the Convention rights in a particular setting – as the Court of Appeal in *X* v. *Y* predicted would be the way the issue was resolved.[129] That setting is that such cases are not in reality a purely private dispute between two private parties. Rather, the court is taking the place of the state in terms of protecting the child from damaging reporting. Under the inherent jurisdiction it had the undoubted power to do so, and, in appropriate cases, a duty to do so. Therefore, the House was not, as such, asserting a new jurisdiction, based solely on Convention rights. Rather, because the duty under the Convention rights is, as Lord Steyn observes, broadly commensurate with its duties under the inherent jurisdiction,[130] the House was *not* using the Convention rights to assert powers that it did not have before, but rather simply taking the more 'simple and direct' route of relying on the Convention rights directly to assert what is in substance the same jurisdiction as previously. It is simply implausible to read this passage in *Re S* as determining anything more than that.[131] It appears, then, that, despite the apparent anomaly of the *Re S* judgment on this point, it in fact represents a continuation of the judicial approach to this issue: a refusal to resolve the issue in general terms, coupled with a finding made as to what is required in the particular context.

The 2005 decision of the Court of Appeal in *Douglas III*,[132] the most recent judgment at the time of writing to deal with this issue in any detail, on its face contains rather more clarity than either of the House of Lords decisions just considered. The case was again concerned with

---

[128] See e.g. the decision of the House of Lords in *Murphy* v. *Brentwood District Council* [1991] 1 AC 398, in which it overruled its previous decision in *Anns* v. *Merton London Borough Council* [1978] AC 728: not only was there full analysis of why this step was taken, but their Lordships also expressly stated that they were overruling *Anns*.

[129] See p. 156 above.

[130] 'I would observe on a historical note that a study of the case law revealed that the approach adopted in the past under the inherent jurisdiction was remarkably similar to that to be adopted under the ECHR': [2005] 1 AC 593, para. 23.

[131] Recent *dicta* of Lord Nicholls also suggest that *Re S* was not intended to make any general finding as to horizontal effect: see below, p. 172.

[132] [2006] QB 125. This is the decision of the Court of Appeal on the appeal from the decision to award damages at final trial made by Lindsay J: [2003] 3 All ER 996 (*Douglas II*), the Court of Appeal having in 2001 declined to grant an injunction in the case: [2001] QB 967.

privacy – specifically whether *Hello!* magazine could be held liable to
Michael Douglas and Catherine Zeta-Jones in respect of the publication
of unauthorised photographs of their wedding.[133] The court first of all
addressed itself to the neglected first level of horizontal effect – the
Strasbourg dimension:

> [It has been observed] that the Strasbourg jurisprudence provides no
> definite answer to the question of whether the Convention *requires* states
> to provide a privacy remedy against private actors. This is no longer the
> case … The ECtHR has recognised [in *Von Hannover* v. *Germany*] an
> obligation on member states to protect one individual from an unjusti-
> fied invasion of private life by another individual and an obligation on the
> courts of a member state to interpret legislation in a way which will
> achieve that result.[134]

It may be that the Court of Appeal dealt with this matter, when others
had not, simply because the judgment in *Von Hannover* had been so
recently delivered, and provided such a clear and unambiguous answer
to the question of the interpretation of Article 8. Nevertheless, it is
welcome to have the matter addressed at all.

The court then turned to the question of the interpretation of the
HRA itself, as an incorporating instrument, and made what is perhaps
the clearest statement so far, by a unanimous appellate court, on the
horizontal effect issue. Lord Phillips MR, speaking for the court, said:

> Some, such as the late Professor Sir William Wade … and Jonathan
> Morgan … contend that the Human Rights Act should be given
> full, direct, horizontal effect. The courts have not been prepared to go
> this far.[135]

Interestingly, the judgment does not even cite Lord Steyn's comments in
Re S, presumably indicating judicial acceptance of the view that they are
confined to the specific context of the (former) inherent jurisdiction,
and do not have wider application. Note also that these *dicta*, rather than
stating that the Wade/Morgan approach is wrong, simply observe that it
has not been judicially followed so far. In other words, again the issue is
not faced squarely. Lord Phillips goes on to cite Lord Hoffmann's
rejection in *Wainwright* v. *Home Office*[136] of 'some high level principle of privacy', and Lord Nicholls' confirmation at paragraph 11 of

---

[133] The decision is discussed in chapter 9, pp. 232–4.   [134] [2006] QB 125, para. 79.
[135] *Ibid.*, para. 50.   [136] [2004] 2 AC 406.

Campbell that: 'In this country, unlike the United States of America, there is no over-arching, all-embracing, cause of action for "invasion of privacy".' Crucially, his Lordship then takes Lord Nicholls' *dicta* in *Campbell*,[137] together with those of Lady Hale,[138] as indicating a clear acceptance by the House of Lords in that case of indirect horizontal effect. Lord Phillips in fact summarises Lady Hale's comments on the matter:

> Baroness Hale said that the Human Rights Act did not create any new cause of action between private persons. Nor could the courts invent a new cause of action to cover types of activity not previously covered. But where there is a cause of action the court, as a public authority, must act compatibly with both parties' Convention rights.[139]

This is an accurate summary. Two points should be noted, however. First, the Court of Appeal continues the fiction promulgated by the House of Lords itself that there was no disagreement on this matter, when, as we have seen, their Lordships expressed markedly divergent views. Secondly, Lord Phillips, whilst citing both Lord Nicholls and Lady Hale, in fact plumps for the view of the latter: 'the court should, insofar as it can, develop the action for breach of confidence in such a manner as will give effect to both Article 8 and Article 10 rights.'[140] This quite clearly does *not* capture Lord Nicholls' stated approach. Lord Nicholls spoke of giving effect to 'the *values underlying* Articles 8 and 10'[141] – an approach which lays a much less precise obligation upon courts and so leaves them much more room for manoeuvre; he also expressly disclaimed any intention to decide the question of whether the effect of the HRA 'extended to questions of substantive [private] law'.[142] The Court of Appeal, in blurring the distinction between the approaches of Lady Hale and Lord Nicholls, thereby failing to distinguish between 'weak' indirect effect – acting in accordance with 'values' underlying an action – and 'strong' effect – acting compatibly with the rights themselves.

The most recent *dicta* on this matter, emanating from the highest level, arose in a case in which the point was moot, the action having been brought against a local authority. In *Kay v. Lambeth; Leeds v. Price*,[143] Lord Nicholls, discussing s.6 HRA, said this:

---

[137] See text to nn. 103, 104 and 107 above.   [138] See text to n. 82 above.
[139] [2006] QB 125, para. 52.   [140] *Ibid.*, para. 53.
[141] [2004] 2 WLR 1232; [2004] 2 AC 457, para. 17 (emphasis added).
[142] *Ibid.*   [143] [2006] 2 WLR 570, para. 61.

The court's own practice and procedures must be Convention compliant. Whether, and in what circumstances, the court's section 6 obligation extends more widely than this, and affects the substantive law to be applied by the court when adjudicating upon disputes between private parties, still awaits authoritative decision.

It is curious that Lord Nicholls speaks of the lack of resolution of this matter with such acceptance; these *dicta* have a curious echo of those in *X* v. *Y*[144] in again adopting the passive voice: rather than saying, 'we the judges have not yet decided this matter', his Lordships observes that it 'awaits . . . decision'. While one would not realistically expect Lord Nicholls to tackle the horizontal effect point in a judgment in which it was not raised, it is interesting that he does go out of his way to remark that the issue is still not resolved. One wonders a little if it ever will be.

Conclusions

What tentative conclusions can we draw from this early assessment of the courts' attempts to tackle this very difficult point? We know that the courts can and have given the Convention rights a strong influence in the common law, particularly in *Campbell* and *Re S*. However, by avoiding proper engagement with the academic debate, save for more or less ruling out the two extreme positions of no and full horizontal effect, the Courts have left themselves the *ability* to bring Convention principles into private law, but have not fully accepted a position in which they are bound to act compatibly with them. The *dicta* of the unanimous Court of Appeal in *Douglas III* cited above come closest to accepting such a clear duty, but their force is undercut by the fact that they are based partly on an assessment of the speeches of Lady Hale and Lord Nicholls as espousing the same position on the matter, when they plainly did not.

This chapter has tentatively suggested that this outcome – of a lack of resolution, thus retaining flexibility in common law reasoning – is in fact one that the judiciary would instinctively have preferred all along. At present, the authorities forbid direct reliance on the Convention rights between private parties in place of the relevant common law cause of action (save in the *Re S* scenario); beyond that, there are *dicta* which could be used to allow reliance on various positions as to the

---

[144] See text to n. 79 above.

applicability of the Convention rights in private law, ranging from effect on remedies and procedures only, to the applicability of Convention 'values' to substantive law doctrines, to a hard-edged duty to act compatibly with Convention *rights* in developing and applying such doctrines. This outcome at present allows the Convention rights to play a greater or lesser part in judicial reasoning, depending, presumably, upon the judge's overall view of the case and where he or she wants the law to go. In other words, there is an additional source of principle to draw upon in common law reasoning, but the judges have so far avoided the possibility of the Convention displacing, in a thorough-going way, the broad consideration of a wide range of factors traditionally used in common law reasoning.

This may be seen as an instance of the judges showing resistance to the incursion of the HRA into what was *par excellence* their own domain: such resistance was mentioned in the Introduction as an important theme of this book; it is illustrated in a different area in the next chapter, by Ian Leigh[145] which delineates the ambivalence displayed by some judges to the prospect of replacement of the common law *Wednesbury* standard of review with the Convention standard of proportionality, while Chapter 11 by Sonia Harris-Short illuminates the resistance to Article 8 shown by the judiciary in the field of child and family law. What is certain is that the approach to the horizontal effect so far has retained a great deal of judicial discretion over the matter – something which may be seen in a number of other areas of judicial reasoning under the Human Rights Act.[146]

---

[145] See Chapter 7.

[146] See for example the analysis of the interpretation given to s.3(1) HRA by the judiciary, discussed by Aileen Kavanagh in Chapter 5, and the ambiguities surrounding the judicial attitude towards the status of the Convention jurisprudence generally in a number of the decisions analysed by Roger Masterman in Chapter 3; the tendency is, interestingly, not so (or not at all) evident in the decisions of the House of Lords he discusses.

7

The standard of judicial review after the Human Rights Act

IAN LEIGH*

Introduction

English administrative law had, prior to the Human Rights Act, failed to develop effective protection for human rights against incursions by public officials and authorities. Much of the blame for the parlous defence of civil liberties and human rights can be attributed to the judges' sentimental attachment to the *Wednesbury* test as the appropriate standard for reviewing official action. Under this test, action was only reviewable if it was so unreasonable that no reasonable decision-maker would have taken it.[1] Long criticised for its circularity, imprecision and excessive deference to the executive, *Wednesbury* nevertheless continues to hold considerable sway.[2]

Its influence can be seen clearly in *Brind*, in which – a mere fifteen years ago – the House of Lords ruled that the Home Secretary was not legally obliged to consider the Convention right of freedom of expression when imposing restrictions on television and radio interviews with people connected with a terrorist organisation.[3] Their Lordships considered that to hold otherwise would amount to what they described as 'back door' incorporation of the Convention and that they should not rush in where (at that time) Parliament had chosen not to. The Convention's relevance was limited to instances of statutory ambiguity – something which in the circumstances of the case (concerning a very wide power to give 'directions' to broadcasters) their Lordships were

---

* This chapter is a revised and updated version of a paper originally presented at a seminar in the Judicial Reasoning and the Human Rights Act series, on 3 December 2003.
[1] *Associated Provincial Picture Houses* v. *Wednesbury Corporation* [1948] 1 KB 223.
[2] Andrew Le Sueur, 'The Rise and Ruin of Unreasonableness' [2005] *Judicial Review* 32.
[3] *R.* v. *Secretary of State for the Home Department, ex parte Brind* [1991] 1 AC 696 (HL).

reluctant to find. At the same time, the House affirmed that proportionality was not part of United Kingdom law and that the broadcasting ban was not open to challenge on conventional grounds for irrationality.

Nevertheless, very belatedly, in the interval between *Brind* and the implementation of the Human Rights Act, a number of judicial techniques were developed which demonstrated greater sensitivity to rights. Where the decision-maker claimed to have considered the Convention, the courts would examine whether he or she had done so correctly.[4] The *Wednesbury* test was modified by the requirement that courts subject administrative decisions with human rights implications to 'anxious scrutiny' or 'most rigorous examination'.[5] Later decisions, notably the litigation in which gay and lesbian service personnel challenged the reasonableness of their discharge from the armed forces, have confirmed that the greater the human rights dimensions of a case the closer the attention the courts will give to the legality of the official decision[6] – described in places as 'substantial objective justification'.[7] Hence, by the time the Human Rights Act came into force, *Wednesbury* had become in effect a variable standard: the more fundamental the right interfered with, the greater the need for justification.

Despite that, as *Smith* shows, before the Human Rights Act the judges regarded themselves (if reluctantly) to be restricted to secondary review of administrative discretion. Even in the period immediately prior to the Act entering into force, there was a continuing reticence to develop administrative law doctrine. In *Kebilene*, the High Court declined to follow the lead of the Australian courts[8] and develop the doctrine of legitimate expectations so as to impose on a prosecutor a duty to exercise the discretion to bring a prosecution in a prospective defendant's favour where a violation of Convention rights might result if there was a conviction.[9]

---

[4] *R. v. Secretary of State for the Home Department, ex parte Launder* [1997] 1 WLR 839, 867, *per* Lord Hope of Craighead.

[5] *R. v. Home Secretary, ex parte Bugdaycay* [1987] 1 All ER 940, 952; and see Lord Templeman (at 956), referring to 'a special responsibility' on the court.

[6] *Smith v. Ministry of Defence* [1996] QB 517, 554, 563, 564–5; *R. v. Secretary of State for Home Department, ex parte Leech* [1994] QB 198.

[7] *Smith*, above n. 6, p. 554; *R. v. Lord Saville of Newdigate, ex parte A* [2000] 1 WLR 1855, 1866–7; and *Launder*, above n. 4, p. 867.

[8] *Minister for Immigration and Ethnic Affairs v. Teoh* (1995) 128 ALR 353, 365.

[9] *R. v. DPP, ex parte Kebilene* [1999] 4 All ER 801, 811, *per* Lord Bingham CJ; the legitimate expectation point was dropped on appeal.

In terms of the European Convention, the pressure to expand judicial review has come from two distinct sources. The first is concern over whether judicial review is an effective domestic remedy for the purpose of Article 13 of the Convention. This is a question that, strictly, arises irrespective of the Human Rights Act. The decision in *Smith and Grady* v. *UK* (the sequel to the domestic litigation in *Smith*) that judicial review had failed to amount to an effective remedy had already demonstrated the need for domestic courts to make review more intensive. As is well known, the European Court found that the domestic courts had set the irrationality threshold so high

> that it effectively excluded any consideration by the domestic courts of the question of whether the interference with the applicants' rights answered a pressing social need or was proportionate to the national security and public order aims pursued.[10]

The Court's ruling stood in contrast to some of its earlier judgments that domestic judicial review satisfied Article 13.[11] Together with the (then imminent) implementation of the Human Rights Act, the judgment prompted a domestic reappraisal of whether even 'anxious scrutiny' went far enough. Even if there had been no HRA, however, the ruling in *Smith and Grady* that judicial review was deficient would still have required the domestic courts to develop the grounds of review to satisfy Article 13 in human rights cases.

The second expansionary pressure arises from Article 6, the right to a fair hearing before an independent and impartial tribunal in determination of criminal charges or civil rights or obligations. Here, the picture has been mixed. In some areas of domestic administrative law, the influence of Article 6 has been to require a reconsideration of long-established standards, for example a reworking of the 'real danger' test in bias into one of 'real possibility'.[12] It strengthens the trend towards an emerging duty to give reasons for decisions,[13] although the courts have yet to find that the effect of the Human Rights Act is to create a general

---

[10] *Smith and Grady* v. *UK* (2000) 29 EHRR 413, para. 138.
[11] Notably *Soering* v. *UK* 11 (1989) EHRR 439 and *Vilvarajah* v. *UK* (1991) 14 EHRR 248.
[12] See *Porter* v. *Magill* [2002] AC 357.
[13] *Stefan* v. *General Medical Council* [1999] 1 WLR 1293, 1301, *per* Lord Clyde. In a number of cases after implementation of the HRA, Article 6 has been cited in support of the duty to give reasons: *R.* v. *Crown Court at Canterbury, ex parte Howson-Ball* [2001] Env LR 36; *Anya* v. *University of Oxford* [2001] EWCA Civ 405; [2001] ELR 711, para. 12.

duty,[14] and the common law will already require reasons in situations where the Strasbourg Court would not consider there was a civil right or obligation.[15] However, in other fields, arguments based on Article 6 have yet to reach their full potential, for example the Court of Appeal has found no apparent bias or violation of Article 6 where a member of a Mental Health Review Tribunal was employed by the same Health Trust that ran the hospital where the applicant was detained.[16]

Article 6 has implications for the remedies available in judicial review. In *Kingsley* v. *UK*,[17] the Strasbourg Court held that Article 6 had been violated by the process under which the Gaming Board had denied the applicant a licence, when the High Court had quashed an initial determination by the Board and remitted it to the Board to redetermine. This aspect of the procedure is a routine feature of administrative law and follows from the fact that the court is a forum for review not of appeal. Nevertheless, the European Court held that Kingsley was denied a fair hearing by an impartial tribunal since the body to which his case was returned was identical in composition to the one which had already found against him. *Kingsley* has yet to make any discernible impact on domestic law and has been cited only occasionally by domestic courts and then in support of the proposition that where a court is able to quash a flawed decision and remit it back to an unbiased decision-maker Article 6 is satisfied.

More attention has been paid, however, to the issue of whether judicial review is capable of correcting deficiencies in administrative processes for determining a person's 'civil rights' that lack the necessary quality of independence and impartiality required under Article 6. The Strasbourg Court has stated in *Albert and Le Compte* v. *Belgium* that trial by an independent and impartial tribunal requires:

> either the jurisdictional organs themselves comply with the requirements of article 6(1), or they do not so comply but are subject to subsequent control by a judicial body that has full jurisdiction and does provide the guarantees of article 6(1).[18]

---

[14] *Gupta* v. *General Medical Council* [2001] UKPC 61; [2002] 1 WLR 1691; *Moran* v. *DPP* [2002] EWHC Admin 89.

[15] *R. (Wooler)* v. *Fegetter* [2002] EWCA Civ 554; [2003] QB 219, *per* Sedley LJ, para. 46.

[16] *R. (PD)* v. *West Midlands and North West Mental Health Review Tribunal* [2004] EWCA Civ 311.

[17] *Kingsley* v. *UK* (2000) 29 EHRR 493; see I. Leigh, 'Bias, Necessity and the Convention' [2002] PL 407–14.

[18] (1983) 5 EHRR 533, para. 29.

In a series of cases, but especially two prominent House of Lords decisions,[19] the issue has been whether domestic courts have 'full jurisdiction' and whether the scope of judicial review is adequate to meet this standard.

Spanning these concerns, the central issue in debate concerning the standard of review after the Human Rights Act has been how to reconcile the more demanding standards of the ECHR where the proportionality test applies with the tradition in English administrative law of deference to the executive. Proportionality had, of course, been mooted as an emerging standard of judicial review as far back as the GCHQ decision.[20] However, Lord Lowry identified the dangers in *Brind* when he stated that to adopt proportionality would leave very little space between conventional judicial review doctrine, emphasising the supervisory nature of the court's task, and the forbidden approach of appellate review.

As we shall see, this conundrum has largely framed the post-Human Rights Act debate over the standard of review among academics and in the courts themselves. Before we turn to it, however, it is worth emphasising that the attention devoted to this question has caused four other important issues to be somewhat neglected. These are: what the Human Right Act itself has to say about the standard of review; the question of the standard of review in *unqualified* rights cases (i.e. where the proportionality test is not part of the Convention standard); the impact of Article 6 on administrative procedure more generally; and the attitude of the Strasbourg Court to English judicial review.

The remainder of this chapter is devoted to considering the patterns of argument used by the courts since the Human Rights Act. We will consider first 'expansionary arguments': those that tend to extending or intensifying the standard of review. Attention will then move to 'limiting arguments': those which tend to maintaining continuity with the standard of review pre-dating the HRA or at least restraining any development of the law. An examination will be made of a recent judicial attempt to reconcile a number of these conflicts. The conclusion evaluates the overall direction of these trends and puts them in the context of further developments at Strasbourg.

---

[19] *R. (Alconbury Developments Ltd)* v. *Secretary of State for the Environment, Transport and the Regions* [2001] 2 WLR 1389; *Begum (Runa)* v. *Tower Hamlets LBC* [2003] UKHL 5; [2003] 2 WLR 388.

[20] *Council of Civil Service Unions* v. *Minister for the Civil Service* [1985] AC 374, 410, *per* Lord Diplock.

Expansionary arguments

A discussion of these techniques should be prefaced by pointing out that the courts have manifestly *not* treated the Human Rights Act as a constitutional springboard from which to launch into 'merits review'. That remains the 'forbidden' appellate or substitutionary method.[21]

It is worth asking what constrains the judiciary. Arguably, it is *not* the text of the Act itself. The wording of s.6 is enigmatic:

> (1) It is unlawful for a public authority to act in a way which is incompatible with one or more of the Convention rights.
> (2) Subsection (1) does not apply to an act if—
>> (a) as the result of one or more provisions of primary legislation, the authority could not have acted differently; or
>> (b) in the case of one or more provisions of, or made under, primary legislation which cannot be read or given effect in a way which is compatible with the Convention rights, the authority was acting so as to give effect to or enforce those provisions.

A court that wished to resort to 'hard-edged' review has several arguments to hand from these provisions.[22] It could emphasise the surprisingly strong wording of s.6(1) and treat it as a duty on public authorities not to breach a person's Convention rights, unless compelled to do so by primary legislation. Such an approach would treat the Act as differentiating sharply between deference to Parliament (which is explicitly maintained by s.6(2)) in contrast to the treatment of the executive. The Act would be treated as a legislative mandate to abandon judicial deference to the executive, which could only then be maintained so far as the Convention itself permitted limitations to rights under the proportionality doctrine in the case of qualified rights.[23] Support for this viewpoint comes from the text of s.6 itself, which makes it *unlawful* for a public authority to *act* in contravention of a person's Convention

---

[21] *R.* v. *Secretary of State for the Home Department, ex parte Brind* [1991] 1 AC 696, 767, *per* Lord Lowry, referring to the 'forbidden appellate approach'.

[22] See further I. Leigh, 'Taking Rights Proportionately: Judicial Review, the Human Rights Act and Strasbourg' [2002] PL 265–87.

[23] M. Taggart, 'Tugging on Superman's Cape: Lessons from Experience with the New Zealand Bill of Rights Act 1990', in University of Cambridge Centre for Public Law, *Constitutional Reform in the United Kingdom: Practice and Principles* (Oxford: Hart Publishing, 1998), p. 85, at p. 92; I. Leigh and L. Lustgarten, 'Making Rights Real: The Courts, Remedies, and the Human Rights Act' (1999) 58 CLJ 509, 517–19.

rights. Elsewhere, Lord Bingham has remarked that the Human Rights Act 'gives the courts a very specific, wholly democratic, mandate'.[24] Further support comes from the architecture of the Act, which applies the same provision (s.6(1)) to both courts and the executive as different types of 'public authority', without making any differentiation in the standard to be applied. This can be seen to call into question the distinction between appeal and review. Since there would be no question of 'deference' to a lower court that acted contrary to s.6,[25] it can be argued that an equally rigorous approach should be applied when the actions of other public bodies are under review under s.6.

This argument has drawn only occasional support from the judiciary in the first five years' operation of the Act. As we shall see, isolated *dicta* can be cited in which judges treat the Act as expanding review for error of law or refer to proportionality as a question of law. Remarkably – and in an almost exact reprise of the Parliamentary debates – when the courts have scrutinised s.6(1), it has been to consider the definition of a public authority.[26] With one exception, they have shown a studied disinterest in the remainder of the wording. In practice, the s.6(1) standard has been treated as requiring no elucidation and few judgments engage in any analysis of whether the text of the Act has any bearing on the standard of review.

A rare exception occurs in the dissenting speech of Lord Hope in *Attorney-General's Reference No. 2 of 2001*.[27] There he points to the differences between the Scotland Act 1998 – which makes violation of Convention rights by members of the executive (including prosecutors) a *vires* question – and the Human Rights Act – which uses the term

---

[24] *A* v. *Secretary of State for the Home Department* [2005] AC 68, para. 42.

[25] *Attorney-General's Reference No. 2 of 2001* [2003] UKHL 68: 'I cannot accept that it can ever be proper for a court . . . to act in a manner which a statute (here, section 6 of the Human Rights Act) declares to be unlawful', *per* Lord Bingham of Cornhill, para. 30.

[26] We are not concerned here with the definition of what constitutes a 'public authority' under s.6 HRA: *Poplar Housing* v. *Donoghue* [2001] 4 All ER 604; [2001] 3 WLR 183; *R. (on the Application of Heather)* v. *Leonard Cheshire Foundation* [2002] 2 All ER 936 (CA); *Aston Cantlow* v. *Parochial Church Council Wallbank* [2001] 3 WLR 393; *R. (on the Application of Hammer Trout Farm)* v. *Hampshire Farmers Markets* [2003] EWCA Civ 1055. See also the report of the Joint Committee on Human Rights, 'The Meaning of Public Authority under the Human Rights Act' (2003–2004), HL 39/HC 382.

[27] [2003] UKHL 68, paras. 73–9. I am grateful to Aidan O'Neill QC for drawing this to my attention. See, however, Lord Bingham of Cornhill, para. 30.

'unlawful'.[28] The crucial difference in his Lordship's view is two-fold. First, under s.6, 'the act is unlawful only against the victim' and not 'all the world'. Secondly, there is no *entitlement* to a remedy – under s.8(1) the court may grant such relief or remedy within its powers as it considers just and appropriate. 'Unless the act (or proposed act) is "unlawful" the court has no jurisdiction under the Act to provide a remedy',[29] but there is no automatic remedy for each unlawful act. This reasoning makes a good deal of sense in relation to central government, where the powers are not in total derived from statute in the same way as the Scottish executive. However, other public authorities – notably local authorities – are fully creatures of statute. It is doubtful whether the discretionary nature of public law remedies[30] generally dilutes the standard of review in their case[31] and, if not, it begs the question why unlawfulness under the Human Rights Act should be regarded as exceptional.

Lord Hope's comments apart, the judicial silence on this issue is curious. It is perhaps indicative of a strong judicial consensus that the Act was not intended to usher in 'merits review'. The White Paper and the parliamentary debates shed no light on this issue so the best that one can say is that there was no intention by the government or awareness in Parliament that the drafting could lead to merits review.

Turning from the wording of s.6 to the cases, three distinct, though overlapping, strategies can be identified by which it has been argued that judicial review should be expanded. These are: distinguishing proportionality from *Wednesbury*; the need for a decision-maker to show 'substantial evidence' and for factual inquiry by the courts; and the treatment of proportionality as a question of law.

---

[28] [2003] UKHL 68, para. 58; and see his speech in *Dyer v. Watson* [2002] 3 WLR 1488, 1523, para. 111. Section 57(2) of the Scotland Act 1998 provides that a member of the Scottish Executive has 'no power' to act in a way that is incompatible with a Convention right. In *Attorney-General's Reference No. 2 of 2001*, above n. 27, Lord Bingham took a contrary view: 'I cannot accept that "compatible" bears a different meaning in section 6 of the Human Rights Act and section 57(2) of the Scotland Act, even though the statutory consequence is unlawfulness in the one instance and lack of power in the other. In each case the act is one that may not lawfully be done.' *Ibid.*, para. 30.

[29] [2003] UKHL 68, para. 54.

[30] Remedies are also discretionary under s.31(1) Supreme Court Act 1981.

[31] I. Leigh, *Law, Politics and Local Democracy* (Oxford: Oxford University Press, 2000), Chapter 2.

Distinguishing proportionality from Wednesbury

Of central importance is Lord Steyn's speech in *ex parte Daly*.[32] There, the House of Lords was concerned with the applicability of proportionality in assessing the legality of the policy for searching prisoners' cells. This required staff to examine the prisoner's possessions, including legally privileged correspondence (which was not, however, normally to be read) in his or her absence. Applying the common law of fundamental rights, their Lordships found the policy to be unlawful. However, they also concluded that the same result would also be reached under the HRA applying the Convention.

Lord Steyn was careful to distinguish proportionality from the modified *Wednesbury* approach and therefore sought to clarify the 'material difference' between the two.[33] The criteria for proportionality were, he argued, 'more precise and more sophisticated'[34] in three respects. It required 'the reviewing court to assess the balance which the decision maker has struck, not merely whether it was within the range of rational or reasonable decisions' and 'may require attention to be directed to the relative weight accorded to interests and considerations'. The third difference concerned the process of reasoning. Taking Article 8 as an example, this required the court to engage with 'the twin requirements that the limitation of the right was necessary in a democratic society, in the sense of meeting a pressing social need, and the question whether the interference was really proportionate to the legitimate aim being pursued',[35] rather than the threshold question for 'anxious scrutiny'. Although using either approach the outcomes would often be the same, sometimes a different conclusion would follow under proportionality, and it was 'therefore important that cases involving Convention rights must be analysed in the correct way'.[36]

While there is no doubt that these comments of Lord Steyn have emerged as the dominant approach to post-HRA judicial review, there is considerable uncertainty over what they require in any particular context. It is no exaggeration to say that proportionality has attracted widespread support as a legal test largely *because* it can be used with equal force by those wishing to maintain the tradition of deference to the executive *and* by advocates of more intensive review.

On the one hand, Lord Steyn was at pains to point out that proportionality did not equate to merits review. This was in keeping with an

[32] *R. (Daly)* v. *Secretary of State for the Home Department* [2001] 2 WLR 1622.
[33] *Ibid.*, paras. 26ff.   [34] *Ibid.*, para. 27.   [35] *Ibid.*, para. 27.   [36] *Ibid.*, para. 28.

emerging academic and professional consensus that the HRA would maintain broad continuity with the tradition of deference. The tasks of judges and administrators would remain distinct. On the other hand, however, his Lordship cited an article by Professor Jeffrey Jowell, which argued that, while the Act would not bring about merits review as such, it nevertheless (together with common law decisions on fundamental rights) pointed towards the development of 'constitutional review' requiring judges to justify their decisions in terms of the necessary qualities of a democratic society.[37]

Among those favouring more intensive review in *Daly*, was Lord Cooke of Thorndon who described *Smith and Grady* as having 'given the quietus'[38] to the argument that *Wednesbury* could be equated with the Convention approach. In practice, proportionality has not wholly supplanted *Wednesbury*. In non-HRA cases, the courts continue to use *Wednesbury*,[39] and the Court of Appeal has held that, although it had difficulty in seeing the justification for retaining the test, only the House of Lords can pronounce it dead.[40] Moreover, as we shall see later, very similar arguments have reappeared even in HRA cases, albeit under different labels.

The need for 'substantial evidence' and factual inquiry by the courts

Traditionally, the courts have seen their role within judicial review as secondary, with the consequence that evidential or factual questions are for the 'primary decision-maker' (the public body subject to review) and not for them. In *Daly*, however, Lord Bingham noted the new approach required under the HRA:

> Now ... domestic courts must *themselves* form a judgment whether a convention right has been breached (*conducting such inquiry as is necessary to form that judgment*) and, so far as permissible under the Act, grant an effective remedy.[41]

---

[37] J. Jowell, 'Beyond the Rule of Law: Towards Constitutional Judicial Review' [2000] PL 671, 682.

[38] *Daly*, above n. 32, para. 32.

[39] See, e.g. *R. (Jones) v. Mansfield DC* [2003] EWCA Civ 1408.

[40] *Association of British Civilian Internees Far Eastern Region v. Secretary of State for Defence* [2003] EWCA Civ 473; [2003] 3 WLR 80, para. 34, *per* Dyson LJ.

[41] *R. (Daly) v. Secretary of State for the Home Department* [2001] 2 WLR 1622, para. 23 (emphasis added).

This passage may imply that this new exercise for the courts requires corresponding changes in *how* they evaluate the effects of the policies and actions of public authorities.[42]

The process can be seen at work in the asylum case of *ex parte Javed* in which Turner J concluded that the minister must have fallen into error in deciding that Pakistan was generally a safe country to which to return asylum seekers.[43] Despite the historical reluctance to do so in judicial review cases, he argued that an effective remedy under the HRA required reconsideration of the evidence before the minister. The judge's scrutiny established that women and religious minorities were liable to face persecution in Pakistani society, and that the Secretary of State's decision to include Pakistan in a designated list of safe countries approved by Parliamentary order could only have been reached on an erroneous view of law or the facts, or both. The Home Secretary was 'plainly wrong', he concluded. Accordingly, he issued a declaration that the minister had erred in law. The Court of Appeal upheld the decision on the more conventional grounds that the Secretary of State's determination was irrational on the available facts, especially concerning persecution of women in Pakistan.[44]

Turner J applied a similar approach at first instance in *Farrakhan*[45] in holding that the Home Secretary had failed to demonstrate objective justification for excluding the controversial Nation of Islam leader, Louis Farrakhan, from the United Kingdom under powers given by the Immigration Rules and the Immigration and Asylum Act 1999, s.60(9) (a). He conducted his own rigorous review of the material before the Secretary of State including the history, teachings and record of the Nation of Islam and the projected speaking programme of Farrakhan. He pointed to the lack of evidence before the court of racial, religious or ethnic tensions between the Muslim and Jewish communities in the UK, and concluded that it was not made out that the community relations would be endangered by Farrakhan's presence in the UK. Accordingly, he quashed the Secretary of State's decision. When this decision was (successfully) appealed by the Secretary of State, the Court of Appeal

---

[42] For discussion of possible procedural changes that may be required, see Leigh and Lustgarten, 'Making Rights Real', above n. 23, pp. 523–6.

[43] R. v. *Secretary of State for the Home Department, ex parte Javed and Others, The Times*, 9 February 2000.

[44] R. *(Javed)* v. *Secretary of State for the Home Department and Another* [2001] 3 WLR 323 (CA).

[45] [2001] EWHC Admin 781.

stressed, however, that in law the decision was a personal one for the Home Secretary, that he was better placed than the court to weigh the competing factors, and was democratically accountable for his actions.[46]

'Substantial justification' can also be seen in operation in another deportation decision, *Mahmood*,[47] where Lord Phillips MR held that the test required adaptation in the new environment: interference with human rights could only now be justified to the extent permitted by the Convention itself.[48] Laws LJ argued, however, that the HRA did not authorise the court to stand in the shoes of the decision-maker: there had to be a 'principled distance' between the court's adjudication and the Secretary of State's decision based on his analysis of the case.[49] In the event, both approaches led on the facts to the same outcome, namely, a refusal to interfere with the deportation order.

The clearest instances of this approach are likely to be where the Convention rights are unqualified.[50] In these instances, it would be expected that the courts would ask themselves the undiluted question whether the public authority has contravened the applicant's Convention rights in fact.[51] Although some commentators have sought to minimise the difference between the unqualified and qualified Convention rights in this regard,[52] the courts can be seen, post-HRA, to be sensitive to the different role that they play in cases of unqualified rights.

The strongest statements to date come in decisions concerning the need for forcible medical treatment of a medical patient. In *R. (on the Application of Wilkinson) v. Broadmoor Special Hospital Authority and Others*,[53] the Court of Appeal held that it was entitled to reach its own view as to the merits of the medical decision and whether it infringed the patient's human rights.[54] As Simon Brown LJ stated, 'the court must

---

[46] *R. (Farrakhan) v. Secretary of State for the Home Department* [2002] QB 1391, paras. 72–4, *per* Lord Phillips MR.

[47] *R. (Mahmood) v. Secretary of State for the Home Department* [2001] 1 WLR 840 (CA).

[48] *Ibid.*, p. 857.   [49] *Ibid.*, p. 855.

[50] See Lord Hope in *R v. DPP, ex parte Kebilene* [2000] 2 AC 326, para. 80, referring to the discretionary area of judgment.

[51] See Leigh, 'Taking Rights Proportionately', above n. 22, pp. 282ff.; P. Craig, *Administrative Law* (4th edn, London: Sweet & Maxwell, 1999), p. 561, arguing that 'primary responsibility' lies with the courts, entailing 'substitution of judgment' over the content of Convention rights and where rights are unqualified.

[52] S. Attrill, 'Keeping the Executive in the Picture: a reply to Professor Leigh' [2003] PL 41.

[53] [2002] 1 WLR 419 (CA).

[54] Note that in *Bloggs 61* Keene LJ (at para. 81) regarded *R. v. Lord Saville, ex parte B (No. 2)* [2000] 1 WLR 1855, as an instance in which the Court of Appeal itself considered directly the various factors relevant to the degree of risk to which the soldiers in

inevitably now reach its own view' both of whether the patient was capable of consenting and of whether the proposed treatment would violate Convention rights under Articles 2 or 3, or in so far as Article 8 was relevant whether it would be a necessary and proportionate restriction.[55] The judgment also demonstrates the need for a new procedural approach. The hospital authority failed in its argument that cross-examination was not permitted because the action had been brought by judicial review. To order that appropriate medical witnesses attend and be cross-examined would also satisfy Article 6 of the Convention. Hale LJ took the view:

> Super-*Wednesbury* is not enough. The appellant is entitled to a proper hearing, *on the merits*, of whether the statutory grounds for imposing this treatment upon him against his will are made out.[56]

Wilkinson was applied, but in some respects restricted, in a later Court of Appeal decision on forcible medical treatment, *R. (N)* v. *Dr M*.[57] There, the court pointed out that judges were free when appropriate to determine the facts for themselves in such cases without oral evidence (which 'should not often be necessary'), and added that 'it should not be overlooked that the court's role is essentially one of review'.[58]

It is apparent, however, that there is judicial reluctance to treat review of alleged breaches of unqualified rights as merits review in fact where no deference is appropriate.[59] In *Bloggs 61*, a prisoner whom the Prison Service had decided to transfer from protected witness accommodation back to the general prison population unsuccessfully argued that to do so would breach his right to life under Article 2 because of the danger of reprisals from his former associates.[60] The Court of Appeal held, in the words of Auld LJ, that:

> despite the fundamental and unqualified nature of the right to life, it is still appropriate to show *some* deference to and/or to recognise the special

question would be exposed, though without expressly deciding whether it should be making a primary judgment of the issue.

[55] [2002] 1 WLR 419 (CA), paras. 26 and 24–5.

[56] *Ibid.*, para. 83 (emphasis added).

[57] [2002] EWCA Civ 1789; [2003] 1 WLR 562.

[58] Dyson LJ, para. 39. See also *CF* v. *Secretary of State for the Home Department* [2004] EWHC Fam 111; [2004] 1 FCR 577, paras. 217–18.

[59] Andrew Le Sueur, 'The Rise and Ruin of Unreasonableness' [2005] *Judicial Review* 32, cites (at n. 18) the comments of Munby J in *R. (IR)* v. *Shetty* [2003] EWHC 3022; and *Claire F* v. *Secretary of State for the Home Department* [2004] EWHC 111.

[60] *R. (Bloggs 61)* v. *Secretary of State for the Home Department* [2003] EWCA Civ 686.

competence of the Prison Service in making a decision going to the safety of an inmate's life.[61]

He continued:

> the degree of deference to, and/or of recognition of the special competence of, the decision-maker is less and, correspondingly, the intensity of the Court's review is greater – perhaps greatest in an Article 2 case – than for those human rights where the Convention requires a balance to be struck.[62]

The Prison Service's 'special competence' comprised its 'experience of prison conditions, options and the relative efficacy of different protective regimes and measures'.[63]

Keene LJ, while emphasising the difference to the court's task in the case of a qualified right, agreed:

> I can see that . . . it could be argued that it is for the court to make its own judgment as to whether there would be an interference with the right to life under Article 2, rather than making a judgment as to the reasonableness of the decision made by the Prison Service. The court is a public authority . . . and cannot therefore act in a way which is incompatible with a Convention right . . .
>
> Even were it to be the case that it is for the court to make that primary judgment . . . the court would have to attach considerable weight to the assessment of risk made by those with professional involvement in the areas with which the case was concerned . . . It may therefore in most cases make little difference whether one describes the court's approach as one of deference or simply as one of attaching weight to the judgment reached by such bodies: the end result would be the same.[64]

There does seem to be a difference in approach between differently constituted benches in the Court of Appeal here. Applying the *Bloggs 61* approach in *Wilkinson* would have required the court to 'attach considerable weight' to the medical opinion, rather than ordering cross-examination. To have adopted the *Wilkinson* approach in *Bloggs*, however, would have taken the court into evaluating for itself the risk to the prisoner by way of evidence. It is noteworthy perhaps that the European Court of Human Rights in *HL* v. *UK*[65] has cited *Wilkinson* as evidence that the UK courts now engage in stricter scrutiny than prior

---

[61] *Ibid.*, para. 65.   [62] *Ibid.*, para. 66.   [63] *Ibid.*

[64] *Ibid.*, paras. 79–81. See also Keene LJ's comments at Chapter 8 below.

[65] *HL* v. *United Kingdom*, App. No. 45508/99, 5 October 2004, para. 139 (concerning the lawfulness of the detention of a mental health patient under Article 5(4)).

to the Act. If it turns out not to be the dominant approach after all, the result is likely to be further excursions to Strasbourg invoking Article 13.

Treating proportionality as a question of law

Section 6 of the Human Rights Act supports an alternative to the line of argument that a court should assess for itself whether the decision of the public authority breaches a person's Convention rights. The language suggests that every statutory and common law discretion of a public authority must now be read subject to a limitation – that the authority cannot, in the absence of clear legislation compelling it to do so, act in contravention of a person's 'Convention rights'. Section 6(1) therefore could be said to create a new form of over-arching *illegality*[66] – in the sense that Lord Diplock used that term in GCHQ: 'the decision-maker must correctly understand the law that regulates his decision-making power and give effect to it'.[67] This approach has received support from Lord Phillips MR in *R. (on the Application of Q)* v. *Secretary of State for the Home Department*,[68] in which he stated:

> courts of judicial review have been competent since the decision in *Anisminic* [1969] 2 AC 147 to correct any error of law whether or not it goes to jurisdiction; *and since the coming into effect of the Human Rights Act 1998, errors of law have included failures by the state to act compatibly with the Convention.*[69]

The implication would be to treat Convention challenges as 'hard-edged' questions on review. Whereas, prior to the Human Rights Act, proportionality had fallen to be considered as an adjunct to the common law grounds for review of discretion, now it could be said to be standing on its own feet. That was the approach taken in an early case. In *B* v. *Secretary of State for the Home Department*,[70] the Court of Appeal quashed the decision to deport an Italian national, following his convictions for gross indecency and indecent assault and the service of a five-year term of imprisonment. It held that the Secretary of State's power to deport on grounds of public policy had to be balanced against B's right of free movement as an EU national and his right to family life under Article 8, and had to be a proportionate remedy. The fact

---

[66] Cf. Craig, *Administrative Law*, above n. 51, pp. 546 and 556–7.
[67] *Council of Civil Service Unions* v. *Minister for the Civil Service* [1985] AC 374, 410–11.
[68] [2003] 2 All ER 903.   [69] Para. 112 (emphasis added).   [70] [2000] Imm AR 478.

that B had lived for most of his life in the UK was sufficient to outweigh public policy considerations and to render deportation a disproportionate punishment.

Simon Brown LJ stated:

> This task is, of course, both different from and more onerous than that undertaken by the court when applying the conventional *Wednesbury* approach. It would not be proper for us to say that we disagree with the IAT's conclusion on proportionality but that, since there is clearly room for two views and their view cannot be stigmatised as irrational, we cannot interfere. Rather, if our view differs from the IAT's, then we are bound to say so and to allow the appeal, substituting our decision for theirs.[71]

However, B had proceeded on the concession that proportionality was a question of law. Later judgments applied a different approach,[72] and the same judge had second thoughts in a later deportation case decided under the revised statutory framework,[73] stating that, in view of the intervening decisions, it would now be 'unhelpful' to characterise the question of proportionality as one of law.

The story would not be complete, however, without reference to what is perhaps the most significant decision of all decided under the Human Rights Act. To long-term students of national security jurisprudence,[74] the Belmarsh decision came as a welcome surprise. As is well known, in *A v. Secretary of State for the Home Department*, a majority of the House of Lords found that the measures providing for detention without trial of foreign nationals under the Anti-Terrorism, Crime and Security Act 2001 violated the Convention.[75] Hence, the derogation entered under Article 15 of the Convention and by an order under the Human Rights Act were not operative. With that hurdle removed, there was a clear

---

[71] Para. 47.

[72] R. (Mahmood) v. Secretary of State for the Home Department [2001] 1 WLR 840; R. (Isiko) v. Secretary of State for the Home Department (C/2000/2939); and Samaroo and Sezek v. Secretary of State for the Home Department [2001] UKHRR 1150.

[73] Blessing Edore v. Secretary of State for the Home Department [2003] EWCA Civ 716.

[74] See L. Lustgarten and I. Leigh, In from the Cold: National Security and Parliamentary Democracy (Oxford: Oxford University Press, 1994), Chapter 12, for a survey of earlier decisions from several jurisdictions.

[75] A (FC) and Others (FC) v. Secretary of State for the Home Department [2004] UKHL 56, Lord Walker of Gestinthorpe dissenting. Lord Hoffmann allowed the appeal on the different ground that there was no public emergency threatening the life of the nation: ibid., paras. 95–7. On which also see the chapter by Aaron Baker in this volume, pp. 366–9.

violation of Article 5, since the detention was prior to neither deportation nor to trial – rather, it was as an alternative to both. The House of
Lords issued a quashing order in respect of the Human Rights Act 1998
(Designated Derogation) Order 2001 and a declaration of incompatibility, finding s.23 of the 2001 Act incompatible with Articles 5 and 14
insofar as it was disproportionate and discriminated on grounds of
nationality.[76] Was the unexpectedly sceptical attitude on the part of
the judiciary attributable to the Human Rights Act? It would appear so.

Two features of the government's stance were fatal to justifying these
powers. First, that they did not apply to those UK citizens (on the
government's estimate, around a thousand) who had engaged in comparable behaviour to the target group of foreign nationals, for example
by attending training in jihaddist camps. Its failure to take any measures
against this group of British citizens cast doubt on the necessity of acting
against non-UK citizens and was, moreover, discriminatory (contrary to
Article 14). Secondly, the foreigners were in a prison with three walls
only – if they could find another state prepared to accept them, they
could leave the United Kingdom at any time. The fact that the UK
government was prepared to allow them to regain their liberty and
freedom of action in this way again cast doubt on the seriousness of
threat assessment in the judges' minds.

In the case of at least some of their Lordships' speeches, the decision
can be seen as a prominent example of treating proportionality (here,
the issue of whether measures were *strictly required* by the exigencies of
the situation) as a question of law. This is clear from Lord Bingham's
rejection of the Attorney-General's argument that this was a constitutional 'no-go zone' for the courts:

> the appellants are in my opinion entitled to invite the courts to review, on
> proportionality grounds, the Derogation Order and the compatibility with
> the Convention of section 23 and the courts are not effectively precluded by
> any doctrine of deference from scrutinising the issues raised . . . It is of course
> true that the judges in this country are not elected and are not answerable to
> Parliament. It is also of course true . . . that Parliament, the executive and the
> courts have different functions. But the function of independent judges
> charged to interpret and apply the law is universally recognised as a cardinal
> feature of the modern democratic state, a cornerstone of the rule of law itself.
> The Attorney General is fully entitled to insist on the proper limits of judicial
> authority, but he is wrong to stigmatise judicial decision-making as in some

---

[76] Para. 73.

way undemocratic ... The 1998 Act gives the courts a very specific, wholly democratic, mandate.[77]

At a later point, criticising the Court of Appeal's refusal to intervene because of reluctance to upset the first instance determination (by SIAC), his Lordship argued:

> The European Court does not approach questions of proportionality as questions of pure fact ... Nor should domestic courts do so. The greater intensity of review now required in determining questions of proportionality, and the duty of the courts to protect Convention rights, would in my view be emasculated if a judgment at first instance on such a question were conclusively to preclude any further review. So would excessive deference, in a field involving indefinite detention without charge or trial, to ministerial decision. In my opinion, SIAC erred *in law* and the Court of Appeal erred in failing to correct its error.[78]

Some caution is necessary, however. This was not the sole basis used to justify the decision: Lord Nicholls and Lord Hope in particular seemed to approach the proportionality question as requiring close scrutiny but as a soft-edged issue nonetheless.[79]

Having reviewed three 'expansionary arguments', we turn now to the arguments that have been made for restraining development of judicial review.

Limiting arguments

The list of potential 'limiting arguments' is rather longer. Identifiable strategies that will be discussed include the following: use of the policy/fact-finding distinction in relation to Article 6; 'indirect deference' to Parliament; use of the different stages of proportionality analysis; and reverting to *Wednesbury*.

Use of the policy/fact-finding distinction under Article 6

As we saw earlier, the Strasbourg case-law allows that deficiencies in administrative process affecting a person's civil rights and obligations under Article 6 can be corrected if there is access to a court of 'full

---

[77] Para. 42.
[78] Para. 44 (emphasis added). And cf. Lord Hope, para. 131; Lord Rodger paras. 173–4.
[79] Paras. 80–1 and 108, respectively.

jurisdiction'. Manipulation of this category gives considerable scope to the courts for widening or narrowing the application of judicial review. In practice, 'full jurisdiction' has been interpreted by the domestic courts primarily to resist efforts at widening judicial review.

In the *Alconbury* litigation,[80] the question was whether the availability of judicial review was a sufficient safeguard to rescue the planning, highways and compulsory purchase processes from an apparent lack of independence for the purpose of Article 6. The House of Lords applied the 'full jurisdiction' test and found, in contrast to the Divisional Court, that overall the procedures under the legislation were compatible with Article 6.[81] The House's own understanding was based on a close reading of the development of the Article 6 jurisprudence in general[82] and a group of cases in which the UK planning regime had been challenged in particular.[83]

Lord Slynn's conclusion was:

> The judgments ... do not require that this should constitute a rehearing on an application by an appeal on the merits. It would be surprising if it had required this in view of the difference of function between the minister exercising his statutory powers, for the policy of which he is answerable to the legislature and ultimately to the electorate, and the court. What is required on the part of the latter is that there should be a sufficient review of the legality of the decisions and of the procedures followed.[84]

Lord Hoffmann agreed:

> the European court ... has never attempted to undermine the principle that policy decisions within the limits imposed by the principles of judicial review are a matter for democratically accountable institutions and not for the courts.[85]

---

[80] R. *(Alconbury Developments Ltd)* v. *Secretary of State for the Environment, Transport and the Regions* [2001] 2 WLR 1389.

[81] Lord Slynn, para. 54; Lord Nolan, para. 58; Lord Hoffmann, para. 136; Lord Clyde, para. 160; Lord Hutton, paras. 196 and 197.

[82] See particularly the speeches of Lord Hoffmann at paras. 84ff. and Lord Clyde at para. 154.

[83] *ISKCON* v. *United Kingdom* App. No. 20490/92, 8 March 1994; *Bryan* v. *United Kingdom* (1995) 21 EHRR 342; *Varey* v. *United Kingdom*, App. No. 26662/95, 27 October 1999; *Chapman* v. *United Kingdom*, App. No. 27238/95, unreported, 18 January; 2001 (Grand Chamber of the European Court of Human Rights).

[84] Para. 49.   [85] Para. 84.

And again:

> Such a requirement would ... also be profoundly undemocratic. The
> HRA 1998 was no doubt intended to strengthen the rule of law but not to
> inaugurate the rule of lawyers.[86]

Both Lord Hoffmann and Lord Nolan[87] saw a delicate interplay between
electoral accountability for matters of policy and issues of legality. This
not only underlay domestic judicial review but was also reflected in the
Article 6 jurisprudence.

This approach was further applied in *Begum (Runa)* v. *Tower Hamlets
LBC*,[88] where the issues before the House of Lords were whether a reviewing
officer (who was an officer of the housing authority responsible for the
decision being reviewed under the Housing Act 1996) constituted an
independent and impartial tribunal and, if not, whether the county court,
to which an appeal lay on a question of law, possessed 'full jurisdiction' so
as to comply with Article 6(1). Assuming for the purpose of argument that
a civil right within Article 6 was at issue, Lord Hoffmann found that the
same considerations which must be considered in applying the rule of law –
'democratic accountability, efficient administration and the sovereignty
of Parliament' – were recognised in the Strasbourg jurisprudence so that
'an English lawyer can view with equanimity the extension of the scope of
art. 6'.[89] Recognition of efficient administration and the sovereignty of
Parliament led to the conclusion that:

> Parliament is entitled to take the view that it is not in the public interest
> that an excessive proportion of the funds available for a welfare scheme
> should be consumed in administration and legal disputes.[90]

In *Begum*, therefore, the House of Lords accepted that, provided the
overall procedure was lawful and fair, it was open to Parliament to deal
with resolving disputes through an adjudicating officer who was not
independent, subject to the safeguard of review by the county court.

'Indirect' deference to Parliament

In a well-known passage in his dissenting judgment in *Roth*,[91] Laws LJ
gave perhaps the most sophisticated account to date of the application of

---

[86] Para. 129.   [87] Para. 61.   [88] [2003] UKHL 5; [2003] 2 WLR 388.
[89] Para. 35.   [90] Para. 46.
[91] *International Transport Roth GmbH and Others* v. *Secretary of State for the Home
Department* [2002] EWCA Civ 158; [2003] QB 728.

judicial deference, setting out four principles.[92] It is the first of these that is especially relevant here:

> greater deference is to be paid to an Act of Parliament than to a decision of the executive or subordinate measure ... Where the decision-maker is not Parliament, but a minister or other public or governmental authority exercising power conferred by Parliament, a degree of deference will be due on democratic grounds – the decision-maker is Parliament's delegate.

Deference is usually referred to in the context of respect for Parliament, and deference to primary legislation is both in-built in the scheme of the Human Rights Act and in continuity with the tradition of Parliamentary sovereignty.[93] We could call this 'direct deference'. This, however, is quite different to deference to *the executive*. In the quotation above, Laws LJ speaks of ministers or other public or governmental authorities exercising power conferred by Parliament and acting as 'Parliament's delegate'.[94] This can be termed 'indirect deference'.

Indirect deference is difficult to justify from the plain wording of s.6 of the HRA, despite the well-known *dicta* that the courts should defer to democratically elected bodies.[95] As we have seen, the wording of s.6(2) requires deference only where a public authority is *compelled* to act in contravention of a person's Convention rights by primary legislation or secondary legislation required to be in that form because of an obligation in primary legislation. This suggests that the courts would be more likely to defer where an executive policy decision has an explicit legislative basis, as opposed to where a broad discretion is granted by

---

[92] On which see further David Keene's comments at pp. 206–12 below.

[93] See generally R. Edwards, 'Judicial Deference under the Human Rights Act' (2002) 65 MLR 859; J. Jowell, 'Judicial Deference and Human Rights: A Question of Competence', in P. Craig and R. Rawlings (eds.), *Law and Administration in Europe* (Oxford: Oxford University Press, 2003); J. Jowell, 'Judicial Deference, Servility, Civility or Institutional Capacity' [2003] PL 592; R. Clayton, 'Judicial Deference and Democratic Dialogue: The Legitimacy of Judicial Intervention under the Human Rights Act 1998' [2004] PL 33; K. D. Ewing, 'The Futility of the Human Rights Act' [2004] PL 829; Lord Steyn, 'Deference: A Tangled Story' [2005] PL 346; F. Klug, 'Judicial Deference under the Human Rights Act' [2003] EHRLR 125.

[94] Note, however, the alternative approach of Lord Walker of Gestingthorpe who in *ProLife Alliance* (at para. 137) described responsibility for the alleged infringement of human rights as shared between Parliament and the executive decision-maker (citing Andrew Geddis, [2002] PL 615, 620–3).

[95] *Kebilene* v. *DPP* [2000] 2 AC 326, 381, *per* Lord Hope; *Brown* v. *Stott* [2001] 2 WLR 817, 834–5 and 842.

Parliament. This would also be consistent with common law presumptions about fundamental rights, which are to be overridden only by the clearest of words.[96]

Despite these powerful objections, one judicial strategy has been to justify deference by reference to Parliamentary sovereignty, even where the power granted by Parliament to the executive is *discretionary*. Two examples of 'indirect deference' in operation can be given.

In *Farrakhan*,[97] the Court of Appeal declined to intervene in the Home Secretary's refusal of entry. Giving the judgment of the court, Lord Phillips MR referred to the exclusion of a right of appeal against the Secretary of State's decision to exclude a person on the grounds that it was conducive to the public good (s.60(9) Immigration and Asylum Act 1999). Far from that leading to the need for added judicial scrutiny of the power, 'the effect of the legislative scheme is legitimately to require the court to confer a wide margin of discretion upon the minister'.[98]

Perhaps the most striking example of 'indirect deference' in operation, however, concerns another public authority rather than an elected organ of government – the House of Lords' judgment in *ProLife Alliance*.[99] That decision – and especially the difference between it and the Court of Appeal's approach – is revealing. The BBC is an unelected body and so no question of direct deference arose. The Court of Appeal found that the BBC's decision to refuse to screen an election broadcast showing film footage of the destruction of foetuses on grounds of taste and decency violated Article 10. The House of Lords, on the other hand, found that the Court of Appeal had addressed the wrong question, and so carried out its own balancing exercise, when Parliament had already decided that the balance lay in favour of restrictions.[100]

To finesse the issue as a question of the broadcasters' *duty* in this way is, frankly, unpersuasive. This is because, despite the apparently strong mandatory words used in the statute, the determination of what is contrary to good taste and decency is largely a matter of judgment in the hands of broadcasters, and this must vary according to context. What *ProLife Alliance* demonstrates, then, is the ease with which a discretionary judgment can be presented as a matter of duty, where Parliament is taken to

---

[96] *R. v. Lord Chancellor, ex parte Witham* [1998] QB 565; *R. v. Secretary of State for the Home Department, ex parte Simms* [2000] AC 115.
[97] N. 46 above.   [98] [2002] QB 1391, para. 74.
[99] *R. (ProLife Alliance) v. BBC* [2002] 3 WLR 1080.
[100] See especially Lord Nicholls, at para. 12, and Lord Hoffmann, at para. 77.

have foreclosed the options open to the decision-maker. This strategy raises the stakes – the issue is not the judgment of the BBC but of Parliament – and invokes Laws LJ's Parliamentary 'delegate' argument.

Whether the 'indirect deference' approach is itself compatible with the Convention is questionable. Although the European Court of Human Rights has treated democracy as one of the foundation stones of the Convention system, it by no means follows that routine deference is due either to legislative or to elected executive bodies. The commitment to democracy has to be considered in the context of the counter-majoritarian nature of Convention rights. It cannot be sufficient to override Convention rights merely to appeal to electoral accountability. Otherwise, the status of unqualified and non-derogable rights would be fatally undermined and the careful restrictions on limitations of qualified rights would be by-passed.

Differential stages to proportionality: prisoners/deportation cases

Another way in which the courts have ruled that some issues are in effect not open to scrutiny is in applying the structure of the proportionality test. In cases involving prisoners and deportees, certain restrictions on rights have been said to *flow axiomatically* from deportation or imprisonment. The courts see themselves as debarred from interfering with these aspects since to do so would fundamentally change the nature of the punishment. Effectively, this rules out one limb of proportionality analysis – whether the infringement of the right is no more than necessary in order to achieve a legitimate aim. While claiming to apply the first limb, the courts appear to be easily satisfied that it has been met. The failure to explore this issue is disappointing: by contrast, Canadian courts applying s.1 of the Charter routinely consider the practice in other countries at this point, rather than merely accepting that to interfere would be to alter the nature of the deliberate and considered choice of the executive.[101] Moreover, deference re-enters in even this slimmed-down proportionality analysis at the second stage.

The approach can be seen in operation in *Samaroo*,[102] in which the claimant challenged the decision to deport him following his conviction

---

[101] See e.g. *Dagenais* v. *CBC* [1994] 3 SCR 835; *RJR-MacDonald* v. *Canada Attorney-General* [1995] 3 SCR 199.

[102] *R. (Samaroo)* v. *Secretary of State for the Home Department* [2001] EWCA Civ 1139; [2001] UKHRR 1622.

for serious drugs offences on the ground that it would interfere with his right to family life under Article 8, since it was likely to result in separation from his wife and children by two marriages. The Court of Appeal accepted the Secretary of State's submission that, although the claimant's rights under Article 8 would be infringed, it was justifiable to prevent disorder and crime and in the operation of a firm but fair immigration policy. Dyson LJ, with whose judgment Butler-Sloss LJ and Thorpe LJ agreed, set out the relevant approach:

> At the first stage, the question is: can the objective of the measure be achieved by means which are less interfering of an individual's rights?
>
> . . .
>
> At the second stage, it is assumed that the means employed to achieve the legitimate aim are necessary in the sense that they are the least intrusive of Convention rights that can be devised in order to achieve the aim. The question at this stage of the consideration is: does the measure have an excessive or disproportionate effect on the interests of affected persons? . . . The issue in such a case is not whether there is a less restrictive alternative to deportation as a means to achieve the objective. The sole question is whether deportation has a disproportionate effect on Mr Samaroo's rights under Article 8.[103]

Elias J followed this two-stage approach in *R. (on the Application of Hirst) v. Secretary of State for the Home Department*,[104] where a serving prisoner who campaigned for prisoners' rights challenged the Prison Service policy to deny prisoners permission to call the media except in exceptional circumstances. The prisoner argued that under Article 10 he had a right to contact members of the media by telephone to discuss matters of legitimate public interest pertaining to prisons and prisoners. The application was granted in part. Although the policy decision was one that the Prison Service was entitled to make, the policy was insufficiently flexible and, therefore, unlawful. In a democratic society, prisoners' concerns as to the monitoring and control of what would be published as a result of prisoners speaking to journalists did not justify imposing a total ban on media interviews. Elias J distinguished carefully between the deference to be shown at different stages of the inquiry. So far as the first stage was concerned:

> where the right is removed as the deliberate and considered response to the need to provide an effective penal policy, there is in truth no room for

---

[103] Paras. 19–20.   [104] [2002] 1 WLR 2929.

> the court to apply the principle of minimum response ... [T]he issue is not whether restricting freedom of speech as part of the penalty is the minimum required to achieve the particular objective sought; that is inherent in what is considered to be the necessary objective. Rather it is whether even if it is the minimum compatible with achieving the desired and legitimate objective, it nevertheless impacts disproportionately on the Convention rights.[105]

However, at the second stage, proportionality applied in a different way:

> There is not simply a general striking of a balance between individual rights and the public interest with deference being shown to the views of the state authorities ... The authority must demonstrate a proper basis for interfering with ... [the Convention right], and show that nothing short of the particular interference will achieve the avowed objective.[106]

The 'inherent restriction' approach is perhaps more easily defensible where Parliament has expressly decreed in legislation that imprisonment shall operate to deprive inmates of certain rights, for example the right to vote, as in *Pearson*.[107] In such cases, there can be said to be a clear and democratic choice (although, as the European Court of Human Rights has noted, that is no guarantee that it is a *considered* choice[108]). However, in other cases, the challenge is to a discretionary decision of the executive which impacts upon the applicant's Convention rights and which is not required by primary legislation, for example, to restrict prisoners' access to journalists or not to make available IVF treatment.[109] In these instances, the finding that the restriction is 'inherent' seems more questionable.

The fair balance approach: reverting to Wednesbury in effect

In contrast to Lord Steyn's speech in *Daly*[110] which emphasised the differences between *Wednesbury* and proportionality, there are other

---

[105] Para. 33.   [106] Para. 40.

[107] R. (Pearson) v. Secretary of State for the Home Department [2001] EWCA Admin 239, finding no violation of Convention rights on grounds of deference.

[108] The European Court of Human Rights held that the disenfranchisement of convicted prisoners violated Article 3 of Protocol No. 1. The Court found no evidence that Parliament had ever sought to weigh the competing interests or to assess the proportionality of the ban as it affected convicted prisoners: Hirst v. United Kingdom (No. 2), App. No. 74025/01, 30 March 2004, para. 51; affirmed by the European Court of Human Rights (Grand Chamber), 6 October 2005.

[109] R. (Mellor) v. Secretary of State for the Home Department [2001] 3 WLR 533.

[110] Notes 32 above et seq.

techniques that can be adopted to maintain continuity by pointing to similarities.

In *Samaroo*,[111] Dyson LJ applied the 'fair balance' test deciding that deportation would not violate Article 8:

> the Court must decide whether a fair balance was struck between the demands of the general interest of the community and the requirements of the protection of the individual's fundamental rights.[112]

This is a markedly less probing standard than *Daly*, and, in an earlier article, it was submitted that it carried the risk of allowing *Wednesbury* to re-enter by the back door.[113] The judgment of Moses J in *Ismet Ala* v. *Secretary of State for the Home Department*[114] illustrates the point by treating the 'fair balance' test in a way virtually indistinguishable from *Wednesbury*. In *Ismet Ala*, an ethnic Albanian from Kosovo, who had illegally entered the country in 1997 but subsequently married a British citizen, applied for judicial review of the Secretary of State's certification that his human rights claim was manifestly unfounded. He contended that his removal would be disproportionate and an infringement of his rights under Article 8, arguing that no reasonable decision-maker would have concluded that his appeal was bound to fail, and that delay had frustrated his chances of being granted refugee status under the policies prevailing at that time. The application was granted. On appeal, Moses J concluded that the adjudicator's task was to decide whether the Secretary of State had 'struck a fair balance between the need for effective immigration control and the claimant's rights under Article 8' or whether the minister's decision was 'outwith the range of reasonable responses'.[115] The language was highly reminiscent of *Wednesbury*:

> A decision-maker may fairly reach one of two opposite conclusions, one in favour of a claimant the other in favour of his removal. Of neither could it be said that the balance had been struck unfairly ... [T]he mere fact that an alternative but favourable decision could reasonably have been reached will not lead to the conclusion that the decision maker has acted in breach of the claimant's human rights. Such a breach will only occur where the decision is outwith the range of reasonable responses to

---

[111] R. (Samaroo) v. Secretary of State for the Home Department [2001] EWCA Civ 1149; [2001] UKHRR 1622. The leading judgment was given by Dyson LJ.

[112] Taken from Sporring v. Sweden (1982) 5 EHRR 35, para. 69.

[113] Leigh, 'Taking Rights Proportionately', above n. 22, pp. 276–7.

[114] [2003] EWHC 521.   [115] Para. 47.

the question as to where a fair balance lies between the conflicting interests.[116]

He continued:

the decision of the Secretary of State in relation to Article 8 cannot be said to have infringed the claimant's rights merely because a different view as to where the balance should fairly be struck might have been reached.[117]

Integrating the approaches: *Huang* v. *Secretary of State*

Having discussed expansionary and limiting modes of reasoning, it is worth examining a recent judicial attempt to reconcile some of the inconsistencies. In *Huang* v. *Secretary of State*,[118] the Court of Appeal had to consider the nature of an appeal to an immigration adjudicator against a decision of the Home Secretary to remove or deport under s.65(1) Immigration and Asylum Act 1999. It found that the adjudicator could allow the appeal because of the effect on Article 8 rights only in exceptional circumstances where 'the imperative of proportionality' required such an outcome notwithstanding that the appellant could not succeed under the Immigration Rules.[119] Laws LJ explicitly rejected the approach adopted in the similar case of *M* v. *Croatia* where Ouseley J had said the test was whether 'the disproportion is so great that no reasonable Secretary of State could remove in those circumstances' and the Secretary of State's own practice should be examined to determine the range of reasonable responses.[120] Laws LJ found this test could not stand with *Daly* and amounted to impermissibly reverting to *Wednesbury*. In the end, however, the difference is unlikely to amount to much in cases like this, since, as Laws LJ himself recognised, cases where the adjudicator could favour an appellant outside the Immigration Rules would be 'truly exceptional'.[121]

Huang is also notable for Laws LJ's comments on deference. It was acknowledged that the balance struck by the Immigration Rules was to be accorded respect as made by democratic decision-makers. However, it was argued that the adjudicator was not required in a case like this to pass judgment on policy given by the Rules since he was concerned with

---

[116] Para. 44.   [117] Para. 45.
[118] [2005] EWCA Civ 105; [2005] 3 WLR 488 (appeal pending to the House of Lords).
[119] Para. 59.   [120] [2004] INLR 327.
[121] *Huang*, above n. 118, para. 60.

the relative importance of immigration control and the individual's right. Rather:

> The adjudicator's decision of the question whether the case is truly exceptional is entirely his own. He *does* defer to the Rules; for this approach recognises that the balance struck by the Rules will generally dispose of proportionality issues arising under Article 8; but they are not exhaustive of all cases. There will be a residue of truly exceptional instances.[122]

The argument involves a variant on the two-stage approach to proportionality, since it distinguishes between the adjudicator's and the court's roles in relation to 'policy' decisions (in effect falling within the routine category here) and those where there is a role for autonomous adjudication. Within the policy realm the courts should recognise that 'principle and practicality alike militate in favour of an approach in which the court's role is closer to review than appeal'.[123] However, even in the policy realm more is now required than the *Wednesbury* approach – the government must provide 'substantial reasoned justification'. Moreover:

> *Wednesbury* review consigned the relative weight to be given to any relevant factor to the discretion of the decision maker. In the new world, *the decision maker* is obliged to accord decisive weight to the requirements of pressing social need and proportionality.[124]

Failure to do so could invite judicial scrutiny, as in *Daly* itself. For cases not involving policy, however, the principle of respect for the democratic powers of the state simply did not apply.

Although inevitably there will be difficulties in delineating what constitutes 'policy' (in *Huang*, it seems to have referred to the need for immigration control), Laws LJ's judgment is a skilful and significant reworking of a number of themes examined in this chapter. If this approach is endorsed by the House of Lords, it will go a long way to establishing a more coherent framework for judicial review in Convention rights cases. It acknowledges frankly that Lord Steyn's twin concerns in *Daly* of setting out a more intensive test than *Wednesbury* (commending 'something close to an autonomous merits decision') but abjuring merits review are in tension.[125] What the judgment does is to make clear that in proportionality analysis that 'first stage' or 'policy' review is intended to be more probing than the conventional *Wednesbury* approach. To underline the point, *Daly* itself is

---

[122] Para. 60. [123] Para. 53. [124] Para. 54 (emphasis added). [125] Para. 49.

classified as concerned with a policy decision. Some of the judicial techniques described above as 'expansionary' find their place in the autonomous decision-making by the adjudicator or the court in non-policy cases.

Conclusion

Murray Hunt has written perceptively that public law's 'big task for the next few years' will be to give practical effect to the difference between proportionality and 'full merits review' without forfeiting the insight that proportionality requires a new and highly structured approach to adjudication which subjects justification for decisions to rigorous scrutiny to determine their legality.[126]

The discussion here has attempted to catalogue some of the techniques at the front line of this battle. To recap, the expansionary arguments are: attempts to distinguish *Wednesbury* and to supplant it with proportionality; the need for a decision-maker to show 'substantial evidence' and for factual inquiry by the courts; and the treatment of proportionality as a question of law. Limiting arguments, on the other hand, include: the use of the fact-finding/policy distinction in relation to Article 6; 'indirect deference' to Parliament; use of the different stages of proportionality analysis; and reverting to *Wednesbury*.

Some of the conflicts of technique surrounding the HRA may in time be settled authoritatively at a doctrinal level – for example, if the House of Lords were to declare *Wednesbury* dead or to adopt the approach of Laws LJ in *Huang* to integrating the tests. Others are likely to persist, perhaps for many years. Several senior judges have indicated their belief that the law is likely to remain in flux for some time as the battle over these approaches continues, and that the present position may simply be a staging post.[127]

Nevertheless, it is already clear that one impact of the Human Rights Act upon administrative law has been to accelerate a pre-existing tendency to treat review as context-specific. Lord Steyn's enigmatic comment in *Daly* that 'in law context is everything' is emblematic.[128] Consequently, the standard of review now appears as a spectrum of different standards

---

[126] M. Hunt, 'Sovereignty's Blight: Why Contemporary Public Law Needs the Concept of "Due Deference" ', in N. Bamforth and P. Leyland (eds.), *Public Law in a Multi-Layered Constitution* (Oxford: Hart, 2003), p. 342.

[127] See Lord Walker in *ProLife Alliance*, at para. 138: 'this is an area in which our jurisprudence is still developing'; Auld LJ and Keene LJ in *Bloggs 61*.

[128] *R. v. Secretary of State for the Home Department, ex parte Daly* [2001] 2 AC 532, para. 28.

applicable to different questions. In this respect, domestic review in the UK has moved significantly towards a conscious recognition of a range of standards as has occurred in other countries. In Canada, for example, applying what is termed a 'pragmatic and functional' approach, review ranges from 'correctness' to 'patent unreasonableness'.[129] Four factors especially are considered in determining the appropriate standard of review in a given context: the presence or absence of privative clauses, whether the question is within the expertise of the respondent, the purpose of the Act and the provision in question and whether a question of law or of fact is involved.[130] In the UK's case, the scale has not been articulated so clearly by the courts. There is at this point much complexity (some points on the range of options have scales within them also) and there is still some dispute over where particular issues are to be placed on the range. Nevertheless, the scale can be discerned in outline.

Prior to the HRA, it was commonplace to talk of 'hard-edged' and 'soft-edged' review. In the former category, the archetype was 'precedent fact' and questions of law. In the exercise of discretion, *Wednesbury* was the archetypical soft-edged question. 'Anxious scrutiny' occupied the middle ground and discretionary decisions involving allocation of public resources or socio-economic policy were softest of all. It is clear that, after the HRA, the hard-edged/soft-edged metaphor is insufficiently nuanced, although judges and commentators have struggled to find an accurate alternative vocabulary that does not have misleading connotations.[131] All metaphors – whether of territory or jurisdiction, competence, deference – tend to break down, and one is hesitant to offer another. Since intensity of scrutiny is what is at stake, possibly an optical analogy is most appropriate, in which case scrutiny might be said to vary from the long-range survey (aided by a telescope) in which the judiciary checks cursorily for obvious odd features in a decision, to external inspection (where the court, as it were, walks around the outside of the decision (cf. inspecting a house, car or horse), to internal inspection, and to microscopic analysis.

On any measure, the Human Rights Act has clearly moved the consideration of human rights questions towards the more intense or detailed end of the range. However, plainly not all rights are alike, and the situations in

---

[129] *Pushpanathan* v. *Minister of Citizenship and Immigration* [1998] 1 SCR 982; *Baker* v. *Canada* [1999] 2 SCR 817; *Suresh* v. *Canada (Minister of Citizenship and Immigration)* [2002] 1 SCR 3. See further D. Dzyenhaus (ed.), *The Unity of Public Law* (Oxford: Hart, 2004).

[130] *Pushpanathan*, above n. 129, paras. 29–38.

[131] The debate about 'deference' being in point.

which they might be limited vary enormously. Unqualified rights attract more intense scrutiny than qualified rights. It could be expected also that some potential limitations on qualified rights (for example, protection of national security) would be treated much more generously than others (for example, prevention or detection of crime) according to the perceived familiarity or competence of the courts.

Finally, what is striking about the present position are two missing pieces of the jigsaw. First, there is the question of what Strasbourg will ultimately make of judicial review post-HRA. There the post-*Smith and Grady* picture is mixed. Five judgments can be cited in which the issue has arisen. In two, one involving removal of an illegal immigrant[132] and another involving refusal of asylum,[133] the domestic proceedings were taken to be adequate. *Smith and Grady* was treated by the European Court as turning on the limited nature of domestic proceedings where national security was involved.

In a further two cases, the European Court has found a violation of Article 13. In *Hatton* v. *United Kingdom*,[134] the defect was the inability of the national courts to consider whether an alleged increase in night flights at Heathrow was a justified limitation under Article 8. In *HL* v. *UK*, the Strasbourg Court held that 'anxious scrutiny' was inadequate in that it did not allow the court to reach its own determination of the lawfulness of the detention of mentally ill persons, in violation of Article 5(4).[135] The domestic proceedings in each ante-dated the HRA but the European Court accepted that the HRA had intensified judicial review.[136] In *HL*, the Court referred to the *Wilkinson* decision to buttress its conclusion that the 'super-Wednesbury' test applicable at the time did not satisfy Article 5(4).[137]

Fifthly, there is *Peck* v. *UK*.[138] The relevant issue so far as Article 13 was concerned was that Peck had unsuccessfully argued in judicial review proceedings that a local authority's decision to disclose footage of him taken from CCTV which had then been broadcast on television was irrational. In terms identical to *Smith and Grady*, the European Court found that Article 13 had been breached. The government had cited *Alconbury*, especially Lord Slynn's comments about proportionality.

---

[132] *Bensaid* v. *United Kingdom* (2001) 33 EHRR 10, esp. paras. 53–8.
[133] *Hilal* v. *United Kingdom* (2001) 33 EHRR 2, esp. paras. 75–9.
[134] *Hatton* v. *United Kingdom* (2003) 37 EHRR 28, paras. 131–42.
[135] *HL* v. *UK*, App. No. 45508/9, 5 October 2004. The domestic proceedings were *R.* v. *Bournewood Community and Mental Health NHS Trust, ex parte L* [1999] AC 458 (HL).
[136] Para. 141.   [137] *HL* v. *UK*, paras. 138–40.
[138] *Peck* v. *United Kingdom* (2003) 36 EHRR 41.

The Strasbourg Court pointed out that *Alconbury* post-dated the coming into force of the HRA (whereas the domestic proceedings pre-dated it) and that the government had accepted that Lord Slynn's comments were *obiter*. It continued:

> In any event, the Government does not suggest that this comment is demonstrative of the full application by domestic courts of the proportionality principle in considering, in the judicial review context, cases such as the present.[139]

Taken in the context of a breach of Article 13, this can be regarded as a hint that domestic courts could go further. However, neither *HL* nor *Peck* is conclusive and it seems that we will have to wait for a case in which the domestic proceedings occurred after the commencement of the HRA[140] to be certain whether judicial review has now gone far enough for Strasbourg.

The second missing piece is the failure of the courts over more than five years to engage with the text of s.6(1). This is puzzling. While counsel and judges have repeatedly succumbed to the fascination of exploring what constitutes a 'public authority', they have shown a remarkable lack of curiosity over the remaining words in the provision. The issue has been systematically ignored, perhaps because of a strong consensus that the Act was not intended to introduce merits review. Nevertheless, within a system which supposedly defers to Parliamentary sovereignty, the wholesale failure to explore the parameters of the words with which Parliament has chosen to express itself in an admittedly constitutional measure[141] is remarkable and suggests a very high degree of collegial thinking.[142]

---

[139] Para. 106.

[140] The *Alconbury* case itself went to the European Court of Human Rights but resulted only in an admissibility decision: *Holding and Barnes plc v. United Kingdom*, App. No. 2352/02, 12 March 2002 (declared inadmissible).

[141] *McCartan Turkington Breen v. Times Newspapers Ltd* [2001] 2 AC 277, 297, *per* Lord Steyn; *Thoburn v. Sunderland City Council* [2002] EWHC Admin 195; [2003] QB 151, paras. 62–4, *per* Laws LJ.

[142] After completion of this chapter, the House of Lords handed down its decision in *Huang (FC) v. Secretary of State for the Home Department* [2007] UKHL 11 (on appeal from the decision discussed at nn. 118 et seq. above). The Appellate Committee agreed with Laws LJ in rejecting the *M v. Croatia* approach (see *ibid.*, para. 13). It emphasised, however, that appellate immigration authorities were engaged in appeal, not review; perhaps, for that reason, the opinion does not discuss Laws LJ's comments on deference.

8

Principles of deference under the
Human Rights Act

SIR DAVID KEENE*

My own view is that the discussion of judicial deference – or the
'discretionary area of judgment' which the judiciary will afford the
democratic arms of the state – is not quite as complex as some commentators might lead one to believe. I think that by now the principles
dealing with the courts' approach to proportionality and deference are
becoming reasonably identifiable in the leading cases. And I think that
most judges would subscribe to the summary given by Lord Justice Laws
in the case of *International Transport Roth GmbH* v. *Secretary of State for
the Home Department*[1] – principles indeed which were generally
approved in the House of Lords by Lord Walker in the *ProLife Alliance*
case.[2] The principles laid down by Lord Justice Laws in *Roth* were as
follows:

1. 'greater deference is to be paid to an Act of Parliament than to a
   decision of the executive or a subordinate measure';
2. 'there is more scope for deference "where the Convention itself
   requires a balance to be struck, much less so where the right is stated
   in terms which are unqualified" (per Lord Hope in *ex parte
   Kebeline*)';
3. 'greater deference will be due to the democratic powers where the
   subject matter in hand is peculiarly within their constitutional
   responsibility, and less when it lies more particularly within the
   constitutional responsibility of the courts'; and

* A Lord Justice of Appeal, Royal Courts of Justice.
[1] [2002] 3 WLR 344.
[2] *R.* v. *British Broadcasting Corporation, ex parte ProLife Alliance* [2004] 1 AC 185,
para. 136.

4. 'greater or less deference will be due according to whether the subject matter lies more readily within the actual or potential expertise of the democratic powers or the courts'.[3]

The first principle suggests that greater deference will be paid to an Act of Parliament than to a decision of the executive or a subordinate measure. It is obvious that in most cases the courts are engaged in striking a balance between the rights of the individual under the Convention and the wider interest of the public. Again, clearly, that requires a judgment to be made as to what that wider public interest is. It is really in that context that the first principle comes into play: that Parliament may have pronounced in some way on what amounts to the public interest in a certain case. That first principle is really therefore based on both a constitutional ground and a practical one. Judges are very conscious – and indeed they ought to be conscious – of the need to respect Parliament's proper function. But the converse is also true: Parliament should respect the judges' role. One sees Lord Justice Laws' first principle in the well-known decision of the Court of Appeal in *R* v. *Lambert*,[4] where Lord Woolf said that, when deciding what is in the interests of the public, generally the court should pay a degree of deference to Parliament as a matter of constitutional principle. Personally, I agree with that.

The Human Rights Act 1998 requires the court, as a public body, to decide whether there is or would be a breach of a Convention right. So it is clearly not mere *Wednesbury* review.[5] The real issue is the extent to which the court, in making its decision, will act as a primary decision-maker on the merits, on the facts. It is clear that, in appropriate cases, a degree of deference will be shown to some other decision-maker.

That brings us quite neatly on to the second principle, which derives from what Lord Hope said in *R.* v. *Director of Public Prosecutions, ex parte Kebilene*:

> In some circumstances it will be appropriate for the courts to recognise that there is an area of judgment within which the judiciary will defer, on democratic grounds, to the considered opinion of the elected body or person whose act or decision is said to be incompatible with the Convention ... [T]he area in which these choices may arise is conveniently and appropriately described as the 'discretionary area of judgment'.

---

[3] [2002] 3 WLR 344, 376–8.   [4] [2002] QB 1112.
[5] See *Associated Provincial Picture Houses* v. *Wednesbury Corporation* [1948] 1 KB 223.

It will be easier for such an area of judgment to be recognised where the Convention itself requires a balance to be struck, much less where the right is stated in terms which are unqualified.[6]

That, I think, raises a particularly interesting point. If one is dealing with Articles 2 or 3 for example, both of which are unqualified rights, the court is principally concerned with, for example, whether there would be a real risk to life from the decision which is in question. One is not seeking to strike a balance, in my view, between that risk and some wider public interest. Now that is not something that one can put in absolute terms; indeed, the passage in *Kebilene* does suggest that even in the unqualified rights cases some deference may have to be paid to the decision-maker. And that passage in *Kebilene* was cited with approval by Lord Walker in the *ProLife* case – although Lord Walker's comments were clearly *obiter* as *ProLife* was dealing with a qualified right, Article 10. When you are dealing with unqualified rights it is much more difficult to see how an issue of proportionality will normally arise because the individual's right to life – or whatever it may be – is not defeasible by any countervailing public interest. I do not know of any case which makes an express decision on this point. My own view is that it is for the court to make its own judgment on the merits in such cases – I see that as flowing from s.6(3) of the Human Rights Act. I say there is no express decision that I know of to that effect, but there is an illustration of it in *R. v. Lord Saville of Newdigate, ex parte B (No. 2)*[7] as the Court of Appeal seems in practice to have itself considered directly the relevant factors as to the degree of risk to which the soldiers in question would be exposed. What it did not do was spell out that that was what it was doing – it did not expressly address the issue of whether it should be making a primary judgment on the merits or not. Nevertheless, that is effectively what it did.

What I would emphasise is that, if it is right that the court make the primary judgment on the merits in such cases of unqualified rights, the end result may not actually be very different from the more deferential approach. I say that because of the problems which the courts face in practice in assessing such things as a risk to life in a certain set of circumstances. When I talk about the problems that the courts face in practice, that is overlapping with Lord Justice Laws' fourth point in the *Roth* case about expertise or lack of it. There is an interesting case called

[6] [2000] 2 AC 326, 381.   [7] [2000] 1 WLR 1855.

R. (on the Application of Bloggs 61) v. *Secretary of State for the Home Department.*[8] That was a case where a prisoner sought to challenge a decision by the Home Secretary to remove him from a protected witness unit in prison and put him back into mainstream prison conditions. He was someone who had provided substantial help to the police about drug smuggling which had been carried out by some former associates of his and had led to his being placed in a protective witness unit and to his anonymity. He alleged that to move him back into the ordinary prison regime would put his life in danger. The Prison Service had decided that there was no real risk by that time as circumstances had changed sufficiently and that as long as certain steps were taken his life would not be at risk. Clearly, this was an Article 2 case. The Court of Appeal recognised that in such cases one is concerned with degrees of risk. It referred to the case of *Osman* v. *United Kingdom*[9] in which the European Court of Human Rights had recognised that not every claimed risk to life automatically prevailed. But the Court of Appeal here said that it was still right to show some deference to the Prison Service on this degree of risk, or to recognise the special competence of the Prison Service in making such judgments. That was the way it was put by Lord Justice Auld in *Bloggs 61*:

> the Prison Service, with its experience of prison conditions, options and the relative efficacy of different protective regimes and measures – and the police, with their expert and close knowledge of the level of risk – are generally better placed than the court to assess the risk to life in such a context.[10]

In my own judgment, I stressed the point that, even where the court was making the primary merits judgment on the degree of risk, it was bound to attach considerable weight to the views of those who actually had expertise in such matters – such as the Prison Service in a case such as this. I suggested that in practice it may actually make little difference to the end result whether one describes the approach that the court is adopting as one of deference to some other decision-maker or simply saying that one is attaching particular weight as a matter of evidence to the judgment reached by the body that has some particular expertise. I have to say that remains my view. I recognise that there is a difference in concept between the two approaches but I think that in reality the end result may not be very different.

[8] [2003] 1 WLR 2724.   [9] (2000) 29 EHRR 245.   [10] [2003] 1 WLR 2724, para. 65.

I now come to comment on Lord Justice Laws' third point – that is the one about greater deference to the democratic powers where the subject matter lies peculiarly within their constitutional authority. That is something which Jeffrey Jowell has described as 'constitutional competence'.[11] It is something which has been taken up by Lord Hoffmann in the *ProLife* case, referring to the separation of powers. Lord Hoffmann stresses there that it is a question of law for the courts which branch of government in the broad sense has the decision-making power under the constitution, saying:

> although the word 'deference' is now very popular in describing the relationship between the judicial and the other branches of government, I do not think that its overtones of servility, or perhaps gracious concession, are appropriate to describe what is happening. In a society based upon the rule of law and the separation of powers, it is necessary to decide which branch of government has in any particular instance the decision-making power and what the legal limits of that power are. That is a question of law and must therefore be decided by the courts.[12]

So in matters such as national defence the courts would show greater deference – and we have seen that of course in *Secretary of State for the Home Department* v. *Rehman*.[13] It seems to me that it is right that they should do so because, if judges do trespass into matters which are constitutionally the province of the executive, then they must do so with very considerable discretion indeed. Apart from anything else, there is likely to be a hostile public reaction to the courts overstepping their proper constitutional role. I believe that most judges accept that they have to recognise the limits of that particular role – something which you will find stressed in Lord Hoffmann's speech in the *ProLife* case.

I see the third point as being very closely linked to the fourth, almost as a corollary of it, namely, that the degree of deference is going to be affected by whether the subject matter lies more readily within the expertise of a democratic body or within the expertise of the courts. This is what Jeffrey Jowell calls 'institutional competence'.[14] It is a

---

[11] J. Jowell, 'Judicial Deference: Servility, Civility or Institutional Capacity?' [2003] PL 592–601.
[12] R. v. *British Broadcasting Corporation, ex parte ProLife Alliance* [2003] 2 WLR 1403, para. 75.
[13] [2003] 1 AC 153.
[14] J. Jowell, 'Judicial Deference: Servility, Civility or Institutional Capacity?' [2003] PL 592–601.

principle on which I place great emphasis and which I think you are bound to see reflected in the decisions of the courts. It is one endorsed by the House of Lords in the *Rehman* case, it is reflected in Lord Steyn's speech in *Brown* v. *Stott*,[15] and it is a practical point which is bound to influence the judges. Think back to pre-Human Rights Act days to how the courts operated in relation to judicial review of decisions made under the royal prerogative – in the GCHQ case for example.[16] Ever since then, the courts have been prepared to review some exercises of the prerogative but not others. The distinction between the two has been essentially on this question of expertise – which matters can fall sensibly within the competence of the court and which do not. That is why, as I think Lord Roskill was saying in the GCHQ case, where the prerogative is concerned with questions of national security or the allocation of national economic resources between one desirable objective and another, and other matters of that kind, such matters of high policy are simply not justiciable.[17] But, where the exercise of the prerogative is related to an area in which the courts feel capable of making an informed and expert decision, there they are much readier to intervene: for example, where the exercise of the prerogative concerns the recommendation of the Home Secretary that a prisoner should receive remission on his sentence for aiding the police authorities on some particular matter. An illustration of this can be found in the 2002 case of *R. (on the Application of B)* v. *Secretary of State for the Home Department*, where the courts were very much prepared to intervene.[18] I would emphasise the point of the inevitability of the courts recognising the limits on their ability to make an informed and reliable judgment on certain issues.

I would also stress the proposition which shines through all of Lord Justice Laws' four points: that it depends on the subject matter. Or, in Lord Steyn's famous words in *Daly*, 'in law context is everything'.[19] When issues are arising under Article 6, for example, generally the courts will feel that they are equipped to intervene. You will see that in *R.* v. *A (No. 2)*,[20] where the Law Lords read down s.41 of the Youth Justice and Criminal Evidence Act, Lord Steyn saying that where the question is whether Parliament's scheme has made an excessive inroad into the

---

[15] [2001] 2 WLR 817.
[16] *Council of Civil Service Unions* v. *Minister for the Civil Service* [1985] AC 374.
[17] *Ibid.*, p. 418.   [18] 22 February 2002, CO/2957/2001, unreported.
[19] *R.* v. *Secretary of State for the Home Department, ex parte Daly* [2001] 2 AC 532, para. 28.
[20] [2002] 1 AC 45.

right to a fair trial the court is – note the word – 'qualified' to make its own judgment and must do so. The case of *Ghaidan* v. *Godin-Mendoza*,[21] was one where we took the same approach. We regarded ourselves as able to intervene there as it was not really a matter of dealing with difficult policy issues which are the province of government, but rather ones about discrimination between individuals where we felt we could properly intervene.

I would conclude with this: I think it is by now obvious that proportionality requires a balance to be struck between an individual's right and the public interest, a 'fair balance' to use Lord Justice Dyson's phrase from *R. (on the Application of Samaroo)* v. *Secretary of State for the Home Department*.[22] Ultimately how much deference the court is to pay to a particular decision-maker must depend on the subject matter and must depend upon the Article with which one is concerned under the Convention. That I think is how you will see the courts developing the law in the months and years to come, very much reflecting those principles set out in the *Roth* case.

---

[21] [2003] Ch 380.   [22] [2001] EWCA Civ 1139.

PART II

The Human Rights Act and substantive law

9

The common law, privacy and the Convention

GAVIN PHILLIPSON*

Introduction

The issue of how the common law has been developed in order to protect a right to privacy[1] against the media under the impetus of the Human Rights Act is, I believe, of great interest to the theme of judicial reasoning under that instrument. As indicated in Chapter 6,[2] it was in response to press fears that the Act would lead to development of such a right that what became s.12 of the Act was introduced by the government. Because of the relatively flexible and inchoate state of the breach of confidence action even prior to the coming into force of the HRA,[3] there was considerable scope for judicial creativity in fusing Strasbourg principles with evolutionary common law reasoning in order to fill a long-lamented lacuna in English law: the provision of a remedy for the unauthorised publication of personal information.[4] It was not surprising, to this author at least, that the judiciary chose this route and firmly declined the alternatives of either giving direct horizontal effect to

---

* The paper given in the Judicial Reasoning and the Human Rights Act seminar series on this subject was presented on 31 March 2003 and published as, 'Transforming Breach of Confidence? Towards a Common Law Right to Privacy under the Human Rights Act' (2003) 66 MLR 726. This chapter was prepared subsequently, although it reflects themes in that article: it also draws in places upon the publications detailed in n. 20 below.

[1] The term is used to denote the right to control personal information about oneself: see G. Phillipson and H. Fenwick, 'Breach of Confidence as a Privacy Remedy in the Human Rights Act Era' (2000) 63 *Modern Law Review* 660, 671–672.

[2] See above pp. 147–9.

[3] G. Phillipson and H. Fenwick, 'Breach of Confidence as a Privacy Remedy in the Human Rights Act Era' (2000) 63 *Modern Law Review* 660, 670–2.

[4] The absence of a remedy for such a practice, absent a breach of confidence, was condemned by the Court of Appeal in *Kaye* v. *Robertson* [1991] FSR 62 (CA), said to give rise to 'serious, widespread concern' by Lord Nicholls in *R.* v. *Khan* [1997] AC 558, 582; and referred to as a 'glaring inadequacy' by the Law Commission, *Breach of Confidence* (Law Com. No. 110), para. 5.5.

Article 8 or 'declaring' the existence of a general tort of invasion of privacy. As far back as 1979, Megarry VC remarked in *Malone* v. *Metropolitan Police Commissioner (No. 2)* in respect of the creation of privacy rights:

> it is no function of the courts to legislate in a new field. The extension of the existing laws and principles is one thing, the creation of an altogether new right is another . . . No new right in the law, fully-fledged with all the appropriate safeguards, can spring from the head of a judge deciding a particular case: only Parliament can create such a right.[5]

Similarly, as Lord Bingham put it, writing extra-judicially around the time of the enactment of the HRA:

> The recognition given by the Convention to the social value of privacy will, I think, encourage the courts to remedy what have been widely criticised as deficiencies in the existing law. But the common law scores its runs in singles: no boundaries, let alone sixes. The common law advances – to change the analogy – like one venturing onto a frozen lake, uncertain whether the ice will bear, and proceeding in small, cautious steps, with pauses to see if disaster occurs.[6]

This refusal to, as it were, hit a six, and declare a general tort of privacy was recently and most emphatically endorsed by the House of Lords in *Wainwright* v. *Home Office*.[7] However, this chapter contends that the decision of their Lordships in *Campbell* v. *MGN Ltd*[8] does gives rise to such a tort, albeit with the proviso that there must be some misuse of 'information' for a cause of action to lie.[9] However, as we shall see, the appearance of having created a 'new' tort is somewhat muted and confused by the continuing references in that case to 'breach of confidence'. I explored in Chapter 6 the manner in which their Lordships in *Campbell* contrived to allow Articles 8 and 10 of the European Convention on Human Rights (ECHR) to have such influence upon

---

[5] [1979] 1 Ch 344, 372.
[6] 'The Way We Live Now: Human Rights in the New Millennium' (1999) 1 Web JCLI (penultimate paragraph).
[7] [2003] 3 WLR 1137.
[8] [2004] 2 AC 457. For comment, see David Lindsay, 'Naomi Campbell in the House of Lords: Implications for Australia' (2004) 11(1) *Privacy Law and Policy Reporter* 4, 4–11; Jonathan Morgan, 'Privacy in the House of Lords – Again' (2004) 120 LQR 563, 563–6.
[9] As Moreham puts it: 'the House of Lords established [in *Campbell*] that there is a right to the protection of private information in English common law': N. Moreham, 'Privacy in the Common Law: A Doctrinal and Theoretical Analysis' (2005) 121 LQR 628.

the judgment, whilst refusing to agree upon or resolve the issue of horizontal effect generally, and I shall return to that paradox below.

In this chapter, I will canvass the argument I have made elsewhere,[10] that the developments in breach of confidence engineered by *Campbell* are significant and justify now referring to the action as the 'tort of misuse of private information'. Essentially, the argument is that the second limb of the breach of confidence action – requiring that there must, in addition to being unauthorised use of confidential information, be 'circumstances importing an obligation of confidence'[11] – has been removed. Meanwhile, the first limb – that the information must have 'the quality of confidence'[12] – has been transformed: the notion that the information must be 'confidential' has morphed into a requirement that it be 'private' or 'personal' information. As Lord Nicholls, one of the dissenters in the judgment, put it: '[t]he essence of the tort is better encapsulated now as misuse of private information'.[13] As I have argued elsewhere, from the perspective of supporting the development of common law protection for privacy, this is, overall, the most persuasive reading of the judgment.[14] In the context of this book, however, my concern is not simply to analyse doctrinal developments, with a view to encouraging recognition of the transformative aspects of the *Campbell* judgment. Rather, it is to unpick the reasoning a little: to examine the rhetorical disagreement amongst their Lordships as to how radical a change was being made to the existing law and ponder its significance; to consider how far the particular circumstances in *Campbell* may have influenced the result, and to examine the ambiguities, therefore, surrounding how far *Campbell* really has replaced the old common law tests with one based on the Convention.

In this respect, it is pertinent to consider the background to *Campbell* and consider how far the changes made by that decision were invited by the common law, rather than, as it were, forced upon it by the HRA and the Convention. In an article published on the eve of the coming into force of the HRA, Helen Fenwick and I considered developments up to 2000 in breach of confidence, concluding that the changes already made to it gave the judges 'a serviceable tool with which to tackle invasions of privacy'. We asked then what would be the role played by the Convention in the future development of this area. Our answer was that 'Article 8 will provide the normative impetus for the consolidation of the [common law

---

[10] See n. 20 below.

[11] The traditional formulation from *Coco v. A. N. Clark (Engineers) Ltd* [1969] RPC 41, 47.

[12] *Ibid.*   [13] *Campbell*, [2004] 2 AC 457, para. 14.   [14] See n. 20 below.

developments we had described]'.[15] In other words, our argument was that at least some of the judges were eager to remedy the much criticised gap in English law. There was, it was plausible to think, a perception of a failure by the common law, a failure that was becoming embarrassing. To recall the words of Lord Bingham quoted above:

> The recognition given by the Convention to the social value of privacy will . . . encourage the courts to remedy what have been *widely criticised as deficiencies* in the existing law.

In other words, the HRA, in this particular instance, provided the justification for doing that which the judges had been wishing to do for some time in any event, and had made some progress towards doing, using breach of confidence; however, pre-HRA, the judges had felt the absence of clear normative justification for bringing about what was bound to be a highly controversial change. The prediction made by Lord Bingham in fact almost exactly captures the approach, five years later, of Lord Hoffmann and Lord Nicholls in *Campbell*, in which the Convention is seen as providing not a set of binding legal principles, but a moral push towards recognition of the proposition that there is:

> no logical ground for saying that a person should have less protection against a private individual than he would have against the state for the publication of personal information for which there is no justification.[16]

Thus was the Convention used in *Campbell* by all their Lordships without any united acceptance by them of its being given any clear binding force in the common law as a whole:[17] the judges wanted to use it *here* – where a need for change had been perceived for many years – but not commit themselves to a general forced acceptance of it into common law.

A further point concerning the treatment of the Convention is of direct relevance to the themes of this book. By a rather extraordinary coincidence, the European Court of Human Rights handed down its first decisive judgment on protection of privacy against the media,[18] in its decision in *Von*

---

[15] 'Breach of Confidence as a Privacy Remedy in the Human Rights Act Era' (2000) 63 MLR 660, 673.

[16] [2004] 2 AC 457, para. 50.   [17] See Chapter 6, pp. 157–67.

[18] The decision in *Peck* v. *UK* (2003) 36 EHRR 41 was of course also of great significance, but, because the complaint in that case related to the decision of a local authority to release private images to the media, it did not settle the issue of the horizontal application of Article 8 in this context.

Hannover v. *Germany*,[19] only a few months after *Campbell*. That decision went much further than simply resolving affirmatively the much disputed point as to whether Article 8 requires a remedy between private persons for misuse of personal information. It *simultaneously* widened the scope of Article 8 in this context quite dramatically: as will be explained below, the decision on its face appears to make Article 8 applicable to any publication of any unauthorised photographs of a person engaged in any activities other than their official duties. In other words, no sooner had the House of Lords developed the common law to meet the standard of protection *thought* to be required by Article 8 than Strasbourg moved the goalposts – and quite some distance too. In terms of the judicial approach to the HRA, and in particular the differences in judicial attitude to the proper treatment of Strasbourg jurisprudence explored by Roger Masterman in Chapter 3 of this volume, the influence – or non-influence – of *Von Hannover* in cases subsequent to *Campbell* provides an interesting case study. Indeed, a fascinating paradox emerges: *Campbell* brought about a significant change in the common law – but *before* the Strasbourg case law clearly *mandated* that change. Conversely, once Strasbourg *did* in *Von Hannover* lay down some categorical guidance in this area, the English courts have proceeded largely to ignore it – preferring simply to 'apply' *Campbell*. This rather curious phenomenon, I tentatively suggest, may be explained by the fact that the courts were happy to draw upon the Convention, in general terms, to provide the needed impetus, the energy, if you like, to drive the transformation of breach of confidence into a real privacy remedy. But, once the House of Lords had achieved that in *Campbell*, very little enthusiasm to audit that decision itself against the evolving demands of the Convention has been evident: instead, old common law values and instincts appear once again to be asserting themselves against Convention principles.

A word or two as to the scope of this chapter is perhaps in order. Because the subject of this book is not legal doctrine as such, but rather the use of the HRA in shaping it, while it will be necessary to explain the changes in English common law that have come about in this area, the primary focus will not be upon analysis of them for their own sake, but rather their use as illustrations of the broader theme of judicial use of the Convention.[20] In addition, and partly for reasons of space, this chapter

---

[19] (2005) 40 EHRR 1.
[20] I have dealt in detail with the doctrinal issues elsewhere: G. Phillipson, see 'The Right of Privacy in England and Strasbourg Compared', in A. Kenyon and M. Richardson (eds.), *New Dimensions in Privacy Law: International and Comparative Perspectives*

will focus upon the normative and doctrinal changes to the confidence action under the impetus of Article 8, rather than upon the reconciliation of privacy protection with the countervailing right of freedom of expression under Article 10, although this issue will be touched upon in places.[21]

Campbell and breach of confidence

The facts of *Campbell* are quite well known, given that the House of Lords decision is the third reported judgment in the case, but, in brief, Naomi Campbell complained in an action both in breach of confidence and under the Data Protection Act 1998 after *The Mirror* newspaper had published details of her treatment for drug addiction with Narcotics Anonymous, including surreptitiously taken photographs of her leaving the clinic and hugging other clients. Importantly, these photographs made the location of the Narcotics Anonymous centre that Campbell had been attending clearly identifiable to anyone familiar with the area.[22] In the trial, the information in question was divided into five classes, as follows:

1. the fact of Miss Campbell's drug addiction;
2. the fact that she was receiving treatment;
3. the fact that she was receiving treatment at Narcotics Anonymous;
4. the details of the treatment – how long she had been attending meetings, how often she went, how she was treated within the sessions themselves, the extent of her commitment, and the nature of her entrance on the specific occasion; and
5. the visual portrayal (through photographs) of her leaving a specific meeting with other addicts.[23]

The applicant had conceded that *The Mirror* was entitled to publish the information in categories (1) and (2) – the vital fact that Campbell was a drug addict and was receiving treatment for her addiction;[24] the dispute therefore centred around whether publishing the further details and the

---

(Cambridge: Cambridge University Press, 2006); and H. M. Fenwick and G. Phillipson, *Media Freedom under the Human Rights Act* (Oxford: Oxford University Press, 2006), Chapters 13–15 and I draw on some of the material here. See also Moreham, 'Privacy in the Common Law', above n. 9.

[21] Helen Fenwick's chapter in this book analyses this topic in depth.

[22] As Lord Nicholls found: *Campbell* v. *MGN Ltd* [2004] 2 AC 457, para. 5.

[23] *Ibid.*, para. 23.

[24] This was because it was accepted that the press was entitled to expose the falsity of Campbell's previous public statements that she did not take drugs and was not a drug addict.

photographs (categories (3) to (5)) could attract liability. The Court of Appeal had found[25] that the extra details in these categories were too insignificant to warrant the intervention of the courts.[26] It was this finding that was overturned by the House of Lords on a three to two majority (Lord Hope, Lord Carswell and Lady Hale in the majority; Lord Nicholls and Lord Hoffmann in the minority).

Breach of confidence is the route the courts have chosen towards achievement of compliance through the common law of the court's own duty to act compatibly with the Convention rights under the Human Rights Act.[27] As Lord Woolf now famously observed in *A* v. *B*:

> Under section 6 of the [Human Rights Act], the court, as a public authority, is required not to act 'in a way which is incompatible with a Convention right'. The court is able to achieve this by absorbing the rights which articles 8 and 10 protect into the long-established action for breach of confidence.[28]

I turn first to the second limb of the action – the requirement that the information be imparted in circumstances importing an obligation of confidentiality.

'Circumstances importing an obligation of confidentiality'

I have dealt elsewhere[29] with the gradual disappearance of the requirement under this limb either of a pre-existing relationship[30] or an express promise or agreement as to confidentiality between the parties to fulfil this requirement, and even of the need for any recognisable *communication* between the parties; this was achieved through cases in which the defendant, with no prior relationship with the plaintiff, surreptitiously acquired the information in question without the plaintiff's awareness[31] and was yet held to be under an obligation of confidentiality. I have also analysed the post-HRA, pre-*Campbell*[32] case-law on this point, pointing out that, while there were *dicta* suggesting that no traditional factors were needed to impose a duty of

---

[25] [2003] QB 633.   [26] *Ibid.*, p. 661.
[27] Under s.6(1) and (3) HRA.   [28] [2002] 3 WLR 542, 546.
[29] G. Phillipson, 'Transforming Breach of Confidence? Towards a Common Law Right of Privacy under the Human Rights Act' (2003) 66 *Modern Law Review* 726, 747–8.
[30] *Stephens* v. *Avery* [1988] Ch 449, 482; the existence of a pre-existing relationship is 'not [now] the determining factor'.
[31] See e.g. *Francome* [1984] 1 WLR 892; *Shelley Films* v. *Rex Features Ltd* [1994] EMLR 134; *Creation Records Ltd* v. *News Groups Newspapers Ltd* [1997] EMLR 444.
[32] That is, prior to the decision of the House of Lords in *Campbell*.

confidence,[33] and at least one first-instance decision which endorsed that view,[34] the courts had clearly not freed themselves from the shackles of traditional confidentiality values.[35] The law stood in a state of uneasy ambivalence between its desire to protect privacy and the continuing pull of its roots in confidence. While the second limb of the action had seemingly been disposed of by *obiter dicta*, in practice it appeared to be in rude health. While Article 8 was said judicially to have reshaped the action, in practice its influence on decisions was negligible or non-existent.[36] This may well have been due to the failure to resolve decisively the 'horizontal effect' conundrum, discussed in Chapter 6, as well as a more general reluctance to take seriously the Strasbourg jurisprudence, even where its relevance was formally accepted,[37] a theme which reoccurs in many of the chapters in this book.

As I have argued elsewhere, *Campbell* has made a decisive contribution in this area. The crucial point to make concerns the *ratio* of the judgment: a majority of the House of Lords found liability in confidence in respect of the publication of surreptitiously taken photographs of the model outside Narcotics Anonymous, in the street. What, then, were the 'circumstances' in which the information was communicated that imposed an obligation of confidentiality'? There was clearly no pre-existing relationship between Campbell and the photographer; no communication between them; no express or implied promise by the photographer of confidentiality – quite the reverse. All these elements were therefore quite clearly disposed of.

---

[33] Most notably, Lord Woolf's bold statement in *A* v. *B plc* [2002] 3 WLR 542, 551B: 'The need for the existence of a confidential relationship should not give rise to problems as to the law . . . A duty of confidence will arise whenever the party subject to the duty is in a situation *where he either knows or ought to know that the other person can reasonably expect his privacy to be protected.*'

[34] *Venables and Thompson* v. *News Group Newspapers* [2001] 1 All ER 908.

[35] This may be seen, in particular, in the way in which the brief sexual relationships in *A* v. *B* and *Theakston* v. *MGN* [2002] EMLR 22 were found not to give rise to a duty of confidentiality, despite the fact that the information in question was clearly of a very intimate nature, and should therefore, according to authorities such as *Dudgeon* v. *UK* (1981) 4 EHRR 149, 165, para. 52, and *Lustig Prean* v. *UK* (1999) 29 EHRR 548, have been treated as a particularly important area of private life, especially deserving of strong protection.

[36] In particular, in the 2004 Court of Appeal decision in *D* v. *L* [2004] EMLR 1, which concerned very intimate information, Article 8 is not even mentioned in the judgment, let alone the Strasbourg jurisprudence on the importance of sexual life within Article 8. Instead, the reasoning is dominated by very traditional notions of equity, conscience and clean hands.

[37] As in *A* v. *B* itself: see the text to n. 28 above.

As Lord Nicholls put it: '[t]his cause of action has now firmly shaken off the limiting constraint of the need for an initial confidential relationship'.[38]

But the *ratio* of this case goes much further: *unlike* in cases like *Shelley Films*, or, more recently, *Douglas v. Hello! Ltd*,[39] in which snatched photographs were made the subject of a duty of confidence, there were no clear indications here that the scene was intended to be confidential, such as warning signs forbidding photography, or other external indications that the scene was confidential, such as the elaborate security precautions to prevent photography taken at the Douglas wedding. In fact, the only thing that could impose the obligation of confidence in relation to the photographs was the obviously private nature of the information itself – the fact that it concerned therapeutic treatment. This was then the first time that an English appellate court had imposed liability for use of personal information, in the absence of any circumstances imposing the obligation save for the nature of the information itself. And, if it is the private nature of the information that can itself impose the obligation, then the second limb of confidence effectively ceases to exist: there has to be information of a private nature to fulfil the first limb in any event, so the second limb no longer has any independent content. It has disappeared. 'Breach of confidence' simply becomes an action that protects against unauthorised publicity given to private facts.[40]

This then is clear, and unarguable, from the *ratio* of the case itself. But there are also *dicta* which suggest a general reformulation of the law which omits the second limb. Lord Nicholls – one of the minority – said:

> Now the law imposes a 'duty of confidence' whenever a person receives information he knows or ought to know is fairly and reasonably to be regarded as confidential.[41]

---

[38] *Campbell v. MGN Ltd* [2004] 2 AC 457, paras. 13–14.

[39] *Douglas v. Hello! Ltd* [2003] 3 All ER 996; *Douglas v. Hello! Ltd* [2006] QB 125; [2005] 3 WLR 881. In that case, stringent security measures, including body searches of the guests and the sealing off of the part of the hotel used for the wedding, had been put in place in an attempt to avoid un-authorised photography of the event.

[40] It should be noted that, whilst the photographs were found to attract liability only by the majority, the minority rejected this finding not on the basis that there was no obligation of confidence, but because of their finding that the photographs contained no information worthy of protection, i.e. that the first limb was not satisfied.

[41] [2004] 2 AC 457, para. 14. Lady Hale also summarises the essential requirement of the new-style action clearly: 'The position we have reached is that [*prima facie* liability is made out] when the person publishing the information knows or ought to know that there is a reasonable expectation that the information in question will be kept confidential': *Ibid.*, para. 134.

It may be noted that this formulation clearly omits the second limb of the confidence action. Lord Hope went further, saying: '[i]f the information is obviously private, the situation will be one where the person to whom it relates can reasonably expect his privacy to be respected'.[42] These *dicta* precisely carry forward the transformative step that the passage from *A v. B* cited above[43] had opened the way to. Those *dicta* allowed for an obligation of confidentiality to be imposed where there was a reasonable expectation of privacy. Lord Hope now suggests that the sole element required to give rise to that expectation is the fact that 'the information is obviously private'. This spells out in clear terms the demise of the second limb. As the New Zealand Court of Appeal put it in *Hoskings v. Runting*:[44] 'In effect, the second element has disappeared.'[45]

What then has happened to the first limb – in other words, what kinds of information are deemed capable and worthy of protection under the new action for breach of confidence.

Article 8 and the reasonable expectation of privacy: the touchstone for deciding what kinds of personal information can be protected and when?

Traditionally, to be afforded protection, information had to have 'the necessary quality of confidence'. Prior to *Campbell*, there had been no detailed discussion in the cases of what the proper scope of this requirement should be, in order to ensure harmony with Article 8 ECHR as interpreted at Strasbourg. Instead, in the typical common law style, decided cases had indicated a number of discrete areas of private life that were worthy of protection.[46] A general test had been recently laid down but it was not, rather surprisingly, one taken from the Strasbourg jurisprudence. Essentially, it involved asking whether disclosure of personal information would be 'highly offensive' to a reasonable person, a test taken from an Australian confidence case.[47] The twin problems that remained were the fact that the general test being used was arguably not in harmony with Article 8 and the persistence of a more general

---

[42] *Ibid.*, para. 96.   [43] Above n. 28.   [44] [2005] 1 NZLR 1.   [45] *Ibid.*, p. 43.
[46] See Fenwick and Phillipson, *Media Freedom*, above n. 20, pp. 740–1, for details.
[47] *Australian Broadcasting Corporation* v. *Lenah Game Meats* (2001) 208 CLR 199, para. 42. The test was taken by the Australian High Court from the US tort. It was used by the Court of Appeal in *Campbell* v. *MGN* [2003] QB 633, 660 and impliedly approved in *A* v. *B plc* [2002] 3 WLR 542, 550G.

tendency, evident especially in the Court of Appeal decision in *Campbell*,[48] to ignore or marginalise Article 8 when making key findings and gravitate instead back to traditional confidentiality concerns. I will concentrate here on the second issue.

The decision of the House of Lords in *Campbell* has gone some way to remedying both these matters. What the House did was first of all recognise that the first port of call in determining whether there are facts worthy of protection should be the Article 8 case-law and, secondly, that the test of high offensiveness was therefore not to be used as a *threshold* test, which had to be satisfied in *all* cases, but rather only as a tie-breaker, to determine marginal or doubtful cases and to be used to help determine the weight or seriousness of the privacy interest when balancing it against the competing interest in publication.

Essentially, the Court of Appeal, applying this test in the *Campbell* case, had asked itself the question, 'would a reasonable person of ordinary sensibilities, on reading that Miss Campbell was a drug addict have found it highly offensive, or even offensive that the details as to her treatment and the photograph of her leaving the meeting were also published?';[49] it answered this question in the negative. In the House of Lords, Lord Hope found this approach to be wrong in law. In a strongly argued passage, his Lordship made two key findings. First, 'the test [of offensiveness] is not needed where the information can easily be identified as private':[50]

> If the information is obviously private, the situation will be one where the person to whom it relates can reasonably expect his privacy to be respected. So there is normally no need to go on and ask whether it would be highly offensive for it to be published.[51]

Secondly, his Lordship found that the information in question in the case was indeed clearly private in nature:

> The private nature of these meetings [at Narcotics Anonymous] encourages addicts to attend them in the belief that they can do so anonymously. The assurance of privacy is an essential part of the exercise. The therapy is at risk of being damaged if the duty of confidence which the participants owe to each other is breached by making details of the therapy, such as where, when and how often it is being undertaken, public. I would hold that these details are obviously private.[52]

---

[48] *Campbell* v. *MGN* [2003] QB 633, 660–1.
[49] *Ibid.*, para. 55.   [50] *Campbell* v. *MGN* [2004] 2 AC 457, para. 94.
[51] *Ibid.*, para. 96.   [52] *Ibid.*, para. 95.

Lord Carswell confirmed this, stating: 'it is not necessary in this case to ask . . . whether disclosure of the information would be highly offensive to a reasonable person of ordinary sensibilities. It is sufficiently established by the nature of the material that it was private information.'[53] Lord Nicholls also expressed strong reservations about the test,[54] while Lady Hale found: 'An objective reasonable expectation [of privacy] test is much simpler and clearer than the ["high offensiveness"] test.'[55]

A further point of significant interest is the manner in which the issue of the photographs accompanying the intrusive article was handled. Their Lordships did not appear to find the fact that the photographs were taken in the street to be problematic in terms of imposing liability *given what they portrayed*. This being the case, the *ratio* of the case inescapably provides that activities taking place in the street – a fully public location – may yet be protected, if sufficiently sensitive. This amounts to full acceptance of the 'public domain' implications of the previous Strasbourg decision in *Peck* v. *UK*[56] and means that the new action provides a generous measure of protection for privacy in public places. This aspect of the finding is particularly important in evidencing the abandonment in *Campbell* of tests based upon the *confidentiality* of the information, as opposed to its private character. It would clearly seem inapt to describe events taking place in the street, witnessed by numerous people, as 'confidential'.[57] The fact that such information *was* protected in *Campbell* establishes that the question now being asked is whether the information relates to private life, *not* whether it is confidential.

Finally, it should be noted that the House of Lords, in dealing with this limb of the action again moved the terminology and the underlying concern of the law away from traditional notions of confidentiality towards a concern with privacy. As Lord Nicholls put it: 'Essentially the touchstone of private life is whether in respect of the disclosed facts the person in question had a reasonable expectation of privacy.'[58] Rather than speaking of whether the information is 'confidential', the question now seems to be whether 'the published information engaged Article 8 at all by being within the sphere of the complainant's private or family life'.[59] Article 8 therefore seems to become the touchstone for the

---

[53] *Ibid.*, para. 166.   [54] *Ibid.*, para. 22.   [55] *Ibid.*, para. 135.   [56] (2003) 36 EHRR 41.
[57] As indeed argued by Jonathan Morgan in 'Privacy, Confidence, and Horizontal Effect: "Hello" Trouble' (2003) 62 CLJ 444, 452.
[58] *Ibid.*, para. 21.   [59] *Ibid.*, para. 20, *per* Lord Nicholls.

fulfilment of the first – now the only substantive – limb of the action. Whilst Lord Hope's speech has a heading, 'Was the information confidential?',[60] his Lordship goes on to identify the 'underlying question' in these confidence cases as being 'whether the information . . . disclosed was private and not public'.[61] His Lordship referred to 'the right to privacy' as lying 'at the heart of the breach of confidence action'.[62] Lord Nicholls declared: 'This tort, however labelled, affords respect for one aspect of an individual's privacy. That is the value underlying this cause of action.[63] Even more boldly, he added:

> Information about an individual's private life would not, in ordinary usage, be called 'confidential'. The more natural description today is that such information is private. The essence of the tort is better encapsulated now as misuse of private information.[64]

Lord Hoffmann was even more sweeping, stating that the cause of action is no longer:

> based upon the duty of good faith applicable to confidential personal information and trade secrets alike, [instead] it focuses upon the protection of human autonomy and dignity – the right to control the dissemination of information about one's private life and the right to the esteem and respect of other people.[65]

Lord Carswell's conclusion does not mention breach of confidence, and holds simply that there had been 'an infringement of the appellant's right to privacy'.[66] 'Breach of confidence', then, seems to be becoming a label only: their Lordships appear to be replacing the values traditionally underpinning the action with those deriving from the human right to privacy.

Campbell *reappraised: does it necessitate a Strasbourg-centred approach?*

The above analysis indicates how far *Campbell* went in discarding both legal tests and values deriving from orthodox notions of confidence. I now wish to introduce a note of caution – further reflections upon *Campbell*, in the light of subsequent case-law. There are two main points here: first, the importance of the particular factual circumstances of this case; secondly, the perhaps surprising degree of rhetorical equivocation,

---

[60] *Ibid.*, para. 88.   [61] *Ibid.*, para. 92.   [62] *Ibid.*, para. 105.   [63] *Ibid.*, para. 15.
[64] *Ibid.*, para. 14.   [65] *Ibid.*, para. 51.   [66] *Ibid.*, para. 171.

given the radical *dicta* just cited, as to how much of a step-change this decision actually represented.

To take the factual issue first: it is worth noting that a significant reason for the finding of the majority of their Lordships in *Campbell* was their belief that the revelation of the details of Campbell's treatment at Narcotics Anonymous was likely to deter her from further treatment and/or diminish the likelihood of that treatment being successful.[67] This may mean that in cases in which the only harm the applicant can point to is the abstract one of violation of individual autonomy, coupled with distress and offence – as for example in cases in which sexual conduct is publicised – the absence of such a substantive harm to weigh in the balance against publication may well result in the judicial scales tipping against the privacy claim. Moreham rightly points out that, whilst the minority in *Campbell* saw the right to privacy as deserving of respect because it was an essential aspect of the individual's dignity and well-being, the majority laid stress on the harm caused by the articles in the particular case.[68]

We have noted above a passage in which Lord Hope emphasises the possible damage the article could do to Campbell's attempt to rehabilitate herself.[69] In fact, his speech more than once stresses this factor:

> there are few areas of the life of an individual that are more in need of protection on the grounds of privacy than the combating of addiction to drugs or to alcohol. It is hard to break the habit which has led to the addiction. It is all too easy to give up the struggle if efforts to do so are exposed to public scrutiny. The struggle, after all, is an intensely personal one. It involves a high degree of commitment and of self-criticism. The sense of shame that comes with it is one of the most powerful of all the tools that are used to break the habit. But shame increases the individual's vulnerability as the barriers that the habit has engendered are broken down. The smallest hint that the process is being watched by the public may be enough to persuade the individual to delay or curtail the treatment.[70]

Lady Hale similarly stressed this factor: the extra details in the complained-of stories, she said, 'all contributed to the sense of betrayal by someone close to her of which she spoke and which destroyed the value of

---

[67] See e.g. *Ibid.*, paras. 157 and 169.
[68] 'Privacy in the Common Law: A Doctrinal and Theoretical Analysis' (2005) 121 LQR 628, 634–5.
[69] See text to n. 52 above.   [70] *Campbell* v. *MGN* [2004] 2 AC 457, para. 81.

Narcotics Anonymous as a safe haven for her'.[71] Her Ladyship indeed focuses strongly upon the importance of what was, for her, at stake here: the struggle by Campbell to overcome a serious threat to her physical and mental health:

> Drug abuse can be seriously damaging to physical health; indeed it is sometimes life-threatening. It can also lead to a wide variety of recognised mental disorders ... [It] needs ... therapy aimed at maintaining and reinforcing the resolve to keep up the abstinence achieved and prevent relapse.[72]

Her Ladyship went on:

> Not every statement about a person's health will carry the badge of confidentiality or risk doing harm to that person's physical or moral integrity. The privacy interest in the fact that a public figure has a cold or a broken leg is unlikely to be strong enough to justify restricting the press's freedom to report it. *What harm could it possibly do?*... But that is not this case and in this case there was, as the judge found, a risk that publication would do harm.[73]

Lord Carswell, the third member of the majority, made the same point: 'It seems to me clear ... that the publication of the article did create a risk of causing a significant setback to her recovery.'[74] Lord Hope and Lord Carswell placed 'a good deal of weight' on the harm factor.

The tentative conclusion then is that, in the *absence* of such evidence of probable damage to such substantive privacy interests, it seems unlikely that the House of Lords would have found in Campbell's favour. This suggests a paradox: the minority, from whom much of the expansive, pro-privacy rhetoric came, found for the newspaper; the majority, who found for the claimant, did so at least partly for reasons quite specific to this particular case, which had little to do with abstract notions of dignity and autonomy and more of a practical concern about the practical ill-effects of intrusive journalism. This may not bode particularly well for future cases, where, although privacy may be invaded, it is difficult to point to any concrete 'harm'. As Moreham points out:

> A couple who are surreptitiously videoed while engaging in sexual activity in a hotel room might be unable to point to any tangible 'harm' suffered

---

[71] *Ibid.*, para. 153.   [72] *Ibid.*, para. 144.
[73] *Ibid.*, para. 157 (emphasis added).   [74] *Ibid.*, para. 169.

as a result but few would dispute that they would nonetheless have suffered a serious affront to their dignity.[75]

To this one could add that newspapers claiming Article 10 rights are not asked to show that restricting their freedom of speech will result in some tangible harm: the restriction upon the flow of speech is assumed to be intrinsically a *prima facie* wrong, to be justified.

The second note of caution I wish to sound is more general. Despite the expansive rhetoric I have cited, there is a possible reading of *Campbell* which plays down its generally radicalising tendencies. There are a number of *dicta* which suggest that the Law Lords did not themselves see this particular case as raising new issues of principle, or breaking new ground. Of some significance in this regard is that the headnote in the law reports does not in fact state that the decision establishes 'reasonable expectation of privacy' as the crucial test under the new action.[76] Lord Hoffmann appeared to regard the case as falling simply within the 'firmly established principle' that no pre-existing relationship of confidence is required. He cited Lord Goff's well-known *dicta* in *Spycatcher* to the effect that:

> a duty of confidence arises when confidential information comes to the knowledge of a person . . . in circumstances where he has notice, or is held to have agreed, that the information is confidential.[77]

It has been said that Gummow J of the Australian High Court is prepared to view *Campbell* as being decided on the orthodox basis that information relating to health and therapeutic treatment has traditionally been seen as axiomatically confidential in nature.[78] There are indeed a number of passages from four of the Law Lords which stress continuity with previous cases of confidence. Thus Lady Hale remarked:

> It has *always* been accepted that information about a person's health and treatment for ill-health is both private and confidential. This stems not only from the confidentiality of the doctor–patient relationship but from

---

[75] N. 68 above, p. 636.

[76] [2004] 2 AC 457. Instead, it states that the threshold test as to whether information is private is 'whether a reasonable person of ordinary sensibilities' in the shoes of the claimant 'would find the disclosure offensive', which is *not* what their Lordships said. See above, pp. 225–6.

[77] *Ibid.*, para. 47, citing Lord Goff in *Attorney-General* v. *Guardian Newspapers Ltd (No. 2)* [1990] 1 AC 109, 281.

[78] Seminar with Australian academics and practitioners, 'The Effect of Article 10 ECHR on Private Law', 12 April 2006, Faculty of Law, University of Melbourne.

the nature of the information itself . . . I start, therefore, from the fact – indeed, it is common ground – that *all* of the information about Miss Campbell's addiction and attendance at [Narcotics Anonymous] which was revealed in the *Daily Mirror* article was both private and confidential, because it related to an important aspect of Miss Campbell's physical and mental health and the treatment she was receiving for it. It had also been received from an insider in breach of confidence.[79]

While Lord Hoffmann spoke of the new recognition of the value of 'human autonomy and dignity'[80] as foundations underlying breach of confidence, he went on: 'In this case, however, it is unnecessary to consider these implications because the cause of action fits squarely within both the old and the new law.' Lord Hope said something very similar: 'The questions that I have just described seem to me to be essentially questions of fact and degree *and not to raise any new issues of principle.*'[81]

His Lordship also said:

> The *language has changed* following the coming into operation of the Human Rights Act 1998 . . . We now *talk about* the right to respect for private life and the countervailing right to freedom of expression. The jurisprudence of the European Court offers important guidance as to how these competing rights ought to be approached and analysed. I doubt whether the result is that the centre of gravity, as . . . Lord Hoffmann says, has shifted. It seems to me that the balancing exercise to which that guidance is directed is essentially the same exercise, although it is plainly now more carefully focussed and more penetrating.[82]

Similarly, Lord Carswell said that the decision 'involved the application of reasonably well settled principles'.[83]

Now it may be that all that is occurring here is the Law Lords setting off a little rhetorical smoke, to disguise the radical nature of the changes the judgment in fact is engineering: as Sedley LJ remarked in the first *Douglas v. Hello* decision, the common law has a 'perennial need . . . to appear not to be doing anything for the first time'.[84] However, there is certainly something strange about this insistence that the actual decision broke no new ground. Such a view simply ignores the significance of the finding of liability in relation to the photographs. While the information provided by the fellow patient at Narcotics Anonymous or staff was clearly stamped with the 'badge of confidentiality', and would have been

---

[79] *Campbell*, paras. 145 and 147.   [80] *Ibid.*, para. 50.
[81] *Ibid.*, para. 85 (emphasis added).   [82] *Ibid.*, para. 86 (emphasis added).
[83] *Ibid.*, para. 163.   [84] [2001] QB 967, 997.

actionable under the traditional cause of action, the photographs, as discussed above,[85] were different: there was nothing in the street scene to give notice of confidentiality, to impose the obligation of confidentiality (i.e. the second limb) beyond the nature of the information being revealed. Moreover, as to the first limb, as Morgan has observed, photographs of someone in the street *cannot* be described as containing 'confidential' information.[86] Why then did not Lord Hoffmann and the others acknowledge that the majority judgment did in fact break new ground – imposed liability, at least in relation to the photographs, where it could not have been imposed before? A possible answer, aside from the consideration suggested by Sedley LJ, is an unconscious desire to mask the radical impact the Convention was having: aside from Lady Hale, the other judges in the *majority* had not taken a clear view on the applicability of Article 8 to the case,[87] while Lord Hoffmann and Lord Nicholls both deny any *direct* relevance of Convention law, seeing it as having only a normative, persuasive force. Their Lordships argued that the values flowing from Article 8 compelled recognition of the value of protecting private information for its own sake as an aspect of the individual's dignity and autonomy. That value could then legitimately be used as a normative impetus to push the common law's development forward (perhaps two runs here, if not a boundary?). But, given that the House of Lords had so recently and firmly disclaimed the wish or ability to introduce a new tort of privacy,[88] it was difficult to acknowledge that this was what was being done: it would not only look a little inconsistent, but also suggest a strong measure of horizontal effect.

The Court of Appeal in its 2005 decision in *Douglas* v. *Hello!*,[89] the only major case so far decided since *Campbell*, was presented, in a sense, with a choice as to how it 'read' or 'presented' the House of Lords decision. While it is of course a subordinate court, it is not unknown for lower courts to 'read down' or 'expand' judgments of higher courts, diminishing or greatly enlarging their transformative effect. In this respect, the clear effect of *Douglas III* is to emphasise the more transformative aspects of the *Campbell* decision. Thus the radical *dicta* of their Lordships are highlighted; more conservative rhetoric and tendencies are not cited. Lord Nicholls' *dicta* as to the awkwardness of referring to confidentiality instead of privacy are foregrounded, as are the expansive *dicta* of Lord Hoffmann that refer to the shift in the values underlying the action from 'the duty of good faith' to

---

[85] See p. 223.   [86] Above n. 57.   [87] See Chapter 6, pp. 157–67.
[88] In *Wainwright* v. *Home Office* [2003] 3 WLR 1137.   [89] [2006] QB 125.

'the protection of human autonomy and dignity'.[90] The court accepts that the basis of the action is now the notion of a 'reasonable expectation of privacy', picking up on the congruence between Lord Hope and Lady Hale in the majority as to the basic test for the action,[91] and its purpose – the protection of 'the individual's informational autonomy'.[92] Finally, the court gives its own succinct summary of the development of this area of law:

> Megarry J in *Coco* v. *A N Clark* identified two requirements for the creation of a duty of confidence. The first was that the information should be confidential in nature and the second was that it should have been imparted in circumstances importing a duty of confidence. As we have seen, it is now recognised that the second requirement is not necessary if it is plain that the information is confidential, and for the adjective 'confidential' one can substitute the word 'private'.[93]

In the result, the court sums up the sole requirement now needed to make out a *prima facie* case:

> What the House was agreed upon was that the knowledge, actual or imputed, that information is private will normally impose on anyone publishing that information the duty to justify what, in the absence of justification, will be a wrongful invasion of privacy.[94]

Remarkably, and in this respect eschewing some of the coyness of the House of Lords in *Campbell*, the Court of Appeal was prepared quite openly to discard even the label of 'breach of confidence'. Thus in a striking phrase, the court referred to 'the cause of action *formerly described as breach of confidence*'.[95]

The label, it appears, has disappeared now also: the Court of Appeal is happy to announce openly the transformation of breach of confidence into what may now be termed 'the tort of misuse of private information'.[96] The court was also much bolder, and more explicit, in suggesting a different treatment in the law for photographs, as opposed to mere written information,[97] and, further, suggested the creation of a new

---

[90] Para. 51 of the House of Lords judgment; cited at para. 79 of the Court of Appeal judgment in *Douglas III*.

[91] *Douglas III*, para. 80.   [92] *Ibid.*, para. 81.   [93] *Ibid.*, para. 83.

[94] *Ibid.*, para. 82.   [95] *Ibid.*, para. 53.

[96] Note, however, that the Court of Appeal took the view that the action was not a tort but an equitable action: *Douglas III*, para. 9.

[97] Essentially, the Court said that republication of even widely circulated photographs could amount to fresh, actionable invasion of privacy, unlike republication of widely publicised information: para. 105.

image right – an intriguing possibility, although one beyond the scope of this chapter.[98] It is a matter of speculation as to *why* the Court of Appeal was so much more fearless than the House of Lords: one reason may simply be that it saw the House of Lords judgment in *Campbell* as providing it with a licence to be bolder rhetorically, the substantial work on doctrine having been already done by a superior court. Another may be that the *Douglas* decision was a fairly simple one to make under even a fairly orthodox approach to breach of confidence, as discussed above.[99] It appears that judges may find it easier to make more radical statements, in terms of *dicta*, when deciding a case that does not *require* the change in the law those *dicta* posit. Whatever the explanation, it is now time to turn to an examination of how Strasbourg has moved the interpretation of Article 8 on since *Campbell* – and how the English courts have reacted since.

The meaning of 'private life' in *Von Hannover* contrasted with *Campbell*

The findings in Von Hannover[100]

It was hinted above that the *Von Hannover* decision represents, to say the least, a radical extension of the Strasbourg Court's jurisprudence. The purpose of the analysis below, however, is not primarily to expound and critique those findings, something that, again, I have done elsewhere.[101] Rather, it is simply to point out the remarkably wide scope that the Court gave to Article 8 in the context of private law, in order to be able to consider how far the English decisions following *Campbell* have shown receptivity to *Von Hannover*, and, in particular, awareness of a possible disjunction between the two key cases. The case concerned an application by Princess Caroline of Monaco in relation to the failure of the German courts to prevent pictures of herself and her children, obtained by paparazzi without consent, appearing in various newspapers and magazines. The pictures themselves were relatively anodyne shots of the Princess engaged in various everyday acts including riding on horseback, being out with her children, canoeing, shopping with her boyfriend and son on a skiing holiday, kissing a boyfriend, leaving her home in Paris, playing tennis, and dressed in a swimsuit at a beach club. These were *not* then photographs that portrayed her engaged in some 'private

---

[98] See para. 113.   [99] See text to n. 39, p. 223 above.   [100] (2005) 40 EHRR 1.
[101] Above n. 20.

act' in the sense in which we have been discussing it so far. Not only was the applicant in a public place, but the activities she was engaged in did not, at first blush, appear to concern private facts at all. Nevertheless, the Court expressed no hesitation at all in making its key finding:

> There is no doubt that the publication by various German magazines of photos of the applicant in her daily life either on her own or with other people falls within the scope of her private life.[102]

It is important to appreciate at this point quite how broadly the notion of 'private life' is being drawn. The word 'private' appears to be being used to describe all those aspects of a person's life that do not relate to their official duties. So, for example, a civil servant is engaged in her private life all the time, except when carrying out her duties as a civil servant. Buying groceries is, in this sense, a part of her private life. There is certainly one sense in which we understand this to be the case: a basic distinction between public (in the sense of 'official') and personal or private life. That this is the sense in which the words have been used is indicated by a passage in which the court 'points out' that 'the photos show her in scenes from her daily life, *thus engaged in activities of a purely private nature* such as practising sport, out walking, leaving a restaurant or on holiday'.[103] The word 'private' here is clearly being used to mean 'non-official'; the word 'public' to mean 'part of one's official life or duties'.

Von Hannover *contrasted with* Campbell *on the scope of private life*

As discussed above, it appears that the sole element that the applicant must now show in English law is that he or she had a 'reasonable expectation of privacy' in the information disclosed by the respondent and that, where the information concerned is 'obviously private', such a reasonable expectation will exist. If it is not, then the issue of whether its disclosure would be highly offensive to the applicant may be examined, presumably along with any other relevant factors, such as the location in which the applicant was when any photographs were taken, the means used to obtain them and the likely effects upon the applicant of publication.

What then is the essential point of difference here between Strasbourg and English law? On its face, it is this: bearing in mind the anodyne nature of the photographs at issue in *Von Hannover*, and the very broad scope to 'private life' given in that case, the Strasbourg decision appears

---

[102] (2005) 40 EHRR 1, para. 53.   [103] *Ibid.*, para. 61 (emphasis added).

to take the view that any publication of an unauthorised photograph specifically taken of a particular person[104] engaged in an everyday activity outside their official duties will involve a *prima facie* violation of Article 8, a reading of the case that I shall refer to as 'the absolutist view'. In contrast, under English law, the applicant must identify information that relates to a specific aspect of private life, as more narrowly understood, such as health, sexuality and the like. The difference is apparent at its starkest in the speech of Lady Hale:

> We have not so far held that the mere fact of covert photography is sufficient to make the information contained in the photograph confidential. *The activity photographed must be private.* If this had been, and had been presented as, a picture of Naomi Campbell going about her business in a public street, there could have been no complaint ... If ... she pops out to the shops for a bottle of milk ... there is nothing essentially private about that information nor can it be expected to damage her private life.[105]

Lord Hoffmann appeared to agree: 'The famous and even the not so famous who go out in public must accept that they may be photographed without their consent.'[106] Lady Hale's comment that publications showing such pictures 'may not be a high order of freedom of speech but there is nothing to justify interfering with it'[107] is particularly significant. It can only be interpreted as meaning that, in such a case, Article 8 would simply not be engaged, precisely the converse of the finding in *Von Hannover*.

Clearly, then, there is something of a gap between the two decisions: the House of Lords appears to take a much more restrictive view of the scope of private life under Article 8 than the Strasbourg Court itself. What is the significance of this for the attitude of English courts after *Campbell* to the *Von Hannover* decision? Of course, it should be recalled that, whilst under the Human Rights Act the UK courts are bound to act compatibly with 'the Convention rights' themselves,[108] they are not bound by the Strasbourg jurisprudence; it is something they must only

---

[104] The words 'specifically taken of a particular person' are used because this judgment would presumably not apply to photographs of normal street scenes in which individuals happen to be caught.

[105] *Campbell* v. *MGN* [2004] 2 AC 457, para. 154 (emphasis added).

[106] *Ibid.*, para. 73.   [107] *Ibid.*, para. 154.

[108] Section 6(1). In fact, of course, the decision in *Campbell* does not make it clear whether this is an absolute duty in the sphere of private common law: see Chapter 6 of this volume.

take into account. However, as Roger Masterman notes in Chapter 3, the House of Lords has itself said that '[t]he duty of national courts is to keep pace with the Strasbourg jurisprudence as it evolves over time',[109] leaving only a very restricted discretion to depart from it, for example where a Strasbourg decision has misunderstood English law,[110] or where its decisions would 'compel . . . a conclusion fundamentally at odds with the distribution of powers under the British constitution'.[111] Neither of these exceptions would appear to apply here.[112] The position of the House of Lords itself is of course different from that of a lower court that is confronted by a clear incompatibility relating to the interpretation of the Convention as between a House of Lords judgment post-HRA[113] and a decision of the Strasbourg Court. In such an instance, it has been held that an inferior court is bound to follow the House of Lords, in preference to a Strasbourg judgment.[114] Therefore, in theory, it would be possible for a judge of a lower court to find that, the House of Lords having definitively determined the parameters for the protection of private information in *Campbell*, she was bound to follow *Campbell*, even if that involved an outcome inconsistent with *Von Hannover*. However, it seems unlikely that the English courts will wish flatly to disobey or disregard *Von Hannover*. Much more probably, they will seek either *genuinely* to reconcile the two decisions, or simply not advert to any difference between them. As will appear below, it is the latter course that has been taken so far. However, if and when the disparity between the two decisions is adverted to, there will be two obvious courses of action. One will be to interpret *Campbell* as simply holding that, for the purposes of the common law action, 'private facts' are those falling within the scope of Article 8, as defined by the Strasbourg jurisprudence, now including *Von Hannover*. This, however, would have the effect of broadening enormously the reach of the common law. Further, it really

---

[109] R. (on the Application of Ullah) v. Special Adjudicator; Do v. Immigration Appeal Tribunal [2004] UKHL 26, para. 20, per Lord Bingham.

[110] See e.g. the remarks of Lord Hoffmann in R. v. Lyons (No. 3) [2003] 1 AC 976, para. 46; for discussion of both exceptions, see Chapter 3.

[111] R. (on the Application of Alconbury Developments Ltd) v. Secretary of State for the Environment, Transport and the Regions [2001] UKHL 23, para. 76.

[112] Section 2(1).

[113] If it were before the HRA, the decision might be found to have been impliedly overruled by the HRA itself.

[114] It has been held that English courts are bound to follow the House of Lords where its post-HRA findings appear to contradict those of the Strasbourg Court: Kay and Others v. Lambeth London Borough Council; Price v. Leeds City Council [2006] UKHL 10.

would make the common law the handmaiden of the Convention: to change the metaphor, the common law would simply become the conduit by which Convention principles were given force in English law – direct horizontal effect disguised as indirect effect, one might say. Given the historic caution of the English judges in relation to privacy, and their clear ambivalence about horizontal effect,[115] such a course seems most unlikely.

I have discussed elsewhere the small signs in *Campbell* that English law may be prepared to accept a further extension, along *Von Hannover* lines;[116] my purpose here, however, is to examine the possibilities of future reconciliation of these two strands of law, and the actual response of English courts to the issue since *Campbell*. Given that a wide gulf between the two decisions nevertheless still exists, the other course of action would be to 'read down' the decision in *Von Hannover* to bring it closer to the approach taken in *Campbell*. Whilst the judgments of the Strasbourg Court cannot strictly be broken down into 'ratio' and 'obiter dicta', it may be observed that the inferences to be drawn from the finding of a breach in the case and the reasoning the Court gives to support that finding, are very different. The holding of the case, *given the facts*, is that the systematic and persistent pursuit and photographing of a person going about their everyday life and the publication of those photographs in mass circulation newspapers can give rise to a breach of Article 8. This is not, perhaps, a particularly radical proposition, given the degree of harassment present in the particular case, and the feeling the applicant had of being under constant, albeit unofficial surveillance. As the Court put it, under the view taken of Princess Caroline's case by the German courts, the Princess simply 'has to accept that she might be photographed at almost any time, systematically, and that the photos are then very widely disseminated'. The Court indeed makes clear that it had this factor very much in mind in coming to the decision it did:

> [The Princess] alleged that as soon as she left her house she was constantly hounded by paparazzi who followed her every daily movement, be it crossing the road, fetching her children from school, doing her shopping, out walking, practising sport or going on holiday.[117]

Indeed, the court makes the influence of this factor on its judgment explicit:

---

[115] See Chapter 6.
[116] Kenyon and Richardson, *New Dimensions*, above n. 20, pp. 209–10.
[117] (2005) 40 EHRR 1, para. 44.

The context in which these photos were taken – without the applicant's knowledge or consent – and the harassment endured by many public figures in their daily lives cannot be fully disregarded.[118]

And again:

Furthermore, photos appearing in the tabloid press are often taken in a climate of continual harassment *which induces in the person concerned a very strong sense of intrusion into their private life* or even of persecution.[119]

The italicised words are of particular significance: they suggest that it is not any one particular photograph, or what it reveals, that induces the sense of intrusion into private life, but, as the court puts it, 'a climate of continual harassment'. This suggests that what we actually have here is a judgment that combines two elements in coming to a finding that Article 8 is engaged: (a) the fact that the pictures relate to the Princess's everyday life, not her official functions, *and* (b) the constant intrusion that the persistent photographing represents. This more restrictive reading would dovetail nicely with the second part of the definition of private facts proposed by Parent: 'information about a person which ... though not generally considered personal, a particular person feels acutely sensitive about'.[120] The photographs, in other words, fall within Article 8 because, while not revealing anything generally considered personal, they induce an acute feeling of intrusion because of the persistent campaign of low-level intrusion of which they are a part. Looked at this way, the judgment in *Von Hannover* does not, necessarily, imply that *any* photograph taken without the consent of a person in their private capacity will engage Article 8; rather, the question will be either whether the photograph taken of the person reveals or exposes some intimate aspect of their life (as in *Campbell* or *Peck*) *or* whether the cumulative impact of the persistent taking and publishing of such photographs is such as to give rise to a level of intrusion sufficient to breach Article 8.

It is conceded immediately that this is only one reading of the judgment: it is quite evident that the Court nowhere states that it is the cumulative effect of the photography that in this case was the decisive factor. Nevertheless, it would be a perfectly defensible course of action for the English courts to interpret *Von Hannover* simply as a finding that the

---

[118] *Ibid.*, para. 68.   [119] *Ibid.*, para. 59 (emphasis added).
[120] W. A. Parent, 'A New Definition of Privacy for the Law' (1983) 2 *Law and Philosophy* 305, 306–7.

systematic pursuit and photographing of a person as they go about their daily life can, in sufficiently serious circumstances, amount to a breach of Article 8. Such a finding could be accommodated within the new law: while the information in the particular photograph might not be 'obviously private', the publication of the photograph could satisfy the alternative test of being 'highly offensive to a reasonable person of ordinary sensibilities'.[121] Thus, if a case were brought in the English courts that concerned a one-off photograph of, for example, a celebrity jogging in the park, the lack of persistent intrusion would clearly be a distinguishing factor that could lead the court to find that the *Von Hannover* principle was not engaged on the facts and that the information was neither obviously private, nor was its publication highly offensive. Interestingly, the Court of Appeal in *Douglas III*, the only appellate decision taken since the two judgments came out, did not even advert to the obvious differences between the two, let alone suggest how they could be resolved. To do so was not necessary in the case in hand; however, the same could not be said of all the later cases, to which we now turn.

Cases since *Campbell* and *Douglas*: resistance to Strasbourg?

In this final part of the chapter, I go on to consider three cases decided since the above, all at first instance. They are significant, I suggest, for two reasons: first, they exhibit the phenomenon noted above – refusal to acknowledge the tension between *Campbell* and *Von Hannover*, or indeed to engage in any real analysis of the latter, despite its obvious significance. Secondly, they indicate strands of common law reasoning actively hostile to Convention principles or at least in strong tension with them. Collectively, although it is too early to say definitively, they indicate that there is no strong desire to embrace the Strasbourg case-law: in the absence of any definitive resolution of the horizontal effect conundrum, the common law continues to exhibit a robust degree of autonomy from Strasbourg.

McKennit v. Ash[122]

McKennit v. *Ash* is the first case to come to trial since the *Douglas* cases. It concerned a book which contained numerous disclosures by a former

---

[121] See the text to n. 47 above.
[122] [2006] EMLR 10; [2005] EWHC 3003 (QB).

intimate friend of the well-known Canadian folk singer on various topics, including her personal and sexual relationships. The applicant was successful in relation to her claim and received £5,000 in damages and an injunction preventing further publication of the passages in the book identified as actionable. In some ways, the case was a straight-forward one: while the judge used the language of privacy, it would have fitted quite nicely under the law of confidence in any case. There was a strong pre-existing relationship between the parties, albeit one of friend-ship, rather than professional status. The confidentiality and trust within the relationship was expressly conceded by the defendant in her book in a number of passages,[123] and the judge had no difficulty in finding that Ms Ash must have known she had infringed the trust and loyalty she owed to McKennit in writing the book.[124]

There was thus a fairly plain case under the orthodox breach of confidence doctrine. However, Eady J takes full account of *Campbell* in his judgment, and takes from it, as the touchstone for liability, the reasonable expectation of privacy test:

> It thus becomes clear that, with respect to any given piece of information, the first task confronting a court is to identify whether there would be a reasonable expectation of privacy such as to engage Article 8 at all.[125]

He also takes note of the de-centring of the 'high offensiveness' test in *Campbell*: he cites Lord Nicholls' concern that the test not be brought in as a threshold requirement,[126] and from this concludes correctly: 'This would strongly suggest that the mere fact that information concerning an individual is "anodyne" or "trivial" will not necessarily mean that Article 8 is not engaged.'[127] Instead, as the judge observed:

> If [the subject matter] is such as to give rise to a 'reasonable expectation of privacy', then questions such as triviality or banality may well need to be considered at the later stage of bringing to bear an 'intense focus' upon the comparative importance of the specific rights being claimed in the individual case. They will be relevant to proportionality.[128]

So far so good, and quite straightforward.

There are, it is suggested, two main points of critical interest about the judgment. The first is the general remarks the judge makes about the

---

[123] See e.g. *ibid.*, para. 72.   [124] *Ibid.*, para. 90.   [125] *Ibid.*, para. 63.
[126] See the text to n. 54 above.   [127] Para. 58.
[128] *Ibid.* It may also be observed that the way in which the speech/privacy clash is reasoned is also quite faithful to Strasbourg principles as laid down in *Campbell*.

Von Hannover decision; the second, his approach to resolving the case in front of him and its consistency with that decision. As to the first, this is the only one of our three judgments to take specific note of *Von Hannover*, save in passing.[129] At one point, indeed, it sounds as if that decision's remarkable nature is being acknowledged: Eady J comments that: '[*Von Hannover*] is notable especially, perhaps, for the width of the notion of "private life" which the European Court of Human Rights is now prepared to recognise.' The judge appears to take this to include the fact that privacy includes 'a zone of interaction with others even in a public context' and also that: 'It is no longer possible to draw a rigid distinction between that which takes place in private and that which is capable of being witnessed in a public place by other persons.'[130] However, what the judge does *not* do is to acknowledge the real potential breadth of the decision, discussed above,[131] and its possible tension with *Campbell*. Instead, he rather blandly observed:

> it would appear that there is consistency between the approach of the court in Strasbourg and that now being adopted in the courts of the United Kingdom.[132]

Perhaps hoping to support such a harmonious conclusion, he recites the Strasbourg Court's own characterisation of the photographs in *Von Hannover* as 'images containing very personal or even intimate "information" about an individual'.[133] However, this amounts to mischaracterisation: as noted above, this is simply not the case. The key point that the judge did not take – perhaps it was not suggested in argument – was that the photographs in question in *Von Hannover* did not disclose 'very personal or even intimate' information about the Princess, but consisted simply of anodyne images of her going about her everyday life. The fact that the judge did not acknowledge the extraordinary breadth of 'private life' consequently recognised in that case, nor alternatively seek to argue (along the lines suggested above)[134] that it may be read as less broad than it first appears, and dependent upon a degree of harassment, is critical for how he then proceeded to dispose of the case in front of him.

The approach of the judge to disposal, an understandable one in many ways, was to examine the various revelations made in the book,

---

[129] In each of the other two decisions considered below, *Von Hannover* is mentioned only once, with virtually no analysis.
[130] *Ibid.*, para. 50.   [131] See pp. 235–40.   [132] Para. 58.
[133] *Ibid.*, para. 52.   [134] See pp. 238–40.

and in each case ask whether they were serious or intrusive enough to attract the protection of the law. Thus one may compile a list, as follows: revelations about the claimant's relationship with her fiancé leading up to his death, her health following that bereavement, detailed descriptions as to the interior of and arrangements relating to her Irish home, details of contractual negotiations with a record company, certain intimate conversations about male friends, and details of a sum of money advanced to the defendant and her partner by the claimant for the purpose of purchasing a home, and which led to subsequent litigation, and of the (non-sexual) behaviour of the claimant in a bedroom after being roused having fallen asleep exhausted. All of these were found, either because of the location (e.g. the home, a hotel room) or the nature of the information itself (grief, bereavement, intimate relationships and so on) to give rise to a 'reasonable expectation of privacy'.

A large amount of other complaints, however, were not: these included various details as to business transactions, 'the panic and stress' of a European tour, details as to the claimant's disputes with staff, including her 'short temper' with them at times, (non-controversial) remarks made by the claimant about Ms Ash's friends and family, details of a shopping trip, a general reference to the fact that at a particular time she was seeing a man who was a friend of Ms Ash, and the fact that she was taken ill and hospitalised in London (without details of her symptoms or treatment). The judge described the details of the shopping trip, for example, as being 'trivial and of no consequence . . . anodyne, and not such as to attract any obligation of confidence'.[135]

The judge may well be praised for an exhaustive and careful examination of the various complaints and his careful attempt to sift them into matters in which there was a reasonable expectation of privacy, and those in which there were not. Further, he did not, as judgments before *Campbell* had done, fall into the error of denying protection for matters plainly related to private life on grounds that were in fact based on confidentiality values (e.g. the duration of the relationships in question).[136] Moreover, the test of 'reasonable expectation of privacy' is, as we have seen, one used by the Strasbourg Court. However, the point that the judge does *not* advert to is the argument derived from *Von Hannover* that *none* of these details related to 'official duties' of any person – plainly impossible in this case – and that therefore, at least on the 'absolutist' reading of *Von Hannover* suggested above, *all* fell plainly

---

[135] *Ibid.*, para. 139.   [136] See n. 35 above.

within the scope of Article 8 and *prima facie* deserved protection. Instead, the finding that certain details were 'anodyne' was repeatedly used by the judge as a reason for finding against a reasonable expectation of privacy, *even though* this is precisely the description that could well be attached to the *Von Hannover* photographs. Now, it could of course be argued that the more intrusive nature of photographs, as opposed to written descriptions, is what distinguished the two cases, an argument which may be right: it seems perhaps doubtful whether Princess Caroline would have won her case had she merely been complaining about a verbal description of what she did in her day. The Court of Appeal in *Douglas III* drew a number of distinctions between the law as it related to photographs and that relating to other modes of communicating personal information,[137] although not on this particular point. Alternatively, the judge could have found that, the House of Lords having definitively determined the parameters for the protection of private information in *Campbell*, he was bound, as judge of an inferior court, to follow the House of Lords, in preference to a Strasbourg judgment.[138] The interesting point for our purposes is that the judge took none of these courses; instead, he simply failed to advert to the apparent tension of the methodology he was undertaking with the approach of the Strasbourg Court in *Von Hannover*, nor to the tension between *Von Hannover* and *Campbell*. In this respect, of course, he followed the Court of Appeal in *Douglas III*. So far, no judge has pointed out the fact that the English privacy emperor is not wearing Strasbourg's clothes.

A v. B[139]

Our second case, also decided by Eady J, is known as *A v. B*, although this is not to be confused with the earlier Gary Flitcroft case of the same name.[140] It should be noted that this was a decision on interim relief (which was emphatically denied), not on final trial; the decision is therefore much shorter, and much less substantially reasoned, than *McKennit*. Nevertheless, it is quite long enough to discern some rather worrying trends. The case concerned an article written by the claimant's former wife, primarily about her own affairs, but which the claimant believed would also contain a

---

[137] See text to n. 97 above   [138] See n. 114 above.
[139] [2005] EMLR 36; (2005) 28(8) IPD 28, 060; [2005] EWHC 1651.
[140] *A v. B plc* [2003] QB 195.

number of disclosures about his private life, in particular about his drug rehabilitation. He had himself admitted to the press on previous occasions his own use of drugs. However, as the judge put it:

> he contended that information about the effect of drugs upon him, his conduct when using drugs and details of his rehabilitation and use of Narcotics Anonymous was not publicly known.[141]

On its face, therefore, there were quite striking similarities with *Campbell*. Indeed, in this case, since there had been no public denial of drug-taking by the claimant, there was no false impression to correct; therefore, the public interest in the story was arguably much weaker. Moreover, it has been established since *Duke of Argyll* v. *Duchess of Argyll*[142] that information obtained about one's spouse in the course of a marriage is, classically, of a confidential character. Nevertheless, and surprisingly, it was found that 'the claimant had failed to establish ... that the ... defendants were proposing to publish anything in respect of which he had a reasonable and continuing expectation of privacy'.[143] While, in relation to some of the claims, this finding was made simply on the basis that the defendants intimated that they did not intend to publish material about which the claimant had had concerns, in relation to others it seemed to be made primarily on the basis of the prior publicity that the claimant had given to the same matters. As the judge put it:

> An important consideration when assessing the background of this case is that the claimant has himself made public through the media a great deal of information that might usually be considered as falling within the protection afforded to private or personal information, including matters concerning [his wife] and the child of the marriage.[144]

Counsel for the claimant had argued that 'the subject matter' of the proposed article 'clearly fell within the category of information which the claimant was reasonably entitled to expect would be afforded protection', and that '[the claimant's] Art.8 rights were ... plainly engaged'.[145]

The judge, however, rejected the notion that 'to pass the threshold' it was sufficient to show that 'the information fell, in general terms, in certain categories'. He conceded that 'no one doubts that at any rate most of the categories which give rise to the claimant's concern in this case would be such as to attract *prima facie* the protection of the law', but went on to put a

---

[141] Above, n. 139, H6.   [142] [1967] 1 Ch 302.   [143] [2005] EMLR 36, para. 38.
[144] *Ibid.*, para. 16.   [145] *Ibid.*, para. 20.

very particular gloss upon the notion of a reasonable expectation of privacy. 'The critical question', he said, was 'whether *the claimant* has a reasonable expectation that such information should be protected', something which, the judge said, 'depends to a large extent upon his own circumstances and conduct'.[146] This, it is suggested, is quite a significant development: the judge uses the inherent flexibility in the term '*reasonable* expectation of privacy' to shift the test from being one that looks primarily at the nature of the information and the circumstances in which it was obtained, to one that puts the claimant's own behaviour under the spotlight. In essence, it asks whether the claimant *deserves* to have his privacy protected. A major factor in deciding whether he does is the extent and nature of his prior revelations. In looking at the significance of previous disclosures, the judge appears to adopt counsel's suggestion that:

> In identifying the scope of material within the public domain, once such a claimant has chosen to lift the veil on his personal affairs, the test will be 'zonal'; that is to say, the court's characterisation of what is truly in the public domain will not be tied specifically to the details revealed in the past but rather focus upon the general area or zone of the claimant's personal life (e.g. drug addiction) which he has chosen to expose.[147]

This does at least reject what I have referred to in the past as the extreme possibility of a 'blanket waiver' – whereby prior revelations about one aspect of private life result in the claimant losing protection for all of it.[148] Nevertheless its calm assertion, without reference to any Strasbourg, or indeed English, authority, that one can lose all Article 8 privacy protection for a particular area of private life by prior disclosures in relation to it is rather startling.[149] There is no attempt at all to examine whether this notion of 'waiver' of privacy rights is compatible with Strasbourg principle, as expressed in cases such as *Van der Mussele*,[150] *Deweer*[151] and *X* v. *Denmark*.[152] Perhaps recognising this, the judge went on:

---

[146] *Ibid.*, para. 21.   [147] *Ibid.*, para. 28.   [148] Above n. 29, p. 740.

[149] For criticism of the notion of 'waiver' of privacy, see *ibid.*, pp. 741–2.

[150] A 70 (1983).   [151] A 35 (1980).

[152] App. No. 7374/76, DR 5. For discussion of these and other cases on the relevance of 'freedom to contract', see E. Alkema, 'The Third Party Applicability, or "Drittwirkung" of the European Convention on Human Rights', in F. Matscher and H. Petzold (eds.), *Protecting Human Rights: The European Dimension* (2nd edn, Cologne, Berlin, Bonn and Munich: Carl Heymanns Verlag, 1990). The basic principle appears to be that Strasbourg requires clear evidence of a genuinely voluntary waiver of Convention rights if a finding of breach is to be avoided.

> I do not take the argument to entail that Art.8 is not engaged at all. I would rather construe [the] submission as being directed towards whether the claimant's *prima facie* right to the protection of such information has been displaced by his own conduct, in the sense that it has rendered it no longer reasonable for that protection to be maintained by legal process.[153]

This is an interesting passage: it seeks to avoid the bold and rather drastic step of denying *prima facie* engagement of Article 8, a point that surely would have required some discussion of Strasbourg case-law. Instead, the judge founds upon the notion that certain behaviour by the claimant disables him from protection of legal process. However, if we take from *Von Hannover* the notion that the requirement for respect for private life *requires* the protection of the legal system, even between private individuals, then what we essentially have here is an attempt to justify a violation of Article 8(1) without reference to paragraph 2 of that Article. Plainly, this won't wash, in Strasbourg terms. Instead, the common law here appears to be going off on a frolic of its own; perhaps the real influence here was the ancient equitable principle that he who comes to equity must come with clean hands,[154] a maxim that, in the context of privacy at least, remains wholly untested against Strasbourg principles.

The judge does then seek some grounding for this remarkable reinterpretation of the notion of a *reasonable* expectation of privacy. It is said to be 'consistent with European jurisprudence' – we are not told which cases. It is also, we are told, in harmony with:

> more recent decisions within this jurisdiction, such as *Douglas* v. *Hello!* . . . to take into account the voluntary revelations on a case by case basis in determining whether any particular information is such that the claimant can any longer *reasonably* expect to keep it private.[155]

Can the judge's approach in *A* v. *B* in fact be reconciled with the *Douglas* case? It seems very doubtful. In that case, it will be recalled, the couple were intending to publicise the entire event to which the disputed

---

[153] [2005] EMLR 36, para. 22.
[154] As the judge said: 'Another important consideration . . . is that for public policy reasons there would be powerful arguments against concealing, with the assistance of the court, information about one's criminal activities' (para. 32). This was not a very persuasive argument in the present case, precisely because the claimant had previously admitted drug-taking: this was not really a revelation of previously unknown criminal conduct, which might indeed attract such a public interest justification.
[155] *Ibid.*, para. 23.

photos related through extensive coverage in *OK!* magazine, yet the Court of Appeal in *Douglas III* not only found that there was a reasonable expectation of privacy in the event, but also that an injunction should have been granted to protect it.[156] Remarkably, however, the judge in *A* v. *B* sought to present the latter case as entirely different from both *Von Hannover* and *Douglas*:

> The claimant's position was to be contrasted to that adopted by Princess Caroline [in *Von Hannover*] ... and by Mr and Mrs Michael Douglas, who had striven to keep the subject-matter of the relevant articles private.

It is difficult to know what to make of this assertion: while it is true that Princess Caroline had, like the claimant in *A* v. *B*, used the courts to fight privacy actions (and thus striven to protect her privacy), the photographs about which she was claiming were not of 'private facts', as the judge here seems to suppose, but of her movements in public. In relation to the *Douglas* litigation, the assertion is even harder to swallow: far from 'striving to keep the subject matter of the relevant articles private', the Douglases had sold the rights to publish pictures of the subject (their wedding) in a mass circulation magazine. This is a particularly unconvincing attempt to justify a conclusion that seems to have no grounding at all in Strasbourg authority, and, it may reasonably be suspected, is based primarily upon the disreputable nature of the activities that the claimant was seeking to conceal.

This indeed leads on to a broader point: a suspicion about what is really influencing the courts in reaching their conclusions in these cases. One can't help noticing that, in the judgments to date, those who have been caught out being 'a bad lot' are denied relief by the courts: *Flitcroft* and *Theakston* (both seeking to conceal sexual impropriety), and the anonymous claimant in *A* v. *B*. In contrast, those who have *blameless* facts revealed about them, by those who have deliberately breached a relationship of trust (as in *McKennit* and in the Prince Charles' diaries case[157]) or effectively 'stolen' an exclusive by subterfuge (as in *Douglas*) are successful. *Campbell* is a borderline case, which is why, perhaps, it so split the judges: on the one hand, *The Mirror* was revealing wrongdoing by Campbell – drug taking, lying and hypocrisy. On the

---

[156] *Douglas III*, paras. 153–9.
[157] [2006] All ER (D) 276 (Mar). The case (discussed below) concerned publication of extracts from Prince Charles' diaries evidently given to the newspaper by a disloyal former employee.

other hand, the newspaper was interfering with a 'virtuous' attempt at rehabilitation by Campbell (possibly risking her relapse into addiction) and also benefiting from a gross breach of trust by staff or patients at Narcotics Anonymous to publish information that, at least to some of the judges, fell into the category of classically confidential information – details about therapeutic treatment. A further category in which the judges are sympathetic to claimants, partially overlapping with the above, are those in which it is possible to point to some real risk of damage to the health or well-being of the claimant or others, over and above the 'nominal' damage caused by interference with privacy: these include *Campbell* itself, the well-known *Venables* case[158] and *Green Corns* v. *Claverley*,[159] in which an injunction was granted to prevent the press from publishing the locations in which vulnerable children in care were being looked after, for fear of disruption and disturbance affecting the children in question. As Eady J put it in *A* v. *B*: 'The potential to cause harm [by the publication] is likely to be "an important factor" for the court to weigh here, as it was in *Campbell*.'[160] While it is perfectly reasonable in privacy cases to take account of the possibility of damage to substantive interests such as health, the rather moralistic considerations also seemingly influential seem to have very little to do with Article 8, and suggest that privacy protection is being granted only to those who appear, in the courts' eyes, 'deserving complainants'.

Prince Charles' diaries

Our final case, *HRH Prince of Wales* v. *Associated Newspapers*,[161] was quite a traditional confidence case, although again it was treated according to the new, *Campbell*-style principles. Essentially, Prince Charles' diaries, detailing not personal information, but his musings upon the hand-over to China of Hong Kong and various related topics, were leaked to the *Daily Mail*, which published extracts. The 'diaries' were slightly unusual, in that they were not kept in a secret journal, but rather were copied and sent to family, close friends and advisers for their

---

[158] *Venables and Another* v. *News Group Newspapers* [2001] 1 All ER 908. A very similar case, also won by the applicant, was *X (A woman formerly known as Mary Bell)* v. *SO* [2003] EWHC 1101.
[159] [2005] EMLR 31. The judge found that there was already substantial evidence of this risk.
[160] *Ibid.*, para. 33, citing para. 118 of the *Campbell* judgment, *per* Lord Hope.
[161] [2006] All ER (D) 276 (Mar).

thoughts, although the covering letter accompanying the copies was marked 'private and confidential'. There was dispute as to the number sent, but it seemed to be somewhere between forty and seventy. The judge, however, did not find the numbers decisive, given the plain intention of Prince Charles to exercise careful control over who was able to read the diaries, the fact that the letters were all marked 'private and confidential', and that the staff handling them were all subject to duties of confidentiality.[162]

This was thus quite a clear case of breach of confidence: the *Daily Mail* had clearly received the fruit of a broken confidence, most probably by a former member of the Prince's staff. Nevertheless, again *Campbell* is quite faithfully applied and the fiction maintained that 'there was no division of opinion [in that decision] over the relevant approach in law'.[163] Thus Blackburne J said:

> Lord Nicholls made clear that the initial question was 'whether the published information engaged article 8 at all by being within the sphere of the complainant's private or family life'. 'Essentially' he said (at [21]) 'the touchstone of private life is whether in respect of the disclosed facts the person in question had a reasonable expectation of privacy'.[164]

There might indeed have been thought to be a possible question mark over the fulfilment of this test, in the sense that the subject matter of the material written in the diaries was not personal, but political. As counsel for the *Daily Mail* put it:

> The material in the Hong Kong journal did not relate to the claimant's private life in any significant way but rather to the public life of a public figure concerning political events, setting out views and impressions which Mr Warby [for the *Daily Mail*] described as 'of a political character'. The information, he said, was obtained and the views were formed by the claimant in the course of official duties carried out on behalf of the nation and at public expense and, to that extent, were of a public and governmental nature rather than of a private and personal character.[165]

This was, then, a slightly unusual instance of a 'privacy' case that did not involve 'private facts' but rather the privacy of the *form* of the information – a diary, or, as it might have been characterised, private correspondence, which of course is specifically protected by Article 8(1).

---

[162] See *ibid.*, para. 101.   [163] *Ibid.*, para. 85.   [164] *Ibid.*, para. 88.   [165] *Ibid.*, para. 104.

There are perhaps two main points of interest here, both of which point in the same direction: that the court was eager to find reasons to find for the claimant, who was seeking – and was granted – summary judgment. The first relates to the way in which the court treated the same argument as to 'waiver' of privacy rights, or loss of a *reasonable* expectation of privacy through prior publicity, that was so successful in the *A* v. *B* case. Here, the argument was dismissed robustly:

> In particular, I dissent from the view that, by speaking out publicly both in speeches and in published articles on issues which in the widest sense are political, the claimant has somehow forfeited any reasonable expectation of privacy in respect of such matters when committed to a hand-written journal not intended by the claimant to be open to public scrutiny. Were it otherwise no politician could ever have any reasonable expectation of privacy in a private diary in which he expresses political views.[166]

Surely, one might equally argue that the claimant in *A* v. *B*, by speaking out to the media about his problems with drug abuse, had not forfeited a reasonable expectation of privacy in relation to such matters when confided in, or witnessed by, his wife. Are not marital secrets as obviously private as those committed to a diary? Moreover, in the *A* v. *B* case, the publication concerned disclosure of intimate and sensitive matters relating to health and physical condition, as opposed to the musings on public affairs of the heir to the throne. But the claimant in that case lost, resoundingly, whereas Prince Charles in this case won, resoundingly, gaining summary judgment.

The second point of interest is the perhaps over-ready dismissal by the court of the competing right of freedom of expression. Admittedly, the case was not an easy one in terms of balancing the two rights. On the one hand, there was a clear breach of confidence by the Prince's staff, while a diary, even if shared with friends, is a classic locus for the development in private of one's thoughts. On the other hand, reading this decision, this author had the rare sensation, in a privacy case, of feeling that he was actually learning something worthwhile about the political attitudes of a genuinely important public figure: in other words, there was, to this reader at least, a real countervailing speech interest. The newspaper argued, with considerably more plausibility than in the numerous cases involving celebrity gossip, that the published material was of real

---

[166] *Ibid.*, para. 115.

public interest, concerning as it did the lobbying activities, as well as the political views, of the future head of state – clearly a significant public figure by any assessment. As the judge put it:

> Mr Warby identified as the legitimate aim the electorate's right to receive information of four kinds: (1) information which will enable it to understand the nature of the lobbying to which their elected leaders are subject; (2) information which will enable it to assess and pass judgment on the political conduct of the heir to the throne; (3) information which will assist it to evaluate the conduct of the claimant in failing to take part in the Chinese Embassy banquet of 1999 and the Buckingham Palace banquet of 2005; and (4) information which corrects the claimant's own public statements about his non-attendance at the 1999 banquet.[167]

In response to this argument, one may detect a certain eagerness on the part of the judge to downplay the importance of the speech in question, which was, after all, of a far more weighty nature than that which prevailed in the *Flitcroft*, *Theakston* and *A* v. *B* cases. There is a general sense that the judge is unreceptive to the arguments as to the importance of the speech in question: it is notable that there is no citation of any of the famous Strasbourg 'political speech' cases, such as *Sunday Times*,[168] *Jersild*,[169] *Lingens*[170] and *Thorgeirson*.[171] Particularly striking is the following passage:

> What then of the claimant's political conduct as Heir to the Throne and in particular any concern that he may be acting contrary to what constitutional convention requires of him? Again, there is nothing in the articles to suggest that his conduct is being assessed and a judgment made about it. There is not a hint of this in the editorial comment.[172]

This is a remarkable comment: it seems to suggest that a court in assessing the 'speech value' of a given article is bound by the way that the newspaper has presented it. In Strasbourg terms, however, the question of whether this is information which the public has a right to receive is not answered by the nature of the editorial comment in the article in question. Certain kinds of publication have strong informational value, whether or not the newspaper expressly comments upon the fact or not.

---

[167] *Ibid.*, para. 123.   [168] *Sunday Times* v. *UK*, A 30 (1979).
[169] *Jersild* v. *Denmark* (1994) 19 EHRR 1.   [170] *Lingens* v. *Austria* (1986) 8 EHRR 407.
[171] *Thorgeirson* v. *Iceland*, (1992) 14 EHRR 843.   [172] [2005] EMLR 36, para. 130.

Such reasoning appears to disclose an anxiety to resolve the case in the Prince's favour: and this, it is hard not to suspect, came from the fact that the Prince was, unlike the unsuccessful claimants we have examined, an 'innocent' and indeed highly respectable victim of a breach of confidence. In the circumstances, one cannot help feeling that the courts' downplaying of the importance of the speech in question in a case in which they had sympathy and respect for the claimant, corresponds, conversely to the rather absurd *attribution* of real public interest to the trivial sexual gossip in *Theakston* and *Flitcroft* in cases concerning figures with whom the court instinctively felt little or no sympathy. Similarly, the easy dismissal of the 'waiver' argument in this case contrasts sharply with the high weight given to it in *A* v. *B* – in the case of a 'non-respectable' figure, seeking essentially to 'cover up' disreputable behaviour. In none of those cases does one sense a dispassionate attempt to apply Strasbourg principles – problematic as they are – to reach a conclusion. Common law reasoning thus continues to wriggle free from the grasp of the Convention.

Conclusions

The House of Lords decision in *Campbell* has given English law a privacy tort; more precisely a cause of action in respect of the misuse of personal information. If the test of 'reasonable expectation of privacy', derived from Strasbourg, is in future applied as it would be at Strasbourg, then, whilst we would notionally have only indirect application of Article 8 through the common law action of confidence, the position arrived at would be more or less the same as it would have been had Article 8 and its associated jurisprudence been directly applied by the courts – an ironic outcome, given the equivocation over horizontal effect in *Campbell*. However, this chapter has pointed out some reasons to be sceptical about such an outcome actually materialising, even though the author remains of the view that *Campbell* provides the guidance necessary to achieve it. First of all, there is the stress placed by the majority judges in *Campbell* upon the particular concrete harm that could have been done by the publication and the equivocation of how far the law was actually being changed. Secondly, the challenges of *Von Hannover* are being ignored: the common law and the Convention continue their elaborate game of flirtation and withdrawal. It is perhaps too early to tell whether the English judges have made only a temporary use of the Convention to bring about a change felt to be necessary anyway to revitalise the common law and remedy the long-standing failure of English law to protect personal privacy. Thirdly, I have sought to trace instances of old common law values and attitudes resurfacing, all under the mantle of assessing whether a given expectation of privacy is 'reasonable', or of 'balancing' speech and privacy interests. In conclusion, it may perhaps be said that the common law and the Convention found a temporary connection in *Campbell* over the issue of privacy: whether the relationship will become a constant and faithful one remains to be seen.

Postscript

Since this chapter was written, the Court of Appeal handed down its decisions in both *McKennit* v. *Ash* and *HRH Prince of Wales* v. *Associated Newspapers*: in both, the media defendants had their appeals dismissed. The latter decision confirms the argument in this chapter: the Court of Appeal was uninterested in the possibility of 'waiver' and dismissed the Article 10 argument even more brusquely than at first instance. Having briefly summarised Blackburne J's stance on that point, the Court merely remarks: 'We agree, for the reasons given by the Judge'. However, the former decision requires more comment. The Court of Appeal *does* confront the implications and width of the decision in *Von Hannover*; indeed, the media bodies put to the Court the author's argument as to the possible 'reading down' of that decision made elsewhere and repeated in this chapter. The Court rejected it, stating: 'While it is quite correct that there is reference in the judgment of the ECtHR to media intrusion, it is not possible to say that the general statements of principle in *Von Hannover* are so limited'. Thus the Court took the opposite view from that predicted here, by apparently embracing the 'absolutist' reading of *Von Hannover*. Three points may be made however. First, the court in *McKennit* was not in fact dealing with a case of anodyne photographs taken in the street: thus its comments were, strictly, *obiter*. No English court has yet imposed liability for such photographs. Secondly, as argued in this chapter, the approach of the first-instance judge was arguably inconsistent with *Von Hannover* in rejecting certain 'anodyne' private facts as unworthy of protection. The Court of Appeal did not dissent from this part of the judgment, or even pick up on the inconsistency. Thirdly, the Court of Appeal did not advert to that decision's apparent inconsistency with *Campbell*. While the author therefore stands to an extent corrected by the Court of Appeal, he modestly maintains some of his criticisms, and his doubts as to the 'absolutist' application of *Von Hannover* in English law.

10

Judicial reasoning in clashing rights cases

HELEN FENWICK*

Introduction

Part I of this book concentrated largely on the mechanics of the Human Rights Act itself, the topic that has understandably tended to form the main preoccupation of the academic literature,[1] while Part II considers aspects of its use in relation to various areas of substantive law, taking some account of its effect in curbing the power of public authorities as it impacts on individual rights.[2] In contrast, this chapter examines judicial reasoning in clashing rights cases, concentrating especially on the intriguing and ambiguous decision of the House of Lords in *Re S (A Child)*.[3] There is not so far a great deal of literature considering the proper

---

* The paper on this topic, which was originally presented at a seminar in the Judicial Reasoning and the Human Rights Act series, on 4 November 2004, was published as 'Clashing Rights: The Welfare of the Child and the Human Rights Act' (2004) 67 MLR 889. This chapter draws on some of the arguments presented in that original paper.

[1] See Chapters 4, 5, 6 and 7 in particular. See further e.g. Justice Arden, 'The Interpretation of UK Domestic Legislation in the Light of European Convention on Human Rights Jurisprudence' (2004) 25 Statute LR 165; A. Kavanagh, 'Unlocking the Human Rights Act: The "Radical Approach" to Section 3(1) Revisited' [2005] EHRLR 259; D. McGoldrick, 'The UK's HRA in Theory and Practice' (2001) 50 ICLQ 901; Lord Lester of Herne Hill QC, 'Interpreting Statutes under the HRA' (1999) 20 Statute LR 218; R. Clayton, 'The Limits of What's Possible: Statutory Construction under the HRA' [2002] EHRLR 559; C. Gearty, 'Reconciling Parliamentary Democracy and Human Rights' (2002) 118 LQR 248; G. Phillipson, '(Mis-)Reading Section 3 of the Human Rights Act' (2003) 119 LQR 183; C. Gearty, 'Revisiting Section 3 of the Human Rights Act' (2003) 119 LQR 551.

[2] See in particular Chapter 13. See further R. Clayton and H. Tomlinson, *The Law of Human Rights* (2nd edn, Oxford: Oxford University Press, 2006); A. Ashworth, *Human Rights, Serious Crime and Criminal Procedure* (London: Sweet and Maxwell, 2002); H. Fenwick, *Civil Liberties and Human Rights* (3rd edn, London: Routledge-Cavendish, 2002).

[3] [2005] 1 AC 593; [2004] 3 WLR 1129; [2004] 4 All ER 683; [2004] UKHL 47.

domestic approach to clashes of Convention rights,[4] and this topic is also somewhat neglected in relation to the Convention itself.[5] The horizontal effects debate has so far dominated the question of the governance of relations between private parties by the Human Rights Act (HRA).[6] But little has been said in relation to instances in which the main question in relation to private parties is not that of the *legal basis* of their claims, but of their resolution in instances where conflicting Convention rights under the HRA enter the arena. At the same time, large numbers of 'clashing rights' cases are already arising before the domestic courts[7] – whether or not they are viewed in those terms – and, as this chapter argues, it cannot yet be said that the Lords' decision in *Campbell* has laid to rest judicial uncertainty as to the proper means of dealing with them.[8] There has been until recently little judicial or even academic recognition of the difference between grappling on the one hand with utilitarian concerns where they conflict with individual rights under paragraph 2 of Articles 8–11, Schedule 1 HRA, and on the other

---

[4] See I. Leigh, 'Clashing Rights, Exemptions, and Opt-Outs: Religious Liberty and "Homophobia"' (2001) 4 *Current Legal Issues* 247; G. Phillipson, 'Transforming Breach of Confidence: Towards a Common Law Right of Privacy under the Human Rights Act' (2003) 66 MLR 726; H. Fenwick and S. Choudhry, 'Taking the Rights of Parents and Children Seriously: Confronting the Paramountcy Principle under the HRA' (2005) 25 OJLS 453, on clashes of rights in the family sphere.

[5] In two of the leading texts on the Convention (D. Harris, M. O'Boyle and C. Warbrick, *Law of the European Convention on Human Rights* (London: Butterworths, 1995); and P. van Dijk and G. van Hoof, *Theory and Practice of the European Convention on Human Rights* (3rd edn, The Hague: Kluwer, 1998)), a very small amount of material appears in various chapters on this issue, but no general discussion of it is attempted at any point. Clapham considers the Convention in the private sphere generally but not the clashing rights issue specifically: A. Clapham, *Human Rights in the Private Sphere* (Oxford: Clarendon, 1993); A. Clapham, 'The Privatisation of Human Rights' [1995] EHRLR 20.

[6] See Chapter 6, pp. 148–54, for references.

[7] See *Ashworth* [2002] 4 All ER 193, which concerned a clash between Articles 10 and 8; and the range of celebrity privacy cases discussed in Chapter 6. Instances also arise in the family context; see e.g. *Payne* v. *Payne* [2001] Fam 473; *R. (Williamson)* v. *Secretary of State for Education and Employment* [2003] 1 All ER 385. See also H. Fenwick and S. Choudhry, 'Taking the Rights of Parents and Children Seriously: Confronting the Paramountcy Principle under the HRA' (2005) 25 OJLS 453. Conflicts between Articles 2, 3 and 10 and between Articles 8 and 10 have arisen in the context of protection for persons convicted of very high-profile crimes after their release (*Venables* v. *News Group Newspapers Ltd* [2001] 1 All ER 908; and *X, A Woman Formerly Known as Mary Bell, Y* v. *SO, News Group Newspapers Ltd and Mirror Group Newspapers Ltd* [2003] 2 FCR 686).

[8] See n. 7 above. See also H. Fenwick and G. Phillipson, *Media Freedom under the Human Rights Act* (Oxford: Oxford University Press: 2006), Chapters 13 and 15.

considering the proper balance to be struck between two such rights when the value of both is assumed. The UK will soon have for the first time an Equality and Human Rights Commission[9] which will inevitably have to grapple with conflicts of rights since its remit will be to provide overarching protection for the Convention rights as well as for rights to freedom from discrimination on the established and the new protected grounds.[10] Essentially, the problem is two-fold. Clashes of Convention rights may go unrecognised in judicial reasoning.[11] Or, even where the clash is acknowledged, there may be a reluctance to accept the equal value of the two rights, except on the rhetorical level. Thus the promotion of debate as to this matter is especially pressing at the present time.

This chapter chooses to concentrate on one particular conflict of rights – that between media free speech and the privacy of children. This particular conflict has been chosen since the clash between the rights appears to be so profound, and until recently elicited such a stark and, this chapter will contend, misguided response from the domestic courts.[12] There are significant differences between this conflict of rights and that between the privacy of adults (in practice, usually celebrities) and media freedom, mentioned in Chapter 6. This clash of rights tends to be far more difficult to resolve since both speech and privacy values tend to be much more strongly engaged. The situations of the children in question often have quite a strong public interest dimension, in contrast to those of adult celebrities where the speech in

---

[9] See the Equality Act 2006 which governs the powers and duties of the new Commission for Equality and Human Rights (CEHR). It will bring together the work of the three existing equality Commissions as well as taking on new responsibilities in relation to the Human Rights Act and the new grounds of discrimination set out in the 'Framework' Directive, Directive 2000/78/EC, and implemented, or in the process of implementation, domestically: see n. 10 below.

[10] Discrimination on grounds of religion and belief in employment was covered from 2 December 2003 by the Employment Equality (Religion and Belief) Regulations 2003, SI 2003 No. 1660; discrimination on grounds of sexual orientation in employment was covered from 1 December 2003 by the Employment Equality (Sexual Orientation) Regulations 2003, SI 2003 No. 1661; both SIs implement European Council Directive 2000/78/EC.

[11] See n. 7 above.

[12] The pre-HRA academic consensus was also to the effect that the jurisprudence in this area was seriously flawed in relation to its failure to probe the limits of free speech in a principled fashion where it conflicts with minors' privacy claims. See I. Cram, 'Minors' Privacy, Free Speech and the Courts' [1997] PL 410; L. Woods, 'Freedom of Expression and the Protection of Minors' (2001) 13 Child and Family Law Quarterly 209.

question normally consists merely of trivial gossip.[13] At the same time, the children concerned have normally come into the limelight due to the effects of a range of critical events, including upheavals in their family life or forms of serious misfortune. Thus arguments as to the extent to which they have exploited their private information are irrelevant and their privacy interests tend to relate to profound and life-changing experiences. Their privacy claims are not therefore contingent and precarious, as they can be in the case of celebrities, but very strongly engage a range of private and family life-based values. So in this instance the clash between the rights can be particularly profound, but it might be anticipated that the courts would show particular sympathy towards the privacy claim. In fact, the clash in question has in general elicited, it will be contended, a misguided response from the domestic courts[14] and there has been a tendency to minimise that claim. Thus the conflict of rights between media free speech and the privacy of children forms an especially significant but somewhat neglected aspect of the post-HRA speech/privacy clash so very pertinent at the present time.[15]

The range of restrictions on what can be published about child welfare matters and disputes concerning children is at an unprecedented level.[16] Where restrictions cover the matter of upbringing, they are enhanced by the 'paramountcy principle' – the principle deriving from s.1(1) Children Act 1989 (CA) that the child's welfare relating to upbringing automatically prevails over the rights of other parties.[17] Some of the restrictions leave no or little room for balancing the two rights against each other and are therefore highly inimical to free speech. In so far as the restrictions leave leeway to the courts to consider free speech considerations the principle stands in the way, if it applies. In other words, it

---

[13] This point is discussed in Chapter 9, pp. 241 and 251–2.   [14] See n. 12 above.

[15] This point is touched upon in Chapter 6 and in Chapter 9. This topic has been extensively considered in relation to the privacy of adult celebrities: see e.g. G. Phillipson, 'Transforming Breach of Confidence: Towards a Common Law Right of Privacy under the Human Rights Act' (2003) 66 MLR 726; H. Tomlinson and H. Rogers, 'Privacy and Expression: Convention Rights and Interim Injunctions' [2003] EHRLR 36 (a special issue on privacy). See also H. Fenwick and G. Phillipson, *Media Freedom under the Human Rights Act* (Oxford: Oxford University Press, 2006), Chapters 13, 14 and 15.

[16] They are discussed below; for comment on their extent, see M. Dodd, 'Children, the Press and a Missed Opportunity' (2002) 14 *Child and Family Law Quarterly* 103, esp. 103; J. Dixon, 'Children and the Statutory Restraints on Publicity' [2001] Fam Law 757, esp. 761.

[17] 'When a court determines any question with respect to: upbringing of a child; or the administration of a child's property or the application of any income arising from it, the child's welfare shall be the court's paramount consideration.'

has the potential to pre-empt a principled resolution of the conflict by ensuring that one side automatically wins out. In the terms of the European Convention on Human Rights, the Article 8 rights of the child to respect for private and family life trump the Article 10 rights of the media, where upbringing is in issue. But judicial unease with this situation, especially in relation to the Human Rights Act, has failed to lead to debate as to what the welfare of the child genuinely requires where a conflict with reporting rights arises; rather, it has manifested itself in a determination in the courts to avoid the issue by the use of exclusionary interpretations of the meaning of the term 'upbringing' so as to avoid an engagement with the conflict in question. It will be contended that the use of such interpretations has meant that judicial reasoning as to welfare is precluded or distorted – since issues relating to the central matter of upbringing are excluded from it. But, conversely, where the paramountcy principle is found *not* to apply, the approach was until recently almost equally flawed in taking a near-converse stance: the Article 8 rights of the child (as encapsulating aspects of the child's welfare) in a number of instances figured merely as exceptions to be narrowly interpreted under Article 10(2). Even after that approach had been abandoned, formally speaking, it lingered on in the judicial stance taken to the child's private life claim. Thus an unprincipled legal oscillation between speech and privacy is occurring, one result being that the child's privacy tends to be under-protected where a reporting restriction leaves leeway for considering the clash of rights in question.

The inception of the Human Rights Act called the judicial approaches to this conflict into question since the stance at the domestic and at the European levels differs. At the domestic level, although post-HRA the presumptive equality of speech and privacy has been accepted, media freedom of expression still tends to win out where the paramountcy principle does not apply. On the other hand, if the principle *was* found to apply in a speech/privacy clashing rights case, it is hard to see how the Article 10 rights of the media could weigh in the scales at all. At the European level, however, the two rights are afforded a much more equal weight. The approach at Strasbourg to clashes between Articles 8 and 10 in general makes it clear that an automatic or near-automatic abroga-tion of one or the other right is unsustainable and entirely opposed to the values underlying the Convention.

This chapter will argue that therefore the established domestic approaches to this conflict of rights can no longer be sustained under the Human Rights Act. They are flawed, since they depend on a refusal

to afford *any* weight to an individual right when it comes into conflict
with another such right, where the paramountcy principle applies. But,
where it does not apply, a similar problem arises – there was, pre-HRA
and in the very early post-HRA years, a refusal to accept that Articles 8
and 10 are of presumptively equal value. It will be argued that, even at
the present time, after the apparent rejection of that approach, there is a
danger that lip-service only will be paid to the presumptive equality of
the two rights in this context, and therefore the private and family life
claim will tend to be minimised. This tendency was exemplified, it will
be argued, in the reasoning of the House of Lords in the recent case that,
as indicated, this chapter centres around, *In Re S (A Child)*.[18]

The comparison chosen – of clashes between Article 8 and Article 10
in this context – is intended to highlight the failure of the UK courts to
adopt a consistent and theorised approach to the broader clashing rights
issue. The key argument is that clashes of rights inevitably raise difficult
moral questions and that therefore, once the value of each individual
right has been recognised, as it must be under a deontological document
such as the European Convention on Human Rights, the issues of
principle at stake should be identified in order to determine how far, if
at all, the moral conflict is incommensurable and irreducible.

A range of statutory restrictions on reporting related to children has
incrementally accumulated. The current complex and chaotic web of
restrictions relates strongly to the Article 8 rights of children to respect
for private and family life, although certain restrictions also have the
intention of protecting the administration of justice. But the statutory
restrictions are not the main subject of this discussion. Below, the
discussion covers the stance taken by the courts in adjudicating on the
restriction founded on the inherent jurisdiction of the court in relation
to conflicts between the welfare of the child and the rights of the media
in the pre-HRA era. It moves on to consider the changed stance under
the HRA, arguing that misunderstandings of the Convention stance on
clashing rights continued to bedevil the jurisprudence until very
recently. Having sought to demonstrate that the domestic courts were
straying away from the approach espoused under the Convention,
despite the inception of the HRA, this chapter will move on to suggest
that, even when those misunderstandings were largely put to rest, it will
be argued that the common law tradition of upholding free speech
values was allowed to overcome the value placed by the Convention

[18] N. 3 above.

upon privacy, in *Re S*. Finally, a suggested model for the proper resolution of such conflicts under the HRA is put forward which, it will be contended, is already emerging at the domestic level and is more firmly rooted in the Convention jurisprudence since it is fully premised on the presumptive equality of Articles 8 and 10 and engages more fully with the justificatory principles underlying those Articles. The particular clashes highlighted here could be viewed as pertinent examples: it is arguable that such a model could and should be used to resolve other issues of clashing rights within the domain of child welfare and outside it.[19]

Reporting restrictions relating to children

A certain group of restrictions affect the reporting of proceedings held in private, and a substantial proportion of such proceedings involve cases concerning children. The common law rule is that all courts, in the exercise of their inherent power to regulate their own proceedings in order to ensure that justice is done, have a discretion to sit in private, but due to the importance of the open justice principle the discretion is to be exercised only in exceptional circumstances.[20] Certain statutes expressly provide for hearings to be held in private in relation to matters involving children.[21] However, the mere fact that a hearing occurs in private does not automatically mean that *reporting* of the proceedings is restricted. Under s.12(1)(a) of the Administration of Justice Act 1960, it will be a *prima facie* contempt to report on proceedings held in private[22] where they relate to wardship, adoption, guardianship, custody or the upbringing of or access to an infant.[23] It has been found that the press cannot report any aspect of wardship proceedings,[24] but this is not an

---

[19] See n. 7, above. Clashes between the Article 8 right of the child to a respect for privacy and the Article 8 right of the parent to respect for family life arise e.g. in respect of disclosures to parents of medical information relating to the child (see J. Loughrey, 'Medical Information, Confidentiality and a Child's Right to Privacy' (2003) 23 LS 510–35, esp. 511–13). See also H. Fenwick and S. Choudhry, 'Taking the Rights of Parents and Children Seriously: Confronting the Paramountcy Principle under the HRA' (2005) 25 OJLS 453.

[20] *Scott* v. *Scott* [1913] AC 417.

[21] Adoption Act 1976, s.64; Magistrates' Court Act 1980, s.69(2) as amended by the Children Act 1989, s.97; Civil Procedure Rules 1998, Part 39.

[22] See further s.12(2).   [23] *Re F* [1977] Fam 58.

[24] See *Re X (A Minor) (Wardship: Injunction)* [1984] 1 WLR 1422 (the Mary Bell case).

absolute restriction:[25] it has been found to cover 'statements of evidence, reports, accounts of interviews' and similar information.[26] In relation to other information linked to the proceedings, the test is whether the information is 'within the mischief which the cloak of privacy in relation to the substance of the proceedings is designed to guard against'.[27]

Section 49 of the Children and Young Persons Act 1933 places restrictions on the identification of children or young persons convicted in the Youth Court, but the restrictions can be lifted where a court is satisfied that this is in the public interest.[28] In relation to any proceedings in any court, the court may make an order under s.39 of the 1933 Act prohibiting publication of particulars calculated to lead to the identification of any child concerned in the proceedings.[29] Section 39 orders are especially problematic for journalists since they frequently provide insufficient guidance as to what can safely be published.[30] Where s.12(1)(a) or s.39 do not apply, the High Court may nevertheless grant an injunction restraining reporting that might reveal a child's identity or other matters relating to a child as an aspect of its inherent jurisdiction to protect minors.[31] After the decision in *Re X (A Minor) (Wardship: Jurisdiction)*[32] (the Mary Bell case), it can be seen that there *was* an increasing recourse to the court's asserted power to grant injunctions to restrain the publication of information about its wards or other children. The invention of this jurisdiction was described by Hoffmann LJ in *R. v. Central Independent Television*[33] in the following terms: 'the

---

[25] See *Pickering* v. *Liverpool Daily Post and Echo Newspapers plc* [1991] 2 AC 370; [1991] 1 All ER 622 (HL), at 423 and 635 respectively.

[26] *Re F (A Minor) (Publication of Information)* [1977] Fam 105.

[27] *Pickering* v. *Liverpool Daily Post and Echo Newspapers plc* [1991] 2 AC 370; [1991] 1 All ER 622 at 422–3 and 634.

[28] Under the Crime (Sentences) Act 1997, s.45, which inserted s.49(4A) into the 1933 Act. See also the Youth Justice and Criminal Evidence Act 1999, s.44. The Anti-Social Behaviour Act 2003 amends the Crime and Disorder Act 1998, s.1, to provide that s.49 does not apply to proceedings for orders under the 2003 Act, but that s.39 does apply.

[29] See also the Children and Young Persons Act 1963, s.57(4); and the Broadcasting Act 1990, Schedule 20, para. 3(2).

[30] See *Briffett* v. *DPP; Bradshaw* v. *DPP* [2001] EWHC Admin 841; and the commentary by M. Dodd, 'Children, the Press – and a Missed Opportunity' (2002) 14 *Child and Family Law Quarterly* 103.

[31] See *Re M and N (Minors) (Wardship: Publication of Information)* [1990] Fam 211, 223, per Butler-Sloss LJ; *Re C (A Minor) (Wardship: Medical Treatment) (No. 2)* [1990] Fam 39, 46, for the finding that wardship 'is the machinery for its exercise'.

[32] [1975] Fam 47.   [33] [1994] Fam 192, 204.

courts have, without any statutory or ... other previous authority, assumed a power to create by injunction what is in effect a right of privacy for children'.

The action for breach of confidence could be utilised in some instances to protect information relating to a child from disclosure by the media.[34] However, due to the availability of the statutory restrictions discussed above and the use of the courts' inherent jurisdiction, recourse to this action tends to be unnecessary in this context.[35] The matter of consent can create difficulties in this context. If a *Gillick*-competent child has given consent to the publication of the information, although the adults around her consider that disclosure may be detrimental to her welfare,[36] the information can no longer be treated as confidential. So for a number of reasons reliance on the doctrine of confidence has not so far been very significant in respect of media disclosures of information relating to children.[37]

Weighing up media freedom against the privacy of the child in the pre-HRA era

Instances in which the High Court is exercising its inherent jurisdiction tend to create the most wide-ranging impact on media freedom to publish, since the reporting is not necessarily linked to court proceedings. The decisions discussed below suggest that the conflict between free expression and privacy is most likely to occur where the inherent jurisdiction is being exercised (after *Re S*, as discussed below, this term was replaced by the term 'the Convention jurisdiction'). But, although the courts have more leeway in this context to consider solutions to this

---

[34] See Chapter 9. See also the findings of the President of the Family Division in *Venables* v. *Mirror Group Newspapers Ltd* [2001] 1 All ER 908, 939. See further J. Loughrey, 'Medical Information, Confidentiality and a Child's Right to Privacy' (2003) 23 LS 510 esp. 511–13.

[35] E.g. the identity of Mary Bell's daughter was protected until her eighteenth birthday by an injunction granted in wardship proceedings: *Re X (A Minor) (Wardship Proceedings: Injunction)* [1984] 1 WLR 1422. Once she was eighteen, an injunction was successfully sought protecting her identity on the ground of the action in confidence: *X, A Woman Formerly Known as Mary Bell, Y* v. *SO, News Group Newspapers Ltd and Mirror Group Newspapers Ltd* [2003] 2 FCR 686.

[36] See e.g. *Nottingham CC* v. *October Films* [1999] 2 FLR 347; *Kelly* v. *BBC* [2001] 1 FLR 197.

[37] However, the fact that the information in question has remained confidential may influence the courts' use of the inherent jurisdiction: see *Re Z (A Minor) (Identification: Restriction on Publication)* [1995] 4 All ER 96.

conflict, the arguments below as to the engagement of Articles 8 and 10 and the discussion of methods of resolving the conflict between them, would apply equally to the automatic reporting restrictions and to orders made under the other current powers. Reporting restrictions engage the 'privacy' of the child in the sense that the injunctions or orders are intended to protect the child's identity or other personal information. Thus, in many instances, her family life, her mental stability and her ability to form and develop relationships are also indirectly protected.[38]

In the pre-HRA era, the courts sought to establish the boundaries between media freedom (recognised as an aspect of a common law right to freedom of expression)[39] and the privacy of the child in a series of decisions, culminating in the decision in *Re Z (A Minor) (Identification: Restrictions on Publication)*.[40] It was accepted that there was no need to strive to create a balance between media freedom and privacy once it was found that the matter at issue related to 'upbringing', and so the paramountcy principle[41] applied: where it did so, it determined the issue without any doubt in favour of the child's 'welfare'.[42] However, where the reporting at issue could be viewed as unrelated directly to 'upbringing', some sort of balancing act had to be undertaken. The tendency was to allow freedom of publication to prevail due to the perceived strength of the value of freedom of expression under the common law. Where a court viewed a case as raising a genuine public interest, it was unlikely to restrain publication, or place only minimal restraints on it. In *Re W (A Minor) (Wardship: Freedom of Publication)*,[43] for instance, it was

---

[38] See *Bensaid* v. *UK* (2001) 33 EHRR 10, para. 47; *A and Byrne and Twenty-Twenty Television* v. *United Kingdom* (1998) 25 EHRR CD 159.

[39] See *R.* v. *Secretary of State for the Home Department, ex parte Simms* [1999] 3 WLR 328; *Reynolds* v. *Times Newspapers* [1999] 4 All ER 609; *Derbyshire CC* v. *Times Newspapers* [1993] AC 534.

[40] [1995] 4 All ER 961 (CA).

[41] As indicated above (text to n. 17), following s.1(1) of the Children Act 1989 (CA), the child's welfare is the court's paramount consideration when it determines any question with respect to the upbringing of the child. In *J* v. *C*, this was explained to mean: 'when all the relevant facts, relationships, claims and wishes of parents, risks, choices and other circumstances are taken into account and weighed, the course to be followed will be that which is most in the interests of the child's welfare.' [1970] AC 668, 710–11, *per* Lord McDermott.

[42] Freedom of publication can be viewed as a 'circumstance' which a responsible parent would take into account; see the discussion of this point in *Re Z (A Minor) (Freedom of Publication)* [1995] 4 All ER 961.

[43] [1992] 1 All ER 794 (CA).

found that the placing of a ward who had previously suffered homosexual abuse, with a male homosexual couple as foster parents, raised public interest questions about the fostering policy of the local authority in question and therefore the newspaper in question had a right to raise such questions, despite the fact that it was accepted as quite possible that the identity of the ward would be disclosed.[44]

An outcome even more favourable to media freedom was reached in *R. v. Central Independent Television*.[45] A programme was made depicting a police investigation into a man subsequently convicted of offences of indecency. His wife, the plaintiff, did not wish her daughter, aged five, who knew nothing of his convictions, to know what had occurred and therefore sought to have the programme altered so that it would not be possible to recognise her husband. The Court of Appeal refused the injunction, finding that the protection for the privacy of children under the inherent jurisdiction would not extend to covering publication of facts relating to those who were not carers of the child in question and which had occurred before the child was born. In other words, the limits of the protection for children's privacy were indicated: no overt balancing exercise between privacy and freedom of expression was found necessary.

These decisions were clearly beginning to establish a spectrum of categories of case covering the balance to be struck between the privacy of the child and freedom of reporting. In the leading pre-HRA case, *Re Z (A Minor) (Identification: Restrictions on Publication)*,[46] these categories were made explicit. A first category of cases was recognised in which freedom of publication would *always* prevail over the welfare of the child. These were cases, it was found, which would fall beyond the proper limit for the invocation of the wardship or inherent jurisdiction since upbringing was not in issue and the risk of harm to the child by invading her privacy could be viewed as incidental;[47] as Ward LJ put it:

---

[44] See also *Re C (A Minor) (Wardship: Medical Treatment) (No. 2)* [1990] Fam 39, 46; *Re W (A Minor) (Wardship: Restrictions on Publication)* [1995] 2 FLR 466 (CA).

[45] [1994] Fam 192.   [46] [1995] 4 All ER 961 (CA).

[47] The court compared *Re X (A Minor) (Wardship: Jurisdiction)* [1975] Fam 47 with *Re X (A Minor) (Wardship: Injunction)* [1984] 1 WLR 1422. In the first case, concerning a book about X's father, the material was not a story about her or about the way she had been brought up, except indirectly since it revealed that her father was a philanderer. By contrast, the story in 1984 about X, Mary Bell's daughter, was directly about the fact that the authorities were permitting her to be brought up by a mother who was viewed by some as too evil to be entrusted with the care of a young child. See also *Re M and N (Minors) (Wardship: Publication of Information)* [1990] Fam 211, 231; *M v. BBC* [1997] 1 FLR 51.

'the freedom of the press is so fundamental that in this category it must triumph over welfare'. A further, second, category of cases was recognised – those in which the court does not have to determine an issue relating to upbringing but where the child's privacy is directly affected. In this category, the child's interests would not be paramount and a balancing exercise had to be performed between the child's privacy and media freedom.[48] The third category covered instances where a question of the child's upbringing or of the exercise of parental responsibility *was* being determined, where the welfare of the child would be the paramount consideration, and her privacy interests would therefore trump competing free expression claims.[49]

In *Re Z* itself, the issue before the court was found to relate to the upbringing of the child. A television company wished to make a film about Z (the daughter of Cecil Parkinson and Sarah Keays) and the treatment she was receiving for her particular educational needs at a specialised institution. It was envisaged that, in demonstrating the methods and results of the institution, Z would be identified and play an active part in the film. The court found that Z would be directly involved and that the proposed publicity would be harmful to her welfare. Therefore the instance was found to fall within the third category of case since the paramountcy principle applied. The court did not therefore need to perform a balancing act and refused to vary the injunction that was already in place preventing commentary on her situation.

The Strasbourg clashing rights jurisprudence

Where rights collide, Strasbourg speaks of taking account of both and striking a fair balance under paragraph 2 of the Article pleaded before the Court.[50] While the reasoning process inevitably follows the structure

---

[48] In *Re W (Freedom of Publication)* [1992] 1 All ER 794, the child's upbringing was a central focus of the publicity, although at the same time the court did not consider that it was determining a question relating to upbringing.

[49] This occurred in *Re C (A Minor) (Wardship: Medical Treatment) (No. 2)* [1990] Fam 39 and in *Re M and N (Minors) (Wardship: Termination of Access)* [1990] Fam 211. In this category the court is seen as exercising its 'custodial' jurisdiction.

[50] See *Otto-Preminger* v. *Austria* (1994) 19 EHRR 34, paras. 47 and 49; see further H. Fenwick, 'Clashing Rights, the Welfare of the Child and the HRA' (2004) 67 MLR 888, 906–7. See also M. Tugendhat QC and I. Christie, *The Law of Privacy and the Media* (Oxford: Oxford University Press, 2002) pp. 420–1; H. Fenwick and G. Phillipson, *Media Freedom under the Human Rights Act* (Oxford: Oxford University Press, 2006), Chapter 13, pp. 690–700.

demanded by the Article(s) invoked by the applicant at Strasbourg, the other Convention right is given greater weight at the stage of determining the necessity of the interference (to support that right) in a democratic society, since it is axiomatic that all the Convention rights must be afforded a high value in such a society.

The Article 8 'family' cases on clashes of rights – where the right of the parent to family life appears to clash with that of the child – have not in general been resolved by reference to a principle of paramountcy – as that is understood domestically. Nor has it been assumed that the child's Article 8 rights can be viewed as exceptions to be narrowly construed. In *Elsholz* v. *Germany*,[51] the applicant father claimed that his Article 8 rights had been breached by the refusal of the national court to allow him access to his child. The European Court of Human Rights, in finding that a violation of the father's Article 8 rights had occurred, reiterated the principle from *Johansen* v. *Norway*[52] that a fair balance must be struck between the interests of the child and those of the parent. Similarly, in *Hansen* v. *Turkey*,[53] a case in which the mother argued that failure to enforce contact had breached her Article 8 right to respect for family life, the Court found, citing *Hokkanen*[54] and *Ignaccolo-Zenide*,[55] that, within the margin of appreciation of the member state, a fair balance must be struck between the Article 8 rights of the child and those of the parent, thereby ruling out the use of a presumption that precludes that balancing exercise, although the welfare of the child will be of especial significance.

The decisions in *Tammer* v. *Estonia*,[56] *Peck* v. *UK*[57] and *Von Hannover* v. *Germany*[58] indicate that Strasbourg is readily able to find interferences with expression justified where a competing Convention right – Article 8 – is

---

[51] [2000] 2 FLR 486.   [52] (1996) 23 EHRR 33.

[53] [2004] 1 FLR 142, App. No. 36141/97. The Court said: 'the rights and freedoms of all concerned must be taken into account, and more particularly the best interests of the child and his or her rights under Article 8 of the Convention. Where contacts with the parent might appear to threaten those interests or interfere with those rights, it is for the national authorities to strike a fair balance between them' (para. 98). Cf. the previous decision in *Yousef* v. *Netherlands* [2003] 1 FLR 210. It is argued that, bearing *Hansen* and the decision in *Hoppe* v. *Germany* (2004) 38 EHRR 15, para. 44, in mind, *Yousef* is out of line with the Court's established and continuing line of reasoning on the interests of the child.

[54] (1994) A 299-A, 22.   [55] *Reports of Judgments and Decisions* 2000-I, 265.

[56] (2003) 37 EHRR 43; (2001) 10 BHRC 543.   [57] App. No. 44647/98.

[58] App. No. 59320/00, judgment of 24 June 2004; see in particular paras. 63–6. See also Chapter 9, pp. 234–40.

at issue. In *Von Hannover*, the Court found quite readily that the private life claim should prevail since the speech in question had no public interest dimension, having the status of mere celebrity gossip. In *Peck*, the seriousness of the private life claim and the immense amount of publicity accorded to the private act in question – attempted suicide – persuaded the Court to allow Article 8 to prevail, even though the act occurred in a public space and the speech did have a public interest dimension. *N* v. *Portugal*[59] and *Barclay* v. *United Kingdom*[60] also support this stance. Indeed, the Court has made it clear that speech which is concerned only with publicising private facts, with no relevance to serious public debate, will generally be afforded a particularly low weight under Article 10, such that interferences with it to uphold Article 8 rights will almost inevitably be justified.[61]

A and Byrne and Twenty-Twenty Television v. *United Kingdom*,[62] although a decision of the Commission only, is of particular significance in this line of authority since it concerned the private life of a child and the paramountcy principle had been found to apply at the domestic level. Decided prior to *Tammer* and *Peck*, it is nevertheless in line with the findings in those decisions, and also reveals the stance taken at Strasbourg to the paramountcy principle where a clash with Article 10 arises. The clash of rights which occurred was resolved in favour of the Article 8 rights of the child (although the case was not argued in those terms), but it was also – most significantly – made clear that, even in respect of a child's welfare, Article 8 does not take *automatic* priority over Article 10. The case concerned the restriction of freedom of expression represented by the refusal to vary the injunction in *Re Z*, discussed above.

The first applicant, the child (C)'s mother, argued that the court's refusal to accept her decision that C should take part in the television programme had constituted a breach of her Article 8 right to respect for family life. The mother and the media applicants both complained of a breach of Article 10. The Commission found that, by continuing the injunctions, the domestic courts prevented all the applicants from making a television programme featuring the education and development of C in an educational and behavioural institute; it found that the continuance of the injunction by the domestic courts constituted an

---

[59] *N* v. *Portugal*, App. No. 20683/92, 20 February 1995.
[60] App. No. 35712/97 (admissibility only).   [61] See *Von Hannover*, n. 58 above.
[62] (1998) 25 EHRR CD 159.

interference with all three applicants' right to freedom of expression within the meaning of Article 10(1).

In relation to the question whether the interference could be considered 'necessary' under paragraph 2 of both Articles 8 and 10, the Commission afforded a certain margin of appreciation in assessing whether the need existed. It conducted the examination of necessity under Article 8(2) but stated that the same principles and considerations would apply under Article 10(2). The applicants submitted that the programme was of significant public interest in that it would inform the educational authorities in the United Kingdom, the families of those who suffer from similar problems as C and those sufferers themselves about other educational and behavioural methods which could significantly improve the latter's potential. The first applicant (C's mother) submitted that, since her decision to allow C to participate in the television programme was taken in good faith, for C's benefit, and with the proper advice, the courts should have followed her decision unless they found it irrational or in bad faith.

The Commission found that it was for the national authorities to strike a fair balance between the relevant competing interests: what would be decisive would be whether the national authorities had made such efforts 'as can be reasonably demanded under the special circumstances of the case' to accommodate the parents' rights.[63] The Commission took into account the fact that the applicant had jointly applied for the first of the injunctions under consideration with the express intention of protecting the privacy of C, and also the High Court's conclusion that the 'overwhelming probability' was that the transmission of the programme would attract extended secondary tabloid publicity largely because of C's parents' high profile. The High Court had taken the view that any short-term benefit for C deriving from the publicity was outweighed by the 'serious consequences' which transmission of the programme would entail for her. The Commission concluded that, in the circumstances of the present case and in view of the margin of appreciation accorded to states in this area, the imposition by the courts of their view as to the best interests of C was supported by 'relevant' as well as 'sufficient' reasons. The domestic courts had made such efforts as could be reasonably demanded to accommodate the first applicant's rights and the interference was accordingly proportionate to

---

[63] *Olsson* v. *Sweden (No. 2)* (1994) 17 EHRR 134, para. 90; and *Hokkanen* v. *Finland* (1995) 19 EHRR 139, para. 57.

the legitimate aim pursued. The restriction was not therefore found to create a breach of Article 10 or – on the particular facts – of the Article 8 right to family life of the mother. The Commission added that the High Court considered that, if it had had to carry out a balancing exercise (for the purposes of Article 10 of the Convention or otherwise) between the welfare of C and the public interest in the programme, it would have 'firmly seen the scales as coming down in favour of there being an order against the programme being made'. Importantly, the Commission did *not* find that, where the UK courts had applied the paramountcy principle, the media's right should be narrowly interpreted or disregarded to avoid an invasion of the child's interests (viewed as aspects of her Article 8 rights).

These decisions, especially those in *Von Hannover* and *Peck*, reveal the stance at Strasbourg in relation to clashes of the qualified rights and particularly to conflicts between Articles 10 and 8. It is clear that neither Article can be viewed as having presumptive priority where such conflicts occur. The protection of both rights is viewed, axiomatically, as necessary in a democratic society. In applying the test of proportionality, Strasbourg engages in something akin to a speech/privacy balancing exercise in which a fairly broad margin of appreciation may be conceded to the national authorities. But the Court is *not* prepared to leave the national authorities with a wide discretion as to the precise balance to be struck in the member state between the two rights where, as in *Von Hannover*, the values underlying one of them are barely engaged, while the other is quite strongly engaged. Thus the Court may be prepared to adopt quite an intensively scrutinising stance when dealing with the proportionality question in relation to clashes of the materially qualified rights.[64]

Clashes between media free expression claims under Article 10 and the child's private and family life under Article 8 in the Human Rights Act era

After the Human Rights Act came into force, a court, in considering a clash between a restriction on publicity – deriving from statute or otherwise – and the private and family life of a child, became bound to

---

[64]   See H. Fenwick and G. Phillipson, *Media Freedom under the Human Rights Act* (Oxford: Oxford University Press, 2006), Chapter 13, pp. 690–700.

adhere to the Convention rights under s.6(1)[65] and had to take the Convention jurisprudence into account under s.2.[66] Under s.12(4), the court had to have 'particular regard' to Article 10. Thus the courts in exercising their inherent discretion to protect children also had to abide by all the Convention rights. Where a restriction on publication was statutory, s.3(1) HRA also required its reinterpretation if necessary, and if at all possible, in order to ensure its compatibility with the rights. The paramountcy principle itself as encapsulated in s.1(1) CA became theoretically subject to such reinterpretation under s.3(1) HRA.

In relation to the inherent jurisdiction, as the cases discussed from the pre-HRA era reveal, the courts had established a method of dealing with conflicts between the child's welfare and media freedom that largely excluded cases involving 'upbringing' from the battleground. It was only in respect of the second category of cases – where the child's privacy was at stake and at risk from media invasion – that the conflict had to be resolved, and in such instances, as indicated, it tended to be resolved in favour of the media, albeit with minimal restrictions on reporting. Doubtful distinctions were relied upon, as *Re Z* reveals, in pursuit of avoidance of the conflict. Once cases could be assigned to the 'upbringing' category on the one hand (the third grouping from *Re Z*) or the 'incidental' category on the other (the first grouping), conflict could be avoided. The general academic view was that adoption of these approaches had led to a failure to deal satisfactorily with the issues of both privacy and free speech at the level of principle.[67] That failure appeared to spring from the resistance of the courts, especially the Family Division, to the notion of individual rights as opposed to welfare.[68]

However, the somewhat simplistic or mechanistic analysis from *Re Z* was thrown into jeopardy by the inception of the Human Rights Act, since where the third category was applicable the Article 10 guarantee was almost automatically abrogated, while, where the first or second applied, the Article 8 rights of the child were likely to be afforded no or insufficient weight. The pre-HRA treatment of both rights appeared

---

[65] Since courts are public authorities under s.6(3)(a).

[66] The jurisprudence is non-binding.

[67] See I. Cram, 'Minors' Privacy, Free Speech and the Courts' [1997] PL 410; L. Woods, 'Freedom of Expression and the Protection of Minors' (2001) 13 *Child and Family Law Quarterly* 209.

[68] See Butler-Sloss LJ in *Re L (A Child) (Contact: Domestic Violence)* [2001] Fam 260 (CA), para. 294.

therefore to become inconsistent with the courts' duty under s.6(1) HRA and also with the interpretative obligation under s.3(1): it might have been expected that s.3(1) would be used to reinterpret the paramountcy principle under s.1(1) CA so that Article 10 no longer suffered automatic abrogation where restrictions on publication related to upbringing.

In what follows certain significant decisions are examined in which the *Re Z* categories were considered in the light of the HRA. However, by subtly manipulating the concept of 'upbringing', either under s.3(1) HRA or by using ordinary principles of interpretation, the courts have managed so far to avoid confronting the most difficult question of all – the compatibility of the paramountcy principle as currently conceived with Article 10. Instead, the courts have succeeded in confining themselves to considering instances falling within the middle category from *Re Z* – wherein a balancing act between the two interests could be performed. But, even in conducting that less difficult exercise, unsatisfactory reasoning processes were followed since there was, at least initially, a reluctance to accord Article 8 its status as a fully fledged Convention right, once it came into conflict with Article 10.

Initial stance: Article 8 rights of children as exceptions under Article 10(2)

The European Convention on Human Rights did not play a significant part in the decisions considered so far since, despite increasing reliance on the Convention in other areas of law pre-HRA,[69] the Family Division was content to balance media freedom against the child's welfare on the basis of common law understandings of those values. In *Kelly* v. *BBC*,[70] however, the imminent inception of the Human Rights Act influenced the court to take Article 10 of the Convention fully into account. The case concerned a boy of 16, Kelly, who was made a ward of court after he disappeared from home to join a religious cult group. The BBC obtained an interview with him, but an order restraining publication of the detail of any report or interview with him or with members of the religious group was made, which the BBC challenged. It was accepted by both sides that the case was one in which the court did have jurisdiction to

---

[69] See e.g. the Court of Appeal decision in *Derbyshire CC* v. *Times Newspapers* [1993] AC 534.

[70] [2001] 1 All ER 323; [2001] 2 WLR 253; [2001] Fam 59.

grant injunctive relief. The dispute between the parties was as to whether the case fell within the second or third of the three categories identified in *Re Z*. Clearly, if it was found to fall within the third, the paramountcy principle would apply and the interest in freedom of expression would be almost automatically overcome. Therefore it was crucial for counsel for the BBC to convince the court that the case fell within the second category and then to argue that the injunction could not be justified as necessary in a democratic society, under Article 10(2).

The court did not find it entirely easy to decide what distinguishes cases in the second category from those in the third. Clearly, this turned on the meaning assigned to the term 'upbringing'.[71] Munby J concluded:

> Upbringing . . . involves a process in which the parent, or other person *in loco parentis*, is the subject and of which the child is the object . . . S.1(1)(a) CA therefore applies only to those processes or actions of which the child is the object, and not to those in which the child is the subject.

Munby J went on to find that *Re Z* had created a distinction between cases such as *Re W*, in which four boys without their father's involvement had given interviews to journalists, and cases in which the parent actively encourages or brings about the involvement of the child with the media. *Re Z*, he found, fell within the latter category in which the child is the object since, as he put it, referring to the words of Ward LJ, Z's mother wished to 'bring up her child as one who will play an active part in a television film'. The *Re W* case was viewed as similar to the instant one since Kelly had given the interview without the involvement of his grandmother or mother. The case was therefore viewed as one not involving upbringing and as a result as within the second category; the paramountcy principle was inapplicable and therefore a 'so-called balancing exercise has to be performed'.[72]

In considering the claim of freedom of expression as compared with the need to safeguard the welfare of the child, Munby J pointed out that this exercise had in general been carried out in an unsatisfactory fashion in the Family Division due to its 'child-centred' approach.[73] He found that there was no question of 'balancing' freedom of expression against

---

[71] See *Re Z* [1995] 4 All ER 961, para. 29.   [72] [2001] 1 All ER 323, 341.

[73] 'As Thorpe LJ [noted] in *In Re G (Celebrities: Publicity)* [1999] 1 FLR 409, 418 . . . Hoffmann LJ rightly said in his judgment in *R* v. *Central Independent Television plc* there is an inevitable tendency for the Family Division judge at first instance to give too much weight to welfare and too little weight to freedom of speech.'

one or more of the interests identified in paragraph 2 of Article 10: those
who sought to bring themselves within the protection of paragraph 2
had to demonstrate convincingly that the protection applied. He went
on to find that the arguments in favour of suppressing the interview
were not sufficiently convincing.[74] Since the arguments were fairly
evenly balanced, and he had already found that Article 10(2) places the
burden on those seeking to make the case for interference with freedom
of expression, he determined that injunctive relief could not be justified.
He further found that the grant of an injunction framed as widely as the
one he was being invited to make would have been wholly disproportionate to any aim that could legitimately be pursued on Kelly's behalf.

A similar instance arose in *In the Matter of X (A Child)*,[75] but the
significant difference was that in the few months since *Kelly* the HRA had
come into force. It prompted the court to go even further than *Kelly* had
done in accepting the primacy of media freedom once it was free to do so,
having once again succeeded in excluding the instance from the third
'upbringing' category.[76] The court proceeded to make the important finding, foreshadowed in *Kelly*, that, while the exercise of its discretion had been
referred to many times before October 2000 as a balancing exercise, such an
exercise was no longer appropriate after the coming into force of the HRA.
The court determined that it must rely on s.12(4) HRA and Article 10 in
reaching its decision, and went on to find: '[This] is not a balancing exercise
in which the scales are evenly positioned at the commencement of the
exercise. On the contrary, the scales are weighted at the beginning so that
Article 10 prevails unless one of the defined derogations applies when given
a narrow interpretation.' The application was, however, granted on the
basis that the injunction was too wide and it was varied accordingly. The
same stance was taken in *Medway Council* v. *BBC*[77] in an instance which

---

[74] It had been argued, *inter alia*, that Kelly would find it harder to reconcile himself with
his family if the interview were broadcast. Munby J found that the argument that further
publicity might be in his best interests was as plausible as the contrary argument put
forward – that it would be opposed to them.

[75] [2001] 1 FCR 541.

[76] A newspaper publisher had applied for an order to vary an injunction granted to the
local authority restraining foster parents from disclosing to the newspaper information
concerning the local authority's policies in respect of trans-racial fostering. Relying on
the analysis of Munby J in *Kelly*, Bracewell J found that in this instance the child should
be viewed as the subject of the process of upbringing, not the object, since the issue
before the court concerned restrictions on media reporting of issues alleged to be raised
by the child's history.

[77] [2002] 1 FLR 104.

once again was not found to involve a question of upbringing – the scales were weighted so that Article 10 prevailed, subject to an application of one of the derogations, narrowly defined.[78] Interestingly, a narrow construction under s.3(1)HRA of s.1(1) CA, allowing the case to be excluded from the 'upbringing' category, was found to accord with the demands of Article 10 and s.12(4) HRA.[79]

Although the recognition of the importance of media freedom in *Kelly*, *In the Matter of X* and *Medway Council* was arguably welcome, when compared to the possibility of an *over*-protective child-centred approach, the analysis in relation to Articles 8 and 10 in this line of authority was quite clearly flawed. This approach meant that Article 8 lost 'its Convention status as a fully fledged right, becoming instead merely a narrowly interpreted exception to the right of freedom of expression'.[80] But, conversely, it is also hard to reconcile *dicta* in this line of authority with the Convention under the HRA since it assumes that, where the paramountcy principle *is* found to apply, Article 10 can be almost automatically abrogated. However, judicial recognition of a need for a proper resolution of the conflict between Articles 8 and 10 in this context under the HRA where the principle does *not* apply was apparent in the most authoritative decision to touch on the issues raised in *Kelly* and in *Re X*.

Re S: acceptance of presumptive equality and recognition of the 'difficult balancing exercise' to be conducted

In *Re S (A Child)*,[81] the Court of Appeal had to adjudicate on an appeal against an order made by Hedley J in the Family Division of the High Court.[82] The appeal raised a short but difficult point: 'can or should the court [under the inherent jurisdiction] restrain the publication of the

---

[78] The case concerned the inherent jurisdiction of the court to restrain a broadcast of a consented-to interview with a boy of thirteen who had been made one of the first subjects of an anti-social behaviour order.

[79] Para. 29.

[80] See H. Fenwick and G. Phillipson, 'Breach of Confidence as a Privacy Remedy in the Human Rights Act Era' (2000) 63 MLR 660, 686.

[81] [2003] 2 FCR 577; (2003) 147 SJLB 873. See also *Harris* v. *Harris* [2001] 2 FLR 895, in which, while there was no detailed consideration of the balancing exercise between Article 10 (and 11) on the one hand and Article 8 on the other, Munby J accepted (at para. 384) that the approach adopted by Sedley LJ in *Douglas* v. *Hello!* [2001] QB 967 should be followed in which Article 10 was *not* given presumptive priority.

[82] 19 February 2003.

identity of a defendant and her victim in a murder trial to protect the privacy of her son who is the subject of care proceedings?' The victim was S's brother, and there was psychiatric evidence to the effect that S, as an already vulnerable child, would suffer greater trauma and be at greater risk of later mental illness if he was subjected to bullying and harassment at school once the identity of his mother became known. Hedley J made an interim order restraining reporting that would identify S but modified it to include in paragraph 8 the proviso that: 'Nothing in this order shall of itself prevent any person (a) publishing any particulars of or information relating to any part of the proceedings before any court other than a court sitting in private.' At the *inter partes* hearing, the newspapers argued that they should be able to publish the names and photographs of both parents and of S's dead brother. In particular, they wanted to publish photographs of S's brother with his mother. Since S was the same age as his brother was when he died and they resembled each other, the photographs would indirectly identify S. The judge decided that the exception in paragraph 8(a) should remain in the order.

On appeal by the child, the Court of Appeal found, unanimously, that the question before them did *not* concern a matter of upbringing since, as Hale LJ found: 'In deciding whether or not to make this order, the court is not exercising its jurisdiction over how CS is to be brought up. That is being done in the care proceedings. Nor is it deciding how any aspect of parental responsibility should be met.'[83] Therefore, this was not an instance in which the paramountcy principle applied. Interestingly, the first-instance judge had considered that, even if the child's welfare *had* been the paramount consideration, he would have decided in the same way. The Court of Appeal disagreed, Hale LJ finding that, when the child's welfare *is* the paramount consideration, 'it rules on or determines the issue before the court. *It* is the trump card' (emphasis in the original).[84]

Despite this finding, it must be asked whether *Re S* was not in fact concerned with upbringing, albeit indirectly. According to the evidence of an expert psychologist, S was more likely to suffer mental illness due to the results of the publicity, and the father, who was his main carer,

---

[83] As she put it: 'Parents cannot prohibit press reporting of criminal proceedings in order to protect their children from harm, however much they might like to be able to do so' (para. 22).

[84] Para. 62, *per* Hale LJ.

would have to deal with those effects. If the child had to move school or home due to bullying after the publicity, that would again affect his upbringing. Perhaps most pertinently of all, the placement of the child with the father was also likely to be affected by the publicity since the father was barely coping with the situation and might have failed to cope with further stress and trauma suffered by an already vulnerable child as a result of the publicity. S might have encountered it himself since he might have seen articles and pictures in the media about his dead brother and his mother. He was also likely to suffer harassment and teasing at school once the identity of his mother and further details of the crime became more widely known, during the period of the trial. That was also the period during which his own trauma and stress due to the loss of his brother were likely to be at their height. In comparison, the upbringing of the child in *Re Z* was unlikely to be directly affected to her detriment or as an indirect effect of the broadcasting of the documentary, although possibly she might have become aware of secondary publicity as a result of it. Thus the only way in which the documentary could have been detrimentally linked to Z's upbringing would have been via the ultimate effects of the publicity. This was also the case in *Re S*. The only difference between the two instances was that in the one instance the child was directly involved in the documentary, while in the other the child was not directly the subject of the press coverage. Taking account of the view of the mother in *Re Z* that the child would *benefit* from participation in the documentary, while all those involved in S's upbringing, and expert opinion, considered that the media coverage would be extremely detrimental to him, it is suggested that the distinction between direct and indirect effects on 'upbringing' is a spurious one.

The *Re S* findings also indicate that it is very unlikely that the welfare principle will ever be found to apply in these instances of indirect effects on upbringing via media reporting. This is clearly the preferred course for the *courts* since it avoids a problematic conflict between s.1(1) CA and Article 10. But it might also mean that the courts are likely to be reluctant to focus too strongly on the effect of reporting on the family and private life of a child, since so doing appears to draw the effects on upbringing back into the equation. It creates tension in the decision since at one stage in the reasoning upbringing is excluded, but at a later stage it potentially re-enters the reasoning process when the private and family life claim is being balanced against the speech claim. This is precisely what occurred, as discussed below, in the House of Lords decision in *Re S*. The better solution, considered further below, is to reinterpret the welfare principle under s.3(1) HRA in order to avoid a conflict with Article 10 and to accept a broad definition of the term 'upbringing'. So doing might encourage the courts to focus strongly on the effects of reporting on upbringing, meaning that the significant issues truly at stake under the private and family life claim manage to obtain a hearing.

The 'ECHR jurisdiction'

Having found that the welfare principle did not apply, the Court of Appeal went on to find that the case fell within the scope of the inherent jurisdiction of the High Court.[85] But, following the House of Lords decision in Re S,[86] it is no longer necessary in these cases to show that the inherent jurisdiction applies. The House of Lords in Re S found unanimously that, since the 1998 Act came into force, the earlier case-law about the *existence* and scope of inherent jurisdiction did not have to be considered in the instant case or in 'similar cases'. Lord Steyn said: 'The foundation of the jurisdiction to restrain publicity in a case such as the present is now derived from convention rights under the ECHR.'[87] In other words, the jurisdiction is not the 'vehicle' allowing for the balancing exercise to occur – the Convention rights themselves provide the vehicle. At first glimpse, this looks like the creation of a form of direct horizontal effect, discussed in Chapter 6, since it would appear that in relation to assertions of a need for restraint to protect the privacy of the child there would be no need for the inherent jurisdiction even to *exist*. Further, the rights under the HRA would not be expected to deliver less than the existing cause of action which could have acted as the vehicle for their delivery. Possibly they could deliver *more* and that would then represent a form of direct horizontal effect since this would mean that there would not be an infusion of the right into the existing cause of action, but a replacement of that existing cause with an extended protection based only on the rights. In other words, Lord Steyn appeared to be stating that the technicalities of the inherent jurisdiction can be discarded and its place taken by the Convention rights. That would be direct horizontal effect as normally understood – the creation of a new cause of action allowing private parties to rely on the rights against each other. There would be no need to rely on an existing cause of action – as was thought to be the case in *Campbell*[88] – in the context of privacy generally.

---

[85] Para. 40.   [86] N. 3 above.   [87] Para. 23.
[88] [2004] 2 WLR 1232; see further Chapter 9, pp. 220–40.

But this part of Lord Steyn's judgment is highly problematic since it was ambiguously expressed; it might appear that *adults* could seek to rely on it in instances in which the action for breach of confidence would not be available, but where a Convention right – normally Article 8 – arguably applies. The obvious example would be in harassment cases where there are difficulties in relying on the Protection from Harassment Act 1997. However, leaving aside the question of Article 8's applicability to harassment, it is suggested that Lord Steyn did not intend that the new 'ECHR jurisdiction' could be extended to adults. The true explanation for the creation of the new jurisdiction is, it is contended, that the court is taking the place of the state in terms of protecting the child and that in this instance alone a form of direct horizontal effect has been created since there is little to be gained in seeking to distinguish the courts' duty under s.6 HRA from its duty under the inherent jurisdiction. It is arguable that at the international level the Convention allows for vindication of the right to private life in instances (such as adopting intrusive means in order to obtain information)[89] where the Human Rights Act provides for no such vindication, due to its inherent limitations – the need to find a public authority to sue, or an existing cause of action, or an applicable statutory provision. But Lord Steyn's remarks, ambiguous as they were, do not appear to provide a basis for affording Article 8 an ability to operate beyond those limitations, at the domestic level. The only instance in which, conceivably, a cause of action could arise outside those limitations after *Re S*, would be one where, had it arisen in the past, the child's welfare would have been viewed as so doubtfully at stake that the inherent jurisdiction could not have been found to apply but where, now, Article 8 could be viewed as applicable.

Thus the simple question in this context is now: is the child's Article 8 right engaged? If it is, it must be balanced against the media's Article 10 right, on the *Campbell* model, as discussed below.

The balancing act between Articles 8 and 10

The Court of Appeal decision in *Re S* is of significance in relation to the balancing act, and its findings that *in general* this balancing act should

---

[89] See *Von Hannover v. Germany*, App. No. 59320/00; the use of intrusive methods by reporters appeared to play a part in the decision to find that a breach of Article 8 had occurred.

occur were not disputed in the Lords. Indeed, they were strongly reaffirmed. Having found that the inherent jurisdiction applied, the Court of Appeal then found, not without difficulty, that the case fell within the second category from *Re Z*. It was found that the 'information in the case lay somewhere in between that in *Re X* and *R.* v. *Central Television* and that in *Re M and N* or *Re W*'.[90] The proposed publication did not relate directly to S's current upbringing. But equally it did not constitute 'the sort of remote and unconnected information about a deceased or long-absent parent' at issue in *Re X* and *R.* v. *Central Independent Television plc*. The reports related to recent events in his family life and therefore could be expected to have a real bearing on his future upbringing.

There was a further important aspect of the case – the information related to the identity of the defendant and her alleged victim in a murder trial. But it was concluded, relying on *ex parte Crook*,[91] that the important public interest in the identification of defendants, in particular those found guilty of serious crimes, can be outweighed in certain circumstances by the need to protect those affected by the crime from further harm. It was accepted that Article 6(1) would not be breached by the concealment of the defendant's identity: it was found that its importance lay in the relationship between the values it protects – the furtherance of the transparency of the administration of justice[92] – and the right to freedom of expression under Article 10(1). Unhampered media reports would play a part in safeguarding the public character of justice. Thus Article 6(1) provided an added dimension in the case.

In seeking to weigh up Articles 8 and 10 against each other, the Court of Appeal found, in a highly significant break with the previous line of authority, that they must be considered as independent elements, on the basis, following *Douglas* v. *Hello!*[93] and *A* v. *B plc*,[94] that s.12(4) HRA does not give one pre-eminence over the other. Having found that the two rights should be considered on a basis of presumptive equality, it was then clearly necessary to conduct a *dual* exercise in proportionality. In other words, Hale LJ found that it was not merely necessary to consider Article 8 as an exception to Article 10 under Article 10(2); it was also necessary to consider Article 10 as an exception to Article 8,

---

[90] Para. 37.
[91] [1995] 1 WLR 139. In that instance, it was found that the likely harm to the surviving children of the defendants outweighed the effect on freedom of expression created by the restrictions on publication.
[92] *Diennet* v. *France* (1995) 21 EHRR 554, para. 33, was referred to.
[93] [2001] QB 967, 1005, para. 24.   [94] [2003] QB 195; [2003] 3 WLR 542, para. 6.

under Article 8(2). She began by considering the proportionality of the proposed interference with freedom of expression, and in so doing took into account not only the importance of press freedom in principle, but also the features of the case which made its exercise of especial importance. Such enhancing features were found to include: the particular importance attached to the reporting of criminal trials; the right of the public to receive the information in question; the important issues raised regarding an unusual and controversial form of child abuse and about the conduct of the world famous children's hospital in which it was allegedly allowed to take place. Thus the public interest in allowing unrestricted reporting was found to be strong. However, that was not found to mean that it was impossible to justify any restriction, however limited, under Article 10(2). The Court had to consider what restriction, if any, was needed to meet the legitimate aim of protecting the rights of S. If prohibiting publication of the family name and photographs was needed, the Court had to consider how great an impact that would in fact have upon the freedom protected by Article 10, taking into account the greater public interest in knowing the names of persons convicted of serious crime rather than of those who are merely suspected or charged.

The important step in the judicial reasoning process, in accordance with the principle of presumptive equality of the two rights, was the next one. Hale LJ then went on to consider the matter from the perspective of S's Article 8 rights, media freedom under Article 10 figuring this time as an exception to them under Article 8(2). In considering the proportionality of the proposed interference with the right of S to respect for his private and family life, she found that account had to be taken of the magnitude of the interference proposed. Factors to be taken into account included the extent to which the additional intrusion would add to the interference which had already taken place; the extent of any further harm that identifying publicity about the trial would do to the child's private and family life, in which his mental health was a 'crucial part'; the impact upon his father, other carers and his school, and the extent to which their task would be made harder by this kind of publicity, and the impact on his relationship with his mother in the short and the longer term. The nature of the publicity would be relevant in minimising the interference: prolonged identifying publicity, with photographs, during the trial, would have a far greater impact than would publicity during the rather shorter period when the family might be identified if there was a conviction. In other words, Hale LJ drew a distinction between the different periods of time during which publicity would occur, if unrestrained: the strength of the free expression claim (bolstered also by the values underlying the guarantee of open justice under Article 6(1)) would be at its greatest at the point at which the argument against publicity would be at its weakest.

Hale LJ came to the conclusion that, since the judge had not considered each Article independently, and so had not conducted the difficult balancing exercise required by the Convention, the appeal should be allowed, in order that the exercise could be properly carried out by the first-instance Family Division court. The two judges in the majority disagreed, finding that, although the balancing exercise outlined by Hale LJ should have been carried out, the result reached – that the restraining order should be discharged – would have been reached even if it had been properly carried out. They considered that the first-instance judge had not carried out the exercise correctly, but had had factors relevant to the question of proportionality under Article 8 sufficiently in mind.

Thus the Court of Appeal decision in *Re S* set out the proper approach to balancing speech/privacy claims (but only within cases in the second category from *Re Z*). This balancing act between Articles 8 and 10 – the dual exercise in proportionality, or 'parallel analysis' – was then endorsed by the House of Lords in their seminal decision in *Campbell*.[95] Lord Hoffmann said of balancing speech/privacy claims: 'There is in my view no question of automatic priority. Nor is there a presumption in favour of one rather than the other.'[96] Any other approach would probably have necessitated a declaration of the incompatibility of s.12(4) with Article 8. The subsection can now be viewed therefore either merely as a (superfluous) reminder of the demands of Article 10, or as a means of drawing in the conflicting right under Article 8 since s.12(4) clearly covers Article 10(2) as well as Article 10(1).[97]

---

[95] [2004] 2 WLR 1232; for discussion of *Campbell*, see Chapter 6.

[96] [2004] 2 WLR 1232; (2004) 154 NLJ 733; [2004] UKHL 22, para. 55. Baroness Hale (at paras. 138–41) made it clear that her own approach in *Re S* should be adopted in order to conduct the balancing exercise, and an exercise based on the presumptive equality of the two Articles was also adopted unanimously by the other Law Lords (see Lord Nicholls at paras. 19 and 18, Lord Hope at paras. 103–11 and Lord Carswell at para. 167).

[97] See Sedley LJ in *Douglas* v. *Hello!* [2001] QB 967, 1003, para. 137. Section 12(4) is not needed to perform the task of drawing Article 8 into the frame since it is performed by s.6; however, Sedley LJ's interpretation accords with the impact of s.3 (which applies to s.12(4)) and refutes the notion that s.12(4) affords presumptive priority to Article 10. Lord Hope in *Campbell* approved of this approach to s.12(4): *ibid.*, para. 111.

Arguably, the former view accords more comfortably with the notion of presumptive equality.

When the House of Lords in *Re S* reached the stage of considering the conflict between Articles 8 and 10 in its reasoning, it strongly endorsed the parallel analysis from *Campbell in general*, confirming that presumptive priority for speech where it competes with another Convention right, not a societal concern, has been decisively rejected. But Lord Steyn went on to make an ambiguous finding as to the strong general rule allowing for the reporting of criminal trials. On one possible reading of his findings, he appeared to suggest that that rule created an exception to the 'ultimate balancing test' (the parallel analysis). The rule, he found, could only be displaced by unusual or exceptional circumstances.[98] Lord Steyn's judgment is confused on this matter since at one point[99] it accepted that both Articles 8(1) and 10(1) are engaged and yet then that Hedley J's analysis should be endorsed.[100] Hedley J had considered that Article 8 would figure only as an exception to Article 10 – an implicit rejection of the parallel analysis model of reasoning. Lord Steyn found that Hedley J's approach at first instance – of affording presumptive priority to Article 10 and then allowing Article 8 to figure only as an exception to it was appropriate in this context. Clearly, as discussed above, this approach denies Article 8's status as a fully fledged Convention right, where there is a clash between private life and the reporting of criminal proceedings. For the reasons given above, and rooted in the Convention clashing rights jurisprudence, it is clear that this is the wrong approach, and that even in relation to such reporting Articles 8 and 10 should have presumptive equality. The creation of this exception is not rooted in the ECHR jurisprudence as

---

[98] Lord Steyn, para. 18: 'the ordinary rule is that the press, as the watchdog of the public, may report everything that takes place in a criminal court. I would add that in European jurisprudence and in domestic practice this is a strong rule. It can only be displaced by unusual or exceptional circumstances. It is, however, not a mechanical rule. The duty of the court is to examine with care each application for a departure from the rule by reason of rights under article 8.' He added, at para. 37: 'In my view [Hedley J] analysed the case correctly under the ECHR. Given the weight traditionally given to the importance of open reporting of criminal proceedings it was in my view appropriate for him, in carrying out the balance required by the ECHR, to begin by acknowledging the force of the argument under Article 10 before considering whether the right of the child under Article 8 *was sufficient to outweigh it*' (emphasis added). He went too far in saying that he would have come to the same conclusion even if he had been persuaded that this was a case where the child's welfare was indeed the paramount consideration under s.1(1) of the Children Act 1989. But that was not the shape of the case before him.'

[99] Paras. 26 and 28.   [100] Para. 37.

Lord Steyn appeared to think. A number of cases were cited that supported the notion of the significance accorded to the open reporting of criminal proceedings,[101] but those cases were not decided in the context of a clash with Article 8 rights. *Tammer* v. *Estonia* demonstrates that, even where a very significant form of expression is in issue, it may have to give way where a significant privacy interest arises. This could also be applied in relation to the form of expression in question in *Re S*. This point is pursued below.

So Baroness Hale's balancing test is to be used in cases where the child's Article 8 right is engaged and clashes with the media's Article 10 right, except – possibly – in instances where the reporting relates to a criminal trial and the child would be indirectly identified. In that instance, on one possible reading of Lord Steyn's judgment, Article 8 appears to figure only as an exception to Article 10; in other words, the House of Lords appeared to go back in this instance to the flawed reasoning adopted in the *Kelly* line of authority. Thus, although the Lords in *Re S* endorsed *Campbell*, there seemed to be no recognition of the fact that the decision departed from the fundamental approach of *Campbell* – that of presumptive equality.

Proper resolution of the conflict under the Human Rights Act

In the Strasbourg clashing rights cases discussed above, a careful examination of the competing claims of each right was undertaken on a basis of the equal value of the two rights.[102] It can now be said with confidence that, where the two rights collide, the notion of affording presumptive priority to Article 10 has been abandoned in favour of affording presumptive equality to the two rights.[103] Thus Hale LJ's judgment in *Re S* – endorsed by the House of Lords in *Campbell* – represents the closest approach yet, not only to a proper understanding of the method of resolving conflicts between Convention rights, but also to a partial acceptance of the need for the Family Division to confront fully the changes in judicial reasoning that the Human Rights Act necessitates.

---

[101] Para. 15.

[102] See the views of Lord Steyn and Lord Cooke in *Reynolds* v. *Times Newspapers* [1999] 4 All ER 609, 631 and 643.

[103] As pointed out in *Campbell* [2004] 2 AC 457 at para. 138, this is consistent with Resolution 1165 (1998) of the Parliamentary Assembly of the Council of Europe, para. 10, which affirms the equal value of the two rights.

It demonstrates a complete break with the mistaken approach adopted in *Kelly*, *X* and *Medway Council* in which freedom of speech was given automatic priority once it was found that the paramountcy principle did not apply. However, highly significantly, by excluding the case on somewhat doubtful grounds from the 'upbringing' category, the Court of Appeal in *Re S* backed away from a confrontation between that principle and Article 10 under the HRA. That principle, if it is to act as a 'trump card', is clearly incompatible with the Convention values. Below, the general question of the proper reconciliation of the conflict between Articles 8 and 10, even where upbringing *is* in issue, or where the child's privacy is only indirectly or inferentially affected, is considered in more detail in relation to all reporting restrictions designed to protect children.

The path forward does not involve, it is argued, continuing to refine the definition of upbringing almost out of existence in this context by the use of exclusionary interpretations under s.3(1) HRA so as to avoid invoking the paramountcy principle (as in *Re S* or *Medway Council*) in order to avoid the difficult questions raised in a conflict with Article 10. Instead, it involves redefining the paramountcy principle under s.3(1) so that, even where it *is* in play, the conflict between Articles 8 and 10 can be properly resolved. At present, resolution of the conflict is merely precluded since, due to the effect of the absolutist presumption of the principle, the Article 8 right to respect for family life of the child[104] will – in effect – always win out where it clashes with Article 10, thereby denying Article 10's status as an individual right. It will be argued below that the Strasbourg approach to clashes between Articles 8 and 10 not only indicates that the paramountcy principle as currently conceived is incompatible with the demands of the HRA, but also underpins and confirms the *Re S* and *Campbell* approach – that Article 10 should not be afforded presumptive priority where the principle does not apply.

The House of Lords in *Re S* endorsed the presumptive equality approach espoused in *Campbell*, but then, on one reading of the findings, appeared to create an exception to it on the basis of the weight traditionally given to the importance of the open reporting of criminal proceedings. However, the more satisfactory explanation of Lord Steyn's judgment in *Re S* was adopted in a significant subsequent case in the

---

[104] It has been accepted in a number of the domestic cases that the welfare of the child can be viewed as an aspect of his or her Article 8 rights. See e.g. *Medway Council* v. *BBC* [2002] 1 FLR 104, para. 29.

High Court, *Re W (Children)*.[105] In that instance, the mother of two children (T, aged 3, and R, aged 6 months), who was HIV positive, had pleaded guilty to knowingly infecting the father of R with HIV; she was awaiting sentence under s.20 of the Offences Against the Person Act. It was apparent that the children were likely to suffer the hostility of the community if it was thought that they might be infected by the disease and their connection with the criminal trial of their mother was fully revealed. It seemed quite possible that their long-term care placement would be jeopardised. The local council therefore sought an injunction to restrict publicity relating to the trial which might connect the children to it. As in *Re S*, the injunction was intended to conceal the identity of the defendant and victim in the trial in order to protect the children, indirectly. Thus the facts of the two cases were very similar.

The President of the Family Division in *Re W* had to determine how to reconcile Lord Steyn's findings as to the presumptive equality of Articles 8 and 10 with his finding as to the strong general rule relating to the open justice principle. As indicated above, it appeared on one reading of Lord Steyn's findings that Article 10 was to be viewed as having presumptive priority where reporting relating to criminal trials was concerned. However, the President managed to find an explanation of Lord Steyn's findings that allowed Articles 8 and 10 to be balanced against each other on a basis of equality:

> the starting point is presumptive parity, in that neither article has pre-cedence over or 'trumps' the other. The exercise of parallel analysis requires the court to examine the justification for interfering with each right and the issue of proportionality is to be considered in respect of each. It is not a mechanical exercise to be decided upon the basis of rival generalities. An intense focus on the comparative importance of the specific rights being claimed in the individual case is necessary before the ultimate balancing test in terms of proportionality is carried out. Having so stated, Lord Steyn strongly emphasised the interest in open justice as a factor to be accorded great weight in both the parallel analysis and the ultimate balancing test . . . However, nowhere did he indicate that the weight to be accorded to the right freely to report criminal proceed-ings would invariably be determinative of the outcome.[106]

---

[105] *A Local Authority* v. *(1) W (2) L (3) W (4) T and R (by the Children's Guardian)* [2005] EWHC Fam 1564.
[106] N. 3 above, para. 53.

In other words, the President interpreted Lord Steyn's findings as meaning that the interest in reporting criminal trials would always be a very weighty factor on the Article 10 side of the balancing act, and very strong Article 8 arguments would have to arise in order for the Article 8 interest to prevail. It is possible that in many – but not all – instances, a clash such as that in *Re S* would result in an outcome favouring Article 10 due to the strength of the open justice principle, but the parallel analysis should still be conducted. The value of reporting criminal trials would be a factor weighing heavily in the balance when conducting it. Thus the discussion will proceed on the basis that Lord Steyn's judgment need not be viewed as creating an exception to the principle of presumptive equality between Articles 8 and 10.

The adoption of presumptive equality means that there are also difficulties in reconciling the findings in the *first* category of cases from *Re Z* with the demands of Article 8 since in that category the privacy of the child is always unable to overcome the freedom of expression claim. *Central Independent Television plc*[107] is the leading authority establishing the boundaries of the inherent jurisdiction of the court in this context. In his judgment, Hoffmann LJ expressed great reservations about any judge-made encroachments upon freedom of speech other than where there were restrictions sanctioned by common law or statute; the principle of a free press was, he found, more important than 'the misery of a five year old child'.[108] His point was not that freedom of expression inevitably overcomes other claims, but that, where no legal restriction already applies, judges should not seek to create one due to the primacy of freedom of expression. However, post-HRA, since the court is a public authority under s.6(1) HRA, it must, in determining *both* the applicability of its inherent jurisdiction and the manner of its exercise, adhere to the demands of Article 8[109] – demands, that is, that could now be viewed in part as aspects of an autonomous *domestic* human rights jurisprudence. As Lord Nicholls said in *Campbell*: 'The values embodied in Articles 8 and 10 are as much applicable in disputes between individuals or between an individual and a non-governmental body such as a newspaper as they are in disputes between individuals and a public authority. In reaching this conclusion it is not necessary to pursue the controversial question

---

[107] [1994] Fam 192.   [108] *Ibid.*, 204.
[109] This at least has been accepted in the area of law with which this chapter is concerned. For discussion of the horizontal effect issue generally, see Chapter 6.

whether the European Convention itself has this wider effect.'[110] The House of Lords' decision in *Re S* in a sense endorsed this approach since it demanded abandonment of the reliance on the inherent jurisdiction in favour of reliance on the Convention rights. Therefore, if a child had an Article 8(1) claim to respect for his or her private life, even if previously the inherent jurisdiction would have been inapplicable, a cause of action appears to arise and the claim has to be tested against the competing Article 10 claim of the media. The problem, however, with speaking of the application of the ECHR jurisdiction, or indeed the extension of the inherent jurisdiction in reliance on s.6 HRA, is that, as touched on earlier, tension between accepting indirect horizontal effect and creating direct effect arises. If it is assumed, in any event, that a cause of action arises, it is clear that, as the Article 8 claim is weak, the Article 10 claim will probably prevail, but this should not be an *automatic* presumption.

Denying the primacy of Article 8, reconfiguring the paramountcy principle and abandoning the *Re Z* categories

Ironically, although the theoretical underpinnings of the paramountcy principle and of Article 8 differ markedly,[111] the principle affords in effect automatic priority to the child's Article 8 rights where matters of upbringing are found to be in issue: had it been found to apply in *Re S*, it would have determined the matter automatically in favour of the Article 8 right. While the Court of Appeal accepted in *Re S* that the presumptive priority approach to Article 10 is flawed and that the two rights must be equally valued, it went on to create impliedly an exception to the principle of presumptive equality which in effect accorded automatic rather than presumptive priority to Article 8 through the operation of the paramountcy principle. The next step to be taken is to recognise the flaws in this approach and to undertake a reinterpretation of the principle in accordance with the demands of the HRA. Such an approach

---

[110] [2004] 2 WLR 1232, paras. 17 and 18. (But see now the post-*Campbell* decision in *Von Hannover* v. *Germany*, App. No. 59320/00, discussed above, which confirmed that the Convention does have this effect.)

[111] There is general acceptance among family lawyers that s.1(1) CA, as it is currently interpreted, reflects a predominantly utilitarian or consequentialist approach. See e.g. S. Harris-Short, in H. Fenwick, D. Bonner and S. Harris-Short, 'Judicial Approaches to the HRA' (2003) 52 ICLQ 549, 580: she speaks of the 'utilitarian welfare' approach of s.1(1).

is supported by the emerging domestic abandonment of presumptive priority for Article 10: if accordance of priority to Article 10 in relation to Article 8 is flawed, it would be inconsistent to continue to accept an unbalanced approach by affording priority to *Article 8* in conflicts with Article 10. *A fortiori*, an approach affording *automatic* priority to Article 8 must be rejected.

Such a stance accords with the Strasbourg decisions discussed above and clearly calls into question the paramountcy principle itself and the *Re Z* categories. Although the categories were developed in the context of the exercise of the inherent jurisdiction of the courts, they have also been referred to as offering guidance in relation to other such restrictions.[112] The decision of the Commission in *Twenty-Twenty Television* gives important guidance under s.2 HRA to domestic courts in situations in which a clash of rights arises, but the child's upbringing *is* in question. The decision, due largely to the margin of appreciation conceded to the domestic courts, fails to confront fully and directly the issue of paramountcy and the automatic abrogation of Article 10 rights envisaged in the Court of Appeal decision in *Re Z*. It takes the stance that, since the same outcome would have been reached taking freedom of expression into account, the absolutist stance of the Court of Appeal, underpinned by the paramountcy principle, did not lead to a breach of Article 10. But, most significantly, the Commission made it clear that the restriction had to be justified within the tests under Article 10(2), thereby implicitly rejecting the paramountcy principle as interpreted domestically and the approach taken in the Court of Appeal in relation to the third category of cases that *Re Z* established. This is in accordance with the settled Strasbourg stance on this matter where clashes between Articles 8 and 10 arise. Where a settled stance can be discerned at Strasbourg, the domestic courts are expected to follow the jurisprudence.[113]

In the post-HRA domestic cases considered here, the tests under Article 10(2) would not have been applicable had the paramountcy principle applied, since it would have operated as a 'trump card': its impact on media freedom would not have had to be justified as

---

[112] See *Oxfordshire CC v. L and F* [1997] 1 FLR 235.
[113] Lord Slynn in *R. (on the Application of Alconbury Developments Ltd) v. Secretary of State for the Environment* [2001] 2 WLR 1389 found: 'In the absence of some special circumstances it seems to me that the court should follow any clear and constant jurisprudence of the European Court of Human Rights.'

necessary and proportionate to the aim pursued – protecting the child's privacy. It may be concluded that, even where a child's upbringing as currently understood is in question, restrictions on reporting must be justified as necessary in a democratic society and as proportionate to the legitimate aim – of protecting the child's privacy – pursued (under the 'rights of others' rubric): a balancing exercise must be conducted. Since the paramountcy principle as currently understood and as applied in *Re Z* – creating the third category of cases – is not compatible with the application of those tests, a declaration of incompatibility under s.4 HRA between s.1(1) CA and Article 10 could be made in a case impossible to exclude from that category, even where s.3(1) HRA was employed to narrow down the meaning of the term 'upbringing'. The case for such a declaration is even stronger than that arising in respect of incompatibility between s.12(4) HRA and Article 8 since the paramountcy principle has a greater abrogating effect on Article 10 than s.12(4) has on Article 8.

The better alternative would be to bring s.3(1) to bear on the principle itself rather than on the term 'upbringing'. The principle could be reconfigured under s.3(1) as an aspect of the child's Article 8 rights, and one that has a highly significant weight, but which is not *paramount*. Given the strength of the interpretative obligation under s.3(1), it is argued that the word 'paramount' can be interpreted as conveying the notion of *primacy*, rather than the meaning the courts have so far given it under the CA, whereby it has in reality meant 'sole'.[114] This reinterpretation of the term 'paramount' would be consistent with the requirements of Article 3(1) of the UN Convention on the Rights of the Child (CRC), under which the best interests of the child are a 'primary', not a paramount, consideration.[115] It follows from this argument that the Article 8 rights of the child would no longer need to be afforded, in effect, automatic priority where a matter of upbringing is at stake; they would be approached on a basis of presumptive equality with Article 10 claims. The term 'upbringing' would not need to be narrowed down or

[114] See S. Choudhry, 'The Adoption and Children Act 2002, the Welfare Principle and the HRA 1998: A Missed Opportunity' (2003) 15 *Child and Family Law Quarterly* 119, 138. She prefers the term 'pre-eminency'.

[115] The CRC has not been incorporated into domestic law, but UK judges are entitled to have regard to it in interpreting legislation on the assumption that Parliament would not have intended to legislate contrary to the UK's international legal obligations. The European Court of Human Rights also uses the CRC as a guide to the interpretation of children's rights under Article 8 (see e.g. *Johansen* v. *Norway* (1996) 23 EHRR 33).

afforded obscure or distorted interpretations. It follows that the second and third categories from *Re Z* should be merged, while the first no longer appears to be necessary at the jurisdictional stage of the argument.

Clearly, once the paramountcy principle has been reconfigured under s.3(1) HRA, concerns might arise that media claims under Article 10 would tend to outweigh claims of privacy for the child under Article 8, even where her welfare was at stake. As indicated above, this occurred in a number of instances post-HRA where the principle was found *not* to apply. There might appear to be a danger that powerful media organisations would acquire an enhanced ability to exploit vulnerable children, sometimes for largely commercial ends. It might have been thought that such fears would be allayed, now that the emerging judicial acceptance of the presumptive equality of Articles 8 and 10, rather than the presumptive priority of Article 10, has become firmly established, in *Campbell*. However, the decision of the Lords in *Re S* is disturbing in this respect since it is indicative of a judicial tendency to minimise the Article 8 claim where free speech is also at stake.

Categories within the ECHR jurisdiction after *Re S*?

The *Re Z* categories still have a residual relevance after this decision since the Lords' findings in *Re S* did not attack the categories themselves as far as the conflict with Article 10 is concerned – indeed, they implicitly reaffirmed the second two. The notion of the protective and custodial jurisdictions appears, however, to have been subsumed in the question of the application of a child's Article 8 right to respect for private life. Assuming that that right is engaged in any particular instance – even arguably in instances in which the inherent jurisdiction would previously have been inexercisable – the position appears now to be as follows. There is a first (very large) category in which the paramountcy principle does not apply since upbringing is not in issue (in the sense that the concept can be interpreted narrowly in order to avoid dealing with the problem of a clash between the principle and Article 10), and the reporting relates to matters unrelated to criminal proceedings. In this category a balancing act between Articles 8 and 10 must be undertaken, on the *Campbell* presumptive equality model. This category now includes weak Article 8 claims which are likely to be readily overcome by the strength of the free expression principle. This new category covers the old first and second categories from *Re Z*. Depending on the reading adopted of the House of Lords judgment in *Re S*, it is arguable that there may then be a second, new category in which the paramountcy principle does not apply since upbringing is not in issue, but the reporting *does* relate to criminal proceedings and a child's privacy would be indirectly affected. This category of case, if it exists, falls within the old second category from *Re Z* since in that category a balancing act of sorts was carried out, but on a basis of presumptive priority for Article 10 – a flawed balancing act, now abandoned for cases within the new first category. However, *Re W* has already found a way of escaping from the creation of this category which is in accord with the Strasbourg jurisprudence. Therefore the better way of delineating this 'second' category of case is merely to view it as a subset of the first category – one concerning criminal reporting in which the child's private life right is highly likely to be displaced, but where presumptive equality is still the starting point for the balancing act. In other words, there can be no presumptive priority for Article 10 even where the rule on open reporting applies.

Finally, there is a second category of cases based on the third category from *Re Z*. This category is unaffected by the decision in *Re S*. In this category, the paramountcy principle applies and therefore, in effect, the Article 8 claim is enhanced – so that it automatically prevails *even if* the reporting relates to criminal proceedings. Lord Steyn made it clear that Hedley J had been wrong to say that even if the paramountcy principle had been applicable he would have decided in the same way – and allowed the reporting. Arguably, this comment was not part of the *ratio* of the House of Lords decision. It is probable that the courts will continue to succeed in excluding cases from this category due to the possibility that a declaration of incompatibility under s.4 HRA between Article 10 and s.1(1) CA might have to be made if a case could not be so excluded. In other words, it may be that this category is almost certainly a merely notional one: in practice, no case is likely to be found to fall within it. The courts have leeway to continue on this exclusionary path since it cannot normally be said that reporting *directly* affects a child's welfare – the direct effect occurs in care or other welfare-based proceedings. But, in taking this stance, the courts have deliberately closed their eyes to the strong *indirect* effect that reporting might have on the child's welfare and therefore ultimately on the long-term outcomes of such proceedings. *Re Z* was exceptional since the child herself was directly involved in the contemplated documentary film.

However, a case might arise in which the facts are so analogous to those from *Re Z* that it is very difficult to avoid assigning it to the 'upbringing' category. If so, the courts might finally have to deal with the confrontation between s.1(1) CA and Article 10. Following the analysis above, the principle would have to be reconfigured under s.3(1) HRA, leading to the abandonment of the third category. Further, if the Lords' decision in *Re S* is either read as in *Re W*, or marginalised and confined to its own facts – on the basis that it is out of line with the Strasbourg jurisprudence and with the values espoused in *Campbell*, a far more persuasive decision – then the *second* category postulated here would become vestigial and virtually redundant.

This would create a far more satisfactory position, since judicial reasoning could concentrate on the true and pertinent issues involved, rather than the distractions offered by artificial categorisations. Once the categories had been abandoned, there would merely be a balancing act between Articles 8 and 10 in all these instances, where the child's private and family life was engaged. It is to the proper way to conduct that balancing act in these clashing rights cases that this chapter now turns. The judicial reasoning model discussed here could of course be used in relation to all clashes of the materially qualified Convention rights.[116]

The parallel analysis or 'ultimate balancing act'

Once the equal value of the rights has been accepted, it follows that the courts should consider the grant of a prior restraint, in instances similar to those mentioned, from the perspectives of both Article 10 and Article 8.[117] Under the proposed reinterpretation of s.1(1) CA, the welfare of the child would be highly significant if s.1(1) *was* found to apply. In all instances in which a power to restrict publicity to protect a child arises, whether based on the ECHR jurisdiction of the court or otherwise, the court should seek if possible to balance the two rights on the *Re S* model in accordance with the demands of the HRA. This process

---

[116] See H. Fenwick and S. Choudhry, 'Taking the Rights of Parents and Children Seriously: Confronting the Paramountcy Principle under the HRA' (2005) 25 OJLS 453.

[117] Other Convention rights may also be relevant. If, for example, the *Re W* case ([1992] 1 All ER 794) had arisen after the HRA was in force, it might have been possible to argue, under Article 14 read with Article 8, that there was also a discriminatory dimension to the findings: had the child been placed with a heterosexual couple after suffering heterosexual abuse, the Court of Appeal might not have concluded so readily that public interest questions arose. The principle of open justice under Article 6(1) may add weight to the Article 10 argument.

may be termed the 'parallel analysis':[118] the steps to be taken under it are considered in more detail below.

Articles 8 and 10: underlying rationales

A number of factors may be taken into account in conducting the parallel analysis in order to resolve clashes between the two guarantees. A starting point is to examine the extent to which the values accepted as underlying either Article are at stake in any particular instance. Where they are not fully at stake, an interference with the primary right is likely to be more readily justifiable. It is clear that claims of media freedom in this context do not necessarily partake fully in the classic justificatory rationales of free speech[119] – a point that is developed below.

As is apparent from Chapter 6,[120] it is clear that both Strasbourg and the domestic courts have accepted a hierarchy of speech, with political speech in the media attracting the most robust level of protection, artistic speech coming something of a poor second. These indications as to the established hierarchy of forms of speech at Strasbourg and domestically, and of the values underlying them, are of utility in seeking to identify underlying harmony between claims of media freedom and those of children to private and family life where they appear to be in competition. But it is also necessary to examine the values underlying Article 8 claims in general and those relating to children in particular, although it is fair to say that a hierarchy of such values is not so readily apparent. Such claims may, especially in the case of children, be viewed as relating to both their private and their family life. As argued in Chapter 9, 'informational autonomy' is the key value underlying privacy in this area, although its protection can also afford indirect support to more substantive autonomy interests.[121]

But self-fulfilment may also be associated with privacy as a free-standing value in the sense that protection for the private life of the individual – which may take many forms – may provide the best conditions under which he or she may flourish. In *Bensaid* v. *UK*, the

---

[118] H. Tomlinson and H. Rogers coined the term 'parallel analysis': 'Privacy and Expression: Convention Rights and Interim Injunctions' [2003] EHRLR 37, 50 (a special issue on privacy).

[119] See H. Fenwick, 'Clashing Rights, the Welfare of the Child and the HRA' (2004) 67 MLR 889, 917–20; E. Barendt, 'Press and Broadcasting Freedom: Does Anyone Have Any Rights to Free Speech?' (1991) 44 CLP 63, 65.

[120] See pp. 159–60.   [121] See Chapter 9, pp. 227–34.

European Court of Human Rights recognised the value of self-development, especially mental development, as an aspect of private life.[122] It is possible to identify further categories of material, in particular those relating to health[123] or sexual orientation or activity[124] that are regarded under Article 8 as 'particularly sensitive or intimate',[125] and, under the Data Protection Act 1998, as requiring especially compelling grounds to justify interference. These values may be particularly pertinent in relation to the privacy of children, as the primacy of the child's welfare, considered above in relation to certain of the 'family' cases under Article 8, indicates. The unauthorised disclosure of personal information relating to children is highly likely to have a greater impact on their personal development, including their ability to recover from traumatic events or sustain or develop beneficial relationships, than it would have on adults. Strasbourg recognised this possibility in the 'family cases' and in *Twenty-Twenty Television*; it has also been recognised domestically as indicated above.[126]

Articles 8 and 10 as mutually supportive guarantees

These findings should, it is argued, inform the parallel analysis. When examining instances in which the media wish to reveal private facts relating to children, it becomes clear that the justificatory arguments underlying media freedom are quite frequently partially or largely inapplicable. In some instances, speech that invades the privacy of children is likely to gain little, if any, support from the arguments from autonomy and self-development, so there will often be little or no justification at the level of principle for allowing it to override privacy. It may also be found that the rationales underlying *both* Articles 8 and 10 come down

---

[122] 'Private life is a broad term not susceptible to exhaustive definition . . . Mental health must also be regarded as a crucial part of private life . . . Article 8 protects a right to identity . . . personal development, and . . . to develop relationships . . . The preservation of mental stability is in that context an indispensable precondition to effective enjoyment of the right to respect for private life.' (2001) 33 EHRR 10, para. 47.

[123] See *Z* v. *Finland* (1998) 25 EHRR 371. See now the findings as to information relating to health matters in the House of Lords in *Campbell* n. 110 above.

[124] See *Lustig-Prean* v. *United Kingdom* (1999) 29 EHRR 548; 7 BHRC 65.

[125] D. Feldman, 'Information and Privacy', in J. Beatson and Y. Cripps (eds.), *Freedom of Expression and Freedom of Information: Essays in Honour of Sir David Williams* (Oxford: Oxford University Press, 2000).

[126] See e.g. *Re Z* [1995] 4 All ER 961; *October Films* [1999] 2 FLR 347; and Hale LJ's judgment in *Re S*, n. 81 above.

on the side of secrecy or, conversely, publicity. The rights to freedom of speech and to privacy are, in many respects, 'mutually supportive',[127] since the principles of autonomy and self-development underlie both Articles.

Millian justificatory arguments based on truth tend to have little application to the paradigmatic child privacy case, in which facts relating intimately to the child's private and family life are revealed. Reporting restraints attempting to prevent the publication of private facts only, and not general expressions of opinion, will pose little threat to that free and unhindered public debate about matters of importance which Mill's argument seeks to protect.[128] However, in certain of the cases considered, such as *Re Z* itself, this argument would support disclosure since the matters sought to be revealed would have formed part of a wider debate about the value of certain forms of education or upbringing.

The justification for speech based on the argument from autonomy may also have an application in this area, depending on whether the child *herself* is seeking publicity as in *Re W (Wardship: Restrictions on Publication)* and *Kelly* v. *BBC*. The value of autonomy underlying Article 8 could *also* speak in favour of publicity: where the child is *Gillick*-competent and seeks publicity, her informational autonomy is at stake in the sense that she is exercising a choice as to disclosure of aspects of her private life. Her informational autonomy would be invaded if disclosure was disallowed. Where a responsible and devoted parent or carer seeks publicity on behalf of the child, as in *Oxfordshire CC*[129] or *Re Z*, invocation of both Articles 8 and 10 could also point in the direction of disclosure. Indeed, in *Twenty-Twenty Television* v. *UK*, the mother as applicant at Strasbourg sought to invoke both Articles in support of her claim for publicity on the ground that her freedom of expression and right to respect for her family life were both at stake. The child herself could have invoked her own Articles 8 and 10 rights in support of publicity.

In such instances, no real conflict between Articles 8 and 10 would arise except in so far as it was arguable under Article 8 that disclosure ran

---

[127] See C. Emerson, 'The Right of Privacy and the Freedom of the Press' (1979) 14 *Harvard Civil Rights – Civil Liberties Law Review* 329, 331. See also H. Fenwick and G. Phillipson, *Media Freedom under the Human Rights Act* (Oxford: Oxford University Press, 2006), Chapter 13.

[128] See E. Barendt, *Freedom of Speech* (Oxford: Clarendon, 1985), p. 191.

[129] See n. 55 above.

counter to the child's own welfare. Where publicity would clearly not further her best interests, a court, affording weight to her welfare in accordance with the stance of the Court of Human Rights discussed in relation to the family cases at Strasbourg and, where applicable, s.1(1) CA (encapsulating the new primacy principle), would uphold non-disclosure. Clearly, even a *Gillick*-competent child might fail to appreciate the harm that publicity could do and could be over-persuaded by reporters or by a parent/carer. In such instances, the court would be expected to consider, not only the autonomy argument and the short-term benefits to the child in terms of, for example, enhanced self-esteem, but also the long-term detriment, including any impact on his development or ability to form or sustain relationships with his peers or others. However, where, as in the *Mary Bell* case,[130] or *Re S*, such arguments are not applicable, the child and her carers are opposed to publicity and there are also weighty welfare grounds for such opposition, it can be argued that disclosures could directly assault the informational autonomy of the child and those caring for her, and indirectly threaten their freedom of choice over substantive issues.[131] In such instances the speech in question, far from being bolstered by the autonomy rationale, is in direct conflict with it. But arguments based on the idea of uncertain and nebulous detriment to the child's welfare would hardly engage Article 8 and would be readily overcome where core values under both Articles 8 and 10 weighed on the other side of the balance. Where the speech was essential to inform a wider debate, the justificatory arguments under Article 10 would be strengthened.

Moreover, it is clearly apparent that the argument for speech from self-development, since it seeks to facilitate human flourishing, far from inevitably opposing the right of the child to privacy, must support it to some extent since a reasonable degree of privacy is a requirement for individual self-development, particularly the ability to form relationships, without which the capacity for individual growth would be severely curtailed. This argument, referred to in *Bensaid* v. *UK*, clearly has an especially significant application in relation to the upbringing and welfare of the child. As indicated above, a version of the paramountcy principle – in which the child's welfare has primacy – is inevitably going to continue to obtain recognition on the basis of

---

[130] *Re X (A Minor) (Wardship Proceedings: Injunction)* [1984] 1 WLR 1422.
[131] Such matters could include choice of abode or of schools. See the discussion on this issue at pp. 276–7 above.

arguments based on the requirements for individual self development under Article 8. Where publicity threatens the welfare of the child, the argument that it should be suppressed would be readily to hand, not only under Article 8, but also under Article 10, on the basis that it would not further the fulfilment of the values underlying its free speech guarantee. This argument could readily have been used successfully in *Re S* to justify the restriction on reporting: the majority judges in the Court of Appeal and the Law Lords assumed too readily in that case, it is contended, that Articles 8 and 10 were entirely opposed in relation to the circumstances.

Conversely, where speech might *further* the welfare of the child, the values underlying both Articles speak in favour of publicity. Such instances arise where she might gain in self-esteem through publicity (as the mother argued in *Re Z*) or where she desires publicity in order to reveal and express feelings of frustration or persecution (as in *Re W (Wardship: Restrictions on Publication)*) or, more controversially, where publication of true facts about the relationship with a parent, as a corrective to the parent's version already successfully placed in the public domain, could vindicate and ratify the child's own stance in respect of that relationship (*Harris* v. *Harris*).[132]

Finally, the argument that prior restraints intended to safeguard the privacy of the child might inhibit journalistic debate on matters of significant public interest must be fully confronted. Clearly, political speech by its nature is unlikely in many instances to conflict with the Article 8 rights of children to private and family life. Such a conflict will not arise where political speech consists of the discussion of political ideas, institutions and policies. The paradigm cases of journalistic invasions of privacy in this context tend to relate to criminal activity involving children or to the children of celebrities and may be driven merely by a desire for sensationalism for purely commercial considerations. Such publications hardly engage the press's right under Article 10 to impart 'information on matters of serious public concern'[133] or more general Convention values such as the furtherance of a democratic

---

[132] Munby J contended in that instance: 'Mr Harris has manipulated the press by feeding it tendentious accounts of these proceedings, enabled to do so because he has been able to ... shelter behind the very privacy which hitherto has prevented anyone correcting his misrepresentations ... [T]he remedy for Mr Harris's antics ... is publicity for the truth ... [T]he children's own best interests will be furthered by the public being told the truth.' [2001] 2 FLR 895, paras. 386–9; and see n. 68 above.

[133] *Bladet Tromso and Stensaas* v. *Norway* (2000) 29 EHRR 125, para. 59.

society. However, far more so than in the typical 'celebrity privacy' cases,[134] political speech, broadly defined, does sometimes come into conflict with the Article 8 rights of children, as where it reveals failings or good practice of state representatives or within state institutions (*Re S*, *Re Z*, *Re C (A Minor)*, *Re W (A Minor)(Restriction on Publication)*, *Re W (A Minor)(Freedom of Publication)*, *Oxfordshire County Council* v. *L and F*), or opposes gendered concepts of parenting (*Re W (A Minor)(Restriction on Publication)*), or the techniques of cult groups (*Kelly*), or concerns criminal activity where there is an arguable public interest dimension (*Central Independent Television*).

Nevertheless, it is only in a fairly narrow category of cases that any genuine and serious conflict arises – those where a publication would reveal material furthering public knowledge or debate about matters of legitimate public concern *and* the privacy or autonomy or family life of the child would be adversely affected. Where a real conflict appeared to arise – as in *Re S* or *Re W* – the privacy interest could frequently be protected while invading the speech interest only minimally by means of a temporary order intended to conceal identity, so long as the order provided sufficient guidance to the media as to the material that could be published.[135] On this basis, it is argued that the factual situations in both *Re S* and *Re W* supported restraint on the media: in *Re S* the revelation of the mother's identity was likely to affect S's ability to recover from the impact on him of his brother's death and mother's trial for the murder, and therefore it was especially crucial that her identity should not be revealed in the immediate aftermath of his brother's death. S was a victim in a very real sense of the alleged offence: he lost his mother (who was later imprisoned for the murder of his brother) and his brother, and his high risk of psychiatric harm was likely to be enhanced, according to expert evidence, depending on the level of publicity.[136] The suffering he was likely to undergo as a result of the publicity in terms of bullying and teasing was thought likely to have such an impact on him in terms of exacerbating the inevitable psychiatric harm he would suffer that the precarious placement with his father was thought to be likely to break down. In other words, the private and family life claims were very strong. The same was clearly true of the

---

[134] Such as *Douglas* v. *Hello!* [2001] QB 967; *Theakston* [2002] EMLR 22; *Campbell* [2002] EMLR 30 (CA); [2004] UKHL 22 (HL); *A* v. *B plc* [2002] 3 WLR 542.

[135] See n. 33 above.

[136] Hale LJ made these points at para. 39 of the Court of Appeal judgment.

claim in *Re W*. But, in contrast to Lord Steyn, the President of the Family Division examined the privacy claims of the children concerned in detail, finding that their Article 8 rights were very strongly engaged.

In contrast to the privacy claim in *Re S*, the speech claim was weak. The interest in open justice and the public interest in the issues surrounding the trial could have been served with relative efficacy at a later date, bearing in mind those compelling arguments for postponement. The speech interest engaged in publishing photographs of the mother with the dead boy and revealing the mother's name was minimal: discussion of the circumstances surrounding the murder could have occurred in the press on a basis of anonymity, at least during the mother's trial. The mother's name would clearly mean nothing to the vast majority of the readers of the newspapers in question. Thus the public interest could have been served, since the case raised certain wider issues, while still protecting S. This was the stance taken towards the speech claim in *Re W*. In granting the injunction in order to protect the children, the President found that:

> granting the injunction is [not] in fact likely to inhibit the press from reporting the case, nor should well-informed debate be significantly impaired simply because of the non-identification of the defendant or victim. It is said that the editor's principal wish is to be free to identify and publish a picture of the defendant *so as to report and convey an adequate understanding to the public*. I do not think the former is essential to the latter.[137]

The structure of the reasoning process and the mechanics of the HRA

In a case such as *Re Z*, arising under the HRA, the court could fulfil its duty under s.6(1) HRA and s.12(4) HRA by adopting an approach which not only weighed up the strength of the Article 10 claim, but also took account under s.2 of the extent to which the values underlying Article 8 were at stake and in harmony with those under Article 10. Where a restriction on publicity was statutory, s.3(1) would bite and would also demand that if possible a reinterpretation of it that took account of both Articles should be adopted. Where the restriction itself allowed

---

[137] N. 122, para. 63 (emphasis in original).

no leeway for the parallel analysis in order to achieve compatibility with Article 10, a declaration of incompatibility should be issued under s.4.[138] Section 12(1) of the Administration of Justice Act 1960 might be likely in future to attract such a declaration since it offers little leeway for consideration of the media freedom claim.

In terms of the *structure* of the reasoning process, the court should begin by considering the issue from the perspectives of both Articles 8(1) and 10(1) in turn, on the *Re S* model. In exceptional instances at the extremes, the matter might be resolvable largely by reference to the scope of media rights under Article 10(1). Speech that invades the privacy of a child, and which relates exclusively to her private life, could be viewed as a form of expression that will inevitably be overcome by the strong Article 8 claim, requiring no justification under paragraph 2 for its suppression.[139] There is perhaps more scope for resolution of the conflict within Article 8(1). Where speech relating to an adult which has only the most incidental and tenuous connection with the private or family life of a child is concerned, on factual bases even less compelling than that in *Central Television*, it might be argued that Article 8(1) is not engaged at all, in which case no conflict arises requiring resolution. Under s.6(1) HRA, as argued above, the ambit of the ECHR jurisdiction arguably extends beyond that of the inherent jurisdiction. Following this argument, a power to restrict publication would *prima facie* be available where the child's claim had the *potential* to fall within Article 8(1); if on close examination it was found that the connection was too tenuous on the particular facts, the case could be resolved in favour of the Article 10 claim without recourse to Article 8(2).

But it is clear that it will only rarely be possible to avoid the conflict within paragraph 1 of either Article by identifying and utilising the underlying values at stake. In most instances, then, the extent to which the rationales discussed are at stake will be relevant, but this time in relation to the exercise of proportionality under paragraph 2 of both

---

[138] See further I. Cram, 'Young Persons, Criminal Proceedings and Open Justice: A Comparative Perspective' (2000) *Yearbook of Copyright and Media Law* 141.

[139] See *Von Hannover* v. *Germany*, n. 110 above, para. 66. The findings in *Von Hannover* would clearly cover the children of celebrities or children who had attracted publicity due to their own or their parents' actions or situation, where the speech related purely to their private life. The term 'private life' was *not* found to cover only especially intimate matters or secluded situations or activities, but also the normal incidents of private life such as shopping expeditions (paras. 49 and 61). See also M. Tugendhat QC and I. Christie, *The Law of Privacy and the Media* (Oxford: Oxford University Press, 2002), pp. 420–1.

Articles. The structure of the reasoning process would follow the con-
tours laid down by Baroness Hale in *Re S* and in *Campbell*, but the
parallel analysis accepted as appropriate would also be used in cases
involving upbringing. The court would consider the issue of any conflict
between Articles 8 and 10 from at least two parallel perspectives.[140] The
court would follow the standard Convention tests under Article 10(2),
asking whether the interference with the primary guarantee proposed
would be prescribed by law, necessary in a democratic society and
proportionate to the legitimate aim of protecting the private and family
life of the child – 'the rights of others' protected under Article 8(1). The
court should then consider freedom of expression as creating an exception to the right to respect for private and family life, under Article 8(2),
again applying the tests of necessity and proportionality. But in each
instance the application of the test of necessity would not require strict
scrutiny in accordance with the findings deriving from the Strasbourg
clashing rights cases such as *Von Hannover* and *Tammer* v. *Estonia*,
since, as argued above, it is axiomatic that there is a pressing need to
protect both rights in a democratic society. The test of proportionality
would clearly be much more significant, as Sedley LJ indicated in a
different context in *London Regional Transport* v. *Mayor of London*,[141]
since, while it is clear that both privacy and speech must be protected,
the particular restriction under consideration must be tailored towards
satisfying this test under both Articles. Useful insights could be gleaned
by asking, for example, both whether the publication in question was
more intrusive than was necessary to further its legitimate aim of
enabling and provoking discussion on matters of public interest, and,
conversely, whether the remedy sought on behalf of the child would
go further than necessary in order to protect the legitimate privacy
interest.

Factors strengthening either the privacy or the speech claim, including those indicated by Hale LJ in *Re S*, could be taken into account in
relation to the exercise of proportionality, as could any harmony that
could be discerned between the underlying rationales of both Articles in
respect of the factors relevant in the particular instance. Where the case
would formerly have fallen within the 'upbringing' category in the
domestic courts this would weigh heavily in the balance in terms of
the child's interests under Article 8, but the factor of upbringing would

---

[140] As pointed out above, other Convention Articles might be relevant.
[141] [2003] EMLR 4, para. 49.

not alone determine the outcome. For example, arguments under both Articles 8 and 10 might favour publicity as in *Re Z*, but there might be countervailing welfare arguments under Article 8 which could be answered to by allowing publication of the material in question but concealing the child's identity, thus allowing for a minimal invasion of the Article 10 guarantee. In terms of Article 10(2), the interference would then be proportionate to the legitimate aim pursued – that of protecting the child's welfare under Article 8(1), while taking into account the value of autonomy which would be served by allowing some publicity. A greater and more nuanced insight into the best interests of the child might be attained; the notion that publicity might in some circumstances serve those interests might begin to take hold. At the same time, the claims of the media in this context would be subjected to greater scrutiny: dissonance between the values of free speech and the commercial interests of the media might be revealed.[142]

Conclusions

This chapter has argued for an approach to conflicts of rights in this context that takes as its starting point a fully equal weighting of Articles 8 and 10. As discussed above, there are a number of statutory restrictions on the reporting of the identity of children and it is hard to see how the parallel analysis can occur in imposing most of them since they leave little leeway for conducting it. Section 49 of the Children and Young Persons Act 1939, as amended, does leave some room for conducting the parallel analysis since the restriction need not be imposed if it is not in the public interest to do so.[143] But certain restrictions, including s.39 of the 1939 Act and s.12(1)(a) of the Administration of Justice Act 1960, may eventually be the subject of a declaration of incompatibility with Article 10 under s.4 HRA since they leave too little, or no, room for the balancing act.[144] The media may be understandably aggrieved at the far-reaching nature of a number of these restrictions, especially when the possibility of 'jigsaw' identification is taken into account.[145]

---

[142] See further on this point I. Cram, 'Minors' Privacy, Free Speech and the Courts' [1997] PL 410, 419; see also *ibid.*, pp. 411–12; see further E. Barendt, 'Press and Broadcasting Freedom: Does Anyone Have Any Rights to Free Speech?' (1991) 44 CLP 63, 65.

[143] See p. 262 and n. 31 above.   [144] See pp. 300–1 and n. 32 above.

[145] See n. 33 above.

The restriction in this context flowing from the paramountcy principle is equally indefensible in free speech terms. In the Human Rights Act
era, a presumption – the principle – that throws a cloak of secrecy over
the workings of the Family Division and over many aspects of decisions
relating to the welfare of children has become increasingly problematic.
The idea that publicity is almost always harmful is an outdated one that
in itself may be inimical to welfare since it tends to stifle a debate that
could otherwise flourish. The judicial determination post-HRA to narrow down the definition of 'upbringing' so as to avoid conflicts between
child welfare and media freedom tends to lead to narrow and sterile
definitions of the notion, to the detriment of debate in courts and in the
media. But, rather than artificially avoiding an engagement with the
notion of 'upbringing' where restrictions on publication are in question
so as to avoid a clash between Article 10 and the paramountcy principle,
the courts could proceed to *expand* the concept (bringing cases such as
Re S within it), since so doing would no longer lead to an automatic
abrogation of speech rights. Such expansion could occur by redefining
the term 'upbringing' in s.1(1) CA under s.3 HRA by reference to the
Article 8 concept of family life. Acceptance of the argument put forward
here would render the courts freer to consider what upbringing involves
in relation to the particular circumstances of a case, and would also
allow the media greater freedom to engage in that debate. The quality of
decision-making in the Family Division and in the courts in general in
cases concerning children might be improved. Hale LJ's judgment in
Re S demonstrates the contradictory nature of judicial reasoning under
the HRA in this field: on the one hand, the decision reveals quite a
sophisticated understanding of the value of individual rights under the
Convention; on the other, it illustrates the determination of the judges
to resist the HRA where a particular strand of consequentialist thinking
has become entrenched in a field of law. In fact, the process of reasoning
in the decision in the Court of Appeal in itself illustrates that movement
towards a rights-based analysis may lead in the long run to a more
sensitive, nuanced and subtle appreciation of welfare, to the benefit of
children.

Most significantly, the changes argued for here would also address the
strange legal oscillation currently occurring between over- and under-
protection for the privacy of children. The anomalies caused by this
oscillation have been exacerbated by the Lords' decision in Re S. Had the
paramountcy principle applied, the decision would presumably have
gone the other way, despite the interest in open reporting. Since it did

not, the decision went almost automatically in favour of media freedom. Lip-service only was paid to the interests engaged by the private life claim. Full use of the parallel analysis in all instances would lead to full scrutiny of the real basis of media free speech claims, with the result, in the wake of *Campbell* and *Von Hannover*, that in instances outside the 'upbringing' category the privacy of the child would nevertheless tend to prevail. This is probably the most significant point emerging from this chapter: the courts are more comfortable with free speech than with privacy claims. The common law accorded a very high value to free speech, elevating it, pre-HRA, to the status of a common law right. In *ex parte Simms*,[146] Lord Steyn referred to free speech as 'the *primary right* . . . in a democracy' (emphasis added). In contrast, the judges failed to create a common law tort of invasion of private life or of the non-consensual use of personal information.[147] Thus, in substantive terms, the strong common law tradition of free speech influenced the decision in *Re S* to the detriment of the more nebulous demands of privacy – demands that appear to have less of a hold on the judicial imagination. Where the judiciary perceive a clash between common law and Convention values, their tendency, despite the inception of the HRA, is to give preference to the former.

Against the backdrop of the traditional weight accorded to free speech, there are real dangers that the marginalisation of the paramountcy principle that has occurred in the media context will enhance the probability that the privacy claim of the child will be minimised, as it was in the House of Lords in *Re S*. That was a case tailor-made for the application of the Human Rights Act: real harm to a vulnerable child could have been averted. If the HRA is about anything, it is about identifying the possibility of such harm and providing a new remedy where common law doctrine and Parliamentary endeavour had failed to do so. Clearly, the HRA's primary role is to protect the citizen against the arbitrary and oppressive use of state power. But the ability of large media

---

[146] [1999] 3 All ER 400 (CA); [1999] 3 WLR 328 (HL).

[147] See *Kaye* v. *Robertson* [1991] FCR 62. The caveat to the above remarks was entered by the author in 1996 in 'Confidence and Privacy: A Re-examination' (1996) 55 CLJ 447 (with G. Phillipson). The article traces the somewhat uncertain steps that the judges were taking towards the creation of such a tort by utilising the action for breach of confidence, and it is fair to point out that post-1996 and pre-HRA further tentative steps were taken (see 'The Doctrine of Confidence as a Privacy Remedy in the Human Rights Act Era' (2000) 63 MLR 660–93, with G. Phillipson). However, it is unlikely that members of the judiciary would claim that private life had attained the same common law recognition as free speech had by the time of the inception of the HRA.

corporations to invade privacy is equal to, or even arguably surpasses, that of the state, since the state does not possess the power *in itself* to create widespread dissemination of private information. Therefore provision of protection for the citizen against the mass media is equally necessary. It is a standing embarrassment to the members of the House of Lords, and in particular Lord Steyn, that that outcome was not achieved in *Re S*.

The far more sensitive and sophisticated reasoning of the President of the Family Division in *Re W*, which succeeded in examining the real weight of both the speech and the privacy claims put forward, may be indicative of the path that judicial reasoning is now likely to take in this context. Clearly, it could be viewed at first glimpse as rooted in the child-centred approach of the Family Division – as merely reflecting the values underpinning the paramountcy principle and therefore as flawed in its desire to afford primacy to privacy as Lord Steyn's approach is in relation to speech. Its claim to be viewed as a model of HRA judicial reasoning – as exhibiting a nuanced and sensitive approach to the clash of rights in question which outdoes the reasoning in a number of Strasbourg cases, including *Twenty-Twenty Television* – is based, however, precisely on its avoidance of the creation or acceptance of a presumption on the lines of those accepted in either *Re S* or *Re Z*.

This chapter has sought to reveal the flaws in judicial reasoning in early post-HRA clashing rights cases. It has suggested that in relation to this speech/privacy clash the inherent or 'ECHR jurisdiction' could develop in a distorted manner: in avoiding the absolutist effects of the paramountcy principle, it could fall into the trap of failing to provide privacy protection even where very strong claims for such protection arise, despite the harmony that can be found between free speech and private life values. The Lords' decision in *Re S* not only fails to demonstrate a strong grasp of the values at stake in difficult clashing rights cases, it also exhibits the tendency of common law judicial reasoning to prefer form over substance. In other words, the judiciary tends to be more comfortable with a fairly mechanistic approach to reasoning, as opposed to the more value-laden type of reasoning demanded by the Convention. *Re S* exemplifies the uneasy fusion in post-HRA judicial reasoning between Convention values and common law ones. We can find in the judgment first a partial abandonment of the needlessly rigid *Re Z* categories, but then a re-entrance of the more mechanistic approach, by way of a device allowing avoidance of an examination of the true values at stake. Clearly, this analysis is complicated by the value-laden nature of that device – a near-automatic presumption in favour of speech based on the value of the open justice principle. But, in Convention terms, any such presumption is flawed since it creates a barrier to the full examination of both the speech and the private life claim, taking account of both speech and privacy values in a democratic society.

11

Family law and the Human Rights Act 1998: judicial restraint or revolution?

SONIA HARRIS-SHORT[*]

Introduction

The implementation of the Human Rights Act 1998 (HRA) in October 2000 was received with mixed feelings by family lawyers. Whilst for some its implementation promised long-overdue changes in the judiciary's approach to legal disputes concerning the family, many were more cautious. Indeed, there were a number of reasons to anticipate that the passage of the HRA into mainstream family law would not necessarily be easy. In particular, it appeared that two key considerations, particularly pertinent to family law, might exert a restraining influence on its use. First, there was, and still is, considerable opposition to the use of rights-based reasoning in the family law context. Secondly, the legal regulation of family life often gives rise to sensitive questions of public policy, including complex socio-economic considerations, which are traditionally regarded as the responsibility of Parliament rather than the courts. It could thus be anticipated that a combination of these two factors would lead to what has been termed a 'minimalist' or conservative approach to the HRA in the family law context.[1]

The purpose of this chapter is not to contend that either judicial conservatism or activism would be the better approach to the HRA. Rather, it is to review the post-implementation case law to determine how, if at all, these two factors have influenced the impact of the HRA on domestic family law. To this end, it focuses on the reasoning employed

[*] This chapter was first published at (2005) 17 *Child and Family Law Quarterly* 329–61. Our thanks are due to the editors and publishers of that journal for permission to reproduce in this volume. I would also like to thank Clare McGlynn, Colin Warbrick and Roger Masterman for their help in preparing this paper.
[1] H. Fenwick, *Civil Liberties and Human Rights* (3rd edn, London: Cavendish Publishing, 2002), p. 186.

by the judiciary with respect to these two issues in a number of leading cases. The chapter begins by exploring the background and potential implications of the prevailing mistrust of rights amongst family lawyers and the problematic public policy issues which arise in the family law context. It then examines how these two restraining influences have impacted on the emerging case-law in three key areas of domestic family law: (i) the legal regulation of intimate adult relationships; (ii) the public law on children; and (iii) private disputes over children.

The case-law is still, of course, in its infancy. It is argued, however, that important trends are beginning to emerge, with the two factors identified playing a significant part in contributing to the overall picture of judicial caution and restraint in the use of the HRA in the family law field.

Potential restraints on the use of the HRA in family cases

Opposition to rights-based reasoning in the family law context

Despite the general growth of, what is now commonly referred to as a 'human rights culture' in the UK, ideological objections to the application of rights-based reasoning in family law cases remain. A perceived alliance between strong liberal values and human rights discourse engenders concern amongst some groups that the human rights paradigm, with its emphasis on individualism, equality and non-discrimination, will be used to gradually undermine and erode the traditional family unit and the values it protects. Thus, the very idea of introducing individualistic rights-based reasoning into the protected sphere of 'the family' is regarded by some as an anathema.[2] Although the benefits of protecting 'the family' against authoritarian, interventionist policies of the state are wholeheartedly endorsed, further penetration of human rights discourse into the private sphere of the family is viewed as deeply problematic. Indeed, strong resistance to penetrating behind the veil of family privacy in an attempt to break down the family unit into its individual 'constituent parts'[3] is by no means constrained to a small

---

[2] See S. Toope, 'Riding the Fences: Courts, Charter Rights and Family Law' (1991) 9 *Canadian Journal of Family Law* 55, esp. 56–63; and S. Boyd, 'The Impact of the Charter of Rights and Freedoms on Canadian Family Law' (2000) 17 *Canadian Journal of Family Law* 292, esp. 297–8. For a good discussion as to how this resistance is beginning to break down, at least as regards relations between the adult parties, see A. Diduck, *Law's Families* (London: LexisNexis UK, 2003).

[3] Diduck, *ibid.*, p. 37.

number of conservative commentators. It is widespread and deeply entrenched within Western societies. The complex realities of contemporary family relationships make many, even the more moderate commentators, sceptical about the utility of trying to divorce the rights and interests of individual family members from the relationships on which they depend – particularly if a strong individualistic view of liberal rights-based doctrine is to be followed.[4]

Nevertheless, such widespread reluctance to introduce the language of rights into the protected family sphere has been fiercely contested by a range of scholars, most notably from the feminist school. A tendency to assimilate the interests of the female partner to the male, and the interests of the child to the parents, has long obscured the harm which can be perpetrated against vulnerable individual family members. Thus, the assumption that 'the family' will provide a loving safe haven for its individual members, despite the known power differentials and abuses which exist, is clearly open to challenge. However, significant concern remains even amongst commentators who can see the *potential* advantages of employing the rights-based discourse contained within the ECHR to address some of the deeply entrenched, and perhaps problematic, assumptions that currently inform English family law. Jane Fortin, for example, when looking at the issue from a children's rights perspective is cautious, pointing out that the 'Strasbourg jurisprudence may not always augur well for British children' and that greater reliance on a rights-based discourse, including the discourse of children's rights, may well be hijacked by the parental rights lobby, particularly fathers, to mask and promote their own claims and interests at the expense of the child.[5] For many family lawyers, to return to the language of parental rights would therefore be a dangerous, retrograde step for a legal jurisdiction which, over the course of the twentieth century, successfully turned its back on the notion of parents holding autonomous 'proprietary' rights over and with respect to their children in favour of a more paternalistic welfare-orientated approach.

Of course, a welfare-based approach to the family also has its critics. Behind the notoriously indeterminate welfare principle, untested

---

[4] See e.g. the concerns of Toope, above n. 2, esp. pp. 95–6, and the concerns of Herring as regards taking an overly individualistic approach to the child in J. Herring, 'The Human Rights Act and the Welfare Principle in Family Law – Conflicting or Complementary?' (1999) 11 *Child and Family Law Quarterly* 223, 232–5.

[5] J. Fortin, 'The HRA's Impact on Litigation Involving Children and Their Families' (1999) 11 *Child and Family Law Quarterly* 217, 251.

assumptions, stereotypes and basic prejudices are able to flourish.[6] However, whilst recognising its flaws, many family lawyers remain deeply loyal to its basic premises. Scepticism as to the reintroduction of a model of family decision-making dominated by the language of parental rights also extends to the rights of the child. Although there have been notable calls by the judiciary to embrace the concept of children's rights as well as the child's welfare,[7] the distinction, if any, between the two concepts and the implications such a distinction may hold for the law's traditional approach to disputes over children remains fiercely contested.

In light of this prevailing scepticism about the value of introducing rights-based reasoning into the family law context, it could be anticipated that the impact of the HRA, particularly in the context of private family law disputes where the ideology of family privacy is particularly strong, would, at least initially, be fairly limited.

Sensitive questions of public policy and family law

The second potentially inhibiting factor in the use of the HRA in family cases is that disputes over the legal regulation of family life often give rise to sensitive questions of public policy. Questions concerning family life strike at the heart of a society's core traditions and values. Any decision which is likely to lead to important changes in the way in which the law responds to fundamental concepts such as 'marriage', 'family' and 'parenthood' are thus likely to invoke a cautious response from the courts, which have traditionally considered these issues more properly to lie within the domain of the duly elected, democratic bodies. This deferential approach derives from an arguably justifiable perception that the courts lack the institutional competence to engage in an informed analysis of complex matters of political, social and economic policy.[8]

---

[6] R. Mnookin, 'Child Custody Adjudication: Judicial Functions in the Face of Indeterminacy' (1975) 39 *Law and Contemporary Problems* 226; and H. Reece, 'The Paramountcy Principle: Consensus or Construct?' (1996) 49 *Current Legal Problems* 267.

[7] Dame Elizabeth Butler-Sloss, 'Are We Failing the Family? Human Rights, Children and the Meaning of the Family in the 21st Century', The Paul Sieghart Memorial Lecture, British Institute of Human Rights, King's College London, 3 April 2003. See further *Mabon* v. *Mabon* [2005] EWCA Civ 634; [2005] 2 FLR 1011; and *R. (on the Application of Axon)* v. *Secretary of State for Health* [2006] EWHC Admin 37.

[8] E. Palmer, 'Courts, Resources and the HRA: Reading Section 17 of the Children Act 1989 Compatibly with Article 8 ECHR' [2003] EHRLR 308, 308–10. On which also see Sir David Keene's comments in Chapter 8 of this volume.

Moreover, a similar constitutional restraint has traditionally operated upon the courts in family law cases which require detailed examination of complex socio-economic questions – a second area of public policy which the legislature has traditionally reserved to itself. This tension between the courts and Parliament most commonly arises, although not exclusively so, in public law proceedings relating to children, where the courts have traditionally displayed a deferential approach to the discretionary decision-making powers of local authorities. The extent to which the HRA now provides the judiciary with the necessary mandate to shift the traditional constitutional boundary between Parliament and the courts on such sensitive questions of public policy is a highly controversial matter, which has not surprisingly been approached with utmost caution by the family law bench.

Consequently, the difficult political, social and economic context in which family law operates again suggested that the impact of the HRA in the family law field would be limited.

The legal regulation of intimate relationships between adults

Since the implementation of the HRA in 2000, there have been significant developments in the law on intimate adult relationships. The important role played by the HRA in pushing forward these developments is clear. At least in this area of family law, the HRA would appear to have had a significant impact in a remarkably short period of time. The two major developments in the area of adult relationships are the decisions of the House of Lords in *Bellinger* v. *Bellinger*[9] and *Ghaidan* v. *Godin-Mendoza*.[10] The *Bellinger* decision (in light of the preceding decision of the European Court of Human Rights in *Goodwin* v. *UK*[11]) was quickly followed by legislation in the form of the Gender Recognition Act 2004. The House of Lords decision in *Mendoza* came against the background of the government's legislative proposals on extending 'familial' rights to same-sex couples now contained in the Civil Partnership Act 2004. These substantive developments in the legal protection of transgendered individuals and same-sex couples have

---

[9] *Bellinger* v. *Bellinger* [2003] UKHL 21; [2003] 2 AC 467.
[10] *Ghaidan* v. *Godin-Mendoza* [2004] UKHL 30; [2004] 2 AC 557.
[11] *Goodwin* v. *UK* [2002] 2 FLR 487.

generally been welcomed by commentators.[12] However, the very different approach which the House of Lords took in the two cases towards the HRA and, in particular, the role of the courts when determining sensitive questions of public policy has proved significantly more controversial. At the heart of these two family cases decided by two differently constituted Houses lies a constitutional dispute about where the line should be drawn between, on the one hand, legitimate judicial interpretation, and, on the other, constitutionally improper judicial legislation, in the exercise of their HRA powers.

Deference to Parliament on a sensitive question of public policy: Bellinger

The *Bellinger* decision concerned an unopposed petition by Mrs Bellinger, a male-to-female transgendered individual, for a declaration that her marriage to her husband of twenty years was valid at its inception and was subsisting. The validity of the marriage turned on whether or not Mr and Mrs Bellinger could be described as respectively 'male' and 'female' for the purposes of s.11(c) of the Matrimonial Causes Act 1973 (MCA).[13] The case thus presented a timely opportunity for the domestic courts to revisit the much-maligned decision of Ormrod J in *Corbett* v. *Corbett*.[14] It is well known that, in the *Corbett* decision, Ormrod J held that the test for determining sex for the purposes of marriage should be restricted to biological characteristics, and that, where the person's biological characteristics were congruent at birth, his/her legal sex would be fixed at birth and could not subsequently be changed, regardless of any later developments in a person's psychological sex and/or gender identity or other medical intervention.

---

[12] See e.g. S. Gilmore, '*Bellinger* v. *Bellinger* – Not Quite Between the Ears *and* Between the Legs – Transsexualism and Marriage in the Lords' (2003) 15 *Child and Family Law Quarterly* 295; R. Sandland, 'Crossing and Not Crossing: Gender, Sexuality and Melancholy in the European Court of Human Rights' (2003) 11 *Feminist Legal Studies* 191; I. Loveland, 'Making It up as They Go Along? The Court of Appeal on Same Sex Couples and Succession Rights to Tenancies' [2003] PL 222; and E. Hitchings, '*Mendoza* v. *Ghaidan* – Two Steps Forward, One Step Back' (2003) 15 *Child and Family Law Quarterly* 313.

[13] Section 11(c) provides: 'A marriage celebrated after 31st July 1971 shall be void on the following grounds only, that is to say – that the parties are not respectively male and female.'

[14] *Corbett* v. *Corbett (Otherwise Ashley)* [1971] P 83.

In light of the European Court of Human Rights' (ECtHR's) decision in *Goodwin* v. *UK*,[15] one question was relatively simple: insofar as s.11(c) of the MCA excluded a transgendered person marrying in his/her acquired gender, it was incompatible with Articles 8 and 12 of the Convention.[16] However, the more difficult question for the House of Lords was whether it could interpret the word 'female' compatibly with Article 12 so as to include a post-operative male-to-female transsexual such as Mrs Bellinger pursuant to its interpretative duty under s.3 HRA. Failing that, it would have to leave the *Corbett* decision in place and consider making a declaration of incompatibility under s.4.

This was a finely balanced case. As Miles has argued, it was clearly *possible* for the House of Lords to depart from *Corbett*'s strictly biological criteria in determining the meaning of 'female' for the purpose of marriage.[17] Indeed, as an interpretative exercise under s.3, it was in many ways straightforward. There was no need to read any additional words into the statute. Advances in medical research and changes in social attitudes were clearly sufficient to support an approach whereby, when determining gender for the purposes of marriage, psychological as well as biological factors could be taken into account. Such a decision, on the facts of *Bellinger*, would be restricted to a 'fully achieved' post-operative male-to-female transsexual at the date of the marriage, leaving Parliament to decide whether it wished to extend recognition beyond this strictly limited context.[18] As the ECtHR argued in *Goodwin*, 'any "spectral difficulties", particularly in the field of family law, [would be] both manageable and acceptable if confined to the case of fully achieved and post-operative transsexuals'.[19] Furthermore, in finding a breach of Article 12, the ECtHR clearly felt that the *Corbett* criteria needed to be revisited:

> The Court is not persuaded that at the date of this case it can still be assumed that these terms [man and woman] must refer to a determination of gender by purely biological criteria ... There have been major social changes in the institution of marriage since the adoption of the Convention as well as dramatic changes brought about by developments in medicine and science in the field of transsexuality. The Court has

---

[15] [2002] 2 FLR 487.

[16] This point was in fact conceded by the Lord Chancellor. See *Bellinger* v. *Bellinger* [2003] UKHL 21; [2003] 2 AC 467, para. 27.

[17] J. Miles, 'Interpretation under HRA Section 3: The Developing Approach of the Courts', Society of Legal Scholars conference, Oxford, September 2003. This was in fact what Thorpe LJ did in his dissenting judgment in the Court of Appeal.

[18] *Ibid.*   [19] *Goodwin* v. *UK* [2002] 2 FLR 487, para. 91.

found above, under Article 8 of the Convention, that a test of congruent biological factors can no longer be decisive in denying legal recognition to the change of gender of a post-operative transsexual.[20]

However, in what is a deeply conservative decision, the House of Lords failed to take this lead.[21] The House of Lords noted that to take a more inclusive approach to the meaning of 'female' would 'represent a major change in the law with far reaching ramifications'.[22] Underlying this observation would appear to be a particular concern that, by reinterpreting the word 'female', the court would be perceived as launching an attack on the traditional institution of marriage itself – more precisely, that they would be opening the door to same-sex marriage. As Lord Nicholls observed, if this was correct, this would be to enter 'deep waters'.[23] Both Lord Nicholls and Lord Hope thus placed great emphasis on the essentially 'biological basis' of the distinction between 'male' and 'female' and the essential link between such a distinction, the ability to engage in procreation and the heterosexual nature of marriage. In a judgment which exactly mirrors the *Corbett* approach, Lord Hope thus concluded that it is simply impossible to interpret the word 'female' for the purposes of s.11(c) MCA to include Mrs Bellinger, on the basis that it would be impossible for any degree of surgical intervention to 'turn a man into a woman or turn a woman into a man'.

Lord Nicholls was more open to the need for a broader, more flexible approach to the notion of gender for the purposes of marriage. However, given the obvious sensitivity of the issue, he was also clearly influenced by the fact that the government, in response to the *Goodwin* decision, had already announced its intention to introduce primary legislation to 'allow transsexual people who can demonstrate they have taken decisive steps towards living fully and permanently in the acquired gender to marry in that gender'.[24] In addition to the perceived sensitivity of the issue, Lord Nicholls put forward a number of persuasive arguments as to why in this instance it would be appropriate for the courts to defer to the legislature.[25] Thus, he pointed out that particularly as

---

[20] *Ibid.*, para. 100.

[21] See e.g. the persuasive critique by Gilmore, above n. 12, esp. pp. 309–11. For a critique of the decision of the European Court in *Goodwin*, see Sandland, above n. 12, esp. pp. 200–7.

[22] *Bellinger v. Bellinger* [2003] UKHL 21; [2003] 2 AC 467, para. 37.   [23] *Ibid.*, para. 42.

[24] *Ibid.*, para. 26. This approach by Lord Nicholls has been the subject of some criticism. See e.g. Gilmore, above n. 12, p. 304.

[25] Again, these purported justifications have been criticised by Gilmore, *ibid.*, pp. 304–6.

regards the validity of marriage – a status which brings with it numerous legal consequences – there is a need for certainty and some kind of 'objective, publicly available criteria by which gender reassignment is to be assessed', which, in his view, the court is simply not well placed to decide. Furthermore, he emphasised that the issue of gender reassignment for the purposes of marriage could not sensibly be isolated from the wider problem of the legal status of transsexuals in the UK. Instead, he considered it to be just one small part of a much bigger problem requiring a comprehensive legislative scheme based on a 'clear coherent, policy' developed following proper public consultation and discussion – a task which could not properly be performed by the courts but was 'pre-eminently a matter for Parliament'.[26] Therefore, rather than engage in a controversial interpretative exercise, the House of Lords made a declaration of incompatibility under s.4 HRA.

As noted above, this was a difficult case, with convincing arguments both for and against such a deferential response. However, whilst one can understand the House of Lords' difficulty in putting aside the broader questions of social policy to which the case on its facts undoubtedly gave rise, there is a strong argument that the House of Lords was wrong to deny Mrs Bellinger her remedy under s.3. As Miles argues, as a 'fully achieved' post-operative female, Mrs Bellinger would almost certainly have met any reassignment criteria the government could have chosen to prescribe.[27] The fact that issues other than marriage would have to be addressed and that other transsexuals at a less advanced stage of their treatment could potentially give rise to much more difficult questions, was strictly irrelevant to Mrs Bellinger's case and could all be addressed at a later date in a more appropriate forum. Moreover, Miles contends that, once a breach of Mrs Bellinger's Convention rights had been established and a Convention-compliant interpretation of the statute shown to be possible, the court was under a clear duty, pursuant to the mandatory language of s.3, to interpret the statute accordingly.[28] The 'substantive deference' shown to Parliament at the interpretative stage of this case was thus unjustified.[29]

The House of Lords decision in *Bellinger* stands as a classic example of a conservative or 'minimalist' approach to the HRA. Only following a clear unequivocal finding of incompatibility by Strasbourg in *Goodwin*

---

[26] *Bellinger* v. *Bellinger* [2003] UKHL 21; [2003] 2 AC 467, para. 37.
[27] Miles, above n. 17.   [28] *Ibid.*   [29] *Ibid.*

v. *UK* did the House of Lords feel empowered to act.[30] Moreover, in doing so it displayed considerable deference to the democratic process by refusing to engage in a controversial interpretative exercise on a matter of considerable sensitivity and public importance. However, if *Bellinger* sits at the conservative end of the spectrum, the decision of the House of Lords in *Mendoza* v. *Ghaidan* arguably sits at the other extreme.

Unexpected judicial activism on a sensitive question of public policy: Mendoza[31]

Mendoza seemed an unlikely case to initiate a strong bout of judicial activism. The applicant in *Mendoza* had lived with his same-sex partner in a 'very close, loving and monogamous relationship' since 1972 and upon his death sought to succeed to the statutory tenancy of the flat they shared. The case raised again the correct interpretation of the word 'spouse' for the purposes of succession to a statutory tenancy under the Rent Act 1977. Just three years earlier, a unanimous House of Lords had held that, whilst a same-sex couple could constitute a 'family' for the purposes of the legislation, the amended definition of 'spouse' to include a person 'living with the original tenant as his or her husband or wife' specifically pointed to a gendered heterosexual relationship between one man and one woman and therefore clearly could not have been intended to include a same-sex couple.[32] The core question in *Mendoza* was therefore whether the subsequent implementation of the HRA now compelled a different conclusion. The applicant argued that, to afford a statutory tenancy to the survivor of a heterosexual relationship when the survivor of an equivalent homosexual relationship was limited to a less beneficial assured tenancy, constituted discrimination on the ground of sexual orientation contrary to Articles 8 and 14 of the Convention. A unanimous House of Lords agreed. Taking a much more 'activist' approach, the House of Lords (Lord Millett dissenting on this particular point) decided to invoke the 'principal remedial measure' under s.3 HRA.[33] Accordingly, paragraph 2 of Schedule 1 to

---

[30] The Court of Appeal judgment which preceded the decision of the European Court of Human Rights in *Goodwin* did not even consider the possibility of making a declaration of incompatibility, the point having apparently not been argued by counsel.

[31] On which also see the discussion in Chapter 5.

[32] *Fitzpatrick* v. *Sterling Housing Association* [2001] 1 AC 27.

[33] *Ghaidan* v. *Godin-Mendoza* [2004] UKHL 30; [2004] 2 AC 557, para. 39, *per* Lord Steyn.

the Rent Act 1977 was interpreted to include the survivor of a homo-sexual relationship as if he/she were the surviving spouse of the original tenant.[34]

In advancing the family rights of same-sex couples, *Mendoza* is clearly a hugely significant decision. The core principle to emerge – that it is contrary to Articles 8 and 14 of the Convention to limit statutory protection in the family law field to unmarried heterosexual couples 'living together as husband and wife' – can be applied to a wide range of existing statutory provisions. The decision thus promises to bring much greater equality to same-sex couples in a number of core areas.[35] This is undoubtedly a welcome development. However, whether or not the decision can be reconciled with the minimalist approach taken in *Bellinger* is an altogether more difficult question.

In stark contrast to *Bellinger*, the *Mendoza* decision is a quite extra-ordinary example of judicial innovation on an issue raising difficult and sensitive questions of public policy. The House of Lords was engaged in interpreting the meaning of 'spouse' and 'living together as husband and wife' – terms which are obviously closely associated with marriage and which only three years earlier the House of Lords had unanimously concluded could only refer to a gendered heterosexual relationship. As Lord Millett pointed out:

> The word 'spouse' means a party to a lawful marriage. It may refer indifferently to a lawfully wedded husband or a lawfully wedded wife, and to this extent is not gender specific. But it is gender specific in relation to the other party to the relationship. Marriage is the lawful union of a man and a woman. It is a legal relationship between persons of the opposite sex. A man's spouse must be a woman; a woman's spouse must be a man. This is the very essence of the relationship, which need not be loving, sexual, stable, faithful, long-lasting or contented.[36]

Lord Rodger downplayed what the majority of the House of Lords were proposing to do, suggesting that it constituted only a 'modest' develop-ment of the law.[37] However, to define heterosexual cohabitation against the benchmark of marriage and then to extend that approach to bring same-sex couples within the meaning of 'spouse' is in many ways a much more direct attack on the traditional heterosexual nature of marriage

---

[34] *Ibid.*, para. 39, *per* Lord Steyn; and *ibid.*, para. 35, *per* Lord Nicholls.
[35] See Civil Partnership Act 2004, ss.81, 82 and 83, Schedules 8 and 9.
[36] *Ghaidan* v. *Godin-Mendoza* [2004] UKHL 30; [2004] 2 AC 557, para. 78.
[37] *Ibid.*, para. 128.

than was ever posed by the *Bellinger* case. The full implication is that, if same-sex couples are capable of living in the manner of husband and wife, then why not simply *as* husband and wife – particularly if, as Baroness Hale argues, the gendered nature of marriage is now a thing of the past:

> Once upon a time it might have been difficult to apply those words to a same sex relationship because both in law and in reality the roles of the husband and wife were so different and those differences were defined by their genders. That is no longer the case. The law now differentiates between husband and wife in only a very few and unimportant respects. Husbands and wives decide for themselves who will go out to work and who will do the homework and child care. Mostly each does some of each. The roles are inter-changeable. There is thus no difficulty in applying the terms 'marriage-like' to same sex relationships.[38]

Could this reasoning not be applied with equal force to s.11(c) MCA, particularly when taken together with Baroness Hale's argument that it is difficult to see how heterosexual marriage-like relationships will be encouraged by denying the equivalent to same-sex couples? If so, in the words of Buxton LJ in the Court of Appeal, the House of Lords really was entering 'deep waters'. This was also a decision that, irrespective of the potential ramifications for the traditional institution of marriage, could have far-reaching effects on a range of important issues from pensions to inheritance. Important questions of social policy were therefore engaged.[39] Furthermore, even within the confines of the statute under attack, this was a case in which deference to Parliament might well have been expected. As Lord Nicholls recognised, this case was essentially concerned with questions of national housing policy involving a delicate balance between the competing interests of tenants and landlords and complex socio-economic issues[40] – territory into which the courts should only enter with 'trepidation'.[41] The House of Lords in *Mendoza* defended its decision not to invoke the s.3 remedy in *Bellinger* on the grounds that *Bellinger* gave rise to 'questions of social policy'[42] and had 'exceedingly wide ramifications raising issues ill-suited for determination by the courts or court procedures'.[43] Following this reasoning, *Mendoza* was arguably also a case in which a more nuanced, informed

---

[38] *Ibid.*, para. 144.   [39] *Ibid.*, paras. 98–101, *per* Lord Millett.   [40] *Ibid.*, para. 19.
[41] *Mendoza* v. *Ghaidan* [2001] EWCA Civ 1553; [2003] 1 FLR 468, para. 19, *per* Buxton LJ.
[42] *Ghaidan* v. *Godin-Mendoza* [2004] UKHL 30; [2004] 2 AC 557, [65], *per* Lord Millett.
[43] *Ibid.*, para. 34, *per* Lord Nicholls.

and comprehensive response from Parliament following widespread
public consultation and discussion was required – a process the government was already engaged in, having introduced the Civil Partnership
Bill to Parliament. Moreover, it is interesting to note that the Civil
Partnership Act avoids some of the potential problems of adopting a
gender-neutral interpretation of the word 'spouse' by defining same-sex
cohabitation against the benchmark of civil partnership, rather than
against the benchmark of heterosexual marriage as demanded by the
Rent Act 1977.[44] It is therefore arguable that a declaration of incompatibility under s.4 HRA would have been a much more measured and
justifiable response in this case and one that was more consistent with
the earlier decision of the House of Lords in *Bellinger*.[45]

The more activist approach adopted by the House of Lords in
Mendoza does, however, give rise to another important question for
the family law bench. A court encroaching into the traditional domain
of Parliament has to have a firm evidential basis on which it can act. In
this respect, it is interesting to compare the Court of Appeal and House
of Lords judgments in *Mendoza* with those of the Canadian Supreme
Court in *M* v. *H*.[46] In *M* v. *H*, which concerned almost identical
statutory wording to that in *Mendoza*,[47] the Supreme Court made
extensive and detailed reference to the original Parliamentary debates,
a wide range of socio-economic research, statistical evidence and academic critique. This impressive review of the available evidence led the
majority to conclude that the goals of the legislation were in fact undermined rather than advanced by the legislature's exclusion of same-sex
couples. In comparison, the evidential basis on which the Court of
Appeal and House of Lords rejected the social policy objectives of the
Rent Act 1977 was feeble. In fact, in the Court of Appeal, Buxton LJ
candidly remarked that, as this part of the argument 'rested simply on

---

[44] Schedule 8, para. 13(3), of the Civil Partnership Act 2004 amends Schedule 1, para. 2, of
the Rent Act 1977 to read: 'For the purposes of this paragraph – (a) a person who was
living with the original tenant as his or her wife or husband shall be treated as the spouse
of the original tenant, and (b) a person who was living with the original tenant as if they
were civil partners shall be treated as the civil partner of the original tenant.'

[45] For an excellent critique of the Court of Appeal's approach to s.3 HRA in *Mendoza*, see
Hitchings, above n. 12, pp. 320–2.

[46] [1999] 2 SCR 3.

[47] *M* v. *H* concerned the exclusion of same-sex couples from spousal support obligations
under s.29 of Ontario's Family Law Act. Under s.29 of the Act, 'spouse' included 'either
of a man and woman who are not married to each other and have cohabited continu-
ously for a period of not less than three years'.

assertion' and 'no actual facts or evidence were available to assist us', the court had to 'fall back on common sense'.[48] Instinct, rather than evidence, was thus called on to dismiss Mr Mendoza's arguments. Moreover, the House of Lords proceeded in exactly the same way. Thus, whilst the conclusion reached by both the Court of Appeal and the House of Lords does *instinctively* make sense, it is clearly questionable whether it is legitimate for a court to declare the original objectives of Parliament improper and thereby embark on a rewriting of statute without a more solid foundation for doing so.

Summary

As regards the legal regulation of intimate adult relationships, the HRA has thus given rise to two hugely significant cases in which the use made of the HRA was strikingly different. In *Bellinger*, the approach of the Lords given the 'sensitivity' of the issue was cautious and deferential; in *Mendoza*, quite the opposite. One explanation for this difference in approach in two family cases dealing with similarly sensitive questions of public policy may lie in the fact that the core liberal values of non-discrimination and equality were more clearly at stake in *Mendoza* values deemed by Baroness Hale to be of high constitutional importance.[49] In contrast, the discrimination point was never argued in *Bellinger*, although interestingly this is how the treatment of transgendered individuals has been dealt with in other forums, such as the ECJ.[50] The fact that the House of Lords in *Mendoza* felt emboldened to take a much stronger stance on a question of discrimination is perhaps not surprising. The Canadian Supreme Court, which has generally taken a similarly deferential approach on sensitive socio-economic issues relating to the family, has also been much more robust in its use of the Canadian Charter where principles of equality and non-discrimination are at stake.[51] However, although the different approaches may be

---

[48] *Mendoza v. Ghaidan* [2001] EWCA Civ 1553; [2003] 1 FLR 468, para. 20. See also the remarks of Keene LJ, *ibid.*, para. 42. In contrast, it should be noted that, in the case of *Evans* v. *Amicus Healthcare Ltd* [2004] EWCA Civ 727; [2004] 3 All ER 1025, the Secretary of State for Health provided comprehensive and detailed evidence as to the legislative history and rationale of the policy considerations underlying the Human Fertilisation and Embryology Act 1990.

[49] *Ghaidan v. Godin-Mendoza* [2004] UKHL 30; [2004] 2 AC 557, para. 132.

[50] Case C-117/01, *KB v. NHS Pensions Service Agency*, judgment of 7 January 2004. Thanks to Clare McGlynn for this point.

[51] See generally, Boyd above n. 2.

rationalised, as they stand, these two key family law cases give rise to a confused and contradictory picture as to the impact of the HRA in the family law context – one supporting the pessimistic predictions outlined above; the other suggesting an unexpected judicial revolution in the family law field.

Public law on children

The importance of protecting 'the family unit' from arbitrary intervention by state authorities constitutes a core principle of liberal doctrine and human rights law. In parallel to the ECHR, it has been a fundamental principle of English domestic law for many years and is now given expression in s.1(5) and s.31 of the Children Act 1989 (CA).[52] One might therefore have expected that the English courts would feel fairly comfortable with the application of Convention values and human rights reasoning to public law cases on children. This, for the English judiciary, is familiar territory and territory in which the doctrine of rights seems particularly appropriate. Indeed, the courts have generally adapted to the HRA and the application of ECHR arguments in the public law context with ease. Since the implementation of the HRA, the demands of the Convention case-law have been taken extremely seriously with some significant changes resulting to both law and social work practice.

An activist approach to the HRA in the public law context

One reason why the domestic courts have had to take the demands of the ECHR in the public law context so seriously is Strasbourg's increasingly robust approach where the state has intervened into private family life on the basis of the child's welfare.[53] It is therefore not surprising that it is in this area of family law that the effects of the Convention were first felt.

---

[52] Section 1(5) of the Children Act 1989 provides: 'Where a court is considering whether or not to make one or more orders under this Act with respect to a child, it shall not make the order or any of the orders unless it considers that doing so would be better for the child than making no order at all.' Section 31(2) of the Children Act 1989 sets a threshold of establishing an existing or a real possibility of future 'significant harm' to the child before compulsory state intervention can be justified.

[53] See e.g. W v. *United Kingdom* (1988) 10 EHRR 29; *Kutzner* v. *Germany* [2003] 1 FCR 249; *Venema* v. *The Netherlands* [2003] 1 FLR 552; *KA* v. *Finland* [2003] 1 FLR 696; and *P, C and S* v. *UK* [2002] 2 FLR 631.

In *Re C and B (Care Order: Future Harm)*,[54] a pre-implementation case, Hale LJ emphasised that in the context of care proceedings the ECtHR requires state intervention to be proportionate. This requires any action taken by the state to be temporary in nature, have the aim of reuniting the family and prevents all contact between the child and his/her family from being terminated unless justified by the 'overriding necessity of the interests of the child'.[55] There have also been particularly strong judicial statements as to the high demands now placed upon local authorities, particularly in terms of the procedural requirements imposed by Article 8 of the Convention. In *Re G (Care: Challenge to Local Authority's Decision)*,[56] Munby J stressed, in a particularly forceful judgment, that the HRA requires urgent changes to 'a "mindset" and "culture" so seemingly oblivious to the imperative requirements of Art. 8 of the European Convention'.[57] Thus he remarked that, 'even some two years after the Human Rights Act 1998 came into force, and, as we shall see, despite no lack of relevant judicial authority, some very important and basic messages have still not worked their way through into day-to-day practice on the ground'.[58] He went on to point out that Article 8 imposes positive obligations on a local authority to ensure that parents are properly involved in the decision-making process, including ensuring that the process is properly documented and that there is proper and timely disclosure to the parents of the relevant documents.[59]

It is therefore evident that the courts are taking the HRA extremely seriously in public law cases and, in particular, are imposing increasingly high standards on local authorities. The substantive changes they are demanding in local authority practices are again to be welcomed – they can only work to the advantage of both the parent and the child. The implementation of the HRA has brought an important new dimension to public law cases and there is some evidence that ECHR arguments will in future form an integral and fairly routine part of the decision-making process. Thus in *Re V (A Child)*,[60] the Court of Appeal set down detailed guidance as to the way in which the HRA should be raised and argued in

---

[54] [2001] 1 FLR 611.   [55] *Ibid.*, paras. 31–3.

[56] [2003] EWHC Fam 551; [2003] 2 FLR 42.

[57] See also *Re L (Care Assessment: Fair Trial)* [2002] 2 FLR 730.   [58] *Ibid.*, paras. 2–3.

[59] *Ibid.*, para. 59. The procedural requirements Munby J imposes on the local authority are extensive: *Ibid.*, para. 45.

[60] [2004] EWCA Civ 54; [2004] 1 All ER 997.

public law care proceedings.[61] However, although the importance of the
HRA to public law care proceedings has generally been accepted by the
family law bench, important pockets of resistance remain in which both
of the two potentially restraining factors identified, have been key.

Continuing pockets of resistance

Opposition to the language of 'rights' in child protection proceedings

Resistance to the introduction of a rights-based discourse in the family
law context is more usually seen in private law disputes. However, this
reason for continuing resistance to the routine application of ECHR
arguments in care proceedings is discernible in the judgment of Charles J
in *Re R (Care: Disclosure: Nature of Proceedings)*,[62] in which, after a brief
summary of the leading domestic and Strasbourg authorities, he throws
doubt on the value of trying to articulate the claims of the parties in
terms of their respective rights.[63] His concern about the use of a rights-
based discourse in this particular context appears based on the fear that
such an approach will obscure what should, in his view, be the central
principle in care proceedings: the paramountcy of the child's welfare.[64]
That concern is understandable. Without a developed jurisprudence on
children's rights capable of counterbalancing the rights-based assertions
of the child's parents, there is a danger that the elevation of the interests
of the parents to that of a 'right' will result in the marginalisation of the
legitimate interests of the child.[65] This concern is to some extent borne
out by the Strasbourg case-law. In the context of care proceedings, it is
clear that Strasbourg considers that Article 8 confers certain protections
on the child's parents which are accurately conceptualised as rights. To
give someone a right is to bring something qualitatively different into
the decision-making process. As Gavin Phillipson points out, rights have
'a special status over other interests';[66] they have an assumed weight and
significance. Thus, although the ECtHR has constantly reiterated that the

---

[61] See also *Re L (Care Proceedings: Human Rights Claims)* [2003] EWHC Fam 665; [2003] 2
FLR 160.
[62] [2002] 1 FLR 755.   [63] *Ibid.*, p. 770.   [64] *Ibid.*, pp. 770–1.
[65] See J. Fortin, 'Rights Brought Home for Children' (1999) 62 MLR 350, 357–9; and
M. Woolf, 'Coming of Age? The Principle of "The Best Interests of the Child"' [2003]
EHRLR 205, 211–12.
[66] G. Phillipson, 'Transforming Breach of Confidence? Towards a Common Law Right of
Privacy under the Human Rights Act' (2003) 66 MLR 726, 750.

best interests of the child are of 'crucial importance' under Article 8(2), the fact that the interests of the child are not elevated to the status of a fundamental right can lead to those interests being treated as somehow less weighty and important than those of the parents. A clear manifestation of this problem can be found in the long line of Strasbourg authority which makes clear that, whilst a fair balance has to be struck between the interests of the child and the potentially competing interests of the parent, there will be some circumstances in which the interests of the child will not be considered sufficiently weighty to justify a particularly serious interference with the rights of the parents.[67] The problem can, however, be addressed without abandoning the human rights discourse altogether. A developed jurisprudence on children's rights which gives clear recognition to the rights of the child, as well as the child's welfare, would ensure that the rights of the child act as an effective counterbalance to the rights of the parents under Article 8(2), whilst constituting a clear basis for the child to bring his/her own action against the state under Article 8(1) or Article 3. Clear recognition of the importance of children's rights would thus help to restore a more acceptable balance to the Convention arguments.[68] An encouraging example of the courts attempting to perform this balancing exercise within the domestic context is provided by *R. (on the Application of Axon) v. Secretary of State for Health*.[69] In this case, Silber J held that, even assuming parents have an Article 8 right to be notified by a medical professional of any advice and/or treatment given to their children on sexual matters, including abortion, such interference could be justified under Article 8(2) to protect children's own rights to confidentiality and to 'make decisions about their own lives by themselves at the expense of the views of their parents'.[70] However, although

---

[67] The guiding principle is taken from *Johansen* v. *Norway* (1997) 23 EHRR 33, para. 78, which provides: 'In carrying out this balancing exercise, the court will attach particular importance to the best interests of the child, which, depending on their nature and seriousness, may override those of the parent.'

[68] This argument is derived from that made by Phillipson and Fenwick in the context of the need to draw a fair balance between the right to privacy and the right to freedom of expression under Articles 8 and 10 of the Convention. See H. Fenwick and G. Phillipson, 'Breach of Confidence as a Privacy Remedy in the Human Rights Era' (2000) 63 MLR 660, 687; and Phillipson, above n. 66, pp. 748–53. For a detailed examination of the issues surrounding balancing rights in the context of media free speech and the privacy of children, see Chapter 10.

[69] [2006] EWHC Admin 37, paras. 144–5.

[70] *Ibid.*, paras. 76–80 and 144–5.

Silber J's approach to the Article 8 arguments, and his conceptualisation of the rights of the child in particular, were encouraging, his suggestion, relying on *Yousef* v. *Netherlands*,[71] that the rights of the child would *always* 'override' the rights of the parent, is more problematic.

Difficult questions of public policy: the socio-economic context and the problem of scarce resources

Predictably, the second factor acting as a restraint on the use of the Convention in public law care proceedings is the socio-economic context in which such cases must be decided and the difficult questions of public policy which thereby arise. Questions of socio-economic policy and, in particular, the allocation of scarce resources is difficult territory for the courts, into which, post-implementation of the HRA, they are increasingly finding themselves drawn. The constitutional and evidential challenges raised by such issues are clearly evident in the public law cases.

A clear indication of how the courts will respond to the 'invitation' provided by the HRA to enter previously protected spheres of local authority decision-making is provided by *Re G (A Child) (Interim Care Order: Residential Assessment)*,[72] *R. (on the Application of G)* v. *Barnet London Borough Council*[73] and *Re S; Re W*[74] – the three leading House of Lords cases which have arisen in this context. In line with the *Bellinger* decision, these cases take a very conservative and cautious approach to the HRA, showing great deference to Parliament's intention in preserving the local authority's protected sphere of discretionary power.

Since the ECHR imposes a clear obligation on the local authority to take positive steps to preserve family ties and reconcile parent and child should removal prove necessary,[75] disputes will inevitably arise over whether the local authority could or should have done more, typically by the provision of services, treatment or therapy, to keep the family together. This issue arose in *Re G (A Child) (Interim Care Order: Residential Assessment)*,[76] where the human rights arguments were

---

[71] (2003) 36 EHRR 345.   [72] [2005] UKHL 68; [2006] 1 AC 576.

[73] *R. (on the Application of G)* v. *Barnet London Borough Council; R. (on the Application of W)* v. *Lambeth London Council; R. (on the Application of A)* v. *Lambeth London Borough Council* [2003] UKHL 57; [2004] 1 All ER 97.

[74] *Re S (Minors) (Care Order: Implementation of Care Plan)* [2002] UKHL 10; [2002] 2 AC 291.

[75] *Kutzner* v. *Germany* [2003] 1 FCR 249, paras. 61 and 65.

[76] [2005] UKHL 98; [2006] 1 AC 576.

summarily dismissed. The case concerned the power of the court under s.38(6) CA 1989 to direct a local authority to undertake and pay for therapeutic treatment for the child's mother under the auspices of an interim care order. A strict reading of the statutory language suggested the court could only direct 'a medical or psychiatric examination' or 'some other assessment' of 'the child'.[77] It was argued that Article 8 placed the state under a positive obligation to provide for the child's mother to receive the proposed therapeutic treatment in order to 'provide [the child] and her family with the optimum chance of being able to live together as a family' and s.38(6) should be interpreted accordingly.[78] Lord Scott dismissed the argument out of hand, simply holding that 'there is no art. 8 right to be made a better parent at public expense'.[79] Lord Clyde gave the human rights arguments even shorter shrift, dismissing them as irrelevant,[80] and, surprisingly, Baroness Hale did not refer to them at all. The House of Lords were clearly concerned by the resource implications of holding the local authority to more expansive duties with respect to the provision of treatment services and firmly rejected the opportunity presented by the HRA to force the local authority to account for its funding decisions.[81]

The prioritisation and appropriate allocation of local authority resources was also a major issue in *R. (G)* v. *Barnet London Borough Council*. The three appeals heard together by the House of Lords were principally concerned with the correct interpretation of s.17(1) CA 1989 and, in particular, whether an assessment carried out pursuant to that provision gave rise to an enforceable duty on the local authority to meet the assessed needs of the child.[82] A second issue arising in two of the appeals was whether a local authority which had assessed a child to be in need of accommodation under s.20 CA 1989 could insist on providing accommodation just for the child rather than for both the child and his/ her mother together. Both Lord Nicholls in dissent and Lord Hope giving judgment for the majority made only cursory reference to the Article 8 arguments. With respect to the local authority's duty under

---

[77] [1997] 1 FLR 1.   [78] *Ibid.*, para. 24.   [79] *Ibid.*   [80] *Ibid.*, para. 33.

[81] *Ibid.*, para. 23, *per* Lord Scott.

[82] Section 17(1) of the Children Act 1989 provides: 'It shall be the general duty of every local authority (in addition to the other duties imposed on them by this Part) – (a) to safeguard and promote the welfare of the children within their area who are in need; and (b) so far as is consistent with that duty, to promote the upbringing of such children by their families, by providing a range and level of services appropriate to those children's needs.'

s.20, both judgments noted in very general terms the positive obligation placed upon the state pursuant to Article 8 to 'secure or protect an effective respect for family life'.[83] However, the wide margin of discretion afforded to the state in this difficult area was also emphasised.[84] Lord Nicholls was alone in simply recording the submission of counsel that 'choosing to accommodate the child only in such a case would be a decision which did not respect the family life of the child or his parent' and that 'such a decision by a local authority would be unlawful: s.6(1) of the Human Rights Act 1998'.[85]

The limited use made of the Convention in this case, particularly with respect to s.17, is disappointing. There are clearly strong human rights arguments which can be made to support the contention that s.17(1) and s.20 should be read compatibly with Article 8 of the Convention to impose an enforceable duty on the local authority to meet the assessed needs of a child, including any need of that child for accommodation with his/her family.[86] The House of Lords, however, made only the briefest reference to the Convention arguments. Their failure to address the issue explicitly means we can only speculate as to their hesitance to give a robust interpretation to the local authority's duties. However, the court's obvious concern not to cross the constitutional divide by embarking upon its own examination of difficult questions of public policy involving complex socio-economic issues, was clearly important. The notorious problems of local authorities' limited resources, and the need to show deference to a statutory scheme carefully constructed by Parliament, were clearly at the forefront of the minds of the judges. Thus Lord Nicholls began his judgment by observing, '[b]ehind the legal questions arising in these appeals is the seemingly intractable problem of local authorities' lack of resources'.[87] He continued:

> The financial resources of local authorities are finite. The scope for local authorities to increase the amount of their revenue is strictly limited. So, year by year they must decide what priority to give to the multifarious competing demands on their limited resources. They have to decide which needs are the most urgent and pressing. The more money they allocate for one purpose, the less they have to spend on another.[88]

---

[83] R. (G) [2003] UKHL 57; [2004] 1 All ER 97, para. 52, per Lord Nicholls.
[84] Ibid., para. 68, per Lord Hope.   [85] Ibid., para. 52, per Lord Nicholls.
[86] See Palmer, above n. 8.
[87] R. (G) [2003] UKHL 57; [2004] 1 All ER 97, para. 10, per Lord Nicholls.
[88] Ibid., para. 11.

Similarly, in dismissing the argument that s.17(1) gives rise to any specific enforceable duty to provide accommodation for a child and his/her family, Lord Hope for the majority pointed out:

> The expenditure of limited resources on the provision of residential accommodation for housing these children with their families would be bound to mean that there was less available for expenditure on other services designed for the performance of the general duty which s.17(1) has identified. A reading of that subsection as imposing a specific duty on the local social services authority to provide residential accommodation to individual children in need who have been assessed to be in need of such accommodation would sit uneasily with the legislation in the Housing Acts. As Mr Goudie pointed out, it could have the effect of turning the social services department of the local authority into another kind of housing department with a different set of priorities for the provision of housing for the homeless than those which s.59 of the Housing Act 1985 lays down for the local housing authority.[89]

The decision of the House of Lords in *Re S; Re W* betrays a similar hesitance to enter the previously forbidden realm of local authority discretion as carefully crafted by Parliament. However, in *Re S; Re W*, the House of Lords did at least explicitly confront the potential impact of the Convention in this area, raising again the constitutional question of where the line between judicial interpretation and improper judicial legislation should be drawn in cases giving rise to difficult questions of public policy. It was well recognised by the profession that the introduction and supervision of starred care plans, as proposed by the Court of Appeal in this case, constituted a radical revision of the division of power, functions and responsibilities between the local authority and the court in public care proceedings.[90] As Lord Nicholls observed:

> First, a cardinal principle of the Children Act is that when the court makes a care order it becomes the duty of the local authority designated by the order to receive the child into its care while the order remains in force . . . While a care order is in force the court's powers, under its inherent jurisdiction, are expressly excluded: section 100(2)(c) and (d) . . . The Act delineated the boundary of responsibility with complete clarity. Where a care order is made the responsibility for the child's care is with the authority rather than the court. The court retains no supervisory role,

---

[89] *Ibid.*, para. 93, *per* Lord Hope.
[90] See *Re W and B (Children) (Care Plan); Re W (Children) (Care Plan)* [2001] EWCA Civ 757; [2001] 2 FLR 582.

monitoring the authority's discharge of its responsibilities. That was the intention of Parliament.[91]

The first question addressed by Lords Nicholls is whether, in accordance with s.3 HRA, it is possible to interpret the Children Act in such a way as to give effect to the Article 8 and Article 6 rights of the child and his or her parents; in other words, to interpret the Children Act to permit the introduction of a starred system. Lord Nicholls answered that question with an unequivocal 'no'. In his view, to introduce rights and liabilities by reading into the Act a completely new scheme not provided for in the express words of the statute would constitute an act of judicial legislation rather than interpretation. As Lord Nicholls pointed out, what the Court of Appeal was proposing cut across the entire legislative scheme for the division of powers between the court and the local authority as originally intended by Parliament and subsequently upheld by the courts. Moreover, there were good policy reasons behind that legislative scheme:

> The particular strength of the courts lies in the resolution of disputes: its ability to hear all sides of a case, to decide issues of fact and law, and to make a firm decision on a particular issue at a particular time. But a court cannot have day to day responsibility for a child. The court cannot deliver the services which may best serve a child's needs. Unlike a local authority, a court does not have the task of managing the financial and human resources available to a local authority for dealing with all children in need in its area. The authority must manage these resources in the best interest of all the children for whom it is responsible.[92]

The Court of Appeal's apparent disregard for the clear legislative intention of Parliament is clearly exacerbated for Lord Nicholls by the fact that any change to the legislative scheme would have far-reaching implications for local authorities in terms of the prioritisation and allocation of their resources – questions the courts are, in his view, ill-placed to judge:

> The starring system would not come free from additional administrative work and expense. It would be likely to have a material effect on authorities' allocation of scarce financial and other resources. This in turn

---

[91] *Re S (Minors) (Care Order: Implementation of Care Plan)* [2002] UKHL 10; [2002] 2 AC 291, paras. 23–35.
[92] *Ibid.*, para. 27.

would affect authorities' discharge of their responsibilities to other
children . . . These are matters for decision by Parliament not the courts.

Lord Nicholls therefore concluded that s.3 HRA cannot be legitimately
employed to achieve the result desired by the Court of Appeal.

Having thus concluded that under s.3 HRA it was not possible to
'interpret' the Children Act in such a way as to permit the introduction
of the 'starring system', the next question for the House of Lords was
whether or not, in light of that conclusion, the Children Act was
incompatible with Articles 6 and 8 of the Convention and a declaration
of incompatibility should be made pursuant to s.4 HRA. Lord Nicholls
accepted the argument that as the Children Act stands it may fail to
provide an adequate remedy for the child and/or his or her parents if the
local authority fails to discharge its responsibilities under a care order
properly. However, he took the view that the Children Act's failure to
provide a remedy to the child if the local authority breaches the child's
Article 8 rights is not itself a breach of Article 8 – it is, if anything, a
breach of Article 13 of the Convention which has not been incorporated
into domestic law.[93] He also accepted that the parents and/or the child's
lack of access to a court in order to challenge the local authority's neglect
of duty may constitute a breach of their Article 6 Convention rights.[94]
However, Lord Nicholls again pointed out that the absence of a provision does not necessarily mean that the Children Act is incompatible
with Articles 6 and 8; it means, at most, that there exists a lacuna in the
statute, not a statutory incompatibility.[95] This raised the difficult question of whether in these circumstances it was appropriate to make a
declaration of incompatibility.[96] Unfortunately, Lord Nicholls failed to
answer the question, having deemed it to be unnecessary for two reasons. As regards the parents he concluded that it was a largely theoretical
question because any violation of their Convention rights could be
protected by taking action under s.7 HRA.[97] The potential breach of
the rights of a child unable to bring an action under s.7 because of the
lack of an appropriate legal representative was ignored. The second
reason relied on was the lack of a 'victim' on the particular facts of

[93] *Ibid.*, paras. 56–60 and 63–4. For criticisms of this approach, see N. Mole and T. Brown,
'Re S (Children) (Care Order: Implementation of Care Plan)' [2003] EHRLR 336, 340.
[94] *Re S, ibid.*, paras. 79–83.
[95] *Ibid.*, paras. 83–6. Again, see the criticisms of Mole and Brown, above n. 93, p. 342.
[96] *Re S, ibid.*, para. 87.   [97] *Ibid.*, paras. 61, 62 and 88.

the case – the local authority in question having been 'galvanised into taking the necessary action'.[98]

The reluctance of the House of Lords to act robustly under s.3 HRA in cases giving rise to sensitive questions of public policy, particularly socio-economic policy, has been the subject of strong criticism.[99] However, in defence of the cautious approach displayed by the House of Lords in all three cases, the implementation of the HRA cannot in and of itself give the courts the institutional competence to simply override Parliament on matters of socio-economic policy, particularly where they are confronted with a comprehensive legislative scheme which has been constructed on the basis of clear, rational policy objectives and the proposed course of action cuts across a fundamental principle of that scheme.[100] That is not to say that there are no means by which the courts could seek to acquire the necessary 'institutional competence' to deal with such matters. There are clearly steps which could be taken in terms of the nature of the evidence typically presented to the court which would help close the current constitutional divide.[101] However, even if one accepts that there are ways to improve the institutional competence of the court, legitimate questions still arise as to the 'constitutional (im)propriety'[102] of using s.3 HRA to fundamentally rewrite a complex statutory code – despite their new and potentially expansive human rights mandate.

Lord Nicholls' refusal to issue a declaration of incompatibility under s.4 HRA is, however, more problematic. Even assuming that Lord Nicholls was right in his analysis of the Convention case-law, his arguments for avoiding the issue and disposing of a case of such importance in this way were disappointing. Having identified a clear potential breach of the Convention rights of the child, Lord Nicholls' refusal to issue a formal declaration of incompatibility to try and ensure this breach was addressed by the government displayed an excessive degree of caution in the use of his powers under s.4. This is particularly so as, much as the Court of Appeal did in *Bellinger*, he concluded his judgment

---

[98] *Ibid.*, para. 88.   [99] Palmer, above n. 8.

[100] See also C. Brennan, 'Third Party Liability for Child Abuse: Unanswered Questions' (2003) 25 *Journal of Social Welfare and Family Law* 23, 31–3.

[101] There is, for example, evidence of this occurring in the Canadian context as the Charter litigation has developed. See Boyd, above n. 2, pp. 295–6.

[102] Palmer, above n. 8, p. 309.

with a strong plea to the government to take the appropriate legislative measures:

> I cannot stress too strongly that the rejection of this innovation on legal grounds must not obscure the pressing need for the Government to attend to the serious practical and legal problems identified by the Court of Appeal or mentioned by me. One of the questions needing urgent consideration is whether some degree of court supervision of local authorities' discharge of their parental responsibilities would bring about an overall improvement in the quality of child care provided by local authorities. Answering this question calls for a wider examination than can be undertaken by a court. The judgments of the Court of Appeal in the present case have performed a valuable service in highlighting the need for such an examination to be conducted without delay.[103]

This resort to informal bidding did indeed achieve the desired response. The government took the legislative opportunity presented by the Adoption and Children Act 2002 to amend the Children Act 1989 and provide much better protection for the rights of a child in care.[104]

Summary

Despite the generally positive reception of the HRA into public law proceedings on children and the generally positive substantive reforms it has initiated, the prevailing mistrust of rights amongst family lawyers, and the complex public policy questions which frequently arise in this context, have clearly exerted a restraining influence in the more difficult cases. In particular, the three House of Lords decisions considered exemplify the continuing caution of the judiciary in applying the HRA given its perceived constitutional limits when applied to sensitive matters of public policy, particularly if the case touches upon difficult questions of socio-economic policy and will have far-ranging administrative and economic effects. Whilst that deference to the democratically elected bodies may disappoint commentators who were hoping for a stronger, more activist approach by the judiciary across all areas of child law, the underlying rationale for that caution, given the institutional limits of the courts, is at least understandable.

---

[103] *Re S (Minors) (Care Order: Implementation of Care Plan)* [2002] UKHL 10; [2002] 2 AC 291, para. 106. See also the speech of Lord Mackay, at para. 112.
[104] Children Act 1989, ss.26(2)(e) and (k) and (2A).

Private law disputes over children

Less understandable is the emerging trend in judicial reasoning in cases concerning private law disputes over children. As expected, it is in this context that the deeply entrenched hostility towards the introduction of rights-based discourse into intra-familial disputes has been most clearly and markedly felt. The suspicion with which the HRA has been greeted in private law cases appears to stem from a genuine concern that the introduction of the Convention's rights-based approach will constitute a damaging step back from a world in which the welfare of the child is the focus of decision-making, to a world in which parental rights are privileged and prioritised.

Disputes falling outside the scope of the welfare principle: a more positive response to the HRA

In some private law disputes where s.1 CA 1989 has been deemed not to apply and the child's welfare is therefore not the paramount consideration, the Convention arguments have generally been quite warmly received.[105] In the case of *Re T (Paternity: Ordering Blood Tests)*,[106] a paternity dispute governed by ss.20 and 21 of the Family Law Reform Act 1969, having held that under domestic law the child's interests were not the paramount consideration but must be weighed against the competing interests of the adults involved,[107] the court went on to undertake a substantive analysis of the various Convention arguments, including making limited reference to the Strasbourg jurisprudence, and concluded:

> [I]n evaluating and balancing the various rights of the adult parties and of
> T under Art.8, the weightiest emerges clearly as being that of T, namely
> that he should have the possibility of knowing, perhaps with certainty, his

---

[105] Section 1 of the Children Act 1989 provides in full: 'When a court determines any question with respect to – (a) the upbringing of a child; or (b) the administration of a child's property or the application of any income arising from it, the child's welfare shall be the court's paramount consideration.'

[106] [2001] 2 FLR 1190.

[107] *Ibid.*, p. 1197. It is still unclear how the amendment introduced to s.21(3) of the Family Law Reform Act 1969 on obtaining consent to the taking of samples from a child for the purposes of DNA tests relates to s.20 on the ordering of tests. It may be that in the future the two questions will be collapsed and a simple welfare test will be applied. The paramountcy principle was not, however, applied in this case.

true roots and identity. I find any such interference as would occur to the right to respect for the family/private life of the mother and her husband, to be proportionate to the legitimate aim of providing T with the possibility of certainty as to his real paternity, a knowledge which would accompany him throughout his life.[108]

The courts have also shown an increasing awareness of the possible impact of Article 8 on procedural issues arising under the Children Act.[109] In the case of *Re J (Leave to Issue Application for Residence Order)*,[110] Thorpe LJ held that the statutory test for determining leave applications under s.10(9) CA 1989 must not be qualified by a requirement to demonstrate 'a good arguable case' given that the applicant grandparents 'manifestly enjoy Art.6 rights to a fair trial and, in the nature of things, are also likely to enjoy Art.8 rights'.[111] The courts have also become increasingly concerned with the issue of how to ensure effective representation for the child given the need to take his or her independent rights and interests into account.[112] Thus, in *Re T (A Child: Contact)*,[113] a difficult contact dispute in which it was alleged that the hostile attitude of the mother towards contact had alienated the child from his father, Thorpe LJ forcefully rejected counsel's 'dismissive' submission that the Strasbourg cases added nothing to the domestic jurisprudence, arguing that the Convention's standards may well be higher than those enshrined within domestic law and there were thus important questions of public policy at stake that Parliament may well have to address:

> Those cases [from Strasbourg] as they stand suggest that the methods and levels of investigation that our courts have conventionally adopted when trying out issues of alienation may not meet the standards that Arts.6 and 8 ... require. There are policy issues here that the Government and the judiciary may need to consider collaboratively. Should judges see children to ascertain their wishes and feelings? If that is to become the norm, what training should judges receive? To what extent should separate representation be made available to the child at the heart of the case

---

[108] *Ibid.*, pp. 1197–8. This point was reiterated by Butler-Sloss P in *Secretary of State for Work and Pensions* v. *Jones* [2004] 1 FLR 282.

[109] It has also impacted upon issues of procedural fairness in adoption. See *Re M (Adoption: Rights of Natural Father)* [2001] 1 FLR 745, 752–5.

[110] [2002] EWCA Civ 1364; [2003] 1 FLR 114.   [111] *Ibid.*, para. 18.

[112] See *Re A (Contact: Separate Representation)* [2001] 1 FLR 715, para. 22; *Mabon* v. *Mabon* [2005] EWCA Civ 634; [2005] 2 FLR 1011, paras. 23–32.

[113] [2002] EWCA Civ 1736; [2003] 1 FLR 531.

in private law proceedings? What services can the Children and Family Court Advisory and Support Service be expected to provide in order to assist the forensic process to satisfy Convention standards?[114]

A similar willingness to engage with the Convention is also evident in the judgment of Munby J in the case of *Re D (Intractable Contact Dispute: Publicity)*.[115] The case was concerned with the enforcement of contact orders, another area of domestic family law in which it is clearly established that the child's welfare is not the paramount consideration.[116] Despite the ECtHR's finding in favour of the UK government on this issue in *Glaser* v. *UK*,[117] Munby J undertook his own detailed and wide-ranging analysis of the relevant Strasbourg authorities and concluded that domestic courts 'can no longer simply complacently assume that our conventional domestic approach to such cases meets the standards required by Art.6 and Art.8'.[118] In his words, the Court of Appeal has 'sounded the wake-up call',[119] and, on the issue of contact, he thus concludes that the Convention now demands a much stronger, more interventionist approach.

The welfare principle and a strong resistance to rights-based reasoning[120]

Unfortunately, the Court of Appeal's 'wake-up call' has not penetrated into substantive disputes concerning the upbringing of a child where the welfare principle applies. In these cases, for those who can see the

---

[114] *Ibid.*, para. 25. However, these comments were based on a chamber judgment of the ECtHR in *Sahin* v. *Germany; Sommerfeld* v. *Germany* [2003] 2 FLR 671, a decision subsequently successfully referred by the German government to the ECtHR's Grand Chamber. It is interesting to note that the child's right to be heard was *not* independently considered by the ECtHR as a right of the child but mitigated through the right of the father to receive a fair hearing.

[115] [2004] EWHC 727; [2004] 1 FLR 1226.

[116] See e.g. *Re M and Others (Minors) (Breach of Contact Order: Committal)* [1999] Fam 263.

[117] (2001) 33 EHRR 1; [2001] 1 FLR 153.

[118] *Re D (Intractable Contact Dispute: Publicity)* [2004] EWHC 727; [2004] 1 FLR 1226, para. 35.

[119] *Ibid.*, para. 35.

[120] This section of the paper draws heavily on previously published work of the author. Please see D. Bonner, H. Fenwick and S. Harris-Short, 'Judicial Approaches to the Human Rights Act' (2003) 52 ICLQ 549, 572–84; and S. Harris-Short, 'Re B (Adoption: Natural Parent) Putting the child at the heart of adoption?' (2002) 14 *Child and Family Law Quarterly* 325.

advantages of a rights-based approach in private family law disputes, the impact of the Convention arguments remains disappointingly weak. The problem derives from the interpretation of the word 'paramount' as set down by the House of Lords in *J* v. *C*.[121] According to the House of Lords, 'paramount' means that, in matters relating to the upbringing of a child, the child's welfare must be the court's *only* consideration.[122] The rights and interests of others, including the child's parents, are deemed irrelevant unless they can be shown to have some direct bearing upon the child's best interests. Although, as Herring points out, the English courts have used a variety of mechanisms to address parental rights and interests through the medium of the welfare test,[123] this approach does not sit easily with the Convention, particularly in light of the requirement under Article 8(1) to give separate and *independent* consideration to the rights of the child's parents. However, in the period immediately preceding implementation of the HRA, clear signs of judicial opposition to any attempt to 'revisit' the paramountcy of the child's welfare in light of the Convention began to emerge.[124] Seven years after implementation, that opposition has not subsided.

One of the most disappointing features of the post-implementation case-law in this context is the apparent reluctance of the courts to confront the issue of the potential incompatibility between the welfare principle and Article 8 of the Convention. Rather than explicitly addressing the possible implications of ss.3, 4 and 6 HRA and providing a convincing defence of the welfare principle in accordance with Article 8 of the Convention, the courts have tended to simply ignore the HRA altogether or to restrict themselves to vague statements as to the need to give effect to the Convention rights of the parties.[125] There is, in short, a marked failure in many of the private law cases to engage with the Convention arguments in any sustained or convincing manner.

---

[121] [1970] AC 668.

[122] *Ibid.*, p. 697, *per* Lord Guest; *ibid.*, pp. 710–11 and 715, *per* Lord MacDermott; and *ibid.*, p. 727, *per* Lord Donovan.

[123] Herring, above n. 4, pp. 225–7.

[124] See e.g. *Re C (HIV Test)* [1999] 2 FLR 1004, 1016G (*per* Wilson J at first instance) and 1021 (*per* Butler-Sloss LJ on appeal); *Re P (Section 91(14) Guidelines) (Residence and Religious Heritage)* [1999] 2 FLR 573, 598–9; *Re A (Conjoined Twins: Medical Treatment)* [2001] 1 FLR 1, 117 (not challenged on appeal, see [2000] 1 FLR 571, 575); *Dawson and Wearmouth* [1999] 1 FLR 1167, 1174 and 1181; and *Re A (Permission to Remove Child from Jurisdiction: Human Rights)* [2000] 2 FLR 225, 226–7 and 229–30.

[125] See *Payne* v. *Payne* [2001] EWCA Civ 166; [2001] 1 FLR 1052, paras. 35–9 and 81–2; and *Re H (Contact Order) (No. 2)* [2002] 1 FLR 22, para. 59.

A strong example of how the process of reasoning has developed in the private law cases is provided by the judgment of Wall J in *Re H (Contact Order) (No. 2)*.[126] The case concerned an application by the child's father for direct contact with the child against the wishes of the mother. The mother was opposed to contact because the father was suffering from Huntingdon's disease and posed a potential risk to the children's safety. In the last paragraph of his judgment, Wall J held:

> Finally, it will be apparent that I have made no mention of the European Convention for the Protection of Human Rights and Fundamental Freedoms 1950 in this judgment. Inevitably, however, every order made under s.8 of the Children Act 1989 represents in some measure an interference by a public authority (the court) in the right to respect for family life contained in Article 8. The court's interference must, of course, be in accordance with the powers given to the court under the Children Act 1989, and proportionate. Every application involves the court balancing the rights of the participants to the application (including the children who are the subjects of it) and arriving at a result which is in the interests of those children (or least detrimental to those interests) and proportionate to the legitimate aims being pursued. However, it seems to me that a proper application of the checklist in s 1(3) of the Children Act 1989 is equivalent to the balancing exercise required in the application of Article 8, which is then a useful cross-check to ensure that the order proposed is in accordance with the law, necessary for the protection of the rights and freedoms of others and proportionate. In my judgment, and for all the reasons I have given, the order I am making in this case fulfils those criteria.[127]

There is no citation of Strasbourg jurisprudence in support of this contention.

As I have argued elsewhere, this rather cursory consideration of the Convention and its case-law is not uncommon.[128] In fact, in what has become a fairly standard approach, the court will typically give detailed and careful consideration to the welfare test and the child's best interests, before turning dismissively in the final paragraph to the Convention arguments and concluding that Article 8 has no material effect on the decision which has already been reached on the basis of

---

[126] *Re H (Contact Order) (No. 2), ibid.*   [127] *Ibid.*, para. 59.   [128] Above, n. 120.

welfare.[129] As in *Re H*, the usual reason given for this conclusion is that the balancing of interests required under s.1 CA 1989 is exactly the same as the balancing of interests required under Article 8 of the Convention. Alternatively, it is simply argued that, whilst the order may constitute a *prima facie* interference with the Article 8(1) rights of one of the parties, the child's welfare will constitute an automatic justification for the interference in accordance with the requirements of Article 8(2). Consequently, if the court reaches a decision in accordance with the best interests of the child, it will automatically be deemed to comply with Article 8. This approach to the Convention is now well established in English law, having been confirmed in clear, unequivocal terms by the Court of Appeal in *Payne* v. *Payne*[130] and, perhaps most significantly, by Lord Nicholls in the House of Lords in the case of *Re B (Adoption: Natural Parent)*:

> The balancing exercise required by Art. 8, does not differ in substance from the like balancing exercise undertaken by a court when deciding whether in the conventional phraseology of English law, adoption would be in the best interests of the child. The like considerations fall to be taken into account. Although the phraseology is different, the criteria to be applied in deciding whether an adoption order is justified under Art. 8(2) lead to the same result as the convention tests applied by English law. Thus, unless the court misdirected itself in some material respect when balancing the competing factors, its conclusion that an adoption order is in the best interests of the child, even though this would exclude the mother from the child's life, identifies the pressing social need for adoption and represents the court's considered view on proportionality.[131]

The strong message from Lord Nicholls in *Re B* that the HRA does not require any change to the traditional understanding and application of the welfare principle in private family law disputes is particularly disappointing given the detailed analysis of the Convention arguments in the judgment of Hale LJ in the Court of Appeal.[132] The approach taken by Lord Nicholls in the House of Lords is, however, telling. It is clearly likely to discourage practitioners who are more enthusiastic about

---

[129] See *Payne* v. *Payne* [2001] EWCA Civ 166; [2001] 1 FLR 1052, para. 82, *per* Butler-Sloss P; *Re B (Adoption: Natural Parent)* [2002] 1 FLR 589, discussed below; and *Re S (Contact: Children's Views)* [2002] EWHC Fam 540; [2002] 1 FLR 1156, 1170.

[130] *Payne* v. *Payne* [2001] EWCA Civ 166; [2001] 1 FLR 1052.

[131] *Re B (Adoption: Natural Parent)* [2002] 1 FLR 589, para. 31.

[132] For further analysis, see Harris-Short, above n. 120, pp. 334–6.

adopting a rights-based approach from trying to reconceptualise the issues in accordance with Article 8 of the ECHR and the Strasbourg jurisprudence. Indeed, there is already emerging evidence of the effects of these judgments on the reasoning employed in substantive private law disputes over children. In the recent cases of *Re C*,[133] *Re B; Re S*[134] and *Re Y*,[135] all of which were concerned with an application by the mother to remove the child from the jurisdiction, there was absolutely no reference made in any of the judgments to the Article 8 arguments, all being decided exclusively on the basis of the judge's determination of the best interests of the child. In a different context, another recent example of the court giving minimal consideration to the Article 8 arguments is *Re C (Welfare of Child: Immunisation)*,[136] in which Sumner J at first instance simply observed: 'I have considered Art. 8 of the European Convention ... The Court may interfere with the rights of both parents and children where to do so is to protect the health of a child.'

Such a dismissive approach to the ECHR cannot be reconciled with the demands of the Convention's normative standards or the Strasbourg jurisprudence. The argument that identical factors will fall for consideration whether one adopts the traditional welfare approach enshrined in English law or the rights-based approach of Article 8 is, with respect, misconceived.[137] As Herring has argued, under the ECHR, individuals have certain entitlements: they have a rights-based claim to which the state must give effect unless it can establish sufficient justification to set the claim aside.[138] One of the entitlements recognised under the Convention is the right of both parents, *and the child*, to respect for their family life: in essence, the right to a meaningful parent–child relationship. This may require the court to differentiate and articulate the rights of all the various parties – that is, to break down the family

---

[133] *Re C (Permission to Remove from the Jurisdiction)* [2003] EWHC Fam 596; [2003] 1 FLR 1066.

[134] *Re B (Removal from Jurisdiction); Re S (Removal from Jurisdiction)* [2003] EWCA Civ 1149; [2003] 2 FLR 1043.

[135] *Re Y (Leave to Remove from Jurisdiction)* [2004] 2 FLR 330.

[136] [2003] EWHC Fam 1376; [2003] 2 FLR 1054, para. 326. No reference at all is made to Article 8 in the judgment of the Court of Appeal, although reference is made in argument to Article 6 of the UN Convention on the Rights of the Child. See *Re C* [2003] EWCA Civ 1148; [2003] 2 FLR 1095, para. 22.

[137] For a particularly good analysis of the difference between the approach taken under the Children Act 1989 and the approach taken under the Convention, see Herring, above n. 4, esp. pp. 228–30.

[138] *Ibid.*

unit into its individual 'constituent parts'[139] – and give separate consideration to the independent rights of all the family members (whether or not those rights are consistent with or even relevant to the child's welfare) before it reaches its final conclusion as to the correct decision on the facts. This may well lead to quite different substantive results than an approach based on the paramountcy of welfare.

At a conceptual level, there is thus a strong argument that the ECHR demands a quite different approach from that which is required in accordance with *J* v. *C* under s.1 CA 1989. Moreover, this approach is now firmly entrenched within the Convention case-law. Of central importance to the balancing exercise to be carried out under Article 8(2) is the concept of proportionality. The Strasbourg jurisprudence on the meaning of 'proportionality' has made it clear that there must exist a 'fair balance' or 'reasonable relationship' between the 'legitimate aim' pursued by the state and the means which are used to achieve it.[140] This would seem to suggest that, whilst action taken to protect the legitimate rights and interests of the child will have the *potential* to justify interfering with the Article 8(1) rights and interests of the child's parent(s), it will not *automatically* do so.[141] In other words, there will be some circumstances in which the interference with the Article 8(1) rights of the parent(s) will be so far-reaching that only particularly strong and weighty welfare considerations will be sufficient to satisfy the 'fair balance' or 'reasonable relationship' requirement of Article 8(2). Although it is important to note that, in conformity with the subsidiary role of the European Court as expressed in the margin of appreciation, Strasbourg has taken a deferential approach to the domestic court's determination of how best to balance the child's best interests against the competing rights of the parent(s),[142] the basic requirements and principles of this balancing exercise and the minimum values and standards to which the courts must adhere have been clearly and consistently stated. The guiding principles as to the balancing exercise to be carried out under Article 8(2) were firmly established in the case of *Johansen* v. *Norway*[143] and, save for the isolated decision of the ECtHR in *Yousef* v. *The Netherlands*,[144] have thereafter been consistently repeated, approved and applied by the ECtHR. The crucial principle to

[139] Diduck, above n. 2, p. 37.   [140] See *James* v. *UK* (1986) 8 EHRR 123, para. 50.
[141] See Herring, above n. 4, p. 230.   [142] Herring, *ibid.*; and Fortin, above n. 5, p. 252.
[143] *Johansen* v. *Norway* (1997) 23 EHRR 33.
[144] *Yousef* v. *The Netherlands* [2003] 1 FLR 210.

be derived from the Court in *Johansen* is found in paragraph 78 of the judgment. Having emphasised the importance of striking a 'fair balance' between the interests of the child and those of the parent, the Court went on to provide:

> In carrying out this balancing exercise, the Court will attach particular importance to the best interests of the child, which, *depending on their nature and seriousness, may* override those of the parent.[145]

The emphasised words are of crucial importance. They make clear that, far from making welfare the paramount consideration in the sense of the *automatic* trump card suggested by Lord Nicholls, welfare *may* override the interests of the parents *depending on their nature and seriousness.* *Johansen* is thus a clear authority against the paramountcy of the child's welfare as it is traditionally understood in English law. It confirms that, under the principle of proportionality, there will be certain situations in which the interference with the rights of the individual are so far-reaching and grave that only very weighty and substantial welfare considerations will be sufficient to justify that interference.[146]

The one isolated decision which provides some scope for defending the paramountcy principle as substantively consistent with the Convention approach is *Yousef* v. *The Netherlands.* The case concerned a mother's refusal to allow the child's father (the parents were unmarried) to recognise the child. The ECtHR held:

> [W]here the rights under Art. 8 of parents and those of a child are at stake, the child's rights *must* be the *paramount* consideration. If any balancing of interests is necessary, the child's interests must prevail.[147]

Yousef is, however, an isolated and weak decision and is therefore unlikely to signal any major shift in the approach of the ECtHR. Significantly, *Johansen* was not discussed by the Court in *Yousef*, the Court relying instead on *Elsholz* v. *Germany*[148] and *TP and KM* v. *United Kingdom*,[149] neither of which actually provides support for the Court's

---

[145] Emphasis added. Although *Johansen* was concerned with an adoption facilitated by the state, the *Johansen* principle has since been reiterated and applied in a number of 'pure' private law disputes. See e.g. *Buchberger* v. *Austria*, App. No. 32899/96, para. 40; *Sahin* v. *Germany; Sommerfeld* v. *Germany* [2003] 2 FLR 671, para. 66; *Gorgulu* v. *Germany* [2004] 1 FCR 410, para. 43.

[146] See Harris-Short, above n. 120, p. 338.

[147] *Yousef* v. *The Netherlands* [2003] 1 FLR 210, para. 73.

[148] *Elsholz* v. *Germany* [2000] 2 FLR 486.   [149] [2001] 2 FLR 549.

approach. Both of the cases cited assert that, in carrying out the required balancing of interests under Article 8(2), the best interests of the child will be of 'crucial importance'. However, the Convention case-law, whilst recognising this fact, does not suggest that 'crucial' equates to 'paramount' as understood in English law. Indeed, *Elsholz* goes on to confirm the approach taken in *Johansen* that 'a fair balance must be struck between the interests of the child and those of the parent . . . and that in doing so, particular importance must be attached to the best interests of the child which, depending on their nature and seriousness, may override those of the parent'.[150] It is also significant to note that, since the Court's judgment in *Yousef*, there have been a number of decisions which have simply affirmed the *Johansen* approach.[151]

The most disappointing aspect of the private law cases is that the domestic courts have generally failed to engage with these crucial decisions from the ECtHR. To date, the use of Convention case-law in private law cases has been limited and, where the Strasbourg jurisprudence has been invoked, the standard of analysis has been disappointingly low.[152] One reason why the English courts may have felt able to take such a casual approach to the ECHR and its case-law in private law family disputes is the perceived improbability of a successful challenge being brought against the UK government at Strasbourg. The Strasbourg jurisprudence has generally accorded a wide margin of appreciation to the state when determining intra-familial disputes. Strasbourg is, however, taking an increasingly interventionist approach in the private family law sphere. In the recent case of *Gorgulu* v. *Germany*,[153] the Court indicated a similar narrowing of the margin of appreciation to that which has occurred in the public law sphere, with the result that domestic decisions may well in the future be subjected to more rigorous levels of scrutiny:

---

[150] *Elsholz* v. *Germany* [2000] 2 FLR 486, para. 50.

[151] See e.g. *Hoppe* v. *Germany* [2003] 1 FLR 384; *Gorgulu* v. *Germany* [2004] 1 FCR 410, para. 43.

[152] For a particularly worrying example of the rather haphazard fashion in which the Convention case-law is being dealt with in the family law context, see the judgment of Thorpe LJ in *Payne* v. *Payne*, discussed in detail in Bonner *et al.*, above n. 120. Gillian Douglas has been similarly critical of the way in which the Convention case-law was applied in the case of *Re J (Leave to Issue Application for Residence Order)* [2002] EWCA Civ 1364; [2003] 1 FLR 114. See G. Douglas, 'Re J (Leave to Issue Application for Residence Order): Recognising Grandparents' Concern or Controlling Their Interference?' (2003) 15 *Child and Family Law Quarterly* 103, esp. 107–8.

[153] *Gorgulu* v. *Germany* [2004] 1 FCR 410.

> The margin of appreciation to be accorded to the competent national authorities will vary in accordance with the nature of the issues and the importance of the interests at stake. In particular when deciding on custody, the Court has recognised that the authorities enjoy a wide margin of appreciation. However, a stricter scrutiny is called for as regards any further limitations, such as restrictions placed by those authorities on parental rights of access, and as regards any legal safeguards designed to secure an effective protection of the rights of parents and children to respect for their family life. Such further limitations entail the danger that the family relations between a young child and one or both parents would be effectively curtailed.[154]

The Court then went on to take the unusual step of going behind the domestic court's evaluation of the best interests of the child, holding that the German court's reasons for refusing the father custody of his child (the risks of separating the child from his foster parents with whom he had bonded) and suspending the applicant's access to his son for one year (the risks of causing tension within the foster family) were insufficient to justify such a serious interference with the applicant's family life.[155] It may therefore be only a matter of time before the welfare principle as interpreted and applied by the English courts is successfully challenged at Strasbourg.

Given the possibility of a successful challenge at Strasbourg, is the move to a more rights-based approach something the domestic courts should be unduly alarmed about? It is of course vital if rights-based arguments are not to work unfairly against particular family members, i.e. that the very vocal calls for better protection of paternal rights are not allowed to hijack the process and obscure the equal importance of the rights and interests of the child and the mother, that the rights of *all* parties are carefully identified and evaluated within the balancing process which is to be performed. However, as more than one commentator has observed, there is nothing objectionable in principle about all the relevant interests of the parties to the dispute being properly and carefully considered in accordance with the rights-based approach. As Eekelaar points out, although the peculiar vulnerability of the child demands that their interests be given especially careful consideration, there is no self-evident reason why the interests of the child should be *automatically* prioritised over the rights and interests of other family

---

[154] *Ibid.*, para. 42.   [155] *Ibid.*, para. 50.

members in *every* case.[156] Such prioritisation at the expense of other rights and interests should therefore be carefully justified on the facts of each individual case. This can only improve the transparency and overall fairness of the decision-making process. The advantages of a rights-based approach to the family should not be too quickly dismissed. Rights-based reasoning has the potential to introduce much greater intellectual rigour and discipline to judicial reasoning in the family law context, ensuring the needs and interests of all family members are clearly articulated and considered in the decision-making process and preventing untested assumptions and prejudices, currently obscured behind the vagaries of the welfare principle, from determining the outcome of common family disputes. Decisions such as that in *Re C (Permission to Remove from Jurisdiction)*[157] are justifiably a matter of some concern. In *Re C*, the clear assimilation of the child's interests to those of the mother was treated as obvious and unproblematic with the decision turning, in the end, almost exclusively on the interests of the mother, her relationship with the father, and her need to come to terms with the breakdown of the marriage.[158] The competing and equally important *rights* of both the child and the father to a continuing and meaningful relationship disappeared almost completely from the decision-making process.

Summary

In cases which stand at the margins of private family disputes, such as those which are principally concerned with procedural or evidential matters, hostility to rights-based reasoning has not been a factor in the post-implementation case-law. The explanation for this may well lie in the fact that issues of this nature do not impact directly on the ideology of the family but engage with matters of a wider public interest, such as the smooth administration of justice or the right to a fair trial, in which the language of rights is more readily accepted. In stark contrast, in those cases where the upbringing of a child is directly in issue, the resistance to a rights-based approach has been at its strongest. Although not

---

[156] J. Eekelaar, 'Beyond the Welfare Principle' (2002) 14 *Child and Family Law Quarterly* 237, 239 and 244.

[157] *Re C (Permission to Remove from the Jurisdiction)* [2003] EWHC Fam 596; [2003] 1 FLR 1066.

[158] *Ibid.*, paras. 24(8)–(10) and 49–50.

articulated as such in the judgments, it is in these cases, where judicial intervention will penetrate down into the heart of the family, that the language of rights is regarded as particularly inappropriate and unhelpful. The impact of the Convention in private family disputes has consequently been marginal at best.

Conclusion

The prediction that two key factors – the prevailing mistrust of rights and the difficult questions of public policy which arise in family disputes – would result in a cautious and minimalist approach to the HRA in mainstream family law, is borne out by the post-implementation case-law. There are of course some vagaries and inconsistencies in the case law, many of which will be due in large part to the individual attitudes of the members of the family bench towards the role of the HRA within family law and the wider constitutional order more generally. It is, for example, clear that, whilst Munby J and Baroness Hale are keen advocates of rights-based reasoning within the family law context, Lord Nicholls is not. However, the emerging overall picture is one of judicial restraint in the family law field, in which the prevailing resistance to rights amongst family lawyers and the difficult public policy questions which arise in family disputes, have clearly been important considerations. Not surprisingly, it has been in the private law field, where the language of rights is regarded as most problematic, that the implementation of the HRA has had least impact. Whilst the poor quality of reasoning employed in these cases is disappointing, the concern of the judiciary at turning their back on the welfare approach is understandable, if essentially misplaced. Strong judicial caution has also been evident in cases where sensitive and difficult questions of public policy are at stake. Where the case raises sensitive questions of public policy, whether because it touches on the 'traditional institution of the family' or because it raises complex socio-economic issues, the courts have preferred to defer to the appropriate democratically elected bodies – bodies who are directly answerable to the electorate for the policy choices they make. In adopting this attitude of caution and deference, the courts have displayed a keen awareness of their own lack of competence to decide on these questions – a lack of competence which is currently not being alleviated by the evidence being put to the court. This important restriction on the court's decision-making capacity has generally prevented the court from adopting a purposive approach to the interpretative obligation under s.3 HRA. It is less clear why it should engender a similar hesitancy to the making of a declaration of incompatibility under s.4 where a clear potential breach of the Convention has been identified. Section 4 already draws a careful constitutional balance between the courts and the legislature. There is thus no self-evident reason why in family law cases the courts should feel unduly constrained from acting under this section.

In contrast to this clear minimalist approach, the courts have been at their most active where human rights discourse is at its strongest and most pertinent. Where core liberal values such as equality and the protection of the family from state intervention have thus been at stake, the implementation of the HRA has initiated some important substantive reforms. It is fair to observe that many of these important reforms have been achieved more by the unilateral action of Parliament than strong action by the courts. However, significant reforms in the law of adult relationships and important changes both to law and practice in the public law field can be viewed with a considerable measure of satisfaction. The one striking example of this more activist thread in the family law field is *Ghaidan* v. *Godin-Mendoza*.

The future? Even taking a 'minimalist' approach to the HRA, Strasbourg's gradual narrowing of the margin of appreciation in the family law field means the domestic courts cannot simply ignore the demands of the ECHR. Particularly within the private law context, the Convention requires a more rigorous and convincing response than that which the courts have so far provided. However, the challenges facing the courts should they choose to adopt a more activist approach to the HRA are clear from the case-law. If the courts are to enter the 'deep waters' of family policy, change is required: change to prevailing attitudes towards the family; change to the nature of judicial reasoning; change to the nature of counsel's argument; and, perhaps most importantly, change to the nature of the evidence relied on. From the cases so far, there would seem to be little appetite for such change within the family law profession.

12

Article 14 ECHR: a protector, not a prosecutor

AARON BAKER*

Introduction

When the Human Rights Act 1998 (HRA) brought the protections of the European Convention on Human Rights (ECHR) into UK law, it entrusted the judiciary with a role with which it had little experience. The HRA asks judges to decide, among other things, whether a notional boundary line defining the outer limits of an individual's portfolio of rights has been crossed by a government measure. The judiciary must determine whether these rights have been encroached upon – even by Parliament – by looking at the impact of state action on an individual or group. By contrast, in exercising judicial review functions, the domestic courts have traditionally focused on whether the actions and decisions of government entities and officials – but generally not Parliament – complied with limits imposed on their conduct.[1] Typically, what has happened to the plaintiff, grievant or victim comes into play only with regard to fashioning a remedy, and could never impugn the acts of Parliament itself. Under the HRA, on the other hand, the negative effect of a statute upon a claimant can form the entire basis for a claim.[2]

This new role for the domestic judiciary could hardly have failed to make judges uncomfortable. After years of submission to Parliamentary intention, where every case has turned on whether the decision of an employer, an administrator or an alleged tortfeasor is reasonable or consistent with a duty

---

* This chapter was originally presented at a seminar in the Judicial Reasoning and the Human Rights Act series, on 18 February 2005. I am grateful to Roger Masterman for his indispensable research assistance. Any errors or omissions are of course my own.

[1] I. Leigh, 'Taking Rights Proportionately: Judicial Review, the Human Rights Act and Strasbourg' [2002] PL 265, 285–6.

[2] P. Craig, *Administrative Law* (4th edn, London: Sweet and Maxwell, 1999), p. 546, at pp. 556–7, 561; I. Leigh, 'Taking Rights Proportionately: Judicial Review, the Human Rights Act and Strasbourg' [2002] PL 265, 282–4.

of care, it must go against the grain to declare that Parliament – expressing the will of the majority and acting with impeccable logic and with good intentions in a way never contemplated to affect human rights – has nevertheless violated ECHR guarantees, and to base that finding on the fact and degree of the impairment of rights suffered by the individual. Yet that is precisely what the HRA requires the UK courts to do. Section 6 HRA makes it 'unlawful for a [court] to act in a way which is incompatible with a Convention right', without express authority from Parliament. Thus, it obliges the judiciary to engage in a protective inquiry, rather than a prosecutorial inquiry. HRA cases ask not whether the acts of legislators or of government officers violate principles of conduct found in the ECHR, but whether such acts have had the effect of burdening the ECHR rights of a protected individual (although many Convention rights bring government objectives and reasoning into the inquiry by way of justification, after a burden on rights has been found). The focus is initially on the alleged victim, not the alleged wrongdoer.

Article 14 of the Convention, as incorporated through the HRA, presents the domestic judiciary with a particular challenge in dealing with this shift in focus. Article 14 requires by its nature a particularly protective approach. This is so because with many Convention guarantees we assume that in general the rights – for example to freedom of expression or privacy, or from torture or slavery – are respected, but that we must hold the line against potential majoritarian transgression. On the other hand, we know that discrimination is widespread in our society, government and legal system, and we can assume that a number of policies, decisions and activities with which the majority would, following its ordinary ways of thinking, be perfectly comfortable are, in fact, discriminatory.[3] In other words, discrimination requires a special focus on the alleged victim because the existing state of affairs tells us that we cannot trust our judgment as to what kinds of decisions or policies are blameless: we must therefore look to the resulting disadvantage to help us understand the discriminatory nature of the decision.[4] Meanwhile, the experience of the domestic judiciary with equality or anti-discrimination adjudication prior to the HRA has involved predominantly statutory schemes, where the intention of Parliament governs, and

---

[3] For example, the Equal Opportunities Commission announced, on 2 February 2005, the results of its research showing that 45 per cent of women who had worked while pregnant believed they had suffered discrimination, that some 30,000 a year are sacked, made redundant or resign owing to discrimination, and that most employers are not aware they have infringed their employee's rights.

[4] See e.g. S. Fredman, 'Equality: A New Generation?' (2001) 30 ILJ 145.

the inquiry tends to focus on the reasons for disparate treatment, not the disadvantage to the alleged victim.[5] Thus, the especially protective and victim-focused approach that I argue is called for by Article 14 under the HRA represents a particularly marked departure from how domestic courts have been accustomed to deal with matters brought before them.

Understandably, therefore, the UK courts have had problems taking their attention away from the reasons for a challenged action, and directing it to whether the action produced effects inconsistent with the protections of Article 14. This chapter focuses on the manifestations of judicial discomfort with the minority-protective function that the HRA and Article 14 ask the judiciary to serve. These manifestations include (1) overly restrictive interpretations of the scope of whether a case 'engages' Article 14 protection and (2) collapsing justification into the concept of an analogous comparator. Both of these problems flow from an inappropriate preoccupation with the reasons for the impugned action, as opposed to its discriminatory effects. To establish this, the first section of the chapter explores the difficulties some domestic judges have had with the question of whether Article 14 is engaged, showing how they have allowed the jurisprudence of other Convention Articles to dominate the interpretation of Article 14, and have drawn the 'ambit' of other Convention rights too narrowly by accounting for the government's objectives at the wrong stage in the analysis. The second section identifies cases in which the domestic judiciary has avoided finding discrimination by collapsing the justification element of the analysis – with its focus on the aims and thinking of the state – into the question of whether the plaintiff suffered less favourable treatment than a chosen comparator. The chapter concludes with an outline of the attributes that an analysis of Article 14 under the HRA must have if it is to take an appropriately protective stand against discrimination in the exercise of Convention rights.

The domestic courts and the 'ambit'

The hegemony of 'helping' rights

It is common ground in Strasbourg, in the domestic courts, and among commentators, that Article 14 provides protection in addition to that afforded by other Convention rights, but that it cannot protect against discrimination beyond the sphere of enjoyment of those

---

[5] See e.g. *Advocate General for Scotland* v. *MacDonald* and *Pearce* v. *Mayfield School* [2003] UKHL 34; *Department for Work and Pensions* v. *Thompson* [2004] IRLR 348; *Smith* v. *Safeway plc* [1996] IRLR 457; *Burrett* v. *West Birmingham Health Authority* [1994] IRLR 7.

rights.[6] However, the fact that Article 14's coverage extends only to the exercise of other rights often leads judges and commentators to call it 'parasitic',[7] and to treat it has having 'no independent existence'.[8] Despite this view of Article 14 as the stepchild of the ECHR, there is no dispute that it protects against categories of state action that other Articles cannot touch, such as rights-promoting policies that are not required by the Convention, but cannot be discontinued selectively.[9] Article 14 thus offers a human rights guarantee of its own; it is a Convention right. It appears in the Convention in the same list as, say, Article 8 and Article 10; it does not have an asterisk next to it, nor has it been relegated to a footnote. It does not, according to the terms of the ECHR or the HRA, feature only as a guide to interpretation. In short, it guarantees the denizens of Europe that:

> The enjoyment of the rights and freedoms set forth in this convention shall be secured without discrimination on any ground such as sex, race, colour, language, religion, political or other opinion, national or social origin, association with a national minority, property, birth or other status.

There is nothing in the language of the Article or of the Convention that explains why this right must suffer the indignity of 'second class' status.[10]

The obvious answer is that Article 14 cannot bite by its own terms unless a case involves the 'enjoyment' of another 'substantive' – or what I prefer to call 'helping' – Convention right. From this it does not follow, however, that Article 14 merely modifies other rights, and that an individual must, in effect, pass through another Convention Article to

---

[6] *Abdulaziz v. United Kingdom* (1985) 7 EHRR 471; *R. (Carson) v. Secretary of State for Work and Pensions* [2003] EWCA Civ 797; R. Wintemute, '"Within the Ambit": How Big *Is* the "Gap" in Article 14 European Convention on Human Rights?' [2004] EHRLR 366; A. Pedain, 'The Human Rights Dimension of the *Diane Pretty* Case' (2003) 62 CLJ 181.

[7] *Whaley v. Lord Advocate*, 2004 SLT 425, para. 93.

[8] *Chassagnou v. France* (1999) 29 EHRR 615, para. 18.

[9] S. Grosz, J. Beatson and P. Duffy, *Human Rights: The 1998 Act and the European Convention* (London: Sweet and Maxwell, 2000), paras. 5–23.

[10] L. Wildhaber, 'Protection Against Discrimination under the European Convention on Human Rights: A Second Class Guarantee?' (2002) 2 *Baltic Yearbook of International Law* 71. The ECtHR has resisted creating a ranking or hierarchy among the rights in the Convention. H. Fenwick, 'Clashing Rights, the Welfare of the Child and the Human Rights Act' (2004) 67 MLR 889, 906.

gain access to Article 14. Yet many view the situation precisely this way. As one judge put it:

> Article 14, which is headed: 'prohibition of discrimination' does not provide a self-standing right ... to the citizen ... What Article 14 does is inform, strengthen and expand other rights which are the subject of independent existence such as Article 8.[11]

When did this happen? The Strasbourg jurisprudence does not compel this conclusion. While the ECtHR requires that the facts in claims under Article 14 fall within the 'ambit' of another Convention right, it has never stated either that Article 14 merely 'expands' other rights, or that the terms of another Article govern whether Article 14 applies.[12] The Strasbourg case-law provides no reason why courts should not determine the scope of Article 14 by reference first to the terms of Article 14 itself, rather than asking how Article 14 might 'inform' the interpretation of another Article, once that Article has been found to apply. This treatment of Article 14 as a mere qualification of other rights without clear guidance in that direction from the ECtHR creates the impression that lawyers in the United Kingdom have become so accustomed to criticising Article 14 for its limitations that they are unable to see its possibilities.

The 'ambit' as the scope of protection of the 'substantive' right

The reason it matters that judges approach Article 14 as a qualifier of other rights is not necessarily that they fail to give it separate effect. Most UK judges who appear to think that Article 14 only comes to life after clearing the technical threshold of another Article do tend to acknowledge that, for example, Article 8 plus Article 14 can apply where Article 8 alone would not.[13] However, by failing to see Article 14 as a guarantee in its own right, these judges incline, as a practical matter, to foreclose any

---

[11] *Clarke* v. *Secretary of State for Environment, Transport and the Regions* [2001] EWHC Admin 800, para. 5.

[12] *Gaygusus* v. *Austria* (1996) 23 EHRR 365; *Petrovic* v. *Austria* (2001) 33 EHRR 307; *Thlimmenos* v. *Greece* (2001) 31 EHRR 15. In *Thlimmenos*, the ECtHR first addressed the claim under Article 14 coupled with Article 9 before dealing with claims based on Article 9 alone, basing its discussion on the meaning of Article 14, not Article 9.

[13] See e.g. *Carson* [2003] EWCA Civ 797; *Michalak* v. *London Borough of Wandsworth* [2002] EWCA Civ 271; but see *Whaley* [2004] SLT 425; *Adams* v. *Scottish Ministers*, 2003 SLT 366.

reflection on the purposes and meaning of Article 14, unless and until they find another right 'engaged'.[14] As a result, the scope of Article 14 often gets treated as Article 8 'lite'[15] or Protocol No. 1, Article 2 'plus'.[16] In essence, many domestic courts assume that one can identify, say, the limits of Article 8 protection, and then determine whether Article 14 applies by asking whether the impugned government action hovers just outside this Article 8 boundary, or is well outside: the former being 'within the ambit' and the latter not. This approach wrongly eschews an interpretation of Article 14's 'enjoyment of the rights and freedoms . . . shall be secured' language in favour of a modified interpretation of what kind of government action is prohibited by other Articles.

For example, in *Whaley* v. *Lord Advocate*, Lord Brodie of the Scottish Outer House took the approach, common in domestic cases, of addressing claims under the 'helping' Articles before addressing the claims under Article 14 taken together with those Articles. Two individuals involved with foxhunting challenged Scotland's ban on that activity on the ground that it violated Articles 8, 9, 10 and 11, and Article 14 taken together with the other helping Articles. I will focus on the Article 8 and Article 14 analyses, because they suffice to make the point. Lord Brodie opted to consider whether Article 8 had been violated before addressing Article 14, probably because it allowed him to deal with the Article 14 claim in the following manner: 'As I have not found any of arts. 8 to 11 to be engaged here, it follows that there can be no breach of art. 14.'[17] However, his analysis of Article 8 focused on whether, under the facts of the case before him, the claimants could avail themselves of Article 8's protection. He never discussed whether this question was the same as an ambit analysis for Article 14 purposes, and did not appear to see the need for a separate assessment. His Article 8 discussion clearly did not deal with the issues pertinent to whether the claimants' enjoyment of their rights had been affected by the challenged measure. The cases the court relied on did not address the ambit of Article 8 for Article 14 purposes, but involved drawing the line beyond which Article 8 afforded no direct guarantees. Indeed, Lord Brodie's conclusion, that he subsequently referred to as a finding that Article 8 was not 'engaged', stated that

---

[14] *Whaley*, 2004 SLT 425; *R. (Douglas)* v. *North Tyneside MBC* [2004] HRLR 14; *R. (Pretty)* v. *DPP* [2002] AC 800; *R. (Erskine)* v. *Lambeth London Borough Council* [2003] EWHC Admin 2479.
[15] *Whaley*, 2004 SLT 425; *Clarke* [2001] EWHC Admin 800.
[16] *Douglas* [2004] HRLR 14.   [17] *Whaley*, 2004 SLT 425, para. 93.

foxhunting 'clearly extends beyond the sphere of purely private life and therefore does not attract *the protection* of art. 8'.[18]

In one sense, Lord Brodie's failure to distinguish clearly between an ambit analysis and the initial 'protection of the substantive article' analysis is just a mistake. It is clearly wrong to treat the two as the same, as even opponents of a broad ambit acknowledge that Strasbourg views the ambit for Article 14 purposes as more extensive than even *prima facie* protection of the helping Article.[19] At the root of the problem, however, lies more than a simple mistake. The error stems from the tendency not to look at Article 14 to determine its scope. Lord Brodie never considered what Article 14 called for. Instead, he did what most domestic judges do: he relied on the mantra that Article 14 has no independent existence, and assumed that Article 14 must be entered through another right. If Article 8 is the gatekeeper to Article 14, then surely one can only unlock Article 14 by applying Article 8 language and precedent. This invites the judge to conflate the scope of Article 8 protection with its ambit for Article 14, or at least to interpret the Article 14 ambit in light of the thinking behind the limits on Article 8 protection. Neither is appropriate.

Using 'helping right' logic to define the scope of Article 14

The latter form of error claimed the House of Lords in the *Diane Pretty* case.[20] The claimant there alleged violations of Articles 2, 3, 8 and 9, and of Article 14 taken together with those rights, and once more I will look to the claim under Articles 8 and 14 to make my point. The House of Lords, like the Outer House, analysed Article 8 before reaching Article 14, again probably because it allowed them to dispense with Article 14 by pointing to their earlier finding that the case did not engage Article 8. It is not as clear from the opinions of Lords Steyn, Hope and Bingham that they equated the limit of Article 8 protection with its Article 14 ambit,[21] but they do seem unequivocally to have concluded that, if Article 8(1) was not *prima facie* 'engaged', Article 14 could not apply.[22] Lord Hope's discussion of why the claimant's case did not 'engage' Article 8

---

[18] *Ibid.*, para. 65 (emphasis added).
[19] *Carson* [2003] EWCA Civ 797, paras. 33–8.   [20] *Pretty* [2002] AC 800.
[21] A. Pedain, 'The Human Rights Dimension of the *Diane Pretty* Case' (2003) 62 CLJ 181, 196.
[22] *Pretty* [2002] AC 800, paras. 34, 35, 64, 104 and 106. These citations were brought to my attention by A. Pedain, 'The Human Rights Dimension of the *Diane Pretty* Case' (2003) 62 CLJ 181, 196.

demonstrates the real danger of this approach. The severely disabled claimant argued under Article 8 that a prohibition on assisted suicide violated her right to privacy by effectively making it impossible for her to choose the time and process of her death, which she deemed a private choice. Lord Hope addressed this claim as follows:

> The way [the claimant] chooses to pass the closing moments of her life is part of the act of living, and she has a right to ask that this too must be respected. In that respect [she] has a right to self-determination. In that sense, her private life is engaged even where in the face of a terminal illness she seeks to choose death rather than life ... [I]t is an entirely different thing to imply into these words [those of Article 8(1)] a positive obligation to give effect to her wish to end her own life by means of assisted suicide. I think that to do so would be to stretch the meaning of those words too far.[23]

By means of the foregoing argument, Lord Hope concluded that Article 8 was not *prima facie* engaged. Yet it is clear from his words that he believed that, if she had the physical capacity to make that choice unassisted, she would in making that choice be enjoying her Article 8 rights, and indeed Lord Hope might say that she would *prima facie* engage Article 8(1). However, because what she sought was lawful assistance with her suicide, that activity fell outside the area of engagement of Article 8(1).

Setting aside the fact that this does not give appropriate effect to Article 8 – a topic for another paper – it clearly cannot form the basis for a sound decision as to the applicability of Article 14. If, as Lord Hope said, in choosing suicide rather than slow, painful death a person is enjoying the right to privacy, then surely a disabled person making the same choice, but carrying it out with assistance, would also be enjoying that right. Article 14 prohibits a state measure (in this case a prohibition on assisted suicide) to imposes an impairment on the ability of one person to make that choice on a basis of equality with other (able bodied) members of society, unless of course the adoption of that measure can be justified. Article 14 is therefore clearly engaged according to Lord Hope's analysis, yet he found that it was not because he had found that Article 8 was not. Article 8(1) was not engaged because the core of protected privacy did not extend to getting assistance with suicide. Yet, if others have the protected freedom to choose suicide,

---

[23] *Pretty* [2002] AC 800, para. 100.

then surely Article 14 must empower those unable to make that choice without assistance to require the state to justify a prohibition which denies that choice to them alone.[24] The Article 8 engagement analysis does not smoothly transfer to the Article 14 analysis, because Article 8 seeks to define the protected core of individual privacy under the ECHR, while Article 14 – a right with its own objectives, logic and defining text – seeks to prevent discrimination with regard to, among other things, what privacy one enjoys in a society protected by Article 8.[25] Ultimately, the mistake in the *Pretty* case was the Lords' unwillingness to interpret and apply Article 14 as a guarantee in its own right.

Importing negative language into Article 14

The danger in requiring the engagement of a helping Article before Article 14 can come to life is nowhere more evident than with the right to education under Article 2 of Protocol No. 1. The negative language of Article 2 invites judges to exclude from the scope of Article 14 any claim involving the discriminatory allocation of positive assistance with education. So, for example, the Court of Appeal in *R. (Douglas)* v. *North Tyneside MBC* found that student loans, in this case discriminatorily denied to persons over the age of 55, did not engage Article 14 because, alluding to the language of Article 2, they did not 'prevent or hamper' anyone in the pursuit of higher education.[26] Surely the state could not, under Article 14, assist white children with school uniforms and not assist non-whites? The facts in *Douglas* contemplate a situation in which a 56-year-old and his or her 54-year-old next-door neighbour enrol in the same university course, at the same time, with the same costs and the same resources, yet one receives loan support and the other cannot and must get a part-time job. The 56-year-old clearly

---

[24] Indeed, the same logic applied in *Thlimmenos* to require an exception, based on religious expression, to the prohibition on persons with serious criminal convictions receiving appointments as chartered accountants. [2000] ECHR 161 (6 April 2000), paras. 39–45.

[25] A similar error is illustrated in *R. (Marper)* v. *Chief Constable of South Yorkshire Police* [2004] UKHL 39, paras. 27, 31 and 44, where the court found that Article 8(1) was not engaged because, despite more privacy-protective cultural traditions in the UK, the protective scope of Article 8(1) must be restricted to the 'floor' of protection prescribed by the Strasbourg jurisprudence. Lord Steyn then observed: 'If my conclusion is right that Article 8(1) is not engaged, it follows that Article 14 is not triggered.' On this point from the perspective of the scope of the primary right, see Roger Masterman's chapter in this volume, at pp. 76–82.

[26] [2004] HRLR 14, para. 56.

suffers an impairment to the equality of his or her enjoyment of the right to education *vis-à-vis* the neighbour. Whether the state measure involves assistance or prevention has nothing to do with it: this characteristic should only inform the justification inquiry. Only the language by which Article 2 outlines the limits of the protection *it* offers brings the negative/positive issue into the ambit analysis, and nothing in the language or case-law of Article 14 suggests that should be so. Again, regardless of which helping right the claimant invokes, the engagement of Article 14 should turn on when a person can be said to be 'enjoying' a Convention right.

State control of the ambit

Why the state chooses to outlaw a certain activity, whether it chooses to assist or prevent, whether it pursues promotion of family life or merely the protection of health and safety, and any other information about the regulatory measure under consideration all relate exclusively to the justification of any demonstrated encroachment on Convention rights. Despite the lack of any sound reason for deciding the meaning of the phrase 'enjoyment of a Convention right' according to what the state is accused of doing to impair the equality of that enjoyment, courts continue to do it.[27] In *Douglas*, for example, the court's conclusion, that Article 2 of Protocol No. 1 was not engaged by age-restricted student loans, received assistance from the observation that the restrictions were not 'aimed' at education, nor did they 'necessarily' affect the claimant's ability to get an education.[28] Thus, somehow, whether the claimant could be said to be enjoying the right set out in Article 2 turned on whether the state intended to affect education, and whether any effects followed 'necessarily' from the measure. In other words, if the state did not intend to involve itself with education rights, then any impairment experienced by the applicant could not have been in the enjoyment of his right to education.

---

[27] Throughout the discussion in this subsection, I am indebted to Kevin Kerrigan and Phillip Plowden for the insight they shared in their paper, 'But the State Didn't *Mean* to Discriminate: Article 14 and the Purposive Heresy', delivered at the Society of Legal Scholars' annual conference in Sheffield in September 2004. I have expanded on their analysis and extended it to cases they did not mention, but I owe the original insight to them.

[28] [2004] HRLR 14, para. 56.

The only support the court cited for this bizarre test came from the ECtHR opinion in *Petrovic* v. *Austria*, where the Court, on its way to finding that discrimination against fathers in the granting of a family leave allowance engaged Article 14 with Article 8, noted that the allowance was 'intended to promote family life and necessarily affects the way in which the latter is organised'.[29] However, the Court in *Petrovic* never suggested that this was the only way or even the usual way that facts might fall within the ambit of a Convention right. Other Strasbourg cases, like *Thlimmenos* v. *Greece*, make it clear that the facts of a case can engage Article 14 even where the state, in enacting the impugned measure, had no intention of involving itself in the invoked right, and where the measure would have the effect complained of in only a handful of cases, completely by accident.[30] The objectives of the state and the kinds of measures it enacts are among the facts that can bring a case within the ambit of a Convention right. If the state seeks to promote a certain right, and in so doing discriminates, a court will properly recite the fact of the state's intended engagement with the right as evidence that the activities affected by the measure are in the area of enjoyment of a Convention right, as the Court in *Petrovic* did. That in no way suggests that such an intention on the part of the state, or a direct relationship of necessity between the measure and the burden complained of, amount to ambit prerequisites.

This importation into the ambit analysis of information more suited to a justification inquiry occurs in far more subtle ways than *Douglas*'s outright reliance on the state's intentions. For example, in two Scottish foxhunting cases, *Whaley*[31] and *Adams* v. *Scottish Ministers*,[32] the analysis of whether the facts engaged Article 8 turned on whether 'foxhunting' was a private activity. However, when the facts are examined more closely, it emerges that several complainants in both cases alleged that the ban on foxhunting affected other areas of their lives that relied on foxhunting. The activities that they claimed the foxhunting ban burdened included their choices about the organisation of home and family life, and their private choices about the lifestyle and vocations they would pursue. With regard to their vocations, they were in situations

---

[29] (2001) 33 EHRR 14. This language was also cited in *Erskine* [2003] EWHC Admin 2479 in support of a similar reliance on the state's health and safety aims to preclude the engagement of Article 8, despite evidence of an unintended impact on home life. See also *R. (Morris)* v. *Westminster CC* [2004] EWHC 2191, paras. 10–15.

[30] *Thlimmenos* (2001) 31 EHRR 15.   [31] 2004 SLT 425.   [32] 2003 SLT 366.

analogous to dismissal for reasons that burden a private lifestyle choice, which has received Article 14 protection.[33] The court in each case, however, refused to consider whether in targeting foxhunting, the state had affected other aspects of life as well. Foxhunting was the activity in question and, according to both courts, foxhunting could not attract the protection of Article 8.

Assuming (without agreeing) that such a focus makes sense under Article 8, it most certainly does not under Article 14. A Roma traveller who chooses to live in a horse-drawn caravan, to earn a living caring for the horses of other similar travellers, and to spend family time travelling on public roads in a horse-drawn caravan does so in the enjoyment of the right to respect for the home and private and family life. Were the government to forbid travel by horse-drawn carriage on all public roads, this would burden and perhaps obliterate the ability to make such choices. The government might properly argue that the fact that the measure only prohibits travel on public roads, and does not prevent living around horses, living in a caravan, moving the caravan from place to place, or earning a living caring for horses means that the burden is not so great as to outweigh the effectiveness of the measure in securing a legitimate aim. This might satisfy the justification analysis under Article 14. It should not, however, be available to the government to argue that, because it sought only to regulate driving on public roads, then that is the activity which must come within the ambit of a Convention right, and that because driving on public roads is not a private, family activity, then no Convention right is engaged. Unfortunately, just such an argument persuaded both courts in the foxhunting cases.

The question for any Convention right is whether the individual right has been burdened, regardless of whether the challenged measure aimed at that right *per se*. Banning foxhunting had the effect, according to some of the claimants in the cases, of depriving them of a livelihood in which they had engaged for most of their lives, eviscerating the usefulness of skills and expertise they had accumulated over a lifetime, blocking avenues of self-improvement and the occupation of leisure time, devaluing the importance of these individuals in their community and social set, and foreclosing activities and enthusiasms shared with their sons and daughters since they were small. That the government did not seek to impact these activities; that the impacts will not occur for most

---

[33] *Smith and Grady* v. *United Kingdom* (2000) 29 EHRR 493; *Vogt* v. *Germany* (1996) 24 EHRR 205.

people; that the ban only eliminates or devalues some but not all such activities; and that the claimants can make choices that limit the negative effects of the ban, are all arguments best heard in justification, and probably successfully. But that is not what the courts did. They held that, if the government only intended to ban foxhunting, and foxhunting is not an activity within the enjoyment of a Convention right, then Article 14 could not be engaged, despite the effects of the ban on other activities in the exercise of protected rights.

The domestic courts and 'analogous' comparators

If Article 14 applies to any situation where a challenged measure impinges on an area of activity within the ambit of a Convention-protected right, and prohibits unjustified impairments to the enjoyment of such rights on an equal basis, then the question remains as to what counts as unequal treatment – or discrimination – and how the aims and reasons of the state – justification – come into the analysis. ECtHR precedent suggests that Article 14 cases will tend to get to the issue of justification: it is unusual for Strasbourg cases to fail before the court has engaged in a justification inquiry.[34] From an academic, almost pedagogic, perspective, it appears clear that courts should adopt distinct steps in the analysis, such that the question whether a person has experienced treatment less favourable than that of an analogous comparator (who lacks the characteristic on the ground of which the person alleges discrimination) is decided without reference to any facts relating to the challenged measure itself which might explain or rationalise the measure, leaving those latter facts to weigh in the separate question of justification.[35] Until recently,[36] the analysis of Article 14 adopted by the UK courts followed the question of ambit (element (1)) with the questions of (2) whether the claimant suffered less favourable treatment than the 'chosen comparator', (3) whether the chosen comparator was in an 'analogous position' to the claimant, and (4) justification.[37]

---

[34] See e.g. D. Feldman, *Civil Liberties and Human Rights in England and Wales* (2nd edn, Oxford: Oxford University Press, 2002), p. 144.

[35] See e.g. *Aston Cantlow Parochial Church Council* v. *Wallbank* [2002] Ch 51 (reversed on unrelated grounds [2003] UKHL 37).

[36] This approach has been questioned, but not completely rejected in all cases, by the House of Lords in *R. (Carson)* v. *Secretary of State for Work and Pensions* [2005] UKHL 37. See nn. 47–51 below and the accompanying text.

[37] *Michalak* [2002] EWCA Civ 271, paras. 20–2.

However, judges have found this too rigid and mechanical, and as a practical matter have been unable or unwilling to keep the steps separated. Brooke LJ, in a passage frequently quoted in domestic Article 14 cases, has opined that the analogous comparator question and justification 'tend to merge'.[38] Case-law suggests that, in the hands of both Strasbourg and domestic judges, they do indeed 'tend' to merge.[39] This tendency is not, however, compelled by any clear authority or by the words of Article 14, and UK judges should resist it.

The justification inquiry, that was read into Article 14 by the ECtHR in the *Belgian Linguistics* case, serves the clear purpose of allowing the state to demonstrate that, whatever discriminatory effect the court accepts as resulting from a given measure, the measure has an objective and rational justification, in that it pursues a legitimate aim, and does not produce negative effects disproportionate to the benefits – in terms of advancement of the legitimate aim – secured by the measure.[40] This inquiry contemplates that, whatever kind or quantum of good intentions and sound reasoning exist to support a challenged act or decision, they can only rescue it from a finding that its effects violate an individual's rights if they represent a social or governmental boon proportionate to the negative impact on an individual or group.[41] It seems obvious, therefore, that for a court to accept, as bearing on a part of the analysis that does not require a proportionality balancing, considerations that are intended to bite only proportionally, allows the state to circumvent the requirements of proportionality. For example, Article 14 intends that the state can justify preferential treatment of persons under 60 years of age only if the reason for the distinction – say, that people over 60 tend to require more medical treatment – discloses a legitimate aim that is sufficiently advanced by the distinction that its benefits outweigh its effect on people – or a given person – over 60. That requirement is evaded if the state can defend an 'under 60' age distinction on the ground that people under 60 are not analogous comparators to people over 60 because they tend to require less medical

---

[38] *Ibid.*

[39] S. Livingstone, 'Article 14 and the Prevention of Discrimination in the European Convention on Human Rights' [1997] EHRLR 25, 30; *Carson* [2003] EWCA Civ 797.

[40] (1968) 1 EHRR 252; see also *A and Others* v. *Secretary of State for the Home Department* [2004] UKHL 56, para. 50; *Ghaidan* v. *Godin-Mendoza* [2004] UKHL 30, para. 133.

[41] A. McColgan, 'Discrimination Law and the Human Rights Act', in T. Campbell, K. D. Ewing and A. Tomkins (eds.), *Sceptical Essays on Human Rights* (Oxford: Oxford University Press, 2001), p. 232.

treatment.[42] The 'analogous comparator' step in the analysis does not require a proportionality balancing, so the state gets its measure off the hook without proving, for example, that the link between age and healthcare costs has sufficient strength to justify the measure applying to those over 60 who do not generate high healthcare costs.

UK judges have not, unfortunately, done a consistent job of containing justificatory considerations within a proportionality review, and keeping them out of the comparison. The disappointing cases have involved not only the application of obvious justification considerations in rejecting a claimant's chosen comparator(s),[43] but the acceptance of government labels – stealth justifications – as decisive factors in a comparison.[44] Fortunately, there have been some glimmers in an otherwise gloomy picture.[45] I will address the patent importation of justification into the comparator question first and then turn to labels.

They can't be the same if the state thinks about them differently

A court could, without a miscarriage of justice, deal with justificatory considerations in the comparator analysis provided it applied legitimate aim and proportionality principles at the same time. However, doing so creates confusion, lacks transparency, and could become a dangerous habit. Identifying the actual ground of distinction used in a challenged decision, or targeted in a challenged policy, is crucial to a proper proportionality review: proportionality weighs the benefits realised by the use of a particular distinction against the burdens imposed by the use of that distinction on those who fall on the wrong side of the line drawn by it.[46] In cases where the ground of discrimination is agreed, the

---

[42] This closely resembles the state's argument in support of a distinction disadvantaging those under 25 in *R. (Reynolds)* v. *Secretary of State for Work and Pensions* [2005] UKHL 37, paras. 37, 39 and 86–91.

[43] See e.g. *R. (Carson)* v. *Secretary of State for Work and Pensions* [2005] UKHL 37; *Carson* (CA) [2003] EWCA Civ 797; *R. (Mitchell)* v. *Coventry University* [2001] EWHC Admin 167; *Michalak* [2002] EWCA Civ 271; *R. (Montana)* v. *Home Secretary* [2001] HRLR 8.

[44] *A and Others* (CA) [2002] EWCA Civ 1502; *MacDonald/Pearce* [2003] UKHL 34.

[45] *A and Others* [2004] UKHL 56; *Ghaidan* [2004] UKHL 30.

[46] Baroness Hale of Richmond, 'The Quest for Equal Treatment' [2005] PL 571, 582 (noting that, in the justification inquiry, 'we are concerned with the aim of the difference in treatment rather than the aim of the treatment given to the more advantaged'); R. Singh, 'Equality: The Neglected Virtue' [2004] EHRLR 141, 152; P. Van Dijk and G. J. H. Van Hoof, *Theory and Practice of the European Convention on Human Rights* (2nd edn, Deventer: Kluwer, 1990), p. 540.

analogous comparator inquiry has no function. Where the parties dispute the ground of discrimination, merger of justification into the comparator inquiry risks justifying discrimination on a ground identified by the state, rather than the actual ground disclosed by a proper comparator inquiry. To use a merged inquiry even where the parties agree on the ground of discrimination is particularly insidious, because a meaningless analytical step can result in a flawed proportionality assessment. Governments commonly use easy distinctions as proxies for harder ones, such as using age to get at high healthcare costs. A court that injects the state's reasons for using a distinction into the comparison risks justifying the reason instead of the distinction – in effect asking whether the state was justified in distinguishing on the ground it put forward as a reason for adopting the proxy, rather than asking whether the state was justified in using the proxy.

Exactly this happened in *R. (Carson)* v. *Secretary of State for Work and Pensions*, where the Court of Appeal upheld a scheme that provided an annual increase in state pension for UK pensioners living in the UK, or those living in countries with which the UK has a reciprocal agreement, but did not pay this increase to UK pensioners living outside the UK in countries without such agreements.[47] The claimant, who lived in South Africa and did not receive the increase under the scheme, claimed the failure to give her the increase discriminated against her in the enjoyment of her rights under Article 1 of Protocol No. 1. The parties agreed that the state denied the claimant the increase on the ground that she lived abroad, and the court accepted 'living abroad' as a status protected under Article 14. There was therefore no distinct purpose to be served by the analogous comparator inquiry: the state had clearly treated the claimant less favourably on the ground of 'living abroad', so the court should have addressed the only remaining question of whether the discrimination was justified. However, Laws LJ opted instead to engage in the comparator inquiry, but to allow clearly justificatory considerations into it, as part of what he called a 'compendious question', which he asked expressly to determine whether to proceed to the next step, which would require a 'positive justification' of the distinction, involving proportionality.[48]

---

[47] *Carson* [2003] EWCA Civ 797.

[48] *Ibid.*, para. 61 ('A possible approach, as it seems to me, is to ask a compendious question in place of [the comparator question]: are the circumstances of [the comparators] so similar as to call (in the mind of a rational and fair-minded person) for a positive

He clearly saw his compendious question as representing a threshold antecedent to a proper justification of differential treatment on the impugned ground.[49] Thus Laws LJ took into account that the claimant lived in a country with lower inflation than the United Kingdom, and concluded that as a result the claimant was not in an analogous position to that of UK resident pensioners, despite the fact that in applying the scheme the state never took into account the rate of inflation in a given pensioner's place of residence. The individual who made the decision as to what pension Carson received did not have the benefit of any information about the cost of living in South Africa, nor would such information have been considered. The question for this notional decision-maker turned on (1) the payments Carson had made into the system and (2) where she lived. Thus, with regard to that decision, she was in an identical position to any other UK pensioner who paid in a relevantly similar amount, except for her place of residence. Nevertheless, the court in *Carson* took account of a circumstance – differences in costs of living – not relevant to the determination of any person's entitlement to any particular amount of pension. The court then found that a 'rational and fair-minded person' would not call upon the state to give a 'positive justification' for giving different pensions to people in countries with different costs of living. The court in so doing committed two significant errors: (1) it justified the state's underlying reason, not the proxy it chose to use instead; and (2) it failed to bring proportionality to bear on either the reason or the proxy.

These errors must be understood together. If the proxy – that is, the actual distinction used to pursue government policy – had been sub-jected to a justification inquiry without a proportionality element, then the court would ignore crucial questions like whether using residence to get at cost of living denies the upgrade to a subset of people who do not benefit from low costs of living, and whether the cost savings realised by using residence – instead of actually taking cost of living into account in pension decisions – outweighs the harm caused to those non-residents who do not enjoy a low cost of living. If, on the other hand, proportion-ality were used, but applied to the reason rather than the proxy, the court would weigh the benefits of distinguishing on the ground of cost of living against the hardship imposed on individuals by such a distinction, and would conclude that taking cost of living into account produces a

---

justification for the less favourable treatment?' The phrase 'positive justification' was used to refer to *Michalak* step four, which incorporated proportionality).

[49] *Ibid.*, paras. 61–3.

minimal hardship and does an excellent job of preventing the state from paying upgraded pensions to those who do not need them – except of course that cost of living was *not* taken into account. It is, in short, a nonsense to apply a proportionality justification to a distinction that the state did not actually employ. *Carson* went beyond that nonsense, justifying a distinction the state did not use, to conclude that the distinction it *did* use need not satisfy the proportionality review required by Article 14.

The court did go on to consider justification *ex hypotheosi*, but it need not have bothered. The House of Lords confirmed the propriety of dispensing with proportionality in Carson's case, although it rejected the compendious question suggested by Laws LJ.[50] The majority, led by Lords Hoffmann and Walker, essentially adopted the 'suspect classification' approach used by the US Supreme Court in cases under the Fourteenth Amendment to the US Constitution.[51] Under this analysis, whether or not a court should engage in a proportionality review depends on whether the ground of discrimination is 'suspect', in that it is associated with a history of invidious discrimination (e.g. race, sex, religion, sexual orientation and so on). If not – and of course place of residence would not constitute a suspect classification – then the state need only have a rational basis for distinguishing between the claimant and the proffered comparator. Courts are to disclose this rational basis through the expedient of a comparison that considers all of the government aims and reasoning that would feature in a proper justification, but they need not weigh those considerations proportionally. This flies in the face of the Strasbourg requirement that every distinction on a ground covered by Article 14 must satisfy proportionality, and it leaves the state free, with regard to grounds of distinction that do not enjoy 'suspect' status, to use any convenient proxy to effect whatever degree of differentiation it chooses without facing scrutiny. Moreover, in cases where the parties disagree on the ground of distinction, the kind of justificatory comparison called for in *Carson*, focusing as it does on the reasons one might have for treating certain groups differently, rather than the attribute actually used to distinguish them, will more often than not reveal that the government did not mean to target a suspect ground. The *Carson* analysis, if it emerges as the domestic orthodoxy, eviscerates the protection afforded by Article 14, by limiting the proper, proportional protection of the Article to those kinds of discrimination that are

---

[50] [2005] UKHL 37, paras. 3, 31, 44 and 79.   [51] *Ibid.*, paras. 15 and 55–70.

already recognised as problems. Meanwhile, the courts are precluded from shining the light of proportionality onto non-suspect grounds of discrimination, assuring that 'suspect classifications' remains a closed category.

'Right of abode' or nationality?

A less depressing example of domestic efforts to apply the comparator analysis comes from the decisions on the cases of the suspected terrorists held in Belmarsh Prison.[52] Although many desponded[53] upon reading the Court of Appeal decision in the case, the House of Lords righted the ship and in so doing illustrated a correct approach to the comparator question. *A and Others* v. *Secretary of State for the Home Department* concerned an order by the Home Secretary to the effect that, under derogation from Article 5 of the Convention, suspected international terrorists who were (1) aliens but (2) could not be deported for fear of torture in their home country, could be detained without trial. Suspected international terrorists who were not aliens, and hence could not be deported, were not subject to similar detention without trial. The claimants in the case alleged that this order discriminated against them on the basis of their nationality under Article 14. The Court of Appeal held unanimously – although expressed in three different opinions – that the order did not violate Article 14 because the Home Secretary did not *base* his choice to detain only alien suspects on their nationality.[54] The Lord Chief Justice, Lord Woolf, identified, as the real reason the Home Secretary had chosen to detain these particular suspected terrorists, the fact that they had only a right not to be removed, whereas British nationals have a right of abode. Brooke LJ identified the reason as the Home Secretary's belief that the alien suspected terrorists posed a greater or more immediate threat than British suspected terrorists. Chadwick LJ reckoned that the Home Secretary based his choice on a factual determination that the state of emergency – which underlay the derogation from Article 5 that made detention without trial permissible in the first place – 'strictly required' only the detention of aliens, but did not go so far as 'strictly' to require the detention of British nationals. Each of these reasons meant, although only Lord Woolf articulated this

[52] *A and Others* (CA) [2002] EWCA Civ 1502; *A and Others* [2004] UKHL 56.
[53] See e.g. K. D. Ewing, 'The Futility of the Human Rights Act' [2004] PL 829, 841–3.
[54] *A and Others* (CA) [2002] EWCA Civ 1502, paras. 47, 103 and 153.

directly,[55] that the 'chosen comparators' – British suspected terrorists – were not in an analogous position to the claimants.

The Court of Appeal thus based its decision on whether discrimination occurred, as opposed to a decision as to whether the measure's objectives and means proportionately justified the discrimination, on the aims and reasoning of the government in making the impugned decision. The question as to the analogous position of the comparators should have turned on whether all of the characteristics relevant to the decision to detain were the same other than the impugned criterion, in this case nationality. Because the Home Secretary based detention decisions on (1) whether the individuals met the pertinent definition of 'suspected international terrorist', (2) whether they could be deported and (3) whether they had a British national's right to remain, the only distinction between those detained and their British comparators was the third criterion. The question posed by that criterion could only be answered one of two ways, and only by reference to nationality. In other words, a proper application of the 'analogous comparator' step in the analysis yields nationality as the only relevant criterion for detention in which the claimants differed from their chosen comparators.

Two interpretations can explain what the Court of Appeal did. First, one could argue that it applied the comparator inquiry properly up to a point, but got stuck on the label of 'right of abode'. Lord Woolf clearly considered that label dispositive, noting the possession of a 'right of abode' as a key relevant characteristic that distinguished the British nationals and made them inappropriate comparators.[56] Such an acceptance of a state-imposed label plastered over the underlying characteristic of nationality would make the inquiry turn on government logic as surely as would open consideration of government aims. The lack of a 'right to remain' is simply one of the many legal consequences attendant to foreign nationality. To treat distinctions based on such legal consequences as being different from distinctions based on nationality would be like treating distinctions based on having different sex organs as different from distinctions based on gender or, worse yet, like allowing the state to distinguish between people based on the fact that they wear a certain kind of hat, where the state requires all members of a minority race to wear that hat. As erroneous as it would have been for the Court of Appeal to base its decision on acceptance of a label, the unfortunate truth is that the court erred even more egregiously. The second

---

[55] *Ibid.*, para. 56.   [56] *Ibid.*, paras. 46–53.

interpretation of its handling of the comparator question, which I suggest more accurately reflects its thinking, is that the Court of Appeal openly considered that the intended object of the Home Secretary's distinction governed the comparator analysis. In short, all three judges decided whether the comparators were analogous based on whether the conscious logic of the Home Secretary's distinction turned on something other than nationality. Each opinion is marked by a discussion of why the Home Secretary chose to draw the line where he did, and focused on how the Home Secretary singled out the claimants for reasons like their lack of a right of abode, the immediacy of the threat posed by them, or the extent to which only their detention was 'strictly required'. If these were the reasons, the logic went, and not nationality, then the claimants were not in an analogous position to their comparators because these reasons applied to them, but not to the comparators.

I have already argued that such an approach does not track with a proper analysis of comparators. It might be suggested, however, that, while the justices got it 'academically' wrong, their approach did nothing more than collapse justification into the comparator analysis, but still applied the justification principles, and no harm was done. The House of Lords, as it happens, was not persuaded that no harm had been done by this approach. As evidenced in the speech of Lord Bingham, the House saw through the use of different immigration statuses to defeat analogous comparison:

> This is, however, to accept the correctness of the Secretary of State's choice of immigration control as a means to address the Al-Qaeda security problem, when the correctness of that choice is the issue to be resolved.[57]

The question of justification should have weighed the threat posed by terrorism, and the effectiveness and reasonableness of the measure employed to combat it, against the burden of nationality discrimination, which requires 'very weighty reasons' for its justification.[58] In essence, not only must the objective of fighting terrorism constitute a 'weighty reason' (which of course it did) but weighty reasons must exist to fight terrorism by discriminating on the basis of nationality (hence immigration) status. Instead, any justification talk in which the Court of Appeal engaged looked at whether the threat of terrorism justified the detention of aliens full stop. By refusing to admit that nationality discrimination

---

[57] *A and Others* [2004] UKHL 56, para. 53.   [58] *Gaygusuz* (1996) 23 EHRR 364, para. 42.

had occurred, and by accepting the immigration labels that the Home Secretary employed, the court skewed the justification analysis away from a proper one – involving whether a good reason existed to use a measure that discriminated on the basis of nationality instead of one that did not – and towards an improper one – involving merely the question whether there was a good reason to detain terrorist suspects with no right of abode who may not be deported. The House of Lords, by applying the correct approach, not only recognised the *prima facie* discrimination for what it was, but focused the justification inquiry on its proper object, and came to the (correct) conclusion that the Home Secretary's order unjustifiably violated the rights of the claimants under Articles 14 and 5.

A *and Others* shows that the domestic judiciary can, when enough is at stake, look beyond government aims and reasoning to the facts as they happened to the claimant, not as the state viewed them. It also shows that some of the Law Lords recognise what the majority in *Carson* did not: that the fact that aliens and citizens are different, in that one has the right of abode and the other does not, and the fact that the state deems this relevant to its decision, provide nothing more than reasons for disparate treatment, which may or may not be a good enough reason for the kind of disparate treatment at issue. That some part of the House of Lords accepts this provides reason for optimism.

The 'homosexual' label

Although the House of Lords pierced the veil of the Home Secretary's 'right of abode' label, it has shown less penetration when confronted with the label 'homosexual'. In *Advocate General for Scotland* v. *MacDonald*,[59] *Pearce* v. *Mayfield School*,[60] and the House of Lords decision on the combined appeals from both,[61] the Scottish Extra Division, the Court of Appeal and the House of Lords wrestled with the question of whether a person discriminated against on the basis of sexual orientation could also prove sex discrimination under the Sex Discrimination Act 1975 (SDA). The central question in each case concerned the application of the SDA test for sex discrimination in employment. The relevant provisions of the SDA provide that 'a person discriminates against a [man/woman] ... if on the ground of [his/her] sex he treats [him/her] less favourably than he treats or would treat a

[59] 2001 SLT 819.   [60] [2001] EWCA Civ 1347.   [61] *MacDonald/Pearce* [2003] UKHL 34.

[person of the opposite sex]', and 'A comparison of the cases of persons of different sex ... must be such that the relevant circumstances in the one case are the same, or not materially different in the other.'[62] The claimants in each case contended that, where, for example, an employer dismisses a man expressly because he is homosexual, under the SDA he should be viewed as having been dismissed because he has or wants to have sex with men, and thus should be compared to a woman who has or wants to have sex with men.[63] Thus the point turned on whether the 'relevant circumstances' for the comparator test include 'homosexuality' or merely the gender of those the claimant has or wants to have sex with. All three courts held, with one dissent from Lord Prosser in the Extra Division, that the relevant circumstance was the 'homosexuality' of the claimant, requiring a comparison of the claimant with a homosexual of the opposite sex.[64] Because, in each case, homosexuals of both sexes would have received the same treatment, this finding foreclosed the claims under the SDA.

These cases were not, strictly speaking, Article 14 claims. Each case involved arguments under Article 14, but the House of Lords determined that, as the facts of each case preceded the effective date of the HRA, none of the decisions turned on an application of Article 14.[65] That leaves us waiting for the other shoe to drop. Although the Employment Equality (Sexual Orientation) Regulations 2003 render the question moot in employment cases like *MacDonald* and *Pearce*, the SDA prohibits discrimination in areas beyond the employment and vocational training covered by the Regulations, such as housing, goods and services. Should an individual who suffers sexual orientation discrimination in the provision of housing, for example, seek to apply the now fully effective HRA to require the SDA to provide a remedy, the question will almost certainly turn on the application of Article 14. It

---

[62] SDA, ss.1(1), 2(1) and 5(3).

[63] This argument drew from a similar argument first put forward (widely) by Robert Wintemute in 'Recognising New Kinds of Sex Discrimination: Transsexualism, Sexual Orientation, and Dress Codes' (1997) 60 MLR 334.

[64] *MacDonald*, 2001 SLT 819, *per* Lord Kirkwood, para. 10, *per* Lord Caplan, paras. 7–10; *Pearce* [2001] EWCA Civ 1347, para. 54; *MacDonald/Pearce* [2003] UKHL 34, paras. 9, 62, 66, 109, 114, 158 and 176.

[65] Lord Prosser in *MacDonald* found that the 'relevant circumstances' included the choice of sex partner – not 'homosexuality' – without assistance from the HRA, but commented that had he concluded otherwise he believed s.3(1) would require him to interpret the SDA as he had (para. 41). The other judges in the case disagreed (Lord Kirkwood, para. 10, Lord Caplan, para. 10).

should be noted in this regard that the then Lady Justice Hale, now in the House of Lords, expressed sympathy with the argument that, if the HRA did apply, s.3(1) would require the interpretation of 'relevant circumstances' to exclude 'homosexuality', in order to avoid a dismissal in violation of Article 14 taken with Article 8.[66] Although in the *MacDonald* and *Pearce* cases the employers were public bodies, under s.6 HRA this issue could arise in the private sector as well.[67] Thus there remains an important question under the HRA whether the courts can and should read the SDA to prohibit sexual orientation discrimination in certain cases.

I maintain, however, that the question goes beyond the SDA to judicial reasoning about discrimination in general. This issue, whether it involves Article 14 or a domestic statute, typifies the kind of issue that calls for a vigilant approach to concepts or conventions with which we have become comfortable, and which otherwise seem obviously reasonable. Although various judges at all levels of the *MacDonald* and *Pearce* cases appeared to make the same mistakes as the Court of Appeal did in *A and Others*, concentrating on the logic and objectives of the relevant decision-makers, the deciding factor in each case was that most of the judges (Lord Prosser and Lady Hale representing notable exceptions) could not let go of the label 'homosexual'. Time and time again, judges referred to this as a fundamental characteristic of the claimant,[68] indeed 'the "critical circumstance"' of the case,[69] referring to the 'subcategories of heterosexual and homosexual'.[70] In so doing, the judges smuggled a discriminatory view into the SDA itself, not because they wanted to discriminate or would consciously suffer it, but through a lack of that vigilance required in all judicial reasoning relating to questions of discrimination. They accepted the view that the claimants received the treatment of which they complained because they were 'homosexual', and they failed to drill down beneath this label to the fact that its use is a form of gender discrimination expressly forbidden by the words of the SDA. To use the label 'homosexual' as a factor in decisions about individuals is to define them in terms of the expectations one has for persons of their gender, and is no more permissible than to use the

---

[66] [2001] EWCA Civ 1347, paras. 14–34.   [67] See e.g. *X* v. *Y* [2004] EWCA Civ 662.
[68] *MacDonald/Pearce* [2003] UKHL 34, para. 83.
[69] *MacDonald*, 2001 SLT 819, *per* Lord Caplan, para. 7.
[70] *Ibid.*, *per* Lord Kirkwood, para. 10.

symmetrical label 'androgynous' to deny benefits or advancement to a 'mannish' woman.

'Homosexuality' is an observation, not a fact

The view of people as being either heterosexual or homosexual, or as being susceptible to distinction from the other members of their gender, and to grouping together with members of their opposite gender such that both male and female are of the separate group 'homosexuals', comes from those who support anti-gay or anti-lesbian policies, and from discriminatory attitudes that the rest of us unwittingly share with them. This view observes facts about people – their sexual partners, whom they claim or appear to be attracted to, particular sexual acts in which they engage – and picks out one specific conclusion that can be drawn from these facts – the conclusion that the individual observed wants to have or at some time in the past has had sex with a person of their own gender – and invests it with a particular salience. The facts about these people and their sexual choices or natural inclinations may have infinite variations. They may have been attracted to members of their own sex exclusively for as long as they can remember, they may have been happily married to a member of the opposite sex for years before first acknowledging a sexual attraction to a particular member of their own sex, or they may never have felt that the gender of a person had any bearing on whether they found them sexually attractive. The people we call 'homosexuals' are people attracted to other people, just as most 'heterosexuals' are. We enshrine with significance, out of the myriad observations one can make about people, the fact that in some cases people happen to be attracted to others of the same gender. This observation has no inherent significance. It is in fact a banal and pedantic notation unless one invests it with importance by contrasting it to a state of affairs presumed 'normal'. That is precisely what most of us do. We bring to the table the assumption that people have sex with members of the opposite sex, and thus when they do not we remark on the significance of the fact. We may have valid reasons for doing this, but there can be no excuse for making our own interest in this neutral fact a fundamental and 'relevant' truth about the person about whom we make the observation.

If Tom has a sexual relationship with John, and Phyllis has a sexual relationship with John, these must, under the law and under any Convention-compatible interpretation of statutes, be neutral facts. Therefore, if an employer sacks Tom because of his relationship with

John, but does not sack Phyllis because of her relationship with John, then Tom has been treated less favourably than a member of the opposite sex. This differential treatment is on the ground of Tom's sex because the employer treats as significant the same conduct by Tom as it did not treat as significant in Phyllis, exclusively because of Tom's gender in relation to John. The employer claims that it did not act on the ground of sex but of 'homosexuality', because a woman who had sex with a woman would also have been treated less favourably than a man who had sex with a woman. However, the motive of a distinction, as opposed to the ground on which it differentiates, has no bearing on the discrimination analysis under the SDA.[71] Moreover, the SDA does not provide employers with a 'symmetry' defence. Nowhere does the statute allow a discrimination claim to fail because the employer would have committed the same kind of discrimination had the claimant's gender been different. This symmetry issue appears to be a problem for many judges,[72] but nobody contends that the Race Relations Act 1976 would allow a 'no-mixed-race couples' policy in a restaurant, simply because black men with white partners would be treated no worse than white men with black partners. The point is that black men with white partners would be treated worse than white men with white partners. Similarly, the SDA cannot allow an employer to operate a 'no androgyny' policy, claiming that in refusing to hire a 'pushy' woman with short hair and a 'masculine' build it treated androgynous women no worse than the androgynous man it refused to hire for having a ponytail, a slight build and good fashion sense.

The comparator analysis in the SDA, as under Article 14, seeks to test whether the decision at issue turned on the impugned characteristic, in this case gender. Therefore the facts taken into account in choosing a comparator must be all of the facts bearing on the employer's decision other than gender, which must be the opposite of the claimant. In deciding what are the 'relevant circumstances' for comparison under the SDA, a court must ask, 'what facts about the claimant led to the decision', not 'what significance did the employer place on those facts in making the decision'. Under such an approach, the woman denied a job for being pushy and having a masculine build would be compared to a man with the same 'pushy' characteristics and build, not a man deemed

---

[71] *James v. Eastleigh BC* [1990] 2 All ER 607.

[72] *MacDonald*, 2001 SLT 819, *per* Lord Caplan, para. 7; *Pearce* [2001] EWCA Civ 1347, para. 54; *MacDonald/Pearce* [2003] UKHL 34, paras. 108 and 167.

'androgynous' in the eyes of the employer. By the same token, a male
SDA claimant openly sacked for 'homosexuality' was sacked because of
the *fact* that he was attracted to or had sex with men. The employer's
focus on his 'homosexuality' connotes nothing more than that the
employer considers it significant that he is a *man* who is attracted to
or has sex with men.

Sexual orientation discrimination is gender discrimination

A theme runs through the opinions of the judges who rejected the
argument that men attracted to men should be compared to women
attracted to men. They complained that this abstract exercise, whereby
we ignore the 'real' reason given by the employer, or are 'persuaded' that
a homosexual man is the same as a heterosexual woman, so departs from
common sense that it distorts the meaning of the SDA from a statute
that prohibits gender discrimination to one that prohibits sexual orientation discrimination as well.[73] On the contrary, this careful, conscien-
tious and, yes, abstract application of the language of the SDA helps us
grope through the darkness of our biased and conventional 'common
sense' to reveal that sexual orientation discrimination is a form of
gender discrimination. In the SDA, Parliament endeavoured to distil
the essence of sex discrimination to a few carefully worded tests.
Parliament almost certainly could not be said to have 'intended' that
the language it used would encompass sexual orientation discrimination, but it did not rule it out. It chose to define sex discrimination
abstractly to include treating a man less favourably than a woman who
was the same, or not materially different, in terms of the 'relevant
circumstances'. It is only through a naïve reading of these words,
coupled with a vigilant insistence on peering behind the curtain of the
employer's reaction to certain facts as manifested in the label 'homosexual', that we discover that treatment based on sexual orientation is
patently gendered treatment. When an employer singles out a 'homosexual', it singles out a member of one sex for doing something it would
be perfectly happy for a member of the other sex to do. It is treatment
based on the failure of an individual to act within the confines of what
the employer expects of persons of that gender. That is sex discrimination. If the domestic judiciary cannot accept such a proposition, or the
kind of thinking that pushes past a label like 'homosexual', it will never
adequately protect individuals against discrimination.

---

[73] *MacDonald/Pearce* [2003] UKHL 34, paras. 109 and 114.

Conclusions

The HRA brought Article 14 into domestic law as part of a new scheme for protecting human rights in the United Kingdom.[74] The fact that s.2 HRA requires the courts to take account of Strasbourg case-law prevents the new scheme from straying too far from its ECHR roots, but the new powers and responsibilities with which it invests the judiciary, as well as the fact that a 'margin of appreciation' has no place in domestic adjudication, dictate that UK Article 14 jurisprudence must take a form of its own.[75] In other words, how UK judges apply Article 14, and indeed all Convention rights, depends not only on what the ECtHR says the Convention requires, but also on the function reserved for the courts in the HRA human rights protection machine.

The HRA has entrusted the judiciary with assuring that the activities of the state do not have the effect of violating Convention rights. Thus the courts in applying Article 14, and indeed any other Article of the Convention, must keep their eyes on the impact of government measures and decisions on the rights of individuals, not on the objectives, processes and reasoning of the government actors. Domestic judges must also beware the temptation to view Article 14 as a mere adjunct of other Articles: it is a Convention guarantee in its own right, and does not call for interpretation according to the limitations written into the other substantive rights. Article 14 therefore applies wherever an impugned measure has a discriminatory impact in the area of enjoyment of rights, an area that cannot be defined according to the scope of protection of Convention Articles as such, or any arbitrary extension thereof. Once engaged, Article 14 calls for a *prima facie* discrimination inquiry cleansed of the taint of justificatory considerations. Only an analysis of relevant circumstances *other than* the intentions of the state will reveal discriminatory *effects*; only when the discriminatory effects of a measure have been identified can a justification inquiry properly

---

[74] See e.g. I. Leigh, 'Taking Rights Proportionately: Judicial Review, the Human Rights Act and Strasbourg' [2002] PL 265; P. Craig, *Administrative Law* (4th edn, London: Sweet and Maxwell, 1999), p. 546, at pp. 556–7 and 561; J. Jowell, 'Beyond the Rule of Law: Towards Constitutional Judicial Review' [2000] PL 671; M. Elliott, 'The HRA 1998 and the Standard of Substantive Review' (2001) 60 CLJ 301.

[75] R. Masterman, 'Section 2(1) of the Human Rights Act 1998: Binding Domestic Courts to Strasbourg?' [2004] PL 725, 727; D. Bonner, H. Fenwick and S. Harris-Short, 'Judicial Approaches to the Human Rights Act' (2003) 52 ICLQ 549, 553; C. McCrudden, 'Equality and Non-Discrimination', in D. Feldman (ed.), *English Public Law* (Oxford: Oxford University Press, 2004), paras. 11.86–11.109.

balance such effects against the objectives and expedience of the state action.

These principles have not, alas, enjoyed consistent adherence in the domestic courts. For example, judicial reasoning on the scope of Article 14 has focused too much on the wording or logic of the other 'substantive' or helping right, putting an inappropriately limiting gloss on Article 14. The courts have also concerned themselves too much with whether the government measure, not the effects on the individual, came within the 'ambit' of a Convention right. Judges have done this openly or by accepting the state's definition of the subject matter of the regulation. Judicial reasoning on the application of Article 14 once engaged has faltered too, especially by allowing justificatory considerations to skew the comparison test and thereby avoid a finding of *prima facie* discrimination. Again, in some cases, this has been done openly, without embarrassment, while in others it happens either surreptitiously or inadvertently through reliance on labels injected by the maker of the impugned decision. For every such example there are corresponding well-decided cases, and several members of the judiciary are leading the way in approaching Article 14 free of the burdens of traditional assumptions. Nevertheless, common threads in the troubling cases tell a story of a judiciary too accustomed to asking whether the state has acted inconsistently with conventional notions of reasonable decision-making. Domestic judges must, in implementing Article 14, tear their attention away from the government, ignoring its justifications and labels, and look exclusively to the effects of challenged measures, considering the government's reasons only in justification of demonstrated differences in the enjoyment of Convention rights. The effects of impugned measures must be examined with a vigilance that acknowledges that some of the most innocuous-seeming and comfortable conventions of governance, and of society in general, must surely hide the seeds of the inequality that flourishes around us. Only through a victim focus and suspicion of the 'normal' can the courts defend the Article 14 right as the HRA intended them to.

13

Criminal procedure, the presumption of innocence and judicial reasoning under the Human Rights Act

PAUL ROBERTS

Preliminaries: objectives, taxonomy and method

Why is criminal procedure relevant to the topic of judicial reasoning under the Human Rights Act 1998? Readers might be forgiven for thinking that the connection between these topics is not self-evident. Indeed, several of the participants in the Durham conference from which the chapters comprising this volume are drawn explicitly posed the question to me: interesting as it might be in its own sphere, what place does a paper on criminal procedure have in a conference or edited collection devoted to exploring the impact of the HRA on judicial reasoning in the United Kingdom?

I hope that this chapter will supply a convincing answer to that question. On one view, it expresses a perfectly reasonable challenge, but it also, I think, betrays misconceptions and even a certain ignorance that I would like to try to dispel. The question has, if not exactly hidden profundity, then at least partly occluded depths. Below its surface lurk other, taxonomic and methodological questions with important theoretical and practical ramifications. To which legal topics or issues is the HRA pertinent? Should an evaluation of its impact consider every eligible example of judicial reasoning or only a sample selection? If a sampling approach is preferred, or dictated on pragmatic grounds, by what criteria should inclusion in the sample be arbitrated? Attention to the grand heights of constitutional law-making might indicate one kind of impact on judicial reasoning, consideration of the role of the HRA in routine appeals or first-instance trials or interlocutory proceedings quite another. My sense is that British human rights scholarship is dominated by constitutional law theorists and public lawyers. This, again, is perfectly understandable: the HRA was intended to be a major constitutional reform. Although evaluations of its early progress and future prospects range from cautious shades of optimism through to black pessimism, few would venture to deny the HRA's constitutional significance as a legal instrument, or the momentousness of its adoption after decades of contentious debate and committed advocacy. Yet it surely does not follow from its indubitably constitutional status that the exclusive, or even primary, juridical significance of the HRA must be located only in the self-consciously constitutional pronouncements of the highest courts. Proponents of constitutional 'Bills of Rights' have long argued that legislative enactment is only the starting point; the real, long-term challenge lies in instilling a culture of respect for human rights through the fabric of law and legal institutions. Senior judges and courts have a pivotal role to play in promoting this agenda through high-profile advocacy and authoritative precedents. But the battle is ultimately won or lost, specifically in relation to nurturing a human rights culture by, in and through judicial reasoning,[1] in the hearts and minds of High Court judges, circuit judges, recorders, district judges, magistrates' clerks and lay magistrates. In assessing the impact of the HRA on 'judicial reasoning', in other words, we may learn more from the legally prosaic and routine than from the constitutionally extraordinary. And here it should be noted that approximately 2 million criminal cases are completed annually in England and Wales,[2] including around 80,000 particularly serious allegations tried on indictment in the Crown Court[3] and fully occupying a dedicated Court of Appeal (Criminal Division) with appeals on points of criminal law, procedure and sentencing.[4]

Criminal law and public law exist in somewhat uncertain relation in British legal scholarship and education. On the one hand, police powers under the Police and Criminal Evidence Act 1984 are a standard

---

[1] Beyond the present focus on judicial reasoning, human rights culture also needs to be fostered amongst legislators, regulators and other law-related professionals and institutions – police, prosecutors, lawyers in private practice, etc. – and throughout public life.

[2] In 2004, 2.02 million defendants were prosecuted in magistrates' courts: Home Office, *Criminal Statistics 2004 – England and Wales*, Home Office Statistical Bulletin 19/05 (Office for Criminal Justice Reform, 2005), http://www.homeoffice.gov.uk/rds/.

[3] In 2004, the Crown Court received 79,232 committals for trial and finalised 81,750 cases: Department for Constitutional Affairs, *Judicial Statistics England and Wales for the Year 2004*, Cm. 6565 (London: TSO, 2005), p. 85.

[4] The Court of Appeal (Criminal Division) received 7,591 applications for leave to appeal in 2004, and actually heard 624 appeals against conviction and 1,937 appeals against sentence: *ibid.*, pp. 17–18.

component of first-year university courses entitled 'Constitutional Law', and criminal law-related topics feature quite prominently in most constitutional and public law textbooks (albeit less so in works devoted specifically to administrative law). But, at the same time, criminal law is generally taught through precedent cases in English law schools and consequently tends to get lumped together with the other predominantly common law foundation subjects, in contradistinction to constitutional law and EU law, with land law something of a statutes-and-cases hybrid. Anecdotally,[5] it appears that criminal law is not generally regarded as a member of the 'public law' family in British scholarship and teaching, though it may confidently be supposed that academic lawyers would readily concur, were the question expressly articulated, that criminal law must necessarily fall on the 'public' side of any illuminating public–private conceptual taxonomy. Certain features of criminal law, broadly conceived to embrace procedure and process as well as substantive prohibitions, must properly be regarded as 'constitutional' norms by any plausible criterion. But, if criminal law has, in general, become estranged from its constitutional and public law conceptual foundations in British legal scholarship and pedagogy, it would not be entirely surprising if constitutional and public law scholars were to overlook the significance of criminal litigation in making global assessments of the impact of the HRA on judicial reasoning.

Proceeding from these assumptions, the primary objective of this chapter is to raise awareness amongst constitutional and public law scholars of the potential significance of decisions in criminal cases, for their researches and theorising in general and for evaluating the impact of the HRA in particular. I refer in the main not to House of Lords decisions on terrorism and torture, in which constitutional and public law scholars are already well versed,[6] but to what might otherwise be

---

[5] The subtle conditioning effected by these pedagogical traditions is eloquently betrayed by an internal memo once circulated amongst undergraduate teachers at Nottingham referring to 'the private law subjects, e.g. tort, contract and crime'! (The author of this chestnut shall remain nameless, but not for any reason connected with the presumption of innocence.)

[6] See e.g. *A v. Home Secretary (No. 2)* [2005] UKHL 71; [2005] 3 WLR 1249; *A v. Home Secretary*; *X v. Home Secretary* [2005] 2 AC 68; [2004] UKHL 56. The comparatively higher profile of these cases amongst constitutional lawyers might well be related to the fact that they are not, strictly speaking, criminal law precedents, though (like the *Kebilene* decision extensively discussed below) they plainly involve alleged criminal conduct and were preceded by criminal investigations.

regarded as 'routine' criminal cases devoid of constitutional merits.[7] It will not be possible in a single chapter to develop every dimension of these expansive and gently provocative introductory remarks. Instead, the discussion will focus on one aspect of the right to a fair trial, the presumption of innocence in criminal proceedings, as a practical case study of judicial reasoning in criminal adjudication. As it happens, this topic does concern major pronouncements of the superior courts regarding a right with evident constitutional status, and for these reasons represents a conservative and relatively uncontroversial choice of illustration.

The second section of this chapter supplies the first part of the case study by summarising five recent appellate court rulings on the presumption of innocence. Even before the HRA had entered fully into force on 2 October 2000, the meaning and scope of the 'presumption of innocence' as a human right had already been argued before the House of Lords *twice*. The point has since been relitigated before their Lordships on a further two occasions, along the way provoking what Ian Dennis has described (erring on the side of understatement) as 'an unusual spat'[8] between the senior Law Lord and the retiring Lord Chief Justice. Such extraordinary appellate activity ought in itself to attract the attention of scholars interested in assessing the impact of the HRA on judicial reasoning. The essentially expository treatment undertaken in the first part of this chapter is intended to introduce these cases, and to indicate some of their complexities, to a new audience beyond the narrow circles of criminal law specialists. Building on this descriptive foundation, the third section of this chapter undertakes an analytically more ambitious if inevitably somewhat speculative exercise, by inferring more general patterns of judicial reasoning and broader jurisprudential trends under the HRA from the courts' newly invigorated engagement with the presumption of innocence. Finally, the chapter draws together the threads of the discussion in a brief conclusion.

---

[7] Cf. Martin Loughlin, *The Idea of Public Law* (Oxford: Oxford University Press, 2003), p. 43: 'In a legal system that exists . . . for enforcing the norms of criminal conduct, it can be assumed that judges perform the important but mundane task of resolving disputes in accordance with the rule system that has been laid down. Concerning matters of constitutional law, however, things are much more complicated.'

[8] Ian Dennis, 'Reverse Onuses and the Presumption of Innocence: In Search of Principle' [2005] Crim LR 901, 903.

Five judgments on the presumption of innocence
as a human right

The 'presumption of innocence' is a standard component of the 'right to a fair trial' declared by international human rights instruments, prominently including the European Convention on Human Rights (ECHR) and the International Covenant on Civil and Political Rights.[9] It is also frequently elevated to the status of a constitutional guarantee in national Bills of Rights and codes of criminal procedure.[10] More specifically for our purposes, Article 6(2) of the ECHR provides that:

> Everyone charged with a criminal offence shall be presumed innocent until proved guilty according to law.

Of course, the presumption of innocence – translated into the burden and standard of proof – was a cherished part of English legal heritage long before the HRA made the ECHR a formal source of law in English criminal proceedings. According to Viscount Sankey LC in his celebrated 'golden thread' speech in *Woolmington* v. *DPP*:

> Throughout the web of the English Criminal Law one golden thread is always to be seen, that it is the duty of the prosecution to prove the prisoner's guilt subject ... to the defence of insanity and subject also to any statutory exception. If ... there is a reasonable doubt ... the prosecution has not made out the case and the prisoner is entitled to an acquittal. No matter what the charge or where the trial, the principle that the prosecution must prove the guilt of the prisoner is part of the common law of England and no attempt to whittle it down can be entertained.[11]

---

[9] ICCPR Article 14(2) provides in almost identical terms to ECHR Article 6(2) that: 'Everyone charged with a criminal offence shall have the right to be presumed innocent until proved guilty according to law.' And see the EU Draft Treaty Establishing a Constitution for Europe (July 2003), Article II-48: Presumption of innocence and right of defence.

[10] In Bassiouni's valuable survey, the presumption of innocence was found to be guaranteed in five of the principal international human rights treaties and sixty-seven national constitutions: M. Cherif Bassiouni, 'Human Rights in the Context of Criminal Justice: Identifying International Procedural Protections and Equivalent Protections in National Constitutions' (1993) 3 *Duke Journal of Comparative and International Law* 235.

[11] [1935] AC 462 (HL), 481–2. Viscount Sankey makes explicit reference to the 'presumption of innocence' only once, and almost in passing, near the end of his speech.

Despite the resounding rhetorical appeal and progressive institutional legacy of these remarks, their doctrinal pedigree has been doubted as a matter of legal history,[12] and the extent of their contemporary application remains controversial. *Woolmington's* golden thread, commentators have lamented, is seriously frayed and even broken in places.[13] The advent of the HRA has provided a pretext for relitigating long-running controversies surrounding the allocation of burdens of proof in English criminal proceedings, now reconceptualised in the terminology of Article 6(2)'s 'presumption of innocence'. It is an opportunity that, for better or worse, English lawyers, aided and abetted by some contentious passages of judicial reasoning, have grasped with both hands.

This section expounds, in chronological order, five post-HRA decisions on the presumption of innocence. Four of these cases went to the House of Lords; the fifth was decided by a specially convened panel of the Court of Appeal (Criminal Division), comprising two Lords Justice of Appeal and three High Court judges rather than the usual panel of three judges, of whom often only one is a Lord Justice of Appeal. The high status of the judiciary involved in these cases serves to make the frequency of disagreements and dissenting opinions all the more striking. Three of the five cases actually involve conjoined appeals, making a total of *twelve* litigated disputes contesting the scope and application of the presumption of innocence under the HRA. The Court of Appeal and the Administrative Court have together heard more than twenty further appeals[14] invoking Article 6(2) since the HRA entered into force.

---

[12] On doctrinal developments preceding *Woolmington*, see J. C. Smith, 'The Presumption of Innocence' (1987) 38 *Northern Ireland Legal Quarterly* 223; George P. Fletcher, 'Two Kinds of Legal Rules: A Comparative Study of Burden-of-Persuasion Practices in Criminal Cases' (1968) 77 *Yale Law Journal* 880. For broader historical context, see Barbara J. Shapiro, *Beyond Reasonable Doubt and Probable Cause: Historical Perspectives on the Anglo-American Law of Evidence* (Berkeley, CA, and Oxford: University of California Press, 1991); Theodore Waldman, 'Origins of the Legal Doctrine of Reasonable Doubt' (1959) 20 *Journal of the History of Ideas* 299.

[13] Andrew Ashworth, 'Is the Criminal Law a Lost Cause?' (2000) 116 LQR 225, 228–9; John Sprack, 'Will Defence Disclosure Snap the Golden Thread?' (1998) 2 *International Journal of Evidence and Proof* 224; Editorial, 'Escaping Liability or a Recipe for Injustice?' [1992] Crim LR 81; Francis Bennion, 'Statutory Exceptions: A Third Knot in the Golden Thread?' [1988] Crim LR 31; Patrick Healy, 'Proof and Policy: No Golden Threads' [1987] Crim LR 355; A. A. S. Zuckerman, 'No Third Exception to the *Woolmington* Rule' (1987) 104 LQR 170.

[14] See nn. 122–3 below.

Ex parte Kebilene[15]

The first of our five cases fell to be determined before the substantive parts of the HRA had even been implemented in England and Wales. Sofiane Kebilene and two co-accused were Algerian nationals resident in London. They were suspected of being members of the Armed Islamic Group, and in this capacity of supplying various articles to assist terrorist associates back in Algeria, including (as specified in the indictment) 'chemical containers, radio equipment, manuals, documents, credit cards and sums of money'.[16] Kebilene was charged under s.16A of the Prevention of Terrorism (Temporary Provisions) Act 1989, a provision since repealed but substantially re-enacted as s.57 of the Terrorism Act 2000.[17] At the time of these proceedings, s.16A provided that:

> (1) A person is guilty of an offence if he has any article in his possession in circumstances giving rise to a reasonable suspicion that the article is in his possession for a purpose connected with the commission, preparation or instigation of acts of terrorism . . .
>
> (3) It is a defence for a person charged with an offence under this section to prove that at the time of the alleged offence the article in question was not in his possession for such a purpose as is mentioned in subsection (1) above.
>
> (4) Where a person is charged with an offence under this section and it is proved that at the time of the alleged offence – (a) he and that article were both present in any premises; or (b) the article was in premises of which he was the occupier or which he habitually used otherwise than as a member of the public, the court may accept the fact proved as sufficient evidence of his possessing that article at that time unless it is further proved that he did not at that time know of its presence in the premises in question, or, if he did know, that he had no control over it.

Section 16A required the consent of the Director of Public Prosecutions before proceedings could be commenced.[18] Consent was duly given, and *Kebilene* eventually[19] came on for trial at the Old Bailey in October 1998.

---

[15] R. v. *DPP, ex parte Kebilene* [2000] 2 AC 326.

[16] 'The Old Bailey was told . . . that the three plotted to smuggle deadly chemicals in tins of baby food from London to Algeria for use in terrorism': *Independent*, 27 July 1999.

[17] With an important twist: by virtue of ss.118(2)–(4), the onus on the defendant to 'prove' innocent possession, etc., is merely *evidential*.

[18] Prevention of Terrorism (Temporary Provisions) Act 1989, s.19.

[19] The first trial date in March 1998 had to be vacated owing to late prosecution disclosure.

After several unsuccessful attempts to have the case thrown out as an abuse of process, the defence argued that s.16A was incompatible with Article 6(2)'s unequivocal guarantee of the presumption of innocence in criminal proceedings.

On the face of it, this was a surprising submission, given the marginal status of the ECHR in English law prior to 2 October 2000. The traditional conception of parliamentary sovereignty coupled with a 'dualist' approach to public international law might have been expected to keep the Convention securely shackled, as nothing more – for the time being – than a subsidiary aid to statutory interpretation in English legal proceedings.[20] Yet the trial judge acceded to defence counsel's submission and ruled that s.16A violated Article 6(2). Lord Hobhouse later expressed surprise that the judge had 'allowed himself to be drawn into listening to argument or into ruling upon incompatibility ... [H]e should have declined to entertain any argument on incompatibility.'[21] But, in fairness to the trial judge, defence counsel's argument was both novel and ingenious: the DPP, it was contended, could not lawfully consent to any prosecution entailing a breach of Convention rights, since a prosecution infringing the ECHR could not be in the public interest[22] and consenting to it would consequently be *ultra vires* for any public official.[23] The DPP sought clarification from independent counsel, and was advised – contrary to the trial judge's finding – that s.16A was compatible with Article 6(2). Thus fortified, the DPP stood his ground, prompting the defence to launch collateral judicial review proceedings challenging the DPP's conduct in refusing to withdraw his consent. The defendants were initially successful before the Divisional Court, but their victory was short-lived. The House of Lords ultimately held (Lord Cooke dissenting) that the DPP's consent to criminal prosecution could only be challenged within the institutional framework of criminal proceedings. Satellite litigation was costly and time-consuming and where, as here, adequate remedies could be pursued through arguments at trial and, if necessary, by routine criminal appeals the

---

[20] R. v. *Home Secretary, ex parte Brind* [1991] 1 AC 696 (HL); cf. R. v. *Navabi*; R. v. *Embaye* [2005] EWCA Crim 2865, para. 28.

[21] [2000] 2 AC 326, 394–5.

[22] All prosecutions in England and Wales must pass the 'public interest' test in addition to satisfying criteria of evidential sufficiency: Code for Crown Prosecutors (CPS, 2004), paras. 5.6–5.11.

[23] HRA, s.6.

proliferation of collateral applications would not be tolerated.[24] This ruling was sufficient to dispose of the case before the House of Lords. Their Lordships nonetheless proceeded to consider, and roundly criticise, the Divisional Court's treatment of the presumption of innocence, setting the tone and framing the juridical context for the flood of Article 6(2)-based appeals which promptly ensued. Meanwhile, with attention diverted to the application for judicial review, the original criminal trial fizzled out ignominiously. The DPP offered no evidence and Kebilene and his co-accused were acquitted by order of the judge, following serial procedural irregularities and amidst allegations that the British government was attempting to conceal its knowledge of atrocities implicating the Algerian security forces.[25]

The nub of Kebilene's incompatibility argument can be summarised succinctly. The offence of possessing ostensibly innocent, everyday objects for a terrorist purpose, created by s.16A of the 1989 Act, was attacked on the basis that it effectively put the accused to the burden of proving innocence in circumstances where the prosecution had done very little to establish blameworthy criminal fault. This lopsided allocation of probative responsibility was said to contravene the presumption of innocence guaranteed by Article 6(2), as well as being irreconcilable with *Woolmington*'s golden thread.[26] The Divisional Court found these contentions compelling, embracing the argument for incompatibility enthusiastically and without reservation. The court reasoned that, because highly equivocal evidence of misconduct might place an accused in peril of conviction of a serious offence unless he could demonstrate his innocence on the balance of probabilities,[27] the section was in effect,

---

[24] Lord Steyn, at 370, for example, was concerned that: '[I]f the Divisional Court's present ruling is correct, it will be possible in other cases, which do not involve reverse legal burden provisions, to challenge decisions to prosecute in judicial review proceedings. The potential for undermining the proper and fair management of our criminal justice system may be considerable.' To similar effect, Lord Hobhouse, at 389 and 394, considered it a 'remarkable proposition' that 'a ruling adverse to the prosecution [should] provide the defence with an opportunity to bypass the criminal process or escape, otherwise than by appeal, other decisions of the criminal court', and concluded that 'it is not correct either as a matter of the construction of s.29(3) or as a matter of principle to use the device of purporting to review the conduct of the Director to obtain the re-litigation in the Divisional Court of an issue in the criminal trial'.

[25] Richard Norton-Taylor, 'Terrorist Case Collapses After Three Years', *Guardian*, 21 March 2000.

[26] *Woolmington* v. *DPP* [1935] AC 462 (HL).

[27] *R.* v. *Hunt* [1987] 1 AC 352 (HL), *per* Lord Griffiths, at 374. Also see *R.* v. *Carr-Briant* [1943] KB 607 (CCA).

if not design, an illegitimate reverse-onus provision. This appeared to follow from subsection (3) which states in terms that it is 'a *defence* for a person charged with an offence under this section *to prove* that at the time of the alleged offence the article in question was not in his possession for such a purpose'.[28] Subsection (4), setting up an explicit reverse-onus defence to a presumption of (constructive) possession, served in the Divisional Court's view only to damn the offence further. Lord Bingham CJ's analysis of s.16A was as succinct as his conclusion was unequivocal:

> The gravamen of the offence charged by section 16A is the possession of articles, in themselves innocent, for terrorist purposes. The crucial ingredients of the offence are in reality possession (the *actus reus*) and the terrorist purpose (the *mens rea*). But neither of these crucial ingredients need be proved by the prosecution to the criminal standard to secure a conviction ... A defendant who chooses not to give or call evidence may be convicted by virtue of presumptions against him and on reasonable suspicion falling short of proof ... It seems to me that on their face both[29] sections undermine, in a blatant and obvious way, the presumption of innocence.[30]

Laws LJ agreed, pausing only briefly to dismiss possible counter-arguments based on the *Edwards*[31] 'third' exception to *Woolmington* for 'exemptions, exceptions, provisos etc.',[32] and on Strasbourg jurisprudence interpreting Article 6(2). His Lordship concluded that the rift between s.16A and Article 6(2) was too wide to be bridged by any conceivable variation of facts, so that the English statute stood condemned as definitively beyond reconciliation with European human rights law.

On appeal by the DPP to the House of Lords, Lord Cooke seems to have inclined to a similar view, opining that 'at best it is doubtful whether Article 6(2) can be watered down to an extent that would leave section 16A unscathed'.[33] But there was otherwise precious little

---

[28] Prevention of Terrorism (Temporary Provisions) Act 1989, s.16A(3) (emphasis added).

[29] The related offence of collecting information for a terrorist purpose, proscribed by s.16B of the 1989 Act and re-enacted as s.58 of the Terrorism Act 2000, was in issue in joint proceedings before the Divisional Court which were not pursued to the House of Lords.

[30] [2000] 2 AC 326, 344.

[31] *R. v. Edwards* [1975] QB 27 (CA), as clarified in *R. v. Hunt* [1987] AC 352 (HL).

[32] See Paul Roberts and Adrian Zuckerman, *Criminal Evidence* (Oxford: Oxford University Press, 2004), § 8.6.

[33] [2000] 2 AC 326, 373.

support for the Divisional Court's conclusion of 'blatant and obvious' incompatibility. Lord Hope and Lord Hobhouse, the two Law Lords who considered the incompatibility argument at greatest length, both thought that s.16A might be saved, whilst Lord Steyn insisted that the point would remain 'undecided and entirely open at all levels in the criminal proceedings'.[34] The courts' divergent conclusions on Article 6(2) incompatibility may be traceable in part to their contrasting approaches to interpreting and applying the ECHR in domestic legal proceedings. Whilst the Divisional Court attempted to interpret the language of the Convention more or less in abstraction, the House of Lords read Article 6(2) in the light of the principles and precedents that have been developed by the Strasbourg organs in their judicial elaborations of the Convention text.

The leading Strasbourg case on Article 6(2) is *Salabiaku* v. *France*,[35] which concerned a smuggling offence under the French customs code. In *Salabiaku*, the ECtHR announced that it would scrutinise presumptions of fact or law in order to ensure that they did not in substance infringe the presumption of innocence, recognising that without this element of European supervision 'the national legislature would be free to strip the trial court of any genuine power of assessment and deprive the presumption of innocence of its substance'.[36] The Court proceeded to formulate the following statement of principle:

> Article 6(2) does not therefore regard presumptions of fact or law provided for in the criminal law with indifference. It requires states to confine them within reasonable limits which take into account the importance of what is at stake and maintain the rights of the defence.[37]

Unfortunately, the precise basis of the Court's holding in *Salabiaku* is obscure. A number of factors were rehearsed in the judgment and it is not clear which, if any, were considered crucial in rejecting Salabiaku's application on the facts of the case. The ECHR-compliance of a domestic law is never evaluated in the abstract under the Convention system. Rather, the question explicitly addressed by the European Court is always whether the applicant's Convention rights have been respected

---

[34] *Ibid.*, p. 372.
[35] (1991) 13 EHRR 379, applied in *Pham Hoang* v. *France* (A/243), 19 August 1992, ECtHR. The presumption of innocence is also considered to be subsumed within Article 6(1)'s general 'fair trial' provision, and there is an uncertain degree of overlap with the privilege against self-incrimination: *Saunders* v. *UK* (1996) 23 EHRR 313.
[36] (1991) 13 EHRR 379, para. 28.   [37] *Ibid.*

in substance, taking into account all relevant circumstances of the legal proceedings in question. Confined to its facts, *Salabiaku* stands for the proposition that Article 6(2) poses no obstacle to convicting a defendant of a non-strict-liability criminal offence where: (i) the defendant is proved to have done a prohibited act; (ii) in circumstances giving rise to a suspicion of guilty knowledge; and (iii) the defendant failed to establish any permitted reverse-onus excuse (in this instance, *force majeure* or non-culpable mistake). Even if this is strictly speaking all that *Salabiaku* decided, however, there are direct implications for the issues confronted in *Kebilene*.

To begin with, it is certainly arguable that s.16A(4) of the 1989 Act was[38] in conflict with Article 6(2) and the principles enunciated in *Salabiaku*. Subsection (4) contemplated that an offence under s.16A might be perpetrated by merely *constructive* rather than actual possession. It explicitly sets up a presumption of fact to this effect, with an accompanying reverse-onus clause. This is exactly the kind of arrangement that the Strasbourg Court indicated would attract close scrutiny for conformity with Article 6(2). Furthermore, s.16A(4)'s factual presumption of possession, in relieving the prosecution of the need to prove one of the offence's two minimalist external elements, might be said to trivialise the prosecution's probative burden to an unacceptable extent. If the s.16A offence had ever been used to obtain a conviction purely on the basis of a defendant's physical proximity to articles which she consistently denied – but could not disprove – knowing anything about, coupled with circumstantial suspicion of terrorist designs, an application to Strasbourg alleging breach of Article 6(2) might well have succeeded. As it turned out, this analysis had limited application to *Kebilene*, since only one of the three co-defendants was actually denying possession of the articles in question. Kebilene himself and the third co-defendant admitted possession, thereby forestalling the operation of subsection (4) in relation to the charges proffered against them.

Lord Hope considered *Kebilene*'s Article 6(2) dimensions at greatest length.[39] His Lordship rehearsed key tenets of Strasbourg jurisprudence,

---

[38] Subsection 16A(4) of the 1989 Act corresponds to subsection 57(3) of the Terrorism Act 2000.

[39] Lord Hope's excursus was motivated in part by his desire to provide guidance to the Scottish Parliament and its ministers, whose devolved powers under the Scotland Act 1998 are, by virtue of s.29(2)(d) of the Act, expressly delimited by Convention rights. This is a sharp point which, though naturally close to the former Lord Justice General of Scotland's heart, went unmentioned by the other Law Lords.

including the margin of appreciation and the principle of proportionality, and underlined the vital significance of factual context in Strasbourg jurisprudence:

> The cases show that, although Article 6(2) is in absolute terms, it is not regarded as imposing an absolute prohibition on reverse onus clauses, whether they be evidential (presumptions of fact) or persuasive (presumptions of law). In each case the question will be whether the presumption is within reasonable limits.[40]

The task for the court, therefore, is to apply the general 'reasonable limits' test to the facts of particular cases, and in contemplating this exercise Lord Hope commended an approach advanced in argument by counsel:

> Mr Pannick suggested that in considering where the balance lies it may be useful to consider the following questions. (1) What does the prosecution have to prove in order to transfer the onus to the defence? (2) What is the burden on the accused – does it relate to something which is likely to be difficult for him to prove, or does it relate to something which is likely to be within his knowledge or (I would add) to which he readily has access? (3) What is the nature of the threat faced by society which the provision is designed to combat? It seems to me that these questions provide a convenient way of breaking down the broad issue of balance into its essential components, and I would adopt them for the purposes of pursuing the argument as far as it is proper to go in the present case.[41]

'The questions were not presented as a set of rules', Lord Hope subsequently elaborated, but rather as 'an indication of an approach which it might be useful to adopt when the interests of the individual are being balanced against those of society'.[42] Without expressing a concluded view, Lord Hope indicated that judicial analysis of the scenario presented in *Kebilene* should revolve around the following countervailing considerations:

> It is not immediately obvious that it would be imposing an unreasonable burden on the accused who was in possession of articles from which an inference of involvement in terrorism could be drawn to provide an explanation for his possession of them which would displace that inference. Account would have to be taken of the nature of the incriminating

---

[40] [2000] 2 AC 326, 385.   [41] *Ibid.*, p. 386.
[42] *McIntosh* v. *Lord Advocate* [2001] 2 All ER 638, para. 46, *per* Lord Hope.

circumstances and the facilities which were available to the accused to obtain the necessary evidence. It would be one thing if there was good reason to think that the accused had easy access to the facts, quite another if access to them was very difficult.

Then there is the nature of the threat which terrorism poses to a free and democratic society. It seeks to achieve its ends by violence and intimidation. It is often indiscriminate in its effects, and sophisticated methods are used to avoid detection both before and after the event. Society has a strong interest in preventing acts of terrorism before they are perpetrated – to spare the lives of innocent people and to avoid the massive damage and dislocation to ordinary life which may follow from explosions which destroy or damage property.[43]

Their Lordships were understandably reluctant to express strong views, on a purely hypothetical basis in collateral judicial review proceedings, about the possible effect of s.3 HRA on the correct interpretation of s.16A in a criminal trial. Lord Cooke displayed a measure of enthusiasm for reading down s.16(3) to a merely evidential burden of production.[44] Lord Steyn (with whom Lord Slynn agreed) likewise thought this 'a respectable argument',[45] whilst Lord Hobhouse was mildly sceptical.[46] In the event, parliamentary intervention pre-empted further speculation about the scope for interpretative 'reading down' or resort to the more drastic remedy of a declaration of incompatibility in relation to this particular offence.[47]

R. v. Lambert

The second of the quartet of Article 6(2) reverse-onus cases to reach the House of Lords was *R. v. Lambert,* in which the accused had been convicted of possession of cocaine with intent to supply having failed to prove an affirmative 'no knowledge' defence. *Lambert* resembles *Kebilene* to the extent that the HRA was not yet in force at the time of Lambert's trial in April 1999. Their Lordships' extended discussion of Article 6(2) and its application to English criminal statutes was therefore technically *obiter dicta,* though patently intended to provide definitive guidance to first-instance tribunals (and the Court of Appeal) just the

---

[43] [2000] 2 AC 326, 387.   [44] *Ibid.,* p. 373.   [45] *Ibid.,* p. 370.   [46] *Ibid.,* p. 398.
[47] Subsections 118(3)–(5) of the Terrorism Act 2000 operate to reduce the defendant's onus of proof under s.57(3) – replacing the old s.16A(4) – to a merely *evidential* burden of production.

same. In *Lambert*, however, there is much fuller judicial consideration of Article 6(2) compatibility and interpretative 'reading down' under s.3 HRA. And, whereas the criminal offence with which Kebilene was charged was subsequently superseded by a toned-down statutory replacement, *Lambert*'s interpretation of ss.5 and 28 of the Misuse of Drugs Act 1971 remains authoritative.

Steven Lambert was apprehended by the police in the booking hall at Runcorn railway station. He had been observed to arrive on the London train and rendezvous with two men whom he apparently knew. One of the men had a duffle bag. All three went out into the car park, and minutes later Lambert returned alone carrying the bag. When the police opened the bag, they recovered two kilos of cocaine with a street value of over £140,000. Lambert denied all knowledge of the drugs. He claimed that he was only a bag man, and mentioned something about collecting and paying for packets of tee-shirts for a man called John. He said that he had queried the contents of the bag with his associates, and had been told that it was 'a bit of scrap ... scrap gold' for John. When he had attempted to rummage around in the bag, he explained, his friends had turned nasty and intimated to him that they had a gun. He had better do as he was told and take the bag and its contents to John.

At trial on a charge of possession of Class A drugs with intent to supply, contrary to s.5(3) of the Misuse of Drugs Act 1971, Lambert repeated his claim of ignorance and insisted, in addition, that he had acted under duress. Neither defence cut any ice with the jury, and he was convicted and sentenced to seven years' imprisonment. He appealed against his conviction on the basis that s.5(3) is incompatible with Article 6(2), inasmuch as s.28 of the 1971 Act contains various reverse-onus clauses requiring an accused to prove, in particular, that 'he neither believed nor suspected nor had reason to suspect that the substance or product in question was a controlled drug'.[48] At the intermediate appellate stage Lambert's case was conjoined with two other appeals, in which the statutory rule requiring an accused to prove diminished responsibility on the balance of probabilities[49] was also attacked for infringing Article 6(2).[50] The Court of Appeal summarily dismissed the Convention-based challenge in relation to diminished responsibility, and was detained by Lambert's arguments only marginally longer. Even on the – rather hesitant and guarded – concession that Article 6(2) was applicable to a criminal trial taking place before 2 October 2000, the Court

---

[48] Misuse of Drugs Act 1971, s.28(3)(b)(i). [49] Homicide Act 1957, s.2(2).
[50] *R. v. Lambert; R. v. Ali; R. v. Jordan* [2001] 1 All ER 1014; [2001] Cr App R 205 (CA).

ruled that s.5(3) was straightforwardly compatible with Convention jurisprudence, and refused leave to appeal to the House of Lords.

Although the House of Lords granted leave for a further appeal, their
Lordships unanimously upheld Lambert's conviction and seven-year
sentence.[51] Given that the jury had rejected Lambert's duress excuse,
which the Crown must be taken to have disproved beyond reasonable
doubt,[52] his conviction was 'a foregone conclusion',[53] irrespective of
the adequacy of the trial judge's direction on the burden of proving
Lambert's knowledge, or otherwise, of the drugs. Despite the absence of
a genuine contest, their Lordships nonetheless took the opportunity to
expound at length on the applicability of Article 6(2). Lord Steyn alone
believed that their Lordships were bound to take this course, in the light
of the injunction in s.6 HRA that 'no appellate court may act incompatibly with a convention right':

> Surely, for an appellate court to uphold a conviction obtained in breach
> of a convention right, must be *to act* incompatibly with a convention
> right. It is unlawful for it to do so. So interpreted no true retrospectivity
> is involved. Section 6(1) regulates the conduct of appellate courts *de
> futuro* ... The language of the statute points in one direction only: the
> House may not *act* unlawfully by upholding a conviction which was
> obtained in breach of a convention right.[54]

None of the other four Law Lords accepted Lord Steyn's interpretation
of s.6(1) as applied, self-reflexively, to their own determination in the
present appeal. Although in form the argument focused on the lawfulness of their Lordships' decision, the majority reasoned, the House was
in substance being invited to say that a conviction that was perfectly
valid and lawful at the time it was entered could no longer be upheld
once the HRA had come into force. The 'reality' of the submission was
apprehended as an attempt to give s.6(1) retroactive effect, against
which Lords Slynn, Hope, Clyde and Hutton presented an implacably
united front.[55] Having pronounced the non-retroactivity of the HRA as

---

[51] *R. v. Lambert (Steven)* [2002] 2 AC 545; [2001] UKHL 37.

[52] Duress being an affirmative defence which the prosecution must disprove, beyond
reasonable doubt, once raised on the facts: *R. v. Gill* (1963) 47 Cr App R 166; *R. v.
Steane* [1947] KB 997.

[53] [2002] 2 AC 545, para. 43, *per* Lord Steyn.

[54] [2002] 2 AC 545, para. 28 (original emphasis).

[55] Lord Hutton, paras. 169 and 175–6; Lord Slynn, paras. 10–13; Lord Clyde, paras.142–3.
Lord Hope reached the same conclusion as a matter of strict construction, and apparently without much enthusiasm, at para. 116.

the strict *ratio decidendi* of the case, their Lordships proceeded to discuss matters of greater jurisprudential substance and more lasting practical effect than this essentially transitional issue.[56]

Lambert's substantive argument was given a noticeably more sympathetic hearing in the House of Lords than it received from the Court of Appeal. Albeit with differences of approach and emphasis, their Lordships (Lord Hutton dissenting) converged on the same two-limb conclusion: ss.5(3) and 28 of the Misuse of Drugs Act 1971 do contravene Article 6(2) of the ECHR, but can be 'read down' into conformity with the Convention by treating the 1971 Act's reverse-onus clauses as imposing only *evidential*, rather than probative, burdens on the accused.[57] This conclusion can be dissected into four discrete propositions.

First, as a matter of statutory construction and settled judicial authority, it is not necessary for an offender to know that she has drugs in her possession in order to be convicted of the s.5 offences. To 'possess' a narcotic for the purposes of subsections 5(2) or 5(3) of the 1971 Act (respectively, possession *simplicter* and possession with intent to supply), one must know that one has control over material later proved to be a controlled substance, but one need not appreciate its properties or nature.[58] In English law, one can possess a drug without knowing that it *is* a drug. Moreover, if the drug is in a box, bag or other container, the accused need only know that he has the container and that there is *something* in it.[59] If that something turns out on subsequent analysis to be a prohibited drug, he is guilty of the offence. The legislative precursors of the 1971 Act[60] imposed strict liability in relation to this aspect of knowledge – or lack of it. Parliament ameliorated the accused's situation to the extent of conceding 'no knowledge' defences in the 1971 Act. In

---

[56] Which is not to deny that the HRA's equivocally retrospective effect has thrown up some fascinating jurisprudential puzzles in the interim: see, for example, *R. v. Kansal (No. 2)* [2002] 2 AC 69 (HL); Kevin Kerrigan, 'Unlocking the Human Rights Floodgates?' [2000] Crim LR 71.

[57] [2002] 2 AC 545, *per* Lord Slynn, para. 17; Lord Steyn, paras. 35 and 39–41; Lord Hope, paras. 76 and 90–4; Lord Clyde, paras. 131–3 and 157. Lord Hutton agreed that the 1971 Act was facially in tension with Article 6(2), but found no contravention in fact, either because (i) reverse-onus clauses were justified as a measure in response to the 'threat posed by drugs to the welfare of society' and compatible with Strasbourg jurisprudence; or in the alternative, (ii) the accused had a fair trial and would have been found guilty, in accordance with Article 6, regardless of the judge's direction on the burden of proving knowledge of the drugs: at paras. 185, 190–2 and 202.

[58] Misuse of Drugs Act 1971, s.28(3)(a).

[59] *R. v. McNamara* (1988) 87 Cr App R 246 (CA).

[60] Dangerous Drugs Act 1965; Drugs (Prevention of Misuse) Act 1964.

particular, s.28(3)(b)(i) provides that the accused 'shall be acquitted ... if he proves that he neither believed nor suspected nor had reason to suspect that the substance or product in question was a controlled drug'. Section 5 of the Misuse of Drugs Act 1971 might conceivably have been read in conjunction with s.28 as making 'knowledge, belief or reason to suspect' a substantive element of the s.5 offences. But, as all their Lordships agreed in *Lambert*, English law did not take that course. The reverse onus clauses of s.28 must therefore be construed as affirmative defences, which extend a previously unavailable lifeline to accused persons who can prove that naivety was their only sin.

The second proposition underpinning their Lordships' conclusions is that s.28, so construed, involves (in the language of the European Court of Human Rights) statutory 'presumptions of fact or of law'.[61] Lord Hutton expressly refers to the 'rebuttable presumption of knowledge created by subsections 28(2) and (3)',[62] and some equivalent idea is implicit in all their Lordships' speeches. Were it otherwise, Article 6(2) analysis could never get off the ground. Orthodox criteria of criminal liability which are satisfied on the facts cannot infringe the presumption of innocence – even in relation to offences of strict liability[63] – unless certain facts are actually being 'presumed' to the detriment of the accused.

Once it has been established that s.28 contains factual presumptions, the third stage in the analysis is to consider the compatibility of this provision with Article 6(2). The overriding proportionality constraints articulated by the Strasbourg Court, as we have seen, are 'reasonable limits which take into account the importance of what is at stake and maintain the rights of the defence'; or, as Lord Hope summarised the position in *Lambert*, 'the test to be applied is whether the modification or limitation of that right pursues a legitimate aim and whether it

---

[61] *Salabiaku* v. *France* (1991) 13 EHRR 379, para. 28.   [62] [2002] 2 AC 545, para. 190.

[63] *Barnfather* v. *London Borough of Islington and Secretary of State* [2003] EWHC Admin 418; [2003] 1 WLR 2318. The extent of Article 6(2)'s application is controversial: see, for example, Victor Tadros and Stephen Tierney, 'The Presumption of Innocence and the Human Rights Act' (2004) 67 MLR 402, taking issue with Paul Roberts, 'The Presumption of Innocence Brought Home?: *Kebilene* Deconstructed' (2002) 118 LQR 41; and the partial rejoinder in Roberts, 'Strict Liability and the Presumption of Innocence: An Exposé of Functionalist Assumptions', in Andrew Simester (ed.), *Appraising Strict Liability* (Oxford: Oxford University Press, 2005). Even those who contest my analysis of the scope of Article 6(2)'s application in English law, however, must – I take it – agree that Article 6(2) cannot be infringed unless the state is illegitimately presuming *something* to the detriment of the accused.

satisfies the principle of proportionality'.[64] In concluding that s.28 failed
this test, Lords Slynn, Steyn, Hope and Clyde stressed that the onus lies
with the state to demonstrate that its aim in derogating from Article 6(2)
was legitimate, and that its chosen means were proportionate to that
end. The objective of combating the 'notorious social evil'[65] of drug
trafficking was, unsurprisingly, accepted as legitimate on all sides. But
s.28 was judged to be a disproportionate measure in pursuit of this
assuredly legitimate objective, inasmuch as it places a probative onus on
the accused to demonstrate absence of knowledge when, their Lordships
said, a merely evidential burden would have sufficed. Various considerations were advanced in support of this conclusion: the increasing
prevalence of reverse-onus clauses in modern criminal legislation, for
which a clear rationale is seldom given;[66] long-standing academic opposition to placing probative burdens on the defence;[67] the non-negligible
probative demands of an evidential burden, which requires the accused
to 'pass the judge' by adducing some evidence in support of her contentions;[68] countervailing probative advantages conferred on the prosecution by criminal legislation of the last decade;[69] Parliament's
expressed preference for evidential burdens in recent enactments;[70]
and persuasive authority from other superior tribunals, especially the
Privy Council,[71] the Supreme Court of Canada[72] and the South African

---

[64] [2002] 2 AC 545, para. 88.   [65] [2002] 2 AC 545, *per* Lord Clyde, para. 156.

[66] Frequent reference was made to the findings of Andrew Ashworth and Meredith Blake,
'The Presumption of Innocence in English Criminal Law' [1996] Crim LR 314. Lord
Clyde, para. 155, suggested that '[t]he 1998 Act should encourage a reconsideration of a
trend which has for over a decade been exposed to powerful criticism'.

[67] Their Lordships also cited the Criminal Law Revision Committee, to the effect that an
evidential burden would always suffice: CLRC Eleventh Report, *Evidence: General*
(London: HMSO, 1972), para. 140.

[68] [2002] 2 AC 545, *per* Lord Slynn, para. 17; Lord Hope, para. 90.

[69] The most significant being ss.34–7 of the Criminal Justice and Public Order Act 1994
(adverse inferences from silence in relation to exculpatory facts, presence at the scene, or
incriminating marks or articles), mentioned by Lord Steyn, para. 39. The defence also
shoulders increased pre-trial disclosure duties pursuant to the Criminal Procedure and
Investigations Act 1996.

[70] Especially ss.57 and 118(2) of the Terrorism Act 2000. Also see Regulation of
Investigatory Powers Act 2000, s.53(3), mentioned by Lord Hope, para. 93.

[71] [2002] 2 AC 545, *per* Lord Hope, para. 90, citing *Vasquez* v. *R.* [1994] 1 WLR 1304; and
Yearwood v. *R.* [2001] UKPC 31; and Lord Clyde, para. 150, quoting from *A-G of Hong
Kong* v. *Lee Kwong-Kut* [1993] AC 951.

[72] [2002] 2 AC 545, *per* Lord Steyn, para. 40, citing *R.* v. *Oakes* (1986) 26 DLR (4th) 200;
R. v. *Whyte* (1988) 51 DLR (4th) 481; *R.* v. *Downey* [1992] 2 SCR 10; *R.* v. *Osolin* [1993] 4
SCR 595.

Constitutional Court.[73] But even this impressive array of factors was incapable of garnering universal assent and consensus. Lord Hutton, dissenting on this point, remained unconvinced:

> In my opinion the threat posed by drugs to the welfare of society is so grave and the difficulty in some cases of rebutting a defence that the defendant believed that he was carrying something other than drugs is so great that it was reasonable for Parliament to impose a persuasive burden as to lack of knowledge on a defendant … I am, with respect, unable to agree with the view that the problem of obtaining a conviction against a guilty person can be surmounted by imposing a[n] evidential burden on the defendant. All that a defendant would have to do to discharge such a burden would be to adduce some evidence to raise the issue that he did not know that the article in the bag or the tablets on the table were a controlled drug, and the prosecution would then have to destroy that defence in such a manner as to leave in the jury's mind no reasonable doubt that the defendant knew that it was a controlled drug in the bag or on the table … In my opinion it would be easy for a defendant to raise the defence of lack of knowledge by an assertion in his police statement or by adducing evidence (which could be from a third person), and the Crown would then have to prove beyond reasonable doubt that the defendant did have knowledge. Therefore I think that in a drugs case, in practice, there is little difference between the burden of proving knowledge resting throughout on the prosecution and requiring the defendant to raise the issue of knowledge before the burden of proof on that matter reverts to the prosecution.[74]

Finally, for the majority who found s.28 to impinge on Article 6(2), the fourth question to be considered is whether the offending statutory provisions can be 'read down' into conformity with the ECHR, by invoking s.3 of the HRA. The reverse-onus clauses of s.28 have always been assumed to impose probative burdens on the accused, and their Lordships did not deny that this is the most natural reading of the section and its legislative history. Lord Clyde, for example, readily acknowledged that 'this approach appears to run counter to what has become generally recognised as the proper construction in England. That approach is fortified by the language of s.28(2) that "it shall be a

---

[73] [2002] 2 AC 545, *per* Lord Steyn, para. 34, quoting from *State* v. *Coetzee* [1997] 2 LRC 593 (Sachs J); and para. 40, citing *State* v. *Mbatha* [1996] 2 LRC 208 and *State* v. *Manamela* [2000] 5 LRC 65.
[74] [2002] 2 AC 545, paras. 190 and 192.

defence for the accused to prove . . .". The ordinary meaning of those words imply a persuasive burden of proof even although the accused has only to establish his defence to the standard of a balance of probabilities.'[75] Yet none of the four-strong majority who concluded that a probative burden would contravene Article 6(2) found any difficulty in interpreting s.28 to impose merely evidential burdens.[76] Perhaps betraying consciousness of the novelty of this reading, Lord Hope went out of his way to insist that constitutional proprieties were being observed even whilst literal meaning and established precedent were relegated to the sidelines:

> Section 3(1) preserves the sovereignty of Parliament. It does not give power to the judges to overrule decisions which the language of the statute shows have been taken on the very point at issue by the legislator . . . [T]he interpretation of a statute by reading words in to give effect to the presumed intention must always be distinguished carefully from amendment. Amendment is a legislative act. It is an exercise which must be reserved to Parliament.[77]

R. v. Johnstone

Underlining the diversity of offences in relation to which Article 6(2) has generated appeals under the HRA, the legislative context of our third trip to the House of Lords was a long way removed from the Misuse of Drugs Act 1971. The charges in *Johnstone*[78] alleged trade mark infringement contrary to s.92 of the Trade Marks Act 1994 (TMA 1994), and the presumption of innocence was implicated, in particular, by s.92(5) which provides 'a defence for a person charged with an offence under this section to show that he believed on reasonable grounds that the use of the sign in the manner in which it was used, or was to be used, was not an infringement of the registered trade mark'. The mischief targeted by s.92 was elucidated in the opening passages of Lord Nicholls' speech,

---

[75] *Ibid.*, paras. 130–2.

[76] *Ibid.*, *per* Lord Slynn, para. 17; Lord Steyn, para. 42; Lord Hope, paras. 90–1; Lord Clyde, para. 157.

[77] *Ibid.*, paras. 79 and 81. Of course, these disavowals are felt necessary precisely because the HRA in general, and s.3 in particular, entrusts unwonted interpretational latitude to the courts.

[78] *R. v. Johnstone* [2003] 1 WLR 1736; [2003] UKHL 28.

with which Lords Hope, Hutton and Rodger agreed (Lord Walker concurring):

> [C]ounterfeit goods and pirated goods are big business. They account for between 5 per cent and 7 per cent of world trade. They are estimated to cost the economy of this country some £9 billion each year ... [I]n the context of music recording, a counterfeit compact disc is an unlawful copy of, say, a Virgin compact disc sold ostensibly as a Virgin product. A pirated compact disc is an unlawful copy of, in my example, a Virgin compact disc which is sold, not as a Virgin product, but under a different brand name. Another type of unlawful trading is 'bootlegging'. Like counterfeit records and pirated records, bootleg records are also big business. They comprise copies of an unlawful recording of a performance at a live concert. The recording is made at an auditorium or taken from a radio or television broadcast ... Nowadays leading performers register their professional names as trade marks in respect of recordings. So, it is said, sales of [bootleg] discs labelled in this way constitute infringements of the performers' registered trade marks.[79]

Robert Johnstone was charged on twelve specimen counts of possessing bootleg CDs of popular music with a view to their commercial distribution, contrary to s.92(1)(c) TMA 1994. Each specimen count related to a different album or artist. However, in total more than 500 CDs and tapes were seized from Johnstone's premises after a package containing '519 compact discs and associated artwork' was mistakenly sent to the wrong address, triggering police interest and official investigation of the accused's bootlegging operation. It was submitted to the trial judge that civil liability for trade mark infringement should be regarded as prerequisite to a criminal conviction, but that Johnstone's activities would not constitute infringing use in civil proceedings because the detailing and design of the CDs in his possession were merely 'indications concerning the kind, quality, quantity ... or other characteristics of goods or services',[80] rather than illegitimate indications of origin. In the alternative, it was contended that Johnstone was entitled to a defence of reasonable belief in non-infringement under s.92(5), since he never claimed to be selling officially sanctioned merchandise and had sought legal advice to ensure that his business practices were lawful. When both these submissions were rejected by the trial judge on a preliminary

---

[79] [2003] 1 WLR 1736, paras. 1–2 and 4.
[80] Specifically designated non-infringing uses by TMA 1994, s.11(2)(b).

ruling, Johnstone pleaded guilty as charged and received six months' imprisonment accompanied by hefty confiscation and forfeiture orders.

Though Johnstone duly served out his sentence, his appeal against these criminal convictions was ultimately successful, first in the Court of Appeal and subsequently before the House of Lords. The appeal was allowed on the relatively slender ground that the trial judge had been in error in withdrawing Johnstone's intended line of defence from the jury. Both as a matter of principle and as an exercise in statutory interpretation, the House of Lords held:

> Parliament cannot have intended to criminalise conduct which could lawfully be done without the proprietor's consent. Parliament cannot have intended to make it an offence to use a sign in a way which is innocuous because it does not infringe the proprietor's rights. That would extend, by means of a criminal sanction, the scope of the rights of the proprietor ... It would make no sense for a reasonable belief in non-infringement to provide a defence if infringement was irrelevant so far as the criminal offences are concerned.[81]

This ruling was sufficient to dispose of the appeal. Criminal offences of trade mark infringement, like their civil law counterparts, are perpetrated only where a registered sign is (mis)used as a (deceptive) indicator of origin, not in circumstances of merely descriptive use. A CD bearing the legend 'Bon Jovi' (as charged in Count 1 against Johnstone), for example, might indicate only that 'this is a recording of the music of Bon Jovi', without also implying that 'Bon Jovi has issued or authorised this recording'. Although recording artists might be expected to have some control over their musical output, this was 'not necessarily indicative that the performer's name is being used on the compact disc as a trade mark or that the average buyer so understands'.[82] The use to which a registered sign was being put on any given occasion could only be determined through properly contextualised inquiry: 'Whether particular labelling and packaging satisfy this test, and consequently are innocuous for trade mark purposes, is a question of fact in each case',[83] and it followed that specifically infringing use 'must therefore be proved by the prosecution'[84] in order to secure a conviction under s.92. 'Mr Johnstone would have had a difficult task in making good the defences on which he wished to rely', Lord Walker ruefully remarked. 'However, he should

---

[81] [2003] 1 WLR 1736, paras. 28–9, per Lord Nicholls.   [82] Ibid., para. 40.
[83] Ibid., para. 36.   [84] Ibid., para. 31.

have been permitted to run them.'[85] If this restrictive interpretation of the scope of trade mark offences appeared to provide insufficient protection for the intellectual property rights of recording artists, studios and labels, the answer was that an elaborate regulatory framework of copyright protection, including criminal prohibitions, has been put in place to safeguard the *content* of original recordings, works and performances.[86]

Although this was all that their Lordships were obliged to say to settle the day's business, Lord Nicholls extended the practice we have already observed in *Kebilene* and *Lambert* by issuing authoritative *obiter dicta* (apparently, no longer an oxymoronic characterisation) in relation to two aspects of the defence provided by s.92(5) TMA 1994.[87] A desire to resolve conflicting authorities in the lower courts provided understandable motivation for stepping beyond the strict boundaries of *ratio decidendi* on this occasion.

On a first, narrow point of construction, it was indicated that s.92(5) should in principle extend to defendants who believed on reasonable grounds – albeit erroneously – that the sign in question was not registered as a trade mark, as well as to those who reasonably believed that their employment of a known trade mark constituted non-infringing use.[88] Lord Nicholls then turned to address the broader issue previously ventilated in *Lambert*, whether the relevant statutory 'defence' imposed a fully probative, or only an evidential, burden on the accused. At the Court of Appeal stage in *Johnstone*, the defence naturally contended for the less exacting standard, which the Court of Appeal accepted, without dispute from the Crown, as the correct interpretation of s.92(5) in the light of Article 6(2). In *R. v. S*,[89] however, a differently constituted Court of Appeal held that s.92(5) imposed a fully probative reverse-onus burden. Adopting different tactics before the House of Lords, the Crown

---

[85] *Ibid.*, para. 89.

[86] *Ibid.*, para. 40, referring to the Copyright, Designs and Patents Act 1988, as amended, and the Copyright, etc, and Trade Marks (Offences and Enforcement) Act 2002.

[87] Lord Walker's concurring speech is confined to the first aspect, and notably silent on any issue relating to Article 6(2) or the burden of proof. The omission is presumably deliberate, but its significance is opaque. This can hardly be regarded as an indication of 'dissent' in the normal sense, since the passages of Lord Nicholls' speech addressing Article 6(2) are technically *obiter dicta* and the 'silent majority' of Lords Hope, Hutton and Rodger all agreed with Lord Walker as well as Lord Nicholls.

[88] [2003] 1 WLR 1736, para. 43, preferring *R. v. Rhodes* [2002] EWCA 1390 to *Torbay Council v. Singh (Satnam)* [1999] 2 Cr App R 451 (DC).

[89] *R. v. S (Trade Mark Defence)* [2003] 1 Cr App R 602; [2002] EWCA Crim 2558.

in *Johnstone* argued that *R.* v. *S* was to be preferred to the Court of Appeal's approach in the instant case, and their Lordships – perhaps surprisingly in view of their holding in *Lambert* – concurred.

The starting point for Lord Nicholls was that s.92(5) patently contemplated imposing a fully probative burden on the accused, as Parliament must certainly have intended:

> I entertain no doubt that, unless this interpretation is incompatible with Article 6(2) of the Convention, s.92(5) should be interpreted as imposing on the accused person the burden of proving the relevant facts on the balance of probability. Unless he proves these facts he does not make good the defence provided by s.92(5). The contrary interpretation of s.92(5) involves a substantial re-writing of the subsection ... [R]aising an issue does not provide the person charged with a defence. It provides him with a defence only if, he having raised an issue, the prosecution then fails to disprove the relevant facts beyond reasonable doubt. I do not believe s.92(5) can be so read. I do not believe that is what Parliament intended.[90]

This interpretation of s.92(5), Lord Nicholls acknowledged, must necessarily entail a *prima facie* breach of Article 6(2) at the next stage of the analysis, since 'this interpretation ... sets out facts a defendant must establish if he is to avoid conviction. These facts are presumed against him unless he establishes the contrary.'[91] The determinative question thus becomes whether a particular derogation from the presumption of innocence is justifiable in the terms indicated by the ECtHR in *Salabiaku*, and previously elaborated by the House of Lords in *Kebilene* and *Lambert*. Lord Nicholls confessed the difficulty of this task, which appeared to him to involve a paradoxical balancing of 'incommensurables':

> In the face of this paradox all that can be said is that for a reverse burden of proof to be acceptable there must be a compelling reason why it is fair and reasonable to deny the accused the protection normally guaranteed by the presumption of innocence.[92]

Derogating from the presumption of innocence in this fashion 'permits a conviction in spite of the fact-finding tribunal having a reasonable doubt as to the guilt of the accused', and this threshold consideration 'should colour one's approach when evaluating the reasons why it is said

---

[90] [2003] 1 WLR 1736, para. 46.   [91] *Ibid.*, para. 47.   [92] *Ibid.*, para. 49.

that, in the absence of a persuasive burden on the accused, the public interest will be prejudiced to an extent which justifies placing a persuasive burden on the accused'.[93] Lord Nicholls then expounded further factors bearing on this determination. Where the punishment on conviction would involve serious hardship, the justification for imposing a probative burden on the accused must be correspondingly weighty. Account should also be taken of the nature and extent of the matters which the prosecution must prove in order to constitute a case to answer and call forth a defence, and the countervailing ease with which the accused might establish facts readily, and perhaps peculiarly, accessible to him.

Turning to the circumstances of the present appeal, manufacturing and distributing counterfeit goods have been shown to involve serious criminality with a major detrimental impact on the global economy. Parliament has responded to what it perceives as a growing menace by enacting offences, including those provided by s.92 TMA 1994, which 'have rightly been described as offences of "near absolute liability"'.[94] These offences require no proof of intent to infringe a trade mark, yet carry severe maximum penalties of up to ten years' imprisonment and unlimited fines, flanked by swingeing confiscation and civil forfeiture provisions. This unflinching penal regime exemplifies Lord Nicholls' 'paradox',[95] that 'the more serious the crime and the greater the public interest in securing convictions of the guilty, the more important the constitutional protection of the accused becomes'.[96] However, two further factors were regarded by their Lordships as decisive in *Johnstone*. First, traders who deal in branded products are well aware of the risks of piracy and counterfeiting and ought to stick to reputable suppliers: should they choose to peddle goods of dubious provenance, they do so at their own peril. Secondly, international supply chains of counterfeit goods are exceedingly difficult for investigators to detect and unravel. Even if the original suppliers are ever traced, their voluntary participation in criminal investigations and prosecutions is seldom forthcoming. Traders can always claim that they received counterfeit supplies in good faith from a trustworthy source. Without the assistance of a reverse-onus clause to lighten its probative load, the prosecution's

---

[93] *Ibid.*, para. 50.   [94] *Ibid.*, para. 52.
[95] *Ibid.*, para. 220, adopting the analysis of Sachs J in the South African Constitutional Court in *State* v. *Coetzee* [1997] 2 LRC 593.
[96] [2003] 1 WLR 1736, para. 49.

task of proving that in reality the trader knew his goods were counterfeit, or that he at any rate lacked reasonable grounds for believing them to be genuine, would be intolerably burdensome in the majority of cases. The constitutional guarantee of the presumption of innocence, their Lordships concluded, must in these circumstances defer to the imperatives of crime control and the practical exigencies of proof:

> Given the importance and difficulty of combating counterfeiting, and given the comparative ease with which an accused can raise an issue about his honesty, overall it is fair and reasonable to require a trader, should need arise, to prove on the balance of probability that he honestly and reasonably believed the goods were genuine.[97]

Since, on closer examination, s.92(5) turned out to be compatible with Article 6(2) after all, the question of 'reading down' under s.3 HRA did not arise in this appeal.[98]

Attorney General's Reference (No. 1 of 2004)

Whilst the House of Lords had been entertaining Article 6(2) cases at comparative leisure, the presumption of innocence had become a regular visitor to the Court of Appeal and the Administrative Court. In the fourth case analysed here, *Attorney General's Reference (No. 1 of 2004)*,[99] the Lord Chief Justice took the opportunity of five conjoined appeals raising essentially the same issues to assemble a full court of experienced judges to consider the existing authorities and identify general principles to guide the application of Article 6(2) to English criminal statutes. The intended recipients of this guidance were not only prosecutors, advocates and trial judges at first instance, but also the House of Lords before whom the appeal in *Sheldrake*, to which we will presently return, was currently pending. Lord Woolf CJ announced:

> [T]he time has now come when it is possible to attempt to pull together the authorities so as to identify the relevant principles to be applied. In addition, we consider that it could be useful to the members of the House of Lords hearing the forthcoming appeals to know the views of the members of this Court. We have, collectively, considerable experience of the problems that are now arising in the courts because of reverse

---

[97] *Ibid.*, para. 53.   [98] *Ibid.*, para. 54.
[99] *Attorney General's Reference (No. 1 of 2004); R. v. Edwards; R. v. Denton and Jackson; R. v. Hendley; R. v. Crowley* [2004] 2 Cr App R 27; [2004] EWCA Crim 1025.

burdens. We hope that the guidance that we will set out can be readily
revised to take into account any views expressed by the House of Lords
when deciding the further appeals.[100]

As we have by now come to expect, the five conjoined appeals in these
proceedings arose in diverse contexts implicating a miscellany of statutory provisions. Two of the cases, *Attorney General's Reference (No. 1 of
2004)* itself and *R. v. Edwards*, concerned s.352 of the Insolvency Act
1986, by which a bankrupt accused of defrauding the official receiver or
trustee in bankruptcy can escape criminal liability if he 'proves that, at
the time of the conduct constituting the offence, he had no intent to
defraud or to conceal the state of his affairs'. The appeal in *R. v. Denton
and Jackson* centred on s.1(2) of the Protection from Eviction Act 1977,
which shields a landlord from charges of unlawfully evicting his tenants
if 'he proves that he believed, and had reasonable cause to believe, that
the residential occupier had ceased to reside in the premises'. *R. v.
Hendley* reprised the question of the correct interpretation of the
reverse-onus provisions of the Homicide Act 1957 which had previously
been ventilated at the Court of Appeal stage in the case conjoined with
Lambert, this time in relation to s.4 suicide pacts rather than, as in
Lambert, s.2 diminished responsibility. Finally, the relevant statutory
provision in *R. v. Crowley* was s.51(7) of the Criminal Justice and Public
Order Act 1994, whereby an accused who knowingly intimidates a
complainant, potential witness or potential juror in criminal proceedings is 'presumed' to have intended thereby to obstruct or pervert the
course of justice 'unless the contrary is proved'.

We need delve no further into the factual circumstances or doctrinal
intricacies of each individual appeal against conviction. The Court of
Appeal's self-consciously future-orientated judgment in *Attorney
General's Reference (No. 1 of 2004)* has two prominent features for our
purposes. First, Lord Woolf CJ detected a 'significant difference
in emphasis'[101] between, in particular, the speech of Lord Steyn in
Lambert and the approach of at least four of their Lordships in
Johnstone; and, since *Johnstone* was the more recent authority, it must
be followed and applied, in accordance with ordinary principles of
precedent, by all inferior tribunals. Moreover, the 'views expressed by
the other members of the House [in *Lambert*] were not as forceful as
those of Lord Steyn',[102] and 'perhaps not sufficient weight had been

---

[100] [2004] 2 Cr App R 27, para. 10.   [101] *Ibid.*, para. 38.   [102] *Ibid.*, para. 30.

given to Lord Hutton's [dissenting] views'.[103] Indeed, in relation to the practical utility of merely evidential burdens, Lord Woolf CJ ventured to suggest that 'it may be of assistance to the Appellate Committee to know that in practice our collective experiences are the same as Lord Hutton's'.[104] Thus was *Lambert*'s general analysis of Article 6(2) stood on its head, and Lord Hutton's dissent elevated to the decision – if it ever makes sense to cast *obiter dicta* in the garb of *ratio*.

The second noteworthy feature of *Attorney General's Reference (No. 1 of 2004)* was the 'general guidance' painstakingly topiaried by the Court of Appeal from the unruly thicket of recent authority. This labour was undertaken 'to ease the task of courts of first instance who have to apply reverse burden provisions'.[105] Any general guidance would naturally require flexible application to the circumstances of particular cases, yet the hope was expressed that, 'if courts bear in mind the following principles, they will not go far wrong':

A) Courts should strongly discourage the citation of authority to them other than the decision of the House of Lords in *Johnstone* and this guidance. *Johnstone* is at present the latest word on the subject.

B) The common law (the golden thread) and the language of Art. 6(2) have the same effect. Both permit legal reverse burdens of proof or presumptions in the appropriate circumstances.

C) Reverse legal burdens are probably justified if the overall burden of proof is on the prosecution i.e., the prosecution has to prove the essential ingredients of the offence, but there is a situation where there are significant reasons why it is fair and reasonable to deny the accused the general protection normally guaranteed by the presumption of innocence.

D) Where the exception goes no further than is reasonably necessary to achieve the objective of the reverse burden (i.e. it is proportionate), it is sufficient if the exception is reasonably necessary in all the circumstances. The assumption should be that Parliament would not have made an exception without good reason. While the judge must make his own decision as to whether there is a contravention of Art. 6, the task of a judge is to 'review' Parliament's approach, as Lord Nicholls indicates.

E) If only an evidential burden is placed on the defendant there will be no risk of contravention of Art. 6(2).

---

[103] *Ibid.*, para. 32.   [104] *Ibid.*, para. 34.   [105] *Ibid.*, para. 52.

F) When ascertaining whether an exception is justified, the court must construe the provision to ascertain what will be the realistic effects of the reverse burden. In doing this the courts should be more concerned with substance than form. If the proper interpretation is that the statutory provision creates an offence plus an exception that will in itself be a strong indication that there is no contravention of Art. 6(2).

G) The easier it is for the accused to discharge the burden the more likely it is that the reverse burden is justified. This will be the case where the facts are within the defendant's own knowledge. How difficult it would be for the prosecution to establish the facts is also indicative of whether a reverse legal burden is justified.

H) The ultimate question is: would the exception prevent a fair trial? If it would, it must either be read down if this is possible; otherwise it should be declared incompatible.

I) Caution must be exercised when considering the seriousness of the offence and the power of punishment. The need for a reverse burden is not necessarily reflected by the gravity of the offence, though, from a defendant's point of view, the more serious the offence, the more important it is that there is no interference with the presumption of innocence.

J) If guidance is needed as to the approach of the European Court of Human Rights, that is provided by the *Salabiaku* case at para. 28 of the judgment where it is stated that 'Article 6(2) does not therefore regard presumptions of fact or of law provided for in the criminal law with indifference. It requires states to confine them within reasonable limits which take into account the importance of what is at stake and maintains the rights of the defence'.[106]

Applying these general principles to the instant appeals, the Court of Appeal concluded that all of the statutory provisions challenged in these proceedings imposed fully probative burdens and that, with one marginal exception, they were all compatible with Article 6(2). It was entirely appropriate and 'proportionate' for Parliament to have taken a hard line with bankrupts, landlords who eject their tenants, survivors of suicide pacts, and those suspected of intimidating witnesses in criminal proceedings. A qualification was entered in relation to s.352 of the Insolvency Act 1986, but only as it applies to the very broadly drawn offence of making fraudulent dispositions within the five years preceding bankruptcy contrary to s.357 of the 1986 Act. The Court of Appeal

---

[106] *Ibid.*, para. 52.

felt that a reverse-onus probative burden in these circumstances went too far:

> The prosecution does not have to establish anything unusual or irregular in relation to the gift or disposition . . . [T]o require the bankrupt against whom it is proved only that he has made a gift or other disposal or created a charge within five years before his bankruptcy to prove that he had no intent to defraud is not justified and infringes Art. 6(2).[107]

The stage was now set for the House of Lords to deliver its authoritative ruling in *Sheldrake*, and nobody can have been more taken aback by their Lordships' speeches than Lord Woolf CJ and his judicial colleagues on the Court of Appeal.

Sheldrake v. DPP

Before the House of Lords, *Sheldrake*[108] involved two conjoined appeals, yet again with strikingly contrasting subject-matter. *Sheldrake* itself concerned the relatively prosaic offence of being drunk in charge of a motor vehicle contrary to s.5 of the Road Traffic Act 1988 (RTA 1988). By s.5(2) of the 1988 Act:

> It is a defence for a person . . . to prove that at the time he is alleged to have committed the offence the circumstances were such that there was no likelihood of his driving the vehicle whilst the proportion of alcohol in his breath, blood or urine remained likely to exceed the prescribed limit.

Sheldrake was discovered at 10.30pm, asleep and slumped over the steering wheel of his stationary vehicle, having consumed more than four times the legally prescribed limit of alcohol for drivers. He claimed that he had made arrangements with a friend to drive him home, but the friend was nowhere to be seen. Sheldrake was convicted at first instance by the magistrates, but a specially convened three-member Administrative Court allowed Sheldrake's Article 6(2)-based appeal, by a majority of two-to-one (and after the original two-member bench had been deadlocked). The House of Lords unanimously allowed the appeal of the Director of Public Prosecutions against the Administrative Court's ruling and restored Sheldrake's conviction. This conclusion was

---

[107] *Ibid.*, paras. 87 and 90.
[108] *Sheldrake v. DPP; Attorney General's Reference (No. 4 of 2002)* [2005] 1 AC 264; [2004] UKHL 43.

supported both in terms of the policy imperative of safeguarding society from the death and destruction wreaked by drunk drivers, and by undertaking close textual analysis of s.5 RTA 1988 and its legislative precursors. Lord Bingham summarised their Lordships' reasoning:

> There is an obvious risk that a person may cause death, injury or damage if he drives or attempts to drive a car when excessive consumption of alcohol has made him unfit (I use that adjective compendiously) to do so. That is why such conduct has been made a criminal offence. There is also an obvious risk that if a person is in control of a car when unfit he may drive it, with the consequent risk of causing death, injury or damage ... The defendant can exonerate himself if he can show that the risk which led to the creation of the offence did not in his case exist. If he fails to establish this ground of exoneration, a possibility (but not a probability) would remain that he would not have been likely to drive. But he would fall squarely within the class of those whose conduct Parliament has, since 1930, legislated to criminalise ... This is not in my view an oppressive outcome, since a person in charge of a car when unfit to drive it may properly be expected to divest himself of the power to do so (as by giving the keys to someone else) or put it out of his power to do so (as by going well away).[109]

Conjoined with the appeal in *Sheldrake* was *Attorney General's Reference (No. 4 of 2002)*, a 'war on terror' decision specifically concerned with the offence of belonging to a proscribed (terrorist) organisation contrary to s.11 of the Terrorism Act 2000. Section 11(2) provides that it shall be 'a defence for a person ... to prove (a) that the organisation was not proscribed on the last (or only) occasion on which he became a member or began to profess to be a member, and (b) that he has not taken part in the activities of the organisation at any time while it was proscribed'. A defence application of 'no case to answer' succeeded at first instance in the proceedings generating *Attorney General's Reference (No. 4 of 2002)*, it having been common ground during the trial, for as long as it lasted, that s.11(2) imposes only an evidential burden on the accused. The Attorney General subsequently disavowed this concession, and success-fully argued before the Court of Appeal that s.11(2) imposes a fully probative burden which, moreover, is nonetheless compatible with Article 6(2).[110] By a narrow three-to-two majority, however, the House of Lords (Lords Rodger and Carswell dissenting) reversed this holding.

---

[109] [2005] 1 AC 264, para. 40.   [110] [2003] 2 Cr App R 22; [2003] EWCA Crim 762.

The decision of Lords Bingham, Steyn and Philips, comprising the majority, was all the more notable in the light of recent legislation. The Terrorism Act 2000 deliberately reduces specified reverse-onus clauses to merely evidential burdens in order to comply with Article 6(2).[111] Ameliorated criminal prohibitions include the statutory successors of the offences prosecuted in *Kebilene*. However, the offences involving membership in terrorist organisations proscribed by s.11 of the Terrorism Act 2000 were, presumably no less deliberately, left unmodified. The inference is irresistible: 'There can be no doubt that Parliament intended s.11(2) to impose a legal burden on the defendant.'[112] Yet opposing and ultimately countermanding Parliament's clearly expressed intention were weighty considerations of principle which, Lord Bingham concluded, required the language of the section to be 'read down' pursuant to s.3 HRA in this instance:

> [A] person who is innocent of any blameworthy or properly criminal conduct may fall within s.11(1). There would be a clear breach of the presumption of innocence, and a real risk of unfair conviction, if such persons could exonerate themselves only by establishing the defence provided on the balance of probabilities. It is the clear duty of the courts, entrusted to them by Parliament, to protect defendants against such a risk. It is relevant to note that a defendant who tried and failed to establish a defence under s.11(2) might in effect be convicted on the basis of conduct which was not criminal at the date of commission ... While a defendant might reasonably be expected to show that the organisation was not proscribed on the last or only occasion on which he became a member or professed to be a member, so as to satisfy subs. (2)(a), it might well be all but impossible for him to show that he had not taken part in the activities of the organisation at any time while it was proscribed, so as to satisfy subs. (2)(b). Terrorist organisations do not generate minutes, records or documents on which he could rely. Other members would for obvious reasons be unlikely to come forward and testify on his behalf ... While the defendant himself could assert that he had been inactive, his evidence might well be discounted as unreliable.[113]

It also had to be borne in mind that this was a serious offence, for which a gaol term of up to ten years' imprisonment could be imposed. The fact that the case raised security concerns could not in and of itself justify wholesale derogations from Convention rights, as the European Court

---

[111] TA 2000, s.118.   [112] [2005] 1 AC 264, para. 50.   [113] *Ibid.*, para. 51

of Human Rights has reminded states parties from time to time.[114] The HRA facilitated this counter-intuitive interpretation of s.11(2) of the Terrorism Act 2000 because 'the interpretative obligation under section 3 is a very strong and far reaching one, and may require the court to depart from the legislative intention of Parliament'.[115] This approach was calculated to serve parliamentary sovereignty in the deeper, richer sense, previously elaborated by Lord Steyn in *R.* v. *A (No. 2)* (another criminal law case, *nota bene*), by giving effect to Parliament's contextualising second-order directive for broad compliance with the HRA in all aspects of legislation and law enforcement – including judicial interpretation of Parliament's own first-order legislative intentions:[116]

> Section 3 places a duty on the court to strive to find a possible interpretation compatible with Convention rights. Under ordinary methods of interpretation a court may depart from the language of the statute to avoid absurd consequences: section 3 goes much further ... In accordance with the will of Parliament as reflected in section 3 it will sometimes be necessary to adopt an interpretation which linguistically may appear strained. The techniques to be used will not only involve the reading down of express language in a statute but also the implication of provisions.

In *Attorney General's Reference (No. 4 of 2002)*, the 'strong and far-reaching' interpretative obligation imposed by s.3 induced a majority of the House of Lords to read the word 'prove' as though it meant 'adduce sufficient evidence to raise an issue in the case', knowing full well that this was not Parliament's immediate intention. But Lord Rodger, dissenting, could detect no infringement of Article 6(2) whatever. Section 11(2) of the Terrorism Act 2000 served to ameliorate what would otherwise be a strict liability offence in favour of the accused, and the distinction between probative and evidential burdens 'has no direct counterpart in civil law systems and is, of course, not mentioned, one way or the other, in any guarantee in Article 6 of the Convention'.[117] This appeal, for Lord Rodger, raised only local issues of criminal procedure law, in which the European Court of Human Rights itself disavows any material jurisdiction.[118]

---

[114] See e.g. *Aksoy* v. *Turkey* (1997) 23 EHRR 553, paras. 76–8; *Fox, Campbell and Hartley* v. *UK* (1991) 13 EHRR 157, paras. 32–6.

[115] [2005] 1 AC 264, para. 28, reciting *Ghaidan* v. *Godin-Mendoza* [2004] 2 AC 557; [2004] UKHL 30.

[116] *R.* v. *A (No. 2)* [2002] 1 AC 45; [2001] UKHL 25, para. 44.

[117] [2005] 1 AC 264, para. 71.

[118] See e.g. *Teixeira de Castro* v. *Portugal* (1999) 28 EHRR 101, para. 34.

More striking, in many ways, than the majority's conclusion in *Attorney General's Reference (No. 4 of 2002)* was their Lordships' barely concealed disdain for the 'general guidance' so recently formulated by the Court of Appeal in *Attorney General's Reference (No. 1 of 2004)*. To begin with, a brief refresher course in the basic arts of case-reading and the theory of precedent was deemed to be required:

> Both *R. v. Lambert* and *R. v. Johnstone* are recent decisions of the House, binding on all lower courts for what they decide. Nothing said in *R. v. Johnstone* suggests an intention to depart from or modify the earlier decision, which should not be treated as superseded or implicitly overruled. Differences of emphasis (and Lord Steyn was not a lone voice in *R. v. Lambert*) are explicable by the difference in the subject matter of the two cases.[119]

So much for the Court of Appeal's attempts to prune back the rambling thicket of precedent by elevating *Johnstone* as the pre-eminent specimen for trial judges to propagate. With the Lord Chief Justice lying bleeding, Lord Bingham (with whom Lord Philips and the now comprehensively rehabilitated Lord Steyn agreed) reached for the salt: 'I would not endorse the guidance given by the Court of Appeal in paragraph [52] of its judgment save to the extent that it is in accordance with the opinions of the House in these cases which must, unless and until revised or supplemented, be regarded as the primary domestic authority on reverse burdens.'[120] Though expressed in superficially equivocal language, this is nothing less than a comprehensive denunciation. 'Guidance' which can only be relied upon to the extent that it comports with – without necessarily fully or faithfully replicating – alternative authoritative sources is not guidance which it would be safe to follow in isolation, or even 'guidance' in any meaningful sense.

Trends and patterns of judicial reasoning under the Human Rights Act

Readers will readily concede that there is plenty in the foregoing litigation histories to occupy the time and to hone the critical faculties of criminal procedure lawyers. I have examined the reasoning in *Kebilene*

---

[119] [2005] 1 AC 264, para. 30.   [120] *Ibid.*, para. 32.

and *Lambert* at greater length elsewhere.[121] The specific claim advanced in this chapter is that post-HRA decisions on the presumption of innocence have broader significance in exemplifying and contributing to more general trends and patterns of judicial reasoning under the HRA. This section highlights and briefly expounds seven notable features of Article 6(2) jurisprudence, setting aside for present purposes knotty transitional problems with temporary curiosity value but limited lasting significance.

(1) Let us begin with the sheer level of judicial activity and its heightened controversy. In addition to engendering dozens of appeals to the Court of Appeal[122] and to the Administrative Court,[123] Article 6(2) has been debated in relation to statutory reverse-onus clauses four times in five years by the House of Lords.[124] Moreover, the frequency and extent of judicial disagreement is extraordinary. The House of Lords disagreed with the court below in *Kebilene, Lambert, Johnstone, Sheldrake* and *Attorney General's Reference (No. 4 of 2002)*. The Administrative Court at the first level of appeal in *Sheldrake* needed

---

[121] Paul Roberts, 'The Presumption of Innocence Brought Home?: *Kebilene* Deconstructed' (2002) 118 LQR 41; Paul Roberts, 'Drug-Dealing and the Presumption of Innocence: The Human Rights Act (Almost) Bites' (2002) 6 *International Journal of Evidence and Proof* 17.

[122] *R. v. Makuwa* [2006] EWCA Crim 175; *R. v. Navabi; R. v. Embaye* [2005] EWCA Crim 2865; *R. v. Barnham* [2005] EWCA Crim 1049; *Attorney General's Reference (No. 1 of 2004); R. v. Edwards; R. v. Denton and Jackson; R. v. Hendley; R. v. Crowley* [2004] 2 Cr App R 27; [2004] EWCA Crim 1025; *R. v. Schofield* [2004] EWCA Crim 369; *R. v. Matthews* [2004] QB 690; [2003] EWCA Crim 813; *Attorney General's Reference (No. 4 of 2002)* [2003] 3 WLR 1153; [2003] EWCA Crim 762; *R. v. Davies (David Janway)* [2003] ICR 586, [2002] EWCA Crim 2949; *R. v. S* [2003] 1 Cr App R 35, [2002] EWCA Crim 2558; *R. v. Daniel* [2003] 1 Cr App R 6; [2002] EWCA Crim 959; *R. v. Kearns* [2003] 1 Cr App R 7; [2002] EWCA Crim 748; *R. v. Drummond* [2002] 2 Cr App R 25; [2002] EWCA Crim 527; *R. v. Carass* [2002] 1 WLR 1714; [2001] EWCA Crim 2845; *R. v. Lambert; R. v. Ali; R. v. Jordan* [2001] Cr App R 205 (CA); *R. v. Benjafield* [2001] 3 WLR 75 (CA); *International Transport Roth GmbH v. Home Secretary* [2003] QB 728; [2002] EWCA Civ 158.

[123] *DPP v. Ellery* [2005] EWHC Admin 2513; *DPP v. Barker* [2004] EWHC Admin 2502; [2006] Crim LR 140; *Dr D v. Secretary of State for Health* [2005] EWHC Admin 2884; *Barnfather v. Islington Education Authority* [2003] 1 WLR 2318; [2003] EWHC Admin 418; *Sheldrake v. DPP* [2003] 2 Cr App R 14; [2003] EWHC Admin 273; *L v. DPP* [2003] QB 137; [2001] EWHC Admin 882; *Parker v. DPP* [2001] RTR 16 (DC); *R. v. DPP, ex parte Kebilene* [1999] 3 WLR 175 (DC).

[124] Further questions concerning Article 6(2)'s scope of application have been argued up to the House of Lords in *R. (Mullen) v. Home Secretary* [2005] 1 AC 1; [2004] UKHL 18; *R. v. H (Fitness to Plead)* [2003] 1 WLR 411; [2003] UKHL 1; and *R. v. Benjafield* [2003] 1 AC 1099; [2002] UKHL 2.

two attempts to reach a decision, splitting three-to-two on aggregate, only for this holding to be reversed, unanimously, on further appeal to the House of Lords. At least one additional Court of Appeal decision applying Article 6(2), which was not argued up to the House of Lords, has been comprehensively disavowed in the short time since the HRA entered fully into force.[125] In the House of Lords itself, there were four-to-one (*Lambert*) and three-to-two (*Attorney General's Reference (No. 4 of 2002)*) split decisions. And their Lordships' treatment of the Court of Appeal's short-lived 'general guidance' from *Attorney General's Reference (No. 1 of 2004)* can only be described as withering. This is not a normal level of appellate scrutiny and disagreement in relation to what is, in essence, the self-same issue relitigated over and over again. Whilst the burden and standard of proof are not exactly strangers to judicial controversy,[126] the HRA has opened up these stalwarts of English criminal procedure to an unprecedented number of appeals litigated in bewilderingly quick succession. Let there be no mistake: this deluge is a direct consequence of human rights legislation. As Lord Bingham remarked in *Sheldrake*, for example, '[u]ntil the coming into force of the Human Rights Act 1998, the issue now before the House could scarcely have arisen'.[127] Anybody wishing to undertake a general assessment of the impact of the HRA on judicial reasoning should surely make room for this remarkable, and still rapidly accumulating, corpus of Article 6(2) jurisprudence in any systematic survey.

(2) If this unwonted level of appellate activity is justifiably ascribed to the HRA, the question naturally arises: how and why have these effects been produced? It was surely not the intention of Parliament to generate endless appeals on previously well-settled points of criminal procedure. The capacity of the HRA to precipitate unpleasant surprises may be attributable, in part, to the complacent assumption that English

---

[125] *R. v. Carass* [2002] 1 WLR 1714; [2001] EWCA Crim 2845, regarded as 'impliedly overruled' by Lord Woolf CJ in *Attorney General's Reference (No. 1 of 2004)* [2004] 2 Cr App R 27, para. 84, and 'wrongly decided' by Lord Bingham in *Sheldrake* [2005] 1 AC 264, para. 32.

[126] In addition to the 'third exception' cases, mentioned above at nn. 13 and 31, a good deal of appellate energy has been expended over the years on trying to provide a juror-friendly elaboration of the phrase 'beyond reasonable doubt': see Paul Roberts and Adrian Zuckerman, *Criminal Evidence* (Oxford: Oxford University Press, 2004), pp. 361–6. The current solution is to avoid the time-honoured expression altogether if at all possible: see Judicial Studies Board Specimen Directions, Part I.2, http://www.jsboard.co.uk.

[127] [2005] 1 AC 264, para. 7.

common law already adequately protects the fundamental rights guaranteed by the ECHR. This assumption is more plausible in relation to certain Convention rights (e.g. prohibition of torture and slavery) than others (e.g. respect for private life), but it particularly flatters common lawyers' sensibilities in relation to Article 6. After all, wasn't fair trial the common law's gift to global jurisprudence, and didn't 'we' write it into the Convention in the first place, and what can 'Europe' teach the heirs of Coke and Blackstone about fairness in legal process? Lord Woolf CJ's remark in *Attorney General's Reference (No. 1 of 2004)* that 'Article 6 does no more than reflect the requirements of fairness which have long been part of English law'[128] is typical of the genre. The expectation that 'incorporating'[129] the ECHR would have little or no material impact on domestic law, since modern rule-of-law democracies can confidently be assumed to have reached and surpassed the Convention's minimum guarantees of fundamental rights, has long since been confounded and abandoned in other jurisdictions.[130] English lawyers would do well to pay heed. Whilst the point has been made specifically in relation to criminal procedure, the lesson for understanding and predicting further developments in judicial reasoning is perfectly generalisable: English law is by no means quite so Convention-proof as English lawyers and judges tend to presume.

(3) We have seen how the HRA, and s.3 in particular, has facilitated judicial activism in defence of Convention rights. In this respect, cases such as *Lambert* and *Sheldrake* exemplify, extend and apply interpretational techniques with which constitutional law and human rights scholars are already familiar. The destabilising impact on orthodox approaches to precedent of novel canons of statutory interpretation was clearly evident in the cases examined in the last section. *Obiter dicta* are liberally dispensed as authoritative directives *per curiam*; dissents are elevated to decisions, in 'general guidance' from the Lord Chief Justice that is denounced by the House of Lords before it can be implemented; and the Court of Appeal finds itself on the wrong end

---

[128] [2004] 2 Cr App R 27, para. 14.

[129] Those of us who still insist, in the name of jurisprudential precision, that the HRA did *not* fully 'incorporate' the ECHR appear to be fighting a losing battle against the irresistible charms of linguistic convenience.

[130] See e.g. Bert Swart, 'The European Convention as an Invigorator of Domestic Law in the Netherlands' (1999) 26 *Journal of Law and Society* 38; Edward A. Tomlinson, 'The Saga of Wiretapping in France: What It Tells Us About the French Criminal Justice System' (1993) 53 *Louisiana Law Review* 1091.

of a lecture reminding its members that decisions of the House of Lords are binding on all inferior tribunals unless and until their Lordships say otherwise. It seems that the HRA, possibly reinforcing parallel developments in judicial practice,[131] may require even very experienced judges and lawyers to take refresher courses in Precedent 101. Or perhaps, to coin a phrase of recent notoriety, the rules of the game have changed?

(4) A more subtle point nicely demonstrated by the Article 6(2) cases is that the Convention invites judges to reason with entirely new concepts, or old concepts newly liberated from their traditional doctrinal moorings. Readers might find it surprising for 'the presumption of innocence' to be invoked as an illustration of this liberating tendency,[132] but the facts speak for themselves. English judges hardly ever referred, in terms, to 'the presumption of innocence' prior to the HRA era. The phrase 'presumption of innocence' occurs only seventy-seven times throughout the entire corpus of the Law Reports, stretching back to 1865.[133] Most of these references are either post HRA cases or appeals to the Privy Council raising points of local constitutional law.[134] The Law Reports contain only seven pre-HRA English criminal cases in which the phrase 'presumption of innocence' appears in the judgment of the court, on no occasion attracting more than a few cursory remarks.[135] Even in *Woolmington* it is mentioned only in passing. There are almost as many

---

[131] Cf. *B (A Minor)* v. *DPP* [2000] 2 AC 428 (HL); *R.* v. *K* [2001] 1 AC 462; [2001] UKHL 41, overruling the very well-settled authority of *R.* v. *Prince* (1875) LR 2 CCR 154, to the surprise of many commentators. (Although *B* v. *DPP* and *R.* v. *K* have been superseded by the Sexual Offences Act 2003, these decisions remain striking examples of recent judicial willingness to depart from settled precedent.)

[132] Cf. *Elfie A. Issaias* v. *Marine Insurance Co.* (1923) 15 Ll.L. Rep 186, 191, where Atkin LJ described the presumption of innocence as 'a principle of English law so well established that it is somewhat surprising to find little reference to it in some recent cases'. (I am grateful to my colleague Howard Bennett for this reference.)

[133] Westlaw search for 'presumption of innocence' in LAW-RPTS database, 30 March 2006. Searching in addition for 'presumed innocent' (which, in any case, is not the same thing) adds only a handful of further citations.

[134] See e.g. *Attorney-General of Hong Kong* v. *Lee Kwong-Kut* [1993] AC 951 (PC); *Haw Tua Tau* v. *Public Prosecutor* [1982] AC 136 (PC); *Ong Ah Chuan* v. *Public Prosecutor* [1981] AC 648 (PC); *Kannangara Aratchige Dharmasena* v. *R.* [1951] AC 1 (PC).

[135] *DPP* v. *Boardman* [1975] AC 421 (HL) (Lord Hailsham); *DPP* v. *Shannon* [1975] AC 717 (HL); *R.* v. *Chapman* [1973] QB 774 (CA); *Callis* v. *Gunn* [1964] 1 QB 495 (DC); *Harris* v. *DPP* [1952] AC 694 (HL); *Woolmington* v. *DPP* [1935] AC 462 (HL); *R.* v. *Lumley* (1865–72) LR 1 CCR 196. The Criminal Appeal Reports contain a few additional citations, but, of the forty-eight references to the 'presumption of innocence' in that series, the vast majority are post-2000 HRA cases.

divorce cases[136] and libel actions[137] referring to the 'presumption of innocence' as criminal appeals in which the presumption might be
expected to predominate. In fact, common lawyers have instead devoted
attention to more practically orientated concepts of the burden and
standard of proof[138] and their modestly prosaic forensic implications.
This is where the accent has changed. The HRA has furnished English
judges with a pristine concept of the presumption of innocence, complete with the interpretational tools to aggrandise its self-consciously
constitutional status. This conceptual innovation was, in retrospect, a
schedule of major works for the Court of Appeal and, as it turned out,
for the House of Lords as well.

(5) Virgin legal concepts require elaboration, elucidation and refine-
ment. Appellate guidance will inevitably be needed to resolve any normative conflicts, clarify linguistic ambiguities, and promote consistency
of approach by first-instance tribunals. Working out the detailed con-
tours of legal concepts may present stern jurisprudential challenges
under the most favourable of conditions. The Article 6(2) cases reviewed
in this chapter testify, however, to the exaggerated perils of attempting
to proceed on an improvised, implicit footing, without ever squarely
confronting the most fundamental conceptual question which echoes as
a deafening silence throughout these appeals: what *is* the presumption of
innocence (in English law)? The challenge of assimilating a novel
European concept of the presumption of innocence into English law
has been compounded by the notoriously imprecise and unstable meanings attributed by judges and scholars to legal 'presumptions' in the
common law tradition. Morgan memorably remarked that 'every writer
of sufficient intelligence to appreciate the difficulties of the subject
matter has approached the topic of presumptions with a sense of hope-
lessness, and has left it with a feeling of despair'.[139]

Working from first principles, some scholars argue for a narrow
conception of the 'presumption of innocence', cashed out in terms of

---

[136] *Robbins* v. *Robbins* [1971] P 236 (DC); *Blyth* v. *Blyth* [1966] AC 643 (HL); *Gorst* v. *Gorst*
[1952] P 94 (PDAD); *Lowndes* v. *Lowndes* [1950] P 223 (PDAD); *Tilley* v. *Tilley* [1949]
P 240 (CA); *Emanuel* v. *Emanuel* [1946] P 115 (PDAD); *Statham* v. *Statham* [1929] P
131 (CA).

[137] *Jameel (Mohammed)* v. *Wall Street Journal Europe* [2005] QB 904 (CA); *R.* v. *Shayler*
[2003] 1 AC 247 (HL); *Alfred Nelson Laughton* v. *Lord Bishop of Sodor and Man*
(1871–3) LR 4 PC 495 (PC); *Spill* v. *Maule* (1868–9) LR 4 Ex 232 (Ex Cham).

[138] As a rough comparator, 'burden of proof' scores 1,414 'hits' in the Westlaw LAW-
RPTS database.

[139] Edmund Morgan, 'Presumptions' (1937) 12 *Washington Law Review* 255.

the burden and standard of proof at trial. For these strict construction-
ists, the presumption of innocence means just that the prosecution must
prove the accused's guilt beyond reasonable doubt in order to secure a
criminal conviction.[140] Other commentators appear to invoke the presumption of innocence with broader connotations, applying the concept
both to aspects of pre-trial process[141] and to limitations on the sources
of evidence and means of proof in criminal adjudication.[142] Exploring
and charting this difficult and expansive jurisprudential terrain is a task
for another occasion. Suffice it here to observe that English law cannot
even begin to resolve the theoretical puzzles and practical tensions
engendered by the presumption of innocence until the urgent need
for elementary conceptual clarification is acknowledged in the highest
judicial echelons. So far from providing authoritative guidance on
the meaning of the presumption of innocence in English law, Lord
Bingham announced in *Sheldrake* that it 'may not be very profitable
to debate' whether the presumption had been breached in that case.[143]
Breach could simply be assumed: the appeal would turn on whether or
not the (assumed) breach was justifiable under the HRA. Small wonder
that the conceptual parameters of Article 6(2) remain obscure if the
senior judiciary places such little store by the discipline of defining and
clarifying basic concepts.

   (6) The liberating impact of the HRA on judicial interpretation has
not been confined to the terminology of the European Convention itself.
Established common law concepts have also been agitated by the Act's
destabilising effect. The familiar procedural device of the 'evidential
burden' supplies a telling illustration in the present context. Though
Glanville Williams, in programmatic mood, once strenuously argued
that the word 'prove' in an English statute could legitimately be interpreted

---

[140] P. J. Schwikkard, 'The Presumption of Innocence: What Is It?' (1998) 11 *South African
Journal of Criminal Justice* 396; P. J. Schwikkard, *Presumption of Innocence* (Kenwyn,
South Africa: Juta, 1999).

[141] Roderick Munday, 'Name Suppression: An Adjunct to the Presumption of Innocence
and to Mitigation of Sentence' [1991] Crim LR 680 and 753, at 756–7 and 760–2;
R. A. Duff, *Trials and Punishments* (Cambridge: Cambridge University Press, 1986), p. 139.

[142] Victor Tadros and Stephen Tierney, 'The Presumption of Innocence and the Human
Rights Act' (2004) 67 MLR 402; Andrew Paizes, 'A Closer Look at the Presumption of
Innocence in Our Constitution: What Is an Accused Presumed to be Innocent *of?*'
(1998) 11 *South African Journal of Criminal Justice* 409; John Calvin Jeffries, Jr, and
Paul B. Stephan III, 'Defenses, Presumptions, and Burden of Proof in Criminal Law'
(1979) 88 *Yale Law Journal* 1325.

[143] [2005] 1 AC 264, para. 41.

as imposing only an 'evidential burden' of production,[144] the better view is that the burden of producing evidence is not a burden of *proof* in any ordinary sense, since it is not necessary to prove anything in order to discharge the onus of adducing evidence. As Lord Bingham declared in *Sheldrake*:

> An evidential burden is not a burden of proof. It is a burden of raising, on the evidence in the case, an issue as to the matter in question fit for consideration by the tribunal of fact. If an issue is properly raised, it is for the prosecutor to prove, beyond reasonable doubt, that that ground of exoneration does not avail the defendant.[145]

Yet the HRA, and in particular s.3's robust interpretative obligation, has afforded a new lease on life to Glanville's pious heresy, most evidently in the reasoning and conclusion of the *Lambert* majority.[146] Some will say that sacrificing the purity of evidentiary concepts is a small price to pay for bolstering the practical significance of the presumption of innocence in criminal adjudication. But the cost is not counted merely in school-room conceptual scruple. After *Lambert*, some judges have readily accepted that statutory references to 'proof' may impose (only) a burden of production,[147] whilst others continue to assert evidentiary orthodoxy and denounce the 'evidential burden of proof' as heretical.[148] This is

---

[144] Glanville Williams, 'The Logic of "Exceptions"' (1988) 47 CLJ 261.

[145] [2005] 1 AC 264, para. 1. Also see *Jayasena* v. *R.* [1970] AC 618 (PC), *per* Lord Devlin, at 624: 'Their Lordships do not understand what is meant by the phrase "evidential burden of proof" ... It is doubtless permissible to describe the requirement as a burden, and it may be convenient to call it an evidential burden. But it is confusing to call it a burden of proof ... The essence of the appellant's case is that he has not got to provide any sort of proof that he was acting in private defence. So it is a misnomer to call whatever it is that he has to provide a burden of proof.'

[146] [2002] 2 AC 545, *per* Lord Slynn, para. 17; Lord Steyn, para. 42; Lord Hope, paras. 90–1; Lord Clyde, para. 157. Also see *R.* v. *DPP, ex parte Kebilene* [2000] 2 AC 326 (HL), at 373, *per* Lord Cooke.

[147] Thus, at the Divisional Court level in *Sheldrake*, Clarke LJ stated: 'There has been some criticism of the use of the expression evidential burden: see e.g. *L* v. *Director of Public Prosecutions* [2001] EWHC Admin 882; [2003] QB 137; [2002] 1 Cr App R 420, *per* Pill LJ, at paras. 22–3 and *Daniel*, *per* Auld LJ, at para. 26. However, both Pill LJ and Auld LJ recognised that it has been used in the cases and it is to my mind sensible to continue to use it provided that it is recognised that all that is required to discharge the burden is to identify evidence raising the issue': *Sheldrake* v. *DPP* [2003] 2 Cr App R 206; [2003] EWHC Admin 273 (DC), para. 47.

[148] Cf. *R.* v. *S* [2003] 1 Cr App R 35, *per* Rose LJ and Davis J, at para. 6; *R.* v. *Daniel* [2003] 1 Cr App R 6; *per* Auld LJ, at para. 26; *L* v. *DPP* [2002] 1 Cr App R 32, *per* Pill LJ, at paras. 22–3.

hardly a recipe for clarity, consistency or sound judgment in judicial elaborations of the presumption of innocence.

(7) An emerging theme of this commentary on Article 6(2) cases is that the HRA has exposed and exacerbated some of the common law's historical uncertainties, and compounded them with fresh interpretational controversies. This is regrettable enough in the abstract, supposing clarity, consistency, generality, accessibility and predictability to be desirable virtues for criminal law. Unresolved legal puzzles have simultaneously contributed, more specifically, to lamentable doctrinal developments in the English courts' post-HRA Article 6(2) jurisprudence. I will not repeat detailed criticisms I have made elsewhere of the courts' Frankenstein creation, 'the gravamen of the offence',[149] and their weakness for conjuring phantom 'presumptions'.[150] It is enough to observe that the presumption of innocence has more often than not been curtailed when its import has been challenged, and that this accommodation has been arrived at through an opaque process of 'balancing' individuals' Convention rights against the public interest. The courts' general approach to Article 6(2), from *Kebilene* onwards, makes the ultimate decision almost inevitable. Little attention is paid to the concept of the presumption of innocence, and its breach can, apparently, simply be assumed in relation to onus-reversing statutes. Everything is then made to turn on the question of the justifiability of the breach. A modern English criminal statute will seldom fail to satisfy the threshold test of pursuing a legitimate objective, if its rationale is to break up terrorist cells, or reduce death on the roads, or prohibit the supply of illegal narcotics, or protect property rights, or safeguard the administration of justice, etc. So, in the end, the justifiability of breaches of Article 6(2) predictably boils down to a single question: are infringing legislative measures *proportionate* to the criminal harm they aim to prevent or punish?

Proportionality is an essentially relative and irremediably contextual concept. As Lord Bingham explained in *Sheldrake*, '[t]he justifiability of any infringement of the presumption of innocence cannot be resolved

---

[149] Cf. *Sheldrake v. DPP* [2005] 1 AC 264, paras. 37–9 (Lord Bingham); *R. v. Lambert* [2002] 2 AC 545, para. 35 (Lord Steyn) and para. 69 (Lord Hope); *R. v. DPP, ex parte Kebilene* [1999] 3 WLR 175 (DC), at 188–90 (Lord Bingham) and 201 (Laws LJ).

[150] See Paul Roberts, 'The Presumption of Innocence Brought Home?: *Kebilene* Deconstructed' (2002) 118 LQR 41; Paul Roberts, 'Drug-Dealing and the Presumption of Innocence: The Human Rights Act (Almost) Bites' (2002) 6 *International Journal of Evidence and Proof* 17.

by any rule of thumb, but on examination of all the facts and circumstances of the particular provision as applied in the particular case'.[151]
This truism goes a long way towards explaining why, having adopted
proportionality as the arbiter of Article 6(2) compatibility, English
appellate courts have found themselves inundated with appeals invoking
the presumption of innocence. There is little that can helpfully be said
about the proportionality of criminal legislation *in general*. The Court of
Appeal and the House of Lords have consequently saddled themselves
with the onerous task of assessing the Convention-compliance of individual statutory presumptions and reverse-onus clauses, one by one,
taking appropriate account of the unique configuration of risks and
regulatory strategies arising in each scenario. Even allowing for the
inevitably contextual nature of a proportionality-based approach, however, it has to be said that precious little guidance can be derived from
the factors which appellate courts have identified as influential in their
decision-making in particular cases. Not only has 'proportionality'
served as a generously capacious receptacle for an expanding catalogue
of miscellaneous considerations, but the comparative weight and,
indeed, direction of influence of the factors identified is often difficult
to predict in advance.

In *Lambert*, the seriousness of the offence and the severity of the
penalty militated in favour of reading down a reverse-onus clause to a
merely evidential burden,[152] yet the fully probative burden was upheld
in *Johnstone* in relation to an offence carrying a maximum sentence of
ten years' imprisonment.[153] More commonly, reverse-onus clauses (and
strict liability offences in general) are justified on the basis that the
offence is *not* serious.[154] The House of Lords in *Johnstone* emphasised
that fraudulent trading was a 'serious contemporary problem',[155] but in
Sheldrake Lord Bingham declared, in relation to a threat – of terrorist
attack – certainly no less serious or contemporary than selling bootleg
CDs, that '[s]ecurity concerns do not absolve member states from their
duty to observe basic standards of fairness'.[156] Sometimes it is said that

---

[151] [2005] 1 AC 264, para. 21.
[152] Cf. *R. v. Davies (David Janway)* [2003] ICR 586, paras. 18–19 and 31, identifying the
absence of custodial sanctions for breaches of ss.3(1) and 33(1) of the Health and Safety
at Work Act 1974 as a reason for upholding the compatibility of s.40's reverse-onus
'reasonably practicable' defence with Article 6(2)'s presumption of innocence.
[153] Also see *R. v. Makuwa* [2006] EWCA Crim 175, para. 36.
[154] *R. v. Davies (David Janway)* [2003] ICR 586, paras. 15–17.
[155] [2003] 1 WLR 1736, para. 52.   [156] [2005] 1 AC 264, para. 21.

the accused is only being called upon to provide information that he can easily procure,[157] whilst on other occasions it is the prosecutor's foreseeable difficulties in satisfying a conventional burden of proof which are said to justify imposing a reverse onus on the defence.[158] There is some judicial recognition that these two related factors are actually distinct,[159] but (I would argue) insufficient allowance for the fact that accessibility of information to the accused cannot be equated with ease of proof, since certain defences and defendants inherently lack credibility in the eyes of fact-finders. Neither relative accessibility of information nor ease of proof appears to require explicit empirical substantiation, beyond the authority of judicial experience and common sense assumptions. The significance of judicial experience in weighing relevant factors was emphasised by the Court of Appeal in *Attorney-General's Reference (No. 1 of 2004)*, but the House of Lords in *Sheldrake* did not seem overly impressed by the 'considerable collective experience' underpinning the Court of Appeal's ill-fated 'general guidance'. Trying to infer a set of clear guiding principles from this riot of arguments and reasons is reminiscent of searching for practical wisdom in a book of proverbs: 'Many hands make light work', but 'Too many cooks spoil the broth'; 'Look before you leap!', though 'He who hesitates is lost'; 'Speculate to accumulate!', yet 'A bird in the hand is worth two in the bush'; and so on, and so forth.

Is it possible to speculate what is really driving post-HRA decisions applying Article 6(2)? There is more than a whiff of results-orientated reasoning in the case-law examined in this chapter, or, in other words, preconceived conclusions decorated with flimsy make-weight arguments and *ex post facto* rationalisations. If gut-reaction is playing a decisive role in these determinations, that might go some way to explaining why appellate judges so often disagree, not only in their

---

[157] *Sheldrake* v. *DPP* [2005] 1 AC 264, para. 41; *DPP* v. *Ellery* [2005] EWHC Admin 2513; *R.* v. *Navabi; R.* v. *Embaye* [2005] EWCA Crim 2865, para. 29; *R.* v. *Davies (David Janway)* [2003] ICR 586, para. 28. These decisions are – problematically – rooted in the well-established common law doctrine that an accused claiming to have acted under the authority of a licence must prove that he possesses a valid licence and conducted himself in accordance with its terms: *Guyll* v. *Bright* (1987) 84 Cr App R 260 (DC); *R.* v. *Edwards* [1975] QB 27 (CA); *John* v. *Humphreys* [1955] 1 WLR 325 (DC); *R.* v. *Turner* (1816) 5 M&S 206; 105 ER 1026.

[158] *R.* v. *Makuwa* [2006] EWCA Crim 175, para. 36; *R.* v. *Johnstone* [2003] 1 WLR 1736, para. 53; *R.* v. *Davies (David Janway)* [2003] ICR 586, para. 30. Cf. *R.* v. *Lambert* [2002] 2 AC 545, *per* Lord Hutton (dissenting), paras. 190–2.

[159] *R.* v. *Davies (David Janway)* [2003] ICR 586, para. 22.

reasoning, but also as to the appropriate result – a spectacle hardly
conducive to inspiring confidence in trial judges, or to reassuring the
accused or potential suspects or, for that matter, anybody who cares
about the presumption of innocence in criminal proceedings. A further
confounding factor may be that expounding and implementing an
abstract concept of 'the presumption of innocence' involves inherently
controversial questions of practical morality, which judges are not
necessarily well qualified to answer; or, if judges are no less well qualified
or constitutionally competent than any other public official to make
these determinations, perhaps they cannot easily explain what they are
doing within the orthodox conventions of judicial reasoning, opinion
and judgment.

   Whatever the deeper institutional, jurisprudential, cultural or even
psychological explanations, the cases surveyed in this chapter tend to
reinforce concerns about the concept of 'proportionality', and in particular English judges' reception of this deceptively familiar-looking
Euro-concept, which are frequently articulated by constitutional law
theorists and human rights scholars. Andrew Ashworth, amongst others,
has long warned of the corrosive impact of 'balancing' on individual
rights in the criminal law context.[160] Perhaps the most important general lesson to be derived from the Article 6(2) cases examined in this
chapter is that 'proportionality' threatens to be a Trojan Horse in
judicial reasoning, a mechanism through which fundamental human
rights are balanced away to vanishing point in a grievously mismatched
contest with the general public interest in security, harm prevention and
law enforcement. In relation to the presumption of innocence, this
process is already well underway, and, though by no means irreversible,
it is rapidly embedding conceptual and doctrinal mistakes in the fabric
of English law which only Parliament, if ever so minded, will be able to
expunge.

Conclusion: human rights and constitutional
criminal procedure

The bulk of this chapter has been devoted to describing five post-HRA
criminal cases in which Article 6(2) of the ECHR figured prominently in
the reasoning and conclusions of senior judges. These cases ought to be

---

[160] Andrew Ashworth, 'Crime, Community and Creeping Consequentialism' [1996] Crim
LR 220, 229 ('[t]he term "balance" should be banned').

better known and discussed beyond the narrow confines of criminal procedure specialists than, I perceive, they are at present. For constitutional law theorists and human rights scholars, no less than for criminal lawyers, *Kebilene, Lambert, Johnstone, Attorney-General's Reference (No. 1 of 2004)* and *Sheldrake* represent a valuable case study illustrating the practical impact of the HRA in one sphere of judicial reasoning and legal practice.

English law's reception of a novel, Convention-based conception of the 'presumption of innocence', and the implications of this doctrinal development for the common law's traditional concepts, doctrines and assumptions, are surely matters of intrinsic legal significance and scholarly interest. As Lord Bingham concluded, after summarising previous authorities in *Sheldrake*: 'The overriding concern is that a trial should be fair, and the presumption of innocence is a fundamental right directed to that end.'[161]

Beyond their intrinsic jurisprudential and constitutional significance, Article 6(2) cases may also be woven into a broader canvas, to illuminate general trends and patterns of judicial reasoning under the HRA. The third section of this chapter identified seven noteworthy features of this rich vein of jurisprudence, highlighting general legal and constitutional developments, broad conceptual issues and pitfalls, trends in adjudication and statutory interpretation which are quite likely to recur within different departments and subfields of law, versatile arguments and counter-arguments, methodological considerations, and useful points of comparison for the purposes of analysis and critical evaluation. This was not intended as an exhaustive roster – most of the points could be subdivided and pursued at greater length – but I hope it suffices to substantiate this chapter's central contention. Criminal cases should not, and must not, be left out of account when assessing the impact of the HRA on English law, legal process and judicial reasoning.

---

[161] [2005] 1 AC 264, para. 21.

14

Concluding remarks

IAN LEIGH

Introduction

Common lawyers tend to be somewhat apologetic about legal reasoning. It is not that they consider it to be an oxymoron. Rather, the subject is seen as too basic – not worthy of advanced investigation. This is perhaps because law students 'cover' 'Legal Method' at an early point in their studies and assume that, having mastered precedent and statutory interpretation, they can leave it behind in favour of more intellectually challenging topics. It is hard to imagine that a professional seminar in the United Kingdom on the topic of Legal Method would attract the involvement of virtually every senior member of the judiciary – as happened in New Zealand in 2001.[1] Likewise, academic attention devoted to legal reasoning is marginal in comparison to substantive analysis, and is mostly reserved for 'Jurisprudence' (the thinking lawyer's diversion) under the guise of theories of adjudication.

However, this is an entirely appropriate focus for a study of the early impact of the Human Rights Act. It is not necessary to believe the New Labour hyperbole (in the days when ministers were still proud of the Act, rather than disowning its progeny) about the biggest legal change since Magna Carta. It is enough to acknowledge that comparing judgments before and after the Act that a major shift has occurred in their style, content and source material.

The Human Rights Act presented a significantly different challenge than the Canadian Charter of Rights, the South African Constitution or even the New Zealand Bill of Rights Act 1990 had for the judiciary in those countries. The task was not that of expounding a virgin constitutional text nor of merely incorporating into domestic law an established

---

[1] Published as R. Bigwood, *Legal Method in New Zealand* (Wellington: Butterworths, 2001).

international treaty. With the treaty text came also a significant body of jurisprudence from the European Court of Human Rights and the European Commission on Human Rights, developed over forty years. The most obvious sign of a change to legal reasoning, then, is the profusion of material drawn from the European Convention jurisprudence that now adorns written judgments whenever Human Rights Act points are raised in argument. This undoubtedly bears witness to the ease with which counsel and the bench have come to terms with a source of law which, if not entirely new (since the Convention had some relevance prior to the Act), has been given considerably added prominence after October 2000. This much is undeniable – any volume of the law reports will confirm it.

It is pertinent to ask, however, how far and how deep this change goes. A major objective of the preceding chapters has been to discuss what it is that the judges are *doing* with all this new law. How do they regard it compared to domestic law? What is its precedential value? What impact has it had on statutory interpretation? What are the prospects that domestic human rights law will itself influence Strasbourg?

Early commentators on the Human Rights Act had high hopes of the overall impact it might have. At a memorable meeting in Cambridge in the spring of 1999, attended by a galaxy of legal luminaries, Lord Lester invoked Wordsworth's account of the French revolution: 'bliss was it in that dawn to be alive, but to be young was very heaven'.[2] It was variously predicted that rights-language and thinking would come to suffuse the law (ushering in a more general 'rights culture'), that the style of statutory interpretation would radically change, that proportionality analysis would drive the courts to consider more social data about the effect of law, and so on. Critics of the Act had their fears too: that Parliamentary sovereignty would be challenged, that the judiciary would become politicised, and that the Act would become a villains' charter.

Have these rosy predictions or the dire warnings been vindicated? One way of mapping the use made by the judiciary of the Act that has become common in the literature is to refer to minimalist and maximalist responses. Giving the Human Rights Act its maximum effect it might be regarded as a proxy Bill of Rights. Some judges have referred to it in this way; Lord Steyn, for example, has described the Act as 'our Bill

---

[2] Published as *Constitutional Reform in the United Kingdom: Practice and Principles* (Oxford: Hart Publishing, 2000).

of Rights'.[3] Others have suggested that there is little practical difference for the courts between the Act and a Bill of Rights.[4] The maximalist 'Bill of Rights' approach suggests two important consequences – a less deferential attitude than hitherto towards the democratically account-able branches and freedom for domestic courts to fashion a distinctive human rights jurisprudence of their own. The minimalist approach, on the other hand, sets the changes under the Act against the fixed point of the constitution – Parliamentary sovereignty. Therefore, while s.3 of the Act allows the courts to go beyond the traditional methods of statutory construction, what they do must still be within the parameters of *interpretation* – if legislative change is needed to achieve Convention compatibility, the declaration of incompatibility should be used to hand the baton back to Parliament. A minimalist reading of s.2, moreover, constrains the freedom of domestic courts to add to Strasbourg principles.

This concluding chapter will attempt to divine between these two approaches, drawing on the lessons of the earlier chapters.

Judicial supremacism and deference

No doubt because of the different constitutional climate in this country, the constitutional role and work of judges has not attracted public attention here in the same way as in the United States (or even, more recently, in Canada). Whereas there are numerous academic and jour-nalistic studies of the United States Supreme Court,[5] the equivalent literature in the United Kingdom comprises two somewhat dated volumes – Alan Patterson's *The Law Lords*[6] and John Griffiths' *The Politics of the Judiciary*.[7] Although the past five years have produced an upsurge of public and professional interest, well-informed understand-ing in the United Kingdom still lags substantially behind both in inten-sity and in sophistication. One cannot imagine the news media in this

---

[3] See Lord Steyn, 'Deference: A Tangled Story' [2005] PL 346, disagreeing with Lord Hoffmann's views on deference expressed in *Secretary of State for the Home Department* v. *Rehman* [2001] UKHL 47; [2003] 1 AC 153 and *R. (on the Application of ProLife Alliance)* v. *British Broadcasting Corporation* [2003] UKHL 23; [2004] 1 AC 185.

[4] *Matadeen* v. *Pointu* [1999] 1 AC 98, 110, *per* Lord Hoffmann.

[5] From a substantial literature: B. Woodward and S. Armstrong, *The Brethren: Inside the Supreme Court* (New York: Simon and Schuster, 2005); E. Lazarus, *Closed Chambers: The Rise, Fall and Future of the Modern Supreme Court* (Harmondsworth: Penguin, 2005); M. Tushnet, *A Court Divided* (New York: Norton, 2005).

[6] A. Paterson, *The Law Lords* (London: Macmillan, 1982).

[7] J. A. G. Griffiths, *The Politics of the Judiciary* (London: Fontana Press, 1997).

country dissecting the record of new appointees to the Appellate Committee of the House of Lords or being concerned to forecast their future voting habits on key legal issues. This is not just because of the absence – even in the new Supreme Court arrangements under the Constitutional Reform Act 2005 – of a power to strike down primary legislation for unconstitutionality. It also reflects a much less sophisticated appreciation of the judiciary's core tasks and skills.

However, a second reason has been the self-imposed institutional modesty of the judiciary – a point not always fully appreciated by successive Home Secretaries (it has invariably been the Home Office which has been the hapless respondent in the more contentious decisions). Deference to Parliament and respect for the executive are quintessential features of the UK legal system that have shaped the role of judges since the Glorious Revolution in the seventeenth century, and it seemed unlikely that this tradition would be transformed overnight. Commentators therefore argued that some equivalent domestic 'proportionality' test or 'margin of deference' would emerge.

Very early in the life of the Act, the tone was set by Lord Bingham in *Brown* v. *Stott*:

> While a national court does not accord the margin of appreciation . . . it will give weight to the decisions of a representative legislature and a democratic government within the discretionary area of judgment accorded to those bodies.[8]

In similar vein were Lord Hoffmann's remarks in *Alconbury*, reflecting a fear that the charge of judicial supremacism would be laid: 'the Human Rights Act 1998 was no doubt intended to strengthen the rule of law but not to inaugurate the rule of lawyers'.[9]

Nevertheless, it was Lord Bingham also who reminded the Attorney-General in the Belmarsh case that the Human Rights Act 'gives the courts a very specific, wholly democratic, mandate'.[10]

The concept of deference[11] featured prominently in the debate among judges, practitioners and academics during the seminars that gave rise to

---

[8] [2001] 2 WLR 817, 835 (PC).

[9] *R. (Alconbury Developments Ltd)* v. *Secretary of State for the Environment, Transport and the Regions* [2001] UKHL 23; [2003] 2 AC 295, para. 129.

[10] *A* v. *Secretary of State for the Home Department* [2005] AC 68, para. 42.

[11] See R. Edwards, 'Judicial Deference under the Human Rights Act' (2002) 65 MLR 859; J. Jowell, 'Judicial Deference and Human Rights: A Question of Competence', in P. Craig and R. Rawlings (eds.), *Law and Administration in Europe* (Oxford: Oxford University Press,

this volume. Lord Justice Keene's contribution to this volume[12] reflects this search by the judiciary to find a middle way[13] and fairly captures the tenor of many of the individual interventions by judges and counsel. Lord Justice Keene expounds the now well-known four principles of deference from the *Roth* case,[14] concluding that the subject-matter of the case and the Article in question are decisive. His own view is that in the case of unqualified rights the court's task is to make its own judgment on the merits,[15] although he concedes that in many Article 2 and 3 cases the result may not differ greatly to deferring to the public authority as decision-maker, since usually what is at stake is an assessment of risk. While in areas such as national defence that fall within the constitutional and institutional competence of the executive deference will be due, in other fields such fair trial rights the judiciary has the home advantage. In a striking aside, he suggests that *Mendoza* (in which s.3 of the Act was used by the House of Lords to extend the benefit of the surviving 'spouse' provision in the Rent Act 1977 to a homosexual partner) fell into the latter category as it involved issues concerning discrimination – on which the judiciary felt competent – rather than difficult policy issues.[16]

In the spirit of democratic egalitarianism and non-deference to the judiciary that characterised the seminars, other contributors to this volume take a different view. Sonia Harris-Short describes *Mendoza* as 'in many ways a quite extraordinary example of judicial innovation on an issue raising difficult and sensitive questions of public policy' and 'a hugely significant decision'.[17] Apart from *Mendoza*, Harris-Short argues

---

2003); J. Jowell, 'Judicial Deference, Servility, Civility or Institutional Capacity' [2003] PL 592; R. Clayton, 'Judicial Deference and Democratic Dialogue: The Legitimacy of Judicial Intervention under the Human Rights Act 1998' [2004] PL 33; K. D. Ewing, 'The Futility of the Human Rights Act' [2004] PL 829; Lord Steyn, 'Deference: A Tangled Story' [2005] PL 346; F. Klug, 'Judicial Deference under the Human Rights Act' [2003] EHRLR 125.

12 See Chapter 8.

13 As Simon Brown LJ has pointed out: 'Constitutional dangers exist no less in too little judicial activism as in too much. There are limits to the legitimacy of executive or legislative decision-making, just as there are to decision-making by the courts' (*International Transport Roth GmbH and Others* v. *Secretary of State for the Home Department* [2002] EWCA Civ 158; [2003] QB 728, para. 54).

14 *International Transport Roth GmbH and Others* v. *Secretary of State for the Home Department* [2002] EWCA Civ 158; [2003] QB 728 (CA), paras. 83–7.

15 Cf. Chapter 7, p. 196.   16 See Chapter 8, p. 212.

17 Chapter 11, pp. 317–22. Just how innovative is made clear in Aileen Kavanagh's chapter dissecting the approach to statutory interpretation, discussed below.

that in the public sphere of family law also the picture is mixed one, with some tendency on the part of judges to 'pass' on sensitive issues that they deem to be within the more appropriate realm of Parliament. This form of deference, based on the courts' modesty about their institutional competence, manifests itself in *Bellinger* in the issue of a declaration of incompatibility, rather than use of the s.3 interpretive obligation.

Statutory interpretation

The interplay or tension between s.3 and s.4 of the HRA has become one of the most intriguing features of the first five years of operation of the Act. David Feldman provides a context for understanding these debates. He points out that legal reasoning engages a wider range of actors than merely the courts.[18] Interpretation, he argues, is not primarily a linguistic matter, but, rather, concerns the effect to be given to words in a particular institutional setting. Hence the duty under s.3 of the Act applies also to anyone who has to read and give effect to legislation. Administrators, legislators, and indeed the public (as part of the wider human rights culture), have to interpret legislation so far as possible in a way that is compatible with Convention rights. It is thus wider in its ambit than the duty laid on public authorities under s.6 (for example, it applies to the interpretation of legislation as part of the Parliamentary process). However, the standpoint from which this interpretation occurs varies according to the institutional role of the interpreter – ministers and parliamentary committees vetting draft legislation on human rights grounds have no final adjudicatory authority (this is reserved to the courts) and are concerned with differing degrees of *probability*. However, the unwillingness of courts to entertain moot questions or to pronounce upon interpretive acts of other bodies that do not affect rights necessarily limits the range of s.3 issues that appear in the law reports.

There is much controversy about s.3 and s.4. On the one side stand those who argue that the courts must not usurp the legislative role and that making a declaration of incompatibility is a way of deferring to Parliamentary sovereignty or of encouraging dialogue between the branches of government. On the other are those who point to the exceptional nature of the s.4 power and its ineffectiveness as a remedy and urge that the interpretive obligation of section 3 should be seen (in

[18] Chapter 4, pp. 89–90.

Lord Steyn's words) as a remedial power in its own right. It would appear that after some initial hesitancy the courts have swung around to the latter view.

In her chapter, Aileen Kavanagh cuts through much of the misunderstanding here and argues that many of the arguments on both sides fail to persuade: Convention compatibility can be achieved as much through legislative reform following a declaration of incompatibility as through a strained interpretation; much inter-institutional 'dialogue' takes place as a result of statutory interpretation and does not hinge upon s.4 orders. In comparing *Fitzpatrick* (decided before the HRA) with *Mendoza* (decided after it) she concludes that rather than ushering a fundamentally different style of judicial reasoning the courts have been emboldened in their use of existing techniques, in part because the Act has given these greater constitutional legitimacy. She argues that the centrality of the interpretive exercise facing the courts under s.3 has thrown into stark relief the lack of attention given to statutory interpretation generally within the English legal system, legal education and legal scholarship.[19] The under-theorised nature of statutory interpretation means that we are some way yet from seeing anything as sophisticated in the literature about the Human Rights Act as the competing theories of constitutional adjudication that hold sway among US judges and academics. Nevertheless, there are signs that this trend could emerge.

It was widely expected that the arrival of the Human Rights Act would herald new techniques of statutory interpretation: 'reading down' (that is, limiting the application of statutory language from the possible or natural meanings to one that is Convention-compatible) and, more controversially, 'reading in' (supplying additional words to achieve the same effect).

In a chapter intended as a case study of legal reasoning with regard to the presumption of innocence, Paul Roberts cites *Lambert* as an example of using the interpretive obligation under s.3(1) of the HRA to read down a statutory provision. In that instance, it was the reverse-onus provisions of the Misuse of Drugs Act 1971 which were treated as imposing only an evidential (rather than a probative) burden on the defendant.[20] Similarly, the majority of the House of Lords in *Attorney General's Reference (No. 4 of 2002)* read down in the Terrorism Act 2000 (a post-1998 Act that Parliament passed in full awareness of the HRA) to

---

[19] Chapter 5, pp. 114–17.   [20] Chapter 13, pp. 390–7.

reduce the burden on a defendant to show that he had not taken part in the activities of proscribed organisations (s.11(2)(b)) – which Lord Bingham described as 'all but impossible' to fulfil.[21] In the process, Roberts argues, these new approaches to statutory interpretation have had a significant destabilising effect on the doctrine of precedent, owing to uncertainty over how to apply the presumption of innocence under Article 6 in cases of reverse burden of proof. After a succession of appeals challenging these provisions with regard to different offences, and an abortive attempt by the Court of Appeal to reconcile the apparently conflicting *dicta* that have resulted and to lay down general guidelines, the House of Lords has strongly reasserted its primacy.[22]

The leading contender for innovative statutory interpretation has, however, to be the House of Lords decision in *Mendoza*. What are we to make of Lord Nicholls' judgment which, with disarming frankness, declares that the language that Parliament uses is not determinative – what matters in determining the limits of s.3 interpretation is 'the concept being enacted'? The freedom with which his Lordship felt able to interpret that concept (referring to a shared life and making a home together) is far from compelling. That this was done on the basis of an apparent appreciation of 'social purpose' of the legislation shows that we are leaving the realm of reasoning altogether and entering into speculation. Denying that s.3 was intended to become a parlour game for lawyers, the court indulged in a different pastime – the judicial equivalent to 'pin the tail on the donkey'. As Sonia Harris-Short points out, there is a marked contrast between the lack of evidential analysis for reaching conclusions in *Mendoza* and the decision of the Supreme Court of Canada in *M* v. *H* on a similar point.[23]

If a court were serious about establishing the 'social purpose' of legislation it was interpreting, there are some simple steps it could take – for example, studying the White Paper or the Parliamentary debates, or considering census data or other statistics that might explain the effect of the legislation in question, both when enacted and (if relevant) contemporaneously. What is striking about a number of leading judgments under the HRA is the extent to which UK judges while purporting to assess such difficult and complex issues as whether measures are

[21] *Attorney General's Reference (No. 4 of 2002)* [2005] 1 AC 264, para. 51.
[22] *Sheldrake v. DPP; Attorney General's Reference (No. 4 of 2002)* [2005] 1 AC 264; [2004] UKHL 43, discussed at pp. 407–11 above.
[23] Chapter 11, pp. 320–1.

'necessary in a democratic society' do so entirely within the closed world of legal argument. Not for them the Brandeis brief or even a historical enquiry into the background of the legislation. Paul Roberts points to the tendency of the judiciary when engaging in proportionality analysis merely to assume the case for combating particular social evils with reverse burdens of proof on the basis of their own knowledge and experience, rather than by consideration of empirical evidence.[24] The promise of more wide-ranging consideration of the effects of policies impinging on human rights simply has not materialised. Judges seem uninterested in anything that has not featured in a law report or a statute. It goes without saying that this gives an impoverished view of social life and public policy.

This then is an intellectual exercise without either roots or limits. In *Ghaidan*, it failed to appear so for two reasons only: that the government colluded in the result by intervening as *amicus curiae* (and so there was no institutional clash), and because most commentators tend to approve of the outcome – recognising the interests of a homosexual partner as against a landlord. If, however, the approach of not violating the concept-as-constructed-by-the-court were to take hold, what, if any, would be the limits to judicial power?

Persistence of common law doctrines

Overt resistance to the Convention among the judiciary has been rare, although one example stands out. Memorably, one senior Scottish judge, Lord McCluskey, wrote in the *Scotland on Sunday* newspaper that the Human Rights Act would be a 'field day for crackpots, a pain in the neck for judges and legislators and a goldmine for lawyers'.[25] The article went on specifically to discuss surveillance against drugs dealers and Article 8 – the very issue at stake in a case that he had heard only days before. The High Court of Justiciary held that his remarks would raise in an informed observer a reasonable apprehension of bias against the Convention and ordered that the appeal be heard by a different bench.[26]

---

[24] Chapter 13, pp. 419–22.   [25] *Scotland on Sunday*, 6 February 2000.

[26] *Hoekstra, van Rijs and Others* v. *HM Advocate (No. 2)*, 2000 SLT 605. Lord McCluskey has been a long-term public opponent of incorporation, since at least his 1986 Reith Lectures: J. H. McCluskey, *Law, Justice and Democracy* (London: Sweet and Maxwell, 1987).

If outright judicial hostility of this kind to the Convention has been unusual, complacency that the common law already conforms to the Convention[27] has been more common. There has also been a consequent attachment to long-established legal standards in some fields, with an unwillingness to re-evaluate them. Paul Robert cites the example of Lord Woolf's wholly unjustified assertion that 'Article 6 does no more than reflect the requirements of fairness which have long been part of English law'.[28] In my chapter, I argue that the same tendency can be seen in the treatment of Article 6 in administrative law cases, notably *Alconbury* and *Begum*.[29]

Likewise, Sonia Harris-Short points to the resistance especially within 'private' family law cases to rights-based reasoning.[30] In part, this is because the 'welfare principle' (giving primacy to the perceived interests of the child) has assumed a dominant legal place and reverting to the language of rights may be seen as a step back to the world of the paterfamilias. In a similar vein, Helen Fenwick argues that the welfare principle has on occasion prevented the courts from correctly balancing free speech and a child's right to respect for private life.[31] From her analysis of the case-law, Harris-Short finds a good deal of unfulfilled promise. Nevertheless, rights-based reasoning, she argues:

> ... has the potential to introduce much greater intellectual rigour and discipline to judicial reasoning ... ensuring the needs and interests of all family members are clearly articulated and considered in the decision-making process and preventing untested assumptions and prejudices ... from determining the outcome of common family disputes.[32]

The persistence of the welfare principle in family law adjudication, despite its apparent inconsistency with the ECHR[33] identified by Harris-Short, finds an echo in public law. There, as I argue,[34] some members of the judiciary have been reluctant after the Human Rights Act to cast off their preference for the *Wednesbury* test as the judicial review

---

[27] For example, it has been repeatedly (and manifestly incorrectly in the light of Strasbourg rulings to the contrary) claimed that the common law protects freedom of expression to the same extent as Article 10: *Attorney-General* v. *Guardian Newspapers (No. 2)* [1990] 1 AC 109, 284–5, *per* Lord Goff; *Derbyshire County Council* v. *Times Newspapers Ltd* [1993] AC 534, 550–1, *per* Lord Keith of Kinkel; *R.* v. *Secretary of State for the Home Department, ex parte Simms* [2000] AC 115, 123–4, *per* Lord Steyn.

[28] *Attorney General's Reference (No. 1 of 2004)* [2004] EWCA Crim 1025, para. 14; p. 414 above.

[29] Chapter 7, pp. 192–3. [30] Chapter 11, pp. 334–46. [31] Chapter 10, pp. 258–61.

[32] Chapter 11, p. 345. [33] Chapter 11, pp. 336–46. [34] Chapter 7, pp. 198–200.

standard of choice. The highest courts have, however, recognised that the traditional common law test required modification in order to be Convention-compliant, while carefully differentiating this new standard from merits review.

A rather different form of judicial resistance has involved the discovery – or, less charitably, the invention – of an independent human rights jurisprudence embedded in the common law. This has allowed the ECHR to be by-passed on occasion.

According to this doctrine, common law fundamental rights will only be taken to be overridden by the clearest of statutory words. The right of access to a court is to be treated as fundamental – Laws J so held in striking down an order by the Lord Chancellor who had used a broadly worded statutory power in order to substantially increase court fees (including those for litigants in person).[35] The crowning achievement of this jurisprudence is said to be the 'legality' principle expressed by the House of Lords in *Simms*, holding that prisoners' rights of access to journalists could not be taken away under Prison Rules.[36] The Appellate Committee stressed the role of journalists in exposing miscarriages of justice where the criminal justice system had failed; some members went so far as to describe it as a 'fundamental and basic right' and relied on a constitutional principle of 'legality' that clear statutory words were necessary in order to displace the right.[37]

This discovery of forgotten treasure in the attic of the common law strains credibility. The chronology of these decisions is strongly indicative of judicial 'rights envy' – the major developments in the United Kingdom occurred only after the High Court of Australia had made similar discoveries of its own[38] and after a series of broad hints from Lord Cooke in the New Zealand courts that the fundamental rights jurisprudence might cross the Tasman Sea.[39] The House of Lords decided *Simms* in the period after the Human Rights Act was passed but before it came into effect. Had the common law contained

---

[35] *R. v. Lord Chancellor, ex parte Witham* [1997] 1 WLR 104.

[36] In *R. v. Secretary of State for the Home Department, ex parte Simms* [2000] AC 115.

[37] *Ibid.*, see especially Lord Steyn, pp. 129–30 and Lord Hoffmann, pp. 131–2.

[38] *Australian Capital Television Pty Ltd v. The Commonwealth* (1992) 177 CLR 106.

[39] Repeated *obiter dicta* questioning whether there are some rights that Parliament could not abridge: see e.g. *Fraser v. State Services Commission* [1984] 1 NZLR 116, 121; *Taylor v. New Zealand Poultry Board* [1984] 1 NZLR 394, 398. See Justice M. Kirby, 'Lord Cooke and Fundamental Rights', in P. Rishworth (ed.), *The Struggle for Simplicity in the Law: Essays for Lord Cooke of Thorndon* (Wellington: Butterworths, 1997), p. 331.

fundamental rights for the previous seven centuries (or even since 1689), it is remarkable that they only came to light in the late twentieth century at the same time as these developments in other countries and when Parliament itself had signalled approval for greater rights protection. It is particularly unfortunate that the House itself was apparently unaware of the fundamental common law right of free speech when denying free speech in *Brind*[40] a decade before *Simms*.

How far this fundamental common law rights jurisdiction complements the Human Rights Act is a difficult question. In *Simms*, the overlap with the Convention was plain – the right appeared to be grounded largely on freedom of expression under Article 10 of the Convention and the principle of legality was virtually identical to the interpretive obligation now contained in s.3 of the Human Rights Act. Masterman notes the intriguing if perverse possibility that the courts might use this route to circumvent their self-imposed ceiling on protection by tying 'Convention rights' to the Strasbourg jurisprudence.[41]

The use of convention jurisprudence and precedent

The great legal historian, Frederick William Maitland, concluded that the English legal system had resisted the reception of Roman law that swept much of the rest of Europe in the sixteenth century because of the influence of the Inns of Court as purveyors and educators in English law: 'taught law is tough law', he argued. One wonders what Maitland would have made of the impact of the corpus of European Convention jurisprudence that has followed the commencement on 1 October 2000 of the Human Rights Act 1998. In 1999, Laurence Lustgarten and I argued that 'a further Europeanisation of the Common law seems imminent'.[42] In a strange way (and in reversal of Maitland's point) the relatively successful integration of Convention jurisprudence can be attributed to another great educational endeavour that sensitised the judiciary – a programme of education under the auspices of the Judicial Studies Board whereby every judge in the country from the House of Lords to District Judges received basic training on the Human Rights Act.[43]

---

[40] *R. v. Secretary of State for the Home Department, ex parte Brind* [1991] 1 AC 696.

[41] Chapter 3, pp. 83–4.

[42] L. Lustgarten and I. Leigh, 'Making Rights Real: The Courts, Remedies and the Human Rights Act' (1999) 58 CLJ 509, 512.

[43] See comments by Lord Justice Sedley in 'Preface', in M. Hill (ed.), *Religious Liberty and Human Rights* (Cardiff: University of Wales Press, 2002), pp. ix–x.

In his chapter in this volume Roger Masterman argues that the duty under s.2 of the Human Rights Act to take account of Convention jurisprudence has been interpreted in a way that sharply diverges from the Parliamentary intention.[44] As he explains, from the Parliamentary debates and from the White Paper, it was clearly envisaged at the time of enactment that domestic courts would be free to go further in their protection of human rights than the minimum set by the Strasbourg Court. In this way, they might make a distinctively British contribution to the development of international human rights law to rival, for example, the claims of the German Federal Constitutional Court. However, following Lord Bingham's speech in *Ullah*,[45] the courts have maintained a minimalist interpretation of the term 'Convention right' that ties it to no less but no more than the Strasbourg Court itself would recognise. As Masterman concludes, this has reduced discretion under s.2 almost to vanishing point.[46] Effectively – and despite protestations to the contrary – the courts have begun to treat European Court rulings over-rigidly as though they were binding precedents, notwithstanding cogent reasons that argue against doing so. In implicit contrast to Masterman's stance, which calls for an expansive and flexible approach towards the 'application' of Strasbourg jurisprudence, Colin Warbrick's chapter is intended to analyse the more basic question of whether domestic courts are using the HRA effectively in its minimal sense – as an instrument allowing for the application, without more, of the Strasbourg jurisprudence in domestic courts. It asks, in other words, not whether the domestic courts could be more *creative* in their use of such jurisprudence, but whether they are discharging their duty of giving faithful effect to it. In particular, Warbrick's critical analysis of the judgment of Laws LJ in *R. (Limbuela)* v. *Secretary of State for the Home Department*[47] clearly points up the *dangers* of judicial activism, or, as Warbrick persuasively characterises it in relation to this judgment, playing fast and loose with Strasbourg principles. As such, it is a useful counterpoint to some of the other viewpoints offered in this book.

Section 2 of the HRA requires courts and tribunals to have regard to Convention decisions '*whenever made or given*, so far as, in the opinion of the court or tribunal, it is relevant to the proceedings in which that

---

[44] Chapter 3, pp. 62–71.
[45] *R. (on the Application of Ullah)* v. *Special Adjudicator* [2004] UKHL 26; [2004] 2 AC 323.
[46] Chapter 3, p. 78.   [47] [2004] QB 1440; [2004] 3 WLR 561 (CA).

question has arisen'.[48] The Convention itself has no system of precedent.[49] The ECtHR has itself stated that the Convention is a living instrument so that the Court should be free to depart from its earlier decisions in the light of changing social conditions.[50] The implication is that interpretations by the domestic courts of Convention jurisprudence, even if correct when given, may be overtaken by later developments at Strasbourg. Consequently, domestic courts may be put in the position of reinterpreting legislation that has already been read at an earlier point to achieve compatibility. The combined nature of the duties *on all courts* under s.2 and s.3 of the Act would suggest that Parliament intended this to be the case and without regard to whether the earlier domestic decision came from a higher court whose decisions are binding under the doctrine of precedent on the court now faced with the issue on the fresh occasion.[51] There is an admission in *Hansard* made during the Committee stage that suggests the government was alert to this issue.[52]

The scenario outlined came to fruition in *Price* v. *Leeds City Council*[53] in which the House of Lords had to consider the effect on one of its own rulings (*Qazi*[54]) of a later Strasbourg decision (*Connors* v. *UK*[55]). In *Qazi*, a majority of the House had held that, where under domestic legislation an occupier had no right to possession (a tenancy having previously been brought to an end by a valid notice served by his joint tenant), this was sufficient to satisfy Article 8(2) and the courts hearing a claim for a possession order against him need not consider his Convention rights. This ruling in itself was highly controversial in view of the position of the county court as a public authority under s.6 of the HRA, although plainly it was much influenced by case-management concerns.[56] In *Connors*, the European Court of Human

---

[48] Emphasis added.

[49] However, the introduction of the Grand Chamber under the reforms of Protocol No. 11 could be seen as moving in that direction.

[50] See e.g. *Tyrer* v. *UK* (1978) 2 EHRR 1, para. 31; *Cossey* v. *UK* (1990) 13 EHRR 622, para. 35.

[51] L. Lustgarten and I. Leigh, 'Making Rights Real: The Courts, Remedies and the Human Rights Act' (1999) 58 CLJ 509, 510–12.

[52] G. Hoon, HC Debs., vol. 313, col. 405 (3 June 1998).

[53] *Kay and Others* v. *Lambeth London Borough Council; Price* v. *Leeds City Council* [2006] UKHL 10.

[54] *Harrow London Borough Council* v. *Qazi* [2004] 1 AC 983.

[55] *Connors* v. *United Kingdom* (2004) 40 EHRR 189; *Blecic* v. *Croatia* (2004) 41 EHRR 185.

[56] Cf. the parallel developments in deportation where the higher courts have sought to limit the scope for Article 8 arguments to exceptional cases.

Rights held the eviction of a family of gypsies from a local authority site by summary process following complaints made against them did not give sufficient opportunity to establish proper justification for the serious interference with his rights under Article 8, and consequently could not be regarded as justified by a 'pressing social need' or proportionate to the legitimate aim being pursued.

The Court of Appeal in *Price* had concluded that *Connors* was unquestionably incompatible with *Qazi* but that, since the latter was a decision of the House of Lords, it was bound to follow *Qazi*.[57]

Intervening in the House of Lords in *Price*, Liberty and Justice had argued that the Court of Appeal was incorrect and that the later Strasbourg ruling should normally be followed by the lower court where four conditions were met:

1) the Strasbourg ruling has been given since the domestic ruling on the point at issue,
2) the Strasbourg ruling has established a clear and authoritative interpretation of Convention rights based (where applicable) on an accurate understanding of United Kingdom law,
3) the Strasbourg ruling is necessarily inconsistent with the earlier domestic judicial decision, and
4) the inconsistent domestic decision was or is not dictated by the terms of primary legislation, so as to fall within section 6(2) of the 1998 Act.[58]

These carefully measured criteria should have been sufficient to allay the fear of insubordinate and anarchic rulings by lower courts enticed by doubtful arguments about Strasbourg jurisprudence. However, the House of Lords came down on the side of legal certainty. Even in the present case there were differing views in the House over whether *Connors* was inconsistent with *Qazi*. Hence, in Lord Bingham's words:

> The prospect arises of different county court and High Court judges, and even different divisions of the Court of Appeal, taking differing views of the same issue ... [C]ertainty is best achieved by adhering, even in the Convention context, to our rules of precedent. It will of course be the duty of judges to review Convention arguments addressed to them, and if they consider a binding precedent to be, or possibly to be, inconsistent with Strasbourg authority, they may express their views and give leave to

---

[57] *Leeds City Council* v. *Price* [2005] 1 WLR 1825, para. 26.
[58] [2006] UKHL 10, para. 41.

appeal, as the Court of Appeal did here. Leap-frog appeals may be appropriate. In this way, in my opinion, they discharge their duty under the 1998 Act. But they should follow the binding precedent.[59]

This aspect of the ruling clearly places a restrictive interpretation on the duty of the lower court under ss.2, 3 and 6 of the HRA. It must be open to question whether the statutory duty of that court not to *act* in a way incompatible with a person's Convention rights (s.6) is adequately discharged by hearing an argument that Convention jurisprudence is incompatible with domestic authority, concluding that it is, but then ruling against the party raising the argument and suggesting an appeal. Apart from anything else, there is the question of why a party invoking Convention rights in this situation must bear the burden, delay and cost of going to the higher court. *Price* is an unwelcome decision that runs directly counter to the scheme of the HRA: Parliament has clearly decreed through applying ss.2, 3 and 6 on *all* courts that they have the task of bringing rights home.

Moreover, when *Price* is taken together with *Ullah* – discussed above – there is a clear inconsistency. Lord Bingham justifies the 'no less/no more' doctrine on the basis that the Strasbourg Court is the authoritative source of the determination of the meaning of Convention rights. Faced with the consequences of his own argument in *Price*, his Lordship reverted to explaining that many Strasbourg decisions leave matters to the domestic courts under the margin of appreciation (and for this reason presumably those courts should be slow to find inconsistency with Strasbourg jurisprudence):

> Thus it is for national authorities, including national courts particularly, to decide in the first instance how the principles expounded in Strasbourg should be applied in the special context of national legislation, law, practice and social and other conditions. It is by the decisions of national courts that the domestic standard must be initially set, and to those decisions the ordinary rules of precedent should apply.[60]

If this is so, however, it plainly contradicts the 'no more' aspect of the *Ullah* doctrine. When the Strasbourg Court invokes the margin of appreciation, there is in truth no objection to a more expansive reading of 'Convention rights' by the domestic courts. It seems clear then, as Roger Masterman suggests in his chapter,[61] that the real objection to

---

[59] *Ibid.*, para. 43.   [60] *Ibid.*, para. 44.   [61] Chapter 3, pp. 85–6.

United Kingdom courts going beyond the minimum protection that the Convention requires is their fear of being tarred judicial activists and legislators, rather than respect for the Strasbourg Court.

Some specific uses of Convention jurisprudence

Gavin Phillipson's chapter on privacy demonstrates the dynamic interplay between Strasbourg jurisprudence and domestic decisions under the Human Rights Act.[62] As he points out, within months of the *Campbell* decision by the House of Lords, the Strasbourg Court pushed the boundaries of what Article 8 required significantly further in *Von Hannover* v. *Germany*.[63] The latter case appears to treat anything not involving the official duties of a public figure as an aspect of their private life in contrast to the more nuanced approach under the emergent common law tort of misuse of personal information. This much-litigated area seems, as Phillipson points out, to be one where the broad influence of the Convention has been more important than precise attention to the detail of Convention jurisprudence – values rather than rights have been determinative in the rapid development of the common law. Indeed, he suggests that this may have been an instance where the Convention was used simply as a 'normative impetus' for developments that the judiciary wished to bring about anyway – something that would account for the lack of attention paid by the English courts to *Von Hannover* since *Campbell* laid down the parameters of the new tort.[64]

Citing the Scottish decision of *Whaley* v. *Lord Advocate*[65] and the House of Lords' speeches in the *Diane Pretty*[66] case, Aaron Baker argues that UK judges have treated Article 14 in a subordinate or second class way, i.e. that it does not merit separate analysis.[67] If no other Convention right has been breached, violation of Article 14 can be summarily dismissed. He argues also that the courts have incorrectly focused on the government's intention in determining the ambit of Article 14 – an issue which is only relevant to the possible issue of

---

[62] Chapter 9.   [63] *Von Hannover* v. *Germany* (2005) 40 EHRR 1.
[64] See Chapter 9, pp. 240–53.   [65] *Whaley* v. *Lord Advocate*, 2004 SLT 425.
[66] *R. (on the Application of Pretty)* v. *Director of Public Prosecutions* [2001] UKHL 61; [2002] AC 800.
[67] Chapter 12, pp. 350–6.

justification[68] – rather than the impact upon the alleged victim of the practice:

> Thus the courts in applying Article 14, and indeed any other Article of the Convention, must keep their eyes on the impact of government measures and decisions on the rights of individuals, not on the objectives, processes, and reasoning of the government actors. Domestic judges must also beware the temptation to view Article 14 as a mere adjunct of other Articles: it is a Convention guarantee in its own right, and does not call for interpretation according to the limitations written into the other substantive rights.[69]

One notable exception to the comment above about a lack of theory must be the question of whether or how the Human Rights Act applies 'horizontally'. Here, as Gavin Phillipson shows, if anything the judges are spoiled for choice when it comes to theoretical literature, largely due to the debate over privacy.[70] The result has been that – except to dismiss the more extreme positions – the courts have neglected much of this learning. Phillipson suggests that this may be due to a semi-instinctive desire on the part of the judges to retain a healthy degree of discretion over how great a role to give the Convention rights in private common law. But perhaps the commentators are themselves partly to blame. It is arguable that an over-attention to cases involving breach of confidence has produced a distorting emphasis in the literature to the neglect of some obvious points about more prosaic forms of horizontal application of the Act – in statutes applying between private individuals (such as landlord and tenant and family members, for example). In these fields perhaps judges have been speaking in prose without always realising it – and without commentators usually noticing either. The question of whether a private contract entered into prior to the Human Rights Act should be interpreted in a way that the parties could not have envisaged is one worthy of theoretical attention.[71] And should it make any difference that the parties might have relied upon earlier precedents from the courts interpreting the statute applying to their arrangements that now might be revisited under the HRA? To answer that question would require a more sophisticated account of private interests, legal certainty and public policy than is permissible now.

[68] See e.g. R. *(Douglas)* v. *North Tyneside MBC* [2004] HRLR 14.
[69] Chapter 12, p. 375.   [70] See Chapter 6.
[71] Particularly in the light of the rather surprising decision of the European Court of Human Rights in *Pla v Andorra* (2006) 42 EHRR 25.

The question of how, if the Convention is given horizontal application, the courts should approach conflicting Convention rights claims is one that is attracting an increasingly sophisticated literature. Strasbourg jurisprudence tends to give few pointers because by definition if the balance between the rights has been left to states then any conflict is subsumed under the margin of appreciation. In her chapter, Helen Fenwick considers the record to date of the courts in one area where this has arisen – the clash between children's rights to respect for their private life and the media's right to freedom of expression.[72] She argues that in early cases the courts have tended either to cling to the paramountcy principle (prioritising the welfare of the child)[73] or to swing away from that approach by avoiding – or attempting to avoid – the issue by 'definitional balancing' (that is, restricting the ambit of one of the rights so that no conflict arises). The result, however, has been unprincipled and chaotic. In contrast to this, she advocates parallel analysis – a process of considering each right in turn and the strength of the arguments for restricting that right and then weighing them against each other. This would allow careful consideration of the principles underlying free speech and privacy to be considered not only in defining the extent to which the rights truly applied but also in weighing the case for the restriction of either.

Conclusion

Laws LJ has remarked on several occasions that the task of the courts under the Human Rights Act is to fashion a municipal human rights jurisprudence in the light of the decisions of the Strasbourg Court:[74]

> The court's task under the HRA . . . is not simply to add on the Strasbourg learning to the corpus of English law, as if it were a compulsory adjunct taken from an alien source, but to develop a municipal law of human rights by the incremental method of the common law . . . case by case taking account of the Strasbourg jurisprudence.[75]

This, of course, reflects a particular perspective on legal reasoning under the Human Rights Act. Nevertheless, it perhaps describes better than

---

[72] Chapter 10.   [73] Cf. Chapter 11.

[74] R. (International Transport Roth GmbH) v. Secretary of State for the Home Department [2002] EWCA Civ 158; [2003] QB 728, para. 81; and cf. R. (M) v. Commissioner of Police for the Metropolis [2001] EWHC Admin 553.

[75] Begum v. Tower Hamlets LBC [2002] EWCA Civ 239; [2002] 1 WLR 2491, para. 17.

anything else from among the ocean of ink applied to the forest of trees felled since October 2000 what it is that collectively the courts are doing.

At times progress appears slow and in some areas of law that the Convention has had less impact than might have been expected. However, one would be hard put to find any field of law that is wholly untouched. The Human Rights Act has unleashed a creative ferment in the law not seen since the time of Mansfield. Although some bold developments have resulted – for example, the Belmarsh decision or the creation of a tort of misuse of personal information – there are many more missed opportunities.

On the whole, the contributions to this volume are critical of the so-far unrealised potential of the Convention in English law and the conservatism with which the judiciary has set about applying the Human Rights Act. Minimalism is the dominant mode of reasoning. An interim term report would be along the lines of 'tries hard, could do better'. Still, these are early days in the life of a constitutional provision whose impact should be judged not over five years but perhaps over five generations.

INDEX

Lightning Source UK Ltd.
Milton Keynes UK
16 February 2011

167667UK00001BB/10/P